Learning to Program with VB .NET

Learning to Program with VB .NET

Patrick G. McKeown
University of Georgia

ACQUISITIONS EDITOR	Beth Lang Golub
SUPPLEMENTS EDITOR	Lorraina Raccuia
EDITORIAL ASSISTANT	Ailsa Manny
MARKETING MANAGER	Gitti Lindner
SENIOR PRODUCTION EDITOR	Ken Santor
COVER DESIGNER	Jeanette Jacobs

This book was set in 10/12 Garamond by Patrick G. McKeown and printed and bound by Courier Westford. The cover was printed by Phoenix Color Corporation.

This book was printed on acid-free paper.

0471-22971-7
Printed in the United States of America

10 9 8 7 6 5 4 3 2 1

To Carolyn
"Still the one ..."

PREFACE

With the introduction of the original Visual Basic for Windows in the early 1990's, Microsoft took a large step toward redefining computer programming. With Visual Basic, instead of writing monolithic programs that are difficult to understand and debug, it was possible to write short sections of code that matched objects on the screen. The newest version of Visual Basic, VB.NET, is a complete rewrite of the earlier versions that is now completely object-oriented, supporting inheritance, encapsulation, and polymorphism. As a result, it is now a language that can be used to teach object-oriented concepts while also being capable of writing "industrial strength" applications. As a part of the larger Microsoft .NET initiative, VB .NET shares the same Microsoft Development Environment as the other .NET languages, Visual Studio .NET.

A Different Type of Textbook

This textbook has been written with the same purpose as my earlier books on Visual Basic 6.0—to demonstrate the many features of the VB .NET interface, while at the same time covering the programming logic required to create information system applications regardless of the computer language used. In my classes and those of my colleagues at the University of Georgia, we have found many students who are capable of creating an interface, but have problems with the programming logic. This textbook approaches this problem by helping students learn how *use* VB .NET to write computer code that works rather than just learning how to use Visual Studio .NET to create attractive interfaces.

To strike the proposed balance between interface and logic, the number of controls introduced in the first five chapters has been kept to a minimum—just enough to enable the students to write interesting projects. By minimizing the number of controls, the emphasis in the first five chapters is on students learning programming concepts that they will need to know regardless of the language they eventually use in the workplace. Four topics are the focus of these five chapters: The fundamentals of the VB .NET development environment; problem solving; using the sequence, decision, and repetition control structures to write programs; and understanding object-oriented concepts. Only after a firm foundation has been laid in these chapters are more VB .NET controls and features added along with more advanced programming topics covered in the next three chapters. These topics include arrays, general procedures, and using and creating classes and objects. In the Chapter 9, using VB. NET to access databases is covered in some detail and Chapter 10 covers a variety of topics including password security, menus, using direct access files and dialog boxes, creating graphics with VB .NET, and printing to the printer are covered.

In this textbook, a specific pedagogy is used: tell the student *what* they are going to be doing, let them know *why* they need to learn this material, and then give them specific instructions on *how* to carry out the programming activities. We believe this is a better approach that avoids long lists of step-by-step instructions while, at the same time, making it very clear what steps need to be taken to create a project.

CHAPTER COMPONENTS

This book has been described as being "feature-oriented with a continuing example." By this, we mean that there is a continuing example that runs throughout the book that is used as an example of the various features introduced in the each chapter. The emphasis is on introducing programming features and concepts and then applying them to the running example as well as to other examples. There are exercises within the chapter and at the end of the chapter. There are also end-of-chapter projects that provide the student with opportunities to solve problems similar to those discussed in the chapter.

Each chapter section includes five key instructional elements:

1. discussions of the solution process as it relates to one or more examples

    1. VB Code Boxes that provide the code to implement the solution of the examples

    2. screen captures that display the result of entering and running the code

    3. *Step-by-Step Instructions* that provide the reader with a detailed sequence of instructions which, if followed correctly, will result in a working VB .NET solution to the example described in the text

    4. *It's Your Turn!* exercises at the end of each section that both test the student's knowledge of the section material and request the student to carry out the *Step-by-Step Instructions*.

The discussion of the solution to the problem posed in an example, VB Code Boxes, screen captures, *Step- by-Step Instructions* and *It's Your Turn!* exercises work together to explain and demonstrate the concept being introduced, provide specific instructions to create an application, test the student's understanding of the material, and then request the reader to create the same application by implementing the VB Code Boxes in VB .NET. All too often, students reading the text assume an understanding of the material without actually testing it. In this system, the instructor can easily assign the students to demonstrate their understanding of the material by completing the end-of-section exercises. Once a student has gone through the chapter and followed all of the *Step-by-Step Instructions*, they will have a working application that solves the example problem. In addition to the *It's Your Turn!* exercises, there are exercises at the end of each chapter that test the student's understanding of chapter material and projects that provide the students with an opportunity to create applications similar to the one covered in the text.

You may think it unusual that, in this day of very colorful textbooks, this textbook has only one additional color beyond black-and-white. However, there is a reason for this. With the continuing rapid release of new versions of Visual Basic, including VB .NET, it is necessary to be able to quickly revise a textbook to keep up with the new versions. We have chosen to do this by desktop publishing this book in a two-color format. This in no way should detract from its usefulness in the classroom and, furthermore, enables us to offer the textbook to students at a lower price than the more elaborate books.

WHAT'S NEW IN THIS EDITION?

In addition to the revised *what-why-how* pedagogy which is introduced in this book, there are a number of new features in this textbook on VB .NET. These include a second color, the addition of the *Step-by-Step Instructions*, a revision of the chapter order, and a reduced number of chapters. In the first case, a second color has been added to both headings and to the VB Code Boxes. While color in headings is attractive, the color in the VB Code Boxes makes it easy for readers to see the keywords in the language the same way they will see them in the development environment. In the second case, the addition of the *Step-by-Step Instructions* provides a clear set of instructions for the reader to follow to create a working project. These instructions are clearly marked and set off from the chapter text so readers will have no problem finding them.

The revision of the chapter order has been made to bring the book more in line with the object-oriented nature of VB .NET. Chapter 8 has been rewritten to cover the use of user-defined data types, the .NET Framework Class Library (FCL), and creating classes and objects. Chapter 9 now covers the new ADO. NET approach to accessing databases and Chapter 10 covers a variety of topics including passwords, menus, direct access files, graphics, and printing to the default printer. While the emphasis on objects and object-oriented programming occurs in Chapter 8, the use of FCL classes such as StreamReader and StreamWriter are discussed as early as Chapter 6. This revised chapter order means that much of the material in Chapter 10 can actually be covered immediately after Chapter 6 if the instructor so desires. Also, with a little discussion of the FCL, the chapter on databases can also be covered after Chapter 7.

SUPPORTING WEB SITE

Rather than including a disk and paper instructor's manual with the text, which would increase the price of the textbook to the student, we have created a supporting Web site at
http://www.wiley.com/college/mckeown
for both instructors and students. The faculty section, which is password-protected, provides all of the support normally associated with a package such as this including lecture slides in PowerPoint for each chapter, a test bank, solutions to end-of-chapter exercises and projects, sample syllabi, and teaching suggestions. The student section of the Web site includes data files needed by student and solutions to the *It's Your Turn!* exercises (instructors will also have access to this section). Students are given access to the *It's Your Turn!* solutions so they can check their work or, if they run into problems with a project, determine their error. The solutions to the *It's Your Turn!* exercises include *all* of the code from the VB Code Boxes presented in the text in a downloadable format. Both sections of the Web site have e-mail access to the author, a bulletin board to display the occasional error that readers may discover, and new information on Visual Basic as it becomes available.

SUPPORTING WEB SITE

Instructors have the option to order this text *with* or *without* a full working version of VB .NET 2003 on a set of five CD-ROMs with the cost of the package of text and software costing somewhat more than the text by itself. The students can install this software on their personal computers and use it to follow the *Step-by-Step Instructions* and in completing the *It's Your Turn!* and end-of-chapter exercises as well as the projects at the end of the chapter. Although VB .NET 2003 is packaged with the book, the text is applicable to either VB .NET 2002 or VB .NET 2003. Instructors wishing to order the combination of textbook and software *must* use an ISBN of 0-471-56577-6; otherwise, only the textbook by itself will be delivered to bookstores.

ACKNOWLEDGMENTS

Completing a textbook such as this one has been made much easier by help from a large number of people and I want to thank each of them here. First, I want to acknowledge the continuing contribution of my coauthor of the previous version of this book, Craig Piercy of the University of Georgia. Though he chose not to work as a coauthor on this version, he provided much needed help on many chapters, including reviewing the first five chapters and helping me write Chapters 8 and 10. In addition, Tianle Tong made a major contribution to the book by helping me rewrite the first five chapters and by checking the *Step-by-Step* exercises in all of the chapters. In addition, Dominic Thomas of the University of Georgia reviewed the last five chapters and made many helpful suggestions. Larry Madeo of the University of Georgia did an excellent job of preparing the testbank and Wendy Ceccucci of Quinnipiac University created the Instructor's Manual. Both also provided me with many corrections to the text, for which I am very grateful.

And last, but far from least, I want to thank my wife, Carolyn, for supporting me throughout this entire effort including the end-stages where I had to spend virtually all of my time on it.

The following individuals reviewed some part of this project and provided many helpful comments:

Teri Butler	Colorado State University
Wendy Ceccucci	Quinnipiac University
Judith Colick	ITT Technical Institute
Tim Jenkins	ITT Technical Institute
Larry Madeo	University of Georgia
Larry Press	CSU-Dominguez Hills
Craig Piercy	University of Georgia
Meenu Singh	Texas Christian University
Suzanne Thompson	Tulsa Community College
Tianle Tong	
Lynn Walker	Jefferson College

Patrick G. McKeown
Athens, GA

TO THE STUDENT

Typically, the Preface to a text book is aimed at the instructor and you may not have read it. For that reason, this *To the Student* page is included to help you make the most of the instructional system that includes this textbook and the associated Web site that are designed to help you learn to program with VB .NET. The key idea behind this system is that the only way to learn how to write computer programs in VB .NET (or for that matter, any computer language) is to "get your hands dirty" by actually writing programs. If you use this system, I think you will easily be able to learn to program and to create fairly sophisticated computer applications in VB .NET.

THE TEXTBOOK

In the textbook, each chapter contains a discussion of one or more programming concepts and the way in which they are handled in VB .NET. There one or more complete examples in each chapter including a continuing example. The chapter sections provide the logic and VB .NET statements for solutions to the examples, give specific VB .NET code to create an application, and then request you to create the same application:

If you read the text discussions of the new concepts which include numerous VB Code Tables and screen captures and then follow the *Step-by-Step Instructions*, you will have a working application that solves the problem posed in each example. To make this work, though, you must make the effort to complete the *Step-by-Step Instructions* exercises *on your own*. In fact, you are directed to follow these instructions in the *It's Your Turn!* exercises that follow each section of text. In addition to the *It's Your Turn!* exercises at the end of each section of the book, there are exercises and projects at the end of each chapter which provide you with the opportunity to create applications similar to the one covered in the text.

Your instructor may have chosen to order this textbook with the accompanying software. If they did, a full, working student version of VB .NET 2003 is included. You will be able to install this software on your own personal computer to use in following the *Step-by-Step Instructions* and in completng the *It's Your Turn* exercises as well as the exercises and projects found at the end of the chapter.

THE WEB SITE

A Web site has been developed as an key part of the instructional system and you may access it at:
http://www.wiley.com/college/mckeown
The Web site includes sections for students and instructors. The student section includes the data files you will need to complete many of the *It's Your Turn!* and end-of-chapter exercises. It also includes the solutions to the *It's Your Turn* exercises in a downloadable format so you can check your work or, if you run into problems with a project, determine your error. The solutions to the *It's*

Your Turn! exercises include *all* of the code from the Code Tables presented in the text which you can use to check your work. Caution: don't use these code samples as a replacement for entering the code on your own; doing so may result in your not learning the necessary coding techniques.

TABLE OF CONTENTS

1 AN INTRODUCTION TO PROGRAMMING AND VISUAL BASIC .NET

After reading this chapter, you will able to

1. Understand the importance of information systems in organizations.
2. List and discuss the six computer operations.
3. Discuss the role of computer programs and programming languages in information systems.
4. Understand the concepts of object-oriented programming in Windows and in Visual Basic .NET.
5. List and discuss the steps in developing an application in Visual Basic .NET.

INFORMATION SYSTEMS IN BUSINESS

Many organizations are finding that, in order to survive, they must be able to collect and process data efficiently and make the resulting information on their operations available to their employees. Successful organizations have found that the key to making this information available is having an effective information system that will carry out these operations. An **information system** is *the combination of technology (computers) and people that enables an organization to collect data, store them, and transform them into information.* To understand the concept of an information system fully, you need to understand the difference between data and information. **Data** are *raw facts that are collected and stored by the information system.* Data can be in the form of numbers, letters of the alphabet, images, sound clips, or even video clips. You are undoubtedly very familiar with many types of data, including names, dates, prices, and credit card numbers. By themselves, data are not very meaningful; however, when data are converted by the information system into **information**, the end result is meaningful. Once again, you are familiar with many forms of information, including written reports, lists, tables, and graphs. Information is what organizational employees use in their work.

To convert or process data into information electronically, software must direct the operations of the computer's operations. **Software** is composed of one or more lists of instructions called **programs**, and *the process of creating* *these lists of instructions* is termed **programming**. Although computer hardware can be mass-produced on assembly lines like other consumer goods, software must be developed through the logical and creative capabilities of humans. Individuals or groups of individuals working together must develop the instructions that direct the operations of every computer in use today. The same is true whether the instructions are for the computer that controls your car's fuel system, the computer that controls the space shuttle, or the computer that prints the checks for the business at which you work.

Programming in Information Systems

Although a great deal of programming work goes on at large software firms like Microsoft or Adobe Systems, much more programming is done at companies that produce non-software goods and services. You may think that these companies could buy off-the-shelf software like word processors or spreadsheets to run their business; however, in most cases companies must develop their own software to meet their particular needs. In fact, it has been said that the "software needed to be competitively different is generally not available from off-the-shelf packages" and that "building . . . systems for unique [competitive] capability is often the single most important activity for an . . . organization."[1] This means that no matter how good off-the-shelf software becomes, there is always going to be demand for programmers to work in businesses and not-for-profit organizations. In fact, the demand for information systems employees is accelerating, and the future is very bright for persons trained in this field.

Programming is actually part of a much larger process known as **systems development.** This process involves a large-scale effort to either create an entirely new information system or to update (maintain) an existing information system. In either case, systems development involves four primary steps: planning, analysis, design, and implementation. In the planning stage, it is decided what must be done to solve a problem or meet a need—create a new system, update an old one, or even purchase a system from an outside source. Once it has been decided what must be done, the next step is to analyze the system that will be created. This may involve analyzing an existing system or analyzing the system that must created. Once the analysis step is completed, the next step is to design the new or updated system. This design must be complete and detailed and leave nothing to chance or guesswork. Once the design is completed, the system can be implemented. It is in the implementation step that programming comes in. Programmers work with the results of the design step to create a series of computer programs that, together, will work as the needed information system. In many cases, the programmers will know little or nothing about the overall problem and must depend completely on the results of the design step. However, without the programming process, the information system will never be built or updated. Visual Basic .NET (VB .NET) and the entire Microsoft .NET framework are aimed at making this process possible.

---

1. Martin, James, *Cybercorp: The New Business Revolution,* New York: AMACOM Books, p. 104

Given that programming is such an important part of building and maintaining information systems for organizations of all sizes, it is easy to see why individuals interested in working in the field of information systems must have some knowledge of computer programming. This book is written with the purpose of helping you become capable of writing computer programs that will solve business-related problems.

COMPUTER OPERATIONS

Before we start our discussion of creating computer programs, it is useful to understand the six operations that all computers can carry out to process data into information. Understanding these operations will help you when you start writing programs. These operations are the same regardless of whether we are discussing multi-user mainframe computers that handle large-scale processing, such as preparing the end-of-term grade rolls or processing the university payroll, or small personal computers that are used today by a large proportion of office workers in the United States and other developed countries. The six operations that a computer can perform are

1. Input data
2. Store data in internal memory
3. Perform arithmetic on data
4. Compare two values and select one of two alternative actions
5. Repeat a group of actions any number of times
6. Output the results of processing

Let's now discuss each of these operations in a little more detail.

Input Data: For a computer to be able to transform data into information, it must first be able to accept input of the data. Data are typically input from a keyboard or mouse, but they can also come from other sources, such as a barcode reader like those used at checkout terminals. Input can also come from some type of sensor or from a data file on a computer disk. For example, with a word processor, the letters of the alphabet, numbers, and punctuation symbols are the data that are processed by the computer. New documents are created by entering data from the keyboard, whereas existing documents are loaded from your hard drive or floppy disk.

Store data in memory: Once data have been input, they are stored in internal memory. Each memory location holding a piece of data is assigned a name, which is used by the instructions to perform the processing. Since the values in a memory location can change as the process occurs, the memory locations are called **variables**. The current balance in your checking account would typically be stored in a single memory location and be identified by a variable name.

The instructions for processing this data are also stored in memory. In the earliest days of computing, the instructions (program) were not stored in memory and had to be entered one at a time to process the data. When the **stored program** concept was developed by John von Neumann, it was a tremendous breakthrough. With a stored program, the instructions can be executed as fast as they can be retrieved from memory to convert the data into usable information.

Perform arithmetic on data: Once the data and instructions have been input and stored, arithmetic operations can be performed on the variables representing the data to process them into information. This includes addition, subtraction, multiplication, division, and raising to a power. The processing chip of the computer carries out these operations by retrieving the data from memory and then performing the processing based on instructions from the programmer.

You may ask how a word processor or computer game works if all the computer can do is perform arithmetic. The answer is that everything in a computer—numbers, letters, graphics, and so on—is represented by numbers, and all processing is handled through some type of arithmetic operation.

Compare two values and select one of two alternative actions: To do anything other than the simplest processing, a computer must be able to choose between two sets of instructions to execute. It does this by comparing the contents of two memory locations and, based on the result of that comparison, executing one of two groups of instructions. For example, when you carry out the spell-checking operation, the computer is checking each word to determine if it matches a word in the computer's dictionary. Based on the result of this comparison, the word is accepted or flagged for you to consider changing.

Repeat a group of actions any number of times: Although you *could* carry out all of the above operations with a typewriter or handheld calculator, repeating actions is something the computer does better than any person or any other type of machine. Because a computer never tires or becomes bored, it can be instructed to repeat some action as many times as needed without fear of an error occurring from the constant repetition. The capability of a computer to repeat an operation is what most clearly sets it apart from all other machines. The spell-checking operation mentioned above is an example of a repeated action: The program repeatedly checks words until it comes to the end of the document.

Output the results of processing: Once the processing has been completed and the required information generated, to be of any use the information must be output. Output of processed information can take many forms: displayed on a monitor, printed on papers, files stored on disk, as instructions to a machine, and so on. Output is accomplished by retrieving information from a memory location and sending it to the output device. For example, when you complete your work with a word processor, the resulting information is displayed on your monitor, and you probably will also print it for distribution to others.

These six operations are depicted in Figure 1-1, where each operation is numbered.

PROGRAMS AND PROGRAMMING

To carry out any of the six operations just discussed, you must be able to provide instructions to the computer in the form of a program. The most important thing about programming is that it is a form of *problem solving,* and the objective is to develop the step-by-step process—the logic—that will solve the problem. Step-by-step logic of this type is referred to as an algorithm. You have worked with algorithms before; a set of directions to a party

FIGURE 1-1. Six computer operations

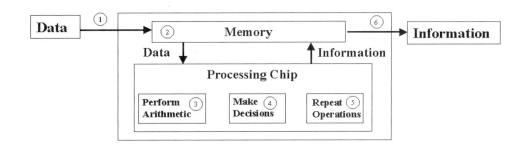

is an algorithm, as is a recipe to make spaghetti sauce or to bake a cake. For a computer program, you must develop a set of instructions for solving a problem using *only* the six operations of a computer. This is the most difficult part of programming.

Many times a program fails to work because the programmer attempts to write the program before developing the correct algorithm for solving the problem. Only after you have developed the logic of the solution can you consider actually writing the instructions for the computer.

Control Structures

Although it can be quite daunting to create the logic to solve a problem, remember that all computer programs can be created with only three types of logic or, as they are known in programming, **control structures.** The three control structures are sequence, decision, and repetition.

The **sequence control structure** includes the input, storage, arithmetic, and output computer operations discussed earlier. It is so called because all four of these operations can be performed without any need to make a decision or repeat an operation. At its simplest, *sequence* means one program instruction follows another in order. Of course, it is up to the programmer to determine the proper sequence order for the instructions.

The **decision control structure** is the same as the decision-making computer operation discussed earlier. It enables the programmer to control the flow of operations by having the user or data determine which operation is to be performed next.

Finally, the **repetition control structure** is used to repeat one or more operations. The number of repetitions depends on the user or the data, but the programmer must include a way to terminate the repetition process.

All algorithms are created using the six operations of a computer within combinations of these three control structures. Once you learn how to create the logic for these three control structures, you will find that writing meaningful and useful programs is a matter of combining the structures to create more complex logic.

Programming Languages

Once you have developed the logic for solving the problem, you can think about writing the actual instructions that the computer will use in implementing the logic. Computer programs must be written in one of various **programming languages** such as VB .NET. These languages use a restricted vocabulary and a very structured syntax that the computer can understand. Although a great deal of research is ongoing to create computers that can accept instructions using conversational English, currently no computers meet this criterion. So, until computers like C-3PO and R2-D2, popularized in the *Star Wars* movies, are created, we are stuck with using these programming languages.

Within the computer, the data and instructions are represented in the binary number system as a series of zeros and ones. This form of representation is used because the computer's only two electrical states—on and off—correspond to 1 and 0. Using a string of transistors that act as switches, the computer can represent a number, character, or instruction as a series of on-off states. All processing is carried out in the binary number system. For example, the computer carries out all arithmetic in binary instead of in the decimal number system that humans use.

The binary form of the instructions is called **machine language,** because this is the language that computers use to carry out their operations. An example of the machine language statements necessary to sum the digits 1 to 100 for a computer using an Intel CPU chip is shown in Figure 1-2.

FIGURE 1-2.
Machine language program

Machine Language Command	Explanation
`10111000 00000000 00000000`	Set Total Value to 0
`10111001 00000000 01100100`	Set Current Value to 100
`00000001 11001000`	Add Current Value to Total Value
`01001001`	Subtract 1 from Current Value
`01110101 11111011`	If Current Value is not 0, repeat

Programming the very first computers, which had to be done in binary, was very difficult and time-consuming. Now, we have English-like programming languages, such as VB .NET, that are referred to as **high-level languages** because they are closer to the level of the human programmer than to the level of the machine. Before the statements in a high-level program can be used to direct the actions of a computer, they must be translated into machine language. Files on a Windows-based computer with an .exe file extension are machine-language programs that have been translated from some high-level language. They can be executed with no translation because they are already in a binary form. Until recently, this was a direct translation from high-level language to machine language by a software program known as a compiler or interpreter, depending on whether the code was translated as a unit or line by line as shown in Figure 1-3.

The problem with this approach is that different types of computers have different machine languages so a program would have to be translated differently for an Apple computer than for a Windows computer. To make it possible for the same program to run on all types of machines, the concept of the **just-in-time (JIT) compiler** was developed. With this approach, the high-level program is translated or compiled into an intermediate form that is machine-independent. The two approaches to this use of a JIT compiler are Java from Sun Microsystems and the .NET framework from Microsoft, of which VB .NET is a part. In the case of Java, the intermediate form is called **bytecode,** and for the .NET framework, it is called **Microsoft Intermediate Language (MSIL).** Once converted, a VB .NET program is compiled into

FIGURE 1-3. Direct translation process

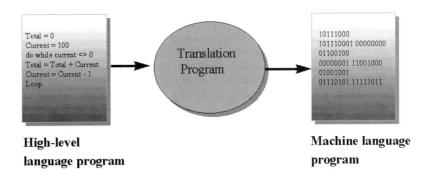

High-level language program

Machine language program

MSIL; the JIT compiler on any computer can convert it into machine language for that particular machine. This process is shown in Figure 1-4 for MSIL.

FIGURE 1-4. Use of MSIL and JIT compilers

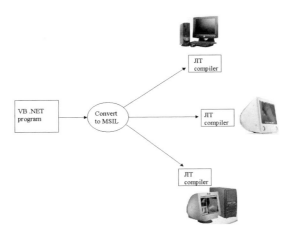

Whereas the Java approach only works for programs written in Java, the .NET framework approach works for all languages that have been revised to work under that framework. At this time, these include VB .NET, C# (pronounced "c-sharp") .NET, and C++ (pronounced "c plus plus") .NET. This means that if you are using one of these languages, it can be compiled in MSIL, and combined with other programs in the MSIL, and then sent to the JIT compiler, which for the .NET framework is called the **Common Language Runtime (CLR)**.

PROGRAMMING IN WINDOWS

As you are probably aware, most personal computers today run some form of the Microsoft Windows operating system, such as Windows 95, Windows 98, Windows ME, Windows 2000, or Windows XP. With Windows being the primary operating system for personal computers, learning to program in the Windows environment has become a critical skill for anybody interested in working in information systems. To program in Windows, you first need to understand a little about how Windows works.

To understand the workings of Windows, you need to understand three key concepts: windows, events, and messages. A **window** is any rectangular region on the screen with its own boundaries. All components run in their own windows. For example, when you use your word processor, a document window displays the text you are entering and editing. When you retrieve a file, you do this from a dialog box that is a window. Similarly, when an error message is displayed, this is done in a window. Finally, the menu bar and all of the icons or buttons on the toolbar across the top or side of your screen are also windows. Figure 1-5 shows a Windows XP screen with several types of windows displayed.

FIGURE 1-5.
Windows in
Windows XP

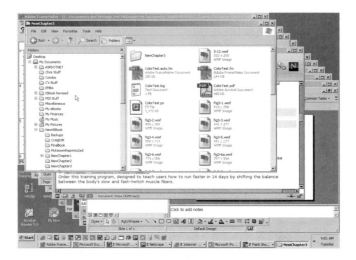

As a part of its operations, the Windows operating system is constantly monitoring all of the windows on the screen for signs of activity termed **events**. An event can be a mouse click or double-click, a keypress, or simply a change in a window caused by an entry of text in it.

When an event occurs, the corresponding window sends a **message** to the operating system, which processes the message and then broadcasts it to other windows. When they receive a message, the other windows take actions based on their own set of instructions. Programming in Windows requires that you learn how to work with windows, events, and messages. For this reason, programming in Windows is usually termed **event-driven programming,** because all actions are driven by events. Although this may sound complicated, languages like VB .NET make it easier to create Windows-based applications that work with Windows by providing you with the necessary tools.

Event-driven programming is quite different from *traditional* approaches to programming where the program itself controls the actions that will take place and the order in which those actions will occur. With traditional programs, execution of the program starts with the first instruction and continues through the remaining instructions, making decisions as to which instructions will be executed depending on the data that are input. The main program may use smaller subprograms to handle parts of the processing. This type of programming is referred to as **procedural programming**, and it works very well for such activities as processing a large number of grades at the end of the term or printing payroll checks at the end of the pay period. However, with the move toward widespread use of graphical user interfaces (GUI), the trend is toward using event-driven programming.

The VB .NET Language

As discussed above, VB .NET is a computer language that has been developed to help you create programs that will work with the Windows operating system. It is an event-driven language that does not follow a predefined sequence of instructions; it responds to events to execute different sets of instructions depending on which event occurs. The order in which events—such as mouse clicks, keystrokes, or even other sets of instructions—occur controls the order of events in VB .NET and other event-driven languages. For that reason, an event-driven program can execute differently each time it is run, depending on what events occur.

In addition to being event-driven, VB .NET is an **object-oriented (OO) language**. It uses software objects that can respond to events. This is an important improvement over previous versions of Visual Basic, which were *almost* object-oriented since they failed to have all of the characteristics of a true OO language. What distinguishes OO programming from earlier languages is that objects combine programming instructions or **code** with data. Previous attempts to structure programs in such a way that large problems could be broken down into smaller problems separated the code from the data. The problem with this approach is that if the data change, then the code may not work with the new data. With OO programming, the combination of code and data avoids this problem. For example, instead of writing code to deal with customers and then using this code with different customer data for each customer, we combine the code and data into an **object** for each customer. The objects for multiple customers are very similar with the exception of the data component, so you can use them in similar ways.

A Primer to object-oriented Programming

Chapter 8 of this book will deal with objects and OO programming in detail, so we will just introduce you to some of the concepts of object orientation. First, consider the fact that each of the windows discussed above as a part of the Windows operating system is an object, as are a wide variety of other shapes, including buttons, click boxes, menus, and so on. There are also many objects in Windows that are unseen, because they are pure computer code, but have the same characteristics as visual objects. The beauty of VB .NET is that, unlike many other OO languages, you do not have to know how to create objects to use them. VB .NET automatically creates for you, the programmer, new instances of many objects from a wide variety of built-in templates.

To understand OO programming, we need to understand a number of concepts and terminology. First, in order to create an object, you must first create a **class**, that is, a *template with data and procedures from which objects are created*. One way of looking at a class is to think of it as the *cookie cutter* and the actual object as the resulting *cookie*.[2] All of the actual work in creating an object is accomplished in creating the class; an object is

---

2. Cornell, Gary, *Visual Basic 5 from the Ground Up* (Berkeley: Osborne/McGraw-Hill, 1997), p. 376.

created by defining it to be an **instance** of a class. Objects have two key concepts: properties and methods. **Properties** of objects are simply the attributes associated with the object, such as their name, color, and so on. **Methods** are a set of predefined activities that an object can carry out. For example, consider the customer objects mentioned earlier; they are instances of a class called *DVDCustomer,* which will have the properties and methods shown in Figure 1-6. Note that the *DVDCustomer* class has *Name, Address, PhoneNumber,* and *LateFees.* The class also has the *Add* and *Delete* methods to add and delete customers. Note that we have also created an object named *DVDCustomer* for a DVD rental store and an instance of this object for *Ashley Hyatt* that contains properties particular to her.

FIGURE 1-6.
Customer class, object, and instance

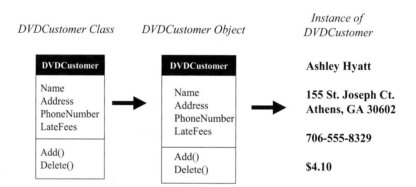

Three key characteristics of OO programming are encapsulation, inheritance, and polymorphism. **Encapsulation** refers to a key concept: It should never be possible to work with variables in an object directly; they must be addressed through the object's properties and methods. This implies a *black-box* view of an object, in which the programmer does not need to know what is going on inside the object, but only needs to know how to work with the object's methods and properties. For example, you would not be able to change the values of the *DVDCustomer* object without going through the properties of the object; you can not get into the object except through the properties.

The second key concept in OO programming, **inheritance**, refers to the capability to create *child* classes that descend from a *parent* class. This capability makes it easier to build new child classes by having them inherit properties and methods from a parent class. For example, the class *DVDCustomer* inherits the properties and methods from a more general *Customer* class, which itself inherits properties and methods from the even more general *Person* class.

Finally, **polymorphism** is related to inheritance in that a child class can inherit all of the characteristics and capabilities of the parent class but then add or modify some of them so the child class is different from the parent class. For example, the *DVDCustomer* class inherits the *Name, Address,* and *PhoneNumber* from the *Customer* class and then adds the *LateFees* property that is particular to the *DVDCustomer.*

As another example of objects, consider a soccer ball. The *SoccerBall* class inherits properties and methods from the more general *Ball* class. These properties include diameter, weight, color, and so on. Methods for the soccer ball include rolling and bouncing. If we apply the KICK event to the soccer ball, then, depending on its diameter and weight, it will roll and bounce a certain distance. It is important to note that the instructions for a method are already a part of VB .NET, but the programmer must write the instructions to tell the object how to respond to an event.

Objects are combined with properties or methods by a period or dot, and objects are combined with events by an underline. Continuing the soccer ball example, we might have a property definition through the following statement:

Ball.Color = White

which defines the color of the ball.

Similarly, the roll method of the soccer ball is referenced by the dot property as shown below:

Ball.Roll

Finally, the Kick event is applied to the soccer ball as follows, causing it to roll:

Ball_Kick

Working with VB .NET involves combining objects with the instructions on how each object should respond to a given event. For example, you might have a button for which the instructions are to display a message; instructions for another button might be to exit the program or, as it is called in VB .NET, the *solution*. These instructions are referred to as the code for the program. The code for VB .NET is written in a much-updated form of one of the oldest computer languages around—Basic, which was first used in 1960. The version of Basic used in VB .NET has been improved in many ways, but it retains one of the key advantages of the original language compared to other languages: It is very easy to use and understand.

PROGRAMMING IN VB .NET

Creating an application using an OO programming language such as VB .NET is much easier than working with a traditional programming language. Instead of having to develop the logic for the entire program as you would with a procedural language, you can divide up the program logic into small, easily handled parts by working with objects and events. For each object, you determine the events that you want the object to respond to and then develop code to have the object provide the desired response. All of the necessary messages between objects in Windows are handled by VB .NET, thereby significantly reducing the work you must do to create an application.

The manner in which you create a VB .NET project is also different from traditional programming. Instead of having to create an entire program before testing any part of it, with VB .NET you can use **interactive development** to create an object, write the code for it, and test it before going onto other objects. For example, assume a store named Vintage DVDs that rents only "old" movies on DVD has asked you to create a VB .NET project that calculates taxes on a DVD rental and sums the taxes and price to compute the amount due. With VB .NET, you can create the objects and code to calculate the taxes and amount due and test them to ensure their correctness, before going on to the rest of the project.

Although creating an application in VB .NET is easier than working with a procedural language, you still need to follow a series of steps to ensure correctness and completeness of the finished product.

1. Define the problem
2. Create an interface.
3. Develop logic for action objects.
4. Write and test code for action objects.
5. Test the overall project.
6. Document the project in writing.

It should be noted that it may be necessary to repeat or iterate through these steps to arrive at an acceptable final solution to the original problem.

In the next sections, we will discuss each of these steps and apply them to a part of the situation just mentioned, that is, creating an application to calculate the taxes and amount due on a DVD rental. We will return to this example and expand it in subsequent chapters.

Step One: Define the Problem

Before we can hope to develop any computer application, it is absolutely necessary to clearly define our objective, that is, the problem to be solved. Only then can we begin to develop the correct logic to solve the problem and incorporate that logic into a computer application. Ensuring that the correct problem is being solved requires careful study of why a problem exists. Maybe an organization is currently handling some repetitive process manually and wants to use a computer to automate it. Or maybe management has a complicated mathematical or financial problem that cannot be solved by hand. Or maybe a situation has occurred or will occur that cannot be handled by an existing program.

The problem identification step should include identification of the data to be *input* to the program and the desired results to be *output* from the program. Often these two items will be specified by a person or an agency other than the programmer. Much grief can be avoided if these input and output requirements are incorporated into the programmer's thinking at this early stage of program development. Unclear thinking at this stage may cause the programmer to write a program that does not correctly solve the problem at hand, or a program that correctly solves the wrong problem, or a combination of both! Therefore the programmer *must* spend as much time as is necessary to truly identify and understand the problem.

Because VB .NET is a *visual* language, a good way to understand what is required to solve the problem is to sketch the interface, showing the various objects that will be part of the project. Not only does this help you understand the problem, it is also a good way for you to communicate your understanding to other people. As a part of this sketch, you should denote the input and output objects and the objects for which code is needed to respond to events, the so-called **action objects.** A sketch of the proposed solution for the DVD rental problem is shown in Figure 1-7.

In looking at the solution, you will see one input—the price of the DVD—and two outputs—the taxes and the amount due. There are also two action objects—a calculation button and an exit button. If there are multiple forms, they should all be sketched with input, output, and action objects denoted as in Figure 1-7.

FIGURE 1-7. Sketch of interface for Vintage DVDs

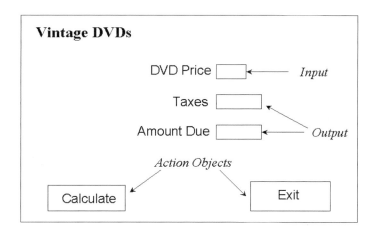

Step Two: Create an Interface

Once you have defined the problem and, using a sketch of the interface, have decided on the objects that are necessary for your project, you are ready to create the interface. Creating the interface with VB .NET is quite easy: You select objects from those available and place them on the form. This process should follow the sketch done earlier. Although you have not yet been introduced to the wide variety of objects available for creating VB .NET projects, we can work on the logic for the Vintage DVDs problem with just four types of objects: the form, buttons for action, textboxes for input and output, and labels for descriptors. The interface in VB .NET is shown in Figure 1-8.

FIGURE 1-8. Interface for Vintage DVDs

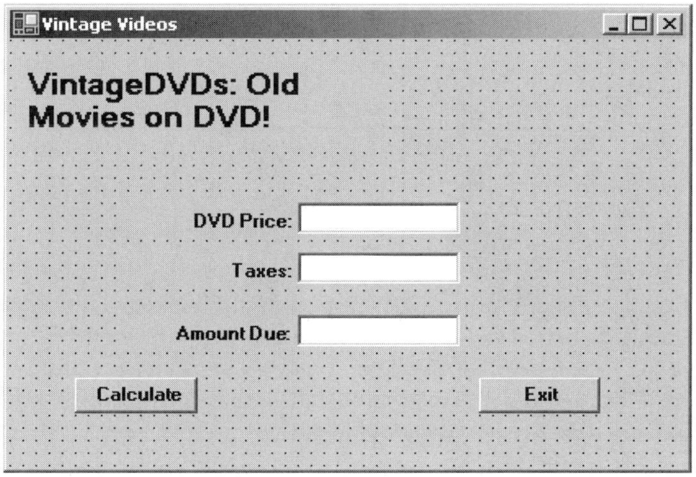

Step Three: Develop Logic for Action Objects

Once the problem has been clearly identified and the interface created, the next step is to develop the logic for the action objects in the interface. This is the step in the development process where you have to think about what each action object must do in response to an event. No matter how good your interface, if you don't develop the appropriate logic for the action objects, you will have great difficulty creating a project that solves the problem defined earlier.

To help with this logical development for the action objects, there are two useful tools for designing programming applications: IPO tables and pseudocode. **IPO** (input/processing/output) **tables** show the inputs to an object, the required outputs for that object, and the processing that is necessary to convert the inputs into the desired outputs. Once you have an IPO table for an object, you can write a pseudocode procedure to complete the logic development step.

Writing **pseudocode** involves writing the code for the object in structured English rather than in a computer language. Once you have developed an IPO table and the pseudocode for each object, it is a very easy step to write a **procedure** in VB .NET that will carry out the necessary processing.

IPO Table

Let's begin by developing the logic for the Calculate button using an IPO table. The IPO table for the Calculate button has as input the price of a DVD. The processing involves the calculation necessary to compute the desired output: the amount of the sale. As mentioned earlier, in many cases the program designer will have no control over the input and output. They will be specified by somebody else—either the person for whom the application is being developed or, if you are a member of a team and are working on one part of the overall application, the overall design. Once you are given the specified input and output, your job is to determine the processing necessary to convert the inputs into desired outputs. Figure 1-9 shows the IPO table for the calculation button. IPO tables are needed for all objects that involve input, output, and processing. We won't do one for the Exit button since it simply terminates the project.

FIGURE 1-9. IPO Table for Calculate button

Input	Processing	Output
Video price	Taxes = 0.07 x Price Amount due = Price + Taxes	Taxes Amount due

Pseudocode

Once you have developed the IPO tables for each action object, you should then develop a pseudocode procedure for each one. Pseudocode is useful for two reasons. First, you can write the procedure for the object in English without worrying about the special syntax and grammar of a computer language. Second, pseudocode provides a relatively direct link between the IPO table and the computer code for the object, since you use English to write instructions that can then be converted into program instructions. Often, this conversion from pseudocode statement to computer language instruction is virtually line for line.

There are no set rules for writing pseudocode; it should be a personalized method for going from the IPO table to the computer program. The pseudocode should be a set of clearly defined steps that enables a reader to see the next step to be taken under any possible circumstance. Also, the language and syntax should be consistent so that the programmer will be able to understand his or her own pseudocode at a later time. As an example of pseudocode, assume a program is needed to compare two values, Salary and Commission, and to output the smaller of the two. The pseudocode for this example is shown on the next page.

In this pseudocode, it is easy to follow the procedure. Note that parts of it are indented to make it easier to follow the logic. The important point to remember about pseudocode is that it expresses the logic for the action object to the programmer in the same way that a computer language expresses it to the computer. In this way, pseudocode is like a personalized programming language.

```
Begin procedure
    Input Salary and Commission
    If Salary < Commission then
        Output Salary
    Else
        Output Commission
    End Decision
End procedure
```

Now let's write a pseudocode procedure for the Vintage DVDs Calculate object. Note that the pseudocode program matches the IPO table shown in Figure 1-9.

```
Begin procedure
    Input DVD Price
    Taxes = 0.07 × DVD Price
    Amount Due = DVD Price + Taxes
    Output Taxes and Amount Due
End procedure
```

We have only one object in our small example for which an IPO table and pseudocode are needed, however, in most situations you will have numerous objects for which you will need to develop the logic using these tools.

Step Four: Write and Test Code for Action Objects

Once you have created the VB .NET interface and developed the logic for the action objects using IPO tables and pseudocode, you must write procedures in VB .NET for each action object. This code should provide instructions to the computer to carry out one or more of the six operations listed earlier—that is, input data, store data in internal memory, perform arithmetic on data, compare two values and select one of two alternative actions, repeat a group of actions any number of times, and output the results of processing. Although creating the interface is important, writing the code is the essence of developing an application.

Since you have not yet been introduced to the rules for writing code in VB .NET for the various objects, we will defer a full discussion of this step until Chapter 3 and beyond. However, you should be able to see the similarity between the VB .NET event procedure displayed in VB Code Box 1-1 and the pseudocode version shown earlier. The differences are due to the way VB .NET handles input and output. Input is from the Text property of the first textbox, named txtDVDPrice. Output goes to the Text property of the two textboxes named txtTaxes and txtAmountDue. There are also statements that begin with the word Dim, to declare the variables, and comment statements that begin with an apostrophe (').

Once you have written the code for an action object, the second part of this step is to test that object and correct any errors; don't wait until the entire project is completed. Use the interactive capabilities of VB .NET to test the code of each and every object as it is written. This process is referred to as **debugging**—trying to remove all of the errors or **"bugs."**

| CODE BOX 1-1. VB .NET computation of Taxes and Amount Due | ```Private Sub btnCalc_Click(ByVal sender As System.Object, _ByVal e As System.EventArgs) Handles btnCalc.Click   Const sngTaxRate As Single = 0.07 'Use local tax rate   Dim decPrice As Decimal, decAmountDue As Decimal   Dim decTaxes As Decimal   decPrice = CDec(txtDVDPrice.Text)   decTaxes = decPrice * sngTaxRate 'Compute taxes   decAmountDue = decPrice + decTaxes 'Compute amount due   txtTaxes.Text = CStr(decTaxes)   txtAmountDue.Text = CStr(decAmountDue)   txtDVDPrice.Text = CStr(decPrice)End Sub``` |

Because VB .NET automatically checks each line of the code of an object for syntax or vocabulary errors, the debugging process is much easier than in other languages. However, even if all the syntax and vocabulary are correct, the code for an object still may be incorrect—either in the manner in which it carries out the logic or in the logic itself. The best way to find and correct such errors is to use **test data** for which the results are known in advance. If the results for the object do not agree with the results from the hand calculations, an error exists, either in the logic or in the hand calculations. After the hand calculations have been verified, the logic must be checked. For example, if the results of the *Calculate* button came out different from what was expected, then we would need to look for a problem in the data or the logic.

In the case of the *Calculate* button, we want to determine if the code shown in VB Code Box 1-1 will actually compute and output to the textboxes the *correct* taxes and amount due for the DVD price entered in the first textbox. Figure 1-10 shows the result of clicking the Calculate button for a DVD with a price of $1.99. Note that the results, while correct, are not *exactly* what you might expect. Instead of rounded values of $.14 for the taxes and $2.13 for the amount due, the answers are the exact values of $.1393 and $2.1293. This is because we have not *formatted* the answers as dollar and cents. This will be done when we revisit this problem in Chapter 3.

Although the answers for this set of test data are correct, this does not mean it will work for all test data. Testing requires that a wide variety of test data be used to assure that the code for the object works under all circumstances.

Since the *Calculate* button appears to work, we can now write the code for the *Exit* button, which consists of one instruction: End . If this command also works, then we are ready to move on to the next step in the application development process: testing the overall project.

FIGURE 1-10.
Testing the
Calculate button

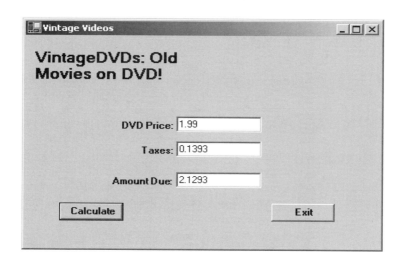

*Step Five: Test the
Overall Project*

Once you have tested the code for each action object individually, the next step is to test the overall project and correct any errors that may still exist or that may be the result of incorrect communication between objects. At this stage it is necessary to determine whether the results obtained from the project meet the objectives outlined in the Problem Definition step. If the project does not meet the final user's needs, then the developer must analyze the results and the objectives to find out where they diverge. After the analysis, the developer should trace through the program development procedure and correct the algorithm, IPO tables, pseudocode, and final code for one or more objects to find the cause of the difference between the objectives and the final project.

*Step Six: Document
the Project in Writing*

An important part of writing any computer software is the documentation of the software. **Documentation** can be defined as *the written descriptions of the software that aid users and other programmers*. It includes both internal descriptions of the code instructions and external descriptions and instructions. Documentation helps users by providing instructions and suggestions on using the software. Documentation helps other programmers who may need to make changes or correct the programs.

Internal documentation usually includes *comments* within the program that are intermingled with the program statements to explain the purpose and logic of the program elements. In VB Code Box 1-1, the statements beginning with an apostrophe (') are examples of internal documentation. This type of documentation is essential to the maintenance of software, especially by someone other than the original programmer. By being able to read the original programmer's purpose for a part of a program or a program statement, a different programmer can make any needed corrections or revisions. Without internal documentation, it can be extremely difficult for anyone to understand the purpose of parts of the program. And, if a programmer is unclear about what's going on in the program, making needed changes will be very difficult. In this text, because we will be explaining the code in detail, we do not include the level of internal documentation that *should* be found in the projects you create both here and in your work.

> **TIP:** Although internal documentation is shown as Step 6 of the program development process, it is more easily carried out if it is done *during* the development process rather than at the end.

Written documentation includes books, manuals, and pamphlets that give instructions on using the software and also discuss the objectives and logic of the software. The documentation should include a user's guide and programmer documentation. The *user's guide* provides complete instructions on accessing the software, entering data, interpreting output, and understanding error messages. The *programmer documentation* should include various descriptive documents that allow for maintenance of the software. These may include pseudocode of sections of the program, a listing of the program, and a description of required input values and the resulting output.

Final Comments on the Programming Process

Creating applications in a language like VB .NET is easy and fun. However, there is one caveat to this statement: You still must be able to develop the logic for the action objects and write the code to make them respond appropriately to events. In this text, we will spend the first five chapters concentrating on two things: showing you how to create a fairly simple interface and discussing the key elements involved in writing code. Although creating the interface can be very interesting, you should not lose sight of the overall goal, which is to produce applications that respond to events in an appropriate manner. The only way to make this happen is to be able to write code that works!

> **TIP:** No matter how good your interface looks, if the code does not work, the application will fail. Helping you create code that works is the purpose of this book.

SUMMARY

At the beginning of the chapter, we said you would be able to do a number of things after reading it. Let's review those things here:

1. **Understand the importance of information systems in organizations.** Developing applications for information systems in organizations is the key job of information technology departments. Although off-the-shelf software is of great use to individuals and organizations, in many cases organizations are finding that they must develop their own software to be competitive in today's world.

2. **List and discuss the six computer operations.** The six operations that all computers can carry out are

1. *Input data* that is then converted into information and output. Input can consist of numbers, text, or even instructions.

2. *Store data in internal memory* for future processing. The data must be stored here so the processing chip can find it and carry out necessary transformations.

3. *Perform arithmetic on data* to convert it into information. Although it may appear that computers can work with text and graphics, in actuality, all they can do is add and compare. However, by sophisticated means, it is possible to manipulate text and graphics by these two operations.

4. *Compare two values and select one of two alternative actions* to make a decision. Without decisions, computing would be very boring since only one sequence of instructions could be carried out. With decisions made by comparing two values, a wide variety of sequences can be followed.

5. *Repeat a group of actions any number of times* to carry out the most sophisticated processing operations. The ability to repeat is what really sets a computer apart from a handheld calculator and what enables it to carry out many of the more complex operations we generally associate with computing.

6. *Output the results of processing* so the user can see the result of the input and processing. Output can be displayed on a monitor, printed to paper, stored as files, or sent as instructions to a machine.

3. **Discuss the role of computer programs and programming in information systems.** All information systems are a combination of people, hardware, and software; their purpose is to collect data, store them, and transform them into information. To convert or process data into information electronically, software must direct the operations of the computer's operations. Software is composed of one or more lists of instructions called programs, and the process of creating these lists of instructions is termed programming. Computer languages can be classified as high-level languages and machine languages. A high-level language uses English-like commands, whereas machine language uses binary instructions that the computer can understand. A high-level language must be translated into machine language before the computer can use it. Most older languages used a direct translation to compile high-level languages into machine language, but the .NET languages use a just-in-time (JIT) compiler. In this process, the high-level language like VB .NET is converted into an intermediate form (MSIL) and then converted into machine language by the JIT compiler on each machine.

4. **Understand the concepts of object-oriented programming in Windows and in VB .NET.** Three key concepts in programming in Windows are windows, events, and messages. On the screen, windows are rectangular regions with boundaries. Signs of activity in the windows are events, and windows send messages when an event occurs. Programming in Windows is known as event-driven programming as compared to older forms of programming, which are procedural. VB .NET is an event-driven language that is also object-oriented since it uses software objects to respond

to events. All objects have attributes, which are known as properties, and predefined activities, known as methods, that they can carry out. Programmers can write instructions to tell an object how to respond to an event.

5. List and discuss the steps in developing an VB .NET application.

Next, we discussed the steps in the VB .NET programming process, which are as follows:

1. Define the problem.
2. Create an interface.
3. Develop logic for action objects.
4. Write and test code for action objects.
5. Test the overall project.
6. Document the project in writing.

Defining the problem involves determining the data to be *input* to the program and the desired results to be *output* from the program. Because VB .NET is a *visual* language, a good way to understand what is required to solve the problem is to sketch the interface showing the various objects that will be part of the project. The sketch should include the input and output objects and the objects for which code is needed to respond to events, the so-called action objects.

Creating the interface in VB .NET involves selecting visual objects from those available and placing them on the form. This process should follow the sketch done earlier.

Developing logic for action objects involves thinking what each action object must do in response to an event. Two useful tools for designing programming applications are IPO (input/processing/output) tables and pseudocode. IPO tables show the inputs to an object, the required outputs for that object, and the processing that is necessary to convert the inputs into the desired outputs. Once you have an IPO table for an object, you can write a pseudocode procedure to complete the logic development step. Writing pseudocode involves writing the code for the object in English rather than in a computer language. Once you have developed an IPO table and the pseudocode for each object, it is a very easy step to write a procedure in VB .NET that will carry out the necessary processing.

The next step is to write and test the computer instructions in VB .NET that will carry out the logic for each action object. This is the most important step since the computer code actually implements the necessary logic to solve the problem.

Once the code for each action object has been tested individually, the next step is to test the overall project and correct any errors that may still exist or that may be the result of incorrect communication between objects. At this stage it is necessary to determine whether the results obtained from the project meet the objectives outlined in the Problem Definition step.

The last step in writing any computer software is the documentation. Documentation can be defined as the written descriptions of the software that aid users and other programmers. It includes both internal descriptions of the code instructions and external descriptions and instructions. Documentation helps users by providing instructions and suggestions on using the software. Documentation helps other programmers who may need to make changes or correct the programs.

KEY TERMS

action objects	information	programming languages
algorithm	information system	programs
bugs	interactive development	project
code	interpretation	properties
compilation	IPO (input/processing/output)	pseudocode
control structures	tables	repetition control structure
data	logic	sequence control structure
debugging	machine language	software
decision control structure	message	stored program
documentation	methods	systems development
event-driven programming	object-oriented language	test data
events	procedural programming	variables
graphical user interface (GUI)	procedure	window
high-level language	programming	

EXERCISES

1. Every month you collect your loose change in a jar on your dresser. At the end of the month, you sort and roll the coins and deposit them in your savings account. Describe what you would do using steps that follow the three basic control structures: sequence, decision, and repetition. By following your steps, you should be able to handle one year's worth of coins.

2. Develop a list of properties, methods, and event for each of the following common objects below.

    a. a pet cat

    b. an automobile

    c. a video tape

    d. a document created using word-processing software

    e. a list of customers and their contact information

3. For the following scenarios, describe the inputs, outputs, and processing steps using an IPO table.

    a. You are balancing your checkbook. You have a stack of items that need to be added to the checkbook record, including deposit slips, ATM withdrawal receipts, and copies of checks used. You need to add the items and keep a running total of the balance for each item.

    b. You are planning your schedule for the next school term. Assume that you will successfully complete your current courses.

    c. You have a personal Web page on which you post a news page about your band, sports team, debate club, or other activity. You wish to automate the creation of your news page.

4. Write the steps that you would take to complete the following tasks or problems.

a. You are going from your home to your first class of the day.

b. You are searching on the Internet for a course research topic.

c. You are attempting to best a friend while playing a simple game (tic-tac-toe, hangman, etc.).

5. Write a brief problem description for the programs that correspond to the following sets of IPO tables and pseudocode. What control structures are used in the logic for each set?

a.

Input	Processes	Output
exchange rate amount in dollars	read exchange rate get amount in dollars calculate amount in foreign currency display amount in foreign currency	amount in foreign currency

```
Begin Procedure
      Read exchange rate
      Get amount in US dollars
      Amount in foreign currency = exchange rate × amount in US dollars
      Display amount in foreign currency
End Procedure
```

b.

Input	Processes	Output
tax rate item 1 price item 2 price item 3 price : item *k* price	read tax rate get prices for items purchased calculate subtotal calculate sales tax calculate total price print subtotal, sales tax, and total cost	subtotal sales tax total price

```
Begin Procedure
      Read tax rate
      Repeat
            Get item price
      Until all item prices obtained
      Calculate subtotal = sum of all prices
      Calculate sales tax = subtotal × tax rate
      Calculate total price = subtotal + sales tax
      Print subtotal, sales tax and total price
End Procedure
```

c.

```
Begin Procedure
```

Input	Processes	Output
grade average 1 grade average 2 grade average 3 : grade average k	get each grade average determine letter grade	letter grade 1 letter grade 2 letter grade 3 : letter grade k

```
Repeat
    Get next grade average
    If grade average >= 90
        letter grade = A
    Otherwise if grade average >= 80
        letter grade = B
    Otherwise if grade average >= 70
        letter grade = C
    Otherwise if grade average >= 60
        letter grade = D
    Otherwise
        letter grade = F
    End Decision
    Output letter grade
Until all grades are assigned
End Procedure
```

PROJECTS

1. Assume that a student takes three quizzes and the score for each quiz is input. The output should be the average score on the three quizzes. Sketch the interface for this problem if textboxes will be used for input and output and a Compute button will calculate the average score. Also, create an IPO Table and pseudocode for the Compute button.

2. Chris Patrick works for the Shrub and Turf Lawn Care Company. He is paid a 10 percent commission on the value of lawn care contracts that he sells. Assume that the input includes the number of sales and the price charged for such contracts (assume it is the same for all contracts). Output should include the total value of the sales and Chris's commission on the sales. Sketch the interface for this problem if textboxes are used for input and output. Assume that two buttons are used: one for computing total value of the sales and one for computing Chris's commission. For each button, develop an IPO table and the pseudocode procedure.

3. Acme, Inc., leases automobiles for its salespeople and wishes to create an application that will determine the gas mileage for each type of automobile. Input should include the make of the automobile, the beginning odometer reading, the ending odometer reading, and the gallons of gasoline consumed. Output should include the miles per gallon for the car being tested. Sketch the interface for this problem if textboxes are used for input and output. Assume that a button is used for computing the gas mileage. Develop an IPO table and the pseudocode procedure for this button. [Note: Gas mileage = (Ending odometer reading – Beginning odometer reading)/Gallons used.]

4. Smith and Jones, Inc., wishes to determine the breakeven production volume for a new product. Breakeven volume is defined as the number of units that must be produced and sold for the total cost of production to equal the total revenue. The formula used to calculate the breakeven point is (Fixed cost of production)/(Selling price per unit – Variable cost per unit). The company also wants to know the Total revenue and Total cost values at the breakeven point where:

Total revenue = Selling price × Number produced

Total cost = Fixed cost + (Variable cost × Number produced)

Input for this problem includes the Fixed cost of production, the Unit price, and the Unit cost for the new product. Output should include the Breakeven volume as well as the Total cost and Total revenue at the breakeven point. Sketch the interface for this problem if textboxes are used for input and output. Assume that one button is used for calculation of Breakeven volume and Total revenue/Total cost at this volume. Develop an IPO table and the pseudocode procedure for this button.

5. Cover-Your-Wall, Inc., specializes in selling wallpaper to "do-it-yourselfers." The company would like a computer program to determine the number of rolls needed to cover a room. This calculation depends on the area to be covered. This value is computed for a rectangular room with an eight-foot ceiling using the following formula:

Area = (2 × Length × 8) + (2 × Width × 8) – (Window area) – (Door area)

Then the number of rolls needed is found by:

Number of rolls = (Room area)/(Roll area)

Design a project that will enable customers to enter data about their room and the type of wallpaper they are using and determine the number of rolls needed. Assume that input includes length and width of the room in feet, window area and door area for the room in square feet, and the roll area in square feet for the type of wallpaper being considered. Output should include the room area and the number of rolls needed to cover the room. Sketch the interface for this problem if textboxes are used for input and output. Assume that one button is for computing the room area and for computing the number of rolls needed. Develop IPO tables and the pseudocode procedures for these buttons.

6. The loan officers of LowHomeLoans.com wish to provide a simple tool for computing the maximum loan payment that a borrower can expect to afford. They want to incorporate two "rules of thumb":

1) The maximum monthly payment should not exceed 28% of the borrower's gross monthly income.

2) The maximum monthly payment should not exceed 36% of the borrower's gross monthly income minus monthly debt payments.

Here the monthly payment will include principle, interest, taxes, and insurance. Assume that input includes the gross monthly income and the monthly debt payments. Output should include the maximum monthly payment based on gross income alone and maximum monthly payment based on gross income minus monthly debt. Sketch the interface for this problem using only textboxes, labels and command buttons. Develop an IPO table and the pseudocode procedures for these buttons.

2 USING VB .NET TO CREATE A FIRST PROJECT

LEARNING OBJECTIVES

After reading this chapter, you will be able to

1. Begin using Visual Studio .NET and then VB .NET.
2. Point out and discuss the elements of the Microsoft Development Environment (MDE) used for VB. NET.
3. Discuss the use of the form in creating a VB .NET project.
4. Understand controls and their properties.
5. Discuss the Code window used to write an event handler to generate a message box.
6. List the different types of files that make up a VB .NET project and be able to save an application.
7. Use the various VB .NET help facilities to answer questions about creating a solution.

GETTING STARTED WITH VB .NET

To start VB .NET in Windows, you first need to understand that VB .NET is a part of Microsoft's Visual Studio .NET development environment as are a number of other languages including Visual C++ and Visual C#. All of these languages use the same environment which is called the **Microsoft Development Environment (MDE)**. To start Visual Studio .NET, select the corresponding menu item from the Programs list on the Start Menu. Once you are in Visual Studio .NET, the first thing you will see is a splash screen showing the languages that are available from Visual Studio .NET and then see a **Start Page** like that shown in Figure 2-1.

In this case, the Start Page shows the projects you've worked on most recently in the center of the page and the help facility on the bottom right of the screen. In this case, three example projects are shown, but you will probably not see any since you are just starting work with VB .NET. Below this list are two buttons, one for opening an existing project and one for starting a new project. We will using the latter button in our initial work.

Depending on how your system has been configured, your screen may look slightly different from this one in terms of what is shown on the right. However, it always has the list of recent projects in the center as well as three

FIGURE 2-1. Start page for VB .NET

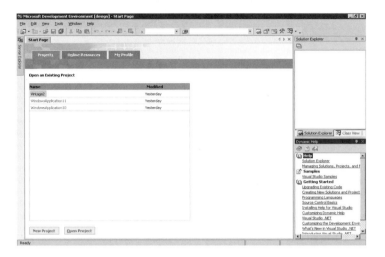

tabs at the top. The first tab, *Projects,* is the current screen. The second tab, *Online Resources,* displays a page with links to Web pages or Internet newsgroups for more information than that provided by the VB .NET Help facility. The third tab, *My Profile,* displays a page on which you can determine parameters for your version of VB .NET. You may actually see this My Profile page instead of the Projects page the first time you use VB .NET. While you could change several of the options on the My Profile page, the only one you really need to change is the **Help Filter** option. Because Visual Studio .NET has a number of languages in it, requesting help on a feature may return information on all of the languages rather than just VB .NET. Using a filter enables you to restrict the help information you receive to just the language you are learning, in this case, VB .NET. For that reason, we suggest you change the Filter option from the default option of No filter to the *Visual Basic* option as shown in Figure 2-2. Doing this will make the help option more useful to you. Once you've have made this change, click on *Projects* tab to return to the Start page.

FIGURE 2-2. Selecting a filter option

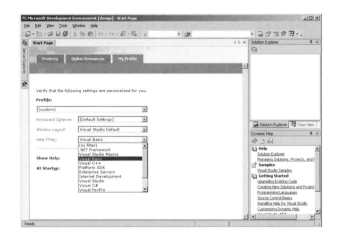

Once you have your Start page configured, you are ready to move on to the actual VB .NET development environment by clicking the *New Project* button. Making this selection displays the dialog box shown in Figure 2-3 from which you can choose a type of project on which to work and a type of template to use. In both cases, we will use the default selections—Visual Basic Projects and a Windows Application. This dialog box also has a default name for the project—*WindowsApplication1,* which we need to change to *Vintage2* to match the project on which we are working. It also shows the default drive and folder in which it will be stored. If this is your home machine on which you have installed Visual Studio .NET, then the default location is *C:\My Documents\Visual Studio Projects.* If you are working on a lab machine, it may have a different default location for the files, or you may be instructed to change the location. For the remainder of this book, we will assume that all files are stored in the default location, whatever that may be. Figure 2-3 shows the dialog box with all of these choices pointed out.

FIGURE 2-3. Dialog box for starting project

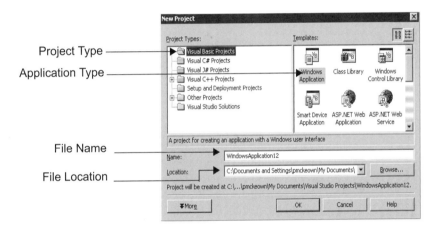

Changing the name of the project to *Vintage2*, accepting the default information for the remainder of this dialog box, and clicking *OK* results in the Windows Form designer for VB .NET being displayed as shown in Figure 2-4. (There are two other modes, Run and Break, which we will discuss later.) Key elements of the Designer window are pointed out in this figure.

The key elements of the VB .NET MDE are the project title bar, the menu bar, the toolbar, the Toolbox (currently hidden), the design window containing one or more forms, the Windows buttons, the Solution Explorer window, the Properties window, and the tabs. The first three of these elements should be familiar to you from other Windows software. The **title bar** shows the name of the project. It also shows that you are in the design mode. The **menu bar** has a variety of menu options, beginning with File and ending with Help, that makes it possible to carry out the operations necessary to create a VB .NET project. As we go through the creation of VB .NET projects, we will discuss the various menu options.

The **toolbar** contains icons that replicate the most commonly used menu options. In VB .NET, as in many Windows applications, there is more than one toolbar available to you; the standard toolbar is what is displayed initially. You can also customize the toolbars by adding or deleting icons. At the

FIGURE 2-4.
VB .NET MDE

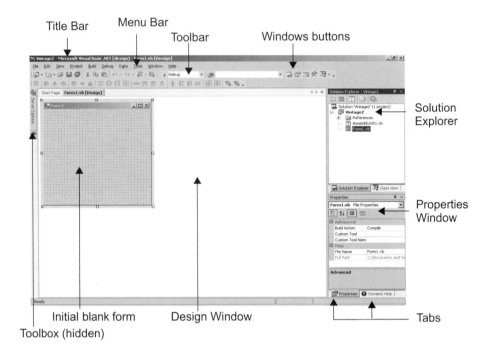

right end of the toolbar are the **Windows buttons** that provide instant access to key windows of the MDE such as the Toolbox and Properties window. As with all buttons on the toolbar, pausing the cursor on them causes a **Tool Tip** to appear displaying the name of that button.

There are a number of tabs of which two are pointed out—the Properties and Dynamic Help tabs. Other tabs on this screen include the Start and Form1.vb [Design] tabs at the upper left side of the Solution Window. We will discuss the Design Window, Toolbox, Solution Explorer, and Properties Windows in separate sections.

You should be aware that the VB .NET MDE shown in Figure 2-4 is the default environment for VB .NET and is referred to as the **tabbed documents environment**. This name comes from the fact that *tabs* are used to switch between pages or windows in this environment. For example, if you clicked on the Dynamic Help tab at the bottom right of the screen, a window with a list of help topics would appear. You could then return to the Properties window by clicking on its tab. You can also close any window by clicking the Close symbol in the upper right-hand corner of the window. However, if you close a window, its tab is no longer visible, and you will need to use selections from the menu bar to display it again. Also, if you select a help topic, information on that topic will be displayed in the Form window and a tab for this topic will remain when you return to the Form designer. For example, if you clicked the Dynamic Help tab and selected *Windows Form Designer*, information on this topic will replace the current form and when you return to the Form Designer by clicking the appropriate tab, the Start Page tab will be replaced with a tab for this help topic.

> **Tip:** The MDE for Visual Studio .NET (and VB .NET) is very flexible both in terms of appearance and ways to carry out the same operation. We will show you the most typical method for carrying out each operation. You can experiment with other methods.

It is also possible in VB .NET to use the older **multiple-document interface (MDI)** environment. If your interface looks differently from that shown above, you are in the MDI interface and you should change back to the tabbed environment by selecting the **Tools** option from the menu and then selecting **Options.** Making these selections will display the dialog box shown in Figure 2-5.

FIGURE 2-5.
Options| General
dialog box

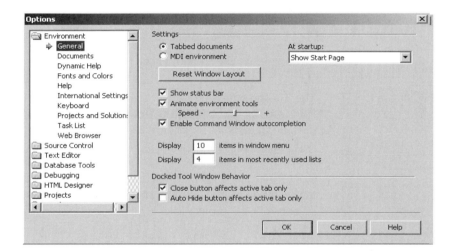

In this case, the **General** option has been selected. In this dialog box, you can select the development environment (tabbed documents or MDI) using option or *radio buttons* and you can set a number of other parameters. The most important of the other selections is the button immediately beneath the environment radio buttons labeled "Reset Window Layout"—this button will return your screen to that shown in Figure 2-4. This is especially important when working a computer lab and a previous user has "rearranged" your screen by moving the windows around.

The Form Window

In the middle of the VB .NET MDE is the **design window** with an initial blank form. This window is key to the creation of any VB .NET project since it enables you to easily create a Windows application by placing objects on the form and writing code for them during the design process. A blank form is shown in Figure 2-6. Note that it also has a title bar, which contains the name of the form (initially Form1). There are also the typical Windows minimize, maximize, and exit controls. More important, the blank form has a grid of dots to help you position objects. When an object is placed on the form, it will automatically "snap" to the nearest dot. Objects can thus be lined up on a row or column of dots to provide a pleasing appearance. You will notice that there are white squares on the bottom, right-hand side, and corners of the form—these are its **sizing handles** which can be used to change the size of the form with the mouse. Because forms are automatically *docked* to the upper left-hand corner of the design window, the upper left-hand sizing handles are grey, indicating you cannot change the dimensions in that direction.

FIGURE 2-6. Blank form

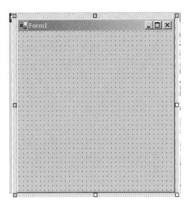

The Toolbox

FIGURE 2-7. Window Forms toolbox

The **Toolbox** holds the objects that are placed on the form to create the VB .NET project. By default, the Toolbox is hidden on the left-hand side of the design window to increase the space in the Design Window and appears only when the mouse pointer is passed over it. You can display it permanently on the left side of the Design window by clicking on the pushpin icon( ) in the Toolbox title bar just to the left of the close icon. The objects in the Toolbox are commonly referred to as **controls**, since they control the response of the project to events such as mouse clicks. Such controls include the four types we used in our example in Chapter 1—buttons, labels, images, and text boxes as well as many more. There are many more controls in this tool box than will be used in this textbook, and they are divided into groups—Data, Component, Windows Forms, Clipboard Ring, and General. In this introductory programming text, we will primarily use the Windows Forms group and the Data group. The *visible* part of the Toolbox is shown in Figure 2-7, and Table 2-1 shows the icons for controls in the Windows Forms toolbox that we will use in this book plus its name and its action. We will also use some controls from the Data toolbox in Chapter 9

> **Tip:** In actuality, all windows in the MDE can be made to auto-hide by using the pushpin icon. The toolbox window is the only one that is set to auto-hide as a part of the default setup.

You may recognize many of the controls in the Windows Forms toolbox from using other applications. If the Windows Form list is not shown when the Toolbox is displayed, simply click the Windows Form tab on the toolbox. More controls can be seen by scrolling down the toolbox. (Depending on the resolution of your screen, you may see more or less icons than shown in Figure 2-7.).

In addition to the controls shown in Figure 2-7 and listed in Table 2-1, there are many **custom controls** that can be added to your Toolbox. Some of these controls are available with VB .NET, but you must add them to the default Toolbox; they can be added individually or as a group.

Table 2-1: Default toolbox controls

Icon	Name	Action
	Pointer	Selects another control; moves controls around screen
	Label	Displays text (read only; no input)
	Button	Responds to events, typically, a mouse click
	TextBox	Displays and inputs text
	MainMenu	Creates menus in applications
	CheckBox	Responds to being checked
	RadioButton	Responds to being on or off
	GroupBox	Acts as container for other controls
	PictureBox	Displays an image; responds to events
	Panel	Acts as container for other controls
	DataGrid	Displays data in a table format
	ListBox	Displays list of text items
	Checked List-Box	Displays list of text items with checks beside selected items
	ComboBox	Acts as drop-down list box
	VScroll (vertical) and HScroll (horizontal) scroll bars	Responds to scrolling by returning a value

Solution Explorer Window

On the right side of the VB .NET development environment are two windows—the Solution Explorer window and the Properties/Help window. The top window is the **Solution Explorer window**. Like the Windows Explorer that is a part of Windows, the Solution Explorer window enables you to view the various parts of the solution to the programming problem. A **solution** contains all files and folders necessary to execute the application including one or more **project** files, which contain the actual code for the application. At the top of the Solution Explorer window are a number of buttons that can be used to display the Code or Designer windows, refresh the current window, show more files in the Solution Explorer window, or display the Properties window. The Solution Explorer window for the new application named Vintage2 containing 1 project and a number of folders or files. The key item is the **form file**, Form1.vb, with which we will work. In Figure 2-8, the Solution Explorer window shows the current project (Vintage2) with one form file (Form1.vb). If there are multiple forms or other objects in the project, they will also be shown here. Note that it has tabs that enable you to switch between the Solution Explorer window and the Class View window that displays the basic building blocks of the solution. For the time being, we will only be interested in the Solution Explorer window as we create projects.

FIGURE 2-8.
Solution Explorer
window

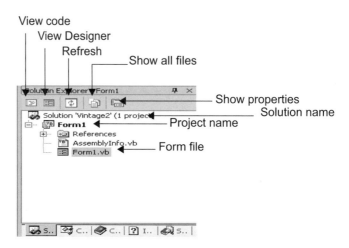

Properties Window

Beneath the Project Explorer window in Figure 2-4 is the **Properties** window with the properties for the VB .NET object that is currently highlighted. Since there is only one object—the form—the properties for it are currently shown in the Properties window with the default text property—Form1—for this form being highlighted. When other objects are added to the form, their properties can also be displayed in the Properties window. However, it is important to note that the properties for only one object can appear in the Properties window and that to view the properties for another object, you must click that object, select it a tab at the top of Design window, or use the combo box at the top of the Properties window.

■ ■

Step-by-Step Instructions 2-1: Starting a project

1. If you received a copy of the VB .NET 2003 student Version, you can install it now on *your own computer*. Caution: it requires Windows 2000 (not ME) or XP to work. If you are using the earlier version, VB .NET 2002, the Start Page will be slightly different, but there will be few other noticeable differences.

2. Using Windows Explorer, go into the *Visual Studios Projects* folder and create a new folder named **Chapter2**. This is where you will save all of your work for this chapter.

3. Regardless of whether you are working from home or in a computer lab, access Visual Studio .NET (or VB .NET if you are using the Student version) by using the Programs option from the Windows Start menu. If you are working from home, set your Start Page parameters to use the Visual Basic Help

filter. Next, select **New Project** and change the name to **Vintage2.** Finally, select **Browse** to find the *Chapter2* folder you created in the previous exercise in which you will be saving the *Vintage2* project.

4. If your screens do not look like Figures 2-1 and 2-3, you may need to use the **Tools | Options | General** option to reset the page reset the window layout. You may also need to select **Show Start Page** for the *At Startup:* option.

5. Take note of the various parts of the opening screen for VB .NET. Where is the Menubar and Toolbar? Find the Windows buttons and click the one that causes the Toolbox to appear. Display it by moving the cursor over it and make sure that the Windows Forms toolbox is displayed. Point out the first six controls from Table 2-1. Turn off the Auto-Hide function of the Toolbox and then turn it back on.

6. Switch from the Properties window to the Help window by clicking on the Dynamic Help tab on the bottom of the window. See if you can make it reappear by clicking the appropriate Windows button at the right end of the toolbar.

Mini-Summary 2-1: Getting started with VB .NET

1. The VB .NET development environment is a typical Windows-based application with title bar and menu bar. It also has a Toolbox and toolbar.

2. The Design window contains the form that is used to create VB .NET applications.

3. The Properties window is used to modify object properties and the Solution Explorer window shows the files that are a part of the project.

It's Your Turn!

1. Of what larger development system is VB .NET a part?

2. What are the three basic modes of VB .NET?

3. List and describe the key elements of the VB .NET MDE.

4. Which of the toolbox controls would be most appropriate for each of the following?

    a. Add text that is a descriptor of another control.

    b. Provide a list of items for the user to select.

    c. Provide a space for users to enter input.

    d. Allow a user to mark one or more from several options.

    e. Provide a means for the user to begin an action.

5. Start VB. NET by following Step-by-Step Instructions 2-1.

FORM
PROPERTIES

As we said earlier, all objects have properties that define them. VB .NET properties include the object's name, its caption, whether it is visible, its size, and so on. To learn about properties in VB .NET, we will use the object that is a part of every project: the form.

When VB .NET is started, it automatically loads a form on the screen. This is the initial form, and for the next few chapters it is the only form we will consider. Since this is the only object on the screen, the Properties window automatically displays the properties for the form, as shown in Figure 2-9. If you click on the form, the name of the form—currently, *Form1*, is displayed in the **Object list box** at the top of the Properties window along with the type of object—in this case, *Systems.Windows.Forms.Form.* If there were other objects on the form, clicking the down arrow on the Object list box would display a drop-down list box of these objects, and clicking on one of these other objects would display its properties.

FIGURE 2-9.
Properties window
for form

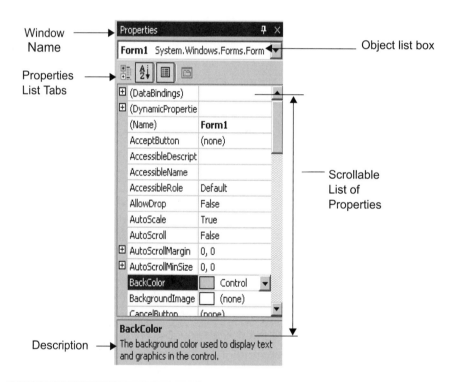

TIP: If the Properties window is not visible on the screen, press the F4 function key or click on the Properties Window button on the toolbar to make it visible.

The Properties List tabs enable you to view the list of properties in one of two ways—categorically or alphabetically—by clicking one of the first two buttons below the Object list box. Even though the default method of listing the properties is to group them by categories, we have shown them in alphabetical order since it is easier to find a property when they are in alphabetical order. Note, however, that the Name property is shown third from the top even though alphabetically it would not come in that location. This makes it easier for you to find and change this property.

If you were to select the Categorized tab, the properties would be grouped by categories, such as Accessibility, Appearance, Behavior, and so on. For example, the background and foreground colors and the font for the object's caption would be included under Appearance. In any case, properties with a plus sign (+) beside them have subproperties, which can be displayed by clicking the plus sign.

Finally, the Description Pane at the bottom of the screen provides a brief description of the property that is currently highlighted in the Properties window—in this case, the BackColor property. If it is not shown, *right*-click the on the Properties window and choose *Description*.

For the current form, we want to change only two properties: the Name and the Text properties. The Name property is used to refer to the object in the VB .NET code that defines the way the object responds to an event, and the Text property is the text that the object displays to the user in the title bar. While they could be the same, in practice they seldom are. You can use almost any text for the object Text property, since its purpose is to identify the control to the user. However, we need to pay close attention to the Name property.

The Name Property

An object's Name property must start with a letter or an underscore (_) and can be as long as you wish, but long names are hard to work with. It can include numbers and score characters, but it cannot include punctuation or spaces. For the name of the form, we should use something that reminds us of the purpose of the project; for example, if we are creating a project for the Vintage DVDs example introduced in Chapter 1, we could simply name the form "Vintage." However, the name should also indicate the type of object being referred to—in this case, a form. For purposes of naming objects, Microsoft has developed a list of prefixes that correspond to types of objects. For example, *frm* is for a form, *btn* for a button, and *lbl* for a label. As we take up each object, we will use the appropriate prefix.

If we take both objectives into account—that is, a name that reminds us of the purpose of the object and a prefix that matches the type of object—a good name for a form for the Vintage DVDs example is *frmVintage*. While VB .NET is not sensitive to the case you use in naming objects, the prefix is usually shown in lowercase letters and the mnemonic part of the name begins with a capital letter.

Changing an Object's Properties

All objects have a set of default properties that are automatically displayed in the Properties window. To change an object's property, you must first give the object the **focus** by clicking on it. Then use the Properties window's scroll bar to find the property you wish to change. In the case of the Name property, if the properties are in alphabetical order, it is already near the top of the list. Next, click in any column for the property you wish to change to highlight it and type a new value, automatically replacing the old value. Finally, press **ENTER**. For example, to change the Name property, highlight it and type the new name: **frmVintage** to replace the default name. (Note: The new name, *frmVintage*, is not actually in boldface or italics in the Properties window, but we will use this method to distinguish text you should input from normal text.) When the Name property of the form is changed, the new name is displayed at the top of the Properties window, in the Object box, and in the right column of the Name property row.

The Text property of the form will be displayed in the title bar of the form, so we want a string of characters that will be in line with the purpose of the project. In this case, the name of the store would be an appropriate caption. To create a new caption for the form, simply highlight the current one in the Properties window (Form1) and change it to **Vintage DVDs**. Notice that the new Text property now appears in the title bar of the form.

Changing the Startup Object

When a VB .NET solution is executed, it immediately looks for the **Startup object**. This is the form or code object that is executed first. The default Startup object is the initial form you add to the project (Form1); if you change the name of the form to something else like *frmVintage*, then you need to also change the Startup object. This is accomplished through the Project Properties dialog box which is accessed by *right-clicking* the Project file in the Solution Explorer window. The resulting Properties dialog box is shown in Figure 2-10 with the new form name, *frmVintage*, highlighted in the Startup object listbox. Failure to change the Startup object to the new form name will result in an error message when you execute the project.

FIGURE 2-10.
Project property page

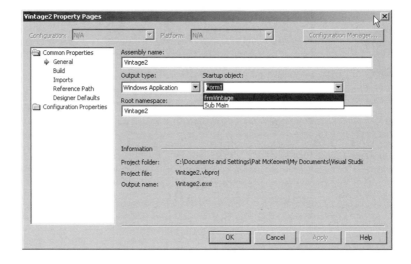

I ■ I

Step-by-Step Instructions 2-2: Creating a form

1. If you have not completed Step-by-Step Instructions 2-1, do so now.

2. Click anywhere in the initial form to ensure that it has the focus. If the Properties window is not visible, press F4 to make it visible or Click the Properties Windows button on the toolbar. If it is not already in alphabetical order, click on the "Alphabetical" button.

3. Highlight the Name property in the Properties window and change it to **frm-Vintage**. Note the effect on the Properties window. Does the form itself change in any discernible way?

4. Note all of the locations on the screen where the new name for the form is displayed.

5. Highlight the Text property for the *frmVintage* form and change it to **Vintage DVDs**. How does the form change?

6. Go to the Properties window and scroll down the list of the properties and highlight the **Enabled** property. What does this property do according to its description in the lower section of the Properties window?

7. To change the Startup object for the project, *right-click* on the Project file name in the Solutions window (typically, the second name from the top in the Solution window.) The Property dialog box shown in Figure 2-10 will be displayed. Click on the Startup object list box and select **frmVintage** as the Startup object. Click **OK** to save this change.

Mini-Summary 2-2: Changing the properties of a VB .NET object

1. To change a property of a control, first select the control by clicking on it. If the Properties window is not visible, you may display it by pressing **F4**.

2. Control properties are changed by moving the cursor to the Properties window, selecting the property to be changed, entering a new setting for the selected item, and pressing **ENTER** to accept the change

3. The Startup object must be changed to the new name of the form using the Project Property page.

It's Your Turn!

1. Which properties primarily affect the form's appearance?

2. Complete Step-by-Step Instructions 2-2 to name the form, change its text property, and the change the project Startup object.

3. Experiment with changing the **BackColor** property for frmVintage by highlighting it and clicking the down arrow. Next, click the **Custom** tab and select a color. To return to the original grey color, click the **System** tab under the **Backcolor** property and select **Control**.

ADDING CONTROLS TO THE FORM

Now that you have seen how to access VB .NET and have become familiar with the opening screen and the Properties window, we are ready to work with controls in the Toolbox to begin creating a project. However, we first need to recall the six-step process for doing this, presented in Chapter 1:

1. Define the problem.
2. Create an interface.
3. Develop logic for action objects.
4. Write and test code for action objects.

5. Test the overall project.

6. Document the project in writing.

Define the Problem

In the Vintage DVDs example discussed in Chapter 1, the owner of Vintage DVDs wants an opening screen that will display the store's name along with some type of picture representing DVDs. He also wants to be able to click a button and display an opening message. Based on this description, we can sketch the interface for this problem. Such a sketch is shown in Figure 2-11.

In Figure 2-11, note that we have three types of controls on the sketch of the opening screen for Vintage DVDs: one control that displays the name of the store and its slogan, a second control that displays a picture of video camera, and a third control that is a button with the caption "Click Me First!" In an actual situation, before we start to create the interface in VB .NET, we would need to have the client approve this sketch. If the owner of Vintage DVDs likes this proposed interface, we can go ahead to the second step, which is to create the interface.

FIGURE 2-11. Sketch of interface for Vintage DVDs opening screen

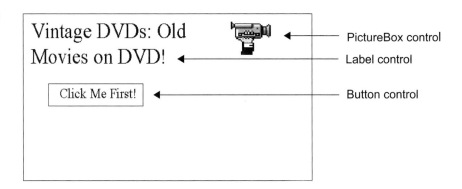

Create the Interface

FIGURE 2-12. Controls for opening screen

Label control

PictureBox control

Button control

To create an interface for the VB .NET project that matches the sketch shown in Figure 2-11, we need to access VB .NET and display the MDE shown earlier as Figure 2-4. Next, we need to decide what controls to use. In this case, we need to use a **Label** control to display the store name and slogan, a **PictureBox** control to display the picture of a video camera, and a **Button** control that will be clicked to display a welcoming message. The Label, PictureBox, and Button controls are shown in Figure 2-12.

There are two ways to select a control and place it on the blank form. You can click it once to *draw* it any size anywhere on the form, or you can double-click it to automatically position the default size on the form. In the first case, if you position the cursor over the control, click it once, and move the pointer back to the form, the cursor becomes a crosshair. The control is then positioned wherever on the form you release the cursor. If you click the left mouse button and *hold* it down, you can "drag" the outline of the control by dragging the crosshairs up, down, left, right, or diagonally. Once you release the mouse button, the control area will be bounded by its sizing handles, with which you can change the size of the control.

> **TIP:** It is easy to determine the control with the focus—it has a dotted border and the sizing handles are highlighted.

In the second case, if you double-click a control, it automatically appears in either the upper left-hand corner of the form or in almost the *same* position as the last control placed on the form. We say *almost*, because you can see both controls and move either control to another location by dragging it or resize either control by use of the handles.

While the choice of whether to draw the control or double-click it on the screen is usually one of personal preference, there are times when you must draw the control. We will point out these situations when they come up.

For example, Figure 2-13 shows the result of drawing the label on the form in preparation for creating the store name and slogan. Note that the default Text property is "Label1," which is also the default name for this label. You will also notice that there are no grid dots in the control area and that there is a default text property in the upper left-hand corner of the label. If you click anywhere within the control area, and hold the mouse button down, you can drag the label control to any other location on the form...

FIGURE 2-13. Label control drawn in form

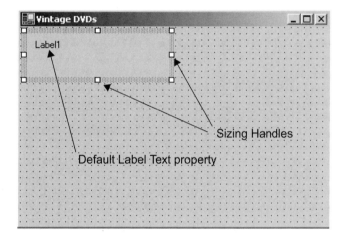

Once the label control is on the form, the next step is to change its Name and Text properties. As with the form, you use the Properties window to change these properties of the label. To do this, first check the Object box in the Properties window to make sure the focus is on the label; if it does not show *Label1*, click the label control to highlight it. Next, click the Name row of the Properties window and change it to **lblVintage**. Notice that we have used the lbl prefix for this object name since it is a label, and that the rest of the name is the same as that of the form. This will not cause any confusion since one name begins with *frm* and the other with *lbl*. When you change the name for the label, notice that the text does not change. Typically, the only time the name and text properties of a control are the same is before you change either of them.

To change the Text property for the lblVintage label, use the same approach as you did for the form: Highlight the Text property and change it—in this case to **Vintage DVDs: Old Movies on DVD!** Note that the actual label text will not change until you press **ENTER**. Notice also that, while the text in the label changes to the new setting, it is not large enough to act as an eye-catching heading for the form. To increase the size of the Text property of the label, we need to change the label **Font** property.

Dialog
box icon

> **TIP:** To force a label to automatically fit its text, change the Autosize property to True.

When you select the Font property for a control, an icon with three dots is displayed. This indicates that clicking on this icon will display a dialog box in which we can make changes to the font of the corresponding label. This dialog box is shown in Figure 2-14 with list boxes that enable you to change the font type (currently MS Sans Serif), the font style (currently Regular), and the font size (currently 8 points). Since we want the label caption to stand out, we need to change the font style to Bold and the font size to 14 points. Clicking **OK** executes these changes. Finally, since the label caption text will "wrap" within the defined label size, we need to use the sizing handles to change the size of the label to display it on two lines like the sketch. The results of these operations are shown in Figure 2-15.

> **TIP:** You can also change the Font property by clicking the plus (+) sign beside it to show the same selections in the Property window as are shown in the dialog box.

FIGURE 2-14. The Font dialog box

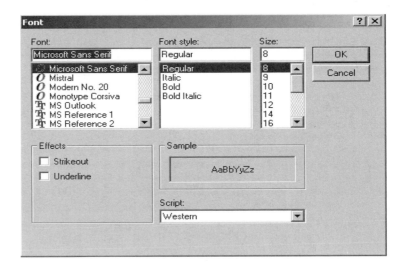

Adding the Image Control

To add the PictureBox control to the form, single-click it and draw it to the right of the existing Label control. Change the Name property to **picVintageLogo** and use the sizing handles to enlarge it so its height and width are the same as the height of the label control. The PictureBox control does not have a Text property, but it does have an **Image** property you can use to insert a graphic image. To do this, select the Image property and click the dialog box icon to display a list of folders from which to choose an image. The image we are going to use (camera.ico) is found in the Program

FIGURE 2-15.
Completed Label
control

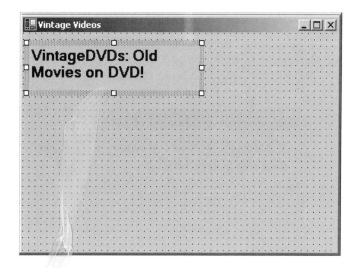

Files\Visual Studio .NET\Common7\Graphics\Icons\Misc folder on your computer's hard disk (your instructor may give you different instructions for where to look for the file.) This will display a variety of icons from which to choose. Find the camera icon and select it to be inserted into the PictureBox control.

When you insert the camera.ico file into the image control, it does not automatically expand to fill the current size of the control; in fact, the Picture-Box control may *shrink* to fit the size of the icon. Even if you resize the Pic-tureBox control, the picture within it may not change. To enlarge the image control and the icon simultaneously, you must use the **SizeMode** property. Clicking this property displays a down arrow indicating that there are multi-ple options from which to chose. Clicking on the down arrow displays these options and you should choose the **StretchImage** option. Doing this will cause the image within the PictureBox control to expand to fit the size of the control. The top portion of the resulting screen will look like that shown in Figure 2-16 .

SizeMode Property
Options

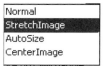

FIGURE 2-16. Result
of adding
PictureBox control

Adding a Button Control

Now that you have added the two controls to the Vintage DVDs form that are primarily for appearance purposes, you are ready to add the Button control that, when clicked, will display a message. To add the Button control, dou-ble-click the corresponding icon in the Toolbox to display it on the form, and then move it to immediately beneath the Label control. Change the Name property of the Button control to **btnMessage** and replace the default Text property with the message **Click me first!** As you did with the Label control, use the Font property to display the text in 12-point boldface type. If the message is too long to be displayed on the button, use the sizing handles to lengthen the button so the text is displayed on a single line. The result of these actions will be a screen like that displayed in Figure 2-17.

Figure 2-17. Result of adding button button control

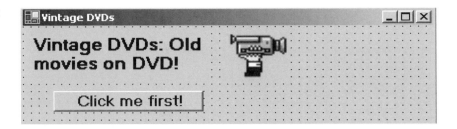

> **TIP:** Often you will use several similar control objects as part of your interface, for example, several labels that have the same font typeface and size. You may be able to save some time by creating the first of these control objects then copying and pasting it as necessary.VB .NET will automatically give them different names.

Step-by-Step Instructions 2-3: Adding controls to a form

1. Add a label control to your form by drawing it in the upper left-hand corner of the form.

2. Click this label and change its Name property to **lblVintage**. Also, move it down from the corner and expand its width.

3. Change the Text property of this label to **Vintage DVDs: Old Movies on DVD!** Change the Font property of this label to have a font style of Bold and a size of 14 points. (Leave the font type as is.) Use the handles on the label to resize it as necessary to make the result appear like that shown in Figure 2-15.

4. Draw a PictureBox control to the right of the existing Label control so that its height and width are approximately the same as the height of the Label control. Use the form grid to help you make this adjustment. Change the Name property for the PictureBox control to **picVintageLogo**.

5. What properties of the PictureBox control may be used to set it to an exact size? Do the Button and Label controls also have these properties?

6. Insert the Program Files\Visual Studio .NET\Common7\Graphics\Icons\Misc\camera.ico file (or wherever you instructor directs you to find it) as the Image property for the PictureBox control and change its SizeMode property to **StretchImage.** The resulting image should be like that shown in Figure 2-16.

7. Add a Button control to the form with a Name property of **btnMessage** and a caption of **Click me first!** Change the Font property to have the text displayed in 12-point boldface type. The result should appear like that shown in Figure 2-17.

Mini-Summary 2-3: Steps for adding a control to a form

1. Select the control you want to add to the form in the Toolbox and either click the control once to draw it on the form, or double-click the control to position it in the center of the form.

2. If you clicked the control once, use the crosshair to "draw" it on the form by holding the left mouse button down. In either case, drag the control to the desired position and use the sizing handles to adjust it to the desired size.

3. Change the properties for the control as discussed earlier.

It's Your Turn!

1. Add a second label to the Vintage DVDs form you created in Step-by-Step Instructions 2-3 by double-clicking the label icon in the Toolbox.

2. Move this second label around the screen with your mouse. Resize it to be approximately one-half the width of the form.

3. If the second label does not have the focus, click on it once. Now press the **DELETE** key to delete the second label. What property of the PictureBox control is used to display a graphic?

4. Where are the graphics that can be added to the PictureBox control found?

5. What property of the PictureBox control must be changed to enlarge the graphic?

6. Follow Step-by-Step Instructions 2-3 to add Picture Box and Button controls to the Vintage DVDs form.

ADDING CODE TO THE PROJECT

Now that you have a completed the interface, the next steps in the application development process are to develop the logic for the action objects in the project and to write and test the code for them. There is only one action object (the button) in the Vintage DVDs project, and the logic is very simple: Display the "Welcome to Vintage DVDs" message when the button is clicked. The only input is the mouse-click event and the only output is the message. There is no processing to speak of.

Write and Test Code for Action Objects

Once you have created the logic for the action objects, the next step is to write and test the code for each of the action objects. There is only one action object in the Vintage DVDs project: the button. The code for this object must display a welcome message when it is clicked.

To do this, we need a very useful VB .NET operation: the **message box.** The message box is a special dialog box with a message placed there by the project developer. When requested by some event, the message box will appear on the screen displaying the message. It will remain on the screen until the user clicks its *OK* button. To write the code that will display a message box in the Vintage DVDs application when the button is clicked, we need to add code for the click event for the Button control. To do this, double-click the button on the form to display the **Code window** as shown in Figure 2-18.

FIGURE 2-18. Code window for Button control

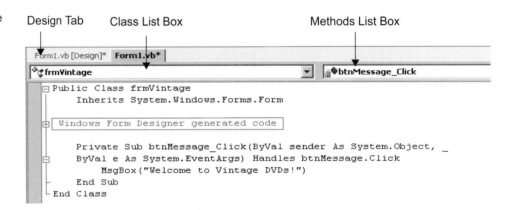

The Code window is the place in the VB .NET development environment where we enter the code that will cause the various objects to respond as we want them to. This code is called an **event handler** because it defines how the object will respond to an event. Note that it shows the name of this new class that we have created—frmVintage in the **Class list box** in the top left side of the code window. It also shows control and the event—btnMessage_Click—in the **Method list box** in the top right of the Code window. Note also that there is a tab for the Design window enabling you to quickly switch back to this view of the project.

When you access the Code window, the first and last lines of the event handler procedure are already displayed with a blank line between them. The first line begins with "Private Sub ..." and last line is "End Sub". When you open the Code window, you will probably not see the end of the first line—"Handles btnMessage.Click", as it may extend off the screen. We have used the underscore (_) continuation character to "wrap" the code so you can see this important part of the first line. It tells us that this is the code procedure that handles the Click event for the btnMessage button. This is the default procedure for the Button control that automatically is displayed when you double-click the Button control. However, as we shall see later, you do not have to use the default event for a control. Because this is a code procedure that handles the event, it is also often referred to as an **event procedure.**

To display a dialog box with a message in it when the btnMessage control is clicked, you should move the cursor to the blank line between the first and last lines of the btnMessage_Click event procedure and add a single line of code to this procedure:

```
MsgBox ("Welcome to Vintage DVDs")
```

as shown in Figure 2-18. As you enter this code, you will probably see a Help Tip window pop up; you may ignore it for the time being.

Note that for better readability you should indent the instruction by pressing the **TAB** key. VB .NET will check lines of code that you enter and alert you to obvious vocabulary and syntax errors. However, it cannot catch all errors, especially errors that are based on invalid logic.

Note that this is the code window for just the btnMessage_Click event. All of the objects in this project—the Form, Label, Button and PictureBox controls can be accessed by clicking the down arrow on the Class list box. The events for those controls can be accessed by clicking the down arrow on the Methods list box. For example, to reach the double-click event for the PictureBox, you would select the PictureBox control from the Class list box and then select double-click from the Methods list box.

To return to the form design window, you can click on the Form1.vb [Design] tab in the Form Design window or click the View Object button in the Solution Explorer window. To return to the Code window, you can double-click the control for which you wish to add code, click the Form1.vb tab, or click the View Code button in the Solution Explorer window.

Once you have entered the single instruction for btnMessage_Click event in the Code window, you are ready to test your project by executing it. You can do this in a number of ways, but we suggest you use the VCR-type Start button on

Start

the toolbar. When you click this button, the grid dots on the form will disappear and you will be in **run time.** You can now click the button to determine if you have entered the code correctly. If you have, the message box shown in Figure 2-19 will appear. Note that there are no grid dots on the form, because the grid disappears when the project is executed. Note also that the title bar of the message box has a caption of "Vintage2" This is the current name of the solution. Any message boxes displayed in the solution use the solution name as their default title. In a later chapter, you will learn how to control the title bar caption for a message box. If you click *OK* on this window, it will disappear.

> **TIP:** You can execute a project by selecting the Start option from the Debug submenu (denoted as **Debug|Start**) or by pressing the **F5** function key. You can stop the execution of a project clicking the close icon in the upper right-hand corner of the form.

When you clicked the Start button on the Standard toolbar, a new Debug toolbar appeared beneath the existing toolbars. We will use this toolbar later to look for errors in your programs. For the time being, we want to use the VCR-type Stop button on this toolbar to terminate the execution of the project.

Stop

FIGURE 2-19.
Message window
displayed

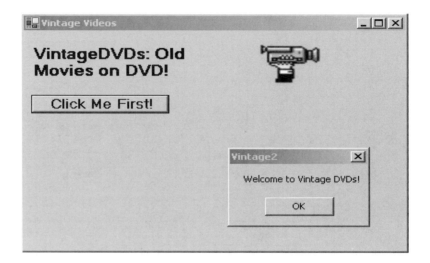

If you have not entered the code correctly, you may receive an error message asking you if you wish to continue. If this occurs, you should choose *not* to continue. This will cause an error message in a new window at the bottom of the screen—the **Task list**. Double-clicking anywhere in this error message will display the Code window with the error highlighted. For example, if we misspelled the Msgbox command as *MgBox*, this will result in an error. Figure 2-20 shows the Code window and Task list resulting from this error.

FIGURE 2-20. Error
in project

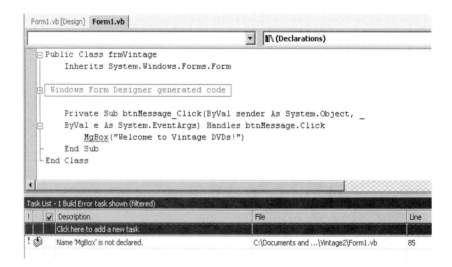

The error can be corrected in the Code window and the project run again. Some errors will not generate an error message; instead they will result in the project not carrying out the desired results. These errors are usually the result of an error in the underlying logic, so you will need to go back and check the IPO tables and pseudocode to find the error. Once you have found it, you must transfer the correction in logic to the code for the control and start the error-checking process again.

> **TIP**: If you receive an error message in the Task List window, try double-clicking the error. In many cases, the line with the error will be displayed.

Test Overall Project and Document It

Normally, after you have coded and tested each individual action object, you are ready to test the overall project and document it. However, in this very simple first project these steps are unnecessary. In later projects, we will discuss the process of carrying out these steps.

Step-by-Step Instructions 2-4: Adding code to a button

1. Double-click the btnMessage button and add the single instruction after the first line in the Code window as shown in Figure 2-18:

```
Msgbox("Welcome to Vintage DVDs")
```

2. Notice that when you clicked the btnMessage button some VB .NET code was automatically generated. How do the automatically generated statements indicate their corresponding action object and event?

3. Click the View Designer button in the Solution Explorer window to display the form. Click the Run button on the toolbar and then click the btnMessage button. Your form should look like Figure 2-19.

4. Click the OK button on the message box and then click the Stop button on the Debug toolbar.

5. Click the View Code button, change the term "Msgbox" in the message box statement to "Msbbox" and run the project again. What happens? Correct your error and run it again to make sure you did not add other errors.

6. Terminate the execution of your project and display the form again.

Mini-Summary 2-4: Writing and testing an event procedure

1. To add code for a control, double-click it to display the Code window with the first and last lines of the event handler already entered.

2. Enter the code for the control between the existing first and last lines of the event handler.

3. Click the View Designer button on the Solution Explorer window or the Design Tab to display the form.

4. Click the Run button on the toolbar to execute the project. Use the Stop button on the Debug toolbar to terminate the project.

5. Test the functionality of the control; if an error occurs, correct it in the Code window.

It's Your Turn!

1. How do you add code to an object on a form?

2. Where does the code for the object go in the code window?

3. How do you switch between the code window and the form design window?

4. What buttons do you use to start and stop a project?

5. Where are errors in a project listed?

WORKING WITH FILES IN VB .NET

Now that you have a little experience working with VB .NET, we will take a closer look at the menu bar and toolbar to work with files in VB .NET. The menu bar contains options that correspond to submenus that contain all of the commands needed for working with the development environment. The toolbar contains icons corresponding to the more commonly used menu commands. As in other Windows applications, you access an option from the menu bar by clicking on the option or by pressing the **ALT** key and, while holding it down, pressing the underlined letter. For example, you can access the File option by clicking on the word *File* in the menu bar or by pressing the **ALT**+**F** key combination. Once you have a submenu, you can select commands or submenus from it in a similar manner. Figure 2-21 shows the top half of the File menu. An icon beside a submenu option indicates that this option is also available on a toolbar.

FIGURE 2-21. A portion of the File submenu

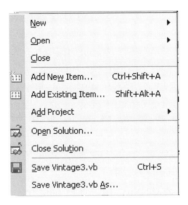

The Standard Toolbar   Clicking an icon on the toolbar is a shortcut way of carrying out the most popular commands. ToolTips are available to help remind you of the purpose of each of the toolbar icons. The icons for the Standard toolbar and their names, corresponding menu options, and use are shown in Table 2-2.

In addition to the Standard or default toolbar, there are other toolbars that contain icons for specialized operations. For example, the Debug toolbar contains icons representing all of the operations you will need to find errors in your projects. You can see what toolbars are open for your project by

TABLE 2-2: Toolbar icons and corresponding menu selections

Icon	Name	Menu Option	Action
	New project	File | New | Project	Starts a new VB .NET application
	Add New Item	Project | New Item	Add a new form or other item to the current project
	Open File	File | Open File	Open a file (solution, project, form, and so on)
	Save Form File	File | Save *formname.vb*	Save current form
	Save All	File | Save All	Save all files in current solution
	Cut	Edit | Cut	Used in code editor to remove a section of code
	Copy	Edit | Copy	Used in code editor to copy a section of code
	Paste	Edit | Paste	Used in code editor to paste a section of code
	Undo	Edit | Undo	Used in code editor to "undo" most previous action
	Redo	Edit | Redo	Used in code editor to "redo" a previously undone action
	Navigate Back	View | Navigate Back	Move to another form in a multiform project
	Navigate Forward	View | Navigate Forward	Move to another form in a multiform project
	Start	Debug | Start	Execute the current project
	Stop	Debug | Stop	
Debug	Solution Configuration		Determines if you are in the debugging process or are ready to release the project
	Find in files	Edit | Find and Replace	Used to find a character or string of characters in the project
	Solution Explorer	View | Solution Explorer	Display Solution Explorer window
	Properties Window	View | Properties Window	Display Properties window
	Toolbox	View | Toolbox	Display Toolbox
	Class View	View | Class View	Display the classes used in this application
	Toolbar options	View | Other Windows	Edit configuration of the toolbar

selecting the **View | Toolbar** menu option and noting those with a check-mark beside them. You can open new ones or close those that are open by checking or unchecking them. For purposes of this book, we will only assume that the Standard and Web toolbars are open.

Files in VB .NET

When you have completed a project or when you have to stop work before finishing, you need to save your work to disk so you can retrieve it later for more work. In addition, you should save your work frequently, especially before attempting to execute your application. To save a project, you first need to understand the files that are a part of it. First, recall that a **file** is *a group of data, instructions, or information to which a name can be applied.* In VB .NET, each solution has one **solution file** with an .sln extension and at least one **project file** with a .vbproj extension. Each project typically has one **form file** with an .vb extension. If the project has multiple forms, then there will be a file with a .vb file for each form in the project. In addition, there is one resource file for each form file. These resource files have .resx extensions. There are also two folders, Bin and Object, that are used in the process of converting a VB .NET solution into a binary form. Finally, for each project, there is utility program named "AssemblyInfo.vb". Figure 2-22 provides an overview of the VB .NET file structure.

FIGURE 2-22. VB .NET file structure

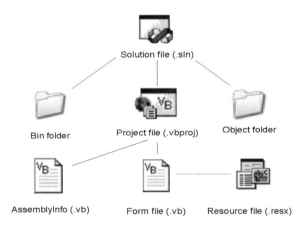

Solution file (.sln)

Bin folder   Project file (.vbproj)   Object folder

AssemblyInfo (.vb)   Form file (.vb)   Resource file (.resx)

Where there a number of files and folders in each VB .NET solution, you need only worry about a few since the remainder are automatically taken care of by the MDE. When you started a new solution named *Vintage2*, VB .NET generated a folder with a name of *Vintage2* for you in the *Chapter2* folder. The solution (.sln) and project (.vbproj) files were also given these same names and your form file was named *form1.vb*. Since we will be using the same solution and project files as we are updating the Vintage DVDs project, we will need to rename them so they can say the same (*Vintage*) throughout the book. Similarly, since the form name is a generic name that does not fit the Vintage DVDs solution on which we are working, we will change it in the next section.

Saving VB .NET Files

To save a VB .NET solution with the default names, simply click the *Save* button on the toolbar. Since all such files are saved in separate folders, there is no problem with overwriting other files with the same name for different solution. However, to change the names of the .sln, .vbproj, and .vb files before saving the project, you must use the *File | Save As...* menu command or rename them from within VB .NET. For example, to change the names of the .sln and .vbproj files to *Vintage* from *Vintage2*, *right-click* on them and select the *Rename* option.

For the form file, you need to actually use the File menu and go to use the *Save Form1.vb as...* option. When you do this, a Save File As dialog box will be displayed for the current folder (*Vintage2*), with the current form file name (initially, *Form1.vb*). We want to change this name to *Vintage.vb*, so simply click on the file name in the dialog box if it is not already highlighted, type in the new name, *Vintage.vb,* and press **ENTER**. Note: Do *not* include the file extension in the file name. VB .NET will automatically add the appropriate extension. If there were additional forms or project elements, their filenames will also be shown here for you to accept or change.

Once you have changed the default filenames, clicking on the Save All icon will automatically save them again without displaying the file dialog boxes. Only if you select the *Save As* option. will the file dialog box be displayed. When you have completed your work on a project, you can exit VB .NET by selecting the Exit option from the File submenu (*File | Exit*).

Retrieving a Saved Solution or Starting a New One

Retrieving a previously saved project from disk is very easy. When you first access VB .NET, the solutions on which you have worked most recently will be listed on the Start Page and you can simply click on the work to open. If a solution is not listed, you can see more solutions by clicking on the *Open Project* button and then selecting the folder you wish to open. You can also open a solution from within another solution by using the *File | Open Projects* menu option and doing the same operation.

Instead of retrieving an existing solution, you will often want to start a new one. If you choose to do this from the Start Page, you simply click *New Project* and enter a name for the project in the New Project dialog box (shown earlier as Figure 2-3). On the other hand, if you want to start from within the VB .NET MDE, you can do this by selecting the *File | New | Project* option. In either case, it is very important to change the generic solution name composed of "WindowsApplication" plus a number to a name that more clearly defines the application. Otherwise, even if you change the name of all files within the solution, they will still all be saved in a folder with this generic name. Naming the name of the application at the beginning defines the name of the folder in which all files are saved.

■ ■ ■ ■ ■ ■ ■ ■ ■ ■ ■ ■ ■ ■ ■ ■ ■ ■ ■

Step-by-Step Instructions 2-5: Saving a project

1. Right-click on Vintage2.sln and change the name to **Vintage.sln**. Similarly, right-click on Vintage2.vbproj and change the name to **Vintage.vbproj**.

2. Select **File|Save Form1.vb As...** from the VB .NET menubar (the file-name is most likely *form1.vb)* and change the file name to **Vintage** and press **ENTER** (it will automatically add the .vb extension.)

3. Click the **Save All** button to save all of the files in the project.

4. Select **Programs|Windows Explorer** from the Windows Start menu and check to make sure the files have been saved in the Vintage2 folder.

5. Use the **File|Exit** menu option to exit the VB .NET MDE. Now start VB .NET again and select the **Vintage2** application from the Start Page. Use the Start icon to execute the project. Terminate it by clicking the Stop icon.

Mini-Summary 2-5: Working with files in VB .NET

1. There are 21 operations that can be executed from the toolbar. All of these operations correspond to commands available from the menu bar.

2. The types of files that make up a VB .NET project include the solution file (.sln), project files (.vbproj), form files (.vb), and resource files (.resx). There are also the bin and object folders.

3. You should save the form files through the File|Save Form1.vb as... menu option.

4. You can save a project though the toolbar Save All icon or through the File|Save All menu option. Similarly, you can open a saved project through Open Project toolbar icon or through the File|Open Project menu option.

4. To start a new project, select the File|New Project menu option and give it a name when you open it.

It's Your Turn!

1. Describe the meaning of each of the following VB .NET file extensions:

    a. .vb

    b. .vbproj

    c. .sln

    d. .resx

2. Why is it necessary to change the form file name and not the other file names?

3. What is the difference between the form file name and the form name?

4. Follow Step-by-Step Instructions 2-5 to change the names of the files in your project and to save them.

USING VB .NET HELP

VB .NET is a very powerful development platform that offers many more capabilities than can be discussed in an introductory programming text such as this. Fortunately, VB .NET also offers developers a powerful Help system that offers help on virtually any possible question. In fact, there are four types of help available to you in VB .NET: the Help menu option, Dynamic help, Web-based help, and Auto help. We will discuss each type of help in a separate section.

> **TIP:** You should be aware that, because VB .NET is a part of the Visual Studio .NET system, unless you select the Visual Basic Help filter on the My Profile page, when you select help on a topic, you will receive help on that topic for all of the languages in Visual Studio .NET. Selecting this filter restricts help to just VB .NET.

Figure 2-22 Using the Help menu option

If you select the Help menu option, the various options shown in Figure 2-22 are displayed. Note that it starts out with one of the other types of help—Dynamic Help, which is a powerful new help system that is a part of VB .NET (it will be discussed separately in the next section). Also listed are options for Contents, Index, and Search in addition to a number of other options. Probably the only other option you might select is the **Show Start Page** option which takes you back to the Start Page from which you can change your Profile if you wish.

With all three of the Contents, Index, and Search Help menu options, selecting an option displays a list of results in the Solution Explorer Window. For example, if you select Index, the results are displayed as shown in Figure 2-23. Note that the usual contents of the Solution Explorer Window are replaced by a list of help items in alphabetical order with a search window at the top, but that there is a Solution Explorer tab at the bottom of the window, which will take you back to it. Note also that this window shows that the help is being filtered by the Visual Basic so only help topics for that language are shown.

FIGURE 2-23. Index Help screen in Solution Explorer Window

The **Contents** Help menu option is an organized to provide a book-like discussion of Visual Studio and VB .NET. In fact the book icon is used to show the various chapters that can be opened with this type help. If you "drill down" far enough, a document icon is displayed, and clicking it will display the actual help in the WinForm Designer window.

The **Index** Help menu option provides an alphabetized list of keywords for Visual Basic (VB .NET), as shown in Figure 2-23. You can select a keyword by clicking it, the corresponding help document will be displayed in the WinForms Designer window. If there are multiple matching documents, they will be listed in a separate dialog box from which you can select the one that best matches your needs. You can also enter a word in the box above the Index list and search for matching keywords. For example, if you chose the Index Help menu option and then entered "button" as a search word, you would receive a number of possible matches. However, since we are working on Windows forms, you would choose the option that matches this type of button. Clicking on *Overview* would display two possible matches in the Task List and selecting *Introduction to the Windows Button Control* displays the screen shown in Figure 2-24 with the list of options in the dialog box (which has been *docked* below the main window by dragging it there) and the help document in the WinForm Design window.

FIGURE 2-24.
Example of Help document

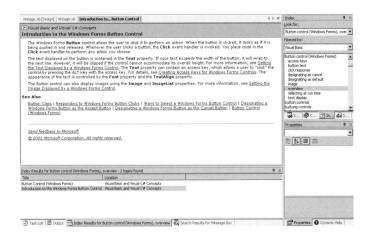

The **Search** Help menu option enables you to search all of the Help documents instead of just the titles or keywords. For example, if you wished to find other examples of the use of the word "clipped," which is found in the fifth line of the document shown in Figure 2-24, you could enter this word in the input box for the Search option and find other documents containing this word.

Between the Contents, Index, and Search options on the Help menu, you can find out how to carry out almost any option in VB. NET. They are undoubtedly extremely powerful help tools.

Dynamic Help

A new and very useful help tool in VB .NET is **Dynamic Help.** When Dynamic Help is selected from either the Help menu or from the tab at the bottom of the Properties window, a list of help topics replaces the existing list of properties in the Properties window. This list of help topics is *context-sensitive* in that clicking a control on a form in design mode or positioning the cursor on a term in the Code window will result in VB. NET attempting to provide context-sensitive help on the item to which you are pointing. While it is not always perfect in matching the help provided to your needs, it does a very good job on most things. For example, if you click the button in the Vintage DVD application, a list of help topics is shown in the Properties window and one of them is the same "Introduction to the Windows Button Control" option that was shown Figure 2-24. Similarly, if you position the cursor on the MsgBox instruction in the Code window, a list of topics, sample code, and general instructions on getting started with VB. NET relating to the MsgBox instruction will be displayed in the Properties window as shown in Figure 2-25. Clicking on one of these topics will result in information about it being displayed in the Window Form Designer window. In many situations, Dynamic Help can be the fastest way to obtain information on a control, code instruction, or other feature of VB. NET.

FIGURE 2-25.
Dynamic Help
screen

TIP: Pressing **F1** will also result in Dynamic Help being activated for the current control or code.

"Think Ahead" Help

In addition to the type of help where you are actively looking for information, VB .NET can automatically provide you several types of information as you work. In the process of entering code, you may have already noticed the little boxes that pop up with information about the statement you are entering. These boxes are a part of Microsoft's effort to have VB .NET "think ahead" and provide you with information you need to complete the statement. There are two primary kinds of "think ahead" help in VB .NET: Auto List and Parameter Information. In the first case, **Auto List** displays a box of items that can be used to complete a statement. For example, if you type a word or phrase in the Code window, the Auto List feature provides you with a list of possible completions from which to choose. Highlighting one the completions in the list and pressing **ENTER** will insert the completion at the end of the current statement.

The **Parameter Information** help feature displays the syntax necessary to complete the statement at the current cursor location. For example, if you enter the first part of a MsgBox statement, say, *MsgBox,* the Parameter Information help will pop up with the syntax for completing the MsgBox statement as shown in Figure 2-26. This means it is not necessary for you to remember the syntax for each and every statement.

FIGURE 2-26. Use of
Parameter
Information Help

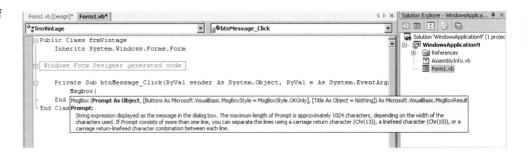

Using Web-Based Help

As a support tool for VB. NET, Web-based help can be useful to you. To access the Web-based help, open Internet Explorer, Netscape, or another Web browser and enter as the URL:

http://msdn.microsoft.com/library/default.asp

This will display the opening MSDN Library page for the Web-based help. Notice the Web interface with a list of items (the Table of Contents—TOC) on the left, a corresponding Web page on the right. The MSDN Welcome item is initially highlighted on the left side and a Welcome page is displayed on the right. To view help on VB .NET (or any other topic), you must drill down by clicking on plus sign next to an item in the TOC. In our case, finding help on VB .NET requires the following sequence of selections:

```
.Net Development
    Visual Studio .NET
        Product Documentation
            Visual Basic and Visual C#|Reference
                Visual Basic Language
                    Visual Basic Language and Run-Time Reference.
```

Once the last link shown above is selected, you can then drill down to find information on a particular item. For example, to find help on the Msg-Box instruction, you would click on *Functions,* and the letter *M*. This will display a list of functions whose names begin with the letter "C." Finally, clicking on *Msgbox* results in a help screen on this function being shown.

Regardless of whether you are using the internal help system or the Web-based systems, VB. NET help is based on the same **hypertext** principles as the World Wide Web: Clicking on an underlined word for which a pointed finger is displayed provides more information on that topic. Many VB .NET help screens will provide information on related topics, examples, and, for objects, information on properties, methods, and events that relate to those objects.

Tip: This Web site is very dynamic and may actually be somewhat different from that described.

■-■

Step-by-Step Instructions 2-6: Using Help in VB .NET

1. Position the pointer on the MsgBox function in the code window for the Vintage DVD application. Now select Dynamic Help from either the Help menu or the tab at the bottom of the Properties window. You should see the similar information to that displayed in the Properties window as shown earlier in Figure 2-25.

2. With the code window for the Vintage DVD application still displayed, position the pointer at the end of the first line of the btnMessage event handler procedure and press **ENTER** to open up a blank line. Type **MsgBox** and press the **SPACEBAR** once. You should now see the same Parameter Information help as was shown in Figure 2-26.

3. Press **ESC** to exit the Parameter Information help and then select **File|Exit** to exit VB .NET without saving the revised Vintage DVDs application.

■-■

Mini-Summary 2-6: VB .NET Help

1. There are three types of help available to you in VB .NET: the Help menu option, Dynamic Help, and "Think Ahead" Help.

2. The Help menu option has three main types of help: Contents, Index, and Search. Contents provides a discussion of major topics while the Index help provides a searchable list of keywords. The Search operation can be used to search for any words in all help documents. Much of this information is shown in the Solution Explorer window. The help documents themselves are shown in the WinForm Design window.

3. With Dynamic Help, you can locate the cursor on a control on the form or word in the Code window and see a list of help topics on that control or code statement in the Solution Explorer window.

4. If you are typing a statement, VB .NET will try to "think ahead" and provide information on completing that statement.

5. Using the Web-based help, you must "drill down" to the information you need through a series of lists of items.

It's Your Turn

1. Select Help from the menu bar, select the Index option from the Help menu, and enter **PictureBox Control** into the input box. Select **Overview** and then **Introduction to the Windows PictureBox Control** to display information on the PictureBox Control. Select the underlined option that will display information on loading an image at design time. Select the Solution Explorer tab at the bottom of the window to return to the Solution Explorer view.

2. Click the Search option Help screen and enter **PictureBox Control** into the input box. How many matches did you find? Click on the exit icon at the top right of the WinForms Design window to exit the Help System. Can you return to the most recent results quickly? How?

3. Use Help to find the answers to the following:

    a. What is the Rnd function?

    b. What does the Inputbox function do?

    c. What does the End statement do?

    d. Which arguments are required for the Msgbox function?

5. Repeat the previous question using Web-based help.

4. Follow Step-by-Step Instructions 2-6 to learn how to use the Help function in VB .NET.

SUMMARY

At the beginning of the chapter, we said you would be able to do a number of things after reading it. Let's review those things here:

1. **Begin using Visual Studio .NET and then VB .NET.** VB .NET is one of several languages that can be used to create applications using Visual Studio .NET. Starting Visual Studio .NET results in the Start Page being displayed, from which the user can create their Profile. The Profile can include setting up a filter to display only VB. NET help topics. New projects can be started or existing projects can be opened. If a new project is being started, it must be named and the type of project selected before the design environment is displayed.

2. **Point out and discuss the elements of the Microsoft Development Environment (MDE) used for VB .NET.** Understanding the MDE is essential to being able to create information system applications in VB. NET. The MDE includes the menu bar, toolbar, Toolbox, Window Forms (WinForm) Designer window, Solution Explorer window, Properties window, and Task List/Output window. The menu bar provides access to all of the commands needed to create applications, and the toolbar has icons corresponding to the more popular commands. The Toolbox has icons corresponding to various controls that can be dragged onto the WinForm window to create an interface. The Solution Explorer window shows the files that make up the project, and the Properties window displays the properties of the controls on the Form. The Task List/Output window displays tasks to be completed by multiple developers, or it displays output messages from executing application when the application is completed.

3. **Discuss the use of the form in creating a VB .NET solution.** The form is the object on which the interface for the application is created. A form can be resized to match the needs of the application. The actual application involves adding instances of controls and writing code for those controls that should respond to an event.

4. **Understand controls and their properties.** Controls are instances of objects that are located in the toolbox and can be positioned on the form to create an interface. An instance of a control can be placed on the form by

selecting it from the Toolbox and drawing on the form or double-clicking the control to display it on the form. Controls used in this chapter included the Label, Button, and PictureBox. All controls have properties or attributes such as the name, text, and image properties that can be set in design mode. These properties distinguish one instance of a control from another on the same form.

5. **Discuss the Code window used to write an event handler to generate a message box.** Once the interface has been created, the next step is to write the code for the action objects on the form to handle an event such as a mouse click. This is done by double-clicking a control and entering the instructions for it in VB .NET in the Code window to respond to a specific event. In this chapter we used the Code window to cause a message box to appear with a specific message when a button was clicked.

6. **List the different types of files that make up a VB .NET application and be able to save an application.** The files that make up a VB .NET application include a solution file with an .sln extension, one or more project files with a .vbproj extension, one or more form files with a .vb extension, a resource file for each form file with an .resx extension, and an assembly info file with a .vb extension. You can save an application through the toolbar Save Files icon or through the File|Save All menu option. You can change the names of files with the Properties window or through the File|Save *formname* As... menu option. Similarly, you can open a saved application through the File|Open Project menu option.

7. **Use the various VB .NET help facilities to answer questions about creating a solution.** There are six types of internal help available to you in VB .NET: the Help menu with the Content, Index, and Search options; Dynamic help; and two types of think-ahead help. You can also access help over the Web. Using the Web-based help, you must "drill down" to the information you need through a series of lists of items.

NEW VB .NET ELEMENTS

Controls/Objects	Properties	Methods	Events
Form object	Name Text		
Label control	Name Text Font		
Button control	Name Text Font		Click
PictureBox control	Name Image		

NEW PROGRAMMING STATEMENTS
MsgBox("message")

KEY TERMS

Auto Help	file	project file
binary form file	focus	Properties window
Class list box	form	run time
Code window	form file	sizing handles
context-sensitive help	hypertext	solution
continuation character	menu bar	Solution Explorer Window
controls	message box	Tabbed Documents Environ-
custom controls	module file	ment
default event	Microsoft Development Environ-	Task List
design mode	ment (MDE)	title bar
Design window	Multiple-document interface	toolbar
event handler	(MDI)	ToolTip
event procedure	Object list box	Toolbox
Events/Procedures list box	Program Design mode	workspace file
	Project Explorer window	

EXERCISES

1. Describe two techniques for adding controls to a form at design time.

2. Suppose that you will be using four command buttons on your form. You would like all four buttons to be the same size. In addition, you would like to line them up vertically along their right edge with equal spacing between them. Which button properties would you set? Provide an example of how you would set these property values.

3. Compare the properties of the form, Button, Label, and PictureBox controls. What properties do they have in common? What properties are different?

4. When will the following code be executed? Describe what occurs when it is executed.

```
Private Sub PicActiveImage_Click(ByVal sender As Object, _
ByVal e As System.EventArgs) Handles PicActiveImage.Click
   Msgbox("Hi Folks. Welcome to my project.")
End Sub
```

5. Using VB .NET, create a simple project that includes a form, a button, and a message that appears when the button is clicked. Test and save your project and exit VB .NET. Using any file utility, such as Windows Explorer, change the file name of the .frm file. Re-enter VB .NET and reload your project. What happens when the project attempts to load? What occurs when you try to run the project? What error did the instructions lead you to make? Why does this error occur? Can you determine how to correct the problem?

PROJECTS

Before beginning the following exercises, create a folder called **Homework** in the *Chapter2* folder you created earlier as a part of completing the *It's Your Turn!* exercises. All of the projects you create here should be saved in the *Chapter2\Homework* folder.

1. Use the **File|New Project** menu option to create a new VB .NET project named **Ex2-1.** The interface for your project should correspond to the sketch shown in Figure 2-27. Give appropriate names to your controls. Assume that when you click the Button control, a message is displayed that reads, "Pro-

fessor Beige's Grading Program." The question mark symbol can be found at ..\graphics\icons\misc\question.ico in the VB .NET directory. Use 16-point Arial font for the label. Test your project and correct any problems. Use the Windows Explorer tool to determine what other files were created when you created the project files.

FIGURE 2-27.
Sketch of interface for Exercise 1

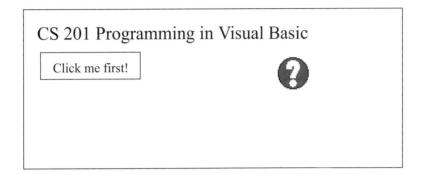

2. Use the **File | New Project** menu option to create a new VB .NET project named **Ex2-2.** The interface for your project should correspond to the interface shown in the sketch shown in Figure 2-28. Give appropriate names to your controls. Assume that when you click the Button control, a message is displayed that reads, "When completed, this button will start the program." The world symbol can be found at ..\graphics\icons\elements\world.ico. Use 18-point Times New Roman font for the label. Test your project and correct any problems.

FIGURE 2-28.
Sketch of interface for Exercise 2

3. Use the **File | New Project** menu option to create a new VB .NET project named **Ex2-3.** The interface for your project should correspond to the interface shown in the sketch shown in Figure 2-29. Give appropriate names to your controls. Assume that when you click the Button control, a message is displayed that reads, "When completed, this program will compute gas mileages." The cars symbol can be found at \graphics\icons\industry\cars.ico. Use 18-point Arial Black font for the label. Create a label with the broken line in it to place the line beneath the company name and information. Change the Backcolor property of the form to yellow using the Palette tab. (Yellow is in the third row, fourth from the left.) Also, change the Backcolor property on the label to the same color. Test

your project and correct any problems.

FIGURE 2-29.
Sketch of interface
for Exercise 3

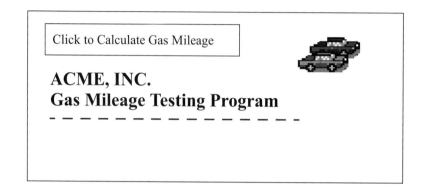

4.   Smith and Jones, Inc., needs you to create a VB .NET interface that will implement the sketch shown in Figure 2-30. Use the **File | New Project** menu option to create a new VB .NET project named **Ex2-4** to carry out this request. Give your controls appropriate names. Assume that when you click the top Button control, a message is displayed that reads, "When completed, this button will calculate breakeven volume and revenue/costs." The graph symbol can be found at ..\graphics\icons\office\graph01.ico.

Use 18-point Impact font for the label. Create a label with the solid line in it to place the line beneath the company name. Change the Backcolor property of the form to white using the Palette tab (white is in the first row, first column). Also, change the Backcolor property on the label to the same color.

FIGURE 2-30.
Sketch of interface
for Exercise 4

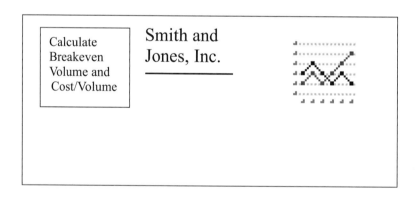

5. Cover-Your-Walls, Inc., has requested your services to create an interface for a VB .NET program that will compute room area and number of rolls of wallpaper needed. A sketch is shown in Figure 2-31. Use the **File | New Project** menu option to create a new VB .NET project named **Ex2-5** to meet this request. Assume that when you click the button control, a message is displayed that reads, "When completed, this button will calculate room area and number of rolls required." The house symbol can be found at ..\graphics \icons\misc\house.ico. Use 16-point Desdemona font for the label. Change the Backcolor property of the form to white using the Palette tab (white is in

the first row, first column). Also, change the Backcolor property on the label to the same color.

FIGURE 2-31.
Sketch of interface for Exercise 5

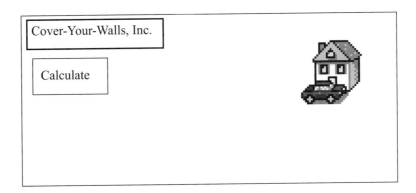

6. Anyone who has watched television late at night has noticed (among other strange programming) various pitches for "get-rich-quick" schemes. Some of these make the outrageous claim that they can help you double your money in a very short time. A simple "rule of thumb" that can be used to estimate the number of years required to double your money is known as the "rule of 72." Using the rule of 72, the approximate number of years to double an investment is equal to 72 divided by the annual percentage returned (for a savings account this would be the interest rate). This rule assumes that the interest is compounded annually and is not taxed. Design a VB .NET program to be used in applying the rule of 72 using an IPO, pseudocode, and a sketch of the interface. Make sure that your interface is intuitive and visually pleasing from a user's perspective. Begin implementing your project by creating a partial interface in VB .NET using the controls that you know. Name this project **Ex2-6** and save it in the Homework folder. Feel free to experiment with other controls on your form.

7. Professional and hard-core amateur athletes often use a heart monitor to check their heart rate during training. The monitor will indicate whether or not the heart rate is within an acceptable range of values. For those of us who are somewhat less than professional in our training, there is a pair of simple formulas that can be used to determine this range called the target heart rate zone. We can then monitor our heart rate during aerobic exercise and try to maintain it within this zone. The lower limit of the zone may be estimated as 60% of the difference between 220 and your age. The upper limit of the zone may be estimated as 75% of the difference between 220 and your age. Design a VB .NET program to determine your target heart rate zone. Use an IPO, pseudocode, and a sketch of the interface. Make sure that your interface is intuitive and visually pleasing. Begin implementing your program by creating a partial interface in VB .NET using the controls that you know named **Ex2-7**. Feel free to experiment with other controls on your form.

8. Have you ever wondered which size of pizza actually provides the most pizza for your pizza-buying dollar? Round pizzas are often identified by their

diameter. The size of the pizza in square inches may be computed using the formula for the area of a circle (area = $\pi \times$ diameter^2/4). The price of the pizza per square inch may then be calculated by dividing the total price by the pizza's area. Design a VB .NET program to be used in determining the area of a pizza in square inches and the price per square inch. Use an IPO, pseudocode, and a sketch of the interface. Make sure that your interface is intuitive and visually pleasing from a user's perspective. Begin implementing your program by creating a partial interface in VB .NET using the controls that you know named **Ex2-8**. Feel free to experiment with other controls on your form.

3 VARIABLES, ASSIGNMENT STATEMENTS, AND ARITHMETIC

LEARNING OBJECTIVES

After reading this chapter, you will able to

1. Understand a four-step process to writing code in VB .NET and its relationship to the six operations a computer can perform.
2. Declare and use different types of variables in your project.
3. Use text boxes for event-driven input and output.
4. Write VB .NET instructions to carry out arithmetic operations.
5. Discuss using VB .NET functions to carry out commonly used operations.
6. Use buttons to clear text boxes and exit the project.
7. Describe the types of errors that commonly occur in a VB .NET project and their causes.

WORKING WITH VARIABLES

Recall from Chapter 1 that a computer can carry out six basic operations:

1. Input data
2. Store data in internal memory
3. Perform arithmetic on data
4. Compare two values and select one of two alternative actions
5. Repeat a group of actions any number of times
6. Output the results of processing.

In Chapter 2, we created a VB .NET project for a company named *Vintage DVDs* that carried out only two of these operations by responding to input in the form of a mouse click to output a message. In this chapter, we are going to expand that project to handle input in the form of the name of the customer, the name of the DVD being rented, and the rental price. The project must then use arithmetic operations on data to compute the sales tax on the DVD and add this amount to the rental price to compute the amount due. The project must output the sales tax and amount due that are calculated and respond to a mouse click to print the form, clear text boxes, and terminate execution of the project.

To do this, we will need to carry out Steps 1–3 and 6; that is, we need to store both data and instructions in the computer's memory, perform arithmetic on the data, and output the results of the processing. In this chapter we will not need to compare two values or repeat a group of actions.

Four-Step Coding Process

After the logic for the problem has been developed using IPO tables and pseudocode, the next step is writing the program in VB .NET or another language. Creating a program in VB .NET follows a four-step process:

1. Decide what variables and constants will be needed and declare them.
2. Input data from text boxes or other input controls.
3. Process data into information using arithmetic or string operations and store in variables.
4. Output values of variables to text boxes or other output controls.

We will follow this four-step process for a simple calculator, the Vintage DVDs example from Chapter 2, and, finally, a monthly payment application. First, we will discuss the use of variables in programming.

Variables

To be able to carry out any type of arithmetic operation, you need to understand the manner in which data are stored in the computer's internal memory. Internal memory can be thought of as a very large number of boxes called **memory cells** arranged in a manner similar to post office boxes. In each memory cell, one and only one data item can be stored at a time. To store a new value in the memory cell, you must destroy the old value. However, you can retrieve and use a value from a memory cell without destroying it.

Because memory cells can have different values stored in them, they are commonly referred to as **variables**. The location of the memory cell remains the same, but different values may reside there at different times during the execution of the program. For example, a memory cell (variable) called Number may begin with a value of 10, have this changed to 0, and then to – 20.

Changing the value of a variable involves destroying the contents of the memory cell and resupplying the cell with a new value. So, in a computer program when we speak of a variable or a variable name, these terms refer to a memory cell in the computer's memory. The *value of a variable* in a program is the *current value* in the memory cell with the same name.

Naming Variables

Because data are stored in variables, in order to perform a desired operation, both you and the computer must be able to refer to a variable. To identify variables, you must assign names to them. Once this is done and a variable name is used in the program, there is no uncertainty as to which variable is being referenced. For example, if you have given a variable a name of Number and it has a value of 10 stored in it, then you can change the value stored in Number by using the appropriate instructions and referring to Number. Note that the name of the memory cell and its contents are *not* the same. If a variable is named B, this does *not* mean it has the symbol "B" stored in it.

Variables are named in VB .NET through a combination of the letters A through Z, the digits 0 through 9, and the underscore (_). Variable names are not allowed to contain any other *special* characters, and they must *always* start with a letter. VB .NET variable names are virtually unlimited in their length, but you will probably never want to create a very long variable name due to the problems in retyping it many times. VB .NET is *case-insensitive*; that is, case is not considered in variable names. For example, a variable named NUMBER is the same as a variable named Number or number. However, it is often useful to use upper- and lowercase letters in variable names, especially when words are combined to create a variable name. Doing this helps you understand the purpose of the variable. For example, InterestRate is easier to understand than interestrate. You should avoid using all capitals for variable names, since they can make the name difficult to understand.

A naming convention is also considered standard when using variables. The standard convention is to prefix the variable name with a three-letter indicator related to the variable data type. Variable data types will be discussed shortly. For example, a variable representing a tax amount that is declared as a decimal data type may be named decTaxes following this convention. This convention will be followed throughout the text.

In addition to these rules about variable names, another rule is that a variable name may not be one of the restricted **keywords** in VB .NET. These are words that VB .NET uses as a part of its language. For example, you could not use the keyword Sub as a variable name. However, it is valid to imbed a keyword in a variable name. For this reason, it would be valid to use SubThis as a variable name. VB .NET is very helpful in alerting you to keywords and errors in variable names. Keywords are displayed in blue and errors with a wavy underline. For example, if you tried to use Sub as a variable name, VB .NET would display an error message and show the word *Sub* with a wavy underline. Positioning the cursor over an error generates a Tool-Tip that explains the problem. If this happens, change the variable name and try again.

A common practice is to choose a name that in some way helps the programmer to remember the quantity being represented by the variable. Such devices that aid the programmer's memory are termed **mnemonic variable names**. The use of mnemonic variable names is considered good programming practice. The only problem with using long variable names is that they can be cumbersome to work with in the programming process. For that reason, it is a good idea to make sure the variable name represents the quantity but does not become too long. Table 3-1 shows quantities and a typical name for the variable corresponding to each of those quantities.

Data Types

Different types of data can be stored in a computer's internal memory. VB .NET supports 13 standard data types as well as user-defined data types. The data types you will use most often for your work include String, Single, Double, Integer, Long Integer, Decimal, Date, and Boolean (true or false).

The **String data type**, prefixed *str*, is used to store any string of ASCII symbols or characters that is enclosed in quotation marks. For example, a String variable might hold "120 Hilltop Rd." All of the remaining data types listed above are considered **numeric data types,** because they store

TABLE 3-1: Example variable names

Item	Variable Name
DVD rental price	decDVDPrice
Amount due	decAmountDue
Taxes due	decTaxes
Interest on home mortgage	decMortageInterest
Year-to-date earnings	decYTDEarnings
Employee's last name	strEmpLastName

numeric data and can be used in arithmetic processing. It is important to remember that Numeric variables are very different from the numbers stored as String variables. Numeric variables can be used in arithmetic operations— addition, subtraction, multiplication, and so on. String variables, on the other hand, *should not* be used in such operations. The primary purpose of String variables is to provide for the input, output, and manipulation of sets or *strings* of characters.

Integers and **Long Integers** are designed to be used only with whole numbers, and they cannot have any fractional portion. **Single** and **Double precision** numbers can contain a decimal point and are used for calculations that require fractional values. They are **floating point operations**, since the position of the decimal point is not fixed. If you need to work with currency or other values in which you need up to 28 decimal places of accuracy, then you would use the **Decimal** data type. You might not think of the **Date** or **Boolean** data types as being Numeric, but both can be used in arithmetic processing. For example, you would store today's data in a variable of the Date data type. Similarly, the Boolean type corresponds to values of 0 (false) or –1 (true), so if a value is multiplied by a Boolean variable, depending on the value of the Boolean variable, its sign may be changed.

Good programming practice calls for the type of variable to be shown as a prefix to the variable name just like prefixes are used as a part control names. For example, we used *dec* as a prefix for a variable that will hold decimal data. We will use these prefixes whenever we declare variables. Table 3-2 displays the characteristics of each Numeric data type along with the standard three letter prefix for each data type and other pertinent information about the data type.

In Table 3-2, the *range* refers to the values that can be represented by this type of constant. A value involving an E followed by a number means that value raised to that power of 10. For example, 2.5E2 is the same as 2.5×10^2. *Precision* in the table refers to how accurately this type of constant can store numbers. For example, Integers and Long Integers cannot store numbers with fractions, so they are accurate to only the whole number part of a value. Similarly, a Single variable can be accurate to only the first seven digits that are stored in it. So, 23,561.1903 is accurate to only the first seven digits, or 23,561.19, with the last two decimal places being lost.

Finally, the *Number of Bytes* refers to the amount of internal memory required to store this constant, where one byte equals eight bits. In general,

TABLE 3-2: Characteristics of numeric data types

Numeric Data Type	Prefix	Range	Precision	Number of Bytes
Single	sng	1.4E-45 to 3.4E38 and −3.4E38 to −1.4E-45	Seven significant digits	4
Double	dbl	4.9E-324 to 1.8E308 and −1.8E308 to −4.9E-324	Fifteen significant digits	8
Decimal	dec	Very large positive or negative numbers to very small positive or negative numbers (too large and small to be shown here)	Twenty-eight places to right of decimal	16
Integer	int	−2,147,483,648 to 2,147,483,647	Whole numbers	4
Long	lng	−9,223,372,036,854,775,808 to 9,223,372,036,854,775,807	Whole numbers	8
Short	sht	−32,768 to 32,767	Whole numbers	2
Date	dtm	Dates between January 1, 0001, and December 31, 9999	Not applicable	8
Boolean	bln	True or false	Not applicable	2

the greater the range and precision, the greater the number of bytes required to store the data type.

In addition to the String and Numeric data types, VB .NET offers the **Object** data type. An Object data type can take on any of the other data types as needed. This generally occurs in the coding process when you fail to declare the type of variable you are using and VB .NET has to "guess" at the data type by using an Object type variable. In general, it is not a good idea to have VB .NET do this, so you should always "declare" the data type for each variable you use in your project. We will discuss this process in more detail next.

Using the coding convention prefixes for objects and variables can provide several advantages including:

* Your code follows a standard that allows anyone who reads the code to immediately determine the data type of the variable;

* Words that are normally reserved as VB .NET keywords may be used as part of an object or variable name, for example strSub;

* You can name different objects and variables with practically the same name. For example, imagine that you have a form with a label and a text box used to enter a user's age. If prefixes are used, you may name your text box *txtAge*, the corresponding label *lblAge*, and even an integer variable that may receive the value of the text box as *intAge*.

Declaring Variables Good programming form requires that you always inform VB .NET of the data type you wish to be used with a given variable. This operation, termed *declaring variables*, is usually the first code instruction that is entered into an event procedure for a control. While variables can be declared in a number of ways, the most common declaration form uses the Dim keyword in combination with the variable name and the data type; that is,

Dim *variable name* As *data type*￼

where you supply both the variable name and the data type (use the data types given in Table 3-2 or, for a String variable, use the keyword String.)

For example, to declare a variable called decMyIncome as Decimal, the statement would be

```
Dim decMyIncome As Decimal
```

Similarly, to declare a variable called strHerName as a String type, the statement would be

```
Dim strHerName As String
```

You may combine multiple declarations on one line by separating them by commas. For example, to combine the two previous declarations on one line, you would enter

```
Dim decMyIncome As Decimal, strHerName As String
```

Multiple declarations of the same type need only have a data type after the last one. For example, the declaration

```
Dim decMySalary, decYourSalary As Decimal
```

will result in both variables being declared to be the type Decimal.

Failure to include any data type declaration with one or more variables on a declaration line will result in all of them being declared as Object type variables. For example,

```
Dim decBigSalary, decSmallSalary
```

will result in both decBigSalary and decSmallSalary being declared as Object type variables.

In VB .NET, you can also *initialize* a variable to some value as well as declaring it in one statement. For example, if you wanted to declare a variable, intCounter, as an Integer and set it to zero in one statement, it would appear as

```
Dim intCounter As Integer = 0
```

> **TIP:** However you declare a variable in terms of upper- and lowercase letters, VB .NET will always change the case of the variable in later references to fit the declaration. This can be useful for a quick check on the variables that you are using.

Using the Option Explicit Statement

Throughout this book, we will always declare variables since it is our belief that the programmer should always be in control. Failure to declare variables leaves it up to VB .NET to use the Object type, which can lead to problems when VB .NET makes the wrong decision as to how a variable should be used. To ensure that you always declare variables, VB .NET automatically turns **Option Explicit** On in every project. This option requires that all variables be declared and generates an error message if any are not. You could turn this option off in every project you create by typing in "Option Explicit Off" *before any other code in the module*, including the Public Class statement.

Mini-Summary 3-1: Variables and data types

1. A four-step coding process should be used to write programs in VB .NET.

2. Variables correspond to memory locations in the computer in which data and results are stored. They are assigned names by the programmer and used in the program.

3. A variety of data types can be stored in the memory locations; all are referred to by their variable names.

4. It is a good idea to declare variables as to the type of data on which they correspond. Variables are declared with the Dim statement.

5. Variables are automatically forced to be declared in VB .NET. To stop this, you must use the Option Explicit Off statement before the Public Class statement (not a good idea.)

It's Your Turn!

1. Give the most appropriate data type for each of the following values:

    a. 23
    b. 7.56
    c. True
    d. $100.87
    e. 9534
    f. 10089.34512

2. Create a variable name for each of the following quantities and give the appropriate data type:

    a. Time until arrival
    b. Take-home pay
    c. Discount rate
    d. Shipping rate per pound
    e. Failure rate per 1000
    f. Pass or fail?

3. Write instructions to declare the variables for which you created names in the previous exercise.

4. Rewrite your declaration from Exercise 3 to initialize the Discount rate to 0.06 as well as declaring it as a single type variable. Do the same for the shipping rate to initialize it to $50 as well as declaring it to be a decimal-type variable.

5. For each of the following short scenarios, list the variables that you would need to solve the problem. In your list include the variable name, its data type, and the declaration statement that you would use.

    a. W. Loman makes a living as a traveling salesman. In order to properly maintain his vehicle, Mr. Loman faithfully records the odometer reading (total miles a car has traveled) and the gallons of gas purchased. He then uses these values to calculate the miles per gallon for his vehicle since the last fill-up.

b. Joe "Bull" Cigar occasionally checks the prices of the shares of stock that he owns in the financial pages of his local newspaper. When he checks, he records the date, the closing price of the stock, and the number of shares traded. Bull would like to be able to save this information in a file on his computer. In addition, he would like to be able to calculate the percent change in stock price since his initial investment.

c. Tiger "Golden Bear" Shark is new to the professional golf circuit. He would like a simple program for his palm device in which he can keep a record of his performance by hole on the various courses that he plays. He will need to enter the name of the course, the date, the hole number, the hole par, his score on the hole, and comments about the hole. In addition, he would like the program to calculate his total score for a round and how far over or under par.

6. Why is it *not* a good idea to include the **Option Explicit Off** statement in your projects?

EVENT-DRIVEN INPUT

Now that you understand the use of variables to represent the contents of a memory cell, the next question is: How do we get data into these variables? This is accomplished through some type of input. By **input** we mean using the keyboard, mouse, or other means to enter data into a variable. There must *always* be some form of input for processing of data into information to take place. In procedural languages, there are some types of input or read statements that enter data directly into a variable. However, for input to occur in event-driven languages like VB .NET, where the user typically enters data into a control on the screen, an event must transfer the data from the control to a variable. This is important to note: While you can enter data into a control, if the appropriate event does not take place, then the data will never be used in the program. (This is not to say that we will never input data directly into variables; it does mean that transferring data from a control to a variable is more in keeping with the event-driven nature of VB .NET).

The control commonly used for event-driven input is the **TextBox control**, into which data can be easily entered into a text box. Once data have been entered into a text box, you can use an event like clicking a button to transfer the data to a variable, which can then be used in some type of computation. The TextBox control can also be used to display processed information. The property of the TextBox control that enables it to be used for input and output is its **Text property**. The Text property is *always* equal to whatever is displayed in the **Edit field** of the TextBox, that is, the area in the text box in which you may enter, edit, or display text. To enter text in a text box, you simply click the mouse pointer inside the blank area to change it to a vertical line and type the text. You may edit existing text by placing the pointer in the text box at the desired location and using the word processing editing keys to change the text.

To add a TextBox control to a form, you select it from the Toolbox, place it on the form, and change its Name and other properties, just like you did with the Label, PictureBox, and Button controls in Chapter 2. The Name property of the TextBox should be changed to begin with a prefix of *txt*. The

TextBox Control

TextBox control
icon

default Text property that is initially displayed in a text box is *text* combined with a number, say, *textbox1*. Figure 3-1 shows a form with a text box cen-tered in the upper half. Note that we have also added a Label control with a Text property that describes this text box as *First Number*. Note also that the text box is empty because we deleted the default value for the Text property. The name of the text box has been changed to *txtFirstNum* and the name of the label to *lblFirstNum*.

FIGURE 3-1. Text box added to form

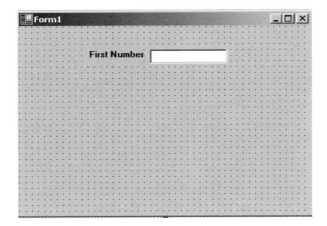

Creating a Simple Calculator

As an example of using the TextBox control for input (and output), let's add two more text boxes and accompanying labels to the form shown in Figure 3-1. Let's also add two buttons and a label for which the Text property can be set equal to the underscore to form a line, to create a very simple calculator that sums the contents of the top two (input) text boxes and displays the result in the third (output) text box. Clicking *Sum* transfers the contents of the two input text boxes to variables, carries out the addition, and transfers the results to the output text box. Similarly, clicking *Clear* clears the text boxes and places the cursor back in the top text box. The resulting form is shown in Figure 3-2 and the Name and Text properties (where appropriate) are shown in Table 3-3. The form has also been made the Startup object for the project and saved as *Simple.vb*. In all cases, the Font properties for the texts have been set to 10 points with bold style .

TIP: The order in which you add text boxes to the form controls the order that the cursor will follow when the **TAB** key is pressed. If the order is incorrect, you can change it in the Properties window with the **TabIndex** property of the text box. Make the TabIndex property for the first text box = 0, the second = 1, and so on.

FIGURE 3-2. Simple calculator design

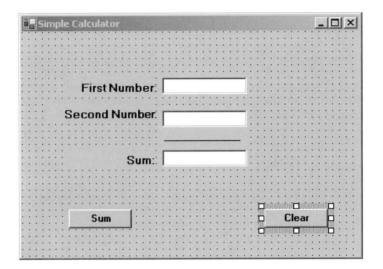

TABLE 3-3: Controls for calculator

Control	Name	Text
Form	frmSimple	Simple Calculator
TextBox	txtFirstNum	
TextBox	txtSecondNum	
TextBox	txtSum	
Label	lblFirstNum	First Number (right-justified)
Label	lblSecondNum	Second Number (right-justified)
Label	lblSum	Sum (right-justified)
Label	lblLine	_____ (multiple underscore)
Button	btnSum	Sum
Button	btnClear	Clear

Using Assignment Statements to Input Data

To transfer the contents of the text boxes to variables, you must use an **assignment statement**. An assignment statement gives a variable a value by setting it equal either to an existing quantity or to a value that is computed by the program. In the case of transferring the contents of a text box to a variable, the variable is set equal to the Text property of the text box. The general form of an assignment statement is

Control property* or *variable* = *value*, *variable*, *expression*, or *property

Note that the control property or variable being assigned a value appears on the left side of the equals sign, with a value, variable, expression, or control property appearing on the right. This is an important rule that must always be followed in the assignment statement. For example, an assignment statement might be

```
decAmountDue = decPrice + decTaxes
```

where decAmountDue is a variable to which the sum of the decPrice and decTaxes variables is being assigned.

To input data from a control property, we simply set a variable equal to the control property. For example, to input the value for intFirst from txt-First.text, the assignment statement is

```
intfirst = txtFirst.text
```

We will discuss other applications of assignment statements in more detail later in this chapter, but for now we are interested in assigning the Text property of the text boxes to variables, summing those variables, and transferring the sum to a third text box. Since all of this is accomplished by the btnSum button, we need to double-click this control to open its Code window and declare three variables—intFirst, intSecond, and intSum—that will be used in the actual summation. Next, we need to use assignment statements to transfer the Text property of the text boxes to the variables intFirst and intSecond as shown above. These statements are shown in VB Code Box 7-1.

VB CODE BOX 7-1. Code to input two numbers	```Private Sub btnSum_Click(ByVal sender As System.Object, _```
	 ```ByVal e As System.EventArgs) Handles btnSum.Click```
	 ``` Dim intFirst, intSecond, intSum As Integer```
	 ``` intFirst = txtFirstNum.Text```
	 ``` intSecond = txtSecondNum.Text```
	 ```End Sub```

> **TIP:** In most places in your project, you can position the pointer on a control, property, function, or other entity and press **F1** to display Dynamic Help about it.

Using Functions

In looking at the assignment statements in VB Code Box 7-1, notice that intFirst and intSecond are Integer variables, but the Text property of any text box is a character string. This means that we have Numeric variables being set equal to String quantities—something that should be avoided since it requires VB .NET to decide how to handle the mismatch of types. While VB .NET *usually* handles this appropriately by converting the quantity on the right to the variable type on the left, it is not wise to leave this conversion up to VB .NET. Instead, we need to use a built-in VB .NET function to carry out the conversion. A **function** is *an operation that returns a single value. It may or may not have any arguments*. The common form of a function with arguments is

variable = functionname(arg1, arg2, ...)
where arg1, arg2, and so on are the arguments of the function and the value
is returned through the function name in an assignment or other statement.
You might want to think of any function as a *black box* into which arguments
are fed and from which a single value is returned, as shown in Figure 3-3. We
do not need to know how it works to use it; we only need to know the name
of the function, the appropriate form of the arguments and the type of value
to be returned.

FIGURE 3-3.
Function as black
box

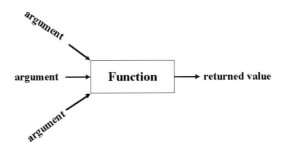

Not all functions require arguments. For example, the **Today** function
returns the system date on your computer with no arguments. Regardless of
whether a function does or does not require arguments, all are used in a similar manner.

In our case, we will use the **CInt( )** function to convert the Text property
from a string to an Integer value number, which is then assigned to a
Numeric variable. For example, instead of

```
intFirst = txtFirstNum.Text
```
the appropriate statement is
```
intFirst = CInt(txtFirstNum.Text)
```
The revised code for the btnSum button using the CInt function is shown
in VB Code Box 7-2.

VB Code Box 7-2. Using CInt( ) function to convert strings to numbers	```Private Sub btnSum_Click(ByVal sender as System.Object, _```
	 ```ByVal e as System.EventArgs) Handles btnSum.Click```
	 ``` Dim intFirst, intSecond, intSum As Integer```
	 ``` intFirst = CInt(txtFirstNum.Text)```
	 ``` intSecond = CInt(txtSecondNum.Text)```
	 ```End Sub```

You might ask, why not use the text boxes directly for this computation?
The answer to this question involves the nature of the Text property of a text
box: It is a String, and as such it must be converted into a Numeric variable
before being used in any type of calculation. If you try to use the Text property in a calculation, in some cases it will be converted into an Object data
type while in others it will remain as a String. In either case, the results can
end up surprising and *wrong!*

Computing and Displaying the Sum

Now that we have the contents of the two text boxes transferred to variables,
the next step is to sum these two variables and assign that sum to a new variable, intSum, which must be declared. The value of intSum is then displayed

in the output text box, txtSum.text. Once again, we use declaration and assignment statements to carry out these operations. First, we declare intSum to be of type Integer and then we use the summation sign (+) to sum the variables intFirst and intSecond, with the result being assigned to the variable intSum. This assignment statement will appear as

```
intSum = intFirst + intSecond
```

In the second case, it might appear that we simply assign the value of the variable intSum to the Text property of the text box txtSum. However, we have the reverse of the problem we had before; we are now assigning the value of an Integer variable to a text box that is a String. To make sure that this conversion is handled correctly, we need to use the **CStr( ) function**, which converts the Numeric argument into a character string. In this case, the assignment statement is

```
txtSum.Text = CStr(intSum)
```

If we add these two statements to the Code window for the btnSum button, we arrive at the code shown in VB Code Box 7-3. This is *all* the code you need to use our simple calculator. If you enter an Integer value in the top text box and a second Integer value in the second text box, and click *Sum*, the sum of the two values will be displayed in the bottom text box. For example, if we enter 20 and 30 and click *Sum* again, the sum, 50, will be displayed.

VB CODE BOX 7-3. Code for btnSum button	```Private Sub btnSum_Click(ByVal sender as System.Object, _ ByVal e as System.EventArgs) Handles btnSum.Click Dim intFirst, intSecond, intSum As Integer intFirst = txtFirstNum.Text intSecond = txtSecondNum.Text intSum = intFirst + intSecond txtSum.text = str(intSum) End Sub```

Properties and Methods

Note that the Text property for the txtSum text box is shown appended to the text box name with a period. This **dot notation** is the way that properties are set at run time. The general form for setting a property at run time is

object.property = value

and for using a property is

value = object.property

The same notation is used to invoke a method for a control. Recall that methods define the actions that a control can carry out. The general form for using a method at run time is

object.method

For example, a method that is associated with a text box is the **Focus( )** method. This method shifts the cursor to the text box whenever it is invoked. If we wanted to put the cursor in the txtFirstNum text box, the statement would be

```
txtFirstNum.Focus( )
```

We will use this method later in the calculator example.

In comparing the use of properties and methods, you should note one crucial difference: *A control* **property** *can be used in an assignment statement, but a control* **method** *can never be used in an assignment statement.*

So, if you ever see a control followed by a period and name in an assignment statement, the name must refer to a property. Conversely, if you see a control followed by a period and name by itself, then the name must refer to a method.

> **TIP:** Note that when you type the name of an object in your code, an Auto List pop-up menu appears just after typing the period. This menu provides a listing of all properties and methods available for the object that you typed.

Clearing Text Boxes   After we use this calculator for one set of numbers, to use it again we need to clear the text boxes and set the focus back to the first text box. To do this, we need to add code to the btnClear button that sets the Text property of each text box to an empty string (`""`) and uses the Focus method to position the cursor in the txtFirstNum text box. The code for this button is shown in VB Code Box 7-4.

| **VB Code Box 7-4.** Code for btnClear button | ```
Private Sub btnClear_Click(ByVal sender As System.Object, ByVal e As
System.EventArgs) Handles btnClear.Click
    txtFirstNum.Text = ""
    txtSecondNum.Text = ""
    txtSum.Text = ""
    txtFirstNum.Focus( )
End Sub
``` |
| --- | --- |

> **TIP:** The null string (`""`) does *not* contain any spaces between the pair of quotation marks.

If 20 and 30 are entered in the top two text boxes of the Calculator project and *Sum* is clicked, the result is shown in Figure 3-4. If *Clear* is then clicked, all three text boxes will be cleared and the focus will be set back to the top text box. The steps to create the simple calculator project are summarized in Step-by-Step Instructions 3-1.

FIGURE 3-4. Running the simple calculator

Simple Calculator

First Number: 20

Second Number: 30

Sum: 50

Sum   Clear
```

Step-by-Step Instructions 3-1: Creating a simple calculator

1. In Window Explorer, create a new folder in the Visual Studio Projects folder named **Chapter3.** Then,

   a. Start VB .NET and select **New Project** from the Start page (or **File|New|Project** if you are already in VB .NET) to create a new project.

   b. Give the new project a name of **Simple** and make sure it is being created in the *Chapter3* folder you just created.

   c. Change the Text property of the form to **Simple Calculator** and change the Name property of the form to **frmSimple**.

   d. In the Solutions Window, *right-click* on the *Simple.vbproj* project file and selecting **Properties.** In the resulting Properties page, select **frmSimple** as the Startup Object.

   e. Finally, use the **File|Save Form1 as...** menu option to save the form as **Simple.vb**.

2. In the Solution Explorer window, *right click* on the **Simple.vbproj** project file (the second one from the top) and select **Properties.** In the Properties dialog box, change the *Startup Object* from **Form1** to **frmSimple**.

3. To the frmSimple form, add three text boxes, four corresponding labels (one for a series of underscores) as shown in Figure 3-2. (You will need to experiment with the number of underscores in the Label control to make it match the width of the text boxes.) Change the font for the labels to **10-point bold**.

4. Add buttons in the lower left-hand and right-hand areas of the form. Use the names and texts (where appropriate) shown in Table 3-3 for the controls on this form.

5. Open the Code window for the **btnSum** button and enter the code shown in VB Code Box 7-3.

6. Open the Code window for the **btnClear** button and enter the code shown in VB Code Box 7-4. Change the font for both buttons to be **10-point bold**.

7. Click the *Start* button. Enter **20** in the top text box and **30** in the second text box and click *Sum.* Your result should look like Figure 3-4. Now click *Clear* to clear all text boxes and set the focus back to the top text box. Test your project with a few other combinations of Integers, both positive and negative. When these are completed, click the *Stop* button.

8. Note: If you receive an error message like "Sub Main was not found ..." when you run the program, double-click on the error message. A window will be displayed from which you can form name **(frmSimple)** and click *OK* to continue. This will occur if you fail to make frmSimple your Startup Object.

9. Click the **Save All** icon to save the files in this project.

Mini-Summary 3-2: Event-driven input

1. Input in a VB .NET program is often event-driven. A value is entered into a text box and then transferred to a variable with an event such as clicking a button.

2. An assignment statement is used to transfer the contents of the text box to a variable and to make arithmetic calculations with the variables.

3. The CInt( ) function is used to convert the string contents of the text box to an Integer variable. The CStr( ) function converts numeric variables into strings for storage in text boxes.

4. Control properties can be used in assignment statements, but control methods cannot.

5. Text boxes may be cleared by setting equal to a null or empty string. The Focus method positions the cursor in a text box.

It's Your Turn!

1. Assume the following variable declarations have been made:

```
Dim intN As Integer
Dim sngPi As Single
Dim sngAlpha As Single
```
Determine which of the following are valid VB .NET assignment statements. If they are not valid explain why they are not.
   a. sngPi = 3.141592
   b. intN + 1 = intN
   c. sngAlpha = 1
   d. sngAlpha = sngAlpha
   e. 3 = intN
   f. intN = intN + 1
   g. intN = "Five"

2. For each of the following, what is the value displayed in txtAnswer after the code completes execution (where we have not shown all of the first statement in each event procedure)?

```
a. Private Sub btnCalculate_Click( )
      Dim intFirst, intSecond, intAnswer As Integer
      intFirst = 5
      intSecond = 3
      intAnswer = intFirst + intSecond
      txtAnswer.Text = intAnswer
   End Sub

b. Private Sub btnCalculate_Click( )
      txtR.Text = CStr(0.07)
       txtS.Text = CStr(4.5)
        txtAnswer.Text= CStr(CInt(txtR.Text) + CInt(txtS.Text))
   End Sub

c. Private Sub btnCalculate_Click( )
      Dim intA As Integer
      Dim intB As Integer
      Dim intAnswer As Integer
```

```
        intAnswer = intA + intB
        txtAnswer.Text = ""
     End Sub
```

3. Explain what is wrong with the following statement:

```
   txtName.Focus = On
```

4. Complete Step-by-Step Instructions 3-1 to create the Simple Calculator example.

5. Experiment with the use of the Text property by adding a new button to the Simple Calculator example with a Text property of **Test** and a Name property of **btnTest**. The Code window for this button should have only one line:

txtSum.Text = txtFirstNum.Text + txtSecondNum.Text

6. Run the project again with values of **20** and **30** and click *Test.* What happens? Note that the two numbers have been concatenated (combined into one string) rather than being summed. Close the project *without* saving the revised version of this project.

USING ASSIGNMENT STATEMENTS FOR CALCULATIONS

Now that you have seen and used assignment statements to transfer input and output to and from text boxes and to carry out a simple calculation, you are ready to consider more complex uses of assignment statements. However, in all cases, the same idea as before applies; that is, you always have the variable or control property on the left side of the equal sign and a value, variable, expression, or Control property on the right side. While the term *expression* in our discussion of assignment statements is a common one in algebra, it needs to be defined for programming: An **expression** is *a combination of one or more variables, constants, or functions with operators.* We already saw one example of an expression when we summed the two variables in the Simple Calculator, that is, intFirst + intSecond. In this discussion, we will cover numerous other situations involving expressions.

To understand our definition of an expression, we need to understand two new terms in it: constants and operators. A **constant** is a quantity that does not change. Numbers are constants, as are strings enclosed in quotation marks. For example, 73 and –0.453 are numeric constants and "VB .NET" is a string constant. Constants are used frequently in expressions when the same value applies to all situations. For example, the circumference of a circle is always 3.14157 times the diameter of the circle (where 3.14157 represents pi).

Operators are symbols used for carrying out processing. The plus sign we used in the Simple Calculator example is an operator. There are four types of operators: arithmetic, concatenation, comparison, and logical. Arithmetic operators are used to carry out arithmetic calculations. Concatenation operators are used to combine String variables and constants. Comparison operators are used to compare variables and constants. Finally, logical operators are used for logical operations. For the time being, we will concentrate on the arithmetic operators shown in Table 3-4.

You should already be familiar with all of these operations, with the possible exception of integer division and the use of the Modulus operator. Inte-

TABLE 3-4: Arithmetic Operators

Operator	Function	Example	Result
( )	Grouping	(A + B)	Groups summation operation
^	Exponentiation	Radius^2	Squares Radius
–	Negation	–Amount	Changes sign of Amount
*	Multiplication	3*Price	Multiplies Price by 3
/	Division	PayRaise/Months	Divides PayRaise by Months
\	Integer Division	Number\3	Performs integer division of Number by 3
Mod	Modulus	15 Mod 2	Remainder from dividing 15 by 2
+	Addition	Price + Taxes	Sums Price and Taxes
–	Subtraction	Salary – Deductions	Subtracts Deductions from Salary

ger division is differentiated from standard division in that with integer division both the divisor and the dividend are rounded to integers and the quotient is truncated to an integer. For example, if A = 7.111 and B = 1.95, then $A\backslash B$ will result in 7.111 being rounded to 7, B being rounded to 2, and the quotient of 7 divided by 2 will be truncated to 3. As a result, 7.111\1.95 yields an integer value of 3.

The Modulus operation finds the integer remainder that results from integer division of the two operands. For example, if we use the same two values of A and B as above, A MOD B will yield a value of 1 (7.111\1.95 = 7\2 = 3 with remainder of 1)

We can construct arithmetic expressions by combining variables, constants, and arithmetic operators. Examples of valid arithmetic expressions in assignment statements are shown in Table 3-5.

All of the examples in Table 3-5 should be clear, with the possible exception of the examples involving the variable intCounter. In these two examples, we first *initialize* the variable to zero and then increment it by one. These two instructions provide two key concepts to remember. First, you should never assume that the value of any variable is automatically zero or anything else. It may retain a value from a previous use, so any variable that will appear later should always be initialized on the *right* side of an assignment statement.

Second, whenever the same variable appears on both sides of an assignment statement, the value of a variable on the *right* side of the equals sign is the *current value* of that variable and the value of the variable on the *left* side of the equals sign is the *new value* of the variable. Having two different values of the same variable in the same assignment statement does not confuse the computer, because it makes any needed calculations on the right side of the equals sign using current values. It then takes the resulting value and places it in the variable on the left side of the equals sign. This way there is no confusion between old and new values of the same variable

At this point, we need to consider a major syntax error that can occur when in the use of an assignment statement: An expression can never appear on the left side of the equals sign. For example, an *invalid* assignment statement is

```
X + Y = Z + Q
```

Note that the expression consisting of two variables and an operator on the left of the equals sign violates the rule about expressions on the left side of the equals sign..

TABLE 3-5: Examples of valid expressions in assignment statements

Expression	Result
decTakeHome = decSalary - decDeductions	TakeHome value is equal to Salary minus Taxes and Deductions.
decInterest = decPrincipal * sngInterestRate	Interest value is equal to Principal times InterestRate.
sngArea = 3.14157*sngRadius^2	Value of pi is multiplied by Radius squared to compute area of a circle.
decUnitCost = decTotalCost/intUnits	Unit Cost is equal to TotalCost divided by number of Units.
intRoundUp = intBig\intTiny + intBig Mod intTiny	The remainder of integer division of Big by Tiny is added to the result of integer division of Big by Tiny to compute the RoundUp value.
intCounter = 0	The variable Counter is set equal to zero.
intCounter = intCounter + 1	The variable Counter is set equal to *old* value of Counter plus 1.

The Hierarchy of Operations

An important question may come to mind when you're using arithmetic operators: In what order will the operators be used? For example, consider the following expression in an assignment statement:

```
Cost = F + V*D + S*D^2
```

Note that there are two summations, two multiplications, and an exponentiation operation. The order in which these operations are carried out will determine the value of the expression, which in turn will be assigned to the variable, Cost, on the left side of the equals sign. However, there is no ambiguity about the order of arithmetic operations in this or any expression on the right side of an assignment statement, because the hierarchy of operations will control the order in which the operations are performed. For VB .NET, the **Hierarchy of Operations** is as follows:

1. Parentheses
2. Raising to a power
3. Change of sign (negation)
4. Multiplication or division
5. Integer division
6. Modulus
7. Addition or subtraction

Note that the arithmetic operators were listed in Table 3-4 in the same order as the hierarchy of operations. In case of a tie, VB. NET works from left to right.

Returning to our example, since there are no parentheses in the expression F + V*D + S*D^2, according to the hierarchy of operations the arithmetic operations will carried out in the following order:

1. *D* will be raised to the second power.

2. *V* will then be multiplied by *D*, and *S* will be multiplied by *D*-squared.

3. F and the two products found in Operation 2 will be summed.

If $F = 100$, $V = 200$, $D = 30$, and $S = 2$, this expression will be evaluated as follows:

1. D^2 = 900

2. V*D = 6000 and S*D^2 = 1800

3. F + V*D + S*D^2 = 100 + 6000 + 1800 = 7900

and the variable Cost will be equal to 7,900.

You should be aware that parentheses can have a dramatic effect on the result of evaluating an expression. For example, consider the same expression as before but with parentheses around $F + V$; that is, the assignment statement is now:

Cost = (F + V)*D + S*D^2

In this case, *F* and *V* will be summed before being multiplied by *D*, yielding a result that is very different from the one we got before. Using the same values as before, we now have:

1. F + V = 300

2. D^2 = 900

3. (F + V) * D = 9000 and S * D^2 = 1800

4. 9000 + 1800 = 10800

and Cost equals 10,800 instead of 7,900.

String Operators

For String variables and constants, the only valid operation is that of combining two strings into one. This operation, which is performed using the plus sign (+) or the ampersand (&), has the effect of adding the second String variable or constant to the end of the first. For example, if we have the assignment statement strBigDay = "May" + " Day" (or "May" & " Day"), the result is that strBigDay is now equal to "May Day" None of the other operators has any meaning for operations with strings.

> **TIP:** While both the ampersand (&) and plus (+) symbols do the same thing when combining strings, they work differently when used with numeric values. This may cause some confusion if you wish to concatenate two numeric values. It may be best to use the ampersand (&) only for concatenation.

Symbolic Constants

In creating an application in VB .NET or any other language, you never work entirely with variables only. Often you are working with constants in expressions or by themselves. While it is possible to use the actual Numeric constant or String constant (enclosed in quotation marks), if a quantity is not going to change in your project, it is advisable to give this quantity a name and data type just like you do for variables. For example, if you are working with an interest rate that is going to remain the same throughout your program at, say, 0.07, you might want to give this value a name of sngIntRate, define it as a Single data type, and use it, rather than the actual value, in your processing. If you decide at a later time that you want to change the interest rate from its current value, you simply change it at the point in your project where you have named it. The same rules and conventions apply to names for constants as apply to names for variables. Named constants are often referred to as **symbolic constants** since you are using a symbolic name for the actual value or string.

Assigning a name to a constant is usually done at the beginning of an event procedure—even before you declare variables. The form of the constant definition statement is much the same as initializing a variable at the same time as declaring it:

Const *constant name* as *variable type* = *value or expression*

where you supply both the constant name and value portions of the statement. For example, to create a symbolic constant called IntRate with a value of 0.07, the statement would be

```
Const sngIntRate as Single = 0.07
```

and if you also wanted to define a constant for the number of years in the investment as being 12, the statement would be

```
Const intNumYears as Integer = 12
```

As with declaring variables, it is possible to define more than one symbolic constant on a line by separating them with commas. For example, the two constant definitions shown above could be combined as

```
Const sngIntRate as Single = 0.07, intNumYears as Integer = 12
```

While the constant and variable declarations look quite similar, they have very different results; a constant should *not* be changed in the code while a variable is *meant* to be changed.

Mini-Summary 3-3: Using assignment statements for calculations

1. Assignment statements are used for calculations by setting variables equal to expressions where an expression is a combination of variables, constants, values from functions, and operators.

2. Arithmetic operators include grouping, exponentiation, negation, multiplication, division, integer division, modulus, addition, and subtraction. The Hierarchy of Operations controls the order in which these operations are carried out.

3. String operators include the plus sign and ampersand for concatenation.

4. Symbolic constants can be defined at the beginning of the program to store values that will not change during the program.

It's Your Turn!

1. Write appropriate assignment statements for the following situations:

   a. The total cost for the sale of multiple items is the unit price times the number of units sold.

b. The net sales price after applying a discount is equal to the gross sales price times (1 − discount rate). For example, if the gross price is $500 and the discount rate is 0.15, the net price is equal to 500 × (1 − 0.15).

c. The value of an amount of money some number of years in the future is equal to the amount of money times (1 + rate of return) raised to the number-of-years power. For example, if the amount of money is $1,000, the rate of return is 0.12, and the number of years is 5, the future value is equal to $1000 \times (1 + 0.12)^5$.

d. The depreciated value of a piece of machinery using straight line depreciation is equal to the original value minus the depreciation, where the depreciation is equal to the original value divided by the life of the machinery times the number of years since it was put into service.

e. The amount due for a sale is equal to the sales price times (1 + tax rate).

2. Evaluate the following expressions to determine the value assigned to the variable on the left of the equals sign.

```
a. Y = 3^2*4-1*2+3
b. X = 3^(2*4)-1*(2+3)
c. sngAverage = ((70 + 80)/2 + 65)/2
d. strState = "New York"
   strCity = strState & " City"
```

3. Declare constants for the following values:

a. Pi (3.14157)

b. The current exchange rate between British pounds and U.S. dollars (1.62)

c. The number of feet in a mile (5,280)

4. Given that sngTwo = 2.0, sngThree = 3.0, sngFour = 4.0, intNum = 8, and intMix = 5 and that the appropriate variable declarations have been made, find the value assigned to the given variable for each of the following

```
a. sngW = (sngTwo + sngThree) ^ sngThree
b. sngX = (sngThree + sngTwo / sngFour) ^ 2
c. sngY = intNum / intMix + 5.1
d. intZ = intNum / intMix + 5.1
```

5. Write variable declaration statements and assignment statements for the following that calculates the given expression and assigns the results to the specified value.

a. Rate times Time to DIST

b. Square root of (A^2+B^2) to C

c. 1/(1/$R1$ + 1/$R2$ + 1/$R3$) to Resist

d. P times $(1 + R)^N$ to Value

e. Area of triangle (one-half base times height) of base B and height H to Area

APPLICATION TO VINTAGE DVDs

So far you have learned about text boxes, assignment statements, and expressions. We are now ready to apply them to the Vintage DVDs example using the six-step development process presented in Chapter 1; that is, define the problem, create an interface, develop logic for action objects, write and test the code for action objects, test the overall project, and document the project in writing.

Define Problem

Assume that the Vintage DVDs store owner wants to extend the project created in Chapter 2 to input the renter's name, the DVD rented, and the price for the DVD and then use this information to calculate the taxes due on the rental price and add these taxes to the rental price to compute the amount due. He also wants to have a way of printing the result of the computations, clearing the text boxes, and exiting the project. To ensure that we understand his request, we need to sketch the interface. In this case, this involves adding additional features to the sketch created in Chapter 2 (Figure 2-8). The resulting sketch is shown in Figure 3-5.

FIGURE 3-5.
Revised Vintage DVDs sketch

> # Vintage DVDs: Old movies on DVD!
> Click me first!
>
> Customer Name [   ]
> Video Name   [   ]
> Video Price   [   ]
> Taxes   [   ]
> Amount Due   [   ]
>
> [Calculate]   [Clear]   [Exit]

Create Interface

Note in the sketch in Figure 3-5 that five text boxes for input and output and five corresponding labels have been added to the form along with a line control to separate the amount due text box from the others. Three additional buttons—to calculate the taxes and amount due, to clear the text boxes, and to exit the project—are required in addition to the existing button that displays a welcoming message. No other controls are required for this project. To add new controls to the existing Vintage form, we must first create the Vintage3 project by copying the Vintage2 project files to a new folder. The steps to do this are summarized in the Step-by-Step Instructions 3-2.

■ ■

Step-by-Step 3-2 Instructions: Modifying an existing project

1. Start Windows Explorer and create a new folder within the *Chapter3* folder (or wherever you have been instructed to save your projects) named **Vintage3**.

2. **Copy** all the files in the *Chapter2\Vintage2* folder to the new *Chapter3\Vintage3* folder. Caution: Do not drag them from the Vintage2 folder—that them instead of copying them. Use the **Edit|Copy** menu command to copy them from Vintage2 folder and the **Edit|Paste** command to paste them to the Vintage3 folder.

3. Start VB .NET and select **Open Project** from the Start Page (if you are already in VB .NET, select **File|Open|Project** menu option.) Now *double-click* the **Vintage3** folder you created in Step 1 to open it. From the resulting dialog box, open the Vintage.sln file by *double-clicking* it also. (It should already be highlighted.)

4. You should now see the Form Design window with the Solution Explorer Window showing the Vintage2 files you copied into this folder, Vintage.sln, Vintage.vbproj, and Vintage.vb.

5. In the Solution Explorer window, *right-click* the **Vintage.vbproj** project file and choose **Properties.** The Vintage Property Pages dialog box will be displayed. Select **frmVintage** from the Startup Object list box and click **OK** to save this choice.

6. Double-click the **Vintage.vb** file in the Solution Explorer window to display the frmVintage form and make the necessary changes.

■ ■

Once you have completed Step-by-Step Instructions 3-2 to create the new Vintage3 folder with the Vintage3 files in it, you are ready to add the new controls that are shown in Table 3-6.

TABLE 3-6: New Controls for Vintage DVDs Application

Control	Name Property	Text Property
text box	txtCustName	
text box	txtDVDName	
text box	txtDVDPrice	
text box	txtTaxes	
text box	txtAmountDue	
label	lblCustName	Customer Name
label	lblDVDName	DVD Name
label	lblDVDPrice	DVD Price
label	lblTaxes	Taxes

TABLE 3-6: New Controls for Vintage DVDs Application (Continued)

Control	Name Property	Text Property
label	lblAmountDue	Amount Due
label	lblLine	_____
button	btnCalc	Calculate
button	btnClear	Clear
button	btnExit	Exit

Once all of the controls shown in Table 3-6 are added to the existing Vintage3 project, it should appear as shown in Figure 3-6 with input text boxes and related labels and three new buttons to calculate the total amount due, clear the input, and to exit the application.

FIGURE 3-6.
Expanded interface for Vintage DVDs

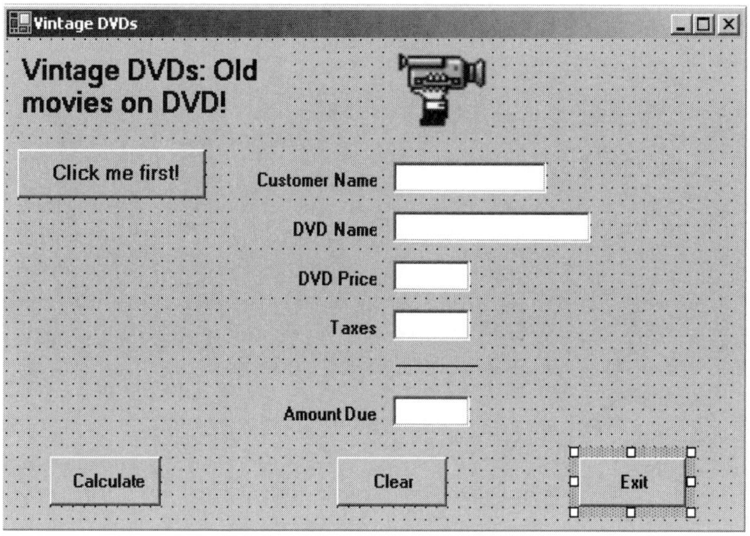

Develop Logic for Action Objects

On the revised Vintage DVDs form, there are three new action objects: the *Calculate, Clear,* and *Exit* buttons. Of these, the *Calculate* button is the only one that involves input, processing, and output. As such, it is the only object for which we need to develop the logic using an IPO table and pseudocode. The *Clear* button clears the text boxes and sets the focus back to the Customer Name text box. The *Exit* button involves only single instructions to exit the application.

Input to the *Calculate* button includes the customer name, DVD name, and DVD price. Processing includes computing the tax on the DVD price and adding it to the DVD price to determine the total amount due. Output should include the tax and the total amount due. The IPO Table for the btnCalc button is shown in Figure 3-7.

The pseudocode for the btnCalc button event procedure shown on the next page converts the IPO into structured English. Note that there is no mention of text boxes in the input and output statements in the pseudocode,

FIGURE 3-7. IPO Table for Calculate button

Input	Processing	Output
Customer name DVD Name DVD Price	Taxes = 0.07 x DVD Price Amount Due = Price + Taxes	Taxes Amount Due

because the pseudocode is intended to present the logic of the operation with no concern for the details of actually how it will be done in the programming code.

```
Begin Procedure Calculate
    Input customer name
    Input DVD name
    Input DVD price
    Taxes = DVD price times tax rate
    Amount due = DVD price + taxes
    Output taxes
    Output amount due
End procedure
```

Write and Test Code   As noted earlier, there are three new action objects for which we need to write code: the click events for the btnCalc, btnClear, and btnExit buttons. The code for the btnCalc button event procedure should follow the pseudocode, except that it should use text boxes for input and output. If we apply the four-step process for writing code to this problem, the resulting code is as shown in VB Code Box 7-5.

VB CODE BOX 7-5. Code for Calculate button

```
Private Sub btnCalc_Click(ByVal sender As System.Object, _
ByVal e As System.EventArgs) Handles btnCalc.Click
    Const sngTaxRate As Single = 0.07 'Use local tax rate
    Dim decPrice, decAmountDue, decTaxes As Decimal
    decPrice = CDec(txtDVDPrice.Text)
    decTaxes = decPrice * sngTaxRate 'Compute taxes
    decAmountDue = decPrice + decTaxes 'Compute amount due
    txtTaxes.Text = CStr(decTaxes)
    txtAmountDue.Text = CStr(decAmountDue)
End Sub
```

Note in the code that a symbolic constant, sngTaxRate, is declared to be equal to the local sales tax rate (0.07). If the sales tax rate changes or the application is used in another jurisdiction, we can easily change the sales tax rate by changing this statement. Since the tax rate does not normally change from use to use, we declare it as a constant rather than inputting it for each use. Note also that the variables are declared as Decimal rather than Single, since the values stored in them will be in dollars and cents. Also, the CDec( ) function is used to convert between the String data type and the Decimal date type, and the CStr( ) function is used in the other direction. Some of the more commonly used conversion functions are shown in Table 3-7.

TABLE 3-7: Commonly Used Conversion Functions

Conversion Function	Purpose
CStr	Converts argument to String data type
CBool	Converts argument to Boolean data type
CDec	Converts argument to Decimal data type
CDate	Converts argument to Date data type
CInt	Converts argument to Integer data type
CSng	Converts argument to Single data type
CDbl	Converts argument to Double data type

Note that in VB Code Box 7-5 we have also added a **comment** to the statement defining the tax rate by beginning it with an apostrophe. Comments are a form of **internal documentation** that is used to explain part of a program. Comments can be on a line by themselves or added to the end of another statement as was done here. Comments are displayed in green on the screen to distinguish them from executable code. Any text begun with an apostrophe or the keyword *Rem* is ignored by the computer and is there for explanation purposes only. You should include comments in your code wherever it will help explain the purpose of the program or a specific statement. As we noted in Chapter 1, since we explain all code in the text, we will add comments here only to explain code that might otherwise be misunderstood. Your instructor may want you to add more comments, and, almost certainly, if you do any coding in your professional life, comments will be *required*.

Figure 3-8 shows an example of running the project with sample data (Customer Name = "George Burdell", DVD Name = *Spartacus*, and DVD Price = 2.99) and clicking *Calculate*. The resulting Taxes value is 0.2093 and the Amount Due is 3.1993.

FIGURE 3-8. Vintage DVDs application

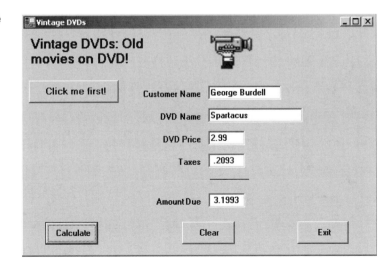

Formatting Output

Note that the values output in the Taxes and Amount Due text boxes are shown not as dollars and cents but with four decimal places. To control the form of *numeric* items or dates in output, we need to use the **Format(*expression, format*) function**. In this function, *expression* is any valid expression that is to be formatted and *format* is a valid **format expression**. The more commonly used Numeric format expressions are shown in Table 3-8, where each format expression is enclosed in quotation marks in the Format function. Note that the Format function has no effect on nonnumeric variables.

TABLE 3-8: Numeric Format Expressions

Format Expression	Abbreviation	Result
Currency	"c" or "C"	Display number with dollar sign, thousands separator, and two digits to the right of the decimal point.
Fixed	"f" or "F"	Display number with at least one digit to the left and two digits to the right of the decimal point.
Standard	"s" or "S"	Display number with thousands separator and at least one digit to the left and two digits to the right of the decimal point.
Percent	"p" or "P"	Display number multiplied by 100 with a percent sign (%) on the right and two digits to the right of the decimal point.
Scientific	"e" or "E"	Use standard scientific notation.

For example, to format a number as currency with two decimal places, the format expression would be "currency"; to format it as percent, the expression would be "percent." These formats can also be abbreviated as "c" for currency or "p" for percent.

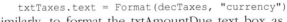

TIP: If you do not include the format expression, the Format( ) function will return the same result as the CStr( ) function.

In the Vintage DVDs project, we will format the txtTaxes text box as currency by replacing the statement involving the CStr( ) function with a statement using the Format( ) function, as shown below:

```
txtTaxes.text = Format(decTaxes, "currency")
```

Similarly, to format the txtAmountDue text box as currency, the statement would be

```
txtAmountDue.text = Format(decAmountDue, "C")
```

It is also possible to format the numeric values using the FormatCurrency function. The **FormatCurrency** function performs the same operation as the Format function with the "currency" or "c" parameter. For example, the input textbox can be formatted by including the same text box on the left side of the assignment statement and on the right side in the FormatCurrency function. To format the contents of txtDVDPrice as currency, the statement might be

```
txtDVDPrice.Text = FormatCurrency(txtDVDPrice.Text)
```

If we replace the two statements in the btnCalc button Code window that use the CStr( ) function with statements that use the Format( ) function and we then add a statement that formats the txtDVDPrice textbox, the final code for this object will appear as shown in VB Code Box 7-6. If we run the revised project with the same sample data as before, the new result will be as shown in Figure 3-9. Note that all monetary values are now shown as currency.

| VB CODE BOX 7-6. Code to compute and display taxes and amount due | ```Private Sub btnCalc_Click(ByVal sender As System.Object, _ ByVal e As System.EventArgs) Handles btnCalc.Click   Const sngTaxRate As Single = 0.07 'Use local tax rate   Dim decPrice, decAmountDue, decTaxes As Decimal   decPrice = CDec(txtDVDPrice.Text)   decTaxes = decPrice * sngTaxRate 'Compute taxes   decAmountDue = decPrice + decTaxes 'Compute amount due   txtTaxes.Text = Format(decTaxes, "c")   txtAmountDue.Text = Format(decAmountDue, "c")   txtDVDPrice.Text = Format(decPrice, "c") End Sub``` |

FIGURE 3-9. Result of running revised project

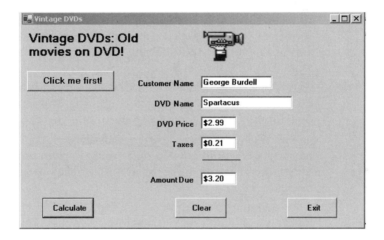

Clearing Entries and Exiting the Application

In addition to computing the taxes and amount due on a DVD rental, we want to make it possible to clear the previous entries in preparation for the next customer, set the focus to the customer name text box, and exit the project. This means that the Text property of the text boxes must be set to an empty string, as was done with the Simple Calculator example, and the Focus method used to place the cursor in the txtCustName text box so the next name can be entered. The complete code for the btnClear button event procedure is shown in VB Code Box 7-7. When *Clear* is clicked, all text boxes are blanked out and the focus set to the txtCustName text box.

The code for the *Exit* button is very simple; it consists of one word: *End.* This will cause the project to terminate, just as if you had clicked the *Stop* button on the toolbar. The steps to create this project are summarized in Step-by-Step Instructions 3-3.

VB CODE BOX 7-7. Code to clear entries	```Private Sub btnClear_Click(ByVal sender As System.Object,_ ByVal e As System.EventArgs) Handles btnClear.Click txtCustName.Text = "" txtDVDName.Text = "" txtDVDPrice.Text = "" txtTaxes.Text = "" txtAmountDue.Text = "" txtCustName.Focus( ) End Sub```

Step-by-Step Instructions 3-3: Adding controls to the Vintage DVDs project

1. Open the **Vintage3** project that resulted from carrying out Step-by-Step Instructions 3-2 and add the five text boxes, five labels, four buttons, and one line control as shown in Figure 3-5.

2. Change the Name properties for all of the new controls to match those shown in Table 3-6. Delete the Text property for the text boxes and add the appropriate texts to the label and button controls. Your resulting form should look like that shown in Figure 3-6.

3. Add the code shown in VB Code Box 7-5 to the Code window for the Click event for the btnCalc button. Add the **End** statement to the Code window for the Click event for the btnExit button.

4. Run the project and test the **Calculate** button by entering a customer name of **George Burdell,** a DVD name of ***Spartacus,*** and a DVD price of **$2.99** (don't include the dollar sign). The result should be the same as shown in Figure 3-8.

5. Change the statements that use the CStr( ) function to use the Format( ) function with the Currency ("c") format expression. Also, format the txtDVD-Price text box with the FormatCurrency function. Your code should be the same as that shown in VB Code Box 7-6. Run your project again with the same data as above. Your result should look like Figure 3-9.

6. Open the Code window for the *Clear* button and add the code shown in VB Code Box 7-7.

7. Exit the project and save the files.

Mini-Summary 3-4: Developing the Vintage DVDs application

1. The Vintage DVDs application can be developed using the six-step process discussed in Chapter 1. The code is written using the four-step process discussed earlier in this chapter.

2. IPO tables and pseudocode are useful for developing the logic of the code.

3. There are a number of other conversion functions that convert String data to a specific Numeric data type including CDec and CInt.

> **Mini-Summary 3-4: Developing the Vintage DVDs application (Continued)**
>
> 4. To convert to numeric data to a string, use CStr function. To control the form of output, the Format function should be used with a variety of format expressions.
>
> 5. The application can be exited with the End command.

It's Your Turn!

1. Describe what appears in the txtAnswer textbox after each of the following is executed. If you are not sure, create a form and write the code in VB .NET to find out.

a.
```
Private Sub btnCalculate_Click( )
    Dim sngValue As Single
    sngValue = 56.789
    txtAnswer.Text = Format(sngValue, "c")
End Sub
```

b.
```
Private Sub btnCalculate_Click( )
    Dim sngValue As Single
    sngValue = 456.7891
    txtAnswer.Text = Format(sngValue, "f")
End Sub
```

c.
```
Private Sub btnCalculate_Click( )
    Dim sngValue As Single
    sngValue = 65.432
    txtAnswer.Text = Format(sngValue, "s")
End Sub
```

d.
```
Private Sub btnCalculate_Click( )
    Dim sngValue As Single
    sngValue = 1.543
    txtAnswer.Text = Format(sngValue, "p")
End Sub
```

e.
```
Private Sub btnCalculate_Click( )
    Dim sngValue As Single
    sngValue = 0.00235
    txtAnswer.Text = Format(sngValue, "e")
End Sub
```

2. Describe what appears in the txtAnswer textbox after each of the following is executed. If you are not sure, create a form and write the code in VB .NET to find out.

a.
```
Private Sub btnCalculate_Click( )
    Dim sngValue As Single
    sngValue = 0
    txtAnswer.Text = CBool(sngValue)
End Sub
```

```
b. Private Sub btnCalculate_Click( )
     Dim sngValue As Single
     sngValue = 3.6
     txtAnswer.Text = CInt(sngValue)
   End Sub

c. Private Sub btnCalculate_Click( )
     Dim strDate As String
     strDate = "3/3/03"
     txtAnswer.Text = CDate(strDate)
   End Sub
```

3. Complete Step-by-Step Instructions 3-2 to modify the file you created in Chapter 2 (Vintage2) to become Vintage3.

4. Complete Step-by-Step Instructions 3-3 to create the Vintage3 project.

5. Run the project again with the previous customer and DVD ("George Burdell", a DVD name of *Spartacus,* and a DVD price of $2.99.) Clear the entries and enter a new customer name of "Sam Cassell", a DVD name of *Sands of Iwo Jima*, and a price of $1.99 and calculate the result. Clear the form and add new data of your choosing and click *Calculate* again.

6. Save the project files and close it.

MORE ON USING FUNCTIONS

You have already used four built-in functions— CStr( ), CInt, CDec( ), and Format( )—in creating the Simple Calculator and the Vintage DVDs application, so you have some knowledge of their use. In addition to these four, there are many other built-in functions that serve a variety of useful purposes. There are built-in functions for converting data types, working with dates and time, performing financial operations, working with strings, and carrying out different mathematical operations. Examples of commonly used built-in functions are shown in Table 3-9. Check the Help operations for others. You will probably recognize many of them from working with spreadsheet software.

TABLE 3-9: Commonly used built-in functions

Function	Type	Purpose
Abs	Mathematical	Returns absolute value of a number
Sqr	Mathematical	Returns square root of a positive number
FV	Financial	Returns future value of an annuity
PV	Financial	Returns present value of an annuity
IRR	Financial	Returns internal rate of return
Pmt	Financial	Returns periodic payment to pay off a loan
UCase/ LCase	String	Converts a string to all upper- or lower-case letters

TABLE 3-9: Commonly used built-in functions (Continued)

Function	Type	Purpose
Len	String	Returns length of string
Datevalue	Date/Time	Returns date for string argument

As an example of using one of the financial functions, we will create an application that will determine the monthly payment necessary to repay a loan. In looking at Table 3-9, you can see that we will need to use the Pmt( ) function for this purpose. The Pmt function has the following form: **Pmt(*rate, nper, pv*)**, where *rate* = the periodic interest rate as a decimal fraction, *nper* = the number of months over which the loan is to be repaid, and *pv* = the present value of the loan which is the *negative* of the loan amount. For example, if you borrowed $10,000 at a 12% annual interest rate for five years, the appropriate form of the function would be Pmt(.01, 60, – 10000), where we have changed the 12% annual rate to a 1% (0.01) monthly rate and have converted the number of years to 60 months. It is important that the number of periods used correspond to the interest rate being used.

> **TIP:** Always be sure to understand completely how a function should be used, what parameters are required or optional, and what it returns before using it in your code. Functions with similar names do not necessarily operate in the same way.

Creating the Interface   To create the interface to compute the monthly payment required to repay a loan, we need to add the three input text boxes for the amount of the loan, the duration of the loan in months, and the interest rate as a percentage. We will also need an output text box for the monthly payment and two buttons, one to compute the monthly payment and one to exit the project. The form is shown in Figure 3-10 and the controls for it are shown in Table 3-10.

FIGURE 3-10.
Interface for
Payment Calculator

![Monthly Payment Calculator interface showing a window titled "Monthly Payment Calculator" with input fields for Loan Amount, Number of Months, Interest Rate (with % symbol), an output field labeled Payment, and Compute and Exit buttons.]

TABLE 3-10: Controls for monthly payment interface

Control	Name	Text	Font/Other
Form	frmMonthPay	Monthly Payment Calculator	Change filename to Monthpay.vb
Label	lblHeading	Monthly Payment Calculator	14-point bold
Label	lblLoanAmt	Loan Amount	Bold
Label	lblNumMonths	Number of Months	Bold
Label	lblIntRate	Interest Rate	Bold
Label	lblPercentSign	%	Bold
Label	lblPayment	Payment	14-point bold
TextBox	txtAmount	N/A	
TextBox	txtMonths	N/A	
TextBox	txtRate	N/A	
TextBox	txtPayment	N/A	14-point bold
button	btnCompute	Compute	Bold
button	btnExit	Exit	Bold

Note that we have added a label with a percentage symbol after the txtRate text box. Doing this will allow us to enter the interest rate as a whole number without formatting it. We do this because formatting a number as a percentage precludes using it later in calculations.

Computing the Monthly Payment

For this project, we need to develop the logic for only one action object—a *Compute* button. For this control, the input includes the loan amount, number of months, and interest rate. The processing involves using the **Pmt( ) function** to generate the required monthly payment, which is then output. Since this is so straightforward, we will dispense with the IPO table and pseudocode for this situation.

For the *Compute* button, the code to compute the monthly payment is very simple: Transfer the contents of the three text boxes to variables, use the variables in the Pmt( ) function to determine a payment value, transfer the result of the payment value to the txtPayment text box, and format all text boxes appropriately. For the interest rate, we need to convert the contents of the txtRate text box to a Single data type variable and divide it by 100 to convert it to a decimal fraction. We then have to divide the result by 12 to convert it into a *monthly* interest rate. With the CSng( ) conversion function, this can be done in one statement (where Rate is the variable):

```
sngRate = (CSng(txtRate.Text)/100)/12
```

The code for the btnCompute_Click event procedure is shown in VB Code Box 7-8.

Several things are of note in VB Code Box 7-8. First, as in the Vintage DVDs application, we declare the decAmount and decPayment variables to be Decimal instead of Single. The intMonths variable is declared to be Integer

VB CODE BOX 7-8.
Code to compute
monthly payment
	``
	Private Sub btnCompute_Click(ByVal sender As System.Object, _ ByVal e
	As System.EventArgs) Handles btnCompute.Click
	    Dim decAmount, decPayment As Decimal
	    Dim intMonths As Integer
	    Dim sngRate As Single
	    decAmount = CDec(txtAmount.Text)
	    intMonths = CInt(txtMonths.Text)
	    sngRate = (CSng(txtRate.Text) / 100) / 12
	    decPayment = Pmt(sngRate, intMonths, -decAmount)
	    txtPayment.Text = Format(decPayment, "currency")
	    txtAmount.Text = Format(decAmount, "currency")
	End Sub
	``

and sngRate is declared to be Single since they are not dollars and cents. Second, we use the CDec( ), CInt( ), and CSng( ) conversion functions to convert the String data into the appropriate type of variable. Finally, we have formatted the contents of the txtAmount and txtPayment text boxes as Currency. However, we have not formatted the contents of the txtRate text box since we want it to remain as an *annual* interest rate instead of being displayed as a monthly interest rate. As mentioned earlier, because of the way the Percent Numeric format expression works, if the txtRate text box had been formatted as percent *before* the calculation or for a new set of values with the same interest rate, it would *not* have been possible to convert the formatted result back to a numeric value and use it in the calculation.

To test the *Compute* button code, we will run the project and enter values for the loan amount, number of months, and interest rate, and then click *Compute.* For example, for a loan of $3,000 for 36 months at 8 percent, the monthly payment is $256.03. The result of using this data is shown in Figure 3-11.

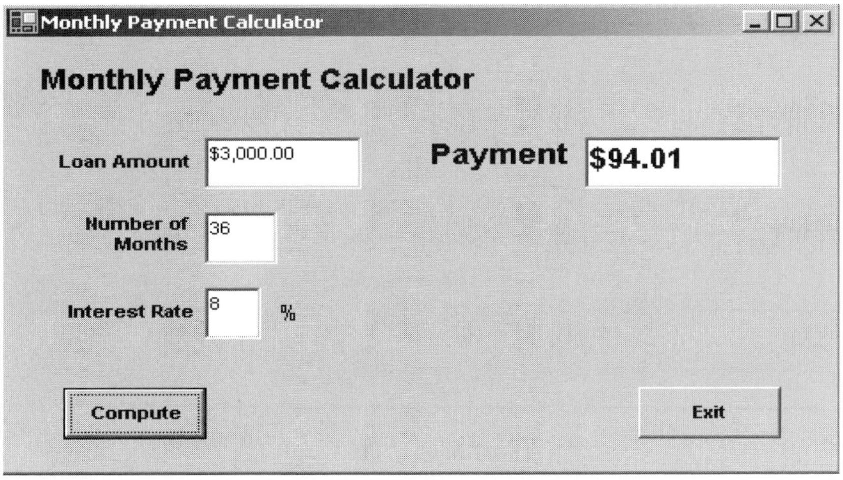

FIGURE 3-11.
Monthly Payment
Calculator

The steps to create the monthly payment project are summarized in Step-by-Step Instructions 3-4.

Step-by-Step Instructions 3-4: Creating a monthly payment calculator

1. Use **Start Page | New Project** or **File | New Project** to start a new project with a name of **MonthPay** in the *Chapter3* folder. Change the filename for the form to **MonthPay.vb** and give it name of **frmMonthPay.** *Right-Click* on the **MonthPay.vbproj** file and select **Properties.** In this dialog box, change the Startup Object to **frmMonthPay.**

2. For this project, add the controls shown in Table 3-10 to create the interface shown in Figure 3-10.

3. Open the Code window for the *Compute* button and add the code shown in VB Code Box 7-8. Also, add the appropriate code for the *Exit* button.

4. Test your project for a loan amount of $**3,000** for **36** months at **8**% interest rate. The results should look like that shown in Figure 3-11. Test it also for a loan amount of $**10,000** for **60** months at **7.3**% (your answer should be $199.43.)

5. If your project runs correctly, save all the files. If there are errors, correct them and then save the files.

Mini-Summary 3-5: More on using functions

1. In addition to the conversion functions (CInt, CStr, and so on), there are many other functions.

2. These include scientific, mathematical, financial, string, and date/time functions.

3. The Pmt function is useful for computing the monthly payment on a loan amount.

It's Your Turn!

1. Describe what is displayed in the text box after the following assignment statements are executed.

```
a. txtAnswer.Text = Abs(-3)

b. txtAnswer.Text = Sqr(25)

c. txtAnswer.Text = UCase("VB is fun")

d. txtAnswer.Text = Len("VB is fun")

e. txtAnswer.Text = Sqr(Len("four"))
```

2. Complete Step-by-Step Instructions 3-4 to create the monthly payment calculator in VB .NET.

ERRORS IN VB .NET

In creating the three projects discussed in this chapter, you may have encountered an error message from VB .NET, or, worse than that, you received no message but your project failed to run correctly. Ideally, in either of those cases, you were able to find your error by comparing your work to the descriptions in the text. Unfortunately, when you begin creating projects with no explicit instructions to follow, you are likely to run into a variety of errors or, as they are commonly known in the programming community, **bugs**. (There is an apocryphal story about the source of this term, which we won't bore you with here!)

Finding errors is a very important part of program development that often takes as long as all the other steps combined, even when special testing software is used to detect errors. Writing bug-free software is inherently difficult, because the logic supporting the program is inflexible. In most engineering projects, a margin of error is built into the design specifications, so a bridge, for example, usually will not collapse if an element is defective or fails. With computer software, on the other hand, *each* program instruction must be absolutely correct. Otherwise, the whole program may fail. This is a significant problem given the ever-increasing complexity of modern programs. For example, between 1983 and 1992, the average size of a typical application software package increased tenfold, from 100,000 lines of computer code to 1 million lines. Today, software like Windows XP have tens of millions of lines of code in them.

Other errors that can occur during execution include the incorrect use of data or the inadvertent request by the user that the computer perform a meaningless operation, for example, dividing by zero. The code for an object will execute until it encounters an error; then it will stop, display a message telling why it has abnormally terminated the program execution, and highlight the line of code that may be causing the error. If possible, test data that can test all portions of the code should be chosen. If this is not done, errors in any untested section of the project will not be discovered. If an error *is* detected, then the programmer must trace through both the logic of the code and the actual language statements to find it. If a logic error goes *undetected,* the results can be catastrophic.

In general, there are three types of errors that you may encounter in creating VB .NET projects: syntax errors, run-time errors, and logic errors. **Syntax errors** are usually caused by incorrect grammar, vocabulary, or usage. Using a keyword for a variable name, using a keyword incorrectly, and entering an assignment statement with an expression on the left of the equals sign are all examples of syntax errors. Fortunately, VB .NET will catch almost all syntax errors when they are entered. For example, if you tried to use the Dim keyword twice in the same declaration statement, VB .NET would immediately alert you to this error when you attempted to press **ENTER** at the end of the line by underlining the error(s) with wavy underline(s). If you then position the cursor over the underlined error, a tooltip will show you the error— "Specifiers valid only at beginning of declaration."—in this case as shown in Figure 3-12. You would receive a similar error message if you tried to use a variable name beginning with a number or a variable name with a period embedded in it. Occasionally, VB .NET will not catch your syntax error until you attempt to run the program, but the result is the same: You must correct the syntax before proceeding. The best way to avoid these errors is to adhere to the rules regarding variable names, use of keywords, and appropriate use of assignment statements and operators in expressions.

FIGURE 3-12.

Incorrect use of keyword

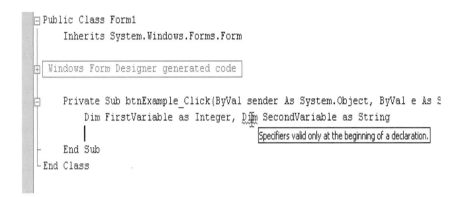

Run-time errors occur when the program is running, and they are almost always associated with an error in programmer logic or input data. For example, if you have a project that requires a division operation and either the data or the logic requires a division by zero, a run-time error will occur. When this occurs, VB .NET will terminate the execution of the project, display the Code window with the line in which the error most likely occurred highlighted, and show a dialog box with a message about the error. At this point, you must stop the program with the Stop icon and correct the error if it involves a problem with the program statement. You may then click the Start icon, and begin executing the program again. If the error is one of input (long experience has shown that a large percentage of all errors are errors of input), then you must terminate execution of the project and enter correct data. Even with VB .NET's help, run-time errors are more difficult to find and correct than syntax errors. For example, dividing by zero will not be caught until Run time and will result in a run-time error as shown in Figure 3-13 ("overflow" indicates that a memory location has filled up beyond its capacity and this event occurs when division by zero is attempted).

To avoid run-time errors, programmers will often include statements to "trap" errors to validate input. For example, a statement will be included that will test a divisor to determine if it is not equal to zero before it gets used in an expression.

Logic errors are errors that result from incorrect program design, and they usually are not caught until the program has been tested extensively or is already in use. The much-discussed Year 2000 (Y2K) problem was a good example of a logic error. This error was caused by the failure of designers of yesterday's programmers to consider the fact that the year 2000 would eventually arrive. Instead, the designers assumed that all date arithmetic could be handled by using just the last two digits of any year. For example, to determine the year a loan would mature, simply add the number of years for the term of the loan to the last two digits of the current year. When it was 1998 and the term of the loan was, say, five years, the maturity date became 03 causing confusion for the computer about whether this referred to 1903 or

FIGURE 3-13. Result of dividing by zero

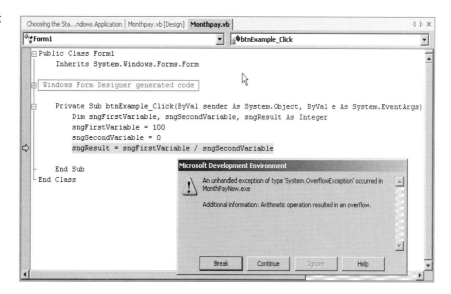

2003. While using only the last two years of the date saved a great deal of disk space at a time when disk space was scarce, it caused a great deal of expense for organizations around the world, not to mention grief for those programmers who were charged with correcting the logic error.

> **TIP:** When error messages appear while you are testing your program, don't simply press End and ignore them. The message will provide valuable clues as to a problem in your code and possibly how to fix it. Selecting Debug will show the line in which your coding error first causes a problem.

Debugging Projects   **Debugging** is the art and science of finding run-time and logic errors in computer programs. We don't include syntax errors in this search, because VB .NET will find almost all of them for you. In debugging a project, you should start by testing each object as it is created, giving special attention to the input statements. Be sure to use test data that will check all possible options in an object; this will catch many of the errors. To help in this process, VB .NET provides a group of debugging tools, which we will discuss in later chapters. Finally, when all else fails, ask someone else to look at your code. Many times fresh eyes can find errors that have evaded you for hours!

Mini-Summary 3-6: Errors in VB .NET

1. There are three major types of programming errors in VB .NET: syntax errors, run-time errors, and logic errors. Programming errors are commonly referred to as *bugs*.

2. Syntax errors are usually found immediately by VB .NET. Run-time errors are also often caught by VB .NET when the program is running. However, logic errors are not found by VB .NET and must be found by the programmer.

3. The process of finding and removing errors is referred to as *debugging*.

SUMMARY

At the beginning of the chapter, we said you would be able to do a number of things after reading it. Let's review those things here:

1. Understand a four-step process to writing code in VB .NET and its relationship to the six operations a computer can perform. To carry out any of the six operations that a computer can perform, it is necessary to write instructions or code. A four-step process for doing this includes determining the variables needed, inputting data, processing it, and outputting the results.

2. Declare and use different types of variables in your project. In terms of storing data in internal memory, variables are used to represent data that are stored in internal memory; they come in many kinds, including integers, strings, decimal, single precision, and so on. In VB .NET, unless you turn Option Explicit Off, you must declare all variables as to their type. One way to declare variables is the Dim statement.

3. Use text boxes for event-driven input and output. Event-driven input involves inputting data when an event occurs, such as mouse click of a button. Often text boxes are used for event-driven input. In this type of input, the user enters data in a text box and then uses an event to transfer the data to a variable using an assignment statement. The variable is then used in the processing step. It is often necessary to use functions such as CDec( ) or CInt( ) to convert from the string form of a textbox to the numeric variables used in processing. The unformatted results of processing can output using the CStr function or formatted through the use of the Format( ) function. For formatting numbers, there are a number of commonly used format expressions, including Currency, Fixed, Standard, Percent, and Scientific.

4. Write VB .NET instructions to carry out arithmetic operations. Assignment statements are used for performing calculations. Arithmetic and string operators are used to create expressions, which can be on the right side of an assignment statement with a variable on the left. The hierarchy of operations controls the order in which arithmetic operations are carried out. Symbolic constants are a method of using a name to represent a constant in a program.

5. Discuss using VB .NET functions to carry out commonly used operations. In addition to the conversion functions and the Format function, other functions enable us to carry out complex operations easily in such areas as converting data types, working with dates and time, finance, and mathematics. The Pmt function is a useful function for computing the monthly payment necessary to repay a loan amount.

6. Use buttons to clear text boxes and exit the project. It is possible to clear text boxes by setting their Text property to an empty value (" ") and the text box Focus method can be used to position the cursor in a text box. The project can be exited through the use of the End command.

7. Describe the types of errors that commonly occur in a VB .NET project and their causes. The various types of errors that can occur in the development of a VB .NET program—syntax errors, run-time errors, and logic errors—were also discussed in this chapter. The process of finding and removing errors is referred to as debugging.

NEW VB .NET ELEMENTS

Controls/Objects	Properties	Methods	Events
TextBox control	Name Text	Focus	

NEW PROGRAMMING STATEMENTS

Statement to declare a variable
Dim variable name **As** type

Statement to assign a value to a constant
Const constant name **As** type = value

Assignment Statement
Control property or variable = value, variable, expression, or control property

Statement to use a function
Variable = functionname(arg1, arg2, ...)

Statement to end execution of a project
End

KEY TERMS

assignment statement
bugs
comments
constant
debugging
Edit Field
fixed point operations
floating point operations
format expression

function
internal documentation
logic errors
memory cells
mnemonic variable names
Numeric data type
operator
prototyping

run-time errors
String data type
symbolic constant
syntax errors
text box
Text property
variables
Object data type

EXERCISES

1. Write a single VB .NET statement to accomplish each of the following:

   a. Declare the variable blnStatus as Boolean.

   b. Assign "Nicolas" to the variable strFirstName.

   c. Assign the value 0.85 to the txtAmount text box to appear in Currency format.

   d. Set the focus to the txtScore text box.

   e. Increment the variable intCounter by 1.

2. What happens when each of the following is executed? Why?

```
a. Private Sub btnCalculate_Click( )
     Dim strAddress As String
     strAddress = "543 Elm Street"
     txtAnswer.Text = CDec(strAddress)
   End Sub
```

```
b. Private Sub btnCalculate_Click( )
     Dim strAddress As String
     strAddress = "543 Elm Street"
     txtAnswer.Text = CInt(strAddress)
   End Sub
```

3. What happens when the following code is executed? Why does this occur? How can it be corrected?

```
Private Sub btnCalculate_Click( )
  Dim intNumber As Short
  intNumber = 42000
End Sub
```

4. Use the VB .NET Help facility to answer the following questions.

   a. What can cause a Type Mismatch error?

   b. What is the data type of the value returned by the Msgbox function?

   c. What does the Microsoft.VisualBasic.Left function do? What are the arguments required?

   d. What is the value and data type of the vbOKOnly constant?

   e. What methods are available for the button?

5. When are two variables that have been assigned the same value not equal? Create an interface with one text box and one button. Write the following code for the button.

```
Private Sub btnCalculate_Click( )
  Dim sngA As Single
  Dim dblB As Double
  sngA = 8.05006
  dblB = 8.05006
  txtAnswer.Text = sngA - dblB
End Sub
```

What is the result in the text box after executing the code? What would it be if the values stored in memory for each variable are equal? Why do you think the result comes out this way? What does this imply for your calculations?

PROJECTS

Create a folder in the *Chapter3* folder named **Homework.** All projects should be saved in this *Chapter3\Homework* folder.

1. Create a new folder named **Ex3-1** in the *Chapter3\Homework* folder. Review your design for Exercise 1 in Chapter 1 and then use **Step-by-Step Instructions 3-2** to copy the *Chapter2\Homework\Ex2-1* files into the new *Ex3-1* folder. Follow those instructions to also rename the files in the folder to be **Ex3-1.vb, Ex3-1.vbproj,** and **Ex3-1.sln.** Be sure to make **Ex3-1.vb** your startup object. Add five text boxes and corresponding labels and modify the properties for the text boxes and labels as needed. The first text box should allow the user to input the student's name, and the next three text boxes are for input of the three quiz scores. The last text box is to display the average of the three quiz scores.

Use a button to sum the three test scores and compute and display the average of the three scores (use the Fixed Numeric format for the average.) Add buttons to clear the text boxes, set the focus back to the student name text box, and to exit the project. Test your project with a student name of **Chris Patrick** and test scores of **71**, **79**, and **85**. Click the **Save All** icon to save the resulting project.

2. Create a new folder named **Ex3-2** in the *Chapter3\Homework* folder. Review your design for Exercise 2 in Chapter 1 and then use **Step-by-Step Instructions 3-2** to copy the *Chapter2\Homework\Ex2-2* files into the new *Ex3-2* folder. Follow those same instructions to rename the files in the folder to be **Ex3-2.vb, Ex3-2.vbproj,** and **Ex3-2.sln** and to make **Ex3-2.vb** the startup object.

Now add four text boxes and corresponding labels to the Ex3-1.vb form and modify the properties for the text boxes and labels as needed. The first text box should allow the user to input the customer's name. The next two text boxes should allow the user to input the square footage for a lawn and the cost per square foot for a given type of treatment. The fourth text box should display the cost of the treatment, which is equal to the square footage times the cost per square foot.

Use a button to compute and display the treatment cost. Format the cost per square foot and treatment cost as dollars and cents. Add buttons to clear the text boxes, set the focus back to the square footage text box, and to exit the project. Test your project with a customer name of **Caroline Myers** with square footage of **3,250** square feet and a treatment cost of $**.002** per square foot. Click the **Save All** icon to save the resulting project.

3. Create a new folder named **Ex3-3** in the *Chapter3\Homework* folder. Review your design for Exercise 3 in Chapter 1 and then use **Step-by-Step Instructions 3-2** to copy the *Chapter2\Homework\Ex2-3* files into the new *Ex3-3* folder. Follow those same instructions to rename the files in the folder to be **Ex3-3.vb, Ex3-3.vbproj,** and **Ex3-3.sln** and to make **Ex3-3.vb** the startup object.

Add four text boxes and corresponding labels and modify the properties for the text boxes and labels as needed. The first text box should allow the user to input the make of the car being tested. The second and third text boxes should allow the user to input the miles driven and the gallons of gas used. The fourth text box should display the miles per gallon, which is equal to the miles driven divided by the gallons used.

Use a button to compute and display the miles per gallon (use the Fixed Numeric format). Add buttons to clear the text boxes, set the focus back to the automobile name text box, and to exit the project. Test your project with a **Toyonda** make of car that was driven **225** miles on **7.3** gallons of gas. Click the **Save All** icon to save the resulting project.

4. Create a new folder named **Ex3-4** in the *Chapter3\Homework* folder. Review your design for Exercise 4 in Chapter 1 and then use **Step-by-Step Instructions 3-2** to copy the *Chapter2\Homework\Ex2-4* files into the new *Ex3-4* folder. Follow those same instructions to rename the files in the folder to be **Ex3-4.vb, Ex3-4.vbproj,** and **Ex3-4.sln** and to make **Ex3-4.vb** the star-

tup object.

Add five text boxes and corresponding labels and modify the properties for the text boxes and labels as needed. The first text box should allow the user to input the fixed cost of production, while the next two text boxes are for input of the unit cost and unit price values. The fourth text box should display the breakeven volume, which is equal to Fixed cost/(Unit price − Unit cost). The fifth text box should display the Breakeven revenue (Cost), which is equal to Breakeven volume times Unit price. Replace the message in the button with the code necessary to make these calculations and display the results. Format the Breakeven volume using the Standard Numeric format. Format all other text boxes to be dollars and cents. Add buttons to clear the text boxes, set the focus back to the Fixed cost text box, and to exit the project. Test your project with a Unit price of $**25**, Unit cost of $**15**, and Fixed cost of $**1,000**. Click the **Save All** icon to save the resulting project.

5. Create a new folder named **Ex3-5** in the *Chapter3\Homework* folder. Review your design for Exercise 5 in Chapter 1 and then use **Step-by-Step Instructions 3-2** to copy the *Chapter2\Homework\Ex2-5* files into the new *Ex3-5* folder. Follow those same instructions to rename the files in the folder to be **Ex3-5.vb, Ex3-5.vbproj,** and **Ex3-5.sln** and to make **Ex3-5.vb** the startup object.

Add seven text boxes and corresponding labels, and modify the properties for the text boxes and labels as needed. The first text box should allow the user to input the customer's name. The next four text boxes should allow the user to input the length of the room, the width of the room, the window area, and the door area. The sixth text box should display the room area, and the seventh text box should display the number of wallpaper rolls needed. Add a line control above this text box.

Replace the message in the button with the calculations to compute the room area and number of rolls of wallpaper needed. **Note:** Because the number of rolls calculated must be an integer, you should use Integer division to calculate the number of rolls and *then* add one (+1) to the result to account for the fractional remainder of a roll. Use the Fixed Numeric format to format all text boxes *except* the number of rolls. Add buttons to clear the text boxes, set the focus back to the customer name text box, and to exit the project. Test your project for a **20' × 15'** room with **2** doors, each of which is **21** square feet, and **4** windows, each of which is **12** square feet. Assume that each roll of wallpaper will cover **45** square feet. Click the **Save All** icon to save the files for this project.

6. Use **Step-by-Step Instructions 3-2** to copy the **SimpleCalc** files that you created in the **Try It Yourself!** exercises into a new folder named **SimpleCalcNew** in the *Homework* folder. Follow those same instructions to rename the files in the folder to be **SimpleCalcNew.vb, SimpleCalcNew.vbproj,** and **SimpleCalcNew.sln** and to make **SimpleCalcNew.vb** the startup object.

Modify SimpleCalcNew form to replace the single button with four buttons: one for addition, one for subtraction, one for multiplication, and one for division (assume you are dividing the contents of the top text box by the contents of the second text box). Use the arithmetic operators (+, −, *, or /) as the Text property for each button. Also, add a button to exit the project. Try your calculator for various values in the two text boxes. Specifically, try to divide by zero and see what happens. Click the **Save All** icon to save the files in this project.

7. Use **Step-by-Step Instructions 3-2** to copy the **MonthPay** files into a new folder named **MonthPayNew** in the *Homework* folder. Follow those same instructions to re-name the files in the folder to be **MonthPayNew.vb, MonthPayNew.vbproj,** and **MonthPayNew.sln** and to make **MonthPay.vb** the startup object. Modify the Month-PayNew.vb form to calculate the future value of a series of fixed value payments into an annuity for some number of months at a fixed interest rate. (Hint: The FV( ) function works *exactly* like the Pmt( ) function except that the fixed payment replaces the loan amount in the function and the future value is returned instead of the payment required.) You will need to modify the button code and the labels. Test your annuity calculator with a fixed payment of $**100** per month for **10** years (120 months) at a **12** percent annual interest rate (1% monthly). Click the **Save All** icon to save the files in this project.

8. The library at Yeehaw Technical Institute needs an application that will compute the overdue fines for books as they are returned. As a first version of this application, as-sume that the borrower's name, the days overdue, and the fine per day (which differs depending on whether the borrower is a faculty member, a grad student, or an under-graduate) are entered in text boxes and that the Total fine due (Days overdue × Daily fine) is output by clicking a button. Create an interface using text boxes, labels, and but-tons. Develop an IPO table and pseudocode for this problem and then create a project that will carry out the logic using VB .NET in your *Homework* folder. Give the project a name of **Ex3-8** and change the name of the form to be **Ex3-8.vb**. The form should have Calculate, Clear, and Exit buttons. Try out your project with the following data:

> Borrower's name: **Jody Silver**
> Days overdue: **10**
> Daily fine: $**.25**

Click the **Save All** icon to save the files in the project.

9. Bob's Bike Factory produces custom-made bikes in four basic models. The price of the basic model plus the price of accessories determine the total price. Some distributors get special discounts, which are subtracted from the price before sales taxes are added. Develop an IPO table and pseudocode for this project, a sketch of the form, and a VB .NET project that has a form with a title and a logo for Bob's Bike Factory (e.g., a bike icon—use graphics/icons/in-dustry/bicycle.ico) plus *Calculate, Clear,* and *Exit* buttons. Create the project in the *Homework* folder. Give it a name of **Ex3-9** and rename the form as **Ex3-9.vb.** The final project should have the following features:

1. The price of the model, the discount rate, and the number of bikes are input via text boxes. The tax rate is set in the code.

2. The discount (if any), taxes due, and total amount due are computed by a Calculate button and are output to text boxes with appropriate labels.

Try out your project with the following data:
Bikes ordered: **10 Model Red Racers**

Price: **$1499.99** each
Tax rate: **7**%
Discount: **15**%
Click the **Save All** icon to save the files in the project.

10. Thinking that they might amuse themselves on their PDAs while waiting in the snow and rain for dangerous weather phenomena, the meteorologists at The Weather Channel need a simple program to allow them to convert temperatures from Fahrenheit to Celsius. The interface would be composed of two text boxes and a button. They would simply type the Fahrenheit temperature (F) into the first textbox, click the button and the corresponding Celsius temperature (C) would appear in the second textbox. The conversion relationship between the two is: $C = 5/9*(F - 32)$. Design and create a VB .NET program for this application in the *Homework* folder. Give your project a name of **Ex3-10** and rename the form as **Ex3-10.vb.** Try out your project with a Fahrenheit temperature of 32 degrees which should result in a Celsius temperature of 0 degrees. Click the **Save All** icon to save the files in the project.

11. A currency trader would like a simple program to calculate the equivalent value of various foreign currencies for a given amount in U.S. dollars. Assume that a VB program would utilize two text boxes to input the amount in U.S. dollars and the exchange rate. Also, an appropriately labeled text box is used to display the equivalent amount of the foreign currency. The amount of foreign currency is calculated by simply multiplying the amount in U.S. dollars by the exchange rate. Assume that the calculation is performed when a button is clicked. Design and create a VB .NET program for this application in the *Homework* folder. Give the project a name of **Ex3-11** and rename the form as **Ex3-11.vb.** Try your project to convert U.S. dollars to U.K. pounds with an exchange rate of 0.60. Check your newspaper for examples of other exchange rates to use in testing your project. Click the **Save All** icon to save the files in your project.

4 THE SELECTION PROCESS IN VB .NET

LEARNING OBJECTIVES

After reading this chapter, you should be able to

1. Understand the importance of the selection process in programming.
2. Describe the various types of decisions that can be made in a computer program.
3. Discuss the statement forms used in VB .NET to make decisions.
4. Use the ListBox control to select from a list of alternatives.
5. Work with complex comparison structures and nested decisions to handle more sophisticated selection processes.
6. Use the scroll bar to input integer values.
7. Use the Form_Load event to execute a procedure when a form is loaded.
8. Work with the debugging toolbar to find program errors.

THE SELECTION PROCESS

In Chapter 1, we listed the six operations a computer can carry out: input data, store data in internal memory, perform arithmetic on the data, compare two values and select one of two alternative actions, repeat a group of actions any number of times, and output the result of processing. In Chapters 2 and 3, we considered using all of the operations in VB .NET *except* for making decisions and repeating a group of actions. In this chapter, we will discuss in detail how to compare two values and then select an action based on the outcome of the comparison; repeating a group of actions will be discussed in the next chapter.

The process of selection is important to the capability of a computer program to carry out useful processing. If a computer could not select between alternatives, its use would be restricted to only those activities for which the order of processing never deviates. As you know, this would be a very unreasonable situation. In our daily lives, we are constantly making decisions to select among alternatives, whether it is something as simple as what to have for lunch or as complex as choosing a career. The same is true for computer programs; to be truly useful, they must be able to select between alternative courses of action. For example, if you were writing a program to compute the weekly payroll for a company, there would be a number of decisions to be made: Is the employee salaried or hourly? Is he or she full- or part-time? Did the employee work any overtime hours this week? Each decision would have some impact on either the employee's gross salary or net (take home) salary, and the program must process the data that are input to make these decisions.

Another way of thinking about the selection process is that it affects the **flow of control** within the program. That is, the selection that is made determines the next statement or set of statements to be executed. In procedural programs, this was virtually the only way a program could be controlled once it was started. However, in event-driven programs, we know that the user has much more control over the flow of control, since nothing happens until either the user or the program causes an event to occur. This does not take away from the importance of the selection process; it just makes it a part of an event procedure.

Anatomy of a Decision

Every decision in a computer program must compare two values to determine which of two alternative statements or sets of statements will be executed. One alternative will be executed if the comparison is true and another alternative will be executed if the comparison is false. In each case, the alternatives to be executed are valid VB .NET statements. The two values to be compared can be variables, constants, expressions, control properties, or any combination of these three. The only restriction is that both values being compared must be of the same broad data type, that is, Numeric or String.

For the salary example discussed above, consider the overtime decision. In this decision, the number of hours worked is compared to 40. If the comparison is true, that is, more than 40 hours were worked, then the employee should be paid at the regular rate for the first 40 hours and should receive overtime pay at the rate of time-and-a-half for hours worked over 40. If the comparison is false—that is, 40 hours or fewer are worked—then the employee should be paid at the regular pay rate for all hours worked. In this case, the values being compared are Single data type variables and constants, and they are being compared for an inequality.

Types of Decisions

In computer programming, there are two basic decision structures: two alternatives and many alternatives. In the above payroll example, the decision as to whether or not the employee worked more than 40 hours is an example of a decision with two alternatives—more than 40 hours worked or 40 hours or fewer worked. On the other hand, a decision involving shipping costs for a letter or parcel is an example of a multiple-alternative decision structure, because the alternatives include standard ground shipment, two-day shipment, and overnight delivery. In a multiple-alternative decision, it is assumed that the alternatives are mutually exclusive and include all possible situations. This may mean that one of the alternatives is "everything else." In either case—two-alternative or multiple-alternative—the true-or-false test is still used and an alternative is executed or not executed.

In the two-alternative decision structure, the **If-Then-Else decision structure** should be used. In this decision structure, there is a single condition that is true or false. If the condition is true, then the true alternative is implemented; if the condition is false, the false alternative is implemented. The general form of the If-Then-Else decision structure in pseudocode is shown here:

```
If condition is true then
        implement true alternative
Else
        implement false alternative
End decision
```

The term *else* means the condition being tested was not true. Note that the true and false alternatives have been indented. This is for ease of understanding only; it has no effect on the decision structure.

In no case are both alternatives implemented; if the true alternative is implemented, the decision structure is exited. If the false alternative is implemented, the true alternative is skipped.

For the payroll example, the pseudocode version of the decision structure is

```
If employee works more than 40 hours then
        employee pay = regular pay + overtime pay
Else
        employee pay = regular pay
End decision.
```

For the multiple-alternative situation, the general form in pseudocode for three possible alternatives is

```
Select one:
        Condition 1 is true: implement alternative 1
        Condition 2 is true: implement alternative 2
        Condition 3 is true: implement alternative 3
End Selection
```

In this situation, the first condition is tested to determine if it is true; if it is, the first alternative is implemented, no other conditions are tested, and the decision structure is terminated. If the first condition is false, the second condition is tested in the same manner and so on until one condition is found to be true. If none of the conditions is true, the decision structure is terminated with no action being taken.

For example, the pseudocode version of the shipping example is

```
Select Shipping Mode
        Standard ground: cost = standard ground cost
        Two-day shipment: cost = two-day cost
        Overnight: cost = overnight shipment cost
End Selection
```

There can be many variations and combinations of these two decision structures. For example, there may be no false alternative for the two-alternative decision structure, or a two-alternative decision structure may be "nested" inside the multiple-alternative decision structure as one of the alternatives. The tests of whether a customer name or DVD name has been entered in the Vintage DVDs application are both examples of a two-alternative decision with no false alternative. We will explore some of these variations as we go through the use of decisions in VB .NET.

THE TWO-ALTERNATIVE DECISION STRUCTURE

Implementing the two-alternative and multiple-alternative decision structures in VB .NET involves learning the correct syntax for the decision statements and the appropriate form for the conditions that are tested to determine if they are true or false. Failure to carry out either of these correctly will result in either a syntax error or a logic error. Since both the statement syntax and the condition forms are different for the two decision structures, we will discuss them in separate sections. However, in both cases the idea is the same: We must determine if a condition is true or false and take appropriate action for each situation.

Recall that the two-alternative decision structure occurs when there is a single condition that must be tested to determine if it is true or false. In VB .NET the If-Then-Else statement for this decision structure is

If *condition is true* **then**
> *statements for true alternative*

Else
> *statements for false alternative*

End if

Notice that the form of the VB .NET two-alternative decision structure is virtually identical to that of the pseudocode version, with the exception that *end if* is used to terminate the decision structure. The results of true and false conditions on the two-alternative decision are shown in Figure 4-1.

FIGURE 4-1. The two-alternative decision

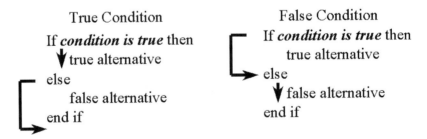

Two Alternative Decision

The If-Then Condition

The main thing you need to understand to use this decision structure is the form of the *condition* part of the statement. In VB .NET, the decision condition has the following form:

> **test expression1** *comparison operator* **test expression2**

where

> **test expression** = variable, constant, or expression

and

> **comparison operator** = one of six comparison operators in Table 4-1.

In this decision structure, the objective is to compare *test expression1* on the left to *test expression2* on the right to determine if the relationship defined by the comparison operator is true. The condition must evaluate to true or false; there is nothing in between.

> **TIP:** Since Boolean variables are either true or false, it is possible to write a condition that consists only of the Boolean variable name.

TABLE 4-1: Comparison operators

Name	Operator Symbol	Example	Meaning
Equal to	=	strEmpCode = "S"	Is employee code equal to "S"?
Greater than	>	intHours > 40	Are hours worked greater than 40?
Greater than or equal to	>=	decRevenue >= decCosts	Is Revenue greater than or equal to Costs?
Less than	<	decThisYear < decLastYear	Is this year's revenue less than last year's revenue?
Less than or equal to	<=	decMySalary <= decYourSalary	Is MySalary less than or equal to YourSalary?
Not equal to	<>	intNumber <> 0	Is Number not equal to zero?

Using the six comparison operators defined in Table 4-1, we can compare any two variables, constants, expressions, or control properties. The only requirement is that the data type for the two expressions being compared be the same; that is, compare strings to strings and numbers to numbers. Trying to compare a string to a number will produce invalid results. For example, we can compare an alphanumeric pay code to the character constant "S" to determine if they are the same. Or we can compare the variable intHours to the constant 40 to determine if the hours worked is greater than or equal to 40. However, trying to compare the string variable strEmpCode to the Integer constant 40 could result in invalid results.

Let's see how we would apply the two-alternative decision structure to the payroll example. To do that, we will create a small project that will compute wages for hourly employees. The project will have four text boxes: one for the employee name, one for the number of hours worked, one for the hourly wage rate, and one for the resulting wage for this employee. If employees work more than 40 hours, then they should be paid at their regular pay rate for the first 40 hours and at their overtime rate for each hour over 40. If employees work 40 hours or fewer, they should be paid at their regular rate for all hours worked. For example, assume that an employee is paid $10 per hour. If the employee works 35 hours, he will be paid 35 × $10 = $350. However, if the employee works 48 hours, he will be paid $10 per hour for the first 40 hours and time- and-a-half for all hours over 40. In this case, the amount paid will be equal to 40 × $10 + 1.5 × (48 − 40) × $10, or $400 for regular time + $120 for overtime = $520 for the 48 hours of work. The decision structure in pseudocode for this situation follows:

```
If Hours > 40 then
        Pay = 40 * PayRate + 1.5 * (Hours - 40) * PayRate
Else
        Pay = Hours * PayRate
End Decision
```

The interface for this example is shown in Figure 4-2, with the four text boxes and corresponding labels and two buttons—one to compute the pay due the employee and one to exit the application. The text boxes are named *txtName, txtPayRate, txtHours,* and *txtPay,* and the corresponding labels are given similar names. These controls are listed in Table 4-2.

FIGURE 4-2.
Interface for payroll computation

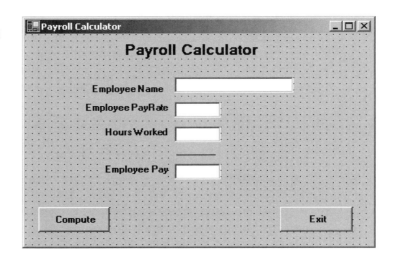

TABLE 4-2: Text boxes and labels for payroll application

Control Name	Text Property	Control Name	Text Property
frmPayroll	Payroll Calculator	txtPay	
btnCompute	Compute	lblName	Employee Name
btnExit	Exit	lblPayRate	Employee Pay Rate
txtName		lblHours	Hours Worked
txtPayRate		lblLine	_____
txtHours		lblPay	Employee Pay

The code for the button to compute the employee's pay (*btnCompute*) is shown in VB Code Box 4-1. Note that we format the rate and pay as currency *after* computation. The *Exit* button (btnExit) has the standard *End* statement.

To test this application, use the data we used earlier, that is, decPayRate = *$10* and sngHours = *35* or *48,* for an employee named *Ben Sibley.* In the first case, the resulting decPay should be $350, and in the second case, the result-

VB CODE BOX 4-1.
Code to compute payroll
	``vb
	Private Sub btnCompute_Click(ByVal sender As System.Object, _
	ByVal e As System.EventArgs) Handles btnCompute.Click
	    Dim decPayRate, decPay As Decimal, sngHours As Single
	    decPayRate = CDec(txtPayRate.Text)
	    sngHours = CSng(txtHours.Text)
	    If sngHours >= 40 Then
	       decPay = decPayRate * 40 + 1.5 * decPayRate * _
	       (sngHours - 40)
	    Else
	       decPay = decPayRate * sngHours
	    End If
	    txtPay.Text = Format(decPay, "currency")
	    txtPayRate.Text = Format(txtPayRate.Text, "currency")
	End Sub
	``

ing curPay should be $520, as seen in Figure 4-3 after the Compute button
has been clicked. You should also test it with some other data for which you
know the resulting pay. The steps to create the payroll calculator are shown
in Step-by-Step Instructions 4-1.

FIGURE 4-3.
Running the Payroll
Calculator

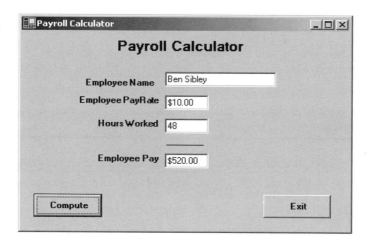

Step-by-Step Instructions 4-1: Creating a payroll project

1. In Windows Explorer, choose to create a new folder named **Chapter4** in
the Visual Studios Projects folder. Start VB .NET and choose a **New Project**
from the Start Page. Choose a Windows Form and browse to find the
Chapter4 folder you just created. Give the project a name of **Payroll** and
rename the form file as **Payroll.vb**.

2. Create an interface for the project like that shown in Figure 4-2. Give the
form a name of **frmPayroll** and a text property of **Payroll Calculator.** Make
frmPayroll your Startup Object.

3. For the controls on the form, use the names and captions shown in Table
4-2.

4. Open the Code window for the Click event for the btnCompute button and add the code shown in VB Code Box 4-1. Also add the **End** instruction to the btnExit button code.

5. Run your project and enter the following data: Name = **Ben Sibley**, Pay rate = **$10**, and Hours worked = **35** (your answer should be $350.00).

6. Change the hours worked to **48** and compare your results to those shown in Figure 4-3. Test your project further by changing the pay rate to **$11.50** and the hours worked to both **38** and **47**. Compare the answer against your hand calculations ($437.00 for 38 hours and $580.75 47 hours).

7. Click the **Save All** icon to save all project files.

I ▬ I

Mini-Summary 4-1: If-Then-Else statements

1. Decisions are an important element of any computer program, because they affect the flow control of a program.

2. There are two types of decision structures: those with two alternatives and those with many alternatives.

3. Two-alternative decisions are handled by the If-Then-Else structure.

4. The two-alternative decision structure uses a comparison condition to determine if a comparison is true or false. The result of this comparison determines which statements are executed.

5. Comparison operators include equal to, greater than, greater than or equal to, less than, less than or equal to, and not equal to.

It's Your Turn!

1. Assuming that intL and intM are integer variables with intL = 9 and intM = −3, and that sngX = −4.25, sngY = 0, and sngZ = 43.5 are Single variables, find the values (true or false) of the following logical expressions:

    a. intL <= intM
    b. −2 × intL <= 8
    c. sngX^2 < Sqr(intZ)
    d. CInt(sngZ) = (5 × intL − 3 × .5)
    e. sngY <> 0

2. Write logical expressions to express the following conditions:

    a. *X* is greater than 5
    b. *R* is negative
    c. *A* is not equal to *B*
    d. *M* is not negative
    e. Half of *Z* is greater than or equal to twice *Y*

3. Write two-alternative decision structures for the following situations (in each case, unless directed to otherwise, do not worry about input and output; just work with the appropriate variables, which we will assume have already been declared).

    a. If taxable income is greater than $30,000, then taxes are $4,500 plus 28% of the taxable income over $30,000. If taxable income is less than or equal to $30,000, taxes are 15% of taxable income.

    b. If the amount to be withdrawn from an ATM is less than the existing balance, subtract the amount from the balance to compute the new balance. Otherwise, use a message box to display an "Insufficient Funds" message.

    c. At the Jones Company, if a salesperson generates $10,000 or less in revenue for a month, she is paid a commission of 10% of the revenue she generates. If she generates more than $10,000 in revenue, she is paid $100 plus a commission of 12% of the revenue.

4. Follow Step-by-Step Instructions 4-1 to create the payroll calculator.

APPLICATION TO VINTAGE DVDs

Assume for the Vintage DVDs example, that the owner wants to make sure that the customer and DVD names have been entered in the appropriate text boxes before continuing the calculation process. This involves determining if either text box is empty—that is, if there is a null string in the text box. To determine this, we need to use a two-alternative decision structure with no false alternative. The form of this decision structure is as follows:

> **If** *condition is true* **Then**
> > *true alternative is implemented*
> **End If**

Note that, in this decision structure, if the condition is true, then the true alternative is executed; otherwise, nothing happens and the decision structure is terminated.

    For the scenario, if either text box is empty, then the project needs to request that a name be entered. One way to do this would be to use a message box to alert the user to the missing entry. However, the user could ignore this message and still not enter a name in the text box. Another way— one that *forces* the user to respond—is the InputBox function. The **Input-Box( )** function has the form

> ***variable or control property* = Inputbox(*prompt, name*)**

where *prompt* is a message enclosed in quotation marks requesting the user to input a certain data item and *name* is the name of the InputBox that will appear at the top of the box. When the project encounters this function, a box is displayed on the screen with the prompt for data. For the scenario, the appropriate use of the InputBox function would be

```
txtCustName.Text = InputBox("Please input the member name.",
_"Vintage DVDs")
```

Note that we have set the Text property of the Customer Name text box equal to the InputBox, so that whatever the user enters in the InputBox will automatically go into the customer name text box. The resulting InputBox is shown in Figure 4-4 with a customer name entered. Note that the name of the Inputbox, "Vintage DVDs," appears in the top of the InputBox.

FIGURE 4-4. Use of InputBox

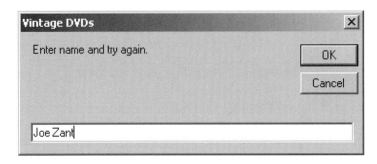

When the user presses **ENTER**, the name will be transferred to the Text property of the txtCustName text box. If the user presses the **Cancel** button, a zero-length string ("") is returned.

It is important to remember that the InputBox function cannot be used by itself like a message box; a variable or control property must be set equal to the InputBox function to receive the user's input. Another important feature of the InputBox function is that it *always* returns a string. This means that if you are entering a number that will be transferred to a Numeric data type variable, you must use the appropriate conversion function, such as CInt( ), to convert the string returned by the InputBox function to a number. For example, if you are using an InputBox function to enter a quiz score, the appropriate statement would be

```
intQuizScore = CInt(InputBox("Please enter a quiz score"))
```

where QuizScore is an Integer data type variable. Note that two right-hand parentheses are needed at the end of the statement to match the two left-hand parentheses earlier in the statement. We don't have to worry about this in the current example, because the Text property of the text boxes is also a string.

> **TIP:** The number of right-hand parentheses in *any* expression **must** match the number of left-hand parentheses.

To test the Customer Name and DVD Name text boxes to determine whether something has been entered in them, the code shown in VB Code Box 4-2 would need to be added to the existing code for the Click event of the btnCalc button in the Vintage DVDs project. This new code would be entered immediately after the existing declaration statements and before the computation of taxes and amount due.

Note in VB Code Box 4-2 that we have checked if a customer name and a DVD name have been entered in the text boxes by comparing the Text property to a zero-length or null string (""). If the comparison is found to be true, then the InputBox function requests the user to enter the appropriate name and click Calculate again. The btnCalc_Click event procedure is then exited via the *Exit Sub* instruction. This precludes the program from continuing until both customer name and DVD name have been input.

| VB CODE BOX 4-2. Additional code to validate input | ```
If txtCustName.Text = "" Then
   txtCustName.Text = InputBox("Enter name and try again.", _
   "Vintage DVDs")
   Exit Sub
End If
If txtDVDName.Text = "" Then
   txtDVDName.Text = InputBox("Enter DVD name and " & _
   "try again.", "Vintage DVDs")
   Exit Sub
End If
``` |
| --- | --- |

These If-Then-Else decisions are examples of an important feature that should appear in all applications: **validation.** In validation, the project developer tries to validate user input *before* it can cause problems for the project. In this case, the validation mechanism checks to see if a name has been entered and, if one has not, requests one. In so doing, it avoids later problems. Any project you create should include some validation to avoid problems later on.

> **TIP:** An empty string is different from one that has blank spaces. If there are spaces in the empty string representation, the comparison will fail.

Note also in VB Code Box 4-2 that the statement to assign a value to txtDVDName.text is sufficiently long that the prompt in the InputBox is continued on the second line using the underscore continuation character (_). However, you *cannot* continue a string constant contained in quotation marks. You must terminate the string constant and concatenate it with the remainder of the string after the continuation. For example, to continue a long string constant, you would do the following:

```
Msgbox("This is an extremely long string " & _
"constant that must be continued to the next line")
```

If there is anything (including spaces) in either text box, then the comparison is false and the corresponding If-Then decision structure is exited with nothing happening. If you run the Vintage DVDs project with this additional code and fail to enter either a customer name or a DVD name, then you will be requested to do so when you click the btnCalc button.

■ ■ ■ ■ ■ ■ ■ ■ ■ ■ ■ ■ ■ ■ ■ ■ ■ ■ ■

Step-by-Step Instructions 4-2: Continuing the Vintage DVDs project

1. Start VB .NET and create a new project named **Vintage4** in the *Chapter4* folder you created earlier. *Copy* the files from the *Vintage3* folder into the *Vintage4* folder.

2. Add the code shown in VB Code Box 4-2 to the Click event for the btnCalc button immediately after the existing declaration statements. Test the resulting project by first failing to enter the customer name and clicking the *Calculate* button. Test it again by failing to enter the DVD name. In both cases, use a DVD price of $**1.99.**
```

3. What happens if the DVD price field is left blank? What could be done to avoid this problem?

4. Click the **Save All** icon to save the files in the Vintage4 folder.

■ ■

Mini-Summary 4-2: Validation of input

1. It is possible to have only a true alternative in the two-alternative decision structure.

2. Validation of input is an important part of any computer program.

3. An InputBox can be used to input data directly to a variable or control property.

It's Your Turn!

1. Assume that as part of a program you wish to obtain the user's age in years. You design the interface so that the user will enter their name in a text box. When a button is clicked, the age will be stored to a variable. You then want to make sure that the value entered for the age is a positive number. If the value entered is not positive, you will ask for and obtain the correct value from the user, store the correct value in the variable, and display it in the text box. Create the pseudocode to carry out this logic.

2. Follow Step-by-Step Instructions 4-2 to continue the Vintage DVDs project.

THE MULTIPLE-ALTERNATIVE DECISION STRUCTURE

When there are more than two alternatives to choose from, the If-Then-Else decision structure is inappropriate. Instead, VB .NET provides two ways to handle the multiple alternatives: If-Then-ElseIf and Select Case decision structures. They work equally well, and you can choose which you want to use (or your instructor may tell you which one he or she favors). In either case, a condition is tested to determine if a given alternative should be executed. If the condition is found to be false, this corresponding alternative will not be executed. If all conditions are found to be false, then none of the alternatives will be executed. As an example involving multiple alternatives, we will use a situation very familiar to all readers: deciding on a letter grade based on a quiz average. (Later, we will apply the multiple-alternative case to the Vintage DVDs scenario.) In this case, the multiple alternatives are usually the grades A, B, C, D, and F and the condition being tested is whether the quiz average is above a certain level. For our purpose, we will assume that the instructor is using the 90-80-70-60 scale for assigning grades. The pseudocode for this decision is shown below (where Integer averages are being used):

If average is 90 or higher then grade is A
    Else if average is 80 or higher then grade is B
    Else if average is 70 or higher then grade is C

```
            Else if average is 60 or higher then grade is D
            Else grade is F
         End decision
```

Note in the pseudocode that we start with the highest grade and move down through the possible breakpoints for grades. Had we started at the lowest grade and tested if the average was 60 or higher, then everybody meeting this criterion, including those with much higher grades, would receive a grade of D and the decision structure would be terminated. For this reason, it is important that the conditions are ordered in the appropriate manner to provide the desired results.

Using the If-Then-ElseIf Decision Structure

For the multiple-alternative situation, the **If-Then-ElseIf** decision structure is a natural extension of the If-Then-Else structure, where there can be multiple ElseIf statements after the original If statement. Each ElseIf statement tests a comparison condition like the one used to test the original If statement and has one or more instructions to execute if it is true. The general form of the If-Then-ElseIf decision structure is shown below for three alternatives and for an alternative when all conditions prove to be false.

> **If** *condition1 true* **then**
>> **first set of statements**
> **ElseIf** *condition2 true* **then**
>> **second set of statements**
> **ElseIf** *condition3 true* **then**
>> **third set of statements**
> **Else**
>> **last set of statements**
> **End if**

As with the If-Then-Else decision structure, the original If statement is tested first. If it is true, then none of the ElseIf statements is tested. If the original If comparison condition is false, then the first ElseIf comparison condition is tested. If it is found to be true, the corresponding set of instructions is executed and the decision structure is terminated. If the first ElseIf condition is false, each subsequent ElseIf statement is tested in order until one is found to be true or until the general-purpose Else statement is encountered. In this situation, the Else is executed when the original If statement and *all* ElseIf statements are false.

In this decision structure, there can be as many ElseIf statements as necessary as long as each one is mutually exclusive of all other ElseIf statements. In other words, overlapping conditions are not allowed. If all test conditions prove to be false, the statements after the Else keyword are executed. Note: The Else statement is not necessary; if it is deleted and all test conditions prove to be false, the decision structure is exited with no statements being executed. The flow of control in this decision structure when *condition3* is the true condition is shown in Figure 4-5.

Determining a Letter Grade

To implement the grade assignment logic, let's create a small project in which we can enter the name and quiz average for a student and determine the corresponding letter grade. The interface for this project is shown in Figure 4-6,

FIGURE 4-5. Flow of control for multiple-alternative decisions

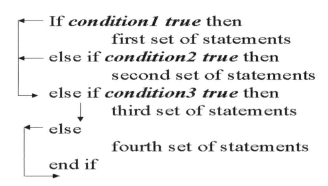

where the form has four labels, three text boxes, and two buttons. The form is named *frmLetterGrade,* and the heading label is named *lblHeading.* The text boxes are named *txtName, txtAverage,* and *txtLetter,* and the labels are given corresponding names. The two buttons, named *btnLetter* and *btnExit,* determine the letter grade and exit the project, respectively. The properties for the text boxes and labels are shown in Table 4-3.

FIGURE 4-6. Interface for letter-grade determination project

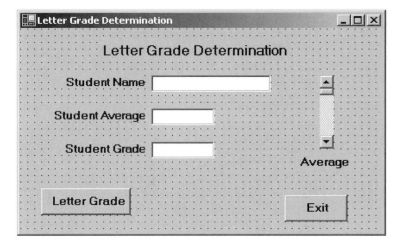

TABLE 4-3: Control names and properties for letter-grade determination project

Control Name	Text Property
frmLetterGrd	Letter Grade
btnLetterGrd	Letter Grade
btnExit	Exit
vsbAverage	
txtName	
txtAverage	
txtLetter	

TABLE 4-3: Control names and properties for letter-grade determination project

Control Name	Text Property
lblName	Student Name
lblAverage	Student Average
lblLetter	Student Grade
lblHeading	Letter-Grade Determination
lblScrollBar	Average

To input the average value, we will use a new control: the **scroll bar.** The scroll bar allows you to use an analog device to input values. There are vertical and horizontal scroll bars that, respectively, begin with *vsb* and *hsb* prefixes. In this case, we will use the vertical scroll bar with a name of *vsbAverage*. The key property of the scroll bar is the **Value** property, which is an Integer. The Value property responds to the **Scroll** event as the scroll bar is moved. The limits on the Value property can be set through the **Maximum** (Max) and **Minimum** (Min) properties. It is also possible to control the amount the value changes when the scroll bar arrows are clicked through the **SmallChange** property. The amount of change that occurs when the interior of the scroll bar is clicked is set through the **LargeChange** property.

For example, to use the scroll bar for a student's average, the Max property would be set to 100 and the Min property set to 0. The LargeChange property might be set to 10 to allow for larger changes in the average and the SmallChange property set to 1 for unit changes. This will result in an Integer average value between 0 and 100. No matter what the SmallChange and LargeChange properties are, the user can always "drag" the scroll bar to any value between the Max setting and the Min setting.

The first event procedure we need to write is to transfer the result of moving the scroll bar to the corresponding text box. As mentioned earlier, this is accomplished in the default scroll bar Scroll event procedure. We need to assign the Value property of the scroll bar to the Text property of the txtAverage text box. The code for this event procedure is shown in VB Code Box 4-3.

VB CODE BOX 4-3. Scroll event code for scroll bar	```Private Sub vsbAverage_Scroll(ByVal sender As System.Object, _ ByVal e As System.Windows.Forms.ScrollEventArgs) Handles _ vsbAverage.Scroll txtAverage.Text = CStr(vsbAverage.Value) End Sub```

The only other code for this project goes in the Click event procedures for the btnLetter and btnExit buttons. The If-Then-ElseIf decision structure is implemented in the btnLetter button to determine and display the appropriate letter grade for this person. This code is shown in VB Code Box 4-4.

Note that no conversion is required to assign the strLetterGrade variable to the Text property of txtLetter, since both are String data types. If the project is run for a sample student, the results are as shown in Figure 4-7.

VB CODE BOX 4-4.
Code for letter-grade
determination
	``
	Private Sub btnLetter_Click(ByVal sender As System.Object, _
	ByVal e As System.EventArgs) Handles btnLetter.Click
	    Dim intAverage As Integer, strLetterGrade As String
	    intAverage = CInt(txtAverage.Text)
	    If intAverage >= 90 Then
	        strLetterGrade = "A"
	    ElseIf intAverage >= 80 Then
	        strLetterGrade = "B"
	    ElseIf intAverage >= 70 Then
	        strLetterGrade = "C"
	    ElseIf intAverage >= 60 Then
	        strLetterGrade = "D"
	    Else
	        strLetterGrade = "F"
	    End if
	        txtLetter.Text = strLetterGrade
	End Sub
	``

The steps to create this project are summarized in Step-by-Step Instructions 4-3.

FIGURE 4-7. Letter Grade project

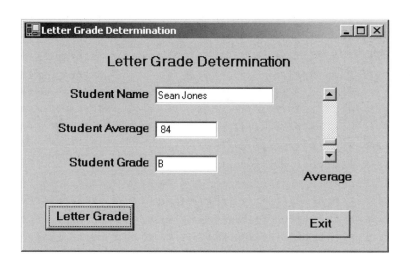

Step-by-Step Instructions 4-3: Creating the letter-grade project

1. Start VB .NET (or select File|New Project) and open a Windows Form project with a name of **LetterGrd** in the *Chapter4* folder. Rename the form file as **LetterGrd.vb,** give it a name of **frmLetterGrd,** and a text property of **Letter-Grade Determination.** Create the interface shown in Figure 4-6 using the control names and properties shown in Table 4-3.

2. Define the properties for the vsbAverage scroll bar to be Max: **100,** Min: **0,** LargeChange: **10,** and SmallChange: **1.**

3. Add the code shown in VB Code Box 4-3 to the Scroll event procedure for the vsbAverage scroll bar. Add the code shown in VB Code Box 4-4 to the Click event procedure for the btnLetter button. Add the **End** instruction to the Click event procedure for the btnExit button.

4. Run your project for Sean Jones with an average of 84, as is shown in Figure 4-7. Try it on Alice West with an average of 58. Try a few other names and averages to ensure the project is running as expected. After you have corrected any errors, save all of the files.

∎ ■ ∎

Using the Select Case Decision Structure

The second decision structure for handling multiple alternatives is the **Select Case** decision structure, in which there can be as many Case statements as necessary so long as there is no ambiguity about which condition will be selected under a given set of circumstances. If all test conditions prove to be false, the statements after the Case Else keywords are executed. Note: The Case Else statement is not necessary; if it is deleted and all test conditions prove to be false, the decision structure is exited with no statements being executed. The form of the Select Case decision structure for three alternatives and an Else alternative is as follows

> **Select Case *expression***
> **Case *condition1 is true***
>   ***First set of statements***
> **Case *condition2 is true***
>   ***Second set of statements***
> **Case *condition3 is true***
>   ***Third set of statements***
> **Case Else**
>   ***Last set of statements***
> **End Select**

The test condition in the Select Case decision structure is different from those in the If-Then-ElseIf decision structure. It can take on one of three forms: a single value or expression, a range of values, or a comparison condition like those used in the If-Then-Else and If-Then-ElseIf decision structures. These three forms are shown in Table 4-4.

TABLE 4-4: Select Case comparison conditions

Test Condition	Condition Format	Example	Condition Is True If
Value or expression	One or multiple values or strings separated by commas	Case 91, 92, 93	Average = 91, 92, or 93.
Range of values	A range of values defined by high and low values separated by keyword To	Case 90 to 100	Average is between 90 and 100 inclusive.
Comparison condition	A comparison condition preceded by the keyword *Is*	Case Is > 89	Average is greater than 89.

In each case, the test conditions refer to a student average, and each must follow the keyword Case. It is also possible to create very complex decision structures by combining all three test condition forms in the same Case statement. In these three forms of the Select Case test condition, it should be obvious that the first form is useful in looking for individual values or letters of the alphabet and the second form is useful in checking to determine if the test expression falls in a range of values. If you use the *To* keyword to define a range, the first value must be less than the second or an error will occur. Finally, the last form is useful for working with comparison expressions of the form discussed earlier.

> **TIP:** When a value may cause more than one condition to be true, only the first True condition will be evaluated and its corresponding action executed.

To apply the Select Case decision structure to the letter-grade example, we need to rewrite the btnLetter event procedure to replace the If-Then-ElseIf decision structure with Select Case. Since we are searching for values that are greater than or equal to some cutoff value, the third Select Case test expression form appears to be the best fit. However, it would also be easy to use the second test expression form. The revised code for the btnLetter_Click event procedure is shown in VB Code Box 4-5.

VB CODE BOX 4-5.
Code for letter-grade determination using Select Case
	<pre>Private Sub btnLetter_Click(ByVal sender As System.Object,_
	ByVal e As System.EventArgs) Handles btnLetter.Click
	    Dim intAverage As Integer
	    Dim strLetterGrade As String
	    intAverage = CInt(txtAverage.Text)
	    Select Case intAverage
	      Case Is >= 90
	        strLetterGrade = "A"
	      Case Is >= 80
	        strLetterGrade = "B"
	      Case Is >= 70
	        strLetterGrade = "C"
	      Case Is >= 60
	        strLetterGrade = "D"
	      Case Else
	        strLetterGrade = "F"
	    End Select
	    txtLetter.Text = strLetterGrade
	End Sub</pre>

Note in the example of the Select Case decision structure shown in Code Table 4-5 that even though a student with an average of, say, 95, fits all of the first four conditions, only the first one, >=90, is executed since it comes first. After a condition is executed, all other conditions are ignored. If the If-Then-ElseIf decision structure used earlier is replaced with a Select Case structure and the project is executed with the same test data as before, the same letter grade should result.

Although we have used numeric values for the Select Case decision structure, the same approach will work with character strings. In that case, the alphabetical ordering must be used to define a range. For example, it would be possible to use Case "A" to "Z" but not Case "M" to "A," because "A" comes before "Z" and "M" in the alphabetical ordering.

Mini-Summary 4-3: If-Then-ElseIf and Select Case decision structures

1. Multiple alternatives can be handled with either the If-Then-ElseIf or the Select Case decision structures.

2. The If-Then-ElseIf decision structure is an extension of the If-Then-Else decision structure in which multiple logical conditions can be tested in the ElseIf statements.

3. Scroll bars can be used to input values through movement up and down or right and left.

4. The Select Case decision structure uses three different types of conditions to test whether an alternative should be implemented: a list of values, a range of values using the To keyword, and a comparison condition using the Is keyword.

5. Either alternative decision structure can be used in almost all situations.

It's Your Turn!

1. Write Select Case conditions to test for each of the following:

    a. An age value is either 10, 20, or 30.

    b. A salary is between $50,000 and $100,000.

    c. A gender is either "m" or "f."

    d. A text box called txtName is not empty.

    e. A weight is below 150 pounds.

2. For each of the following, determine the result that is displayed in txtResult.

    a. If sngX = 0.5? If sngX = –1.8? If sngX = 53.9?

```
Private Sub btnCalculate_Click()
    Dim sngX As Single
    If (sngX <= 0) Then
        txtResult.Text = -sngX
    ElseIf (sngX < 1) Then
        txtResult.Text = sngX ^ 2
    Else
        txtResult.Text = 1
    End If
End Sub
```

    b. If strResponse = "g"? If strResponse = "H"? If strResponse = "Y"?

```
Private Sub btnCalculate_Click()
    Dim strResponse As String
    Select Case strResponse
    Case "g", "G"
        txtResult.Text = "50% discount"
    Case "h", "H"
        txtResult.Text = "30% discount"
    Case "i", "I"
```

```
                              txtResult.Text = "10% discount"
                    Case Else
                              txtResult.Text = "No discount"
                    End Select
              End Sub
```

c. If intZ = −4? If intZ = 2? If intZ = 4? If intZ = 1? If intZ = 0? If intZ = 8?

```
              Private Sub btnCalculate_Click()
                    Dim intZ As Integer
                    Select Case intZ
                    Case 1, 2, 3
                          txtResult.Text = 5
                    Case 2 To 5
                          txtResult.Text = 5 / intZ
                    Case Is >= 0
                          txtResult.Text = 5 * intZ
                    Case Else
                          txtResult.Text = 0
                    End Select
              End Sub
```

3. Write If-Then-ElseIf and Select Case statements for the following situations:

a. Assume that the property tax on a home on South Beach is based on the market value of the home: 10% for homes over $200,000, 8% for homes over $100,000, and 6% for homes $100,000 or less. Write statements to determine the appropriate tax if the market value is known.

b. Assume that the FAST Parcel Service charges according to the distance a package is shipped: $1.00 per pound for over 1,000 miles; $.75 per pound for over 750 miles, and $.50 per pound for 750 miles or less. Write statements to determine the shipping charge if weight and distance shipped are known.

4. Follow Step-by-Step Instructions 4-3 to create the Letter Grade project.

5. Revise the code in the Click event procedure for the btnLetter button in the Letter Grade project to use the Select Case decision structure shown in VB Code Box 4-5. Test your project with the same data as before. After you have corrected any errors, save all files.

APPLICATION TO VINTAGE DVDs EXAMPLE

In the Vintage DVDs example, assume that in addition to validating input to the Web page, the owner of the store is interested in adding features that will make it possible to enter the type of DVD and to automatically compute a price. Currently, Vintage DVDs rents three types of DVD: Kids, Regular, and Classic. Kids DVDs rent for $.99, Regular DVDs rent for $1.99, and Classic DVDs rent for $2.99. We will address this request in this section.

While we could use an InputBox to input the type of DVD, there is an easier way to do this that does not require the user to type anything. As mentioned in Chapter 3 on programming errors, a large percentage of all run-time errors can be traced to errors on input. It is all too easy for a user to misspell a word or to reverse the capitalization. Even if a single letter is being entered, there can still be problems with capitalization. For this reason it is always wise, if at all possible, to avoid having the user key in data, especially where the data concerns text.

Fortunately, VB .NET provides a variety of controls that enable projects to be created that do not require the user to key in large amounts of data. You have already seen one of these controls earlier in this chapter—the scroll bar. Recall that the scroll bar allows the user to input numeric data by moving the scroll bar either vertically or horizontally. Other controls that are useful for displaying textual or numeric data in a list format are the ListBox and ComboBox controls. With a **list box,** a list of data is displayed at all times. With the **combo box,** it is possible to display the data in a drop-down list box of the type you have probably used with the Windows operating system. Although both controls can be used for input and output, in this chapter a list box will be used to input the DVD type instead of having the user enter it. In the next chapter, we will use a combo box as well.

The ListBox Control

The ListBox control is much like an extended TextBox control in that it displays multiple text entries in a list. If the size of the list box as defined by the user is insufficient to display all items in the list, a scroll bar is automatically added that enables the user to scroll up or down to see the remaining list items. The SelectedItem property refers to the item in the list that the user has highlighted by clicking on it.

The list box icon in the Toolbox looks like a list with a scroll bar on the right-hand side. It is added to the form just like any other control. When a list box is placed on the form, the default name (*ListBox* plus a number; for example, *ListBox1)* is displayed. When you change the name, the new name will be displayed in the list box until list items are added. The three-letter prefix for list box names is *lst*. For example, if you wanted a list box to display the DVD types, an appropriate name would be *lstTypes*.

> **TIP:** You can change the SelectionMode property from One to MultiSimple if you want to allow for multiple items to be selected at the same time.

In addition to the number of text items displayed, one key way that the list box differs from the text box is in how data or information are placed in it. With the text box, we usually set the Text property to a null string at design time and then change it with an assignment statement at run time. With the list box, you can create the list of items either at design time or at run time. If you are creating a list of items that will be the same every time you run the project and that is fairly short, you will probably want to create it at design time. On the other hand, if the contents of the list box will change from use to use, then you must add the items to the list in run time through a list of program instructions. Similarly, if the list of items to be added to the list box is long, then you will probably want to add them at run time by reading from a file (discussed in the next chapter.)

Since for Vintage DVDs we have a short list of items that will be the same for every execution of the application, we will add the items to the list box at design time through the **Items** property of the list box. When you click on the Items property in the Properties browser and then click on the dialog button, a dialog box is displayed into which you can enter items to go on the list. You can edit your list of items in the dialog box as you normally would in a text editor.

Figure 4-8 shows the new list box added to the Vintage DVDs form, with items being added to the Items property in the Properties browser. Note that when the name of the list box is changed to lstTypes, it will be displayed in the list box. Note also that we have entered two items, "Kids" and "Regular." Since we have not clicked on the **OK** button yet, they do not yet appear in the list box. When the third Item, "Classic," is input and **OK** is clicked, the Items property items will replace the Name property in the list box.

FIGURE 4-8. List box and use of List property

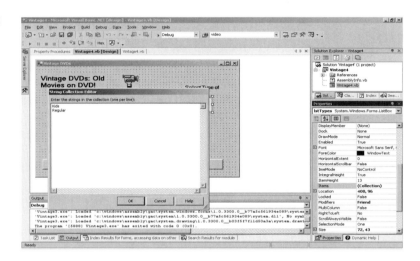

Adding Code

Once all three DVD types have been entered in the lstTypes list box, the next step is to add code to respond to the SelectedIndexChanged event for the list box. We also need to modify the code in the btnCalc button to ensure that the user has selected a type of DVD by clicking on it to highlight a type in the list box. Earlier we said that when an item is highlighted, the list box SelectedItem property is automatically set equal to that item. For example, if *Regular* is highlighted in the lstTypes list box, then the SelectedItem property for the list box is set equal to *Regular.*

To add the code for the SelectedIndexChanged event for the lstTypes list box, we need to double-click it to display the Code window for the SelectedIndexChanged event. While either of the two multiple-alternative decision structures could be used in this situation, the Select Case decision structure is more appropriate because of the efficient manner in which it selects a single code or word from among several possibilities and executes the corresponding statements. The code for the pricing decision is shown in VB Code Box 4-6.

Note in VB Code Box 4-6 that the DVDType String variable has been set equal to the (default) SelectedItem property of lstTypes. We then check to see which of the three possibilities—"Kids," "Regular," or "Classic"—the DVDType variable matches and set the price accordingly. This price is then formatted as Currency and transferred to the txtDVDPrice text box.

| VB CODE BOX 4-6. Code for lstTypes SelectedIndex-Changed event | ```
Private Sub lstTypes_SelectedIndexChanged(ByVal sender As _
System.Object, ByVal e As System.EventArgs) Handles _
lstTypes.SelectedIndexChanged
    Dim strDVDType As String, decPrice As Decimal
    strDVDType = lstTypes.SelectedItem
    Select Case strDVDType
       Case "Kids"
          decPrice = 0.99
       Case "Regular"
          decPrice = 1.99
       Case "Classic"
          decPrice = 2.99
    End Select
    txtDVDPrice.Text = Format(decPrice, "c")
End Sub
``` |

TIP: When comparing strings, everything, even the case, must match exactly.

If this section of code is entered in the lstTypes list box SelectedIndex-Changed event Code window, we are almost finished. However, what if the user fails to select a DVD type from the list box? In this case, the SelectedItem property for lstTypes does not equal any of the three DVD types and the price in the txtDVDPrice text box will not change. To check for this, we need to insert a validation statement in the code for the btnCalc button. Like the previous validation statements, it will be a single-alternative If-Then-Else statement that checks for an empty string for the SelectedItem property of the lstTypes list box. In this case, if an empty string is found, a message box alerts the user to this condition and instructs the user to make a selection from the list box and to press the btnCalc button again. Until the user selects a DVD type from the list box, he or she will not be able to calculate any values for this DVD. The new validation code is shown in VB Code Box 4-7 (where the DVDType variable has been declared as a String). This code should be inserted immediately before the price assignment in the btnCalc event procedure. The complete revised code for the btnCalc_Click event procedure button is shown in VB Code Box 4-8.

| VB CODE BOX 4-7. Additional code for btnCalc | ```
strDVDType = lstTypes.SelectedItem
If strdvdtype = "" Then
    MsgBox("Select a DVD type and try again.", ,"Vintage DVDs")
Exit Sub
End If
``` |

It is also necessary to clear the list box at the same time that the text boxes are cleared. The statement to do this uses the ClearSelected() method and is

```
lstTypes.ClearSelected()
```

This statement should be added to the btnClear_Click event procedure.

Figure 4-9 shows the project being executed where the customer's name is Shelli Keagle and she is renting *Bambi,* which is classified as a "Kids" type DVD. The steps to revise the Vintage DVDs project to use a list box are shown in Step-by-Step Instructions 4-4.

VB CODE BOX 4-8.
Complete code for
btnCalc_Click event
procedure
	``
	Private Sub btnCalc_Click(ByVal sender As System.Object, _
	ByVal e As System.EventArgs) Handles btnCalc.Click
	    Const sngTaxRate As Single = 0.07 ' Use local tax rate
	    Dim decPrice As Decimal, decAmountDue As Decimal
	    Dim decTaxes As Decimal, strDVDType As String
	    If txtCustName.Text = "" Then
	        txtCustName.Text = InputBox("Enter name and try again.", _
	        "Vintage DVDs")
	        Exit Sub
	    End If
	    If txtDVDName.Text = "" Then
	        txtDVDName.Text = InputBox("Enter DVD name and " & _
	        "try again.", "Vintage DVDs")
	        Exit Sub
	    End If
	    strDVDType = lstTypes.SelectedItem
	    If strdvdtype = "" Then
	        MsgBox("Select a DVD type and try again.", ,"Vintage DVDs")
	        Exit Sub
	    End If
	    decPrice = CDec(txtDVDPrice.Text)
	    decTaxes = decPrice * sngTaxRate ' compute taxes
	    decAmountDue = decPrice + decTaxes ' compute amount due
	    txtTaxes.Text = Format(decTaxes, "C")
	    txtAmountDue.Text = Format(decAmountDue, "C")
	    txtDVDPrice.Text = FormatCurrency(txtDVDPrice.Text)
	End Sub
	``

FIGURE 4-9.
Execution of project
with list box

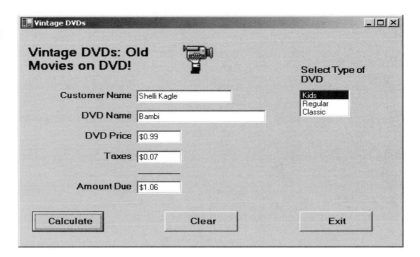

Step-by-Step Instructions 4-4: Revising Vintage DVDs

1. To revise the Vintage DVDs project to use a list box, open the *Vintage4* project and add a ListBox control named **lstTypes** in the upper right-hand section of the frmVintage form and a label to describe it. Change the **Items**

property for lstTypes to include the entries **Kids, Regular,** and **Classic.** Remember to press **ENTER** after each entry and click **OK** to save all entries. The resulting list box should look like Figure 4-8.

2. Add the code shown in VB Code Box 4-6 for the lstTypes SelectedIndex-Changed event. Run your project and test this code to ensure that the correct price is being shown in the price text box. Remember, the String constants in the Select Case statements must be *exactly* the same as the items in the lst-Types list box or the decision structure will not work correctly.

3. Modify the code for the btnCalc button to insert the code shown in VB Code Box 4-7. Your final code should appear like that shown in VB Code Box 4-8.

4. Add a statement to the btnClear_Click event procedure to clear the lst-Types list box.

5. Test your modified project with a customer name of **Shelli Kagle,** a DVD name of ***Bambi,*** and a DVD type of **Kids.** Your result should appear like that shown in Figure 4-9. Also, try it for another type of DVD.

6. Save the files in the project.

┃ ■ ┃

Mini-Summary 4-4: Using list boxes

1. A ListBox control can be used to display multiple lines of text, each of which can be selected by clicking on it. The Items property can be set at design time to the items in the list box.

2. The default property of the list box is the SelectedItem property, which is equal to the selected item.

3. The list box SelectedIndexChanged event can be used to check which value has been selected.

It's Your Turn!

1. What property do we use to add items to a list box at design time?

2. What property is equal to the item in the list box that has been clicked?

3. Update the Vintage DVDs project by completing the following Step-by-Step Instructions 4-4.

4. Modify the Payroll project to use a ListBox control by completing the following exercises:

    a. Open the **Payroll** project and add a ListBox control named **lst-PayRate** to the frmPayroll form. Change the Items property to include four payrates: **$5.25, $8.50, $10.00,** and **$12.50.**

    b. Add code for the lstPayRate SelectedIndexChanged event to input the pay rate value from this list box to the txtPayRate text box.

c. Test this project with all four pay rates and the number of hours worked both below and above 40 hours. Once you are sure everything is correct, save all of the files in the project.

MORE COMPLEX DECISIONS

So far, we addressed only fairly simple decision structures in that only one condition was being considered. However, it is possible to encounter situations with more complex decision conditions. For example, in the Payroll Computation project, we may need to consider both salaried and hourly workers. Since salaried workers are typically not paid for overtime hours, we would need to pay them for 40 hours regardless of how many hours they actually worked. To do this, we would first need to check if a worker is salaried or hourly; if she is hourly, we would then need to make a decision as to how much she would be paid by checking the number of hours worked. If she is salaried, she is paid for 40 hours. This is an example of a decision as an alternative for another decision, a so-called **nested decision.**

Another situation that you might encounter would be one in which the alternative selected depends on more than one condition. This situation is referred to as a **compound condition,** since we combine multiple conditions. For example, in the Letter-Grade Determination project, assume the professor considers both the quiz average and the number of absences in assigning a letter grade. A student must have an average of at least 90 *and* have no more than 3 absences to make an A grade, 80 and have no more than 5 absences to make a B, 70 and have no more than 7 absences to make a C, and so on. We will discuss both nested decisions and compound conditions in this section.

Nested Decisions

Whenever a decision structure is one of the alternatives of a decision, this is referred to as a nested decision, since one decision is said to be *nested* in another decision. For example, in the payroll situation mentioned above with salaried and hourly employees, it must be decided if an employee's pay status is hourly *before* the decision about overtime versus regular time can be made. If the employee is not hourly, then no decision needs to be made.

In working with nested decisions, the key point to remember is that any nested decisions must be completely carried out within a true or false alternative; it is not possible to have a nested decision completed outside of the alternative in which it appears. For the payroll example, the overtime decision must be completely handled within the true alternative of the hourly/salaried decision. This is shown, as follows, in pseudocode form:

```
If PayStatus = Hourly Then
    If Hours > 40 then
        Pay = 40 * PayRate + 1.5 * (Hours - 40) * PayRate
    Else
        Pay = Hours * PayRate
    End Decision
Else
    Pay = 40 * PayRate
End Decision
```

Note in the pseudocode for the nested payroll decision that PayStatus is checked first; if it is found to be Hourly, then, and only then, is the number of hours checked to make the overtime decision. If PayStatus is *not* Hourly, then the employee is paid for 40 hours regardless of the number of hours he actually worked. It is in nested decisions such as this that indenting is of great use, because it clearly shows the level of each decision. In this case, the overtime decision is indented one level and its alternative is indented to a second level. This clearly shows these statements are alternatives for this decision and not for the pay status decision. On the other hand, the false alternative for the pay status decision is indented only one level to show its relationship to that decision structure. We will use the same type of indentation in the VB .NET code.

In VB .NET, let's add a list box named lstPayType to the frmPayroll form in the Payroll project. The list box should have two items: *Hourly* and *Salaried*. Now we can select one item from the list box and use it to determine the employee's pay. In this case, the code to compute a value for the variable decPay is shown in VB Code Box 4-9 (where strPayType has been previously declared as a String type variable.)

VB CODE BOX 4-9. VB .NET code for nested payroll decision	```
	strPayType = lstPayType.SelectedItem
	If strPayType = "Hourly" Then 'Check pay status
	    If sngHours > 40 then 'Pay status is hourly
	        decPay = decPayRate * 40 + 1.5 * decPayRate * (sngHours - 40)
	    Else
	        decPay = decPayRate * sngHours
	    End if
	Else 'Pay status is salaried
	    decPay = decPayRate * 40
	End if
	``

Compound Conditions

When a decision depends on a condition that involves two or more expressions, we have a compound condition. The modified grading condition mentioned earlier is an example of just such a condition, in which a student must achieve an average of at least 90 *and* have no more than three absences in order to earn a grade of A. In this case, the *and* is referred to as a **logical operator** because it operates on the logic of the true-or-false condition.

There are six logical operators, four of which are shown in Table 4-5. (We have not shown the other two—Imp and Eqv—because they are seldom used except in very specialized situations.) In addition to the name of the logical operator, Table 4-5 also contains a short description of each logical operator and an example using the operator (it is assumed that $X = 20$, $Y = 10$, and $Z = 50$).

It is important to note that each condition in a compound condition must be independent of the other conditions so it can be evaluated on its own. This means you could *not* have a statement of the form

```
If X > 15 and < 25
```

because the second half of the statement cannot be evaluated independently of the first half.

To rewrite our letter grade example to include the number of absences in the requirement for a grade, we need to use the And operator. We will

TABLE 4-5: Logical operators

Operator	Description	Example
And	Both conditions must be true for the entire condition to be true.	$X > 15$ *And* $Z < 100$ is true because both conditions are true.
Or	One or both conditions must be true for the entire condition to be true.	$X > 15$ *Or* $Y > 20$ is true because one condition ($X > 15$) is true.
Not	Using this reverses a condition.	*Not* ($Y > 5$) is false because $Y > 5$ is true.
Xor	One and only one condition is true.	$X > Y$ *Xor* $Y > Z$ is true because the first condition is true and the second is false.

assume that a second scroll bar named *vsbAbsences* is being used to input the number of absences and that the appropriate code has been added to its Change event to transfer the number of absences to a text box called txtAbsences. With these additions, the revised code for the btnLetter button for the Letter Grade example is shown in VB Code Box 4-10.

Mini-Summary 4-5: Complex decisions

1. Complex decisions can be implemented as nested decisions or compound conditions.

2. Nested decisions involve a decision being one of the alternatives of another decision.

3. Compound conditions combine conditions using one of the logical operators: And, Or, Not, or Xor.

4. Each condition in a compound decision must be able to be evaluated by itself.

| **VB CODE BOX 4-10.** Revised code for grade decision | ```
Private Sub btnLetter_Click(ByVal sender As System.Object, _
ByVal e As System.EventArgs) Handles btnLetter.Click
    Dim intAverage, intAbsences As Integer
    Dim strLetterGrade As String
    intAverage = CInt(txtAverage.Text)
    intAbsences = CInt(txtAbsences.Text)
    If intAverage >= 90 And intAbsences <= 3 Then
        strLetterGrade = "A"
    ElseIf intAverage >= 80 And intAbsences <= 5 Then
        strLetterGrade = "B"
    ElseIf intAverage >= 70 And intAbsences <= 7 Then
        strLetterGrade = "C"
    ElseIf intAverage >= 60 And intAbsences <= 9 Then
        strLetterGrade = "D"
    Else
        strLetterGrade = "F"
    End If
        txtLetter.Text = strLetterGrade
End Sub
``` |
```

It's Your Turn!

1. For each of the following, write a compound condition or nested decision that will allow the appropriate alternative to be selected:

a. When the value of an integer variable intAge is between 20 and 65, output the result "Employment Age," otherwise do nothing.

b. When a Single variable sngTemp is less than 32, output the result "Very Cold"; when sngTemp is from 32 to less than 50, output the result "Cold"; when sngTemp is from 50 to less than 65, output the result "Cool"; when sngTemp is from 65 to less than 80, output the result "Warm"; otherwise output the result "Hot."

c. When a marital status code, strMarStatCode, is "m" or "M," output the result "Married"; when the code is "s" or "S," output the result "Single"; otherwise give a message about an incorrect code and exit the subroutine.

d. When a Single variable, sngSales, is less than $50, the value of the Single variable sngCommission is $0; when sngSales is between $50 and $500, inclusive, the value of sngCommission is 10% of sngSales; when sngSales is greater than $500, the value of sngCommission is $50 plus 8% of sngSales above $500.

2. For the following, determine the value that is displayed in the txtResult text box:

a. When txtX.Text = 5 and txtY.Text = 3? When txtX.Text = –5 and txtY.Text = 3? When txtX.Text = 5 and txtY.Text = –3? When txtX.Text = –5 and txtY.Text = –3?

```
Private Sub btnGo_Click()
    Dim intX As Integer
    Dim intY As Integer
    intX = CInt(txtX.Text)
    intY = CInt(txtY.Text)
    If intX > 0 And intY > 0 Then
        txtResult.Text = intX * intY
    ElseIf intX < 0 And intY < 0 Then
        txtResult.Text = -intX * intY
    ElseIf intX > 0 And intY < 0 Then
        txtResult.Text = intX * intY
    ElseIf intX < 0 And intY > 0 Then
        txtResult.Text = -intX * intY
    End If
End Sub
```

b. When txtX.Text = 5 and txtY.Text = 3? When txtX.Text = –5 and txtY.Text = 3? When txtX.Text = 5 and txtY.Text = –3? When txtX.Text = –5 and txtY.Text = –3?

```
Private Sub btnGo_Click()
    Dim intX, intY As Integer
    intX = CInt(txtX.Text)
    intY = CInt(txtY.Text)
```

```
        If (intX > 0 And intY > 0) Or (intX > 0 And _
          intY < 0) Then
            txtResult.Text = intX * intY
        End If
        If (intX < 0 And intY < 0) Or (intX < 0 And _
          intY > 0) Then
            txtResult.Text = -intX * intY
        End If
End Sub
```

c. When txtX.Text = 5 and txtY.Text = 3? When txtX.Text = –5 and txtY.Text = 3? When txtX.Text = 5 and txtY.Text = –3? When txtX.Text = –5 and txtY.Text = –3?

```
Private Sub btnGo_Click()
    Dim intX As Integer
    Dim intY As Integer
    intX = CInt(txtX.Text)
    intY = CInt(txtY.Text)
    If intX > 0 Then
        If intY > 0 Then
            txtResult.Text = intX * intY
        Else
            txtResult.Text = -intX * intY
        End If
    Else
        If intY > 0 Then
            txtResult.Text = -intX * intY
        Else
            txtResult.Text = intX * intY
        End If
    End If
End Sub
```

3. For each of the following compound conditions, write two conditions that are its opposite—that is, conditions that will be true when the original is false, and vice versa. Write one of your conditions using the Not operator and one without.

```
    a. intW > 10 And intW < 20
    b. intK = 5 Or intJ <= 5
    c. (intM < 0 or intN < 0) And intP < 0
    d. Not ((intA > 0 Or intB > 0) Or Not (intA > 0 Or intB > 0))
```

4. Nick's mom is making videos of Nick's favorite television reruns while he is on duty with the National Guard in Iraq. She wants to create a program that, when a day and time are entered, will remind her which show to record and what channel it is on. Write a selection structure that will implement the data in Table 4-6.

5. The local hobby shop is starting a club for collectors of wooden railway system products. For each $10 purchase, a club member will receive a point. After 5 points have been accumulated, the member will receive a 3% discount on each subsequent purchase. After 10 points have been accumulated, the member will receive a 5% discount on each subsequent purchase. After 20 points have been accumulated, the member will receive a 7.5% discount

TABLE 4-6: Nick's show schedule

Day	Time	Show and Channel
Monday	11:00 A.M.	MASH, Ch. 43
Monday	12:00 noon	Law and Order, Ch. 39
Wednesday	9:00 A.M.	Frazier, Ch. 24
Wednesday	1:00 P.M.	ER, Ch. 29
Friday	11:00 A.M.	Cheers, Ch. 35

on each subsequent purchase. Finally, a club member who accumulates 50 points will receive a 10% discount on each purchase. Write a selection structure that will determine the discounted price of an item based on the actual price and the number of points accumulated. Additional points should be added based on the discount price.

Completing the remaining questions will enable you to create the revised VB .NET Payroll project discussed in the text.

6. Modify the Payroll project to include types of employee by completing the following exercises:

    a. Open the *Payroll* project and display the **frmPayroll** form. Add a ListBox control named **lstPayType** and a label to describe the list box. Use the Items property to add two items to the list box: **Hourly** and **Salaried.** Declare a variable **strPayType** as string.

    b. Modify the code for the btnCompute button control so the payroll decision matches that shown in VB Code Box 4-9.

    c. Test your new Payroll project by selecting **Hourly** for both **35** and **45** hours worked at a payrate of **$10.00** per hour. Do the same again except select **Salaried** as the pay type. You should get different answers for the two pay types for 45 hours.

    d. Save the revised Payroll project.

7. Modify the Letter Grade project to handle number of absences by completing the following exercises:

    a. Open the *LetterGrd* project and display the **frmLetterGrd** form. Immediately below the txtAverage text box on this form, add a new TextBox control named **txtAbsences** with an appropriate label. Also, add a second scroll bar control named **vsbAbsences** with a Max property of **10** (if they have more than 9 absences it won't change their grade) and a Min property of **0**. Set both the LargeChange and SmallChange properties to **1**. Finally, add appropriate labels for the new scroll bar.

    b. Add the necessary code to the Change event procedure for the vsbAbsences control to transfer its Value property to the txtAbsences text box. Modify the code for the btnLetter button control to match that shown in VB Code Box 4-10.

c. Test the revised grading project with various values for the average and number of absences. In particular, test the effect of the number of absences on the letter grade. For example, what letter is assigned a student with an average of 95 and 5 absences? Two absences?

d. Save the letter grade assignment files.

8. Look at the form of the Select Case decision structure. Is there any reason why we could not use nested decisions in it? How about using compound conditions in a Select Case decision structure?

USING THE LOAD EVENT

Assume that the owner of Vintage DVDs has requested that the welcome message appear automatically when the project begins, rather than only when the user remembers to click the "Click me first!" button. To cause any code to be executed when the project is initiated, you must use the Load event for the form (commonly referred to as the **Form_Load event**). As the name implies, the Form_Load event occurs when the form is loaded. This event is triggered for the main form when you first start the project and is triggered for any other form when it is loaded into memory. To enter code for the Form_Load event for a specific form, you simply double-click anywhere on the form to open the event procedure Code window for this event. Just as the Click event is the default event for buttons, the Load event is the default event for the form.

Our objective for using the Load event for the frmVintage form is to enter the same code that now exists for the Click event for the btnMessage button. For any form, the name of this procedure is *frmFormName_Load,* so for the frmVintage form, the name of the event is frmVintage_Load.

Actually, rather than retyping the code in the frmVintage_Load event procedure, we want to *move* the code from the btnMessage_Click to it and then delete the button altogether. To do this, we can also use the editing capabilities of the Code window to expedite the process. When you open the Code window for the frmVintage_Load event, you can display the code for the btnMessage Click event procedure (if it is not displayed already) by using the vertical scroll bar. When the code for this event procedure is visible, use the mouse to highlight it, the Cut icon on the toolbar to *cut* it (shortcut keys: **Ctrl-x**), and the Paste icon to *paste* it (shortcut keys: **Ctrl-v**) in the frmVintage_Load event Code window. [If you want to copy only a section of code, you would use the Copy icon (shortcut keys: **Ctrl-c**) instead of the Cut icon.] Figure 4-10 shows the line of code for the btnMessage Click event procedure highlighted and ready to be moved to the Form_Load event procedure.

Cut

Paste

Copy

Once you have moved the code from the btnMessage Click event procedure to the frmVintage_Load event procedure, it will be executed every time the form is loaded when the project is started. Since we don't need the btnMessage button any more, we need to delete it. To do this, display the form and click on the button to highlight it. You can then delete it by pressing the **DELETE** key or by using the **Edit|Delete** option. You should delete the beginning and ending lines of code in the Code window for the now

FIGURE 4-10.
Moving code from
one event
procedure to
another

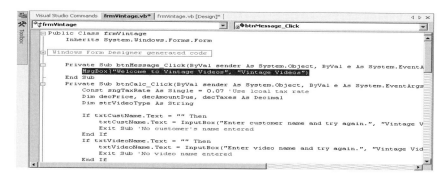

nonexisting btnMessage button to keep the Code window from being filled with extraneous lines of code.

Most of the code for the Vintage DVDs project from this chapter is shown in VB Code Box 4-11 (the btnExit and frmVintage_Load event procedures are now included.)

Step-by-Step Instructions 4-5: Using the frmVintage_Load event

1. Open the *Vintage4* project and then open the **frmVintage_Load** event procedure Code window. Move the welcoming message from the btnMessage_Click event procedure to the frmVintage_Load event procedure.

2. Delete the btnMessage button and delete the corresponding event procedure code.

3. Test the frmVintage_Load event by starting the project several times. If it works, save the form and project under the same name as before.

It's Your Turn!

1. Modify the Vintage DVDs project by completing Step-by-Step Instructions 4-5.

2. Why did we use the "cut-and-paste" approach to move the code from the btnMessage button to the frmVintage_Load event rather than deleting and retyping it?

A FIRST LOOK AT VB .NET's DEBUGGING TOOLS

As we noted in the last chapter, VB .NET has a wide array of debugging tools. To help you with your projects as they become more complex and have a greater chance of including errors, we will introduce these debugging tools in this chapter. In later chapters, we will extend this discussion to other tools.

| **VB CODE BOX 4-11.** Code for Vintage DVDs project | ```vb
Private Sub btnCalc_Click(ByVal sender As System.Object, _
ByVal e As System.EventArgs) Handles btnCalc.Click
    Const sngTaxRate As Single = 0.07 ' Use local tax rate
    Dim decPrice decAmountDue, decTaxes As Decimal
    Dim strDVDType As String
    If txtCustName.Text = "" Then
        txtCustName.Text = InputBox("Enter name and try again.", _
        "Vintage DVDs")
        Exit Sub
    End If
    If txtDVDName.Text = "" Then
        txtDVDName.Text = InputBox("Enter DVD name and " & _
        "try again.", ,"Vintage DVDs")
        Exit Sub
    End If
    strDVDType = lstTypes.SelectedItem
    If strdvdtype = "" Then
        MsgBox("Select a DVD type and try again.", ,"Vintage DVDs")
        Exit Sub
    End If
    decPrice = CDec(txtDVDPrice.Text)
    decTaxes = decPrice * sngTaxRate ' compute taxes
    decAmountDue = decPrice + decTaxes ' compute amount due
    txtTaxes.Text = Format(decTaxes, "C")
    txtAmountDue.Text = Format(decAmountDue, "C")
    txtDVDPrice.Text = FormatCurrency(txtDVDPrice.Text)
End Sub
Private Sub btnClear_Click(ByVal sender As System.Object, _
ByVal e As System.EventArgs) Handles btnClear.Click
    txtCustName.Text = ""
    txtDVDName.Text = ""
    txtDVDPrice.Text = ""
    txtTaxes.Text = ""
    txtAmountDue.Text = ""
    txtCustName.Focus()
End Sub
Private Sub lstTypes_SelectedIndexChanged(ByVal sender As _
System.Object, ByVal e As System.EventArgs) Handles _
lstTypes.SelectedIndexChanged
    Dim strDVDType As String, decPrice As Decimal
    strDVDType = lstTypes.SelectedItem
    Select Case strDVDType
        Case "Kids"
            decPrice = 0.99
        Case "Regular"
            decPrice = 1.99
        Case "Classic"
            decPrice = 2.99
    End Select
    txtDVDPrice.Text = Format(decPrice, "c")
End Sub
``` |

A primary aid to debugging is the Debug toolbar, which you can display by selecting Toolbars from the View menu item. In the **View|Toolbars** submenu, you will see the various toolbars that are available with VB .NET:
```

View Toolbars submenu

Debug, Edit, Form Editor, and Standard. There is also an option to customize a toolbar but we will not discuss that here. To view the Debug toolbar, click the check box at the left of the Debug option. The resulting toolbar is shown in Figure 4-11 with the various icons labeled. Although you will not understand all of these now, their purpose will become clear to you in later chapters. Some of these options are also on the Standard toolbar.

> **TIP:** If you prefer the keyboard to using the mouse, there are several hot keys that can be used for the debugging features. These include F11 (Step Into), F5 (Run), Shift-F10 (Step Over), and CtrlB (Toggle Breakpoint).

FIGURE 4-11. Debug toolbar

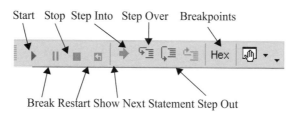

Using Breakpoints

The primary way to debug a VB .NET program is to use breakpoints. A **breakpoint** is a statement in the code window where you want execution to stop so you can inspect the variables and statements and learn why the program is not working as desired. In a sense, it's like a time-out in a sports event; all of the players stay on the field, and the game can be restarted when the time-out is over. In programming, all of the variables retain their values and the program can be restarted whenever you want it to.

Adding a breakpoint to a program is very easy; you simply click in the gray margin to the left of the statement to place a large red dot (called a **glyph**) in the margin and to highlight the statement in red. When this line of code is encountered in the project during execution, the execution pauses and you are put into **break mode** until you click the Start icon again. This will enable you to look at information in the Code window as well as a variety of other windows below the Code window. However, for the time being, we will concentrate on using the Code window to determine the value of variables.

For example, assume that in the Vintage DVDs project, you made a mistake in the lstTypes_SelectedIndexChanged event procedure: Instead of *Classic,* you used *Classics* (with an *s*) in the Case statement. Then, when you run the project and click on the *Classic* option, a price of $0.00 is displayed because there was no match for *Classics* in the Case statement. To find the cause of this error, you need to stop the program, go into the Code Window, and set a breakpoint at the beginning of the Select Case statement as shown in Figure 4-12. Note the glyph in the left margin and the highlighted statementt.

Once the breakpoint is set, you can start the program again. The program will run until you click on any option in the list box, at which point it will stop at the breakpoint you set and display the Code window with the

FIGURE 4-12.
Setting a
breakpoint

```
frmVintage                                    ▼   (Declarations)
          Private Sub lstTypes_SelectedIndexChanged(ByVal sender As Sys
              Dim strDVDType As String
              Dim decPrice As Decimal
              strDVDType = lstTypes.SelectedItem
              Select Case strDVDType
                  Case "Kids"
                      decPrice = 0.99
                  Case "Regular"
                      decPrice = 1.99
                  Case "Classics"
                      decPrice = 2.99
              End Select
              txtDVDPrice.Text = Format(decPrice, "c")
          End Sub
```

breakpoint highlighted in yellow. To view the value of the variable strDVDType, which has been set equal to the SelectedItem property for lstTypes, simply position the cursor over this variable in the Select Case statement. Doing this causes the value of the variable to be displayed as a tooltip as shown in Figure 4-13. Note that it is seen to be *Classic,* while the Select Case statement in the Code window uses *Classics.* After seeing this, you can stop the program, change the Select Case statement to match the value of lstTypes.SelectedItem (*Classic*), and click on the Run icon to start the project with the correct code. If you click again on the *Classic* item in the lstTypes list box, the correct price is displayed in the DVD Price text box.

FIGURE 4-13.
Displaying variable
value at breakpoint

```
          Private Sub lstTypes_SelectedIndexChanged(ByVal sender As Syst
              Dim strDVDType As String
              Dim decPrice As Decimal
              strDVDType = lstTypes.SelectedItem
              Select Case strDVDType
                  Case "Kids"   strDVDType = "Classic"
                      decPrice = 0.99
                  Case "Regular"
                      decPrice = 1.99
                  Case "Classics"
                      decPrice = 2.99
              End Select
              txtDVDPrice.Text = Format(decPrice, "c")
          End Sub
```

It's Your Turn!

1. If it is not already open, open the *Vintage4* project and modify the lstTypes_SelectedIndexChanged event procedure to change the **Case "Classic"** statement to **Case "Classics"** and run the project. Enter a customer name of "Joe Smith", a DVD name of *Spartacus,* and click on **Classic.** When a value of $0.00 is displayed, click the Stop icon.

2. In the Code window, click the left gray margin next to the Select Case statement to create a breakpoint on this statement. Run the project again and click **Classic** again. You should see the screen shown in Figure 4-13 and, if

you position the cursor over the highlighted statement, you should see that the value of the strDVDType variable is *Classic* and not *Classics* that is used in the Select Case statement.

3. Stop the program, modify the Case statement back to **"Classic,"** and click the Run icon. Click the **Classic** option again and you should see $2.99.

SUMMARY

At the beginning of the chapter, we said you would be able to do a number of things after reading it. Let's review those things here:

1. Understand the importance of the selection process in programming. The selection process of programming involves comparing two values and, on the basis of that comparison, selecting one of two or more alternatives to execute. The selection process is very important in programming, because it allows the program to make decisions based on the data. Without the selection process, all programs would simply execute the code straight through, with no deviation from a set procedure.

2. Describe the various types of decisions that can be made in a computer program. The types of selection processes that we discussed involved two alternatives and many alternatives. In the two-alternative decision type, there is one comparison condition and two alternatives: one for the true comparison condition and one for the false condition. Only one of the two alternatives can be executed, and then the decision structure is terminated. It is also possible to have a one-alternative decision type by including only a true alternative. In this case, if the comparison condition is false, no alternative is implemented and the decision structure is terminated. For the many-alternative decision type, there are multiple conditions with an alternative for each condition. The conditions are tested, and when a true condition is encountered the corresponding alternative is selected. There may also be an alternative that is implemented if *all* conditions are found to be false. In any case, when a condition is found to be true and an alternative is executed, no other conditions are tested and the decision structure is terminated.

3. Discuss the statement forms used in VB .NET to make decisions. The two-alternative decision type is implemented in VB .NET through the If-Then-Else decision structure. The one-alternative case is implemented in VB .NET through the If-Then decision structure with no false alternative. The multiple-alternative decision type is implemented in VB .NET through the If-Then-ElseIf and Select Case decision structures. In all cases other than the Select Case form, six comparison operators are used: greater than (>), greater than or equal to (>=), equal to (=), not equal to (<> or ><), less than (<), and less than or equal to (<=).

4. Use the ListBox control to select from a list of alternatives. The list box, which can be used as a means of displaying several alternatives, was also discussed. In a list box, you can select an alternative by clicking it. The SelectedIndexChanged event for this control was used in combination with the Select Case decision structure to select a type of DVD and display its price in the corresponding text box.

5. Work with complex comparison structures and nested decisions to handle more sophisticated selection processes. Two types of more complex decisions were also discussed: nested decisions and compound conditions. With nested decisions, at least one alternative of a decision structure is itself a decision structure. Only if this alternative is executed will the nested decision be implemented. An important feature of nested decisions is that decisions cannot overlap; the inner decision must be completed totally within the alternative in which it is found. With complex conditions, one or more of the logical operators (And, Or, Not, and Xor) are used to combine two or more conditions to make a decision. It is important to remember that each condition in a compound condition must be able to be evaluated by itself.

6. Use the scroll bar to input integer values. The scroll bar is an analog control that returns an integer value depending on the movement of the slider bar. The Scroll event is the default event for both vertical and horizontal scroll bars.

7. Use the Form_Load event to execute a procedure when a form is loaded. The Form_Load event is a way of executing instructions every time the project is started. This event procedure is executed whenever the form is loaded. Each form has its own Form_Load event, which is named *frmFormName_Load*.

8. Work with the debugging toolbar to find program errors. The debugging toolbar has a number of operations associated with it. The use of breakpoints is a good way to check the value of variables in the project that may be causing errors to occur.

NEW VB .NET ELEMENTS

Controls/Objects	Properties	Methods	Events
ScrollBar control	Name Value Maximum/Minimum/LargeChange/ SmallChange		Scroll
ListBox control	Name SelectedItem List		SelectedIndex- Changed
Form object			Load

NEW PROGRAMMING STATEMENTS

> *Statements for two-alternative decision*
> **If** *condition is true* **then**
>   *statements for true alternative*
> **Else**
>   *statements for false alternative*
> **End if**

NEW PROGRAMMING STATEMENTS (CONTINUED)

Statements for one-alternative decision
If *condition is true* **then**
  statements for true alternative
End if

Statement to use InputBox *variable or control property* = **InputBox**(*"prompt"*, *"name"*)

Statements for multiple-alternative decision using If-Then-ElseIf form
If *condition1 is true* **then**
  first set of statements
Elseif *condition2 is true* **then**
  second set of statements
ElseIf *condition3 true* **then**
  third set of statements
Else
  last set of statements
End if

Statements for multiple-alternative decision using Select Case form
Select Case *expression*
Case *condition1*
  First set of statements
Case *condition2*
  Second set of statements
Case Else
  Last set of statements
End Select

KEY TERMS

Break mode	If-Then decision	logical operator
Breakpoints	If-Then-Else decision	nested decision
Combo Box	If-Then-ElseIf decision	Select Case decision
compound condition	glyph	scroll bar
Form_Load event	list box	validation

EXERCISES

1. Based on what you have read and your practice with VB .NET, answer the following questions
   a. What are the various types of decisions in a computer program?
   b. What statement forms are available in VB .NET to make decisions? When should each be used?
   c. What are comparison operators? List those that are available in VB .NET.
   d. What are logical operators? List those that are available in VB .NET.
   e. Describe the new controls that were presented in this chapter.

2. What will be shown in txtResult after each of the following is executed?

```
a. Private Sub btnGo_Click()
      Dim strResponse As String = "Hiya!"
      If strResponse <> "" Then
         txtResult.Text = "Not Empty"
         Exit Sub
      End If
      txtResult.Text = "Empty"
   End Sub

b. Private Sub btnGo_Click()
      If txtResult.BackColor = vbRed Then
         txtResult.BackColor = vbGreen
         txtResult.Text = "Green"
      Else
         txtResult.BackColor = vbRed
         txtResult.Text = "Red"
      End If
   End Sub

c. Private Sub btnGo_Click()
       Dim intDist As Integer
       Dim sngCost As Single
       intDist = 23 * 5
       If intDist <= 100 Then
         sngCost = 5
       ElseIf intDist > 100 And intDist <= 500 Then
         sngCost = 8
       ElseIf intDist > 500 And intDist < 1000 Then
         sngCost = 20
       Else
         sngCost = 12
       End If
       txtResult.Text = sngCost
    End Sub

d. Private Sub btnGo_Click()
       Dim strGender As String
       Dim strMarStatus As String
       Dim strCode As String
       strGender = "F"
       strMarStatus = "m"
       If strGender = "m" Or strGender = "M" Then
         If strMarStatus = "s" Or strMarStatus = "S" Then
           strCode = "AA"
         Else
           strCode = "AB"
         End If
       End If
       If strGender = "f" Or strGender = "F" Then
         If strMarStatus = "s" Or strMarStatus = "S" Then
           strCode = "BA"
         Else
           strCode = "BB"
         End If
       End If
```

```
        txtResult.Text = strCode
    End Sub
```

3. Write Select Case blocks for the following scenarios:

   a. In the Spring, a certain city classifies a pollen index of less than 10 as "pleasant," 11 to 20 as "slightly unpleasant," 21 to 30 as "unpleasant," and over 30 as "stay inside." Write a Select Case block that uses a variable intPollenIndex to generate the appropriate message.

   b. The local library checks out more than just books these days. With the different types of media available for checkout, a more complex mode of determining overdue charges is required. Write a Select Case block that will determine the amount of a fine based on the item and the number of days overdue. The late fees for each item are listed in Table 4-7.

TABLE 4-7: Library late fees

Item	Fine per Day
General books	Each day, $0.10
New books	First 10 days, $0.10 Over 10 days, $0.20
Video tape	First 3 days, $0.25 4 to 6 days, $0.50 Over 6 days, $1.00
Audio tape	First week, $0.20 Over 7 days, $0.40

   c. Tropical storms are classified as hurricanes based on their wind speeds and storm surges. Generally, a minimum hurricane has sustained winds of at least 74 miles per hour (mph). A storm that is a hurricane can be classified into 5 categories based on the Saffir-Simpson classification scale: Category 1—sustained winds of 74 to 95 mph; Category 2—sustained winds of 96 to 110 mph; Category 3—sustained winds of 111 to 130 mph; Category 4—sustained winds of 131 to 155 mph; Category 5—sustained winds above 155 mph. Write a Select Case block that will determine the hurricane category based on the wind speed in mph.

   d. If you have eaten at a Chinese restaurant, you may have noticed placemats depicting the Chinese zodiac. Each year in the Chinese calendar is associated with a particular animal. The 12-year cycle is rat, ox, tiger, rabbit, dragon, snake, horse, ram, monkey, rooster, dog, and boar. The year 1900 is a year of the rat, 1901 is a year of the ox, and so on, with 1912 being another year of the rat. If you know when someone was born, you can calculate the difference between their year of birth and 1900 and use this to determine in which year of the Chinese zodiac the person was born. Write a Select Case block that will determine the Chinese year based on the difference between a year of birth and 1900.

4. For each of the following, explain what is wrong with the code. What error

messages would you see, if any? What can you do to fix it?

```
a. Private Sub btnGo_Click()
     Dim intX As Integer
     intX = 5
     If intX = txtInput.Text Then
       txtResult.Text = "They are the same"
     End If
   End Sub
```

```
b. Private Sub btnGo_Click()
     Dim intX As Integer
     intX = CInt(txtX.Text)
     intY = CInt(txtY.Text)
     If intX > 0 And (intY < 0 And intX < 0) Then
       txtResult.Text = "Hurray, it's True!"
     End If
   End Sub
```

5. Use the VB .NET Help facility to answer the following questions.

   a. What can the LCase and UCase functions be used for?

   b. What is the value of the list box SelectedItem property if no item is selected? If the first item in the list box is selected?

   c. What is the difference between the Form_Load and Activated events?

PROJECTS

Create a folder in the *Chapter4* folder named **Homework.** All projects should be saved in this *Chapter4\Homework* folder.

1. Copy the files from the *Chapter3\Homework\Ex3-1* folder into a new folder named **Ex4-1** in the *Chapter4\Homework* folder. Rename the files in the new folder to be **Ex4-1.vb, Ex4-1.vbproj,** and **Ex4-1.sln.** Be sure to make **Ex4-1.vb** your startup object. Open the code window and add validation statements to the code for the button that sums and averages the three quiz scores. These validation statements should check that the user has entered a student name and three quiz scores. If the name or a quiz score is missing, use an InputBox to request an entry from the user. Test your revised project with a student name of **Ashley Hyatt** and quiz scores of **75, 90,** and **80.** However, do not enter the name or the last quiz score until requested to do so by the project. Save the revised project.

2. Copy the files from the *Chapter3\Homework\Ex3-2* folder into a new folder named **Ex4-2** in the *Chapter4\Homework* folder. Rename the files in the new folder to be **Ex4-2.vb, Ex4-2.vbproj,** and **Ex4-2.sln.** Be sure to make **Ex4-2.vb** your startup object. Open the code window and add validation statements to the code for the compute button that check that a customer name and the number of square feet have been entered. If the name or square footage has been omitted, an InputBox should request this information. Also, assume that there are two types of treatment: **Pre-emergence** at **$0.004** per square foot and **Fertilizer** at **$0.001** per square foot. Add a list box with the two types of treatments, from which the user can select one. Based on the selection, the project should compute the cost. Test your revised project with a

customer name of **Todd Allman,** a square footage of **4,000,** and **Pre-emergence** treatment. However, do not enter the name until requested to do so by the project. Save your revised project.

3. Copy the files from the *Chapter3\Homework\Ex3-3* folder into a new folder named **Ex4-3** in the *Chapter4\Homework* folder. Rename the files in the new folder to be **Ex4-3.vb, Ex4-3.vbproj,** and **Ex4-3.sln.** Be sure to make **Ex4-3.vb** your startup object. Open the code window and add a validation statement to the code for the button that computes the miles per gallon to ensure that the miles driven is not zero. If it is zero or has not been entered, display an error message and terminate the computation of the miles per gallon. Test your project with an **Altissan** make of car that used **10.5** gallons of gas. Do not enter the miles driven until after you have first clicked the button. At that time, enter **285** miles and click it again. Save your revised project.

4. Copy the files from the *Chapter3\Homework\Ex3-4* folder into a new folder named **Ex4-4** in the *Chapter4\Homework* folder. Rename the files in the new folder to be **Ex4-4.vb, Ex4-4.vbproj,** and **Ex4-4.sln.** Be sure to make **Ex4-4.vb** your startup object. Assume that the company makes only two products: Widgets and DoHickeys. The unit price and unit cost for each of these items is shown in Table 4-8, and the fixed cost of production is the same for both products. A list box should display the names of the products. The user should select the item for which the breakeven cost is being computed. Based on this selection, the unit price and cost information shown below should be used to compute the breakeven amount. Test your project to compute the breakeven cost for both products if the fixed cost is $**1,000.** Test it again if the fixed cost is $**5,000.** Save your revised project.

TABLE 4-8: Unit price and costs

Product	Unit Price	Unit Cost
Widgets	$25	$15
DoHickeys	$35	$30

5. Copy the files from the *Chapter3\Homework\Ex3-5* folder into a new folder named **Ex4-5** in the *Chapter4\Homework* folder. Rename the files in the new folder to be **Ex4-5.vb, Ex4-5.vbproj,** and **Ex4-5.sln.** Be sure to make **Ex4-5.vb** your startup object. Assume that the wallpaper company sells two types of wallpaper: Standard, which has 50 square feet per roll at a cost of $15 per roll, and Premium, with 37.5 square feet per roll at a cost of $25 per roll. A list box should display the types of wallpaper from which the user can choose. Add the capability to clear the list box selection to the Clear button. Test your project to compute the number of rolls needed and cost to wallpaper the room for both products if the room is **12.5** feet by **20** feet with a door area of **42** square feet and a window area of **36** square feet. Save your revised project.

6. Copy the files from the *Homework\Ex4-1* folder into a new folder named **Ex4-6.** Rename the files in the new folder to be **Ex4-6.vb, Ex4-6.vbproj,** and

Ex4-6.sln. Be sure to make **Ex4-6.vb** your startup object. Add a text box to display the letter grade earned by the student. Also add a corresponding label to describe the contents of the text box. Add the necessary code to the button that computes the average score to assign the student a letter grade based on Table 4-9. Also, add a welcoming message that is displayed when you start the project. Test the resulting project for the data shown in Project 1. Also text your project for a variety of other quiz scores. Save your revised project.

TABLE 4-9: Grading scale

Average	Letter Grade
93 and above	A
At least 85 but less than 93	B
At least 77 but less than 85	C
Less than 77	F

7. Copy the files from the *Homework\Ex4-2* folder into a new folder named **Ex4-7,** rename them to match their new folder, and make **Ex4-7.vb** your startup object. Add (or modify) a list box with types of treatments and a descriptive label. Assume that users will input the square footage directly into the text box or from a scroll bar. They will then choose a type of treatment from the list box and determine a price per square foot based on Table 4-10. Also, add a welcoming message that is displayed when you start the project and add the capability to clear the list box selection to the existing Clear button. Test your revised project with a customer name of **Todd Allman,** a square footage of **4,000,** and **Premium Grass Fertilizer** treatment. Test it for the other treatments. Save your revised project.

TABLE 4-10: Product data

Treatment	Price per Square Foot
Pre-emergence	$0.004
Broadleaf weed	$0.002
Regular fertilizer	$0.001
Premium grass fertilizer	$0.005

8. Copy the files from the *Homework\Ex4-6* folder into a new folder named **Ex4-8,** rename them to match their new folder, and make **Ex4-8.vb** your startup object. Modify the project to consider the number of quizzes taken. To receive a grade of A, in addition to the quiz score requirement, the student must have taken all 3 quizzes; for a B, they must have taken at least 2 quizzes; and for a C, they must have taken at least 1 quiz. (If no quizzes are taken, the grade is an F.) Test your project for the same data as for Exercise 1 (where 3 quizzes were taken). Also test it on a student with quiz scores of **92** and **96** for **2** quizzes. Save your revised project.

9. Copy the files from the *Homework\Ex4-4* folder into a new folder named

Ex4-9, rename them to match their new folder, and make **Ex4-9.vb** your startup object. Revise the project to use a list box to handle four products. The four projects and their unit costs and unit prices are shown in Table 4-11. Also, add a welcoming message that is displayed when you start the project. Finally, add the capability to clear the list box selection in preparation for the next product. Test your project to compute the breakeven cost for all products if the fixed cost is $**1,000**. Test it again if the fixed cost is $**5,000**. Save your revised project.

TABLE 4-11: Product data

Product	**Unit Price**	**Unit Cost**
Widgets	$25	$15
DoHickeys	$35	$30
Whatzits	$9.50	$4.50
ThingaMabobs	$12.25	$9.75

10. Copy the files from the *Homework\Ex4-5* folder into a new folder named **Ex4-10,** rename them to match their new folder, and make **Ex4-10.vb** your startup object. Revise the project to use a list box to handle five types of wallpaper. The five types of wallpaper and the square feet per roll are shown in Table 4-12. Also, add a welcoming message that is displayed when you start the project. Finally, add the capability to clear the list box selection in preparation for the next type of wallpaper to the existing Clear button. Test your project to compute the number of rolls needed for each type of wallpaper for the data given in Project 5. Save the revised project.

TABLE 4-12: Wallpaper data

Wallpaper Type	**Square Footage per Roll**	**Cost per Roll**
Standard	50	$15
Premium	37.5	$25
Jumbo	60	$20
Double	75	$45
Triple	112.5	$65

11. John Galt has been concerned over his amount of his gas bill and wants to build a VB .NET program to check the gas company's calculations. John has found that the meter, which is read once a month, displays a four-digit number representing cubic meters of gas. The difference between the current month's reading and the previous month's reading is used to calculate the amount used. Note that, since only four digits are available on the meter, the current reading may be less than the previous reading. For example, the previous reading may be 9780, and the current one may be 0408. The company charges for gas based on the rates shown in Table 4-13.

TABLE 4-13: Gas rate chart

Gas Used	Rate
First 80 cubic meters	$10.00 minimum cost
Next 120 cubic meters	$0.10 per cubic meter
Next 200 cubic meters	$0.05 per cubic meter
Above 400 cubic meters	$0.025 per cubic meter

Design and create a VB .NET program for calculating John's gas bill in the *Chapter4\Homework* folder. Give the project folder a name of **Ex4-11.**

12. Architect Howard Roark has recently turned his attention to ensuring that his buildings conform to the Uniform Federal Accessibility Standards (UFAS). The purpose of these standards is to make sure that public areas, such as lobbies and corridors, are accessible for all users, including those in wheelchairs. A couple of the standards involve the dimensions required for a turn around an obstacle in a corridor. If the obstacle at least 48 inches wide, then the both the aisle width and the turn width of the corridor must be at least 36 inches. If the obstacle is less than 48 inches, then the aisle and turn widths must be at least 42 inches and at least 48 inches, respectively. Design a VB .NET program that will determine whether or not a design specification for a turn meets the UFAS requirements. Howard should be able to enter the widths of the obstacle, the aisle, and the turn. Then a message should appear notifying him whether or not the design is within specifications. Create this project in the *Chapter4\Homework* folder and give the project a name of **Ex4-12.**

13. Mr. Roark's architecture firm is interested in energy conservation in the houses they build. He knows that sunlight through a window during the day can contribute significantly to a rise in the daily indoor temperature of a room. The Average Indoor Temperature in a well-insulated room may be calculated in terms of the *Heat Gain Factor (HGF)* and the *Heat Loss Factor (HLF)* as (HGF × Window Area)/(HLF × Room Area) + Average Outdoor Temperature.

The area of the window is calculated using its width in feet times its height in feet. Similarly, the area of the room in square feet is calculated using its width in feet times its length in feet. The heat gain and loss factors depend on whether the window is single- or double-paned according to Table 4-14. Design and create a VB .NET program that computes the average daily temperature in a well-insulated room. What is the average daily indoor temperature in a 20-by-25-foot room with a single-paned, 5-by-5-foot window and an average outdoor temperature of 35.4 degrees? Create this project in the *Chapter4\Homework* folder and give the project a name of **Ex4-13.**

TABLE 4-14: Window heat factors

Window Type	Heat Gain Factor (HGF)	Heat Loss Factor (HLF)
Single-paned	1540	13
Double-paned	1416	9.7

5 THE REPETITION PROCESS IN VB .NET

LEARNING
OBJECTIVES

After reading this chapter, you will be able to

1. Understand the importance of the repetition process in programming.
2. Describe the various types of loops that can be carried out in VB .NET.
3. Discuss the statement forms used in VB .NET to handle repetition, and understand the use of pre- and post-test loops.
4. Understand the concepts of variable scope and static variables.
5. Use the ComboBox control to select from a list of alternatives.
6. Understand the use of files to store data and information.
7. Describe the creation and use of executable files in VB .NET.
8. Use debugging tools in VB .NET to find and correct errors.

INTRODUCTION
TO LOOPS

In the first four chapters of this book, we have discussed five of the six operations that computers can carry out. In this chapter, we will discuss the sixth and final computer operation: Repeat a group of actions any number of times. This operation is the one that really makes the computer a useful tool, because a computer can repeat an operation as many times as needed without making mistakes due to boredom or tiredness, like a human being might. Whether it be processing thousands of payroll checks, simulating millions of years of geological development, or searching for a name in a list, computers can repeat an operation over and over again with great ease.

You should be familiar with repetition, because you have had to repeat operations in many situations. For example, when you balance your checkbook, you must repeatedly determine if a check has cleared and, if not, subtract that check's amount from the balance shown on your bank statement. You must also do this for each deposit during the last month and, if it is not shown on your statement, add the amount of the deposit to your bank balance. In both cases, there is an action to be repeated—commonly referred to as the *body of the loop*—and some condition that indicates the end of the repetition process—a *termination condition*. If the loop does not have a body, then nothing happens in the repetition process. If the loop does not have a valid termination condition, then the loop will continue until stopped by the user either aborting the loop or turning the computer off. This last situation is often referred to as an **endless** or **infinite loop** and is something you should guard against in your programming.

Types of Loops

Loops can be classified into three types: event-driven, determinate, and indeterminate. The latter two types of loops occur in both event driven languages like VB .NET and procedural languages, but the first type is restricted to an event driven language. An **event-driven loop** is one in which the repetition is driven by an event occurring—say, by a button being clicked. A **determinate loop** is one for which you *know* in advance how many repetitions will occur, and an **indeterminate loop** is one for which you *do not know* how many repetitions will occur.

An event-driven loop with which you should be familiar occurs at the grocery checkout counter. In this case, the event that activates the repetition is the checkout clerk passing a grocery item over the laser beam to determine its price. This loop is terminated by the clerk ceasing the checkout operation, printing a receipt, and clearing the register for the next customer.

An example of a determinate loop would be a loop that computes the outstanding balance for a loan for each month of the repayment period. Recall that we used the Pmt() function to find the monthly payment on a loan in Chapter 3. With a determinate loop, we can compute and display the balance after each payment. In this case, the number of months determines the number of repetitions.

On the other hand, an example of an indeterminate loop is one that computes the balance for each month *until* the balance is less than some predefined amount. In this case, we do not know in advance how many repetitions it will take for the balance to reach the desired amount.

It should be noted that an event-driven loop is actually a form of indeterminate loop since the number of events usually is not known in advance. If we compare it to the traditional indeterminate loop, we see that it uses events to control the number of repetitions, whereas the traditional form of the indeterminate loop uses either input data or values generated by the program to control the number of repetitions. In a sense, the traditional indeterminate loop is *data-driven*.

We will discuss each of these types of loops using the same simple examples before proceeding to the Vintage DVDs scenario.

Repetition Example

To help you understand the repetition process, we will use a simple example to demonstrate various loop structures. This example will involve entering, counting, and summing Integer values. We will also add them to a list box. In this situation, the repetition involves repeatedly entering a number, increasing a counter by one, and adding the number to the current sum to arrive at a new sum. It also involves adding the value to a list box so there will be a record of the values entered. When the loop is terminated, the number of integers and their sum should be displayed in text boxes.

The summing process involves inputting a value and adding it to the current sum. The counting process involves adding one to a counter for each value that is input and summed. The only difference between summing and counting is that counting always adds one to a counter, whereas summing adds some value to an existing sum.

In the process of working with this example, you should become comfortable working with loops. We will then turn our attention back to the Vintage DVDs scenario to develop the application for it.

Initializing Variables

Anytime you sum or count values, it is important that the variables be *initialized* to some value before the repetition process, usually zero. Although all variables are initialized to zero when they are declared, unless initialized to some other value, if a summing or counting variable is used in a second loop, its initial value will be whatever it was after the execution of the previous loop. For this reason, we will initialize all summing and counting variables prior to their use in a loop if they are used in a second loop or computation.

> **TIP:** Initializing variables can be even more important when variables have a higher-level scope (discussed in next section).

It's Your Turn!

1. Give an example, other than the one given in the text, of a process in your daily life where repetition is important.

2. List the types of loops that are possible in VB .NET. Which one is not possible in a procedural language? Why?

3. Which type of loop would work best for each of the following everyday scenarios: determinate, indeterminate, or event-driven?

    a. Keeping score for a 10-frame game of bowling.

    b. Recording the results of a set of baseball pitches until the batter is out.

    c. Adding up the prices for each item on an order form.

    d. Increasing an auction bid as long as the bid amount is less than a predefined maximum.

4. Why is it important that your loops have a stopping mechanism?

EVENT-DRIVEN LOOPS

With procedural programming, it was necessary to write code to create a loop, but in event-driven programming we can actually create a loop just by repeating an event, say, clicking a button. We will start our discussion of summing and counting integers by using an event-driven loop that uses a button to repeat the summation process. The form for this example is shown in Figure 5-1. Notice that it has an input text box, a text box for the sum, a text box for the number of values, and a list box to display the values that were entered. There are also three buttons: one for calculating the current sum and counter value, one to clear the text boxes, and one to exit the project.

FIGURE 5-1. Form for event-driven loop

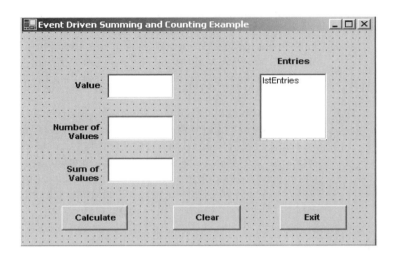

The first button, which we will name *btnCalc*, adds the contents of the first text box (*txtTheValue*) to the sum of all previous values and displays the sum in the last text box (*txtSum*). It also adds one to the previous number of entries and displays this value in the second text box (*txtNumValues*). This button also adds the value to the list box (*lstEntries*) and, finally, clears the existing value in *txtTheValue*.

The second button (*btnClear*) clears all values from the text boxes, clears the list box, and sets the variables that sum and count the values back to zero. The final button (*btnExit*) exits the project.

Variable Scope

Note that, in this project, we have a new situation: The variables that sum and count the number of input values appear in two event procedures—btnCalc and btnClear. If we simply declare them as usual in each event procedure, the processing in one event procedure will have *no* effect on the processing in the other event procedure. This is due to a concept in Visual Basic known as **variable scope,** which does not allow one procedure to "know" about variables declared in another procedure. Variables declared in an event procedure are referred to as **local** or **procedural level variables,** and they are protected from *contaminating* local variables in other event procedures. Within an event procedure, it is possible to declare **block variables** in a *block* of statements, such as a decision block or a loop. Block variables are only "known" within that block, but local variables are known everywhere in the event procedure.

Outside of an event procedure, variables can be declared as **form-level variables** such that all event procedures that are a part of this form will be aware of them. This concept is shown in Figure 5-2 for a single form where both procedures "know" about the form-level variables. If there are multiple forms that need to know about a variable, then this needs to be declared at the *project level* using a Code module. This will be discussed in more detail in Chapter 7, when we discuss multiple forms.

In the case of the sum and counting variables that appear in both the btnCalc and btnClear event procedures, we need to declare them at the form level by placing their declaration immediately after the *Inherits* statement and

FIGURE 5-2.
Concept of variable scope

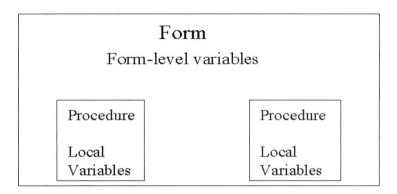

> **TIP:** If the same variable is declared at both the form level and the procedure level, the procedure-level declaration will override the form-level declaration. You should *avoid* double-declaring of variables!

the Windows generated code, but prior to *any* of the event procedures, as shown in Figure 5-3. In this case, *intSum* and *intNumValues* are declared as Integer variables. Like all declarations, whether at the procedure level, the form level, or the project level, this declaration also automatically initializes the declared variables to zero, and it is not necessary to explicitly initialize them.

FIGURE 5-3.
Form-level variable declaration

```
Friend Class frmEventDriven
    Inherits System.Windows.Forms.Form
Windows Form Designer generated code
    Dim intSum, intNumValues As Integer
```

Code for the Calculate Button

The pseudocode for the Calculate button to input, sum, count, and add the entries to a list box is shown below:

```
Sum and count procedure
    Input Value
    Add Value to Sum
    Increment Number of values by 1
    Display Sum and Number of values
    Add value to list box
End procedure
```

Note that there is no reference to *repeating* the loop or to a loop termination condition, because all repetition will be controlled by the user clicking the Calculate button. We also do not need to explicitly initialize the summing and counting variables to zero, because this is done in the Form_Load procedure and when they are declared at the module level.

The complete VB .NET code for the Calculate button is shown in VB Code Box 5-1. In looking at this code, you will notice that, after the summation and counting statements, there are two additional statements that clear the txtNumValues text box and put the cursor back into it. To carry out this latter action, the Focus method is appended to the name of the text box. When you click the Calculate button, the txtNumValues text box will be cleared and the cursor will be placed there by the Focus method for the next value to be entered. You should also notice that although the intTheValue variable is declared in this event procedure, the intSum and intNumValues variables are not, since they were declared at the module level.

| **VB Code Box 5-1.** Code for Calculate button | ```
Private Sub btnCalc_Click(ByVal sender As System.Object,_
ByVal e As System.EventArgs) Handles btnCalc.Click
    Dim intTheValue As Integer
    intTheValue = CInt(txtTheValue.Text)
    intSum = intSum + intTheValue
    intNumValues = intNumValues + 1
    txtSum.Text = CStr(intSum)
    txtNumValues.Text = CStr(intNumValues)
    lstEntries.Items.Add(CStr(intTheValue))
    txtTheValue.Text = ""
    txtTheValue.Focus()
End Sub
``` |
| --- | --- |

We have used a new method in this procedure: The **Items.Add()** method. This method is used to add items to a list box at run time, instead of at design time as we did in Chapter 4. The Items.Add() method is used with list and combo boxes to add String data to the list. Like all methods, it is appended to the object with a period followed by the item to be added. Note that because a list box is made up of strings, we convert the Integer variable intTheValue to a String before adding it to the list box

The code for the Clear button shown in VB Code Box 5-2 is very simple; it clears all text boxes and the list box, sets the variables intSum and intNumValues to zero, and sets the focus back to the txtTheValue text box in preparation for the next use. Clearing the list box requires us to use a second new method: the **Items.Clear()** method, which applies to list and combo boxes. As with the other methods, you simply append it with a period to the object to be cleared.

| **VB Code Box 5-2.** Code for Clear button | ```
Private Sub btnClear_Click(ByVal sender As System.Object,_
ByVal e As System.EventArgs) Handles btnClear.Click
    txtTheValue.Text = ""
    txtNumValues.Text = ""
    txtSum.Text = ""
    intSum = 0
    intNumValues = 0
    lstEntries.Items.Clear()
    txtTheValue.Focus()
End Sub
``` |
| --- | --- |

Executing an Event-Driven Loop

To run the event-driven loop project, you simply enter an integer in the txtTheValue text box and then click the *Calculate* button to add this integer to the current sum and to add one to the number-of-values variable. The sum will appear in the txtSum text box and the number of entries (including this one) will appear in the txtNumValues text box. Also, when you click the Calculate button, the txtTheValue text box will be cleared and the cursor will be placed back there.

To make the use of this project even easier, the TabIndex property of some controls can be set at design time. You can do this in such a way that, when the project begins, the cursor is automatically located in the txtTheValue text box, and when you press the **TAB** key after entering a number, the focus jumps to the Calculate button. When the focus is on the *Calculate* button, a dotted line is displayed around the caption, and you can simply press the **ENTER** key on the keyboard instead of having to click the button with the mouse. To have this occur, at design time set the TabIndex property to zero for the txtTheValue text box and to one for the btnCalc button. If you run your project for values of 123, 456, 789, –135, and 246, the result will appear as shown in Figure 5-4. The complete code for this project is shown in VB Code Box 5-3 (where we have left out the reference to the Windows Designer generated code.).

Button with focus Calculate

FIGURE 5-4.
Execution of summing and counting example

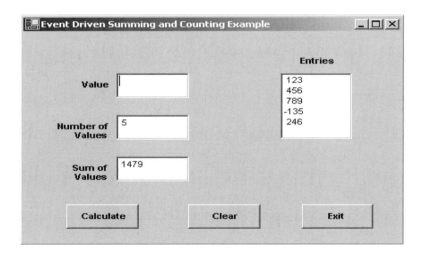

Static Variables

In addition to declaring variables to be form-level variables so they will be known to all procedures in the form, you can also declare a local variable to be *Static*. A **Static variable** is one that retains its value between executions of an event procedure. Normally, a local variable will be reset to zero between events, but when it is declared Static, the variable retains its value until the project is terminated. The form of the Static declaration statement is

Static *variable* as *type*, *variable* as *type*, etc.

For example, if we had declared the intSum and intNumValues variables as Static variables instead of as form-level variables, they would have retained their values between clicks of the Calculate button. However, we would not have been able to set them to zero at the end of the event-driven

| VB CODE BOX 5-3. Complete code for event-driven input loop | ```
Dim intSum, intNumValues As Integer
Private Sub btnCalc_Click(ByVal sender As System.Object,_
ByVal e As System.EventArgs) Handles btnCalc.Click
        Dim intTheValue As Integer
        intTheValue = CInt(txtTheValue.Text)
        intSum = intSum + intTheValue
        intNumValues = intNumValues + 1
        txtSum.Text = CStr(intSum)
        txtNumValues.Text = CStr(intNumValues)
        lstEntries.Items.Add(CStr(intTheValue))
        txtTheValue.Text = ""
        txtTheValue.Focus()
    End Sub
    Private Sub btnExit_Click(ByVal sender As System.Object,_
    ByVal e As System.EventArgs) Handles btnExit.Click
        End
End Sub
Private Sub btnClear_Click(ByVal sender As System.Object,_
ByVal e As System.EventArgs) Handles btnClear.Click
        txtTheValue.Text = ""
        txtNumValues.Text = ""
        txtSum.Text = ""
        intSum = 0
        intNumValues = 0
        lstEntries.Items.Clear()
        txtTheValue.Focus()
End Sub
``` |

loop. For the event-driven loop, the Clear button was used to reset the values.

It is also possible to make *all* variables in an event procedure static by replacing the Private keyword in the sub name statement with the Static keyword. The general form of this is

Static Sub *control name_event name()*

> **TIP:** If the project screen disappears from sight when you display the Immediate window, you will find it as an icon on the Windows task bar at the bottom of the screen. You can redisplay it by clicking the icon.

■ ■

Step-by-Step Instructions 5-1: Event-driven input

1. Use Windows Explorer to create a **Chapter5** folder in the Visual Studios Project folder. Start VB .NET (or select **File|New Project**) to create a project to input, count, and sum a series of values using a Windows Form project within the *Chapter5* folder as **EventDriven.** Rename the form file as **Event-Driven.vb,** give it a name of **frmEventDriven,** and a form text property of **Event-Driven Summing and Counting Example.** Create the interface shown in Figure 5-1 using the control names, labels, and text properties (where necessary) discussed in the text.
```

2. Add the code shown in Figure 5-3 to declare the **intSum** and **intNumValues** variables as *form-level* as Integer variables.

3. Add the code for the btnCalc_Click and btnClear_Click event procedures as shown in VB Code Box 5-1 and VB Code Box 5-2. Also, add the **End** statement to the btnExit_Click event procedure. Finally, set the **TabIndex** properties for txtTheValue to be **0,** btnCalc to be **1,** btnClear to be **2,** and btnExit to be **3.** For all other controls, the **TabStop** property should be **False.**

4. Run your project with the data shown in the text, that is, **123, 456, 789, –135,** and **246.** Your result should appear like that shown in Figure 5-4. Can you see why we call this an *event-driven loop?* Clear the text boxes and test your project with the following values: **101, 73, –451, 23,** and **–202.** (Your answer should be –456).

Mini-Summary 5-1: Event-Driven Loops

1. Event-driven loops are a special type of loop that are possible with event-driven languages. Repetition is controlled by the user repeating an event, such as a mouse click.

2. Variable scope determines the level at which a variable is known—block, procedure, form, or project level.

3. The Focus method is used to position the cursor in a text box.

4. The Items.Add() method is used to add items to a list box or a combo box at run time, and the Items.Clear() method is used to clear the contents.

5. A variable can be defined to be *static* so that it will retain its value between executions of the event procedure.

It's Your Turn!

1. Why are form-level variables defined before any of the event procedures?

2. Why aren't all variables defined as form-level variables rather than within each event procedure?

3. Define a variable for miles-per-hour as static. How are static variables different from form-level variables, although they seem to have some of the same characteristics?

4. Create the project for event-driven input, summing, and counting by following Step-by-Step Instructions 5-1 and save it.

5. For the EventDriven project you just created, add the following declaration to the btnCalc_Click event procedure:

Static intSum as Integer, intNumValues as Integer

6. Now run your project again with the two sets of data used previously. What happens when you click the Clear button after the first data set? What happens when you begin to enter the second set of data? Were the intSum

and intNumValues variables reset to zero? Why or why not? Exit your project and run it again with a new data set. Are the variables reset to zero this time? Exit your project again but do *not* save this revised version.

DETERMINATE LOOPS

As mentioned above, the second loop type is the *determinate loop,* for which you *know* the number of repetitions in advance. Although you could create an event-driven loop like the one discussed previously and repeatedly click a button until the number of repetitions has occurred, this can quickly become tedious. Instead, we will use a type of loop that is available in VB .NET to handle this situation.

For-Next Loops

When the number of repetitions is known in advance, the **For-Next loop** is appropriate. The form of this loop is as follows:

> **For *variable* = *start value* to *end value* Step *change value***
> ***statements that compose body of loop***
> **Next *variable***

where ***variable*** = the counter variable in the loop

start value = the beginning value of the counter variable

end value = the ending value of the counter variable

change value = the amount the counter variable changes each time through the loop

and **Next *variable*** = the end of the For loop

If there is no ambiguity about which For-Next loop is being terminated, the *variable* part of the Next statement is optional. However, if it appears, it *must* match the variable name in the For statement. Also, if the Step part of the statement is omitted, the change value is assumed to be one.

Figure 5-5 points out these parts of the For-Next loop for a simple example where the objective is to sum the first 10 integers (1–10). It is also assumed that all variables have been previously declared and the summation variable, intSum, has been initialized to zero.

FIGURE 5-5. Parts of a For-Next loop

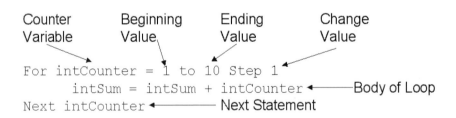

```
For intCounter = 1 to 10 Step 1
        intSum = intSum + intCounter        Body of Loop
Next intCounter        Next Statement
```

In a For-Next loop, the Next statement adds the change value to the current value of the counter variable on each repetition. This new value is compared to the ending value to determine whether or not the loop should be terminated. The loop is terminated when the counter variable is greater than the end value. If the loop is *not* terminated, the Next statement transfers control back to the For statement after the body of the loop has been executed. If the loop is terminated, control is transferred to the statement in the program that immediately follows the Next statement. Notice in Figure 5-5 that the body of the loop is indented. Just as in decision structures, indenting the body of a loop is a good way to make it clear what the loop is repeating.

Note that the Step part of the statement was equal to one in our first example of the For-Next loop. Since the change value was one, it was not required but was shown for demonstration purposes. On the other hand, if we wished to count backward from 10 to 1, we would need to use a change value of –1 and begin and end values of 10 and 1, respectively. The For statement in this case is

```
For intCounter = 10 to 1 Step -1
```

The *Step –1* part of this For statement is necessary to have the loop count backward. Otherwise, the loop will *not* be executed at all. For example, if we changed the For statement to leave out *Step –1*, that is,

```
For intCounter = 10 to 1
```

then there would be *no* output. The loop would terminate immediately because the beginning value, 10, is greater than the ending value, 1, and the Step value is positive. In this case the loop would not repeat at all.

> **TIP:** Although it is allowed by VB .NET, it can be dangerous to modify the loop counter variable within the loop. This should usually be avoided.

Application to Summing and Counting Example

To apply the For-Next loop to the summing and counting example discussed previously, we will use the Calculate button to input and sum the values, assuming that we know in advance the number of values that will be entered. We must also use an InputBox to input the values to be summed. This is because the For-Next loop, once initiated by a button or other event, will *not* pause to allow you to enter a new value in the txtNumValues text box. If you tried to use a text box for input with a For-Next loop, the value you input before initiating the loop would be summed as many times as the loop repeats, and no other values would be entered.

With the For-Next loop in this example, the only input outside of the loop is the number of values from the txtNumValues text box. The For-Next loop will handle the input and summing of the values; there is no need to count because the For-Next loop also handles this task. It was not necessary to declare any form-level variables in this event procedure, because all of the inputs and calculations are being done in one event procedure—btnCalc.

To modify the event-driven loop project, delete the txtTheValue text box and add a button named *btnPrint* with a caption of *Print*. This button will be used later in the application. At the code level, delete the form-level declaration of intSum and intNumValues, since they are declared at the procedure level, and replace the existing code in the btnCalc with the code in VB Code Box 5-4.

In looking at the code, we see that after the summation variable is initialized, a validation If-Then decision structure is used to check whether the user has entered a value in the txtNumValues text box. If not, a MsgBox warns the user that the text box is empty, and the sub is exited. This keeps the For-Next loop from trying to run a zero number of times.

If the txtNumValues.Text value is not zero, then the intNumValues variable is set equal to it, and the For-Next loop takes over. It runs from 1 to int-

| **VB CODE BOX 5-4.** Code for btnCalc event procedure | ```
Private Sub btnCalc_Click(ByVal sender As System.Object, ByVal e As
System.EventArgs) Handles btnCalc.Click
    Dim intTheValue, intSum, intNumValues As Integer
    Dim intCounter As Integer
    intSum = 0
    If txtNumValues.Text = "" Then
       MsgBox("Please enter number of values to be summed.")
       Exit Sub
    End If
    intNumValues = CInt(txtNumValues.Text)
    For intCounter = 1 To intNumValues
       intTheValue = CInt(InputBox("Enter next value:"))
       intSum = intSum + intTheValue
       lstEntries.Items.Add(Str(intTheValue))
    Next
    txtSum.Text = Str(intSum)
    lstEntries.Items.Add("Sum is " & Str(intSum))
End Sub
``` |

NumValues, inputting each value with an InputBox, adding it to the sum, and adding it to the list box. The last two lines move the sum to a text box and to the list box. Note that a label ("Sum is ") is concatenated using an ampersand with the String version of the sum variable (Str(intSum)). This alerts the user to the fact that this value is the sum.

The btnClear_Click event procedure for the For-Next loop example is shown in VB Code Box 5-5. The code for it is very similar to that for the event-driven example, except that no variables are reset to zero and the focus is set to the txtNumValues text box rather than to the now-nonexistent txtTheValue text box. When this project is run for the same data as before—that is, five values, which are 123, 456, 789, –135, and 246—the result is as shown in Figure 5-6.

| **VB CODE BOX 5-5.** Code for btnClear event procedure | ```
Private Sub btnClear_Click(ByVal sender As System.Object, _
ByVal e As System.EventArgs) Handles btnClear.Click
    txtNumValues.Text = ""
    txtSum.Text = ""
    lstEntries.Items.Clear()
    txtNumValues.Focus()
End Sub
``` |

Printing the Contents of a List Box

For-Next loops are not always used to input data; actually they are more often used for working with lists of items. One such use of a For-Next loop is to print the contents of a list or a combo box. In printing the contents of a list or combo box, there are issues that we must face: first, where will the printing occur and, second, how will we print the contents of the list or combo box?

In the first case, VB. NET provides us with two ways of printing the contents of a list or combo box: to the Output window or to a printer. Printing to the Output window is a good way of creating a semipermanent printed copy during the development process because it does not require a printer and avoids wasting paper. Printing to a printer is appropriate when the system is completed and a "hard copy" of the output is required. We will discuss print-

FIGURE 5-6. Result of running project with For-Next loop

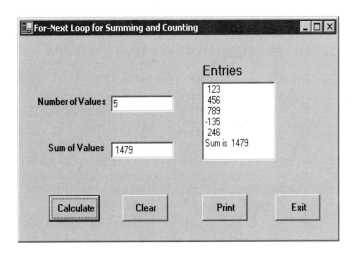

ing to the Output window in this chapter and printing to a printer in a later chapter.

To print to the Output window, you first need to recall from Chapter 2 that at design-time, the **Output window** shares the window beneath the Design window with the Task list as indicated by the tab beneath this window. However, at run time when a project is executed, the Output window is changed so that it takes up the right half of the entire lower portion of the screen, with the Autos window taking up the left half of this area. This arrangement is shown in Figure 5-7, at run time for the current project with the Output window pointed out. We will discuss more about the Autos window later on in this chapter, in our discussion of debugging.

FIGURE 5-7. Output and Autos windows

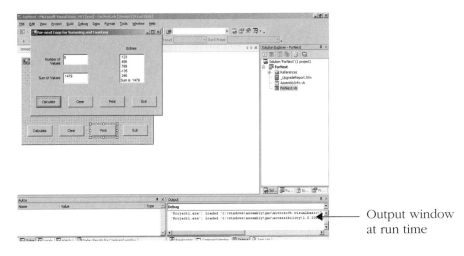

Output window at run time

Initially the Output window displays the **Debug pane** with information about the files that were used to run this project, but you can change this to show the **Build pane,** which will display information about the process of compiling this project. Note from the tabs beneath the Output window that it shares this space with a number of other windows, including a list of breakpoints that have been set like those discussed in Chapter 4; the **Command window,** which can be used to input a command directly or to display the value of specific variables; and the same Task list discussed in Chapter 2. For the time being, we will only be concerned with the Debug pane of the Output window, because this is where we can "print" the contents of a list box.

Now that we know "where" our printing will occur, the next question is "how" do we actually carry out the printing. To answer this question, we first need to determine the number of items in a list box. You can use the **Items.Count** property of the list box; this property keeps up with how many items have been added to a list box. For example, in Figure 5-6, the value of lstEntries.Items.Count would be six, because there are six items in the list box (five values and the sum).

To identify the items in a list box, we can use the run-time Items() property of the list box. We used the design-time version of the Items() property to add items to the list box, but the run-time version of this property specifies an item in the list box. The first item is always numbered as zero and goes up to the number of items in the list box (Items.Count) *minus 1.* Because Items.Count is equal to the number of items in the list box, and the index of Items() starts at zero, the index of Items() property of the last item is Items.Count − 1. This means that the first item is identified as Items(0), the second item as Items(1), and so on to the last item, which is identified as Items(Items.Count − 1). In the example in Figure 5-6, lstEntries.Items(0) is 123, lstEntries.Items(1) is 456, lstEntries.Items(2) is 789, and so on down to lstEntries.Items(5), which is "Sum is 1479."

Now that you know how many items there are in any list box (Items.Count) and how to identify items in the list box with the run-time Items() property of the list box, the only thing we do not yet know is how to communicate with the Output window. This is accomplished with the **Writeline** method of the **Debug** class; that is, to write anything to the Output window from the project, the form of the statement is

Debug.Writeline*(variable or constant as a string)*

Note that the argument of the Debug.Writeline function *must* be a string, so you may need to concatenate multiple values separated by a space in order to output them.

For the list box, the item to be printed is the one of the items in the list box. Since these items are identified by the run-time Items() property of the list box, we can use a For-Next loop to print all items in the lstEntries list box in the example with the following three statements (assuming intCounter has been declared as an Integer variable):

```
For intCounter = 0 to lstEntries.Items.Count - 1
    Debug.Writeline(lstEntries.Items(intCounter))
Next
```

In this For-Next loop, the intCounter variable goes from 0 to lstEntries.Items.Count − 1 and the lstEntries.Item(intCounter) property is equal to each item in the list box. As a result, all items are printed. If the code in VB Code Box 5-6 is added to the btnPrint event procedure, then clicking the Print button will print the six items displayed in the list box to the Debug pane of the Output window, as shown in Figure 5-8 (where we have expanded the Output window to show all six items).

VB CODE BOX 5-6. Code for btnPrint_Click event procedure	```Private Sub btnPrint_Click(ByVal eventSender As Object, _ByVal eventArgs As EventArgs) Handles btnPrint.Click Dim intCounter As Integer For intCounter = 0 To lstEntries.Items.Count - 1 Debug.WriteLine(lstEntries.Items(intCounter)) NextEnd Sub```

FIGURE 5-8. Use of Output window for printed output

The results of printing to the Output window will remain there even after exiting the program, and you can use the vertical scroll bar to view them. Although you *cannot* delete the contents of the Output window at any time, it will automatically be cleared when you begin a new execution of the project! The complete code for the For-Next input loop is shown in VB Code Box 5-7.

> **TIP:** If your Output window is not visible when you run your project, you can make it visible with the **View | OtherWindows | Output window** menu selection.

▬▬▬▬▬▬▬▬▬▬▬▬▬▬▬▬▬

Step-by-Step Instructions 5-2: Summing and printing using a For-Next loop

1. To create a project to input, sum, and print a series of values using a For-Next loop, use Windows Explorer to create a new folder in the *Chapter5* folder named **ForNext.** *Copy* the files in the *EventDriven* folder to this new folder and rename them as **ForNext.sln, ForNext.vbproj,** and **ForNext.vb.** Give the form a name of **frmForNext,** and a form **text** property of **For-Next Loop for Summing and Counting.**

2. Use the Design tab to display the frmForNext form and delete the text box used to enter values (txtTheValue) and the corresponding label. Add a button with a name of **btnPrint** and a text property of **Print.** Finally, set the **TabIndex** properties for txtNumValues to be **0,** btnCalc to be **1,** btnPrint to be **2,** btnClear to be **3,** and btnExit to be **4.** For all other controls, the **TabStop** property should be **False.**

3. Delete the existing code for the btnCalc and btnClear buttons and the form-level declarations of the summing and counting variables (intSum and intNumValues). Add the code in VB Code Box 5-4 to the btnCalc event procedure and the code in VB Code Box 5-5 to the btnClear event procedure.

| VB CODE BOX 5-7. Complete code for For-Next input loo | ```
Private Sub btnCalc_Click(ByVal sender As System.Object, _
ByVal e As System.EventArgs) Handles btnCalc.Click
    Dim intTheValue, intSum, intNumValues As Integer
    Dim intCounter As Integer
        intSum = 0
    If txtNumValues.Text = "" Then
        MsgBox("Please enter number of values to be summed.")
        Exit Sub
    End If
    intNumValues = CInt(txtNumValues.Text)
    For intCounter = 1 To intNumValues
        intTheValue = CInt(InputBox("Enter next value:"))
        intSum = intSum + intTheValue
        lstEntries.Items.Add(Str(intTheValue))
    Next
    txtSum.Text = Str(intSum)
    lstEntries.Items.Add("Sum is " & Str(intSum))
End Sub
Private Sub btnClear_Click(ByVal sender As System.Object, _
ByVal e As System.EventArgs) Handles btnClear.Click
    txtNumValues.Text = ""
    txtSum.Text = ""
    lstEntries.Items.Clear()
    txtNumValues.Focus()
End Sub
Private Sub btnPrint_Click(ByVal sender As System.Object, _
ByVal e As System.EventArgs) Handles btnPrint.Click
    Dim intCounter As Integer
    For intCounter = 0 To lstEntries.Items.Count - 1
        Debug.WriteLine(lstEntries.Items(intCounter))
    Next
End Sub
Private Sub btnExit_Click(ByVal sender As System.Object, _
ByVal e As System.EventArgs) Handles btnExit.Click
    End
End Sub
``` |

4. Test your project with the data given in the text—five values: **123, 456, 789, –135,** and **246** (your answer should be 1,479).

5. Click the Clear button and enter the following data—six values: **–34, 107, –301, 202, 782,** and **15** (your answer should be 771).

6. Add the code in VB Code Box 5-6 to print the contents of the list box to the Output window with the Print button. Run your project again with the same data as in Exercise 4, and click the Print button to print to the Output window. Exit the project to clear the contents of the Output window, and run your project again with the same data as in Exercise 5, printing to the Output window.
```

Mini-Summary 5-2: For-Next Loops

1. If the number of repetitions is known in advance, then you can use a For-Next loop. For-Next loops have a For statement, statements in the body of the loop, and a Next statement.

2. A For statement has a numeric counter variable, a beginning value, an ending value, and an optional Step value. The Step value must be negative to count down.

3. For-Next loops are often used to work with lists such as list or combo boxes. With list or combo boxes, the Items.Count property indicates the number of elements in the list and the run-time Items() property is used to designate which element is being printed.

4. It is possible to print to either a printer or the Output window. The Writeline method of the Debug class can be used to print to the Output window.

It's Your Turn!

1. For each of the For-Next loops shown on the next page, what values will be displayed in the text boxes, txtRes1 and txtRes2, after the loop has been completely executed?

```
a.    Private Sub btnGo_Click()
          Dim intCounter, intSum As Integer
          For intCounter = 1 To 10
              intSum = intSum + intCounter
          Next intCounter
          txtRes1.Text = intCounter
          txtRes2.Text = intSum
      End Sub
b.    Private Sub btnGo_Click()
          Dim intCounter As Integer
          Dim intSum As Integer
          For intCounter = 2 To 8 Step 2
              intSum = intSum + intCounter
          Next intCounter
          txtRes1.Text = intCounter
          txtRes2.Text = intSum
      End Sub
c.    Private Sub btnGo_Click()
          Dim intCounter As Integer
          Dim intSum As Integer
          For intCounter = 20 To 10 Step -2
              intSum = intSum + intCounter
          Next intCounter
          txtRes1.Text = intCounter
          txtRes2.Text = intSum
      End Sub
d.    Private Sub btnGo_Click()
          Dim intCounter As Integer
          Dim intSum As Integer
          For intCounter = 3 To 20 Step 5
              intSum = intSum + intCounter
          Next intCounter
          txtRes1.Text = intCounter
          txtRes2.Text = intSum
```

```
                    End Sub
```

2. For each of the following For-Next loops, what error has been made? How should it be corrected?

```
a.    For intCounter = 5 To 1
          intSum = intSum + intCounter
      Next intCounter
b.    For intCounter = 2 To 6 Step 2
          intSum = intSum + intCounter
      Next intSum
c.    ' sum the numbers from 1 to 10
      For intCounter = 1 To 10
          intCounter = intCounter + intCounter
      Next intCounter
```

3. Follow Step-by-Step Instructions 5-2 to create the ForNext project from the EventDriven project

---

INDETERMINATE LOOPS

The third classification of loops is the indeterminate loop, for which the number of repetitions is not known in advance. Although the number of repetitions for an event-driven loop can be known or not known in advance, in this section we will consider loops that are data-driven, either by values generated in the code or by input. In all cases, the loops will be executed within a single control rather than in multiple controls.

There are four types of indeterminate loops in VB .NET:

1. Looping *until* some condition is true, with the termination condition *before* the body of the loop.
2. Looping *while* some condition is true, with the termination condition *before* the body of the loop.
3. Looping *until* some condition is true, with the termination condition *after* the body of the loop.
4. Looping *while* some condition is true, with the termination condition *after* the body of the loop.

Classifying Indeterminate Loops

The four types of indeterminate loops listed above can be classified in two ways: as pretest or posttest loops, or as While or Until loops. The first two types of loop are referred to as **pretest loops** because the termination condition comes *before* the body of the loop, and the second two types of loop are referred to as **posttest loops** because the termination condition comes *after* the body of the loop. The choice of a pretest loop or a posttest loop depends on whether or not the loop should always execute at least one repetition. Because the termination condition comes after the body of the loop, a posttest loop will always execute at least once. A pretest loop, on the other hand, may not execute at all, because the termination decision before the body of the loop may keep the loop from executing.

The first and third types of loop listed above are also referred to as **Until loops,** and the second and fourth types of loop are referred to as **While loops.** The difference between the two types is that in an Until loop, the loop continues *until* a termination condition *becomes true*, but in a While loop, the loop continues *while* a termination condition *is true*. In general, either type of loop can be used for any situation so long as the termination condition is set up correctly.

The form of the pretest loops is
Do Until (or While) *condition*
    body of loop
Loop
and the form of the posttest loops is
Do
    body of loop
Loop Until (or While) *condition*

The *condition* part of these statements is the same as the comparison conditions used in the If-Then-Else statement. In a pretest Do While loop, if the condition being tested is true, then control is transferred to the body of the loop for another repetition of the loop. If the condition is false, control is transferred out of the loop and to the statement immediately following the Loop statement.

> **TIP:** The statements within an indeterminate loop must eventually cause the termination condition to be satisfied; otherwise an infinite loop results.

On the other hand, in a pretest Do Until loop, if the condition being tested is false, then control is transferred to the body of the loop for another repetition of the loop. If the condition is true, control is transferred out of the loop and to the statement immediately following the Loop statement. Figure 5-9 shows the Do While and Do Until processes for a pretest loop.

In a posttest loop, the body of the loop is executed and then the *condition* is tested. If the condition being tested in the Loop While statement is true, control is transferred back to the Do statement at the top of the loop and then to the body of the loop for another repetition of the loop. If the condition is false, control is transferred out of the loop and to the statement immediately following the Loop While statement.

> **TIP:** If the program appears to be doing nothing when you run it, and does not respond to mouse clicks or key presses, you probably have an infinite loop in progress. You should terminate it by pressing the Ctrl+Break key combination.

For the posttest Until loop, if the condition being tested in the Loop Until statement is false, control is transferred back to the Do statement at the top of the loop and then to the body of the loop for another repetition of the loop. If the condition is true, control is transferred out of the loop and to the statement immediately following the Loop Until statement.

As an illustration of indeterminate loops, consider the case of initializing a variable to 10 and repeatedly subtracting 2 from it *while* the variable is greater than zero. When the variable becomes less than or equal to zero, the loop terminates and control passes to the statement immediately following the Loop statement. The statements to do this for a pretest While loop are shown in VB Code Box 5-8 (note that the body of the loop is indented; this helps a reader understand what is being repeated):

FIGURE 5-9. Pretest
indeterminate loop

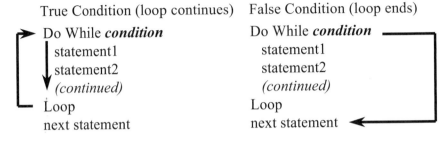

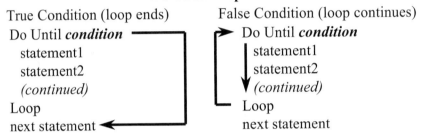

| **VB CODE BOX 5-8.** Using While loop to count backwards | ```
intValue = 10
Do While intValue > 0
   MsgBox("Value = " & CStr(intValue))
   intValue = intValue - 2
Loop
``` |
| --- | --- |

If a project is created with a single button, and these statements are entered in the Code window for that control, the values 10, 8, 6, 4, and 2 will be displayed in a series of message boxes. The values that are displayed are all positive, since the loop is terminated by the Do While statement when intValue variable becomes less than or equal to zero.

Note that the Do While statement in this example can be replaced with an equivalent Do Until statement that will continue to subtract 2 from the variable *until* the intValue variable is less than or equal to zero; that is,

```
Do Until intValue <= 0
```

This same loop can also be created as a posttest While loop with the following statements:

```
intValue = 10
Do
    MsgBox("Value = " & Str(intValue))
    intValue = intValue - 2
Loop While intValue > 0
```

An equivalent Loop Until statement would be

```
Loop Until intValue <= 0
```
```

Processing an Unknown Number of Values from a File

One way to input, sum, count, and display values when the number of values is unknown is to use an event-driven loop like the one discussed earlier. In that case, the user entered values in a text box and clicked a button to process each value. Essentially, the user entered an unknown number of values, using the button event to continue the process *while* values remained to be summed (or *until* no more values remained).

We could also input and process an unknown number of values using a pretest Do While loop or Until loop, with input coming from an InputBox like that used for the For-Next loop. However, with the event-driven loop capability of languages like VB .NET, this is unnecessary. This does not mean that indeterminate loops will never be used for keyboard input; it just means we will not use them in this text for this type of input. Instead, we will use them to input values from a data file.

A **data file** is a *collection of data stored on magnetic or optical secondary storage in the form of records.* A **record** is a *collection of one or more data items that are treated as a unit.* Files are identified by the computer's operating system with **filenames** assigned by the user. Files are important to processing data into information because they provide a permanent method of storing large amounts of data that can be input whenever needed for processing into information. There are three types of data files in widespread use: sequential access files, direct access files, and database files. **Sequential access files** are files from which the data records must be input in the same order that they were placed on the file. **Direct-access files** (also known as **random access files)** are files that can be input in any order. Although **database files** are widely used for data storage, they must be accessed with a database management system and cannot be input directly into a VB .NET project. In this chapter, we will discuss reading from and writing to sequential access files. Database files will be discussed in Chapter 9 and direct access files will be discussed in Chapter 10.

Sequential access files replicate the action of entering data from a keyboard, since you enter data from a keyboard one after the other just like they would be read from a sequential access file. The number of records on a sequential access file is often unknown, but there is an invisible binary marker at the end of the file called the **EOF** (end of file) **marker.** Although this precludes the use of a For-Next loop for inputting data from a sequential file, it does not affect the use of a Do While loop or a Do Until loop, because these loops can input data until the EOF marker is encountered (or while it has not been encountered).

> **TIP:** As your program code gets longer, splitting the screen enables you to look at widely separated parts of the code. Do this by dragging the small separator just above the right scroll bar of the code window into position. To remove the split, simply double-click it.

Data Input from Sequential Access Files

To input data from a sequential access file, such a file must first exist. The easiest way to create a sequential access file is to use a text editor like Notepad. When you type data into a text editor and then save it as a *text* file (not a *Word* file), an EOF marker is automatically placed at the end of the file. Figure 5-10 shows a sequential access file being created in Notepad, where each record consists of a single Integer value. (We recommend using an editor like Notepad instead of a processing program like Word or WordPad to create data files, because Notepad automatically saves them as text files. Word-processing programs generate files that contain special formatting characters, which will not work as data files.)

FIGURE 5-10.
Creating a sequential file in Notepad

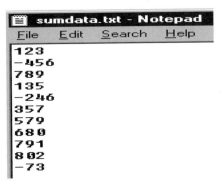

Once you have a sequential access file, you must first *open* it in the project before data can be input from it. This is accomplished with a file-Open statement of the form

FileOpen (*n*, "*filename*", OpenMode.Input)

where *filename* must include the drive and folder where the file is located and *n* is a number between 1 and 511. This is the number that VB .NET will use to refer to the file. The last parameter of the FileOpen statement, Open-Mode.Input, indicates that the file is being opened for input from a text file. For example, from a floppy disk in drive a:, opening a file named "Sum-Data.txt" as number 10 would require the following statement:

```
FileOpen(10, "a:\SumData.txt", OpenMode.Input)
```

The FileOpen statement must be executed before any data can input from or output to a sequential file. At some point before the project is terminated, the file should be closed with the Close statement:

FileClose(*n*)

For example, to close the same file opened earlier, the statement would be

```
FileClose(10)
```

To input data from a sequential file once it has been opened, you use the Input statement:

Input(*n*, *list of variables*)

where *n* must match the number assigned earlier to the file, and *list of variables* is a list of variable names for which data will be entered. There must be a one-to-one match between the list of variables and the data on the file, in terms of both data type and number of items being input. For example, to input data into a variable called intTheValue from the sequential access file opened earlier as 10, the statement would be

```
Input(10, intTheValue)
```

As an example of using a Do Until loop to sum and count values that are input from a sequential file on the a: drive, we will use the same form as we

> **TIP:** If errors occur when reading a file, they may be caused by the file instead of your code. Check for such things in the file as: an extra line at the end of the file, string values that are not enclosed in quotes, and missing delimiters (for example, a missing comma).

did for the For-Next loop. However, the code will be decidedly different; instead of inputting the number of values to be input, we will count them as they are input from the sequential access file and display this number in the text box. The btnCalc event procedure to accomplish this is shown in VB Code Box 5-9.

| **VB CODE BOX 5-9.** Code for btnCalc_Click event procedure | <pre>Private Sub btnCalc_Click(ByVal sender As System.Object, _
ByVal e As System.EventArgs) Handles btnCalc.Click
    Dim intTheValue, intSum, intNumValues, intCounter As Integer
    FileOpen(10, "a:\SumData.txt", OpenMode.Input)
    intSum = 0
    intNumValues = 0
    Do Until EOF(10)
        Input(10, intTheValue)
        intSum = intSum + intTheValue
        intNumValues = intNumValues + 1
        lstEntries.Items.Add(Str(intTheValue))
    Loop
    txtNumValues.Text = Str(intNumValues)
    txtSum.Text = Str(intSum)
    lstEntries.Items.Add("Sum is " & Str(intSum))
    FileClose(10)
End Sub</pre> |

The code necessary to clear the form is almost the same as that for the For-Next example. The only difference is that there is no need to set the focus to the txtNumValues text box, because all input comes from the sequential file. The code for the btnClear event procedure is shown in VB Code Box 5-10.

| **VB CODE BOX 5-10.** Code for btnClear_Click event procedure | <pre>Private Sub btnClear_Click(ByVal sender As System.Object, _
ByVal e As System.EventArgs) Handles btnClear.Click
    txtNumValues.Text = ""
    txtSum.Text = ""
    lstEntries.Items.Clear()
End Sub</pre> |

Note that we do not need to change the code for the Print button, because it used the Items.Count property of the list box to determine the number of items in the list box and does not depend on the Calculate button or the Clear button for any information. If this project is executed with the sequential data file called a:\SumData that was shown in Figure 5-10, the results are as shown in Figure 5-11. The complete code for a project using an indeterminate input loop is shown in VB Code Box 5-11.

FIGURE 5-11.
Results of using
Until loop to input,
sum, and count
values

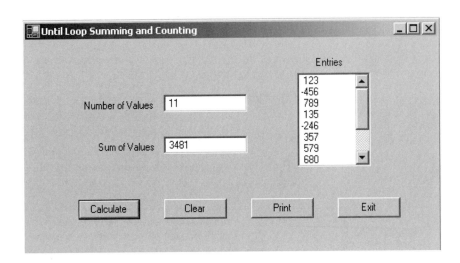

| VB CODE BOX 5-11. Complete code for indeterminate input loop | ```
Private Sub btnCalc_Click(ByVal sender As System.Object, _
ByVal e As System.EventArgs) Handles btnCalc.Click
    Dim intTheValue, intSum, intNumValues, intCounter As Short
    FileOpen(10, "a:\SumData.txt", OpenMode.Input)
    intSum = 0
    intNumValues = 0
    Do Until EOF(10)
        Input(10, intTheValue)
        intSum = intSum + intTheValue
        intNumValues = intNumValues + 1
        lstEntries.Items.Add(Str(intTheValue))
    Loop
    txtNumValues.Text = Str(intNumValues)
    txtSum.Text = Str(intSum)
    lstEntries.Items.Add("Sum is " & Str(intSum))
    FileClose(10)
End Sub
Private Sub btnClear_Click(ByVal sender As System.Object, _
ByVal e As System.EventArgs) Handles btnClear.Click
    txtNumValues.Text = ""
    txtSum.Text = ""
    lstEntries.Items.Clear()
End Sub
Private Sub btnPrint_Click(ByVal sender As System.Object, _
ByVal e As System.EventArgs) Handles btnPrint.Click
    Dim intCounter As Integer
    For intCounter = 0 To lstEntries.Items.Count - 1
        Debug.WriteLine(lstEntries.Items(intCounter))
    Next
End Sub
Private Sub btnExit_Click(ByVal sender As System.Object, _
ByVal e As System.EventArgs) Handles btnExit.Click
    End
End Sub
``` |
```

■ ■

Step-by-Step Instructions 5-3: Using an Until loop to input data from sequential access file

1. To create a project to input, sum, and print a series of values from a sequential access file using an Until loop, use Windows Explorer to create a new folder in the *Chapter5* folder named **UntilLoop.** Copy the files in the *ForNext* folder over to this new folder and rename them as **UntilLoop.sln, UntilLoop.vbproj,** and **UntilLoop.vb.** Change the form name to **frmUntil-Loop** and make it the StartUp object for the project. Finally, change the form text property to be **Until Loop for Summing and Counting**.

2. Modify the code for the btnCalc event procedure to match that shown in VB Code Box 5-9. Also, change the code for the btnClear event procedure to match that shown in VB Code Box 5-10.

3. Create a data file by opening Notepad from the Windows Accessories folder and enter the data shown in Figure 5-10. Be sure not to add extra blank lines at the end of the file, as this will lead to an incorrect value for the number of values in the data file. Save this file to the root folder of a data disk as **a:\SumData.txt**.

4. Run your project and click the **Calculate** button. The result should appear like that shown in Figure 5-11.

■ ■

Nested Loops

Just as decision structures can be nested, loops also can be nested. In the case of nested loops, there is an outer loop and an inner loop. As with decision structures, the inner loop *must* be completely contained within the outer loop. Nested loops are used whenever it is necessary to repeat an inner loop all of the way through for each repetition of the outer loop. An analogy may be drawn between nested loops and the way an automobile's odometer works. Recall that the tenths wheel on the odometer must make one complete revolution before the miles wheel advances one mile. In this analogy, the tenths wheel is the inner loop, and the miles wheel is the outer loop.

Although there can be any combination of nested For-Next, While, and Until loops, to combine any of these loops with an event-driven loop requires that the event-driven loop be the outer loop. In this brief discussion of nested loops, we take a look at nested For-Next loops. In future chapters, there will be situations where other combinations of loops are required.

Nested For-Next loops have a For-Next loop within a For-Next loop. When this combination is used, the inner For-Next loop will go through all its values for each value of the outer For-Next loop. There are three key programming rules to remember about using nested For-Next loops:

1. Always use different counter variables for the outer and inner For-Next loops.

2. Always have the Next statement for the inner For-Next loop *before* the Next statement for the outer For-Next loop.

3. Always include the counter variable in the Next statements to distinguish between the loops.

As an example of nested For-Next loops, consider the situation where the outer loop counts from 1 to 5 and the inner loop counts from 10 to 100 by 10s. The values of the inner and outer counter variables are summed as the bodies of the loops. This code is shown in VB Code Box 5-12.

| **VB CODE BOX 5-12.** Nested For-Next loops | ```
Private Sub frmNestedLoops_Load(ByVal sender As Object, _
ByVal e As EventArgs) Handles MyBase.Load
    Dim intInside As Integer, intOutside As Integer
    Dim intInnerSum As Integer, intOuterSum As Integer
    intInnerSum = 0
    intOuterSum = 0
    For intOutside = 1 To 5 'Start outer loop
        For intInside = 10 To 100 Step 10 'Start inner loop
            intInnerSum = intInnerSum + intInside 'Find Inner Sum
        Next intInside 'End inner loop
        MsgBox("Inner sum = " & Str(intInnerSum))
        intOuterSum = intOuterSum + intOutside 'Find Outer sum
    Next intOutside 'End Outer loop
    MsgBox("Outer sum = " & Str(intOuterSum))
End Sub
``` |
|---|---|

If the code in VB Code Box 5-12 is executed, the result will be an outer sum of 15 and an inner sum of 2,750. Note that the inner loop results in a sum of 550, but the inner loop is repeated five times, resulting in the larger value.

■ ▬ ▬ ▬ ▬ ▬ ▬ ▬ ▬ ▬ ▬ ▬ ▬ ▬ ▬ ▬ ▬ ▬ ▬ ▬ ■

Step-by-Step Instructions 5-4: Using nested loops

1. Use the **File|New Project** menu option to create a new project in the *Chapter5* folder. The name of the new project should be **Nested Loops,** with a form file named **NestedLoops.vb.** Give the form a name of **frmNested-Loops** and make it the Startup Object. Change the form text property to be **Using Nested Loops.**

2. Open the **frmNestedLoops_Load** event and enter the code shown in VB Code Box 5-12.

3. Run your project and you should have a series of message boxes; the first five showing the various inner sums and the last showing the outer sum.

4. Save all files in this project.

■ ▬ ▬ ▬ ▬ ▬ ▬ ▬ ▬ ▬ ▬ ▬ ▬ ▬ ▬ ▬ ▬ ▬ ▬ ▬ ■

Mini-Summary 5-3: While, Until, and Nested Loops

1. Do While and Do Until loops can be used when the number of repetitions is not known in advance and the termination of such loops depends on a comparison condition.

2. Do While and Do Until loops can be pretest or posttest loops, depending on where the decision condition is located relative to the body of the loop.

3. Sequential access files can be used to work with data that must be processed in the same order that it was input. Values are input from a sequential access file with the Input statement.
```

> **Mini-Summary 5-3: While, Until, and Nested Loops (Continued)**
>
> 5. A sequential access file must be opened and assigned a number between 1 and 511. The file is referred to by this number in the code. The file must also be closed.
>
> 6. Nested loops are created by having one loop completely inside of another with the inside loop completing all of its repetitions for each repetition of the outer loop.

It's Your Turn!

1. For each of the following loops, what values will be displayed in the text boxes, txtRes1 and txtRes2, after the loop has been completely executed?

```
a. Private Sub btnGo_Click()
      Dim intCounter As Integer
      intCounter = 0
      txtRes2.Text = 0
      Do While intCounter < 5
         txtRes2.Text = txtRes2.Text + intCounter
         intCounter = intCounter + 1
      Loop
      txtRes1.Text = intCounter
   End Sub
b. Private Sub btnGo_Click()
      Dim intCounter As Integer
      intCounter = 0
      txtRes2.Text = 0
      Do While intCounter <= 5
         txtRes2.Text = txtRes2.Text + intCounter
         intCounter = intCounter + 1
      Loop
      txtRes1.Text = intCounter
   End Sub
c. Private Sub btnGo_Click()
      Dim intCounter As Integer
      intCounter = 0
      txtRes2.Text = 0
      Do
         txtRes2.Text = txtRes2.Text + intCounter
         intCounter = intCounter + 1
      Loop Until intCounter = 5
      txtRes1.Text = intCounter
   End Sub
d. Private Sub btnGo_Click()
      Dim intCounter As Integer
      intCounter = 0
      txtRes2.Text = 0
      Do
         txtRes2.Text = txtRes2.Text + intCounter
         intCounter = intCounter + 1
      Loop While intCounter <= 5
      txtRes1.Text = intCounter
   End Sub
```

2. For each of the following loops, make corrections so that they will work as the comments indicate.

a.
```
Private Sub btnGo_Click()
  ' add numbers from 1 to 10
    Dim intCounter As Integer = 0
    Do
       intCounter = intCounter + 1
       txtRes2.Text = txtRes2.Text + intCounter
    Loop While intCounter <= 10
  End Sub
```
b.
```
Private Sub btnGo_Click()
  ' calculate 5 factorial
    Dim intCounter As Integer
    intCounter = 5
    txtRes2.Text = 0
    Do
       intCounter = intCounter - 1
       txtRes2.Text = txtRes2.Text * intCounter
    Loop Until intCounter = 0
  End Sub
```
c.
```
Private Sub btnGo_Click()
  ' add even numbers between 0 and 10
    Dim intCounter As Integer
    intCounter = 0
    txtRes2.Text = 1
    Do While intCounter = 10
       txtRes2.Text = txtRes2.Text + intCounter
       intCounter = intCounter + 2
    Loop
  End Sub
```

3. For each of the following loops, convert the While condition to an equivalent Until condition or vice versa.

a.
```
intCounter = 0
Do While Not (intCounter = 10)
   intCounter = intCounter + 1
Loop
```
b.
```
intCounter = 5
blnFlag = True
Do
   intCounter = intCounter - 1
   If intCounter = 3 Then blnFlag = False
Loop Until Not blnFlag And intCounter = 0
```
c.
```
intCounter = 10
Do Until intCounter = 0
   intCounter = intCounter - 1
Loop
```

4. For each of the following nested loops, what values will be displayed in the text boxes, txtRes1 and txtRes2, after the loop has been completely executed?

a.
```
Private Sub btnGo_Click()
    Dim intLoop1 As Integer
    Dim intLoop2 As Integer
    txtRes1.Text = 0
    txtRes2.Text = 0
    For intLoop1 = 1 To 3
       For intLoop2 = 1 To 3
```

```
            txtRes1.Text = txtRes1.Text + intLoop1
            txtRes2.Text = txtRes2.Text + 1
        Next intLoop2
     Next intLoop1
  End Sub
b. Private Sub btnGo_Click()
     Dim intLoop1, intLoop2 As Integer
     txtRes1.Text = 0
     txtRes2.Text = 0
     For intLoop1 = 1 To 2
        For intLoop2 = 3 To 1 Step -1
            txtRes1.Text = txtRes1.Text + intLoop1
            txtRes2.Text = txtRes2.Text + 1
        Next intLoop2
     Next intLoop1
  End Sub
c. Private Sub btnGo_Click()
     Dim intLoop1 As Integer, intLoop2 As Integer
     txtRes1.Text = 0
     txtRes2.Text = 0
     For intLoop1 = 1 To 3
        For intLoop2 = intLoop1 To 4
            txtRes1.Text = txtRes1.Text + intLoop1
            txtRes2.Text = txtRes2.Text + 1
        Next intLoop2
     Next intLoop1
  End Sub
```

5. Assume that you have a sequential file with an unknown number of records. Each line in the file contains the following information in this order: first name, second name, age, gender, and marital status. Design and write code that will read this file and display each line in a list box.

6. Follow Step-by-Step Instructions 5-3 to create a project that will input data from a sequential access file.

7. It is very easy to make the Until loop project more flexible by inputting the name of the file using an InputBox. To do this, modify the code for the btnCalc event procedure to declare **strTheFileName** as a String variable and to add the following line of code before the FileOpen statement:

```
strTheFileName = InputBox("Input filename for data file")
```

Also, modify the FileOpen statement to replace "a:\SumData.txt" (including the quotation marks) with **strTheFileName** (with no quotation marks) as shown below:

```
FileOpen(10, strTheFileName, OpenMode.Input)
```

This will allow you to input the filename for the data file. Note: The file name stored in strTheFileName *must* include the complete path for the file.

7. Run your revised project and input **a:\SumData.txt** as the filename of the data file. Use Notepad to create another text data file similar to SumData.txt with a different name. Run your project with new data file.

APPLICATION TO VINTAGE DVDs

Now that you have a good understanding of the repetition process in VB .NET, we are ready to apply this understanding to create a multiple-DVD Vintage DVDs application. In this application, instead of assuming that each customer will only rent one DVD, the project needs to be capable of allowing a customer to rent multiple DVDs, each of which will be listed on a receipt that can be printed. The revised project will also determine whether a customer is a member of Vintage DVDs. If the customer is not a member, then he or she will be enrolled as a member for future reference. To add this increased functionality, we need to be able to repeat actions in VB .NET.

As with all project designs, we need to begin by designing the interface, which is an extension of the existing Vintage DVDs interface, to include new features. The revised interface is shown in Figure 5-12, with the new elements pointed out.

FIGURE 5-12. Form for multiple-DVD application

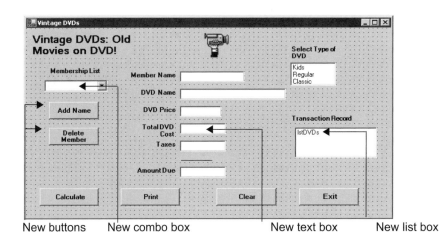

Note that we have added a sixth text box that will display the total cost of the DVDs this customer rents. In addition, we have added a drop-down list (combo) box that will display the names of all Vintage DVD's members. We have also included buttons to add a customer name to this list in the text box or to delete a name from the list. A list box has been added that will display a list of DVDs rented, and the Calculate button will handle the process of summing the prices, computing the taxes on the sum, and adding the taxes to the sum to compute the amount due. This will be done for each DVD that is rented.

To help you understand how this interface will operate, here is a list of steps that will be followed in renting DVDs:

1. Check the combo box to see if the customer is a member. If they are, add their name to the customer name text box from the combo box and go to Step 3 below; otherwise go to Step 2.

2. If the customer is not a member, enter their name in the *Customer Name* text box and then add it to the membership list by clicking the *Add a member* button and continue with the next step.

3. Enter the name of the DVD in the *DVD Name* text box and click the DVD type to display the price.

4. Click the *Calculate* button to
   a. add the price of this DVD to the previous total DVD cost;
   b. compute taxes, add them to the total DVD cost, and display the total in the *Amount Due* text box;
   c. add the name and price of the DVD to the *Transaction List* list box.
5. When all DVDs have been added to the list, click the *Print* button to add the total cost of DVDs, the taxes on the DVDs, and the amount due to the *Transaction List* list box and print the contents of this list box to the Output window.
6. Click the *Clear* button to clear all information from the list boxes in preparation for the next customer.
7. If the customer is a member, but his or her name needs to be removed from the membership list, select it in the combo box and then remove it from the membership list by clicking the *Delete Member* button.
8. Click the *Exit* button to save the revised list of members and to exit the application.

Note that in this revised project all of the buttons at the bottom of the form have been modified, and additional controls need to be added to the form. This will require modifying your existing single-DVD Vintage DVDs project to add the new controls—a combo box, a list box, a text box, and two buttons—to the form and to revise the code for existing controls. With the exception of the combo box, you should already know how to add all of the new controls and set their properties. We will assume that an empty list box with a name of *lstDVDs*, buttons named *btnAdd* and *btnDelete*, a text box named *txtTotalCost*, and appropriate labels have also been added to the form as shown earlier in Figure 5-12.

Combo Boxes

A **combo box** is a combination of a text box and a list box. It has a text box portion that is displayed at all times and a drop-down list of items that can be displayed by clicking on the down arrow. One property of note for the combo box is the **DropDownStyle** property, which can be set at design time to DropDown (the default), Simple, or DropDownList. With the default DropDown style, you can use the drop-down list to select an item or you can type a value into the text box. In either case, the Text property is set equal to the selected item or typed value. With the Simple style, the list portion of the combo box is always displayed like a list box, but the top-most item is still a text box. Finally, with the DropDownList style, there is no text box portion, and you must select from the drop-down list. We will use the default style for this application.

combo box

To add a member-names combo box, select the combo box icon from the toolbox. It looks much like the list box icon with the addition of a drop-down arrow on the top. The prefix for the combo box name is *cbo*, so we will give it a name of *cboMembers*. Finally, since this combo box will have a list of members that will change from day to day, we will add them at run time instead of at design time. The final version of the revised form is shown in Figure 5-12.

Required Operations   As noted at the earlier, there are a variety of new operations that must be included in the multiple-DVD application. Let's discuss how we will handle each of these requirements.

Adding a list of members to a combo box. To create the combo box of member names, we need to input names from a sequential file and add them to the cboMembers combo box. Since the number of members may change each day, it will be unknown and we will need to use a Do Until EOF() loop to input the names from the file. The pseudocode for this operation is shown below:

```
Open file
Repeat Until end of file encountered
    Input Name
        Transfer name to combo box
End of loop
Close file
```

Since the combo box must be filled before any other events can occur, we need to write the code for it in the Form_Load event procedure by double-clicking on the form to display the event procedure. The code that needs to be entered follows the logic of the pseudocode and is shown in VB Code Box 5-13, where the file that stores the member names is named *members.txt* and is in the same directory as the executable version of the project.

VB Code Box 5-13. VB .NET code for the Form_Load event	```Private Sub frmVintage_Load(ByVal sender As System.Object, _ ByVal e As System.EventArgs) Handles MyBase.Load Dim strName As String Dim strFileName As String lstDVDs.Items.Add("Welcome to Vintage DVDs") strFileName = CurDir() & "\members.txt" FileOpen(1, strFileName, OpenMode.Input) Do Until EOF(1) Input(1, strName) cboMembers.Items.Add(strName) Loop FileClose(1) End Sub```

With the exception of the location of the text file, this code is the same as you saw earlier for the Until loop project. Since most data is stored on the hard disk rather than a floppy disk on the a: drive, we shown this code using the hard disk. The lines of code

```
strFileName = CurDir() + "\Members.txt"
FileOpen(1, StrFileName, OpenMode.Input)
```

enable us to do this. The first line stores the combination of the current location of the executable version of the project and the name of the data file in the string variable strFileName. We say *executable* version because the binary version of any VB .NET project that is actually executed when the project is run is stored in the **Bin** folder within the project folder. This means that the data file must also be stored in the Bin folder for these two lines of code to work. The second line of code actually opens the data file using the File-Open sub.

To make the search for a customer's name easier, we will assume that the customer's full name is listed in last-name-first fashion with the last and first names separated by a comma. Since VB .NET takes a comma as the delimiter between variable items, we must do something to make sure VB .NET gets the entire name and not just the last name. One way to do this would be to input two String variables—say, strLastName and strFirstName—and then concatenate them when they are added to the cboMembers combo box. However, since we are going to save this combo box back to the file, this would require "unconcatenating" the names before writing them to file, something we would like to avoid.

Another way to handle the two names is to enclose the entire name in quotation marks to force VB .NET to interpret it as one string rather than two. For example, instead of entering

```
Watson, Betsy
```

as a name in the file, the employee must enter it as

```
"Watson, Betsy"
```

so the first name is not interpreted as another string. Since this matches our need to write the names back to the file, we will use this approach.

Another helpful feature of combo and list boxes is that they can be **sorted**, that is, arranged in alphabetical or numerical order. Since we are listing names with the last name first, if the **Sorted** property of the combo box is set to true, then the names will appear in alphabetical order according to last name.

Transferring name from combo box to customer name text box. To check if the customer is a member, the user can manually search the cboMembers combo box. If the customer's name is in the list, it can be quickly transferred to the customer name text box using the combo box Click event (the default event for a combo box). The only statement in the event procedure will be the one that sets the Text property of the txtCustName text box equal to the Text event of the cboMembers combo box. This statement is

```
txtCustName.Text = cboMembers.Text
```

Adding customer name to combo box. If the customer's name is not found in the cboMembers combo box, then we want to enter it in the txtCustName text box in last name first form and use the *Add a member* button to transfer it to the combo box. This name in the text box is added to the combo box with the following statement:

```
cboMembers.Items.Add(txtCustName.Text)
```

When the name is added to the list, since the Sorted property of the combo box is turned on, the name is automatically added in the appropriate alphabetical order. As with any type of input, we need to validate that a name is actually in the txtCustName text box before we try to add it to the combo box.

Processing multiple DVDs. After the customer name has been checked, the project must be able to process multiple DVDs using the Calculate button. This is an event-driven loop of the type used earlier to sum and count multiple values. As in the single-DVD project, the name of the DVD must be entered in the txtDVDName text box and the price must be determined by selecting the DVD type from the lstTypes list box. The Calculate button will not continue if the customer name, DVD name, or DVD price is missing.

Once the necessary information has been entered, the btnCalc event procedure adds the rental price to the sum of the prices to find the total price, calculates the taxes for this total price, and finds the amount due by adding the taxes to the total price. To do this, the decTotalCost variable is declared at the module level as a Decimal data type variable to retain its value between calculations and to make it available to other event procedures. It will be initialized to zero in the FrmVintage_Load event. The btnCalc event procedure will also add the name and price of the DVD to the lstDVDs list box as well as clearing the DVD name and DVD price text boxes and the text property of the lstTypes list box. Finally, the focus is set back to the DVD name text box.

The statement to add the DVD name and price to the lstDVDs list box uses concatenation to combine the DVD name, two spaces, and the previously formatted contents of the txtDVDPrice text box before adding the combined string to the list box. The statements to do this are

```
lstDVDs.Items.Add() strDVDName & "  " & txtDVDPrice.Text
```

The revised portion of the btnCalc event procedure that sums the prices of the multiple DVDs, formats the text boxes, adds the DVD names to the list box, clears the text boxes, and sets the focus to the DVD name text box in preparation for the next DVD is shown in VB Code Box 5-14 (some statements are not changed).

Note: To make processing multiple DVDs easier, you should set the TabIndex properties of the txtCustName and txtDVDName text boxes, the lstDVDs list box, and the btnCalc button to be 0, 1, 2, and 3, respectively. Doing this enables the user to input the customer name and then easily tab between the three other controls from which input originates.

VB Code Box 5-14. Revised code for end of btnCalc event procedure	```decPrice = CDec(txtDVDPrice.Text)``` `decTotalCost = decTotalCost + decPrice` `decTaxes = decTotalCost * sngTaxRate ' compute taxes` `decAmountDue = decTotalCost + decTaxes ' compute amount due` `txtTotalCost.Text = Format(decTotalCost, "c")` `txtTaxes.Text = Format(decTaxes, "C")` `txtAmountDue.Text = Format(decAmountDue, "C")` `txtDVDPrice.Text = Format(decPrice, "c")` `lstDVDs.Items.Add(txtDVDName.Text & " " & txtDVDPrice.Text)` `lstTypes.Text = ""` `txtDVDName.Text = ""` `txtDVDPrice.Text = ""`

Printing the lstDVDs list box and clearing entries. Printing the lstDVDs list box is accomplished with a For-Next loop like that used earlier to print the list of values. However, before printing the list box, we need to add the total DVD cost, the taxes on this amount, the total amount due, and a message of the form "Thanks for your business!" to the list box after the existing entries. The code for this is shown in VB Code Box 5-15.

Note that we have used the Output window. As mentioned earlier, we will cover using the printer later. To clear the entries, we simply need to set

VB Code Box 5-15. Code for btnPrint event procedure	```
	Private Sub btnPrint_Click(ByVal sender As System.Object, _
	ByVal e As System.EventArgs) Handles btnPrint.Click
	    Dim intNumber As Integer
	    Dim intCounter As Integer
	    lstDVDs.Items.Add("Total DVD price " & txtTotalCost.Text)
	    lstDVDs.Items.Add("Taxes " & txtTaxes.Text)
	    lstDVDs.Items.Add("Total Price = " & txtAmountDue.Text)
	    lstDVDs.Items.Add("Thanks for your business")
	    intNumber = lstDVDs.Items.Count - 1
	    For intCounter = 0 To intNumber
	        Debug.WriteLine(lstDVDs.Items(intCounter))
	    Next
	End Sub
	``

all text boxes to a null string (""), set the decTotalCost variable to zero, and clear the lstDVDs list box with the following statements:

```
txtTotalCost.Text = ""
decTotalcost = 0
lstDVDs.Items.Clear()
```

Removing names from the membership list. While the ability to delete individuals from the membership list is not needed just as Vintage DVDs is opening its doors for business, it will be necessary as the membership list grows. To remove an item from a combo box or list box, use the Items.RemoveAt() method. This method is the reverse of the Items.Add() method with one exception: Instead of giving the string to be added, you must provide the index of the item to be removed through the **SelectedIndex** property of the list box or combo box. This property is equal to the index of the item currently selected in the list box or combo box. For example, cboMembers.SelectedIndex is equal to the index of the currently selected item in the cboMembers combo box.

To be able to click the Remove Member button to remove the currently selected item in the cboMembers combo box, the only statement needed is

```
cboMembers.Items.RemoveAt(cboMembers.SelectedIndex)
```

However, if the combo box is empty or no item has been selected, attempting to remove a member will result in an error message. For that reason, we need to check the value of cboMembers.SelectedIndex to ensure that it is greater than –1 (if the combo box is empty or no name has been selected, the SelectedIndex property is equal to –1). The resulting code for the btnDelete_Click event procedure is shown in VB Code Box 5-16.

VB Code Box 5-16. Code to delete name from list	```
	Private Sub btnDelete_Click(ByVal sender As System.Object, _
	ByVal e As System.EventArgs) Handles btnDelete.Click
	    If cboMembers.SelectedIndex > -1 Then
	        cboMembers.Items.RemoveAt(cboMembers.SelectedIndex)
	    Else
	        MsgBox("No name selected or empty list", ,"Vintage DVDs")
	    End If
	End Sub
	``

Saving membership list to file and exiting project. The membership list may change during the day as customers are added to it. We need to be able to save it to disk so that the revised membership list will be used the next time this project is run. Just as we can input data from a file, we can also save data and information to a file. As with inputting data from a file, the file must first be opened. However, the FileOpen statement is different, with *Open-Mode.Output* replacing *OpenMode.Input*. The general form of the FileOpen function for output is

FileOpen(*n*, "*filename*", OpenMode.Output)

For example, to output to the same file **members.txt** as was used for input, the statements are

```
strFileName = CurDir() + strFileName
FileOpen(10, strFileName, OutputMode.Output)
```

Once a file has been opened for output, to store the revised membership list to the file, we need to use the WriteLine statement of the following form:

Writeline(*n*, *variable list*)

This function will insert commas between items and quotation marks around strings as they are written to the file and a carriage-return linefeed to the end of the file. This will allow the file to be input later using the *Input* statement, which requires that values be separated by commas. Note that the Writeline function to write to a file is very different from the Debug.Writeline statement in terms of its arguments.

To output the entire list of names in cboMembers to a file, we will use a For-Next loop to repeat the Writeline statement for each name on the list. The code to do this is shown in VB Code Box 5-17; it includes the End statement to exit the project.

VB Code Box 5-17. Code for btnExit event procedure	<pre>Private Sub btnExit_Click(ByVal sender As System.Object, _
	ByVal e As System.EventArgs) Handles btnExit.Click
	    Dim intNumMembers As Integer, strMemberName As String
	    Dim intcounter As Integer, strPath As String
	    strPath = CurDir() & "\members.txt"
	    FileOpen(10, strPath, OpenMode.Output)
	    intNumMembers = cboMembers.Items.Count
	    For intcounter = 0 To intNumMembers - 1
	       strMemberName = cboMembers.Items(intcounter)
	       WriteLine(10, strMemberName)
	    Next
	    FileClose(10)
	    End
	End Sub</pre>

Running the Project

After the code for all of the event procedures has been input, we are ready to run the project for a customer named Ben Dyer who is renting two movies—*Bambi* (Kids) and *Spartacus* (Classic). Figure 5-13 shows the form after the data for *Bambi* and *Spartacus* have been entered but before the *Print* button has been clicked to end the transaction. Figure 5-14 shows the Output window after the *Print* button has been clicked.

FIGURE 5-13.
Running multiple-
DVD project with
sample data

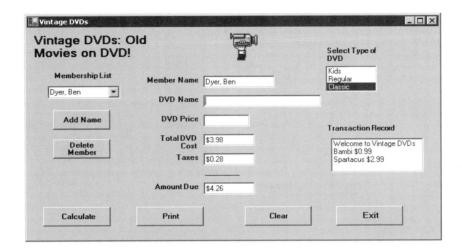

FIGURE 5-14.
Printing to Output
window

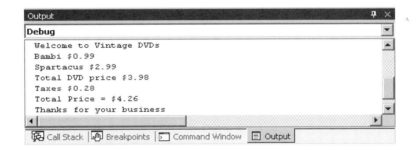

Step-by-Step Instructions 5-5: Handling multiple rentals at Vintage DVDs

1. Create a new folder within *Chapter5* folder named **Vintage5** and copy all of the files and folders in the *Chapter4\Vintage4* folder into the new folder.

2. Start VB .NET (or use File | Open) and open the new *Vintage5* project. Click on **Vintage.vb** to display the form and add the controls shown in Table 5-1 in the locations shown in Figure 5-12.

TABLE 5-1: Controls added to Vintage DVDs form

Control	Name	Text Property	Control	Name
button	btnAdd	Add Name	combo box	cboMembers
button	btnDelete	Delete Member	text box	txtTotalCost
			list box	lstDVDs

3. Change the control names and, where appropriate, add a text property. Also, change the label beside the customer name text box to have a text property of **Member Name** and the text property for the label beside the DVD price text box to be **Price.**

4. Open the frmVintage_Load event and delete the existing code there. Enter the code shown in VB Code Box 5-13 to input the names from a **members.txt** file (to be created) to the combo box.

5. Double-click the *cboMembers* combo box and enter this line of code into the Click event procedure:

```
txtCustName.Text = cboMembers.Text
```

5. Double-click the btnAdd button and enter these three lines of code into the Click event procedure:

```
If txtCustName.Text <> "" then
   cboMembers.Items.Add() txtCustName.Text
End If
```

6. Double-click the *Delete* button and enter the code shown in VB Code Box 5-16 to remove members from the combo box.

7. Declare the variable **decTotalCost** as a form-level Decimal data type variable. Next, double-click the *Calculate* button to modify the existing event procedure so that the lines *starting* with **Price = CDec(txtDVDPrice.Text)** match the code shown in VB Code Box 5-14.

8. Exit the project, double-click the *Print* button, and erase the existing code. Replace it with the code shown in VB Code Box 5-15. Double-click the Clear button and add the following lines to its event procedure:

```
txtTotalCost.Text = ""
curTotalCost = 0
lstDVDs.Items.Clear()
```

9. Double-click the *Exit* button and add the code shown in VB Code Box 5-17 (don't re-enter the **End** statement) Finally, set the TabIndex properties so that it is easy to tab between essential input controls. Save your project.

10. The complete code for the Vintage DVDs project up to this point is shown in VB Code Box 5-18.

∎ ■ ∎

Executable Files

When you click the Run icon, VB .NET compiles a project and places the resulting **executable (.exe) file** in the Bin folder of the project. It is this .exe file that is actually executed. This is the reason that the members.txt file had to be placed in the Bin folder in order for it to be found when the project was found. Once an executable file has been created, it can be installed and run on computers that do not have VB .NET installed. Because it does not have to be recompiled and is already in a binary form, an executable file runs much faster than the original VB .NET file from which it was created. Finally, you can run an executable file in Windows just by double clicking it. For example, once you have your project running correctly, you can close the VB .NET MDE and use Windows Explorer to open the Bin folder. Once there, double-clicking the Vintage5.exe file you find there will cause it to execute immediately.

It is now possible to copy the executable file to any other location or computer and run it there. The only caveat in the case of the Vintage DVDs project is that the members.txt data file must be in the same folder as the executable file.

| VB CODE BOX 5-18. Complete code for Vintage DVDs | ```
Dim decTotalCost As Decimal
Private Sub btnCalc_Click(ByVal sender As System.Object, _
ByVal e As System.EventArgs) Handles btnCalc.Click
    Const sngTaxRate As Single = 0.07 ' Use local tax rate
    Dim decPrice, decAmountDue, decTaxes As Decimal, strDVDType As String
    If txtCustName.Text = "" Then
        txtCustName.Text = InputBox("Enter name and try again.", _
        "Vintage DVDs")
        Exit Sub
    End If
    If txtDVDName.Text = "" Then
        txtDVDName.Text = InputBox("Enter DVD name and " & _
        "try again.", "Vintage DVDs")
        Exit Sub
    End If
    strDVDType = lstTypes.SelectedItem
    If strdvdtype = "" Then
        MsgBox("Select a DVD type and try again.", ,"Vintage DVDs")
        Exit Sub
    End If
    decPrice = CDec(txtDVDPrice.Text)
    decTotalCost = decTotalCost + decPrice
    decTaxes = decTotalCost * sngTaxRate ' compute taxes
    decAmountDue = decTotalCost + decTaxes ' compute amount due
    txtTotalCost.Text = Format(decTotalCost, "c")
    txtTaxes.Text = Format(decTaxes, "C")
    txtAmountDue.Text = Format(decAmountDue, "C")
    txtDVDPrice.Text = Format(decPrice, "c")
    lstDVDs.Items.Add(txtDVDName.Text & " " & txtDVDPrice.Text)
    lstTypes.Text = ""
    txtDVDName.Text = ""
    txtDVDPrice.Text = ""
    txtDVDName.Focus()
End Sub
Private Sub btnAdd_Click(ByVal sender As System.Object, _
ByVal e As System.EventArgs) Handles btnAdd.Click
    cboMembers.Items.Add(txtCustName.Text)
End Sub
Private Sub btnDelete_Click(ByVal sender As System.Object, _
ByVal e As System.EventArgs) Handles btnDelete.Click
    If cboMembers.SelectedIndex > -1 Then
        cboMembers.Items.RemoveAt(cboMembers.SelectedIndex)
     Else
        MsgBox("No name selected or list is empty", ,"Vintage DVDs")
     End If
End Sub
Private Sub btnClear_Click(ByVal sender As System.Object, _
ByVal e As System.EventArgs) Handles btnClear.Click
    txtCustName.Text = ""
    txtDVDName.Text = ""
    txtDVDPrice.Text = ""
    txtTaxes.Text = ""
    txtAmountDue.Text = ""
    txtTotalCost.Text = ""
    decTotalCost = 0
    lstDVDs.Items.Clear()
    lstTypes.SelectedIndex = -1
    txtCustName.Focus()
End Sub
``` |
```

| VB CODE BOX 5-18. Complete code for Vintage DVDs (continued) | ```vbnet
Private Sub btnExit_Click(ByVal sender As System.Object, _
ByVal e As System.EventArgs) Handles btnExit.Click
    Dim intNumMembers As Integer, strMemberName As String
    Dim intcounter As Integer, strPath As String
    strPath = CurDir() & "\members.txt"
    FileOpen(10, strPath, OpenMode.Output)
    intNumMembers = cboMembers.Items.Count
    For intcounter = 0 To intNumMembers - 1
        strMemberName = cboMembers.Items(intcounter)
        WriteLine(10, strMemberName)
    Next
    FileClose(10)
    End
End Sub
Private Sub lstTypes_SelectedIndexChanged(ByVal sender As _
System.Object, ByVal e As System.EventArgs) Handles _
lstTypes.SelectedIndexChanged
    Dim strDVDType As String, decPrice As Decimal
    strDVDType = lstTypes.SelectedItem
    Select Case strDVDType
        Case "Kids"
        decPrice = 0.99
        Case "Regular"
        decPrice = 1.99
        Case "Classic"
        decPrice = 2.99
    End Select
    txtDVDPrice.Text = Format(decPrice, "c")
End Sub
Private Sub frmVintage_Load(ByVal sender As System.Object, _
ByVal e As System.EventArgs) Handles MyBase.Load
    Dim strName, strFileName As String
    lstDVDs.Items.Add("Welcome to Vintage DVDs")
    strFileName = CurDir() & "\members.txt"
    FileOpen(1, strFileName, OpenMode.Input)
    Do Until EOF(1)
        Input(1, strName)
        cboMembers.Items.Add(strName)
    Loop
    FileClose(1)
End Sub
Private Sub cboMembers_SelectedIndexChanged(ByVal sender As _
System.Object, ByVal e As System.EventArgs) Handles _
cboMembers.SelectedIndexChanged
    txtCustName.Text = cboMembers.Text
End Sub
Private Sub btnPrint_Click(ByVal sender As System.Object, _
ByVal e As System.EventArgs) Handles btnPrint.Click
    Dim intNumber, intCounter As Integer
    lstDVDs.Items.Add("Total DVD price " & txtTotalCost.Text)
    lstDVDs.Items.Add("Taxes " & txtTaxes.Text)
    lstDVDs.Items.Add("Total Price = " & txtAmountDue.Text)
    lstDVDs.Items.Add("Thanks for your business")
    intNumber = lstDVDs.Items.Count - 1
    For intCounter = 0 To intNumber
        Debug.WriteLine(lstDVDs.Items(intCounter))
    Next
End Sub
``` |
```

It's Your Turn!

1. Follow Step-by-Step Instructions 5-5 to modify the Vintage DVDs application to handle multiple DVDs.

2. Test the multiple-DVD application by following these steps:

   a. Open Notepad and create a *text* file called **members.txt** in the **Bin** folder with the following names entered one to a line in last-name-first order with the entire name enclosed in quotation marks: **Ben Dyer, Lonnie Stams, Alice Goodly, Betsy Watson, Suzy Arons, Ann Carroll, Jimmy Triesch, Ashley Hyatt, Chris Patrick, Sam Jones, Carolyn Myers, Pat George, Margo Kidd, Ben Sibley,** and **Joe Smith.** For example, the first name would be entered as "Dyer, Ben". Also, do not add an extra line to the end of the file.

   b. Run the project and check that these names have been added to the combo box. If they have, note that **Adams, Bill** is not found in the combo box. Since he is not in the member list, add his name to the customer name text box and click the *Add Name* button to add him to the list.

   c. Check the combo box for **George, Patrick** and highlight it. Click the *Delete* Member button to remove him from the list. Go back to the combo box and verify that **Adams, Bill** has been added to the list and that **George, Patrick** has been removed.

   d. Verify that **Ben Dyer** is a member and use the *Calculate* button repeatedly to add these three DVDs: *Bambi* (Kids), *Spartacus* (Classic)**,** and *Stripes* (Regular). The sum of DVD prices should be $5.97, the taxes should be $0.42, and the amount due should be $6.39.

   e. Click the *Print* button. The Output window should appear like that shown in Figure 5-14.

   f. Exit your project and then run it again to ensure that Bill Adams's name was added to the end of the membership file and that Patrick George's name was deleted by checking the combo box.

3. If any of the operations do not work as described in the text, determine the error and correct it and test the project again. Once your project is running correctly, close the VB .NET MDE and use Windows Explorer to run the executable version of the project (*Vintage5.exe)* that you will find in the **Bin** folder of the *Vintage5* folder.

DEBUGGING LOOPS

It can easily be said that projects that involve loops are an order of magnitude more difficult to debug than projects without loops. Because these projects involve repetition, there are multiple values to check for correctness. Input using loops can easily run into errors, especially when files are involved. There are also problems with infinite loops when the termination condition is incorrectly stated. To find and correct errors in projects with loops, VB .NET has provided a variety of tools. We will consider some of these tools in this chapter and others in subsequent chapters. The tools we consider in this chapter are printing to the Output window object and using the Watch window and the Locals window combined with a program breakpoint.

Using the Output Window

One easy way to find out what's happening inside a loop is to print values for each repetition of the loop to the Output window. If you are not displaying input values in a list box, then this is an excellent way of checking the input. Remember: Input errors cause a large proportion of the errors you will encounter, and this is even more true when loops are used to input data from files.

For example, in the project we created earlier to use an Until loop to input values from a file and sum and count those values (*UntilLoop*), assume that the sum of those values is equal to zero. To find the error, you could insert the following statement in the event procedure for the *Calculation* button immediately before the end of the loop:

```
Debug.Writeline(intTheValue & " " & intSum & "  " & intNumValues)
```

If your error involves using the multiplication sign (*) instead of the addition sign (+) in the assignment statement in which the value intSum is calculating, that is,

```
intSum = intTheValue * intSum
```

the result of using the Output window is shown in Figure 5-15. Note that the input values appear to be correct; but the intSum value remains at zero throughout the loop, indicating that the error is somewhere in the calculation. The Output window can be resized as necessary to allow you to view more of the output.

FIGURE 5-15. Use of Output window to display values in loop

Using the Autos, Locals, and Watch Windows

When the project is running, there are three tabs at the bottom of the window at the bottom of the screen to the left of the Output window—the Autos tab, the Local tab, and the Watch tab. Each of these tabs displays a different window containing specific values of variables when the project is in break mode. Recall from Chapter 4 that a good way to put a project in break mode is to set a breakpoint somewhere in the event procedure of interest or on a specific statement of interest.

The **Autos window,** which is displayed by clicking the Autos Tab, can be used to display the values of all variables in the current statement plus three statements on either side of the current statement. On the other hand, the Locals window, which is displayed by clicking the Locals Tab, can be used to display the values of *all* variables that are *local* to the current event procedure; that is, they are known to it. For example, in the btnCalc event procedure discussed in the previous section, where two values are multiplied rather than being added to compute the intSum variable, we might want to use the Autos window to look at the value of variables the variables in this assignment statement plus three statements on either side of the statement. Or, we might want to use the Locals window to display all variables local to the btnCalc_Click event procedure. Figure 5-16 shows the Autos and Locals windows for the btnCalc_Click event procedure for the third input value. In both cases, a breakpoint was set on the assignment statement in which the intSum value is calculated. Note that, in both cases, the counter variable, intNum, is 3; the input value, intTheValue is 135; and the intSum value is 0. The Locals windows shows more values including the path of the input file.

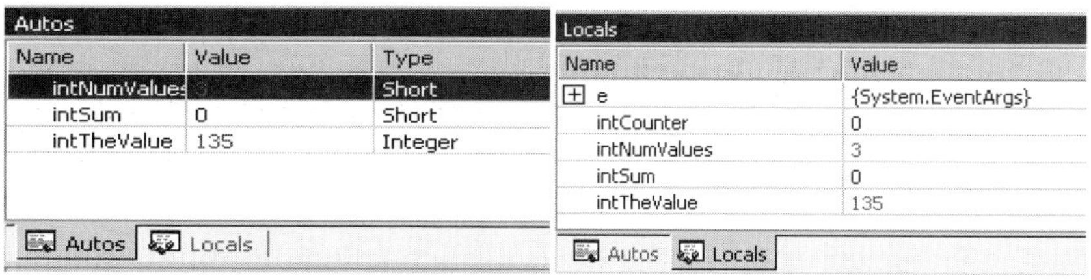

FIGURE 5-16. Autos and Locals windows

Autos		
Name	Value	Type
intNumValues		Short
intSum	0	Short
intTheValue	135	Integer

Locals	
Name	Value
⊞ e	{System.EventArgs}
intCounter	0
intNumValues	3
intSum	0
intTheValue	135

Finally, the Watch window allows us to *watch* the values for a specific variable or expression as the project is executed. The easiest way to watch a variable is to set a breakpoint somewhere in the procedure containing the variable of interest and, when the breakpoint is encountered, position the cursor on a variable and select the Quick Watch menu option on the Debug menu option. This will display a window like the one shown in Figure 5-17 in which the selected variable will automatically appear as it does in the top of the figure. You can also enter some other value by typing it into the input box. Regardless of the variable in the input box, you can select *Add Watch* to add this variable or expression to the list of variables or expressions to be watched. Each time the breakpoint is encountered in the procedure, the value of the Watch variables will be shown in the Watch window as shown at the bottom of Figure 5-17.

By repeatedly clicking the Run icon, we can watch the variables in all three windows—Autos, Locals, and Watch—to see how they change for each repetition of the loop. Since the value of intSum never changes from zero, we know that the problem must be in the statement that calculates this value. The breakpoint can be toggled off by clicking the appropriate icon again.

Breakpoints are also useful for debugging infinite loops—loops that never stop. If you encounter a situation where a project with a loop appears to do *nothing* when you run it, you probably have an infinite loop. When this occurs, you should press the **CTRL+BREAK** key combination to stop the endless loop. You should add a breakpoint and some watches on the variables to determine why the loop is not encountering a termination condition.

FIGURE 5-17.
Adding a Watch on
a variable

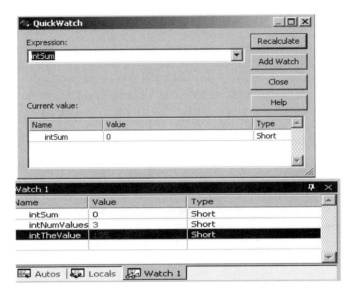

It's Your Turn!

1. Open the **UntilLoop** project and change the line that calculates the sum to be

```
intSum = intSum * intTheValue
```

2. Run the project and note the value that is displayed for the sum of the values. It should be zero. Now, add this statement before the end of the loop:

```
Debug.Writeline(intTheValue, intSum, intNumValues)
```

and run your project again. Your output should look like that shown in Figure 5-15.

3. Set a breakpoint within the loop by positioning the cursor on the last line before the loop instruction. Run your project again and repeatedly click the Run icon to view different values in the Autos and Locals windows as the loop progresses.

4. Stop the project and start it again. When you encounter the breakpoint set in the previous exercise, use the select **Debug | QuickWatch** option to add a watch on the three variables in the btnCalc event procedure (intTheValue, intSum, and intNumValues). Click the Run icon to repeat the loop again.

5. Terminate execution of the project, turn the breakpoint off, and close the Watch and Locals windows. Do *not* save the modified project.

SUMMARY

At the beginning of the chapter, we said you would be able to do a number of things after reading it. Let's review those things here:

1. Understand the importance of the repetition process in programming. Without loops, computer programs would be of little use, since loops are what enable users to repeat an action as many times as desired or needed. All loops have a body that is repeated and a termination condition that causes the loop to stop. Without a correct termination condition, the loop could continue endlessly, resulting in an infinite loop.

2. Describe the various types of loops that can be carried out in VB .NET. There are three types of loops in an OOED language like VB .NET: event-driven loops, determinate loops, and indeterminate loops. Event-driven loops, which are possible only in an OOED language, are repeated by the user repeatedly performing an event such as a mouse click. Determinate loops are loops for which the number of repetitions is known in advance. Indeterminate loops are those for which the number of repetitions is not known in advance.

3. Discuss the statement forms used in VB .NET to handle repetition, and understand the use of pre- and posttest loops. In VB .NET, determinate loops are implemented with the For-Next loop, where the For statement includes a counter variable; the beginning and ending values for the counter; and the Step value, which is the amount by which the counter variable is increased each time through the loop. You can count up or down with a For-Next loop depending on the parameters in the For statement. Indeterminate loops are implemented by the While loop and the Until loop. In both types of loop, the termination condition uses a condition like that used in If-Then-Else decision structures. Both types of loops can be either pretest loops, in which the termination condition occurs *before* the body of the loop, or posttest loops, in which the termination condition occurs *after* the body of the loop.

4. Understand the concepts of variable scope and static variables. Variables can be declared at the procedural level as local variables, as form-level variables that are known to the entire form, or at the project level as global variables. Static variables are those that retain their value between executions of an event procedure.

5. Use the ComboBox control to select from a list of alternatives. Combo boxes, which are a combination of a text box and a list box, were also introduced in this chapter. For-Next loops can also be used to print the contents of a list box or combo box or to write them to a file.

6. Understand the use of files to permanently store data and information. Three types of files in are widespread use for permanently storing data and information: sequential access files, direct access files, and database files. Sequential access files are files from which the data records must be input in the same order that they were placed on the file. Direct access files are files that can be input in any order. Database files are widely used for data storage, but must be accessed with a database management system. Sequential access files replicate the action of entering data from a keyboard, since you enter data from a keyboard one after the other, just like they would be read from a sequential access file. The number of records on a sequential access file is often unknown, but there is an invisible binary marker at the end of the file called the EOF (end-of-file) marker. An Until loop is a good way to input data from a sequential access file when there are an unknown number of records. Files must be opened before data can be input from them or output to them.

7. Describe the creation and use of executable files in VB .NET. Executable (.exe) files are automatically created in VB .NET whenever you choose to compile and run the project. The executable file, which is found in the Bin folder, can then be run on any Windows computer regardless of whether or not it has VB .NET loaded on it.

8. Use debugging tools in VB .NET to find and correct errors. Debugging of loops can be handled by writing values to the Output window. Loops can also be debugged by using the Auto, Locals, and Watch windows. The Auto window shows the value of variables near the current statement, whereas the Locals window shows the value of all variables in the current event procedure. The Watch window is used to show the values of variables being watched. In all cases, setting a breakpoint in the loop is the best way of stopping it to the value of the variables.

NEW VB .NET ELEMENTS

Controls/Objects	Properties	Methods	Events
ComboBox control	ListIndex Name Text Sorted Style	Items.Add() Items.Remove()	Change Click
Output Window		Debug.Writeline	
ListBox control	ListCount List() ListIndex Sorted	Items.Add() Items.Remove() Items.Clear()	

NEW PROGRAMMING STATEMENTS

Statement to define a variable as being Static **Static** variable as type
Statements for For-Next loop **For** variable = start value **to** end value **Step** change value   statements to compose body of loop **Next** variable
Statements for While or Until pretest loop **Do While** (or **Until**) condition   body of loop **Loop**

NEW PROGRAMMING STATEMENTS (CONTINUED)

Statements for Until or While posttest loop **Do**   body of loop **Loop Until** (or **While**) condition
Statement to open a sequential access file for Input **FileOpen(**n, "filename", **OpenMode.Input)**
Statement to close a sequential access file **FileClose(**n**)**
Statement to input a list of values from a sequential access file **Do Until EOF(**n**)**   **Input(**n, variable**)** **Loop**
Statement to open a sequential access file for Output **FileOpen(**n, "filename", **OpenMode.Output)**
Statement to output a known number of list items to a file **For intCounter = 0 to intNumItems – 1**   **WriteLine(**n, variable**)** **Loop**

KEY TERMS

break mode	executable file	posttest loop
breakpoint	filename	pretest loop
data-driven loop	form-level variable	procedural-level variable
data file	general object	record
database file	indeterminate loop	sequential access file
determinate loop	infinite loop	static variable
direct access file	initialize	Until loop
endless loop	local variable	variable scope
EOF Marker	nested loop	While loop
event-driven loop		

EXERCISES

1. Write VB .NET program segments to

   a. Print the first 50 positive numbers.

   b. Print the value of intX and decrease intX by 0.5 as long as intX is positive.

   c. Obtain a list of names using a loop and input box until the Cancel button is clicked.

   d. Print the square roots of the first 25 positive integers.

   e. Calculate and display the squares of consecutive positive integers until the difference between a square and the preceding one is greater than 50.

2. Any looping structure may be written in several ways. For each of the following, convert the given looping structure into the requested looping structure that will achieve the same results. Additional variables and selection statements may be required.

a. Convert the following to use a Do While loop.

```
Private Sub btnGo_Click()
   Dim intLoop As Integer
   Dim intResult As Integer
   intResult = 0
   For intLoop = 10 To 0 Step -1
      intResult = intResult + intLoop
   Next intLoop
   txtResult.Text = intResult
End Sub
```

b. Convert the following to use a For-Next loop.

```
Private Sub btnGo_Click()
   Dim intLoop As Integer
   Dim intResult As Integer
   intResult = 0
   intLoop = 0
   Do Until intLoop = 10
      intResult = intResult + intLoop
      intLoop = intLoop + 2
   Loop
   txtResult.Text = intResult
End Sub
```

c. Convert the following to use a For-Next loop. The variable intMax will be a nonnegative number that is entered into a text box by the user. Your new code should work the same as the original no matter what nonnegative value has been entered.

```
Private Sub btnGo_Click()
   Dim intLoop As Integer, intMax As Integer
   Dim intResult As Integer
   intResult = 0
   intLoop = 0
   intMax = txtMax.text
   Do
      intResult = intResult + intLoop
      intLoop = intLoop + 1
   Loop Until intLoop = intMax
   txtResult.Text = intResult
End Sub
```

3. Write VB .NET code segments for each of the following:

a. A sequential data file called dogs.txt contains a listing of dogs and their stats. Each line contains the dog's name, weight, and age, respectively. Code is needed to read this file as input to a VB .NET program.

b. Code is needed to write a listing of television programs to a sequential data file called TV.txt. On each line of the file a program's name, day of week, time of day, and length in minutes should be written.

c. Code is needed that will allow a new program to be added to the file of part b. Each new program should be added to the end of the file without losing the current data in the file.

4. For each of the following, explain what is wrong with the code. What error messages would you see, if any? What can you do to fix it?

a. This code should add the numbers from 1 to 10.

```
Private Sub btnGo_Click()
   Dim intLoop As Integer
   intLoop = 0
   txtResult.Text = 0
   Do
     txtResult.Text = txtResult.Text + intLoop
   Loop Until intLoop = 10
End Sub
```

b. This code should find the product of the numbers from 1 to 10.

```
Private Sub btnGo_Click()
   Dim intLoop As Integer
   Dim intResult As Integer
   intResult = 1
   For intLoop = 1 To 10
      intResult = intResult * intLoop
   Next intLoop
   txtResult.Text = intResult
End Sub
```

c. The following code should write the contents of a list box to a file called EmpData.dat on the a: drive when the Save button is clicked. Then, when the Load button is clicked, the list box should be loaded from the file. Each line of the list box currently holds information about an employee, including name, age, gender, and salary. For example, the first line might be Joe Smith 30 m 50000.

```
Private Sub btnSave_Click()
   Dim intLoop As Integer
   Open "a:\Empdata.dat" For Output As #1
   For intLoop = 0 To lstDisplay.ListCount
     Write #1, lstDisplay.List(intLoop)
   Next intLoop
   Close #1
End Sub
Private Sub btnLoad_Click()
  Dim intLoop As Integer, strName As String
  Dim intAge As Integer, strgender As String
  Dim intsalary As Integer
  lstDisplay.Items.Clear()
  Open "a:\Empdata.dat" For Input As #1
  Do While Not EOF(1)
    Input #1, strName, intAge, strgender, intsalary
    lstDisplay.Items.Add() strName & " " & intAge & " " & _
    strgender & " " & intsalary
  Loop
  Close #1
End Sub
```

5. Use the VB .NET Help facility to answer the following questions.

a. What VB .NET statement may be used to exit a Do loop prematurely?

b. What is the difference between the debug commands Step Into and Step Over?

c. How can you write a For-Next loop that will print all available screen fonts?

d. What built-in VB .NET function will return an integer that represents the next file number available for use by the Open statement?

PROJECTS

1. Create a folder named **Homework** in the *Chapter5* folder. In this *Homework* folder, create a project named **Ex5-1.** Give the form the same name and make it the StartUp object. The project should enable an instructor to input a student's name and quiz scores. The name should be posted to a list box before any quiz scores are input. There should be a button that will input the quiz scores and sum, count, and post the quiz scores to a list box as they are entered. Based on these quiz scores, a second button should compute the student's quiz average and assign a letter grade using the typical 90-80-70-60 cutoff values. The average grade and quiz score should also be posted to the list box. Be careful—if a student takes zero quizzes, he or she automatically receives a letter grade of F. You should be able to print the information in the list box and clear all information in preparation for the next student. Test your project with the student names and quiz scores in Table 5-2.

TABLE 5-2: Student data

Name Quizzes>>	1	2	3	4	5	6	7	8
Ashley Patrick	73	82	69	77	81	73		
Ben Oakes	88	83	92	79	85			
Nancy Wilson	88	91	89	93	87	90	89	93

2. Copy the files from the *Chapter4\Homework\Ex4-2* folder (or the *Ex4-7* folder if you completed it) into a new folder named **Ex5-2** in the *Chapter5\Homework* folder. Rename the files in the new folder to be **Ex5-2.vb, Ex5-2.vbproj,** and **Ex5-2.sln.** Be sure to make **Ex5-2.vb** your startup object. Modify the project to count the customers and to keep a running total of the sales for each day. An existing button should enable the user to input the name and use the price and square footage to compute the amount of the sale. Customer names and the amount of the sale should be posted to a list box. The total sales for the day and the number of customers served should also be added to the list box by clicking a new button. It should also be possible to print the list box and to clear all entries in preparation for the next business day. Test your project with the data in Table 5-3.

TABLE 5-3: Customer data

Name	Square Footage	Treatment
John Jarret	3,000	Pre-emergence
Beth Anderson	5,500	Broadleaf weeds
Kelly Smith	6,500	Regular Fertilizer

TABLE 5-3: Customer data (Continued)

Name	Square Footage	Treatment
Sally Jones	3,500	Regular Fertilizer
Andy Silverman	5,000	Premium Fertilizer

3. Copy the files from the *Chapter4\Homework\Ex4-3* folder into a new folder named **Ex5-3** in the *Chapter5\Homework* folder. Rename the files in the new folder to be **Ex5-3.vb, Ex5-3.vbproj,** and **Ex5-3.sln.** Be sure to make **Ex5-3.vb** your startup object. Modify the project to count the number of automobiles tested and to keep a running sum of the average gas mileage computed for each vehicle. An existing button should enable the user to input the type of automobile, the miles driven, and the gallons of gas used. It should then compute and display the miles per gallon. Automobile types and their gas mileage should be posted to a list box. Another button should compute the average miles per gallon for *all* vehicles tested, and this value should also be posted to the list box along with the total number of vehicles tested. It should be possible to print the contents of the list box and to clear all entries. Test your project with the data in Table 5-4. (Hint: Be careful of zero cars!)

TABLE 5-4: Automobile data

Type of Automobile	Miles Driven	Gallons of Gas Used
Atlissan	270	10.5
Lexiadillac	400	20.5
Meruick	425	22.3
Toyonda	300	9.8
Chrysillis	350	20.0

4. Copy the files from the *Chapter5\Homework\Ex5-1* folder into a new folder named **Ex5-4** in the same *Chapter5\Homework* folder. Rename the files in the new folder to be **Ex5-4.vb, Ex5-4.vbproj,** and **Ex5-4.sln.** Be sure to make **Ex5-4.vb** your startup object. Modify the project to allow the instructor to input the number of quizzes taken by a student from a scroll bar and then input the individual quiz scores using a For-Next loop and InputBox. Your output for the project should be the same as that for Exercise 1. Use the data given in Table 5-2 to test this project. Warning: Watch out for zero quizzes being entered!

5. Copy the files from the *Chapter5\Homework\Ex5-2* folder into a new folder named **Ex5-5** in the same *Chapter5\Homework* folder. Rename the files in the new folder to be **Ex5-5.vb, Ex5-5.vbproj,** and **Ex5-5.sln.** Be sure to make **Ex5-5.vb** your startup object. Modify the project you created for Exercise 2 in this chapter to allow the user to input the number of customers from a scroll bar and then input the name, treatment type, and square footage for each customer using a For-Next loop and input boxes. Your output for the

project should be the same as that for Exercise 2. Use the data given in Table 5-3 to test this project.

6. Copy the files from the *Chapter5\Homework\Ex5-3* folder into a new folder named **Ex5-6** in the same *Chapter5\Homework* folder. Rename the files in the new folder to be **Ex5-6.vb, Ex5-6.vbproj,** and **Ex5-6.sln.** Be sure to make **Ex5-6.vb** your startup object. Modify the project you created for Exercise 3 in this chapter to allow the user to input the number of automobiles tested from a scroll bar and then input the automobile type, miles driven, and gallons of gas used for each automobile type using a For-Next loop and input boxes. Your output for the project should be the same as that for Exercise 3. Use the data given in Table 5-4 to test this project. Also, use the executable file in the Bin folder to run the project.

7. Copy the files from the *Chapter5\Homework\Ex5-1* folder into a new folder named **Ex5-7** in the same *Chapter5\Homework* folder. Rename the files in the new folder to be **Ex5-7.vb, Ex5-7.vbproj,** and **Ex5-7.sln.** Be sure to make **Ex5-7.vb** your startup object. Modify the project you created for Exercise 1 in this chapter to allow the instructor to input the quiz scores for the first student (Ashley Patrick) from a sequential access file. Your output for the project should be the same as that for Exercise 1. Use the data given in the first row of Table 5-2 to create this file and give it name of *Ashley_Patrick.txt* (where an underscore is used to connect the first and last names) and save it to the root folder of your data disk. Test your project to ensure you get the same results as you did for Ashley in Exercise 1. Also, use the executable file in the Bin folder to run the project.

8. Copy the files from the *Chapter5\Homework\Ex5-7* folder into a new folder named **Ex5-8** in the same *Chapter5\Homework* folder. Rename the files in the new folder to be **Ex5-8.vb, Ex5-8.vbproj,** and **Ex5-8.sln.** Be sure to make **Ex5-8.vb** your startup object. Modify the project to allow the instructor to input the quiz scores for the students from a series of sequential access files; that is, there is a separate sequential file for each student with his or her name as the name of the file, as was done in Exercise 7. Your output for the project should be the same as that for Exercise 1. Use the data given in Table 5-2 to create the remaining files needed to test this project on your data disk. Hint: You will need to input the filename for each student's data file before you open it and input data from it. Also, use the executable file in the Bin folder to run the project.

9. Copy the files from the *Chapter5\Homework\Ex5-2* folder into a new folder named **Ex5-9** in the same *Chapter5\Homework* folder. Rename the files in the new folder to be **Ex5-9.vb, Ex5-9.vbproj,** and **Ex5-9.sln.** Be sure to make **Ex5-9.vb** your startup object. Modify the project to input a list of customers to a combo box from a file called *customer.txt* in the Bin folder. Then compare a customer's name to the names in the combo box to determine if this is a new customer. If the customer is new, alert the user and add the customer's name to the combo box and the customer-name text box. Add statements to the btnExit event procedure as needed to save the contents of the combo box to the file for use the next day. Your output for the project should

be the same as that for Exercise 2. Use the data given in Table 5-3 to create the data file, and then test this project with those same names and data. Also test it with a name of **Lance Motowick** and **3,600** square feet of **Premium Fertilizer.** Also, use the executable file in the Bin folder to run the project.

10. Create a VB. NET project to automatically input an unknown number of golfer names and golf scores from a file called *golfer.txt* in the Bin folder. Give the project a name of **Ex5-10** in *Chapter5\Homework* folder. Create this file using the data shown in Table 5-5. Hint: To input a name and a value from a file, the Input statement should be of the form:

```
FileInput(n, variable1, OpenMode.Input)
FileInput(n, variable2, OpenMode.Input)
```

and the data should be entered in the file with a name and the score on the same line, separated by a comma.

These names and scores should be loaded into a list box, and the number of golfers and average of all scores should be computed and displayed in text boxes with appropriate labels. There should also be a second list box of all golfers with a score less than 90. You should also add an Exit button. Hint: To see how to add a name and score to a list box, review how the DVD name and price were added to a list box.

TABLE 5-5: Golfer data

Golfer	Score
Fred Smith	93
Larry Vinings	101
Hugh Smith	88
Al Nimmi	79
Archie Card	83
Ben Brown	98

11. Create a project that will allow the user to select a personal computer from among the five listed in Table 5-6. Give the project a name of **Ex5-11** in the *Chapter5\Homework* folder.

TABLE 5-6: Computer data

Type of PC	Price
Basic	$595
Standard	$795
Standard Plus	$995
Special	$1,195
Special Plus	$1,395

These computer types should be input into a list box from which the user can select the one that is being sold. Depending on which computer type is selected, the project should display the product's name in one text box and the price in a second text box. The user should be able to select the number of items sold using a scroll bar (minimum = 1 and maximum = 10). Based on the price and number sold, the application should display the sale amount in a text box and add the computer type and number sold to a "Computers Sold" list box. This project should be able to handle multiple customers, keep a running total of sales, and count the number of each type computer sold. At the end of the day, a summary of number of each type sold and total sales volume should be added to the list box. It should be possible to print the contents of the list box and exit the project with buttons.

12. The net present value (NPV) of a project may be calculated using the formula

$$\text{NPV} = -I_0 + F_1/(1 + k) + F_2/(1 + k)^2 + \cdots + F_n/(1 + k)^n + S/(1 + k)^n$$

where I_0 is the initial investment, k is the minimum required rate of return, n is the lifetime of the project, F_i is the cash flow in period i, and S is the salvage value for the project after period n. Create a VB .NET project that will calculate and display the NPV for any project. Give your project a name of **Ex5-12** in the *Chapter5\Homework* folder on your data disk. This means that your code must accommodate any number of periods in a project's lifetime. A project with an initial investment of $5,000, a minimum rate of return of 6%, a seven-year lifetime with the cash flow for each year equal to $1,000, and no salvage value, will have an NPV of $582.30.

13. Depreciation of assets is a real-world accounting problem that requires computer assistance to do it in the volume that large corporations require. Depreciation is the allocation of the cost of an asset over a period of time for accounting and tax purposes. There are several methods available for making these allocations. Each method takes the original value of the asset (*depreciation basis*), the number of years over which the asset is to be used (*useful life*), and a calculation rule to determine the amount to depreciate each year. The *book value* is the current value of the asset after depreciation has been subtracted each year. For example, if the asset cost $10,000 and the depreciation in the first year is $2,000, then the book value after the first year is $8,000 (equal to $10,000 minus $2,000). The book value for a given year is calculated by simply subtracting the depreciation from the previous year's book value. The original book value is equal to the depreciation basis:

Book Value = Book Value – Depreciation

Three classic methods of depreciation are

Straight-Line depreciation: Straight-line depreciation is the simplest method; it uses the basis of an asset and the useful life of the asset to assign equal depreciation to each period, or

Depreciation = Depreciation Basis / Useful Life

Sum-of-the-years'-digits: The sum-of-the-years'-digits method computes a different fractional depreciation for each year. The denominator of each fraction is the sum of the digits from 1 to N, where N is the useful life of the asset. The denominator is the same each year. The numerator is $N - Y + 1$, where Y is the period number. The formula for this is

Depreciation = Depreciation Basis × (Useful Life – Year + 1) / Sum of digits in Useful Life

Double declining balance: The double declining balance uses a fixed percentage of the prior year's book value to calculate depreciation. The percentage rate is $2/N$, where N is the useful life of the asset. The formula may be written:

Depreciation = Book Value for previous year × 2 / Useful Life Loan Amortization

Create a VB .NET project that will allow a user to select a depreciation method from a list box, and enter the depreciation basis, useful life, and lifetime of the asset in years into text boxes. Give your project a name of **Ex5-13** in the *Chapter5\Homework* folder. When a button is clicked, the year, amount depreciated, and book value will be displayed in a list box for each year of the asset's life. The results for a $10,000 asset depreciated over eight years for each method are shown in Table 5-7.

TABLE 5-7: Depreciation data

Straight-Line			Sum of Years' Digits			Double Declining Balance		
Yr.	Dep.	B.V.	Yr.	Dep.	B.V.	Yr.	Dep.	B.V.
1	$1250	$8750	1	$2222.22	$7777.78	1	$2500	$7500
2	$1250	$7500	2	$1944.44	$5833.34	2	$1875	$5625
3	$1250	$6250	3	$1666.67	$4166.67	3	$1406.25	$4218.75
4	$1250	$5000	4	$1388.89	$2777.78	4	$1054.69	$3164.06
5	$1250	$3750	5	$1111.11	$1666.67	5	$791.02	$2373.05
6	$1250	$2500	6	$833.33	$833.34	6	$593.26	$1779.78
7	$1250	$1250	7	$555.56	$277.78	7	$444.95	$1334.83
8	$1250	$0	8	$277.78	$0.0	8	$333.71	$1001.12

14. If a loan with a beginning balance of X dollars, which carries a monthly interest rate of k percent, is to be paid off in n months, the monthly payment M may be calculated using

$$M = X \times k \times (1 + k)^n / ((1 + k)^n - 1))$$

During this time period, some of each monthly payment is used to repay that month's accrued interest, and the rest is used to reduce the balance owed. The amount of accrued interest I for any month is

I = Current Balance × k

Write a VB .NET program to display an amortization table that displays the payment number, the amount of the monthly payment, the interest for that month, the amount of the payment applied to the principle, and the new balance. Give your project a name of **Ex5-14** in the *Chapter5\Homework* folder. Use your program to produce an amortization table for a $120,000 loan to be repaid in 20 years at 7% APR. Note: Assume 12 months per year.

15. If you save $100 per year at 5% interest compounded yearly, how much money will you have in 5 years? What about 10 years? What if you save at 6% interest instead? It is often beneficial to prepare a table that can be used to help compare possible scenarios such as these. An example of such a table for equal investments of $100 at the beginning of each year is shown in Table 5-8. The balance at the end of any year using an interest rate k may be calculated using

End of Year Balance = $(1 + k) \times$ Beginning of Year Balance

For a 5-year term, one could start with a balance of $100, calculate the end-of-year balance, add $100 for the next year's investment, then use this new balance as the beginning of year balance for year 2. This process may then be repeated until the balance at the end of year 5 is obtained. (The values in the table reflect the balance before the next year's investment is made.)

Write a VB .NET program that will create a table like that in Table 5-8 for any amount of yearly investment provided by the user. What would be the balance after investing $500 for 20 years at 7% interest? Save your project as **Ex5-15** in the Chapter5\Homework folder.

TABLE 5-8: Compound interest table

Yearly investment = $100							
	5 Years	10 Years	15 Years	20 Years	25 Years	30 Years	35 Years
5%	$581	$1,322	$2,268	$3,474	$5,015	$6,981	$9,491
6%	$597	$1,396	$2,466	$3,897	$5,813	$8,377	$11,808
7%	$614	$1,477	$2,687	$4,385	$6,766	$10,105	$14,787
8%	$634	$1,565	$2,933	$4,944	$7,898	$12,239	$18,616
9%	$653	$1,657	$3,201	$5,578	$9,234	$14,860	$23,516
10%	$671	$1,752	$3,494	$6,297	$10,814	$18,086	$29,799

6 WORKING WITH ARRAYS IN VB .NET

LEARNING OBJECTIVES

After reading this chapter, you will be able to

1. Understand the use of list and table arrays in VB .NET projects and the difference between arrays and combo boxes, list boxes, and similar controls.

2. Declare the maximum index value for a list array and understand the errors that occur when declared upper limits on index values are exceeded.

3. Input data into an array from a file using loops and the StreamReader object and redimension it to match the number of elements input.

4. Work with array data to find the sum and average of array values, the largest or smallest value in an array, match values in one array to those in another, and find a particular value in an array.

5. Add forms to a project and display or hide them.

6. Declare, input, process, and output two-dimensional arrays.

7. Use Step operations to step though an array operation to find and correct an error.

WORKING WITH LISTS AS ARRAYS

In Chapters 4 and 5 we discussed the use of list and combo boxes for displaying and working with lists of names and other types of information. The capability to display lists of data and information is one of VB .NET's strengths, because so much of the information you work with in business applications—client names, prices, part numbers, and so on—is in the form of lists. Working with lists can include arranging them in a desired order, finding a particular item in the list, and working with values on two or more lists. VB .NET's abilities extend to yet another area: tables of information. Although working with tables may be new to you, it involves many of the same operations as working with lists. In this chapter we will discuss working with both lists and tables.

Introduction to Arrays

Although it is possible in VB .NET to display and work with lists using controls like combo and list boxes, there comes a time when there are simply too many items to depend on visual tools. Instead, you need to store the data or information in memory as a list or table or, as it is termed, an **array**. Arrays provide a way of working with long lists in memory in the same way as working with shorter lists using the VB .NET ListBox and ComboBox controls. We can input items into the list, initialize them to some value, process them to find their sum and average, find the largest or smallest item in a list, look up an item in a list, or rearrange a list in alphabetical or numerical order.

One difference between lists stored as arrays and lists stored as controls is that list and combo boxes respond to control properties, such as *Sorted*, but arrays do not respond to any control properties. Another difference is that whereas VB .NET controls such as combo boxes and list boxes store only text in the form of character strings, arrays can be declared to hold any type of data you wish. However, it is important to note that an array can store *only* one type of data. For example, an array can store String data or Decimal data, but not both. Finally, there is no array operation that corresponds to the Items.Count property of the list and combo boxes, so the number of elements in the array must be input or calculated whenever the array is to be processed. There is no way to look this value up as you can with a list and combo boxes.

Arrays hold multiple values or strings the same way combo and list boxes do—by giving each value or string a number (or numbers) that defines its position in the list or table. In a combo box or list box, the position of an item is determined by the Items() property, but in an array the position is determined by the index or **subscript** of the array element. As an example of this, consider a list box called lstPrices and an array called decPrices, as shown in Figure 6-1.

FIGURE 6-1.
Comparing arrays and list boxes

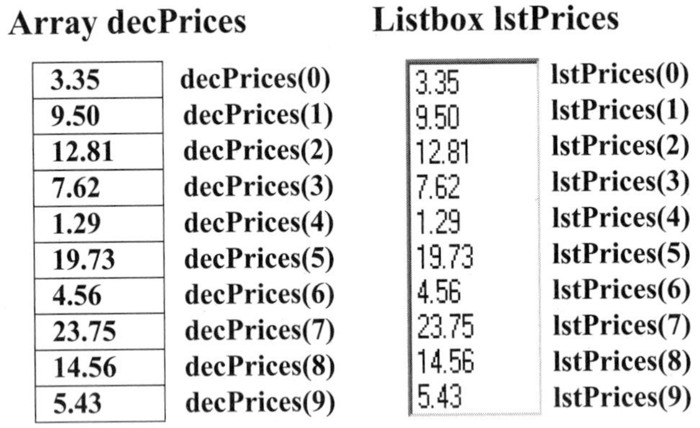

Array decPrices

3.35	decPrices(0)
9.50	decPrices(1)
12.81	decPrices(2)
7.62	decPrices(3)
1.29	decPrices(4)
19.73	decPrices(5)
4.56	decPrices(6)
23.75	decPrices(7)
14.56	decPrices(8)
5.43	decPrices(9)

Listbox lstPrices

3.35	lstPrices(0)
9.50	lstPrices(1)
12.81	lstPrices(2)
7.62	lstPrices(3)
1.29	lstPrices(4)
19.73	lstPrices(5)
4.56	lstPrices(6)
23.75	lstPrices(7)
14.56	lstPrices(8)
5.43	lstPrices(9)

In this example, the list box holds a series of character strings, but the decPrices array holds a series of Decimal type values. The strings in the list box are designated as lstPrices.Items(0), lstPrices.Items(1), lstPrices.Items(2), and so on, whereas the Decimal type array values are designated as decPrices(0), decPrices(1), decPrices(2) and so on, where the numbers in parentheses after the variable names are the index values. That is, the index for the first decPrices value is 0, the second is 1, and so on. When you want to refer to an element of an array, you *must* always give the index value for that element.

In summary, each item in an array is identified by two things:

1. The name of the array
2. The position of the item in the array (its index), which must be an Integer constant, variable, or expression.

Declaring an Array

Before using an array, you must *declare* any array you use so that VB .NET knows that it is a list of variables and not a single-value variable. While declaring single-valued variables is a good practice to use in programming, you *must* declare an array for it to be used in the project. If an array is declared in an event procedure, then only that procedure will know about the array, and, unless the array is declared with the *Static* keyword, its values will be reset to zero each time the event procedure is terminated. If the array is declared at the form level, then all procedures on that form will be aware of the array and will be able to use it in computations. The array values will not be reset to zero *unless* you leave that form. Finally, as will be discussed in the next chapter, an array can be declared globally so that all forms and other code elements can use it.

> **TIP:** VB .NET will generate a "Subscript out of Range" error if you try to refer to an array element that has not been declared.

Arrays are declared the same way as any other type of variable except that you declare the *maximum* number of elements the array will contain. The general form of a fixed-size array declaration statement for a list array is

Dim *ArrayName(max index value)* **as** *variable type*

This declaration statement defines the upper limit on the index for the array, with the lower limit being set to zero by default. Attempting to go outside of these limits will result in an error.

For example, if the decPrices array discussed earlier has an upper limit on the index of 99, then the declaration would be

```
Dim decPrices(99) as Decimal
```

Note that this allows a total of 100 prices to be stored, with the index starting at zero.

When you declare the upper limit on the index value, you are putting an absolute restriction on the value of the index. If you try to use an index above the declared upper limit, an error message will be displayed indicating you have attempted to reference an index value higher than the declared upper limit. If this occurs, you have the option of attempting to continue execution or viewing the code by clicking on *Break*. If you select Break, you can then view the code and try to determine the cause of the problem, change it, and recompile the code to run it.

It is possible to change the upper limit on the subscript of an array with the ReDim statement. Reducing the size of an array to match the actual number of elements needed is a good way to conserve memory within the computer. The **ReDim statement** is used to change the upper limit on the array size to the actual maximum subscript that will be used. For the decPrices example, if the maximum required number of elements is determined to be only 50, the ReDim statement would be

```
ReDim decPrices(49)
```

If data has already been stored in a dynamic array that is to be redimensioned, it can be retained by using the **ReDim Preserve statement.** For example, if data has been stored in the decPrices array that is being redimensioned, it can be saved with the following statement:

```
ReDim Preserve decPrices(49)
```

If the *Preserve* keyword is not included, the ReDim statement zeros out the entire array.

The ReDim Preserve combination can be used to declare a **dynamic array** with no upper limit on the array size. This is useful if you have no idea how large it may become. For example, if we initially dynamically declared the array decPrices() with no upper limit

```
Dim decPrices() as Decimal
```

then, we could use the ReDim Preserve statement to increase it each time a new element is added to the array. This will be discussed more as we demonstrate array input in the next section.

Mini-summary 6-1: Using arrays

1. Like list and combo boxes, arrays store lists of data; however, arrays store the data in memory and are unseen. Each element in an array is identified by its index value which is an integer variable or constant.

2. All arrays can declared as to the maximum number of elements they will contain or they can be declared dynamically with no initial upper limit.

3. The size of an array can be changed as needed using the ReDim statement. Including the Preserve keyword with the ReDim statement retains any existing data in the array and allows the array to grow as necessary.

It's Your Turn!

1. List the similarities and differences between a list box and a one-dimensional array.

2. By what two things is every array element defined?

3. How many array elements are in each array declared by the following dimension statements?

    a. Dim intNum(10) As Integer
    b. Dim intCount() as Long
    c. Dim decSalary(100) As Decimal
    d. Dim sngTemp(120) As Integer

4. Write statements for the following declarations:

    a. A Decimal type array named *decDollars* that will hold no more than 51 elements
    b. An Integer type array named *intPoints* that will hold no more than 101 elements
    c. A String type array named *strTeams* for which the upper limit is unknown

5. Write the statements to declare the following arrays:
   a. A list of names with a maximum index of 50
   b. A list of prices with a maximum index of 100
   c. A list of the number of quizzes taken by students where there will be an unknown number of students in the class

6. Change the maximum number of elements for each of the arrays in Exercise 3 to have double the number of the original declaration.

7. Change the maximum number of elements for each the arrays in Exercise 3 to have triple the number of the original declaration while retaining any data already saved in the array.

ARRAY INPUT, DISPLAY, AND INITIALIZATION

Once the array is declared, you either input or create the items in the array just as you would with a combo or list box. Even if you do not see the values in an array, they are there and can be displayed using a list or combo box. Finally, an important operation that is frequently required is *initializing* all elements of an array to some value prior to using them in calculations.

Inputting Values to an Array

Once you have declared an array, values can either be input or assigned to it. In this section, we will discuss inputting values to an array; in the next section, we will consider assigning values to an array. An important rule about input to an array is that inputting data to an array must always be done one element at a time. It is not possible to input an entire array in one operation.

Inputting a value into a single element of an array is just like inputting a value to a single-value variable, except that you *must* include the index for the array element. For example, to use an input box to input a value to decPrices(3), which was declared earlier as an array of the Decimal data type, the statement is

```
decPrices(3) = Cdec(InputBox("Please input a price"))
```

Although you can input data into a single element of the array, most arrays are sufficiently large that keyboard input becomes very tedious. For that reason, loops are usually used to input the entire array, one element at a time. If the number of elements to be input is known, then a For-Next loop can be used. However, this is not a good way to input array elements if the number of elements may change or is unknown. A more realistic situation is one in which an unknown number of array values are input from a sequential access file, as was done in Chapter 5. For these reasons, we will concentrate on file input for an unknown number of elements using an Until loop.

An Until loop for inputting data into an array works very much like the loop in Chapter 5 that input and counted an unknown number of values from a file, except that the file values will be input into an array in memory instead of being added to a list box. The index for the array will correspond to the value of the counting variable for each value that is input, and, since we may no idea how big the array will be, we declare it with no upper limit and revise the size of the array prior to each input. The general form of the Do Until input loop for array input from a file is

> **Dim** *ArrayName( ) as data type, intCounter as Integer*
> *intCounter = 0*
> **Do Until EOF(*n*)**
>   **ReDim Preserve** *ArrayName(intCounter)*
>   **Input** *n, ArrayName(intCounter)*
>   *intCounter = intCounter + 1*
> **Loop**

Note in this general form that the data values are input directly from the file into the array element defined by *ArrayName(intCounter),* where the variable intCounter has been defined as an Integer variable. There is no need to input the data value to a variable and then add this variable to a combo box or list box.

To demonstrate this type of array input, assume that a list of prices is to be stored in an array called decPrices, as shown earlier in Figure 6-1, and that a form named *frmArrayInput* similar to that used to input and sum values in Chapter 5 will be used to input and display the array of decPrices, as shown in Figure 6-2.

FIGURE 6-2. Form for working with decPrices array

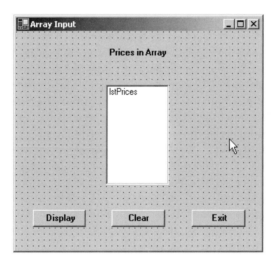

This form has a list box for displaying the array *after* it is completely input using the frmArrayInput_Load event. There are also buttons to display prices, clear prices, and exit the project. The *Display* button transfers the array values into the list box, and the *Clear* button clears the list box using *lstPrices.Items.Clear.* Finally, the *Exit* button exits the project. The decPrices array and the intNumPrices variable are declared at the form level, since they must be known to more than one event procedure (frmArrayInput_Load and btnDisplay_Click).

The decPrices array is declared to be a Decimal data type with no maximum number index value because we don't know how many prices will be stored in the array. The declarations at the *form* level are shown below:

```
Dim intNumPrices As Integer, decPrices() As Decimal
```

In the frmArrayInput_Load event procedure, each item from the sequential access file are assigned to the decPrices array with an index of intNumPrices. The variable intNumPrices is then incremented. Because its initial value is zero from the declaration at the form level, intNumPrices is incremented *after* each price from the file is assigned to an element of the array. The code for the Form_Load procedure is shown in VB Code Box 6-1.

| **VB Code Box 6-1.** frmArrayInput_ Load event procedure to input array elements from a file | ```
Private Sub frmArrayInput_Load(ByVal sender As Object, _
ByVal e As EventArgs) Handles MyBase.Load
   Dim strMyPath As String
   IntNumPrices = 0
   strMyPath = CurDir()
   FileOpen(5, strMyPath + "\Prices.txt", OpenMode.Input)
   Do Until EOF(5)
      ReDim Preserve decPrices(intNumPrices)
      Input(5, decPrices(intNumPrices))
      IntNumPrices = intNumPrices + 1
   Loop
   FileClose(5)
End Sub
``` |
|---|---|

Displaying an Array

Once an array is input and stored in memory, it can then be displayed in a list box or other control using a For-Next loop. For example, in the btnDisplay_Click event procedure, a For-Next loop is used to display the contents of the decPrices array by adding them to a list box. Note that the For-Next loop starts at zero and runs to *intNumPrices – 1* and not intNum-Prices. This is true because intNumPrices counts the absolute number of elements in the array, but the array index starts at zero. This makes intNumPrices one more than the index value of the last array element. In fact, this will be true in general for all For-Next loops that involve the intNum-Prices value. Finally, the *Clear* button clears the list box and the *Exit* button exits the project as before. The remainder of the code for the project to display the contents of the array in a list box, clear the list box, and exit the project are shown in VB Code Box 6-2.

| **VB Code Box 6-2.** Code to display array contents, clear list box, and exit project | ```
Private Sub btnDisplay_Click(ByVal sender As Object, _
ByVal e As EventArgs) Handles btnDisplay.Click
   Dim intCounter As Integer
   For intCounter = 0 To IntNumPrices - 1
      lstPrices.Items.Add(Format(decPrices(intCounter), _
      "currency"))
   Next
End Sub
Private Sub btnClear_Click(ByVal sender As Object, _
ByVal e As EventArgs) Handles btnClear.Click
   lstPrices.Items.Clear()
End Sub
Private Sub btnExit_Click(ByVal sender As Object, _
ByVal e As System.EventArgs) Handles btnExit.Click
   End
End Sub
``` |
|---|---|

If you create a file named *Prices.txt* containing the prices shown earlier in Figure 6-1 and save it to the Bin folder of the project, you can use this as input for the project. When you run the project, it appears nothing has happened (unless you see an error message), but clicking on the *Display* button results in the contents of the array being displayed in the lstPrice list box as shown in Figure 6-3. Note that clearing the list box *does not* clear the array as evidenced by the fact that you can display again by clicking the *Display* button.

FIGURE 6-3. Result of displaying array of prices

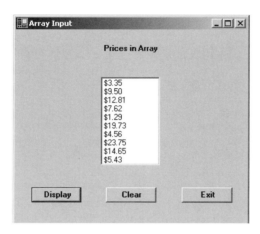

Initializing Array Elements

Instead of inputting an array, it can be created using a For-Next loop to refer to each value of the array. Although all values of an array are automatically set to zero when it is declared, it may be necessary to *initialize* all values to some other value. For example, if a list array of Single values called sngScores has a declared upper limit of 100, then all values in this array can be set to some value less than zero, say, –1.0. The statements would be

```
For intCounter = 0 to 100
    sngScores(intCounter) = -1.0
Next
```

Using the For-Next and For-Each Loops

As you have probably already noticed, processing arrays often requires the use of a For-Next loop. In fact, working with arrays is a very important use for For-Next loops. The Integer counter variable in a For-Next loop matches up very well with the Integer index values of the array elements. If you want to go through the elements of a list array, then you need only use a For-Next loop with starting and ending values that match the declared lower and upper limits of the array index values. If the actual number of array elements is less than the declared number (a common occurrence), the index value of the last used array value can be used in the For-Next loop instead of the declared upper limit. For example, even though the Scores array presented earlier had all of its elements initialized to –1, if the last index of an element that actually is used is only 25, then the For-Next loop to process the array would be

```
For intCounter = 0 to 25
```

For-Next loops are so important for processing arrays that VB .NET has included a special version of the For-Next loop just for working with arrays: the **For-Each Loop.** In this type of loop, it is not necessary to know the maximum number of elements in the loop, since each element will be processed in order. The form of the For-Each Loop is shown below:

For Each *variable* in *ArrayName*
    array processing using variable
Next

where the *variable* in the For-Each statement is of the same data type as the array identified by *ArrayName*.

For example, the sngScores array discussed earlier can be declared to be equal to minus 1.0 using a For-Each loop as shown below:

```
Dim sngValue as Single
For Each sngValue in sngScores
    sngValue = -1.0
Next
```

Note the variable to be of the same type as the array (Single) is used to carry out all of the processing and there is no need to refer to the array subscript to identify each value in the array. The variable in the For-Each loop, sngValue in this case, sequentially takes the place of each element of the array in the processing or initialization. This type of loop continues to work even when the size of the array is changed.

The primary shortcoming of the For-Each loop is that it processes *every* element in the array up to the declared maximum number of elements. This can cause problems when there are empty elements in the array that are processed by the For-Each loop. However, if the array is redimensioned using the ReDim statement to the actual number of elements in the array as you enter the data, this is not an issue. Or, if you have declared the array to be of a certain size, you can change that size with the ReDim Preserve statement at the end the event procedure. For example, had we declared the decPrices array to hold 200 elements and there were fewer than that number, we could change the array size with the following statement:

```
ReDim Preserve decprices(intNumPrices - 1)
```

Note that we redimensioned decPrices to have intNumPrices − 1 maximum elements, since we will be counting from zero and not one. The *Preserve* part of the statement ensures that we preserve the data that is already there. Failure to include this portion of the statement will result the existing data being lost.

In general, we will be using arrays with no initially declared size and resizing them as data are input with the ReDim Preserve statements as was done in VB Code Box 6-1.

> **TIP** The For-Each loop should only be used to process an array if the size of the array has been redimensioned to be equal to the actual number of elements in the array. Otherwise, many "empty" array elements may be processed leading to potentially incorrect results.

Once we know that the array is dimensioned to exactly the number of elements in it, we can then redo the display of the decPrice array in a listbox using a For-Each loop as shown in VB Code Box 6-3.

Once arrays are declared and input, they must be processed like any other data. Although we could process arrays directly in an event procedure, since they are stored in memory, we don't have to process them as they are

| VB CODE BOX 6-3. Using the For-Each loop to display an array | ```Private Sub btnDisplay_Click(ByVal sender As Object, _
ByVal e As System.EventArgs) Handles btnDisplay.Click
    Dim decOnePrice As Decimal
    For Each decOnePrice In decPrices
        lstPrices.Items.Add(Format(decOnePrice, "currency"))
    Next
End Sub``` |
| --- | --- |

input. The important thing to remember is: once an array is input, there is *no* need to input it again in order carry out processing on it.

Step-by-Step Instructions 6-1: Inputting and displaying an array

1. Use Windows Explorer to create a new folder named **Chapter6** in the Visual Studios Project folder. Start VB .NET and choose to create a new project with a name of **ArrayInput** in the Chapter6 folder. Create the form shown in Figure 6-2, using the control properties shown in Table 6-1. Name the form **frmArrayInput** and give it the text property shown in the figure. Right-click on the Project file in the Solution Explorer and click on Properties. Change the Startup object to be **frmArrayInput**.

TABLE 6-1: Control properties for Until loop input form

Control Name	Text Property	Control Name	Text Property
lstPrices		lblPriceList	Prices in Array
btnDisplay	Display	btnExit	Exit
btnClear	Clear		

2. Declare the decPrices array and the intNumPrices variable at the form level. The decPrices array should have *no* maximum index value.

3. Add the code shown in VB Code Box 6-1 to the frmArrayInput_Load event procedure to input the contents of a file to the decPrices array.

4. Add the code for the btnDisplay_Click, btnClear_Click, and btnExit_Click event procedures, as shown in VB Code Box 6-2.

5. Use Notepad to create a text file in the Bin folder of the **ArrayInput** project folder called **Prices.txt,** with the prices shown in Figure 6-1.

6. Run your project and click the *Display* button. The results should look like Figure 6-3.

7. Modify the btnDisplay_Click event procedure as shown in VB Code Box 6-3 to use a For-Each loop to display the contents of the decPrices array.

8. Run your project and click the *Display* button. The results should still look like Figure 6-3. Save all the files in your project.

Mini-Summary 6-2: Array input and initialization

1. Arrays must be input one value at a time using the index value of each element. They can be input as single elements or using any of the three types of loops discussed earlier.

2. Until loops are good for array input from a file, with a counter variable being incremented to determine the index value.

3. Many arrays must be initialized to some value other than zero.

4. For-Next loops are useful for working with arrays. For-Each loops are specifically designed for working with arrays and do not require a knowledge of the maximum index for an array.

It's Your Turn!

1. Why is file input often the best way to input data to an array?

2. Why is a For-Next loop *not* appropriate for file input?

3. Why is a counter variable that is being incremented on each repetition of the loop needed for array input from a sequential access file?

4. Why would it be necessary to initialize an entire array to some value?

5. Why does the For-Next loop for displaying the contents of an array run to the number of elements in the array *minus* one?

6. Explain why clearing a list box displaying the contents of an array does not clear the array itself?

7. Follow Step-by-Step Instructions 6-1 to create a the UntilLoopInput project and test it with the Prices.txt file.

8. Modify the array limits on the decPrices array in the ArrayInput project to have a maximum index of five. Run your project again. What happens? Do *not* save the modified project.

9. How is the For-Each Loop different from the For-Next Loop? Which would you use if only a portion of the array is going to be processed? Why?

PROCESSING ARRAYS

Inputting data into an array is only the first step in using it. There are a large number of processing activities that can be handled best by arrays, including summing and averaging the values in an array, finding the largest or smallest value in a list, working with multiple lists, finding a particular value in a list, and sorting a list into a desired order. In this chapter, we will cover the first four of these operations; all of them plus the last operation, sorting a list, will also be covered in Chapter 7 using subs and functions.

Summing and Averaging Values

Once you have an array of values, it is very easy to sum and average them using a For-Next or For-Each loop to add each array element to the sum and then divide the sum by the number of elements. To implement this procedure in VB .NET, we will use the same file of 10 prices as before (Prices.txt). We will modify the ArrayInput project used to input an unknown number of values and add a button to find and display the sum and average (btnSumAverage) in text boxes (txtSum and txtAverage) with corresponding labels. The code for the btnSumAverage_Click() event procedure is shown in VB Code Box 6-4. The result of running this project and clicking the *Display* and *Sum and Average* buttons is shown in Figure 6-4.

| **VB CODE BOX 6-4.** Code to compute the sum and average of array elements | ```
Private Sub btnSumAverage_Click(ByVal sender As Object, _
ByVal e As EventArgs) Handles btnSumAverage.Click
    Dim decSum As Decimal, intCounter As Integer
    Dim decAverage, decOnePrice As Decimal
    decSum = 0
    For Each decOnePrice In decPrices
      decSum = decSum + decOnePrice
    Next
    If IntNumPrices > 0 Then
       decAverage = decSum / IntNumPrices
    Else
       MsgBox("No values to average!")
       Exit Sub
    End If
    txtSum.Text = Format(decSum, "currency")
    txtAverage.Text = Format(decAverage, "currency")
End Sub
``` |

Note in VB Code Box 6-4 that we have used a For-Each loop to compute the sum for the same reason that we used it in the btnDisplay_Click() event procedure. Note also that the average is computed by dividing the sum by intNumPrices, since this value is the actual absolute number of elements in the array. Finally, we check to ensure that intNumPrices is *not* zero before we try to divide by it. Attempting to divide by zero is a very common error that is often caused by input errors resulting in no values being input.

FIGURE 6-4. Form to compute the sum and average of array values

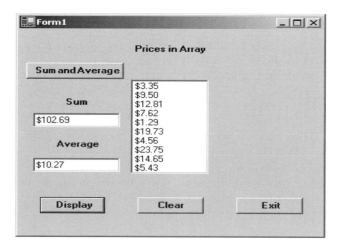

> **TIP**: Whenever computing averages or other values that depend on the number of elements in an array, to avoid computation errors, it is critical that you use the most recent value for the number of elements.
```

Finding the Largest (Smallest) Value in a List

A common operation in working with lists is finding the largest or smallest value in the list. By *value*, we mean a numeric value or a character string. For numeric values, it is obvious what larger and smaller mean, but what about for character strings? For character strings, the alphabetical ordering holds; that is, the letter A is *smaller* than the letter B because it comes first in the alphabetical ordering. Similarly, lowercase letters come *after* uppercase letters, and digits come before the alphabetical characters. The order of characters is known as the **collating sequence,** and it includes all 256 characters that VB .NET recognizes. You can see the complete collating sequence by entering and running the code shown in VB Code Box 6-5 in the Form_Load event for a new project with a form named frmCollate.

VB CODE BOX 6-5. Displaying the collating sequence	```
	Private Sub frmCollate_Load(ByVal sender As Object, _
	ByVal e As EventArgs) Handles MyBase.Load
	    Dim intCounter As Integer
	    For intCounter = 0 To 255
	        Debug.WriteLine(Chr(intCounter))
	    Next
	End Sub
	``

This code uses the **Chr( )** function to convert the Integer values of the For-Next counter variable into the corresponding characters. To reverse this operation and find the position of a particular character in the collating sequence, you would use the Asc( ) function with the character as the argument of the function. For example, if we entered

```
Debug.Writeline Asc("A")
```

the number 65 would be printed in the Immediate window.

Regardless of whether you are working with characters or numbers, finding the largest value in an array requires that each item in the list be compared to the currently known largest value. If an item in the list is larger than the currently known largest value, the item in the list becomes the largest known value. This comparison process continues until all items in the list have been compared to the currently known largest value, at which time the comparisons end and the largest value is known. The pseudocode for this logic is shown on the next page (to find the smallest value, simply reverse the direction of the inequality from greater than to less than):

Note that the largest value is initialized to the first item in the list and then compared to every item in the list, starting with the second item. The largest value must be compared to something, and the first item in the list is a convenient value to be used.

Begin procedure to find largest value
   Set largest value to first item in list
   Repeat beginning with second item to last item
      If item in list > largest value then
         Largest value = item in list
      End decision
   End repeat
   Display largest value
End procedure

To see how this works, assume you have the same list of 10 prices as shown in Figure 6-4 and you want to find the largest value. If we walk through the pseudocode shown above for these prices, the results are as follows:

Set Largest = decPrices(0) = $3.35
Set intCounter = 1
Is decPrices(1) = $9.50 > $3.35? Yes, so Largest = decPrices(1) = $9.50
Is decPrices(2) = $12.81 > $9.50? Yes, so Largest = decPrices(2) = $12.81
Is decPrices(3) = $7.62 > $12.81? No, so no change
Is decPrices(4) = $1.29 > $12.81? No, so no change
Is decPrices(5) = $19.73 > $12.81? Yes, so Largest = decPrices(5) = $19.73
Is decPrices(6) = $4.56 > $19.73? No, so no change
Is decPrices(7) = $23.75 > $19.73? Yes, so Largest = decPrices(7) = $23.75
Is decPrices(8) = $14.65 > $23.75? No, so no change
Is decPrices(9) = $5.43 > $23.75? No, so no change
End of array, so Largest = $23.75

To implement this procedure in VB .NET, we will use the same file of 10 prices as before (Prices.txt) and extend the project used earlier to input, sum, and average an unknown number of values (ArrayInput). A button to find the largest value (btnFindMax) and a text box (txtMaxPrice) to display the largest value in the array with a corresponding label should be added. The code for the btnFindMax_Click() event procedure is shown in VB Code Box 6-6, and the result of clicking the *Display* and *FindMax* buttons is shown in Figure 6-5.

VB Code Box 6-6. Code to find the maximum price in the decPrices array	```
	Private Sub btnFindMax_Click(ByVal sender As Object, _
	ByVal e As System.EventArgs) Handles btnFindMax.Click
	   Dim intCounter As Integer, decLargest As Decimal
	   Dim DecOnePrice As Decimal
	   decLargest = decPrices(0)
	   For Each DecOnePrice In decPrices
	      If DecOnePrice > decLargest Then
	         decLargest = DecOnePrice
	      End If
	   Next
	   txtMaxPrice.Text = Format(decLargest, "currency")
	End Sub
	``

■ ■

Step-by-Step Instructions 6-2: Processing arrays

1. To modify the ArrayInput project to process arrays, start by adding the **btnSumAverage** button to the form with a text property of **Sum and Average.** Also add the **txtSum** and **txtAverage** text boxes with corresponding labels. The resulting form should look like Figure 6-4.

2. Add the code shown in VB Code Box 6-4 to the btnSumAverage_Click event procedure. Run the project and click the *Sum and Average* button. You should see a sum of $102.69 and an average of $10.27.

FIGURE 6-5. Form to find maximum value

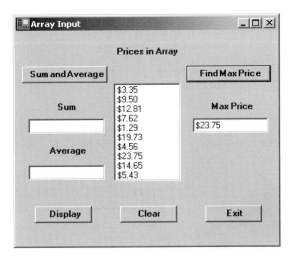

3. To modify the current project to find the maximum price in the list, begin by adding the **btnFindMax** button to the form with a text property of **Find Max Price**. Also add the **txtMaxPrice** text box, with a corresponding label. The resulting form should look like Figure 6-5.

4. Add the code shown in VB Code Box 6-6 to the btnFindMax_Click event procedure. Run the project and click the *Find Max Price* button. You should see a maximum price of $23.75.

5. Save all of the files for this project before exiting VB .NET.

Mini-Summary 6-3: Processing with arrays

1. Typical array operations include initializing all array elements to sum value, summing and averaging the array values, and finding the largest or smallest value in the array.

3. Summing and averaging involve adding each value of the array to a summation variable while counting the number of elements. The number of elements should always be checked to ensure it is not zero before dividing by it.

4. Finding the largest or smallest value involves multiple comparisons of array elements to the current largest (smallest) value until all elements have been checked.

It's Your Turn!

1. What is the collating sequence and what does it have to do with decisions?

2. What operations do the Chr( ) and Asc( ) functions carry out?

3. Assume that the following declarations have been made:

```
Dim intArray1(4) As Integer
Dim intArray2(4) As Integer
```

Also assume that the intArray2 initially contains the following values:

0	1	2	3	4
10	13	7	24	2

Describe the contents of the arrays after each of the following VB .NET code segments have been executed.

```
a. Private Sub btnGo_Click()
     Dim intI As Integer
     For intI = 0 To 4
       intArray1(intI) = 1
     Next intI
   End Sub

b. Private Sub btnGo_Click()
     Dim intI As Integer
     Dim intTemp As Integer
     intTemp = intArray2(0)
     For intI = 0 To 3
       intArray2(intI) = intArray2(intI + 1)
     Next intI
     intArray2(4) = intTemp
   End Sub

c. Private Sub btnGo_Click()
     Dim intI As Integer
     Dim intTemp As Integer
     For intI = 0 To 4
       intArray1(intI) = intArray2(intI) + 10
     Next intI
   End Sub

d. Private Sub btnGo_Click()
     Dim intI As Integer
     Dim intTemp As Integer
     For intI = 0 To 4
       If (intArray2(intI) Mod 2) > 0 Then
         intArray1(intI) = intArray2(intI)
       Else
         intArray1(intI) = intArray2(intI) + 1
       End If
     Next intI
   End Sub
```

4. Follow Step-by-Step Instructions 6-2 to modify the ArrayInput project to sum and average the prices as well as find the maximum price in the list.

5. How would you modify the ArrayInput project to find the *minimum price* in the data file?

6. To display the VB .NET collating sequence, start VB .NET or select **File|New Project** and choose to create a new project with a name of **Collate** in the Chapter6 folder. Give the form a name of frmCollate and change the Startup object to be **frmCollate.** Double-click the form and enter the code shown in VB Code Box 6-5 in the frmCollate_Load event procedure. Run the project and, if the Output window is not already displayed, use

View | Other Windows | Output to display it. Note that the first characters are not printable. What character precedes the letter *a*? The letter *A*? Save the form as **Collate.vb** and then save all the files in the project.

FINDING ITEMS AND WORKING WITH MULTIPLE LISTS

As mentioned earlier, in addition to finding the largest or smallest value in a list, typical processing operations include finding a particular item in a list and working with multiple lists. In this section we will take up these two operations, and then in the next section we will apply them to the Vintage DVDs scenario. To discuss these two operations, we will assume that instead of the prices being just a random list, each price in the list is associated with a part identifier as shown in Table 6-2.

TABLE 6-2: Part identifiers and prices

Part Identifier	Price	Part Identifier	Price
V23-5W	$3.35	V24-5V	$19.73
X37-3K	$9.50	X44-8T	$4.56
Q55-8S	$12.81	Q49-3K	$23.75
R12-7T	$7.62	V24-2T	$14.65
T17-6Y	$1.29	R13-8W	$5.43

For example, the part with identifier V23-5W has a price of $3.35, whereas the part with identifier X37-3K has a price of $9.50. Since the part identifier is a character string and the price is a Decimal data type, they must be stored in separate arrays. This will also allow us to find the item with largest or smallest price easily by searching the price array or to find a particular item in the list by searching the identifier array. If the data in this table were input into a data file named *Parts.txt,* then the first two lines of data on the file would appear as follows, where the data items are separated by commas:

```
V23-5W, 3.35
X37-3K, 9.50
```

Project Objectives

The objective of this project will be twofold:

1. Find the part with the maximum price and display the part identifier and price;
2. Find the part with a specified identifier and display the part identifier and price; if the part is not on the list, display a message.

To work with two arrays to achieve these objectives, we need create a new folder named *MultipleLists* and copy all of the existing files from the ArrayInput folder into it. All of the files should be renamed from within the VB .NET environment to match the project name and the form should be named as *frmMultiple* with an appropriate text property. You will also need to rename the Form_Load procedure to be *frmMultiple_Load.*

Once the new project is set up, we are ready to modify it to handle multiple lists. Specifically, we need to expand the width of the list box used to display the prices so that both the identifier and the price can be displayed on one line in the list box. We also need to widen the text box that was used to display price to now display the part identifier and the price for the highest priced item in the list. Since we also want to search the list for a particular identifier, we need to add another button (btnFind) to execute the search and add a text box (txtFound) to display the identifier and price for the item once it is found. This may require that the form itself also be widened and the existing buttons moved down to handle these changes and additions. Finally, the labels need to be modified to describe the revised or new text boxes, and the name of the list box needs to be changed to *lstParts*. The final form should look like Figure 6-6.

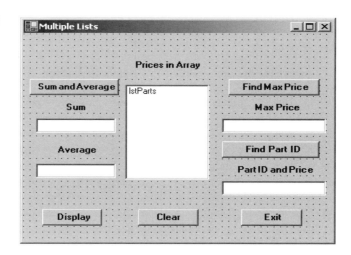

FIGURE 6-6. Form to display part identifier and price

Using the StreamReader Object to Input Data

To input the part identifiers and prices from the PartList.txt file, we need to declare a second array, *strPartID*, at the form level as a String data type. We also need to modify the frmMultiple_Load event procedure in a number of ways, starting with the use of a **StreamReader object.** The StreamReader object enables us to read the entire stream of data from a line of the sequential access file in one statement. If there are multiple data items in the string, we will then need to **parse** that string to find the data items. But first, let's look at the creation of the StreamReader object.

You have used many *visual* objects in the first six chapters of this textbook and should be ready to use your first code object. Such code objects have many advantages over writing your own code to carry out activities, including that they come with useful properties and methods and have been extensively tested before being released for use by VB .NET programmers such as you. Throughout the rest of this book, you will be seeing and using a large number of objects as well creating your own in Chapter 8.

As discussed in Chapter 1, all objects are created from a class. For example, when you drag a new text box onto the form, you are creating a new text box object from the text box class in the toolbox. This is referred to as creating an **instance** of the object because you can create many objects from one class. The general form of the statement to create a new instance of an object from a class is shown here:

Dim *instance of object* AS *object class* = New *object class*

Although this is actually two statements in one, it is easily understand in that form; the left side of the assignment statement declares the instance of the object of a certain class. The assignment then actually creates the instance. It is like declaring a variable to be of a certain data type and then assigning a value to that variable. For example, to declare an instance of the Stream-Reader object, the statement is

```
Dim srdReadFile as IO.System.StreamReader = IO.System._
StreamReader(strFileName)
```

where *srd* is the prefix for the StreamReader object, and the strFileName variable indicates the name of the file to be read and the IO.System prefix on the StreamReader class indicates the library in which this class is found.

If we also declare a String variable, say, strLine, we can read the contents of each line of the sequential access file into the variable with the ReadLine() method of the StreamReader object as shown below:

```
strLine = srdReadFile.Readline()
```

As with the use of the Input() statement to input data from a file, we need to include the srdReadFile.Readline() method in a loop that can check when the end of the file has been encountered. However, this loop structure is a little bit different with the general format being shown below:

Do Until *srdReadFile*. Peek = −1
    strLine = srdReadFile.ReadLine()
    Process strLine
Loop

(The line "process strLine" will be discussed in a moment.) The key idea in this loop is that the lines of the file are input until the Peek method of the StreamReader object returns a value of −1, indicating no more characters to be read.

The part of the loop that processes the contents of the String variable, strLine, can vary from situation to situation but, for array input, will include increasing the size of the array with ReDim Preserve, setting the array element equal to the contents of strLine, and incrementing the array counter. If there are multiple data items embedded in the string, then we must use the **Split method** of the String data type to separate out the various items. This method uses some programmer-defined delimiter, say a comma, and breaks the string into substrings whenever it encounters that delimiter. These substrings are automatically added to an array with first string going into the array element 0, the next string into the array element 1, and so on. For example, if the strLine variable contains

```
"Jon Standly", "OL", "JR", 305
```

and chrComma = "," then StrLine.Split(chrComma) would parse strLine into the array elements in the array Player shown in Figure 6-7.

Processing strLine

In our case, to process the strLine variable we use the comma delimiter in the Split method to generate elements of the strFields array from the strLine String variable and then set the elements of the strPartID and decPrices arrays equal to the two elements of the strFields array, that is,

```
strFields = strLine.Split(strDelimiter)
strPartID(IntNumPrices) = strFields(0)
decPrices(IntNumPrices) = CDec(strFields(1))
```

FIGURE 6-7. Result of using String Split method

Player(0)	Jon Standly
Player(1)	OL
Player(2)	JR
Player(3)	305

This entire process of reading from a sequential access file into multiple arrays is shown in VB Code Box 6-7.

> **TIP** The Split method is one of the few situations where you can create an entire array with a single assignment statement.

VB CODE BOX 6-7.
Revised Form_Load event procedure

```
Private Sub frmMultiple_Load(ByVal sender As _
System.Object, ByVal e As System.EventArgs)_
Handles MyBase.Load
    Dim strPathName As String, strLine As String
    Dim chrDelimiter As Char, strFields() As String
    Dim intNumPrices As Integer = 0
    chrDelimiter = ","
    strPathName = CurDir() + "\Parts.txt"
    Dim srdReadFile As System.IO.StreamReader = New _
    System.IO.StreamReader(strPathName)
    Do Until srdReadFile.Peek = -1
       ReDim Preserve decPrices(intNumPrices)
       ReDim Preserve strPartID(intNumPrices)
       strLine = srdReadFile.ReadLine
       strFields = strLine.Split(chrDelimiter)
       intNumPrices = intNumPrices + 1
    Loop
    FileClose()
End Sub
```

New things about the code shown in VB Code Box 6-7 from that used earlier in this chapter to input data from a sequential access file (VB Code Box 6-1) include the variable strLine to hold the line of data from the file and the Char data type variable, chrDelimiter, which will hold the delimiter (a comma in our case) on which the parsing will be based. We also define an array, strFields(), to hold the parts into which the strLine variable will be parsed. The object srdReadFile is also declared and set equal to an instance of the StreamReader object. In the loop itself, we use the ReDim Preserve statement twice to enlarge the decPrices and strPartID arrays prior to reading the next line from the array, which is handled with the strReadFile.ReadLine method. The resulting strLine is then parsed into two fields and saved to the strFields array. These two elements are then assigned to the corresponding array elements of strPartID and decPrices. Finally, the number of elements in the strPartID and decPrices arrays is increased by one.

When the StreamReader object ReadLine() method in the code box reads the first line in the data file, strLine is set equal to "V23-5W, 3.35". This is then parsed into two strings, strFields(0), which is equal to "V23-5W", and str-Fields(1) which is equal to "3.35". Finally, the strPartID(0) is set equal to str-

Fields(0), that is, "V23-5W", and decPrices(0) is set equal to the decimal conversion of "3.35", or simply 3.35. Similarly, strPartID(1) is set equal to "X37-3K", decPrices(1) is set equal to 9.50, and so on for the 10 sets of part IDs and prices in the file.

Note that for a given part, the index values for the strPartID and decPrices array elements are the same. This means that the array index acts as a *link* between the two arrays, and if you find a price, you can find the corresponding part ID through the index value and vice versa. To display the two items on the same line in the list box, we need to modify the statements in the btnDisplay_Click event procedure to add items to the newly named lstParts list box in such a way that the part identifier is concatenated with the formatted part price. To do this, we must dimension and use a counter variable with the strPartID array. This is necessary because there is no automatic link between elements of the decPrices array represented by the decOnePrice variable and elements in the strPartID array. The only link is the index of the array represented by the counter variable. The resulting event procedure is shown in VB Code Box 6-8.

VB Code Box 6-8. Revised btnDisplay event procedure	```
	Private Sub btnDisplay_Click(ByVal eventSender As Object, _
	ByVal eventArgs As System.EventArgs) Handles btnDisplay.Click
	    Dim decOnePrice As Decimal, intCounter As Integer = 0
	    For Each decOnePrice In decPrices
	        lstParts.Items.Add(strPartID(intCounter) & " " & _
	        Format(decOnePrice, "currency"))
	        intCounter = intCounter + 1
	    Next
	End Sub
	``

Finding a Specified Part Identifier

To search for a part identifier in the parts list to find its price, we need to use a For-Each loop to compare the part identifier to every part identifier in the parts list. Before the loop, the user enters the part identifier that is to be found in an input box. Prior to the loop, a **Flag** variable is set to *false*. Within the loop, if a match is found between the part identifier that was input and a part identifier on the parts list, an If-Then decision saves the index of the part identifier, sets the Flag to *true*, and the loop is exited. The pseudocode for this operation is shown here.

```
Begin procedure to find part identifier
    Input part identifier
    Set Flag to False
    Repeat for each part in parts list
        If part identifier = identifier on parts list then
            Flag = True
            Save index of part identifier on parts list and exit the loop
        End decision
    End repeat
    If Flag = True
        Use saved index to display part identifier and price
    Else
        Display message that part not on parts list
    End decision
End procedure
```

The flag variable in the VB .NET version of the above pseudocode will be a Boolean variable that is initially set to *false* and then set to *true* if a match is found in the loop. After the loop, the status of the flag variable is checked; if it is true, the part identifier and price are displayed in a text box. If the flag variable is false, a message is displayed that the part is not on the parts list. Another variable is set to the array index of the part identifier that is a match. This variable is then used to display the part identifier and price after the loop. The code for the btnFind_Click event procedure is shown in VB Code Box 6-9.

| **VB Code Box 6-9.** Code to search for part identifier in parts array | ```
Private Sub btnFind_Click(ByVal sender As Object, _
ByVal e As EventArgs) Handles btnFind.Click
    Dim intCounter As Integer, intResults As Integer
    Dim strFindPartID As String, blnFound As Boolean
    Dim intPartIndex As Integer
    strFindPartID = InputBox("Input identifier to find")
    blnFound = False
    For intCounter = 0 To IntNumPrices - 1
        If UCase(strFindPartID) = UCase(strPartId(intCounter)) Then
            blnFound = True
            intPartIndex = intCounter
            Exit For
        End If
    Next
    If blnFound Then
        txtFound.Text = strPartId(intPartIndex) & "   " & _
        Format(decPrices(intPartIndex), "currency")
    Else
        MsgBox("Part not found", vbExclamation, "Price Search")
    End If
End Sub
``` |

Several things are of note in this code. First, if the part identifier is found, the For-Next loop is exited with the *Exit For* instruction. This has the same effect as if the loop had ended normally. This saves processing time by not looking for the part identifier after it has already been found. Second, to check the status of the Boolean variable blnFound, you do *not* need to actually compare it to *true*; Boolean variables are already true or false, so no comparison is necessary. Finally, we have added second and third parameters to MsgBox, and it is now being used as a function to assign a value to the variable Results. The new parameters are a VB .NET constant that displays an exclamation sign—VBExclamation— and a title, "Price Search."

> **TIP** Be careful that the delimiter you choose for your sequential access file does not appear in the file itself. If it does, you will receive erroneous results when the Split method is applied. For example, if a comma appears in your file, you might want to use a tab as a delimiter.
```

More on the Message Box

Up to this point, we have used MsgBox as a statement to display a message in a dialog box. However, it is possible to include other parameters with Msg-Box to display a designated title as well as icons and buttons. The form of the message box with additional parameters is

MsgBox(*message, buttons, title*)

where *buttons* is one or more internal VB .NET constants, such as vbExcla-mation or vbYesNoCancel, that display one or more buttons or an icon. Simi-larly, *title* is a title string for the dialog box. For example, using the MsgBox function in VB Code Box 6-9 will result in the dialog box shown in Figure 6-7.

FIGURE 6-7.

Message Box with exclamation mark

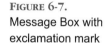

In addition to adding a title, icons, and buttons to MsgBox, it is also pos-sible to treat it as a *function* and use it to learn which of the buttons the user clicked. As with any function, the parameters must be enclosed in parenthe-ses and the MsgBox function must appear in an expression as shown below:

***intVariable* = MsgBox(*message, buttons, title*)**

The value of *intVariable* can be checked to determine which button on the dialog box the user clicked.

For example, assume you used the following instruction in a project:

```
intResults = MsgBox("Write over old file?",vbYesNoCancel, "File")
```

In this case, the user would be presented with a dialog box with the prompt and three buttons—*Yes, No,* and *Cancel*—one of which must be clicked. It would then be possible to use an If-Then-ElseIf or Select Case decision struc-ture to check the status of the Integer variable *intResults* to determine which button the user clicked: *Yes* to write over the old file, *No* to not write over the old file, or *Cancel* to cancel the entire operation. If the user clicks *Yes* to overwrite old file, the intResults variable will be equal to 6; if the user clicks *No* to not overwrite the old file, the intResults variable will be equal to 7; and if the user clicks *Cancel* to cancel the entire operation, then intResults will be equal to 2. However, you do not have to remember these values, since they can be replaced with the MsgBox constants vbYes, vbNo, and vbCancel. The code to check if the user clicked the *Yes* button would be

```
If intResults = vbYes then
```

Table 6-3 shows the most commonly used internal VB .NET constants, along with commonly used buttons and the values they return.

TABLE 6-3: MsgBox constants and values returned from the MsgBox function

Button Constant	Description	Value Returned	MsgBox Constant	Operation
vbOKOnly	Display **OK** button only	**1**	**vbOk**	**OK** button clicked
vbOKCancel	Display **OK** and **Cancel** buttons	**2**	**vbCancel**	**Cancel** button clicked
vbYesNoCancel	Display **Yes**, **No**, and **Cancel** buttons	**3**	**vbAbort**	**Abort** button clicked
vbYesNo	Display **Yes** and **No** buttons	**4**	**vbRetry**	**Retry** button clicked
vbCritical	Display **Stop sign**	**5**	**vbIgnore**	**Ignore** any buttons

TABLE 6-3: MsgBox constants and values returned from the MsgBox function (Continued)

Button Constant	Description	Value Returned	MsgBox Constant	Operation
vbQuestion	Display a **question mark**	6	vbYes	**Yes** button clicked
vbExclamation	Display an **Exclamation mark**	7	vbNo	**No** button clicked
vbInformation	Display **Information Message** icon			

If the code in VB Code Box 6-9 is entered in the btnFind_Click() event procedure, this button is ready to test. To do this, run the project, click the *Find Part ID* button, and enter (for example) "V24-5V". If this is done, the following will be displayed in the txtMaxPrice text box:

```
V24-5V    $19.73
```

However, if you enter "Z93-Q1", a message like that shown in Figure 6-7 will be displayed, because this part identifier is not on the parts list.

> **TIP:** It is possible to use the plus sign (+) to combine two or more of the VB .NET constants to display both icons and buttons, say an exclamation mark and the Cancel button.

Finding the Part Identifier with the Highest Price

To find and display the part identifier and price corresponding to the part with the highest price, it is only necessary to modify the btnFindMax_Click event procedure to save the array index for the maximum price, as was done when a matching part identifier is found. This requires adding a statement that stores the index of the current largest price to the loop that searches for the maximum price. This statement will store the array index at the same time that the value of the largest price is saved. We will also need to include a statement that adds the part identifier and price to the txtMax-Price text box. The revised btnFindMax_Click() event procedure is shown in VB Code Box 6-10.

VB CODE BOX 6-10. Code to save index for part with highest price	```Private Sub btnFindMax_Click(ByVal sender As Object, _```
	```ByVal e As EventArgs) Handles btnFindMax.Click```
	``` Dim intCounter As Integer, decLargest As Decimal```
	``` Dim DecOnePrice as Decimal, intMaxIndex As Integer```
	``` decLargest = decPrices(0)```
	``` For Each DecOnePrice In decPrices```
	``` If DecOnePrice > decLargest Then```
	``` decLargest = DecOnePrice```
	``` intMaxIndex = intCounter```
	``` End If```
	``` intCounter = intCounter + 1```
	``` Next```
	``` txtMaxPrice.Text = strPartID(intMaxIndex) & " " & _```
	``` Format(decPrices(intMaxIndex), "currency")```
	```End Sub```

If the project is run and the *Find Max Price* button is clicked, the part identifier and price for the highest priced part will appear as shown below:

```
Q49-3K    $23.75
```

This has been a fairly big project, so to help you with the code, we have shown all of the code for the MultipleLists project in one place in VB Code Box 6-11.

VB Code Box 6-11. Complete code for MultipleList project	<pre>Public Class frmMultiple
	Inherits System.Windows.Forms.Form
	Dim IntNumPrices As Integer, decPrices() As Decimal
	Dim strPartID()
	Private Sub frmMultiple_Load(ByVal sender As System.Object, ByVal e _
	As System.EventArgs) Handles MyBase.Load
	        Dim strPathName As String, strLine As String
	        Dim chrDelimiter As Char, strFields() As String,
	        Dim intfields As Integer
	        IntNumPrices = 0
	        chrDelimiter = ","
	        strPathName = CurDir() + "\Parts.txt"
	        Dim srdReadFile As System.IO.StreamReader = _
	        New System.IO.StreamReader(strPathName)
	        Do Until srdReadFile.Peek = -1
	            ReDim Preserve decPrices(IntNumPrices)
	            ReDim Preserve strPartID(IntNumPrices)
	            strLine = srdReadFile.ReadLine
	            strFields = strLine.Split(chrDelimiter)
	            decPrices(IntNumPrices) = CDec(strFields(1))
	            strPartID(IntNumPrices) = strFields(0)
	            IntNumPrices = IntNumPrices + 1
	        Loop
	        FileClose()
	End Sub
	Private Sub btnSumAverage_Click(ByVal sender As Object, _
	ByVal e As EventArgs) Handles btnAverage.Click
	    Dim decSum As Decimal, intCounter As Integer
	    Dim decAverage, decOnePrice As Decimal
	    decSum = 0
	    For Each decOnePrice In decPrices
	        decSum = decSum + decOnePrice
	    Next
	    If IntNumPrices > 0 Then
	        decAverage = decSum / IntNumPrices
	    Else
	        MsgBox("No values to average!")
	        Exit Sub
	    End If
	    txtSum.Text = Format(decSum, "currency")
	    txtAverage.Text = Format(decAverage, "currency")
	End Sub
	Private Sub btnClear_Click(ByVal sender As Object, _
	ByVal e As EventArgs) Handles btnClear.Click
	    lstParts.Items.Clear()
	End Sub
	Private Sub btnExit_Click(ByVal sender As Object, _
	ByVal e As EventArgs) Handles btnExit.Click
	    End
	End Sub</pre>

| **VB CODE BOX 6-12.**<br><br>Complete code<br>for MultipleList<br>project (cont.) | ```
Private Sub btnDisplay_Click(ByVal sender As Object, _
ByVal e As EventArgs) Handles btnDisplay.Click
    Dim decOnePrice As Decimal, intcounter As Integer
    For Each decOnePrice In decPrices
        lstParts.Items.Add(strPartID(intCounter) & " " & _
        Format(decOnePrice, "currency"))
        intCounter = intCounter + 1
    Next
End Sub
Private Sub btnFindMax_Click(ByVal sender As Object, _
ByVal e As EventArgs) Handles btnFindMax.Click
    Dim intCounter As Integer, decLargest As Decimal
    Dim DecOnePrice as Decimal, intMaxIndex As Integer
    decLargest = decPrices(0)
    For Each DecOnePrice In decPrices
        If DecOnePrice > decLargest Then
            decLargest = DecOnePrice
            intMaxIndex = intCounter
        End If
            intCounter = intCounter + 1
    Next
    txtMaxPrice.Text = strPartID(intMaxIndex) & "   " & _
    Format(decPrices(intMaxIndex), "currency")
End Sub
Private Sub btnFind_Click(ByVal sender As Object _
ByVal e As EventArgs) Handles btnFind.Click
    Dim intCounter As Integer, intResults As Integer
    Dim strFindPartID As String, blnFound As Boolean
    Dim intPriceIndex As Integer
    strFindPartID = InputBox("Input identifier to find")
    blnFound = False
    For intCounter = 0 To IntNumPrices - 1
        If UCase(strFindPartID) = UCase(strPartID(intCounter)) Then
            blnFound = True
            intPriceIndex = intCounter
            Exit For
        End If
    Next
    If blnFound Then
        txtFound.Text = strPartID(intPriceIndex) & "   " & _
        Format(decPrices(intPriceIndex), "currency")
    Else
        MsgBox("Part not found", vbExclamation, _
        "Price Search")
    End If
End Sub
End Class
``` |

Step-by-Step Instructions 6-3: Working with multiple lists

1. Use Windows Explorer to create a folder named **MultipleLists** and *copy* the contents of the *ArrayInput* folder into it. Rename all of the files in the *MultipleLists* folder to match the name of the name of the folder. Rename the
```

form to be **frmMultiple** and give it a text property that matches the folder name. Right-click on the project file and select **Properties.** Change the Startup object to be **frmMultiple.**

2. On frmMultiple, rename the listbox as **lstParts** and make it wide enough to display both the part ID and the price. To the right of the list box, add a new button and a new text box named **btnFind** and **txtFound,** respectively. The text box should be wide enough to display a part identifier and price. In addition, modify existing labels and captions and add new labels and captions so your form looks like that shown in Figure 6-6.

3. Open the Code window for the form and add the following to the form-level declaration:

```
Dim strPartID() as string
```

4. Change the name of the Form_Load event procedure to be frmMultiple_Load and modify the part identifier and price in the Do Until loop as shown in VB Code Box 6-7. This will require extensive modification to the current Form_Load event procedure so be careful to make all of the changes (or better yet, retype the entire procedure.

5. Modify the btnDisplay_Click event procedure so the statement that adds the part identifier and price to the list box appears as shown below:

```
lstParts.Items.Add(strPartID(intCounter) & " " & _
    Format(decOnePrice, "currency"))
```

Also, dimension the intCounter variable as an Integer and increment it in the loop as shown in VB Code Box 6-8.

6. Modify the btnClear_Click event procedure to be

```
lstParts.Items.Clear()
```

7. Use Notepad to modify the *Prices.txt* data file to include part identifiers and prices separated by commas. Save the revised data file as **Parts.txt** in the Bin folder of the project.

8. Run the project and click the *Display* button. All 10 part identifiers and prices should now be in the list box. You may have to scroll down to see all of them.

9. Add the code shown in VB Code Box 6-9 to the btnFind_Click event procedure. Run the project, click the *Find Part ID* button, and enter "T17-6Y". What price is displayed? Click the button again and enter "R73-0S". Is this part identifier in the list?

10. Modify the btnFindMax_Click event procedure so that it is like that shown in VB Code Box 6-10. Run your project and click this button. You should find that the part identifier for the highest priced part is Q49-3K.

11. Modify the btnClear_click event procedure to reflect changing the name of the list box to *lstParts* and the addition of the txtFound text box.

12. When every element of the project executes correctly, save all of the files.

Mini-Summary 6-4: Finding array elements and working with multiple lists

1. It is possible to work with multiple list arrays by matching the index values for the arrays. The For-Each loop is still appropriate for working with multiple arrays, but a counter must be added to track the array index.

2. Finding a specific array value involves comparing each array element to the desired value. A flag is often used to indicate whether a match has been found.

3. MsgBox can be used with multiple parameters to display a title and icons or buttons. By treating MsgBox as a function, it is possible to determine which button the user clicked.

It's Your Turn!

1. Assume that the following declarations have been made:

```
Dim strArray1(4) As String
Dim decArray2(4) as Decimal
```

Also assume that the arrays initially contain the following values:

TABLE 6-4: strArray1

0	1	2	3	4
Thomas	Henry	Percy	Gordon	Skarlooey

TABLE 6-5: decArray2

0	1	2	3	4
10.99	12.65	11.55	12.65	9.69

Describe the contents of the txtAnswer text box after the following VB .NET code segment has been executed:

```
Private Sub btnGo_Click()
  Dim strSearch As String
  Dim intI, intPos As Integer
  Dim blnFound As Boolean = False
  strSearch = InputBox("Enter name:")
  For intI = 0 To 4
    If UCase(strArray1(intI)) = UCase(strSearch) Then
      blnFound = True
      intPos = intI
      Exit For
    End If
  Next intI
  If blnFound Then
    txtAnswer.Text = strArray1(intPos) & _
      " costs " & decArray2(intPos)
  Else
    txtAnswer.Text = "Item not found"
  End If
End Sub
```

2. Follow Step-by-Step Instructions 6-3 to create the MultipleLists project to work with two lists.

3. Modify the MsgBox function used in the btnFind_Click procedure so that it displays *Yes, No,* and *Cancel* buttons. Add instructions that will display another MsgBox indicating which button was clicked when a part identifier is not found. Test your project with a part identifier that is not in the parts list. Modify this further to also include a stop sign icon. Do *not* save this version of your project.

USING ARRAYS WITH VINTAGE DVDs APPLICATION

Now that you have some understanding of arrays, we can turn our attention to the Vintage DVDs application. When we left it in Chapter 5, the member names were being input from a data file and stored in a combo box from which one was selected and transferred to the customer name textbox. In this chapter, we will turn our attention to searching for DVDs using a complete or partial name. For example, a customer may want to rent the DVD "Ghost" or they may only know part of the name, say, that the title has "ghost" in it. In looking at the current frmVintage form, it is obvious that there is no room on it for the controls that would be needed to enter a DVD name, search for and display the names of DVDs that are like the one entered, and then display the price of the DVD in which the customer was interested and its location in the DVD rental store. About the best he can do on the current form is add a button that requests the name of the DVD to be found and transfers control to a second form where the actual information is displayed.

Working with Multiple Forms

In the first five chapters of this book, we have restricted our attention to projects that involve only a single form. However, VB .NET gives you the capability to easily create and manage projects that involve multiple forms. You can create projects in which new forms are displayed when the user requests additional functionality as in the scenario or projects in which new forms automatically "pop up" as needed to respond to a user or program request.

Add Item

To add a second form to an existing project, use the *Project | Add Windows Form...* menu selection, or click on the *Add Item* icon on the toolbar and select *Add Windows Form*. In either case, the Add New Item dialog box will be displayed as shown in Figure 6-8.

This dialog box contains a wide variety of types of forms that you can add to your project and modify to fit your needs. In our case, we are only interested in adding a Windows Form. At the bottom of the dialog box, you can change the file name for the form.

When a new form is added to a project, the existing form is replaced by a blank form and the new form's name (initially Form1) is added to the Solution Explorer window above the original form (frmVintage), as shown in Figure 6-9. To view the original form again, simply double-click its name in the Solution Explorer window or click on one of the tabs at the top of the design window. Do the same to return to the new form. The new form should be named with a *frm* prefix and saved as a part of the overall project. In our

FIGURE 6-8. New
Item Dialog Box

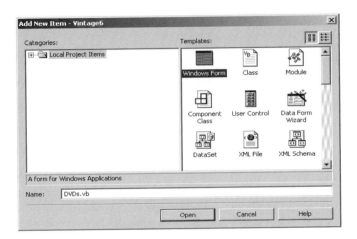

case, the new form will be named *frmDVDs* and will be saved as *DVDs.vb* as
a part of the Vintage project in the Chapter6 folder.

Once you add a new form to the project, you may add controls and code
to it as you did with the original form. This form also has its own Form_Load
event, which occurs when it is loaded and displayed. The control names for
the second and successive forms can be the same as for the main form, since
they are attached to a different form. In fact, the complete name of any control is:

FIGURE 6-9. Solution
Explorer window

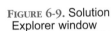

formname.controlname

but you do not need to include the *formname* portion of the name unless a
control on another form is being referred to.

The question is, then, how do you load and display a second form?
Since a new form is nothing but another instance of the form class, we need
to create a new instance of the second form and then display it. Creating an
instance of another form requires a type of declaration statement of the form
that is very similar to that used earlier to create the new instance of the
StreamReader class:

Dim *frmNewFormName* as New *frmFormName*

For example, to create a new instance of the frmDVDs form on the frm-
Vintage form, the declaration statement would be

```
Dim frmNewDVDs as New frmDVDs
```

which is entered as a form-level declaration.

Once a new instance of the second form has been created, it can be displayed with with the **Show** method in a single instruction of the form:

***frmNewFormName*. Show**

where *frmNewFormName* is the name of the instance of the form to be displayed and Show is the method that handles this operation. If the form is not
already loaded into memory, the Show method loads it too.

For example, to display the DVD form, a new button named *btnFind-
DVD* should be added to the frmVintage form. This button have a text prop-
erty of *Find DVD* and should be placed beneath the button with the *Add
Name* text property. The statement

```
frmNewDVDs.Show
```

should be added to the corresponding event procedure, btnFindDVD_Click.

If this new button is added to the main form, it will allow the clerk to switch to the DVD form to answer a customer's question regarding whether the store carries a particular DVD and, if it does, how much the rental on it is and where it is located in the store. There should be a button on this new form to hide it so the main form is once again displayed. The resulting main form is shown in Figure 6-10.

FIGURE 6-10.
Revised frmVintage
to access second
form

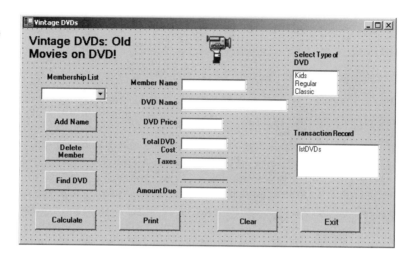

The DVDs Form

Now that a new form has been added to the project and a button to display it has been added to the main form, we are ready to design and program this form. There should be a way for the clerk to type in a name or part of a name and have all DVDs that match the entry displayed in a list box, or, if no matching entries are found, then a message to that effect should be displayed. From the list of matching entries, the clerk can ask which one the customer is looking for and then display the name, price, and location of that DVD. For example, if a customer is looking for a DVD that has the word *ghost* in the title but is not sure of anything beyond that, the clerk can enter this word and display three DVDs with *ghost* in the title: *The Ghost and Mrs. Muir, Ghost,* and *Ghostbusters.* If the customer decides that the movie he is interested in is *The Ghost and Mrs. Muir,* then the clerk can click on this movie and find that it rents for $1.99 and is in the Drama section of the store. The design for a form to handle this operation is shown in Figure 6-11.

This form does not need to be as large as the main form because it contains only a list box (lstDVDs), two buttons (btnSearch and btnBack with text properties of *Search* and *Back,* respectively), and various labels. The name or partial name of the DVD to be searched for is entered in an input box when the *Search* button is clicked. A list of DVDs matching the entry is listed in lst-DVDs, and if one is clicked, the list is replaced with more information about that particular DVD.

This form will require code in the btnSearch button to search for DVDs matching a DVD name from the input box and code for the Selected-Index_Changed event of lstDVDs to find the DVD matching the one selected from the list. Entering this code on the second form is just like entering it for

FIGURE 6-11.
Design for DVDs
form

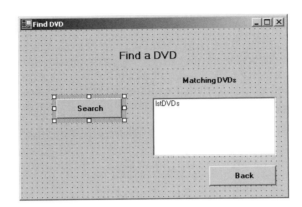

the main form—you simply double-click the control and enter the code in
the Code window.

Because it is necessary to store information on the DVD name, DVD
price, and DVD location, three arrays are needed. These arrays will be used
in two different event procedures, so the arrays and the number of elements
in the arrays must be declared at the form level. The DVD name array and
DVD location array will be String data types, but the DVD price array will be
a Decimal data type array. Declaring form-level variables for the frmDVD
form is the same as doing it for any other form—you declare them prior to
any of the event procedures. The necessary declaration statements are shown
in VB Code Box 6-13, where we have not given the arrays in maximum size
because they will be input from a file and we will not know in advance how
many there are.

VB CODE BOX 6-13. Form-level declaration of arrays in frmDVDs	```Dim strDVDs() As String, intNumDVDs As Integer``` ```Dim decDVDPrice() As Decimal, strDVDLoc() as string```

Once the arrays have been declared at the form level, the next step is to
write the code to input the list of DVDs when the form is loaded in the
frmDVDs_Load event procedure. This code is very similar to that used earlier
to input the part identifiers and prices from a file. If the file name is *DVDs.txt,*
and it is stored in the Bin folder within the Vintage folder, the code to input
names, prices, and locations into the *strDVDs, decDVDPrice,* and *strDVDLoc*
arrays is shown in VB Code Box 6-14.

Step-by-Step Instructions 6-4: Using multiple forms

1. Create a new folder within the *Chapter6* folder named **Vintage6** and copy
all of the files and folders in the *Chapter5\Vintage5* folder into the new
folder.

| VB CODE BOX 6-14. Code for frmDVDs_Load event procedure | ```
Private Sub DVDs_Load(ByVal sender As System.Object, _
ByVal e As System.EventArgs) Handles MyBase.Load
    Dim strOutput, strLine As String, strFields() As String
    Dim strMyPath As String, chrDelimiter As Char = ","
    strMyPath = CurDir() & "\DVDs.txt"
    Dim srdReadDVDs As System.IO.StreamReader = New _
    System.IO.StreamReader(strMyPath)
    Do Until srdReadDVDs.Peek = -1
        ReDim Preserve strDVDs(intNumDVDs)
        ReDim Preserve decDVDPrice(intNumDVDs)
        ReDim Preserve strDVDLoc(intNumDVDs)
        strLine = srdReadDVDs.ReadLine
        strFields = strLine.Split(chrDelimiter)
        strDVDs(intNumDVDs) = strFields(0)
        decDVDPrice(intNumDVDs) = CDec(strFields(1))
        strDVDLoc(intNumDVDs) = strFields(2)
        intNumDVDs = intNumDVDs + 1
    Loop
    FileClose()
End Sub
``` |

2. Start VB .NET (or use File | Open) and open the new *Vintage6* project and add the **btnFindDVD** button to the frmVintage form below the Delete button. Use **Find DVD** as the text property. The resulting form should look like Figure 6-10.

3. Use the **Project | Add Windows Form** menu selection or the **Add Item** icon to add a new form to the Vintage project. Give the new form a name of **frmDVDs** and give it a text property of **DVD List.** Add the controls shown in Table 6-6. The result should look like Figure 6-11.

TABLE 6-6: Controls for frmDVDs form

Control Name	Text Property	Control Name	Text Property
btnSearch	Search	lstDVDs	
btnBack	Back	lblDVDs	Find a DVD

4. Resize the form to be as small as possible while keeping the list box wide enough to display DVD names, prices, and locations.

5. Go into the Code window for the frmVintage form and add the form-level declaration statement to create an instance frmDVDs as shown below:

```
Dim frmNewDVDs as New frmDVDs
```

6. Add the instruction

```
frmNewDVDs.Show
```

to the btnFindDVD_Click event procedure.

7. Now go to the frmDVDs form and add the form-level declarations shown in VB Code Box 6-13.

8. Add the code shown in VB Code Box 6-14 to the frmDVDs_Load event procedure to input the DVD names, prices, and locations.

9. Use Notepad to create a file called **DVDs.txt** with the DVDs shown in Table 6-7 plus 20 or so other pre-1990 DVDs of your choosing.
```

TABLE 6-7: DVDs for DVDs.txt data file

DVD Name	DVD Price	DVD Location
Ghost	1.99	Drama
Ghostbusters	1.99	Comedy
Sons of Katie Elder	1.99	Western
Bambi	0.99	Kids
Star Wars (original)	2.99	Sci-Fi
The Ghost and Mrs. Muir	1.99	Drama

Be sure and include the DVD name and location in quotation marks with the price in between them, all separated by *commas*. For example, the first entry should be

```
"Ghost", 1.99, "Drama"
```

(You may also download this data file from the Chapter 6 section of the textbook Web site.)

10. Add the following two instructions to the frmDVDs_Load event procedure immediately prior to the statement to increment the variable intNumD-VDs to output the arrays read from the file and run your project

```
strOutput = strDVDs(intNumDVDs) & "  " & strDVDs(intNumDVDs) & _
" " & format(decDVDPrice(intNumDVDs), "currency")
debug.Writeline(strOutput)
```

11. Click the *Find DVD* button on the main form to display the DVD List form. All of the DVD information should appear in the Output window.

12. When your project works correctly, remove the two statements you just added and save all of the files in the project.

■ ▬ ■ ▬ ▬ ▬ ■ ▬ ■ ▮

Mini-Summary 6-5: Using multiple forms

1. It is possible to have multiple forms in a project. A new form can be added using the Project | New Windows Form menu option or the New Item icon on the toolbar.

2. To display one form from another, you must create an instance of the other form. Once a new instance has been declared, the Show method can be used to display another form.

It's Your Turn!

1. What two ways can be used to add a new form to a project?

2. How is a new instance of a form created?

3. What method is used to display an instance of a form?

4. To modify the Vintage DVDs project to use a second form, follow Step-by-Step Instructions 6-4.

SEARCHING FOR DVDs

The logic to search for the DVD name or partial name is very much like that used earlier to search for a part identifier, with one exception: Since we are searching for a partial name, we need to use a String function that will determine if a word or sequence of characters is a **substring** of a longer string sequence. This is the **InStr( )** function. The form of this function is

InStr(*string to search, search string*)

where *string to search* is the character string that is being searched for an occurrence of the second parameter *search string*. If the search string is found as a substring of the string to search, InStr( ) returns the position at which it begins. If no match is found, InStr( ) returns zero. Thus, to determine if a match was found, all that is necessary is to determine if InStr( ) returned a nonzero value.

For example, InStr("Ghostbusters", "Ghost") returns a nonzero value of 1, since "Ghost" is a substring of "Ghostbusters" that begins at the first character. Similarly, InStr("Ghostbusters", "bust") also returns a nonzero value. However, since InStr( ) does a case-sensitive comparison, InStr("Ghostbusters", "Bust") returns zero because "Bust" is not in "Ghostbusters." One way to avoid this problem is to use the UCase( ) function to convert all strings to upper case before doing any comparisons. If this is done, InStr(UCase("Ghostbusters"), UCase("Bust")) returns a nonzero value, because "BUST" is a substring of "GHOSTBUSTERS."

If the user enters a partial title, such as "ghost," then multiple titles may be returned. Each title should be added to the list box—unless there are too many, in which case a message should be displayed requesting a more specific search word. For example, to search for all DVDs with "the" in their title would result in far too many DVDs being listed to be of any help. The code for the btnSearch_Click event procedure to search for DVDs matching the search string is shown in VB Code Box 6-15.

Note in VB Code Box 6-15 that a For-Next loop is used to compare the character string entered from the InputBox to each DVD name entered earlier. If the character string is found to be a substring of the DVD name, the DVD name is added to the list box and the number of matches counter is incremented. After the For-Each loop, the number of matches is checked to determine if no matches were found or if too many (> 5) matches were found. If too many were found, the list box is cleared when the *OK* button on the message box is clicked.

If one to five DVDs that matched the search string were found, the user can then click on any one of them in the list box to display price and location. The code is similar to that shown in VB Code Box 6-15, except that since an exact match is desired here, the InStr( ) function is *not* used. The code for the lstDVD_SelectedIndex-Changed event is shown in VB Code Box 6-16.

In this code, lstDVDs is cleared, and once the match is found, the name, price, and location are displayed in the list box. Figure 6-12 shows the frmD-

| **VB Code Box 6-15.** Code to search for DVD name | ```
Private Sub btnSearch_Click(ByVal eventSender As Object, _
ByVal eventArgs As System.EventArgs) Handles btnSearch.Click
    Dim strDVDName, strOneDVD As String
    Dim intCounter, intNumMatches As Integer
    strDVDName = InputBox("Input DVD name.", "Vintage DVDs")
    lstDVDs.Items.Clear()
    lstDVDs.Items.Add("DVD Name")
    For Each strOneDVD In strDVDs
        If InStr(UCase(strOneDVD), UCase(strDVDName)) > 0 Then
            intNumMatches = intNumMatches + 1
            lstDVDs.Items.Add(strOneDVD)
        End If
    Next
    If intNumMatches = 0 Then
        MsgBox("No matching DVDs found! Try again.", _
        vbExclamation, "Vintage DVDs")
    ElseIf intNumMatches <= 5 Then
        lstDVDs.Items.Add(Str(intNumMatches) & " DVDs found")
    Else
        lstDVDs.Items.Clear()
        MsgBox("Too many matching DVDs", _
        vbExclamation, "Vintage DVDs")
    End If
End Sub
``` |
|---|---|

| **VB Code Box 6-16.** Code to search for exact match of DVD name | ```
Private Sub lstDVDs_SelectedIndexChanged(ByVal _
eventSender As Object, ByVal eventArgs As System.EventArgs)_
Handles lstDVDs.SelectedIndexChanged
    Dim strDVDName, strOneDVD As String, intCounter As Integer
    strDVDName = lstDVDs.SelectedItem
    lstDVDs.Items.Clear()
    intCounter = 0
    For Each strOneDVD In strDVDs
        If strDVDName = strOneDVD Then
            lstDVDs.Items.Add(strDVDName & " " & _
            Format(decDVDPrice(intCounter), "currency") & " " _
            & strDVDLoc(intCounter))
            intCounter = intCounter + 1
            Exit For
        End If
    Next
End Sub
``` |
|---|---|

VDs form after the string "ghost" is searched for and after "Ghostbusters" is clicked.

The only thing left to do in this project is to add an instruction to the btn-Back button to clear the information on the DVDs form and hide it. Hiding a form is accomplished with the **Hide** method of the form to be hidden. That is, to hide the current form without removing it from memory, the statement form is

Me.Hide

where "Me" refers to the current form. This code is shown in VB Code Box 6-17..

FIGURE 6-12.
frmDVDs after
search and after
selecting a DVD

VB CODE BOX 6-17. btnBack_Click event procedure	```Private Sub btnBack_Click(ByVal eventSender As Object, _```

```
Private Sub btnBack_Click(ByVal eventSender As Object, _
ByVal eventArgs As EventArgs) Handles btnBack.Click
    lstDVDs.Items.Clear()
    Me.Hide()
End Sub
```

Step-by-Step Instructions 6-5: Searching for DVDs

1. Add the code shown in VB Code Box 6-15 to the btnSearch_Click event procedure on the frmDVDs form.

2. Add the code shown in VB Code Box 6-16 to the lstDVDs_SelectedIndex-Changed event procedure on the frmDVDs form.

3. Add the code shown in VB Code Box 6-17 to the btnBack_Click event procedure on the frmDVDs form.

4. Run your project, switch to the frmDVDs form, and enter "ghost" in the txtSearch text box. Click the *Search* button to display the DVDs shown on the left side of Figure 6-12. Click on the *Ghostbusters* selection in the list box to display the information on this DVD shown on the right side of Figure 6-12. Click on *Back* to return to the main form.

5. When the project is working correctly, save all files. The complete code for the new DVDs form operations is shown in VB Code Box 6-18

Mini-Summary 6-6: Searching for DVDs

1.The Instr() function can be used to search a string for the occurrence of a substring and return the location of the beginning of the substring if it is found and zero, otherwise. The UCase() function can be used to convert strings to uppercase.

2. To hide a form, the Hide method of a form can be used. The Me keyword can use used in place of the current form name.

| **VB Code Box 6-18.** Complete code for DVDs form | ```
Dim strDVDs() As String, intNumDVDs As Integer
Dim decDVDPrice() as Decimal, strDVDLoc() As String

Private Sub DVDs_Load(ByVal sender As System.Object, _
ByVal e As System.EventArgs) Handles MyBase.Load
    Dim strOutput, strLine As String, strFields() As String
    Dim strMyPath As String, chrDelimiter As Char = ","
    strMyPath = CurDir() & "\DVDs.txt"
    Dim srdReadDVDs As System.IO.StreamReader = New _
    System.IO.StreamReader(strMyPath)
    Do Until srdReadDVDs.Peek = -1
        ReDim Preserve strDVDs(intNumDVDs)
        ReDim Preserve decDVDPrice(intNumDVDs)
        ReDim Preserve strDVDLoc(intNumDVDs)
        strLine = srdReadDVDs.ReadLine
        strFields = strLine.Split(chrDelimiter)
        strDVDs(intNumDVDs) = strFields(0)
        decDVDPrice(intNumDVDs) = CDec(strFields(1))
        strDVDLoc(intNumDVDs) = strFields(2)
        intNumDVDs = intNumDVDs + 1
    Loop
    FileClose()
End Sub
Private Sub lstDVDs_SelectedIndexChanged(ByVal eventSender _
As Object, ByVal eventArgs As System.EventArgs) _
Handles lstDVDs.SelectedIndexChanged
    Dim strDVDName, strOneDVD As String, intCounter As Integer
    strDVDName = lstDVDs.Text
    lstDVDs.Items.Clear()
    For Each strOneDVD In strDVDs
        If strDVDName = strOneDVD Then
            lstDVDs.Items.Add(strDVDName & " " & _
            Format(decDVDPrice(intCounter), "currency") & " " _
            & strDVDLoc(intCounter))
            intCounter = intCounter + 1
            Exit For
        End If
    Next
End Sub
Private Sub btnBack_Click(ByVal eventSender As Object, _
ByVal eventArgs As EventArgs) Handles btnBack.Click
    lstDVDs.Items.Clear()
    Me.Hide()
End Sub
``` |
```

| VB CODE BOX 6-19. Complete code for DVDs form (Cont.) | ```Private Sub btnSearch_Click(ByVal eventSender As Object, _ ByVal eventArgs As System.EventArgs) Handles btnSearch.Click   Dim strDVDName, strOneDVD As String   Dim intCounter, intNumMatches As Integer   strDVDName = InputBox("Input DVD name.", "Vintage DVDs")   lstDVDs.Items.Clear()   lstDVDs.Items.Add("DVD Name")   For Each strOneDVD In strDVDs   If InStr(UCase(strOneDVD), UCase(strDVDName)) > 0 Then   intNumMatches = intNumMatches + 1   lstDVDs.Items.Add(strOneDVD)   End If   Next   If intNumMatches = 0 Then   MsgBox("No matching DVDs found! Try again.", _   vbExclamation, "Vintage DVDs")   ElseIf intNumMatches <= 5 Then   lstDVDs.Items.Add(Str(intNumMatches) & " DVDs found")   Else   lstDVDs.Items.Clear()   MsgBox("Too many matching DVDs", _   vbExclamation, "Vintage DVDs")   End If End Sub``` |

It's Your Turn!

1. Why is the InStr() function needed to add DVDs to the lstDVDs list box but is not needed to display the information for a particular DVD?

2. Why is the UCase() property often combined with the Instr() function?

3. What property of the form is used with the Hide function to cease displaying a form.

4. To complete the frmDVDs form to search for DVDs, follow Step-by-Step Instructions 6-5.

WORKING WITH TWO-DIMENSIONAL ARRAYS

Now that we have worked with one-dimensional arrays of lists of items, we will consider situations where a two-dimensional array or table is needed. There are many situations in business where tables are used, including tables of intercity shipping charges, income tax tables, and tables of unemployment statistics by month and city, and many more.

Two-dimensional arrays share many characteristics with one-dimensional arrays, so much of this discussion will be an extension of the earlier part of this chapter. The first thing to note is that these tables require two index values or subscripts for the array, with the first index giving the row position and the second subscript giving the column position.

Declaring Two-Dimensional Arrays

To declare a two-dimensional array (a table), you must provide the maximum row and column index values. The general form for declaring a table array is

Dim *ArrayName(max row index, max column index)* as *var type*

For example, if the maximum row index is 10 and the maximum column index is 20 for an array that will hold Single data type values, the declaration statement is

```
Dim sngNumberTable(10, 20) as Single
```

Like lists, table arrays start both the row and column index values at zero; therefore, in the example, sngNumberTable will hold 11 rows and 21 columns for a total of 11 × 21 = 231 elements.

To illustrate, assume we have a table of revenues for products and regions (in millions of dollars) for a computer company, as shown in Table 6-8.

TABLE 6-8: Product revenues by region (in millions of dollars)

Product	Northeast	Southeast	Midwest	West
PCs	53.5	62.1	27.1	41.5
Storage	24.7	23.5	27.3	20.3
Memory	15.1	11.3	17.9	20.7

If we wanted to store this information in a two-dimensional array, we would first declare the maximum row index in the first position, and then the maximum column index in the second position. For our example this would be

```
Dim decRevenue(2,3) as Decimal
```

As in list arrays, the index values for the first row and first column are zero.

In the table above, the revenue for PCs in the Northeast region is in the element decRevenue(0,0), because PCs is the first row and Northeast is the first column. Likewise, the element decRevenue(2,3) gives the revenue for memory in the West region. Each element of the table is uniquely defined by its row and column position.

Input for Two-Dimensional Arrays

All of the methods for handling input with lists also work for tables. The most commonly used method of input for tables is a nested For-Next loop, where the outer loop is used to input the rows of an array and the inner loop is used to input the columns. This means that all of the elements of the first row are input first, followed by all the elements of the second row.

For example, in the product revenues table above, the statements necessary to read the revenue data from a file on an item-by-item basis for each row in the frmRevenue_Load event procedure are shown in VB Code Box 6-20 preceded by the form-level declaration of the decRevenue array. The input assumes that revenue.txt has only one value per line.

The Input statement will read all of the first row, then all of the second row, then all of the third row, as shown in Table 6-9.

If we reverse the row and column counters in the For-Next loop, then the order of input would read all of the first column, then all the second column, and so on through all four columns.

| VB CODE BOX 6-20. Form_Load event procedure to input data for two-dimensional array | ```
Dim decRevenue(2, 3) As Decimal
Private Sub frmRevenue_Load(ByVal sender As Object, _
ByVal e As EventArgs) Handles MyBase.Load
   Dim intProduct As Integer, intRegion As Integer
   FileOpen(10, CurDir() + "\revenue.txt", OpenMode.Input)
   For intProduct = 0 To 2
      For intRegion = 0 To 3
         Input(10, decRevenue(intProduct, intRegion))
      Next intRegion
   Next intProduct
End Sub
``` |
|---|---|

TABLE 6-9: Revenue data

Read first	53.5	62.1	27.1	41.5
Read second	24.7	23.5	27.3	20.3
Read third	15.1	11.3	17.9	20.7

Processing Tables

As in one-dimensional arrays, data manipulation on two-dimensional arrays is performed on an element-by-element basis. Although these operations were performed with a single For-Each loop for list arrays, tables often require nested For-Next loops, especially if all values in the array are involved in the operation. For-Each loops are inappropriate because you need to specify exactly which element of the table is being input or processed.

For example, suppose we want to know the total revenues by product and by region. To make these calculations, we need to use nested For-Next loops to cover all elements. Assume that we have a form with three buttons—one for product totals, one for regional totals, and one to exit the project—and a list box for output.

To find the product totals, we need to sum across the rows and add the sum to the list box with an appropriate message. To find the regional totals, we need to sum down columns, adding the sums to the list box. The Code window for this form is shown in VB Code Box 6-21, and the form after the *Total by Product* button has been clicked is shown in Figure 6-13 .

■ ■

Step-by-Step Instructions 6-6: Working with two-dimensional arrays

1. To create a project to work a two-dimensional array, start VB .NET or select **File | New Project** and choose to create a new project with a name of **Revenues** in the Chapter6 folder. Give the form a name of **frmRevenue** and change the Startup object to be **frmRevenue.** Double-click the form and enter the code shown in VB Code Box 6-5 in the frmRevenue_Load event procedure.
```

FIGURE 6-13.
Results of finding
sums by product

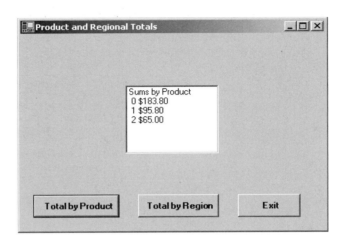

VB CODE BOX 6-21. Working with two- dimensional arrays	

```
Private Sub btnProduct_Click(ByVal sender As Object, _
ByVal e As EventArgs) Handles btnProduct.Click
    Dim decProductSum As Decimal, intProduct As Integer
    Dim intRegion As Integer
    lstSums.Items.Clear()
    lstSums.Items.Add("Sums by Product")
    For intProduct = 0 To 2
        decProductSum = 0
        For intRegion = 0 To 3
            decProductSum = decProductSum + _
            decRevenue(intProduct, intRegion)
        Next intRegion
        lstSums.Items.Add(Str(intProduct) & " " & _
        Format(decProductSum, "currency"))
    Next intProduct
End Sub
Private Sub btnRegion_Click(ByVal sender As Object, _
ByVal e As EventArgs) Handles btnRegion.Click
    Dim decRegionSum As Decimal, intProduct As Integer
    Dim intRegion As Integer
    lstSums.Items.Clear()
    lstSums.Items.Add("Sums by Region")
    For intRegion = 0 To 3
        decRegionSum = 0
        For intProduct = 0 To 2
            decRegionSum = decRegionSum + _
            decRevenue(intProduct, intRegion)
        Next intProduct
        lstSums.Items.Add(Str(intRegion) & " " & _
        Format(decRegionSum, "currency"))
    Next intRegion
End Sub
```

2. Add buttons to compute and display the product and region tables named **btnProduct** and **btnRegion,** respectively with text properties of **Total by Product** and **Total by Region**. Also add a button, **btnExit,** to exit the project. Add the text properties for the buttons shown in Figure 6-13.

3. Add the code shown in VB Code Box 6-20 to declare the array at the form level and to input the revenue data into a two-dimensional array.

4. Enter the code shown in VB Code Box 6-21 for the two buttons, btnProduct and btnRegion. Add the code to exit the project to btnExit.

5. Create a data file named **Revenue.txt** for the data shown in Table 6-3. Enter the numeric data (not the headers) one per line for the first row (press **ENTER** after each one), then the second row, and, lastly, the third row. Save this file to the Bin folder for this project.

6. Run this project to compute and display the product and region totals shown in Figure 6-13.

Mini-Summary 6-7: Two-dimensional arrays

1. In VB .NET, tables are processed as two-dimensional arrays, with the first index referring to the row and the second referring to the column of the table.

2. Nested For-Next loops are usually the best way to input and process two-dimensional arrays.

It's Your Turn!

1. How many array elements are in each array declared by the following dimension statements?

    a. Dim intNum(4, 4) As Integer
    b. Dim strID(3, 5) as String
    c. Dim sngData(2, 10) as Single

2. Declare two-dimensional arrays as follows:

    a. Salaries in five departments for the four quarters of the year.
    b. Sales for 10 companies for each of the 12 months of the year.
    c. Unemployment percentages for each of the 50 states for the last 10 years.

3. Why is the For-Each loop not appropriate for input and processing of two-dimensional arrays?

4. What would you do to add a button that would compute the grand total of all sales for the Revenue project?

5. To complete the Revenue project, follow Step-by-Step Instructions 6-6.

USING THE STEP COMMANDS FOR DEBUGGING

In Chapter 5, we discussed the use of watches, breakpoints, and windows to debug your projects. In addition to these tools, VB .NET allows you to *step* through your code one line or one event procedure at a time. When combined with the Output, Locals, Auto, and Watch windows, this capability allows you to view the changes that occur in variables as each line of code is executed. You can also step around event procedures that contain long loops or code that you believe to be correct. You can also step out of a procedure if you do not want to continue to watch it one line at a time. The three Step commands are available from the Debug submenu or from the Debug toolbar. The Debug toolbar icons are shown in Figure 6-14.

FIGURE 6-14. Step commands on Debug toolbar

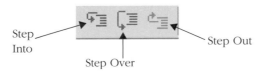

Step Into

Step Over

Step Out

If you click the Step Into icon in Break mode, you can then *step through* the code by repeatedly clicking the **Step Into** icon. If you turn on the Locals or Autos windows using the **Debug|Windows** menu, you can watch their values as you step through the code. You can also display the values for variables by positioning the cursor over a variable while stepping through the code.

For example, assume that instead of using the greater-than sign (>) in the search for DVDs that match the search string in the Vintage DVDs project, you inadvertently entered the greater-than-or-equal-to sign (>=) in the line of code, as shown below:

```
If InStr(UCase(strDVDs(intCounter)), UCase(strVidName)) > = 0 Then
```

When the project is executed with this line of code, no matter what you enter as the search string, you always receive the message *Too many matching DVDs!* To find this error, we first need to set a Breakpoint at the beginning of the btnSearch_Click event procedure in the frmDVDs Code window. This will put the project into Break mode and you can then step through the code.

We set a breakpoint at the beginning of the btnSearch_Click event procedure because this is where the error appears to be occurring. If we had no idea where the error was occurring, we would set a breakpoint at the beginning of the Form_Load event procedure for the initial form, in this case, frmVintage_Load, and then step through the entire program. Procedures can be skipped by selecting the Step Over option.

> **TIP:** When debugging, it is often helpful to set a breakpoint at a point past code that has already been tested and then step into the code from that point.

Recall that the Locals window shows the value of all variables that are declared in this event procedure, and the Autos window shows variables in the current statement plus those in the previous statement. Each type of window can be very useful, but for looking for the error in btnSearch_Click event procedure, we have chosen to use the Autos window since it shows the variables we need to see without forcing us to look through all of the variables declared in this procedure. It will also show form level variables in addition to local variables. With the Autos window displayed along with the Code window, you are ready to start stepping through the program.

If you start the project by clicking the Run icon or pressing **F5** and then clicking the *Find DVD* button on the main form, the DVDs form is displayed. If you then enter a partial DVD name, say, "ghost," in the DVD Name textbox and click the *Search* button, the first line of the btnSearch_Click event procedure for the DVDs form is displayed with yellow highlighting. By repeatedly clicking the *Step Into* icon, you can watch the values for variables in the Autos window as the procedure executes. You can also view the value of a variable by hovering the cursor over it. Although it is not the case in this situation, you may notice that there is a plus sign in the Autos window beside a variable name; this indicates that this variable is an array, and clicking the plus sign will display the items in the array. Figure 6-15 shows the screen after one iteration of the search loop. Note in the Autos window that even though strDVDName("ghost") is not contained in StrOneDVD("101 Dalmations"), the If-condition is still found to be true and the value of the intNumMatches variable has been set to one. This means that *every* DVD name matches the search string, which indicates a problem with the search criteria in the If-Then statement. Note that we have also hovered the cursor over intNumMatches to display a value of one—the same value as shown in the Autos window.

> **TIP** When stepping through a project, you still need to carry out all of the operations of the project by, say, clicking on buttons or entering data. If the form becomes minimized, you can display it by clicking the corresponding icon on the Windows task bar.

FIGURE 6-15.
Stepping through an event procedure

```
Private Sub btnSearch_Click(ByVal eventSender As System.Object, ByVal eventArgs As Syste
    Dim strDVDName, strOneDVD As String
    Dim intCounter, intNumMatches As Integer
    strDVDName = txtSearch.Text
    lstDVDs.Items.Clear()
    lstDVDs.Items.Add("DVD Name")
    For Each strOneDVD In strDVDs
        If InStr(UCase(strOneDVD), UCase(strDVDName)) >= 0 Then
            intNumMatches = intNumMatches + 1
            lstDVDs.I intNumMatches = 1 OneDVD)
        End If
    Next
    If intNumMatches = 0 Then
        MsgBox("No matching DVDs found! Try again.", vbExclamation, "Vintage DVDs")
    ElseIf intNumMatches <= 5 Then
        lstDVDs.Items.Add(Str(intNumMatches) & " DVDs found")
    Else
        lstDVDs.Items.Clear()
        MsgBox("Too many matching DVDs", vbExclamation, "Vintage DVDs")
    End If
End Sub
```

Name	Value	Type
intNumMatches	1	Integer
strDVDName	"ghost"	String
strOneDVD	"101 Dalmations"	String

We have only shown you one of the many ways that you can use the Step process to look for errors in a project. You can also use the Locals and Watch windows as well as the Command and Output windows to display the value of variables within a procedure while looking for errors.

■ ■

Step-by-Step Instructions 6-7: Use the Step commands for debugging

1. Modify the **Vintage** project so that the If-Then statement in the btnSearch_Click event procedure in the frmDVDs form uses a greater-than-or-equal-to sign (>=) instead of a greater-than sign (>).

2. Set a breakpoint at the beginning of the btnSearch_Click event procedure and turn on the Locals window.

3. Start the execution of the project. Go as directly as possible to the DVDs form and enter some character string in the Search textbox. Click the *Search* button to activate the btnSearch_Click() event. Step through it watching the Autos window and hovering the cursor over the various variables. Note the values of the variables, especially that of the intNumMatches variable.

4. Stop the execution and correct the error you introduced earlier. Follow the same steps as before and step through the btnSearch_Click event procedure to see how the search procedure should work. Stop the execution of the project, but do not save it.

■ ■

SUMMARY

At the beginning of the chapter, we said you would be able to do a number of things after reading it. Let's review those things here:

1. Understand the use of list and table arrays in VB .NET projects and the difference between arrays and combo boxes, list boxes, and similar controls. In this chapter, we have studied list arrays and table arrays. A *list array* is a list of values or strings that are referred to as a single entity. A *table array* is an array with both rows and columns. As a list box, the index for a list array starts at zero. Unlike a list box, however, a list array must have the value of the index known or computed in the code. Also, unlike a list or combo box, in a list array, the array name is declared, along with the maximum value for the index or subscript that is used to distinguish between the array elements. Finally, a list array can contain data types other than the string type.

2. Declare the maximum index value for a list array and understand the errors that occur when declared upper limits on index values are exceeded. List and table arrays must be declared as to the maximum index value that will be accessed in them. Arrays can be redimensioned to a smaller or larger maximum index number as necessary using the ReDim Preserve statement. Through the use of the ReDim Preserve statement, it is possible for arrays with an unknown number of elements that are being input one at a time to not be given a maximum index value. The maximum index is redimensioned after each input of an array element.

3. Input data into an array from a file using loops and the StreamReader object and redimension it to match the number of elements input. To input the elements of an array from a file, the Input statement can be used as was done in Chapter 5. However, a more object-oriented approach is to create an instance of the StreamReader class and use it to read the sequential access file as a stream of data. This data must then be parsed using the Split method of the String data type to create an array of data items on each line.

4. Work with array data to find the sum and average of array values, the largest or smallest value in an array, match values in one array to those in another, and find a particular value in an array. Many operations can be accomplished using an array, including initializing them to some value, summing and averaging values in a list, finding the maximum or minimum value in a list, finding a particular value in a list, and working with multiple lists. For-Next and For-Each loops are the most common ways to process arrays. Finding the sum or average uses a loop to add each array value to a sum. Finding the maximum or minimum value (or string) in a list involves using a loop to compare each value in the list to the current maximum or minimum value and, if the current value is larger or smaller, replacing the maximum or minimum value with the current value.

Multiple lists can be handled by matching the index values in each list to corresponding elements of the array. If a maximum or minimum value or a search string is found in one list, the corresponding elements in the other lists are found by the matching index. If a For-Each loop is used to process of the arrays, a counter must be used to access arrays other than the one involved in the loop.

Finding a particular value or string in a list involves using a loop to search for matches between the search value or string and each value in the list. Flag variables are used to indicate that a match has been found and to indicate the index of the value in the list that matches the search string.

5. Add forms to a project and display or hide them. Forms are added to a project via the New Item icon or the Project|New Windows Form menu option. The additional forms enable you to place groups of operations on individual forms rather than crowding them onto a single form. To display a new form, it is necessary to instantiate it via the Dim New as a declaration statement. To hide the form, you use the Hide method of the current form.

6. Declare, input, process, and output two-dimensional arrays. Two-dimensional or table arrays allow you to work with tables in the same way that list arrays are used to work with lists. Working with two-dimensional arrays usually involves using nested For-Next loops for input and manipulation.

7. Use Step operations to step though an array operation to find and correct an error. Arrays can be debugged using the Step commands on the Debug menu or toolbar. These commands enable you to step through the code in an event procedure, watching the values of variables as each instruction is executed. You can also use these commands to step out of a procedure or to step over procedures rather than going through them.

EXERCISES

1. Declare an array for each of the following scenarios:

   a. A hobby shop sells a popular wooden railway system that includes 150 different items. The proprietor needs an array to store an alphanumeric product ID for each different item.

NEW VB .NET ELEMENTS

Control/Object	Properties	Methods	Events
StreamReader		ReadLine Peek	
String		Split	
Form object		Hide/Show	

NEW PROGRAMMING STATEMENTS

Statement to declare the size of an array **Dim** ArrayName(max index value) as variable type

Statement to input an array from a sequential access file
intCounter = 0
Do Until EOF(n)
  Input #n, ArrayName(intCounter)
  intcounter = intcounter + 1
Loop

Statement to redimension an array while preserving existing contents **Redim Preserve** ArrayName(new number of elements)
Statement to carry out a For-Each loop **For Each** variable **in** ArrayName   processing statements **Next**
Statement declare an instance of a class **Dim** instance of object **AS** object class = **New** object class

Statement to read from a sequential access file using a StreamReader object
Do Until srdReadFile.Peek = −1
    strLine = srdReadFile.ReadLine( )
    Process strLine
Loop

Statement to process string output (strLine) from StreamReader object into an array strFields = strLine.Split(strDelimiter) ArrayVariable0(intCounter) = strFields(0) ArrayVariable1(intCounter) = strFields(1) . . . intCounter = intCounter + 1
Statement to display a message box with buttons/icons and a title **MsgBox(**message, buttons, title**)**
Statement to determine which button on the message box is clicked variable = **MsgBox(**message, buttons, title**)**
Statement to declare a new instance of a form **Dim** *frmNewFormName* **as New** *frmFormName*
Statement to display an instance of form *frmNewFormName*.**Show**

NEW PROGRAMMING STATEMENTS (CONTINUED)

Statement to declare the size of an array **Dim** ArrayName(max index value) as variable type
Statement to determine if search string is a larger string variable = **InStr(**string to search, search string**)**
Statements to hide the current form **Me.Hide**
Statement to declare a two-dimensional array **Dim** ArrayName(max row index, max column index) as variable type

KEY TERMS

array
collating sequence
For-Each loop

flag
index
instance

parse
subscript

b. A survey has questions with responses ranging from –3 (strongly disagree) to 3 (strongly agree). The survey analyst needs an array to store a count of each possible response.

c. A department store chain has six stores, and each store has the same 10 departments. The chain would like to store the weekly sales of all departments in one array.

2. Write a VB .NET code segment for each of the following scenarios:

a. Myleig Hiers, a regional furniture chain, is going out of business and needs to close out its inventory. It decides to begin by offering 20% off for all furniture models. Prices for each of its 1,200 furniture models are stored in a one-dimensional array called decFurnPrices(). Write a VB .NET program segment that will calculate values for a new array called decDiscFurnPrices() that will hold the new discount price for each model.

b. Lens Makers creates custom eye wear quickly and at a reasonable price. Its inventory includes 220 frame styles. Information about the frames is stored in three different arrays: strProductID(), strFrameStyle(), and decPrice(). Write a VB .NET program segment that will allow the user to enter a product ID and then display the corresponding frame style and price.

c. The Big Chips Cookie Company records the number of cases of cookies produced each day over a four-week period. These values are stored in an array, intCases(3, 4), which includes the number of cases for each day (five per week) of the week. Write a code segment that would request a week number and a day from the user and then display the corresponding number of cases produced.

3. Describe the output displayed in txtResult after each of the following code segments is executed.

```
a. Private Sub btnGo_Click()
       Dim strLetters(10) As String, intJ As Integer
       Dim strTemp As String, intPos As Integer
```

```
      strTemp = strLetters(0)
      intPos = 0
      For intJ = 1 To 10
        If strLetters(intJ) < strTemp Then
          strTemp = strLetters(intJ)
          intPos = intJ
        End If
      Next intJ
      txtResult.Text = strTemp & " in pos. " & intPos
    End Sub
```

b.
```
Private Sub btnGo_Click()
    Dim intArr1(4) As Integer, intArr2(4) As Integer
    Dim intI As Integer, intJ As Integer
    txtResult.Text = 0
    For intJ = 0 To 4
      txtResult.Text = txtResult.Text +  _
        intArr1(intJ) * intArr2(intJ)
    Next intJ
End Sub
```

c.
```
Private Sub btnGo_Click()
    Dim intArr1(3, 3) As Integer
    Dim intArr2(3, 3) As Integer
    Dim intI As Integer, intJ As Integer
    Dim intTemp As Integer
    txtResult.Text = 0
    For intJ = 1 To 3
      For intI = 1 To 3
        If intArr1(intI, intJ) > intArr2(intI, intJ) Then
          strTemp = strTemp + intArr1(intI, intJ)
        Else
          strTemp = strTemp + intArr2(intI, intJ)
        End If
      Next intI
    Next intJ
    txtResult.Text = strTemp
End Sub
```

4. For each of the following, explain what is wrong with the code. What error messages would you see, if any? What can you do to fix it?

   a. The following code should initialize each item in the array to zero:

```
Private Sub btnGo_Click()
    Dim intArray(4) As Integer
    Dim intI As Integer
    For intI = 1 To 5
      intArray(intI) = 0
    Next intI
End Sub
```

   b. The following code segment should load intArray2 with the values of intArray1:

```
Private Sub btnGo_Click()
    Dim intArray1(4) As Integer
    Dim intArray2(4) As Integer
    Dim intI As Integer
```

```
        For intI = 0 To 4
           intI(intArray1) = intI(intArray2)
        Next intI
     End Sub
```

c. The code segment on the next page should load intArray2 with the values of intArray1 times 10:

```
     Private Sub btnGo_Click()
        Dim intArray1(4, 4) As Integer
        Dim intArray2(4, 4) As Integer
        Dim intI As Integer
        Dim intJ As Integer
        For intI = 0 To 4
          For intJ = 0 To 4
            intArray1(intI, intJ) = intArray2(intJ, intI * 10)
          Next intJ
        Next intI
     End Sub
```

PROJECTS

Before starting any of these projects, use Windows Explorer to create a folder within the *Chapter6* folder named **Homework.** Store all of the projects in the *Chapter6\Homework* folder.

1. Assume that a sequential file named **Students.txt** is created from the list of student names and quiz averages shown in Table 6-10. Create a project named **EX6-1** in the new *Chapter6\Homework* folder. This project should input data from Students.txt and store it in two arrays. The project should also determine the appropriate letter grade on a 90-80-70-60 scale and add it to a corresponding array. Rename the form file as **EX6-1.vb** and give it a name of **frmEX6-1** with an appropriate text property. To the form, add a button to display the name, quiz average, and letter grade in a list box. Add another button that will display the name, quiz average, and letter grade in text boxes for the students with the highest and lowest quiz scores. Add another button to find the average of the quiz averages.

TABLE 6-10: Student quiz averages

Student	Quiz Average
Booker, Alice	77
Bounds, Nancy	83
Carter, Jay	92
Ertel, Dean	63
Spafford, Phil	55
Boatright, Ann	66
Patrick, Chris	88
Burgell, George	93

2. Assume that a sequential file named **CustSales.txt** is created from the list

of customer names and sales shown in Table 6-11. Create a project named **EX6-2** in the *Chapter6\Homework* folder. Rename the form file as **EX6-2.vb** and give it a name of **frmEX6-2** with an appropriate text property. Add a button to the form so that it displays the customer name and sales amount in a list box. Add buttons that will display the name and sales amounts in text boxes for the customers with the highest and lowest sales and the average sales.

TABLE 6-11: Sales for customers

Customer Name	Sales
Calfos, Dennis	$3,456
Batson, Rick	$5,120
Jones, Mary	$7,490
Hitchcock, April	$5,435
Abernathy, Ann	$9,710
Smith, Jeff	$8,604

3. Assume that a sequential file named **Golfer.txt** is created from the list of golfers and golf scores shown in Table 6-13. Create a project named **EX6-3** in the *Chapter6\Homework* folder. Rename the form file as **EX6-3.vb** and give it a name of **frmEX6-3** with an appropriate text property. The project should input an unknown number of golfer names and golf scores from a the Golfer.txt file and store them in two arrays. The project should also determine the appropriate designation for the golfer according to Table 6-12.

TABLE 6-12: Golfer categories

Score	Designation
70 or less	Professional
71–79	Club Champ
80–89	Good
90–99	Fair
100 and above	Duffer

Add a button to the form so that it displays the golfer name, score, and designation in a list box. Add another button that will display the name and scores in text boxes for the golfers with the highest and lowest scores.

TABLE 6-13: Golf scores

Golfer	Score
Fred Smith	93
Larry Vinings	101
Hugh Smith	88

TABLE 6-13: Golf scores

Golfer	Score
Al Nimmi	79
Archie Card	83
Ben Brown	98

4. Assume that a sequential file named **ZipCodes.txt** is created from the list of cities and Zip codes shown in Table 6-14. Create a project named **EX6-4** in the *Chapter6\Homework* folder. Rename the form file as **EX6-4.vb** and give it a name of **frmEX6-4** with an appropriate text property. Assume that the name and Zip code for each city are input into two arrays from ZipCodes.txt. The project should find the Zip code for a city name that the user inputs. The user inputs a city for which she wants the Zip code and clicks a button to display it in another text box.

TABLE 6-14: Zip codes

City	Zip Code
Bishop	30621
Athens	30601
Bogart	30622
Comer	30629
Hull	30646
Watkinsville	30677

5. Assume that a sequential file named **Premium.txt** is created from the age ranges and associated insurance premiums shown in Table 6-15. Create a project named **EX6-5** in the *Chapter6\Homework* folder. Rename the form file as **EX6-5.vb** and give it a name of **frmEX6-5** with an appropriate text property. The project should input a list of age ranges and associated insurance premiums into two arrays from the Premium.txt file. Add a button to the form so that it displays the age ranges and premiums. Then add text boxes to input a person's name and age and a button to display the corresponding insurance premium in a third text box. For example, if the data in Table 6-15 were input and a person had an age of 39, his premium would be $95.

TABLE 6-15: Insurance categories

Age	Premium
20 or younger	$50
21–30	$65
31–40	$95
41–50	$135

TABLE 6-15: Insurance categories (Continued)

Age	Premium
51–60	$195
61 or older	$250

6. Create a project named **EX6-6** in the *Chapter6\Homework* folder. Copy all files form your *EX6-1* folder into the new folder. Add a second form to the project with filename of **EX6-6Two,** a name of **frmEX6-6Two,** and an appropriate caption. The user should be able switch to this new form by clicking a new button on the main form. When loaded, the second form inputs the same file as does the main form. On the second form, the user should be able to input a student name in a text box and click a button to display the student's name and average score in text boxes. Also, the user should be able to click another button to input a value from an input box and have a list box display the names of all students with a score above that value. (Don't change the name of the main form.)

7. Create a project named **EX6-7** in the *Chapter6\Homework* folder. Copy all files form your *EX6-2* folder into the new folder. Add a second form to the project with filename of **EX6-7Two,** a name of **frmEX6-7Two,** and an appropriate caption. The user should be able to switch to this new form by clicking a new button on the main form. When loaded, the second form inputs the same file as the main form. On the second form, the user should be able to input a customer's name in a text box and click a button to display the customer sales in another text box. Also, the user should be able to click another button to input a value from an input box and have a list box display the names of all salespeople selling less than this value. (Don't change the name of the main form.)

8. Create a project named **EX6-8** in the *Chapter6\Homework* folder. Copy all files form your EX6-3 folder into the new folder. Add a second form to the project with filename of **EX6-8Two,** a name of **frmEX6-8Two,** and an appropriate caption. The user should be able to switch to this new form by clicking a new button on the main form. When loaded, the second form inputs the same file as the main form. On the second form, the user should be able to input a golfer name in a text box and click a button to display the golfer's name and score in text boxes. The user should be able to click another button to input a score from an input box and have a list box display the names of all golfers with a score above that score. (Don't change the name of the main form.)

9. Assume that a sequential file named **Payroll.txt** is created from the payroll values shown in Table 6-16. Create a project named **EX6-9** in the *Chapter6\Homework* folder. Rename the form file as **EX6-9.vb** and give it a name of **frmEX6-9** with an appropriate text property. Create a project to declare a two-dimensional array that contains the total employee salaries for three departments for each of the first six months of the year. Input the data from the PayRoll.txt file by using the Form_Load event procedure. Add but-

tons and a list box to the form. The buttons should compute and display the average monthly salaries for each department and the total salaries for each month.

TABLE 6-16: Payroll data by month

Dept.	January	February	March	April	May	June
Personnel	$24,500	22,800	23,100	25,600	24,900	24,100
Engineering	$33.800	33,900	33,100	32,500	34,900	35,200
Sales	$28,300	27,900	26,500	29,500	30,100	29,300

10. Mega-Home Warehouse sells, among other things, lawn mowers. Past experience has indicated that the selling season is only six months long, lasting from April 1 through September 30. The sales division has forecast the sales for next year as shown in Table 6-17.

TABLE 6-17: Lawn mower demand each month

Month	Demand
April	40
May	20
June	30
July	40
August	30
September	20

All lawn mowers are purchased from an outside source at a cost of $80.00 per lawn mower. However, the supplier will sell them only in lots of 10, 20, 30, 40, or 50; monthly orders for fewer than 10 mowers or more than 50 are not accepted. Discounts based on the size of the lot ordered are shown in Table 6-18.

TABLE 6-18: Discounts

Lot Size	Discount (%)
10	5
20	5
30	10
40	20
50	25

For each order placed, the store is charged a fixed cost of $200 to cover shipping costs, insurance, and so on, regardless of the number ordered (except no charge for a month if no order is placed). Assume that the orders are placed at the first of the month and are received immediately. The store also incurs carrying charges of $12.50 for each mower that remains in stock at the end of any month.

Assume that a sequential file named **LawnMower.txt** is created from demand data shown in Table 6-17. Create a project named **EX6-10** in the *Chapter6\Homework* folder. Rename the form file as **EX6-10.vb** and give it a name of **frmEX6-10** with an appropriate text property. The project should calculate the total seasonal cost, the price that must be charged per mower in order for Mega-Home Warehouse to break even, and the price that must be charged to realize a profit of 30% based on the data in LawnMower.txt and Table 6-18. Try your program with various ordering policies (different combinations of orders per month) and determine which is best.

11. Suppose that in a certain city in the South, the pollen count is measured at two-hour intervals, beginning at midnight. These measurements are recorded for a one-week period and stored in file. The first line of the files contains the pollen count for day 1, the second line for day 2, and so on. An example file is shown in Table 6-19.

TABLE 6-19: Pollen count file

Day1	32	33	31	35	37	42	44	45	47	45	41	39
Day 2	33	32	31	36	42	51	47	50	55	50	46	39
Day 3	38	35	36	37	37	41	42	42	40	39	37	36
Day 4	32	33	35	37	42	44	46	47	49	51	47	43
Day 5	39	40	42	45	47	47	48	49	51	53	52	50
Day 6	38	39	39	42	43	43	45	46	47	48	47	44
Day 7	37	39	40	40	41	44	46	46	47	47	46	45

Assume that a sequential file named **Pollen.txt** is created from the data shown in Table 6-19. Create a project named **EX6-11** in the *Chapter6\Homework* folder. Rename the form file as **EX6-11.vb** and give it a name of **frmEX6-11** with an appropriate text property. Write a VB .NET program to produce and display a weekly report of the pollen count using the data in Pollen.txt. The report should consist of a table showing the pollen count for each day and time. In the margins of the table, display the average pollen count for each day and the average pollen count for each sampling time.

7   USING FUNCTIONS, SUBS, AND MODULES

After reading this chapter, you will be able to

1. Understand the importance of general procedures and modules in programming with VB .NET.

2. Describe the difference between the two types of general procedures: sub procedures and functions.

3. Describe the relationship between arguments and parameters in general procedures.

4. Understand the difference between passing by value and passing by reference in sub procedures.

5. Write functions to return single values and sub procedures to process multiple values.

6. Understand the types of errors that can occur in the use of general procedures.

7. Use the Code module to declare variables globally or create global general procedures.

8. Understand the use of string functions to work with string constants and variables.

9. Be able to write general procedures to add to arrays, delete from arrays, and print arrays in a desired order.

USING GENERAL PROCEDURES

Up to this point in the book, we have concentrated on the fundamentals of programming using assignment statements, decision structures, loops, and arrays. You are now ready to consider more complex programs that carry out a variety of activities. Creating projects for more complex situations like those that involve arrays requires that we use the Julius Caesar approach to programming: Divide and conquer! By this we mean that instead of trying to think about the entire project all at one time, we should divide it up into pieces that are more easily programmed. You have already been doing this with the VB .NET event procedures that you have been writing for each control on your forms. Each event procedure carries out a piece of the project, thus dividing it up into small pieces. For example, when you write an event procedure for the Click event of a button, you are taking care of that part of the overall project without having to worry about other controls and events. This is one of the reasons the Visual Basic family of languages, including VB .NET have become so popular.

Although event procedures are extremely useful in creating projects, they are associated with a particular event, and unless you remove the word *Private* that precedes an event procedure, it is not available to other forms. There will be many situations where you will want to write code that is *not* associated with a particular event or that will be available to multiple forms or both. To do this, we need to use **general** (rather than *event*) **procedures.**

A general procedure tells the project how to carry out a specific task that is not associated with an event. General procedures must be defined in the General object of the form and then *invoked* elsewhere on the form. Invoking a general procedure involves referring to it in another general or event procedure. For example, if you wrote a general procedure called FindMax to find the maximum value in a list in the form of an array, you could use Find-Max in the code whenever you wanted it to find the maximum value. Compare this to an event procedure, which reacts to some event caused by the user or by the system.

There are two types of general procedures that the user can write and include in the project: sub procedures (also called *subroutines*) and function procedures. Figure 7-1 shows the relationship between event procedures and the two types of general procedures.

FIGURE 7-1.
Relationship between general and event procedures

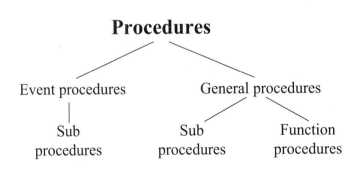

General procedures are *general* because they are not associated with any specific event or control and can be invoked by any part of the project. They are a form of **reusable code** since they can be invoked repeatedly throughout the project or saved and installed in other projects where a specific task is required. Rather than writing the same code over again in each location, you could create a general procedure that is invoked every time you want to do this. For example, the general procedure FindMax mentioned earlier could be used to find the maximum value in a list in several different places in a project. It could also be saved and used in other projects where finding the maximum value in a list is needed.

Another reason for using a general procedure is to reduce the complexity of event procedures. Instead of placing all of the input, output, and logic in an event procedure, it is possible to place some or all of the logic in one or more general procedures and have just the input and output statements in the event procedure. This is another way of dividing up the work that can enable you to separately test and debug parts of an event procedure.

Types of General
Procedures

As mentioned above, there are two types of general procedures: functions and sub procedures. A **function procedure** (or more simply, a **function**) is similar to the built-in functions that we have been using since Chapter 3 in that arguments are passed to it and are processed to compute and return a single value. The FindMax general procedure discussed earlier should be written as a function, since a single value—the maximum value in the list—is returned.

On the other hand, a **sub procedure** (hereafter referred to simply as a **sub**) is similar to an event procedure in that it is a unit of code that performs a specific task within a program but *returns* no value. Like event procedures, general sub procedures begin with the word *Sub* plus a name and end with *End Sub*. Although they return no value, subs can have arguments passed to them, the values of which can be changed in the sub and passed back to the calling procedure. For example, a sub to sort a list of names will have the list and the number of names in the list passed to it, and those names will be rearranged in the sub and passed back. Figure 7-2 shows the primary purposes of a sub and a function.

FIGURE 7-2.

Primary purposes
of sub and function
procedures

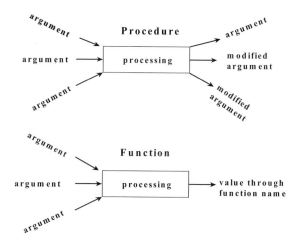

Note that two of the arguments passed to the sub are modified by it, and one is not. It is possible for none, some, or all of the arguments to be modified by the sub. On the other hand, although it is possible to modify the arguments of a function, this is not its primary purpose, so none are modified here.

Whether to use a function or a sub depends on whether a single value is to be returned. If it is, then a function should be used; otherwise, a sub should be used. Although both built-in functions and subs are available, in this chapter we will be discussing **programmer-defined general procedures,** that is, subs and functions that are created by the person developing the project.

Working with General Procedures

In either type of general procedure—that is, function or sub—you must first decide where the procedure will be used (invoked). Once you have made this decision, then you can design and write the general procedure to accomplish the desired purpose. Deciding where the general procedure will be invoked is a part of the overall design of the project. If an operation will be repeated in a project or if the logic in an event procedure is complicated, then a general procedure can be of great help in reducing both the amount of code to be written and the complexity of the programming. For example, if the membership list for Vintage DVDs needs to be searched for a single name, a function would be useful for handling this operation since only a single value is returned. On the other hand, if the list of names needs to be sorted, this may be a job for a sub since the entire list is being rearranged.

Designing a general procedure is much like designing an event procedure: You must decide what you want it to do, what the input and desired output are, and what logic is required to convert the input into the desired output. Input for a general procedure is usually through the arguments that pass values to it, but it is possible to use other forms of input. Similarly, output for a function is usually through its name, and output from a sub is usually through the arguments. However, in both cases it is possible to use other forms of output. Pseudocode is very important for developing the logic of a function or sub, and we will demonstrate its use here.

Mini-Summary 7-1: Working with functions and subs

1. General procedures are units of code that are not associated with a specific event and that can be used anywhere on a form or in the project as needed.

2. There are two types of general procedures: function procedures and sub procedures.

3. Function procedures return a value through their names, whereas subs do not return a value. However, subs can be used to modify the arguments passed to them.

It's Your Turn!

1. List the differences between an event procedure and a general procedure.

2. Give some reasons for using general procedures in a VB .NET project.

3. Why would you use a general procedure even if the operation occurs only once in the project?

4. List the primary purposes of functions and subs. Also, list the main differences between them.

5. Why is the name important in a function but not in a sub procedure?

6. For each of the following situations, tell whether you should use a function or a sub and why.

    a. Determine the number of occurrences of the letter *A* in a list of strings.

    b. Input a list of strings and create a new list of all the strings that begin with the letter *A*.

    c. Input a list of integers and find their sum.

    d. Input a list of integers and place them in order from largest to smallest.

7. How can you refer to another event procedure from within an event or general procedure?

8. When referring to a sub with arguments, how is it different from the reference to functions with arguments? (There are at least two differences.)

ADDING AND INVOKING SUBS AND FUNCTIONS

To work with subs and functions, you must first add them to the project and then invoke them. To add a function or sub, go to the end of any event or general procedure in the Code window and press **ENTER** to open up a line. Then enter the word *Function* or *Sub* plus the procedure name and press **ENTER** to create the first and last lines of the general procedure.

Once you have created the first and last lines of the function, you must include the list of parameters that will be used in the general procedure between the parentheses in the first line. **Parameters** are name and type specifiers of data being passed to and from the general procedure. They are separated by commas and must include the data type in the same way as declaration statements do.

The **Function definition statement** includes the name of the function followed by the list of parameters with type specifiers. Also, since function returns a value, the name must be declared as a data type. The general form of the Function definition statement is

Function *FuncName(parameter1* as *type, parameter2* as *type, ...)* as *type*

For example, the Function definition statement for a function to accept two string parameters and return the number of letters in the longest string would be

```
Function intMost(strWrd1 as String, strWrd2 as String) as Integer
```

Note that we have used a data type prefix for the function. This is done because functions return a value of a specific type, and using the data type prefix tells us what type value will be returned. It is important to note that the parameter types and the type of the function don't have to be the same. In the example shown above, the parameters are strings and the value returned is an Integer.

An important rule for creating functions is that, since the value of the function is returned, the function name should be assigned a value in the function or a value returned by the Return operation. In the first case, this means that the function name would appear on the left side of an assignment statement or a value for it should be input, for example, the statement

```
intMost= intLongWord
```

would assign a value to the function name in the intMost function example (where intLongWord contains the number of letters in the longest word).

In the second case, the variable containing the value to be returned must be included in the Return operation, for example, the statement

```
Return(intLongWord)
```

would return the value of intLongWord in the case of the intMost function.

Failure to assign a value to the function name or to return the value will result in the function not returning a value. We will return to this key point when we go into functions in more detail using the intMost function as well as others.

The general form of the Sub definition statement is similar to that of the Function definition statement, with the keyword *Sub* instead of *Function*:

Sub *SubName (parameter1* as *type, parameter2* as *type, ...)*

Note that there is no data type definition for a sub because it returns no value through the name. In fact, the name of a sub has no meaning other than to link the Sub definition statement to the statement invoking the sub. Since no value is returned through the sub name, it is *incorrect* to define a data type for the sub.

For example, the Sub procedure definition statement for a sub named Reverse that reverses two values would be

```
Sub Reverse(decFirst as decimal, decSecond as decimal)
```

where decFirst and decSecond are the parameters for this sub.

Invoking a Function or Sub

You invoke a function that you have written just like you invoke a VB .NET built-in function—by placing it on the left side of an assignment statement or by including it in any statement that would use a variable, say, a Debug.Writeline statement. In any case, you invoke the function by referring to the function name with the arguments in parentheses (where *arg1, arg2, ..., argn* are the arguments passed to the function):

variable = functionName(arg1, arg2, ..., argn)

For example, if you have created the intMost function described earlier, the statement to invoke this function with two string variables (strOne and strTwo) and display the result in a text box (txtMostLetters) would be

```
txtMostLetters.text = intMost(strOne, strTwo)
```

On the other hand, you invoke a sub by referring to its name and arguments in a separate line of code, with the arguments listed after the name separated by commas. The arguments are enclosed in parentheses in the same way as they are with functions. The general form of a sub reference is shown below:

subName(arg1, arg2, ..., argn)

For example, assume you have created the sub called Reverse, mentioned earlier, to reverse the values in two Decimal data type variables, decFirst and decSecond. After this sub is invoked, the variable decFirst is now equal to the old value of decSecond and decSecond is equal to the old value of decFirst. Invoking Reverse would be done as follows:

```
Reverse(decFirst, decSecond)
```

Matching Parameters and Arguments

The parameters in Function and Sub definition statements must match the arguments that appear in the statement invoking the function or sub, in terms of position, number, and data type. That is, the first argument must match the first parameter, the second argument the second parameter, and so on. Similarly, number of parameters should match the number of arguments. Finally, the data type of a parameter should match the data type for the corresponding argument. This is required because the parameters and arguments constitute the linkages between the definition statement and the statement invoking the function or sub. (Although it is possible to have optional arguments, we won't consider that situation in this text.)

For example, if there are three parameters in a Sub definition statement, with the first two being Integer data types and the last one being a String data type, then there must be three arguments in the statement invoking the sub, with the first two being integers and the third one being a string. Figure 7-3 shows the relationship between the Sub definition statement and the statement invoking the sub. In this figure, the name of the sub (SubName) must be the same in the statement invoking the sub and in the Sub definition statement. Also, the number of arguments matches the number of parameters and their types match. That is, the first argument (arg1) must be an Integer data type and the second argument (arg2) must a Decimal data type.

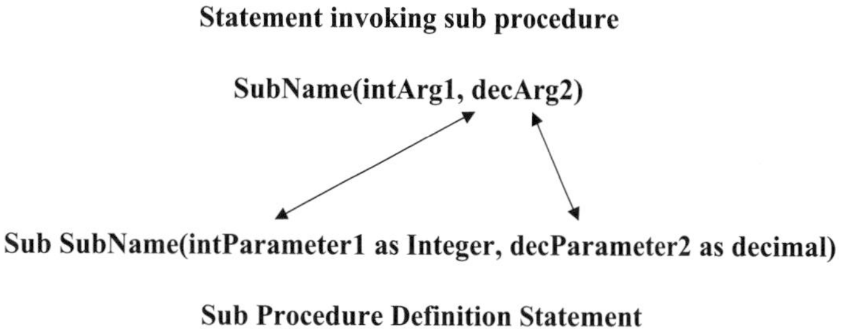

FIGURE 7-3.
Relationship between Sub definition statement and statement invoking the sub

Statement invoking sub procedure

SubName(intArg1, decArg2)

Sub SubName(intParameter1 as Integer, decParameter2 as decimal)

Sub Procedure Definition Statement

This type of argument-parameter matching holds for functions as well. This is shown in Figure 7-4 for a function that has one Integer parameter and one Decimal parameter and returns a Single data type value.

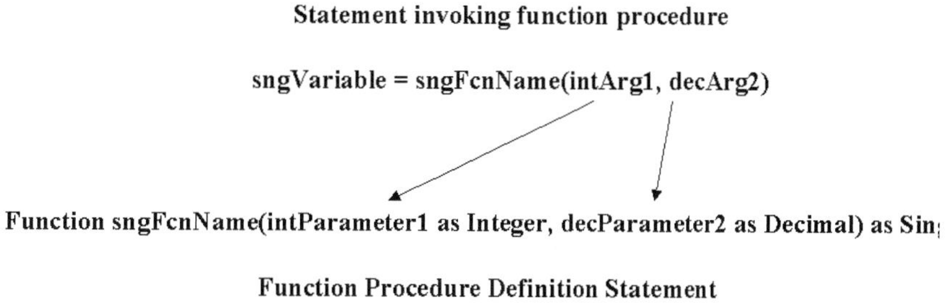

FIGURE 7-4.
Relationship between Function definition statement and statement invoking the function

Statement invoking function procedure

sngVariable = sngFcnName(intArg1, decArg2)

Function sngFcnName(intParameter1 as Integer, decParameter2 as Decimal) as Sin

Function Procedure Definition Statement

You have undoubtedly noticed in our examples that the variable names used as parameters in the functions and subs are not the same as the names used in the argument list. The reason for this is that the parameter names are local variables in the sub or function to which the value of the corresponding arguments are passed from the arguments in the invoking sub or function. This means that the same sub and function can be used with different arguments as long as the arguments match the parameters. For example, you could use the Reverse sub shown earlier to reverse another pair of Decimal values by calling it with a different set of arguments, as shown here:

```
Reverse(decMySalary, decYourSalary)
```

> **TIP:** You can define some parameters as optional by placing the **Optional** keyword in front of the corresponding parameter. If it is used, all parameters listed after the first Optional keyword must be optional, too.

Passing by Value or by Reference

As we mentioned earlier, parameters in functions and subs are local variables to which the value of the corresponding arguments in the invoking statement. These values can be passed in one of two ways: by value or by reference. **Passing by value** means that argument values are passed into a sub or function but *not* passed out; that is, the passing is a one-way street, and the arguments are protected from being changed in the sub or function. When a parameter is defined as being passed by value in a sub or function, it becomes a local variable in the sub that is initialized to the value of the corresponding argument. In essence, it is a *local copy* of the argument that cannot leave the sub.

On the other hand, **passing by reference** means that the argument in the calling procedure and the parameter in the sub or function occupy the same memory location. When a parameter variable is modified within the sub, the corresponding argument variable is also modified. The argument-parameter pair creates a *two-way* communication link between the sub or function and the statement that invokes it. We will show examples of passing by reference when we discuss processing arrays. In this case, any changes to a parameter inside the procedure are communicated back to the corresponding variable outside the procedure.

Passing by value is preferred when there is no need to communicate changes to variables inside a procedure to the corresponding argument. This is almost always the case with a function because the name of the function is assigned to the result of processing in the function. On the other hand, it is often useful to pass variables by reference in subs. For example, in the Reverse sub discussed earlier, passing by reference would be required to change the values of the arguments.

Passing by value is the default method of VB .NET. This is indicated by the fact that whenever a sub or function is created, the keyword, *ByVal,* is automatically inserted prior to every parameter in the sub or function definition statement, as shown in Figure 7-5. For this reason, the arrows in Figure 7-3 and Figure 7-4 are one way from the invoking statements to the function or sub definition statements. Although passing by value is the default method, it is easy to change to passing by reference by simply changing the

keyword *ByVal* to *ByRef*. It turns out that it is possible to have it both ways—
to pass some parameters by reference and to pass other parameters by value
by using ByVal for some parameters and ByRef for others. Figure 7-5 shows a
case where we have changed the second parameter to passing by reference
by changing *ByVal* to *ByRef* by typing over ByVal.

FIGURE 7-5. Default
use of passing by
value

```
Sub intmost(ByVal strWord1 As String, _
ByRef strWord2 As String)
```

It's Your Turn!

1. How are sub and functions different in the way in which they return values?

2. For each statement below, write a corresponding general procedure definition statement. The variable prefixes indicate the appropriate data type.
    a. blnAge = blnAgeValidate(strAge)
    b. intCount = intCntChar(strPhrase, strChar)
    c. LongAverage(intArr(), intNum)
    d. MatInv(intArr(), intSize, intArrInv())

3. Write a statement to invoke each of the following general procedures.
    a. Public Function sngConvert(intFeet as Integer)
    b. Public Function strBldMsg(strWords() As String, intNum As Integer)
    c. Public Sub Random(intSeed As Integer, sngRNum As Single)
    d. Public Sub Merge(intArr1() As Integer, intArr2() As Integer)

4. Using the sub Reverse discussed in the text, write the statement to invoke
it with two Integer variables, intHigh and intLow.

5. Rewrite the statement to invoke a function named intFindMaxList in if an
array of integers called intNumbers() and the number of integers called
intHowMany are passed to the function. Write the Function definition statement for intFindMaxList.

6. What is the difference between passing a variable by reference and passing a variable by value? When should you pass a variable by value?

**USING FUNCTIONS
TO PROCESS
ARRAYS**

In Chapter 6, we used event procedures to process arrays by summing and
averaging values in the array and finding the max value or a particular value
in the array. In looking at these operations, we can note that in all cases, a
single value is being returned—the sum, the average, the maximum value, or
the index of a particular item. This means that these operations are appropriate for functions. So, to introduce you to functions, we will rewrite all of
these processing operations as functions and then invoke the functions in the
event procedures.

    To do this, we must first create a new folder for this chapter named
Chapter7. To this new folder, we need to copy the *MultipleList* folder with all

its subfolders and files from the *Chapter6* folder. It is not necessary to modify any file or form names because we are only interested in changing the programming instructions, not the design of the project.

Functions for Summing and Averaging Values

Once you have an array of values, it is very easy to sum and average them using a function since a single value is being returned—the sum or average of the array values. To sum the values, we can use For-Next or For-Each loops to add each array element to a summation variable. To find the average, we simply divide the sum by the number of elements.

Let's start with a function to find the sum of the prices and follow with a function to find the average of the prices. The logic behind the decSum function used to find the sum of the prices is the same as that used in the existing btnSumAverage_Click event procedure; in fact, we can move the code from the event procedure into the function and then the modify the event procedure to reference the function. To create the function to find the sum of prices, you start by going to the beginning of any event procedure in the Code window for frmSumAverage and pressing **ENTER** to "open" an empty line in the Code window. In this open line, enter the word *Function* followed by the function name and a list of parameters in parentheses (even if there are no parameters, still include the parentheses) followed by the data type of the function as shown here:

```
Function decSum(ByVal decValues() as Decimal, _
    ByVal intNumValues as Integer) as Decimal
```

In this case, we have declared the function to be of type Decimal, which matches the prefix we have given the name. Note that the array parameter, decValues(), must have a set of parentheses associated with it to indicate it is an array. Note also that VB .NET automatically adds *ByVal* to indicate we are passing by value. VB .NET will also automatically add an "End Function" statement leaving room for you to start entering the code for the function.

The next step is to enter (or copy from the event procedure) the code to carry about the logic of the function. For the decSum function, the code is shown in VB Code Box 7-1 where the processing is handled by a For-Each loop that computes the sum by adding the values of the variable decOneValue (which sequentially takes on the value of each array element) to the summation variable decSumValues, which is returned after the loop is completed.

VB CODE BOX 7-1. Code to compute the sum and average of array elements	```Function decSum(ByVal decvalues() As Decimal) As Decimal
	    Dim decSumValues As Decimal, intCounter As Integer
	    Dim decAverage, decOnePrice As Decimal
	    decSumValues = 0
	    For Each decOnePrice In decPrices
	        decSumValues = decSumValues + decOnePrice
	    Next
	    Return (decSumValues)
	End Function```

To reference this function in the btnSumAverage_Click event procedure, the reference statement is

```
txtSum.text = decSum(decPrices,intNumPrices)
```

where the text property of the txtSum text box is set equal to the decSum function with the decPrices Decimal array and the intNumPrices Integer variable as arguments. Note that these arguments match the parameters in the function definition statement.

The function to compute the average of the prices, decAverage, is created in the same manner as the decSum function. The logic for this function involves dividing the value generated by the decSum function by the intNum-Values variable, since this value is the actual absolute number of elements in the array. Note that we need check to ensure that intNumPrices is *not* zero before we try to divide by it. Attempting to divide by zero is a very common error that is often caused by input errors in which no values were input. The resulting function is shown in VB Code Box 7-2.

| **VB CODE BOX 7-2.** Code for Average function | ```
Function decAverage(ByVal decValues() As Decimal, ByVal _
intNumValues As Integer) As Decimal
   If intNumValues > 0 Then
      decAverage = decSum(decValues, intNumValues) / IntNumPrices
   Else
      MsgBox("No values to average!")
      Exit Function
   End If
End Function
``` |
|---|---|

This function is also called by the btnSumAverage_Click event procedure by the following statement:

```
txtAverage.text = decAverage(decPrices,intNumPrices)
```

To format the output from the decSum and decAverage functions, we simply use the Format function on them as we would on a variable or constant. The revised code for the btnSumAverage_Click event is shown in VB Code Box 7-3, and when the project is run the output is the same as in Chapter 6.

| **VB CODE BOX 7-3.** Code for BtnSumAverage event procedure | ```
Private Sub btnSumAverage_Click(ByVal sender As Object, _
ByVal e As EventArgs) Handles btnSumAverage.Click
   txtSum.Text = Format(decSum(decPrices), _
   "currency")
   txtAverage.Text = Format(decAverage(decPrices, _
   intNumPrices), "currency")
End Sub
``` |
|---|---|

TIP: It is good programming practice to put the processing in general procedures, which are then referred to or called from event procedures.

Using Functions to Find the Maximum Value in an Array

To find the largest value in an array and the matching part identifier, the logic is the same as was used in Chapter 6 for the btnFindMax_Click event procedure for multiple lists (VB Code Box 6-11) and much of the code is the same. As with the decSum and decAverage functions, the function is created by pressing **ENTER** at the beginning of any existing procedure and entering the name of the function, **intMaxValue.** We precede this function with *int* to indicate it is an integer function. We only pass the intMaxValue function a

Decimal array, and it returns the index of the highest-valued element in the array. The code for the multiple list btnFindMax_Click event procedure is copied into the intMaxValue function and a Return instruction added; the result is shown in VB Code Box 7-4.

VB CODE BOX 7-4. Code to find the maximum price in the decPrices array	```Function intMaxValue(ByVal decValues() As Decimal) As Integer
Dim decMaxMin, decOneValue As Decimal, intMaxMin As Integer
Dim intCounter As Integer
decMaxMin = decValues(0)
intMaxMin = 0
For Each decOneValue In decValues
If decOneValue > decMaxMin Then
decMaxMin = decOneValue
intMaxMin = intCounter
End If
intCounter = intCounter + 1
Next
Return (intMaxMin)
End Function```

As with displaying the sum and average values, the contents of the btnFindMaxMin_Click event procedure are simply setting the txtMaxprice textbox equal to elements of the strPartID and decPrices arrays that match the highest-priced element, with formatting as shown in VB Code Box 7-5.

VB CODE BOX 7-5. Code for btnFind-MaxMin event procedure	```Private Sub btnFindMax_Click(ByVal sender As Object, _
ByVal e As EventArgs) Handles btnFindMax.Click
Dim intFoundMax As Integer
intFoundMax = intMaxValue(decPrices)
txtMaxPrice.Text = strPartID(intFoundMax) & " " & _
Format(decPrices(intFoundMax), "currency")
End Sub```

Note that we use a temporary variable, intFoundMax, in this code to avoid a very long assignment statement. The result of clicking all of the buttons on the form is the same as it was in Chapter 6; that is, the highest-priced part is Q49-3k at $23.75.

Using Functions to Find a Specific Item

As with the previous examples, we can also use a function to replace the code in the btnFind_Click event procedure to find the price for a specific part identifier. The process is almost identical: Create a function named intFindID and use the same logic we used in Chapter 6. The primary difference between this and previous examples of functions is that we will leave the input and output processes in the event procedure. The resulting intFindID function and btnFind_Click event procedure are both shown in VB Code Box 7-6. Note that the function returns a value of −1 if no match is found. The calling event procedure then checks if the returned value is negative and, if it is, does not attempt to output a value.

| VB CODE BOX 7-6. Function and event procedure to find a price | ```Function intFindID(ByVal strOneID As String, _
ByVal strList1() As String, ByVal decList() As Decimal, _
ByVal intNumList As Integer) As Integer
    Dim intFound As Integer, strItem As String
    Dim intCounter As Integer
    For Each strItem In strList1
        If UCase(strItem) = UCase(strOneID) Then
            intFound = intCounter
            Return (intFound)
            Exit Function
        End If
        intCounter = intCounter + 1
    Next
    MsgBox("No matching part ID found", VbExclamation, _
    "Price Search")
    Return (-1)
End Function
Private Sub btnFind_Click(ByVal sender As Object, _
ByVal e As EventArgs) Handles btnFind.Click
    Dim intCounter As Integer, intResults As Integer
    Dim strThePartID As String, decThePrice As Decimal
    Dim intResult As Integer
    strThePartID = InputBox("Input a Part ID", "Find Part ID")
    intResult = intFindID(strThePartID, strPartID, _
    decPrices, IntNumPrices)
    If intResult > -1 Then
        decThePrice = decPrices(intResult)
        txtFound.Text = strThePartID & "   " & _
        Format(decThePrice, "currency")
    End If
End Sub``` |

Step-by-Step Instructions 7-1: Using functions

1. Use Windows Explorer to create a new folder named **Chapter7** in the Visual Studio Projects folder. To this folder, copy the *MultipleList* folder and all of its files and subfolders from your *Chapter6* folder. There is no need to rename any of the files or forms in this folder.

2. Go into the Code window for the **frmMultiple** form and add the code shown in VB Code Box 7-1 to create the decSum function. Also, add the code shown in VB Code Box 7-2 to create the decAverage function.

3. Replace the existing code for the btnSumAverage_Click event procedure with the code shown in VB Code Box 7-3 to reference the decSum function and the decAverage functions. Run the project and click the btnSumAverage button. You should see the same sum of $102.69 and an average of $10.27 as before.

4. Go into the Code window and add the code shown in VB Code Box 7-4 to create the intMax function. Replace the existing code in the btnFindMax_Click event procedure with the code shown in VB Code Box 7-5

to reference the intMax function that determines the array index of the highest-priced part. Run the project and click the btnFindMax button to display the part with the highest price (Q49-3k and $23.75).

5. Add the code shown in VB Code Box 7-6 to the intFindID function and to replace the code in the btnFindID_Click( ) event procedure. Run the project, click the btnFind button, and enter **T17-6Y.** The same price as before should be displayed. Click the button again and enter **R73-0S.** You should determine that this is not a part identifier in the list.

6. Click the **Save All** icon to save the files in this project.

▪ ▬ ▪

Mini-Summary 7-2: Using functions

1. A common use of a function is to create a single value that is assigned to a variable or is output.

2. A function may or may not have arguments passed to it but must always have a value assigned to its name or a value returned.

3. Functions are useful for processing arrays because they can be used for specific operations.

It's Your Turn!

1. Why do we say that, in many cases, the For-Each loop is the best way to process an array? When is it not a good idea to use the For-Each loop?

2. Assume that the following form level declarations have been made:

```
Dim intMyArray(4) As Integer
```
Also assume that the intMyArray initially contains the following values:

0	1	2	3	4
10	13	7	24	2

and the following statements are executed:
```
MsgBox(intGetSumOdd(intMyArray))
MsgBox(strCorrChar(intMyArray, 2))
MsgBox(intProd(intMyArray))
MsgBox(intCount(intMyArray))
```
What value will be displayed if the following VB .NET functions are included in the project?

```
a. Function intGetSumOdd(ByVal intAnArray() As Integer) As Integer
      Dim intI As Integer
      For intI = 1 To 4 Step 2
         intGetSumOdd = intGetSumOdd + intAnArray(intI)
      Next intI
      Return intGetSumOdd
   End Function
```

```
b. Function strCorrChar(ByVal intAnArray() As Integer, _
     ByVal intNum As Integer) As String
          Dim intI As Integer
          strCorrChar = ""
          For intI = 0 To 4
              If intI = intNum Then
                  strCorrChar = Chr(intAnArray(intI))
              End If
          Next intI
          Return strCorrChar
     End Function
c. Function intProd(ByVal intAnArray() As Integer) As Integer
          Dim intI As Integer
          intProd = 1
          For intI = 0 To 4
              intProd = intProd * intAnArray(intI)
          Next intI
     End Function
d. Function intCount(ByVal intAnArray() As Integer) As Integer
          Dim intI As Integer
          For intI = 0 To 4
              If (intAnArray(intI) Mod 2) > 0 Then
                  intCount = intCount + 1
              End If
          Next intI
          Return intCount
     End Function
```

3. Follow Step-by-Step Instructions 7-1 to modify the *MultipleList* project to use functions to compute the sum, average, and maximum of a numeric array as well as finding a specific item.

USING SUBS: SORTING EXAMPLE

As mentioned earlier, programmer-defined subs are useful when the arguments will be modified by the general procedure and no value will be returned through the general procedure name. If the processing is executed multiple times, reusing the sub will reduce the amount of code that must be written. Even if the processing is carried out only once in a project, a sub is often still very useful in reducing the complexity of the programming. The Sub definition statement is like that shown earlier and includes the name of the sub and the parameter list with type specifications.

For example, assume you wanted to use a sub to sort the lists of part identifiers and prices in the MultipleList project in order of the prices. Figure 7-6 shows the form for that project after a button is added to sort the list according to price. Recall that there are two arrays associated with this project—strPartID() and decPrices()—and the number of items in both arrays is equal to intNumPrices.

You may ask, why not just use the Sorted property of the lstPrices list box to sort this list? That would work if the parts were to be sorted according to their identifier, since it appears first in the list box. However, to sort them according to the price, which appears second in the list box, we need to write a sub to rearrange the arrays themselves. This also has the advantage of rearranging the actual arrays, which is not done when the list box is sorted.

Since the decPrices() and strPartID() arrays and the number of items in both arrays, intNumPrices, were declared at the form level, they are known

FIGURE 7-6.
Modified parts list
form

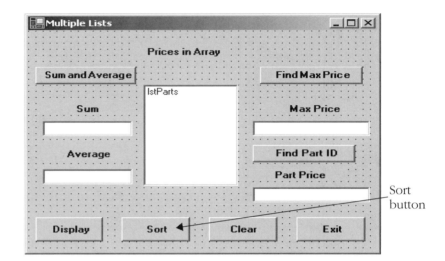

Sort button

to all event procedures on the form. That means we can pass them to a Sort sub called from within the btnSort_Click event procedure, as shown in VB Code Box 7-7.

VB CODE BOX 7-7. Event procedure for Sort button	`Private Sub btnSort_Click(ByVal sender As Object, _`
	`ByVal e As EventArgs) Handles btnSort.Click`
	`   Sort(decPrices, strPartID, intNumPrices)`
	`End Sub`

The Sorting Process

FIGURE 7-7.
decPrices Array

Prices(0)	$3.35
Prices(1)	$9.50
Prices(2)	$12.81
Prices(3)	$7.62
Prices(4)	$1.29
Prices(5)	$19.73
Prices(6)	$4.56
Prices(7)	$23.75
Prices(8)	$14.65
Prices(9)	$5.43

Sorting an array is a commonly used operation in processing data into information. This operation is similar to finding the maximum (or minimum) value in an array or finding an element in the array, because it involves pairwise comparisons. However, it goes further in also requiring repositioning of array elements. To help you understand the sorting process, we will use the list of 10 prices (decPrices()) from the PartsList project discussed earlier. This array is shown in Figure 7-7.

There are a variety of algorithms for sorting lists, but we will use a sort procedure that, while not very fast, is easy to understand. Called the **Bubble Sort,** this sorting process uses a For-Next loop to compare each array element to the next one, and if they are out of order, it reverses them. For example, if the decPrices() array is being ordered from smallest to largest, the decPrices(0) element is compared to decPrices(1). Since decPrices(0) is less than decPrices(1), no changes are made. Next, decPrices(1) is compared to decPrices(2), and once again, no changes are made. Next, decPrices(2) is compared to decPrices(3), and since decPrices(2) is greater than decPrices(3), they are reversed. The result of this reversal is shown in the *leftmost* set of prices in Figure 7-8 along with the remaining comparisons and reversals for the array.

Note in Figure 7-8 that, including the reversals of decPrices(2) and decPrices(3), which are not shown, there are five reversals of array elements due to a price being higher than the next price in the list. Note also that after this loop the largest value is at the bottom, but the array is not completely sorted. Even though this sorting algorithm is called the *Bubble Sort* because the lowest values *bubble* their way to the top of the list, in actuality, the largest values *sink* to their relative positions at the bottom of the list on each pass through the loop.

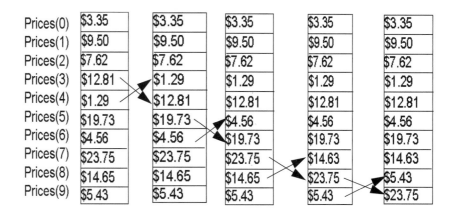

To completely sort the array, the comparison-reversal loop must be repeated as many times as necessary to sort the array. How do we know when the array is sorted? Note that if no reversals are made in the comparison-reversal loop, then the array is sorted. This indicates that we need a loop to repeat the comparison-reversal loop *until* no reversals are made. This is a situation where we use nested loops, with the outer loop being a Do Until loop and the inner loop being a For-Next loop. The pseudocode for this process is shown below:

```
Begin Sort procedure
Repeat until no reversals made
        Repeat for each pair of values
            If value > next value then
                Reverse values
            End decision
        End repeat
End repeat
End Procedure
```

Implementing this pseudocode in VB .NET requires that we address several programming issues:

1. How do we handle the For-Next loop and decisions to carry out the pairwise comparisons on array elements?

2. How do we reverse two array elements?

3. How do we handle the nested DoUntil and For-Next loops so that the array is repeatedly searched until no reversals have been made?

TIP: You can use Exit Sub or Exit Function to cause VB .NET to immediately terminate the current procedure. However, they should be used sparingly.

Carrying Out Pairwise Array Comparisons

To carry out the pairwise comparisons for the decPrices( ) array with index values that run from 0 to intNumPrices − 1, the For-Next loop runs from the first array element to the next to last, with each element being compared to the one that follows it. Since we are not processing every element in the array, we cannot use the For-Each loop. Note that the loop stops at the next-to-last array element because there is no *next* element after the last one. If the last element of the array has index intNumValues − 1, the index for the next to last array element will be intNumPrices − 2. This means that the first statement of the For-Next loop will be

```
For intCounter = 0 to intNumPrices - 2
```

Using the intCounter variable for the decPrices( ) array, the current value is decPrices(intCounter) and the *next* value will be decPrices(intCounter + 1). This means that the pairwise comparisons are of the following form:

```
If decPrices(intCounter) > decPrices(intCounter + 1) then
```

If the comparison is found to be true, and the two array elements are out of order, then they should be reversed. The forms of the For-Next loop and comparisons are as shown in VB Code Box 7-8 (where it is assumed that a sub will be used to reverse the two array elements).

VB Code Box 7-8. Code to reverse two price elements	```For intCounter = 0 To intNumList - 2 If decList1(intCounter) > decList1(intCounter + 1) Then Reverse(decList1(intCounter), decList1(intCounter + 1)) End If Next```

Using a sub to reverse the array elements is an example of reducing the complexity of code. Even though we do not yet know the logic that will go into the sub, we can write the statement to invoke it and handle creating the sub later.

Reversing Array Elements

The key to the sorting process is being able to reverse two array elements when they are found to be out of order. Reversing two array elements is not as simple as just setting one element equal to the other. That is, these two statements will *not* reverse two string array elements:

```
strList(intCounter) = strList(intCounter + 1)
strList(intCounter + 1) = strList(intCounter)
```

In fact, all these two statements will accomplish is setting the two array elements to the *same* value, the original value of strList(intCounter + 1). For this reason, we need to use a *temporary* variable to carry out the reversal—as shown in Figure 7-9 for decPrices(3) and decPrices(4), which are initially out of order.

In Step 1 of the reversal process, the temporary variable is set equal to decPrices(3). In Step 2, decPrices(3) is set equal to decPrices(4). Finally, in Step 3, decPrices(4) is set equal to the temporary variable. In the process, the value of decPrices(3) is changed to $1.29, and the value of decPrices(4) is changed to $12.81. In each case, the *old* value for the array element is replaced by the *new* value, as shown by the values being struck out. This process can be generalized by replacing decPrices(3) and decPrices(4) with decPrices(intCounter) and decPrices(intCounter + 1).

FIGURE 7-9. Use of a temporary variable to reverse two values

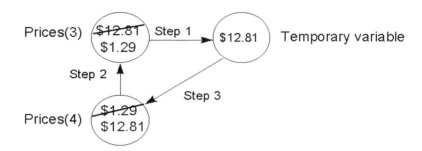

The Reverse sub to handle reversing two elements in the For-Next loop is shown in VB Code Box 7-9. It is not necessary to use arrays in the sub, because two specific array elements—decPrices(intCounter) and decPrices(intCounter + 1)—are passed to the array. They match the decFirst and decSecond parameters in the Sub definition statement. Note that the parameters in the Reverse sub are passed by reference because we are going to change their values and want this information passed back to the calling sub. Finally, the temporary variable, decTemp, is declared as a Decimal data type local variable.

VB CODE BOX 7-9. Sub to reverse two values	```Sub Reverse(ByRef decFirst As Decimal, ByRef decSecond As Decimal) Dim decTemp As Decimal decTemp = decFirst decFirst = decSecond decSecond = decTemp End Sub```

Repeating the For-Next Loop until the Array Is Sorted

The last issue to be dealt with in the sorting process is using nested loops with a Do Until outer loop that repeats a For-Next inner loop until the array is sorted. We already know that the array will be sorted when there are no reversals in the For-Next loop, so we can use this fact to terminate the Do Until outer loop. One way to do this is to use a Boolean variable called bln-NoReversal that is set to False *before* the Do Until loop and then reset to True within the Do Until before the start of the For-Next loop. Within the For-Next loop, if any reversals occur, then blnNoReversal is set to *False*. If blnNoReversal is still *True* after the For-Next loop, this means there were no reversals; the Do Until loop can be terminated, and the array is sorted. The assignment of blnNoReversal to *False* before the Do Until loop ensures that the Do Until loop will complete at least one repetition. The pseudocode for this process is shown below.

```
Begin Sort procedure
    Repeat until no reversals made
        If value > next value then
            Reverse values
        End decision
    End repeat
End procedure
```

The corresponding VB .NET code for the complete Sort sub that will go in the Code module is shown in VB Code Box 7-10.

| **VB CODE BOX 7-10.** Code for sub to sort an array | ```
Sub Sort(ByRef decList1() As Decimal, ByRef strList2() As _
String, ByVal intNumList As Integer)
   Dim blnNoReversal As Boolean, intCounter As Integer
   blnNoReversal = False
   Do Until blnNoReversal
      blnNoReversal = True
      For intCounter = 0 To intNumList - 2
         If decList1(intCounter) > decList1(intCounter + 1) Then
            Reverse(decList1(intCounter), decList1(intCounter + 1))
            ReverseStr(strList2(intCounter), strList2(intCounter + 1))
            blnNoReversal = False
         End If
      Next
   Loop
End Sub
``` |
|---|---|

Note in VB Code Box 7-10 that the parameters called decList1(), strList2(), and intNumList are defined to match the arguments in the statement that invokes the sub—decPrices, strPartID, and intNumPrices. Also, since the decPrices() array is being used to sort both the decPrices() and strPartID() arrays, whatever is done to the decPrices() array should also be done to the strPartID() array. This requires a second sub called ReverseStr to reverse the String data type strPartID() array, because the Reverse sub was created to reverse Decimal data type elements. The ReverseStr sub will look *exactly* like the Reverse sub for Decimal type data variables except that the decFirst, decSecond, and decTemp variables will be String data type instead of Decimal type. Finally, to check the status of the Boolean variable blnNoReversal, you do *not* need to actually compare it to True; Boolean variables are already True or False, so no comparison is necessary.

When the btnSort button and the associated code is added to the project, and the Sort, Reverse, and ReverseStr subs are added to the MultipleList project, the project can be executed. If this is done, the form shown in Figure 7-10 will result from clicking on the btnSort and btnDisplay buttons in that order.

FIGURE 7-10. Displaying part identifiers and prices

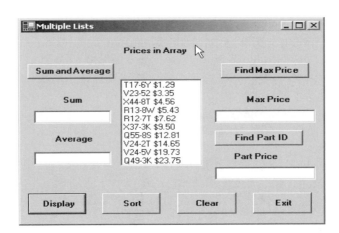
```

Note in VB Code Box 7-10 that the parts are displayed in increasing order of price, starting with the part that has ID number T17-6Y with a price of $1.29.

Using Array Methods

Now that you have some understanding of how a general procedure works with arrays, we can show you how to use the *Sort* method of the *Array* class. This method can be used to sort one list array or two list arrays based on values in one of them. In the first case, the form of the statement would be (where the array name is in the parentheses.)

Array.Sort*(list1)*

For example, to sort just the decPrices array, the statement would be:

```
Array.Sort(decPrices)
```

For two arrays, they are both enclosed in the parentheses with the first array controlling the order of the sorting, so for our case where we want to sort both decPrices and strPartID based on the order of decPrices, the statement would be:

```
Array.Sort(decPrices, strPartID)
```

Since the Sort method of the Array class is based on much faster sorting methodology than the bubble sort, it would be able to sort much bigger lists in much less time than the routine we created.

In addition to the Sort method, the Array class has a very fast search method, a method to reverse the order of the array, and a number of other methods, all of which can be found in the VB .NET Help system.

Common Errors in Using General Procedures

General procedures have their own special set of errors of which you should be aware, including the number of arguments and parameters not matching, the data types of the arguments and parameters not matching, and arguments being out of order.

In the first case, unless you have defined one or more parameters as optional, then the number of arguments must match the number of parameters. If this error is encountered, one of several error messages referring to a type mismatch will be displayed. Figure 7-11 shows a possible error message.

Figure 7-11. Type mismatch error message

In the second case, unless you have defined parameters as the data type, then the data type of the arguments *must* match the data type of the parameters. If this error occurs, the error message will likely be the same as that for an incorrect number of arguments, since both errors can result in the same situation—a mismatch in the data types. The same type of error can occur when arguments are out of order and data types do not match. However, a worse case is when arguments are out of order but the data types still match. This will *not* result in an error message, but it will result in incorrect results. Using breakpoints and watches along with the Locals window and Watch window is often the only way to find this error in programmer logic.

■ ■

Step-by-Step Instructions 7-2: Using subs to work with multiple lists

1. Working with the **frmMultiple** form in *MultipleList* project in the Chapter7 folder, add the **btnSort** button with a text property of **Sort.** The resulting form should look like Figure 7-6.

2. Open the Code window for the btnSort_Click event procedure and add the single line of code:

```
Sort(decPrices, strPartID, intNumPrices)
```

to sort the decPrices( ) and strPartID( ) arrays as show in VB Code Box 7-7.

3. While still in the Code window, create the first and last lines of the **Reverse** sub by entering

```
Sub Reverse
```

The last line will be automatically added.

4. Enter the code shown in VB Code Box 7-9 for the Reverse sub. Be sure to change the *ByVal* modifiers for the parameters to be *ByRef* so that they are being passed by reference. Do the same to create the first and last lines of ReverseStr sub and copy the code from the Reverse sub into it. Change all declarations from the Decimal data type to the String data type for the ReverseStr sub.

5. Start another sub by entering the words **sub Sort** and enter the code shown in VB Code Box 7-10. Once again, make sure the decList1 and strList2 parameters are being passed by reference instead of by value. Run your project and sort the arrays with the Sort button. Display the resulting arrays in the list box. Be sure and clear the list between applications of the Display button.

6. All of the *new* code for the MultipleList project is shown again in VB Code Box 7-11.

7. Save all files in the project.

■ ■

It's Your Turn!

1. What is accomplished by the following sub procedures? Which variables and data types should be passed to them when they are invoked? Describe what is passed back as the result.

```
a. Public Sub ASub(ByVal intArr() As Integer, ByVal _
intTop As Integer, ByRef intX As Integer, _
ByRef intY As Integer)
    Dim intN As Integer
    intX = intArr(0)
    intY = intArr(0)
    For intN = 1 To 4
      If intArr(intN) < intX Then
```

| **VB CODE BOX 7-11.** New code for the frm-Multiple form in the MultipleList project | ```vb
Private Sub btnSort_Click(ByVal sender As Object, _
ByVal e As EventArgs) Handles btnSort.Click
    Sort(decPrices, strPartID, intNumPrices)
End Sub
Sub Sort(ByRef decList1() As Decimal, ByRef strList2() As String, _
ByVal intNumList As Integer)
    Dim blnNoReversal As Boolean, intCounter As Integer
    blnNoReversal = False
    Do Until blnNoReversal
        blnNoReversal = True
        For intCounter = 0 To intNumList - 2
            If decList1(intCounter) > decList1(intCounter + 1) Then
                Reverse(decList1(intCounter), decList1(intCounter + 1))
                ReverseStr(strList2(intCounter), strList2(intCounter + 1))
                blnNoReversal = False
            End If
        Next
    Loop
End Sub
Sub Reverse(ByRef decFirst As Decimal, ByRef decSecond As Decimal)
    Dim decTemp As Decimal
    decTemp = decFirst
    decFirst = decSecond
    decSecond = decTemp
End Sub
Sub ReverseStr(ByRef strFirst As String, ByRef strSecond As String)
    Dim strTemp As String
    strTemp = strFirst
    strFirst = strSecond
    strSecond = strTemp
End Sub
``` |

Mini-Summary 7-3: Using subs to work with multiple lists

1. A sub is often used for manipulating the arguments passed to it. A sub can invoke another sub; for example, a sub to sort an array can invoke a sub to reverse two array elements.

2. It is possible to work with multiple list arrays by matching the index values for the arrays.

3. Sorting an array requires that nested loops be used to repeat the comparison-reversal process until the array is sorted. A Boolean variable can be used to determine when to stop the reversal process.

4. Reversing two array elements requires the use of a temporary variable.

```vb
            intX = intArr(intN)
        End If
        If intArr(intN) > intY Then
            intY = intArr(intN)
        End If
    Next intN
End Sub
```

```vb
b. Public Sub BSub(ByVal intArr1() As Integer, ByVal_
intArr2() As Integer, ByVal intSize as Integer,
ByRef intArr3() As Integer)
    Dim intN As Integer
    For intN = 0 To (intSize * 2) Step 2
```
```

```
              intArr3(intN) = intArr1(intN / 2)
           Next intN
           For intN = 1 To (intSize * 2 + 1) Step 2
              intArr3(intN) = intArr2((intN - 1) / 2)
           Next intN
      End Sub
   c. Public Sub CSub(ByVal strOne As String, ByVal strTwo _
         As String, ByRef strThree as String, _
         ByRef blnStatus as Boolean)
         If strOne < strTwo Then
            strThree = strOne & strTwo
            blnStatus = True
         Else
            strThree = ""
            blnStatus = False
         End If
      End Sub
```

2. Write sub procedures to do each of the following:

   a. Return the name of a month and the number of days in the month based on an integer passed to it (1 = Jan., 2 = Feb., etc.).

   b. Calculate the new monthly balance of a checking account after passing it the following: a beginning balance; an array of deposits and the number of deposits for the month; and an array of withdrawals and the number of withdrawals for the month. Assume that there are service charges of $5 per month, $0.05 for each withdrawal, and $0.02 for each deposit.

   c. Print a table stored in a two-dimensional array that is passed to it. Assume that the number of rows and the number of columns will also be passed to the sub.

3. Modify the *MultipleList* project to sort both lists based on price by following Step-by-Step Instructions 7-2.

4. How would you change the Sort sub to create a sub named **PartSort** that will sort on the basis of the strPartID() array rather than on the decPrices() array?

GLOBAL DECLARATIONS AND THE CODE MODULE

As projects grow and more forms are added, like we did in Chapter 6 with the addition of the frmDVDs form to the Vintage DVDs project, it is often the case that at least two forms must *know* about variables and general procedures. Because of this need to share variables between forms, we need to use a different type of declaration for them—global declarations in which all forms and general procedures are aware of the declared variable. Similarly, if we want all forms to know about a general procedure, the easiest way to make this possible is create a global general procedure.

In a **global declaration**, the scope of global variables, as compared to form-level variables or procedure-level variables, includes all parts of the project. Recall that the scope of a form-level variable is the current form, and the scope of a procedure-level variable is the current procedure. Global declarations are carried out in the Code module portion of the project. The **Code module** is a section of pure code that is known to all forms in a project. It contains only declarations and general procedures, no controls or event procedures. Figure 7-12 shows the concept of scope for global, form-level, and procedure-level variables. In each case, the elements below a variable declaration *know* about those variables but not in the other direction. That is, procedures know about the form-level variables, and the forms and procedures all know about the global variables, but the Code module does not know about the variables at the form level or procedure level. This is a way of protecting variables from inadvertent contamination.

FIGURE 7-12.
Scope of global
variables

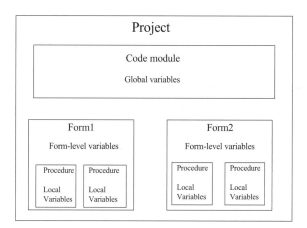

We add a Code module to the project by using the **Project | Add Module** menu selection, and it has a *.vb* extension just like the forms we have already added. When this menu option is selected, a dialog box will be displayed from which you can select a new or existing module. The only indication that a module has been added is the addition of the module name to the Solution Explorer window beneath any existing forms and the appearance of a blank Code window with the module file name in the in the title bar. For example, if a module named *modVintage* is added to the Vintage project, the Solution Explorer window will appear as shown in Figure 7-13. As with any other object, you can rename a module in the Properties window, and it is saved along with other files when you save all files.

The actual declaration of global variables occurs in the *Declarations* procedure of the Code module. Initially, this is the procedure in the Code module, so it is the one that is automatically displayed when you add the Code module or select it from the Solution Explorer window. Declaring a variable globally is just like declaring it at the form level or control level, except that the keyword *Public* is used instead of the keyword *Dim* in the declaration. The general form for globally declaring variables is

Public *varName1* as *type*, *varName2* as *type*, ...

For example, if you wanted to declare an Integer data type variable int-NumMembers so that it would be known to all forms and procedures in a project, the appropriate statement in a Code module would be

```
Public intNumMembers as Integer
```

FIGURE 7-13. Addition
of module

Although declaring variables globally is necessary for multiple forms to know about them, declaring a variable globally means that any changes to that variable in a procedure will change it everywhere in the project. In other words, you must be careful when you change a global variable, because the change may have far-reaching effects.

Once global variables are declared globally in the Code module, it is not necessary or even useful to declare them again in a general or event procedure. In fact, if a global variable is declared again in any type of procedure, then all values will be zeroed out when this procedure is executed, and it will not know about the contents of the global variables. For this reason, once a variable is declared globally, declaring the same variable locally in a procedure is generally a *bad* idea.

Global Variables vs. Passing Variables

You may ask, why pass variables to a general procedure rather than just declaring everything as global variables? There are two reasons for passing variables instead of using global variables. First, if we used global variables instead of passing variables, there would be the possibility of inadvertently changing a global variable within a procedure. Second, using global variables instead of passing variables would mean that subs or functions could not be used in multiple locations in the project. If functions and subs used a specific global variable rather than a local variable corresponding to the argument variable, it would work only with that specific global variable.

In general, global variables are useful for making multiple controls aware of a variable, but care should be taken when they are used within functions and subs. If the value of a global variable is changed within a function or sub, then it is changed everywhere—even if that was not intended! You can avoid this potential problem by copying the global argument variable to a local parameter variable to protect it from contamination and to allow a function or sub to be used in multiple situations.

Global General Procedures

Just as variables declared globally in the Code module are known to all forms in the project, general procedures created in the Code module are also known to all forms. Although a function or sub created in a form with a *Public* keyword is known to other forms, invoking it is more difficult because you must include the form name as a part of the function or sub name. It is easier and more straightforward to create the function or sub in the Code module so it can be invoked with just its name.

Subs and functions are created in a module the exact same way as in a form—creating an empty line in the existing code and typing the *Function* or *Sub* keyword plus the procedure name. We will demonstrate this shortly in the Vintage DVDs project.

Mini-Summary 7-4: Global declarations and the code module

1. Global variables are declared in a Code module in a module, which is saved with a *.vb* extension. Variables declared globally with the *Public* keyword are known everywhere in the project.

<table>
</table>

> **Mini-Summary 7-4: Global declarations and the code module**
>
> 2. Any change to a global variable is reflected everywhere in the project.
>
> 3. Global general procedures can also be declared in a Code module and can be used in any other form or module.

It's Your Turn!

1. Why can global variables and procedures be necessary in a project?

2. Why should you be careful about declaring variables as global level variables?

3. Under what circumstances would it be appropriate to declare a variable as a global variable rather than passing it between procedures?

APPLICATION TO VINTAGE DVDs

In Chapter 6, we discussed using arrays to store and process information. Now, assume that several extensions to the existing Vintage DVDs project are required, including:

1. A way of adding DVDs to the system as they come into the store.

2. A better system for managing the membership list to check if a customer is a member, add new members, and delete old ones.

3. The capability to add late fees to a customer's bill.

4. A system to print an alphabetical list of members or DVDs as needed.

5. Customer phone numbers should be made a part of each customer's record so that customers with similar names can be differentiated.

General subs and functions will be useful in handling the new requirements for the Vintage DVDs project. In addition, a number of changes are required. First, the names, phone numbers, and late fees will also be stored in arrays that can be searched for names in a manner similar to that used for searching for DVDs. To respond to the request for an alphabetical printing of the membership list or list of DVDs, both lists will have to be sorted. Although it is possible to sort a list in a list box or combo box using the *Sorted* property, this only works to sort on the first item on each line. If you want to sort the list based on another part of the line, you will need to use arrays that are sorted by the code rather than by the Sorted property of the list box.

In considering the new requirements, it is obvious that more forms, controls, and general procedures will be needed to handle the additional functionality. For example, instead of the store clerks manually scanning the combo box of member names, a form like that used to search for DVDs can be used. This requires us to think about the overall design of the project. A design that matches the requirements for the revised project is shown in Figure 7-13.

Note that in Figure 7-13 there are now two secondary forms instead of just one. The secondary form on the right is for managing the membership

FIGURE 7-13.
Design for
expanded Vintage
DVDs project

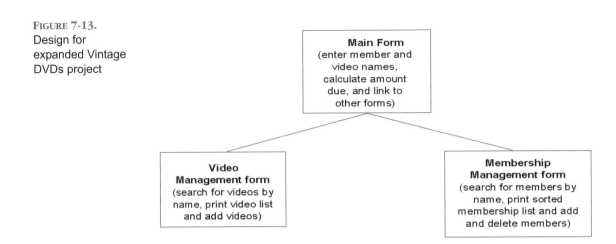

list, and the secondary form on the left is for managing the list of DVDs. In both cases, the forms provide the capability to search for items on the list and display matching items in a list box, add items to the list, and print the list in alphabetical order.

The new membership management form *(frmMembers)* is shown in Figure 7-14, with a list box to display the names *(lstMembers)*, a text box to enter the search string *(txtSearch)*, and a button to initiate the search *(btnSearch)*. In addition, there are buttons to add names to the list *(btnAdd)*, delete names from the list *(btnDelete)*, to print the list of names *(btnPrint)*, and to return to the main form *(btnBack)*. If one of the member names in the list box is clicked, then that person's name and late fees are transferred to the main form.

FIGURE 7-14.
Membership
management form

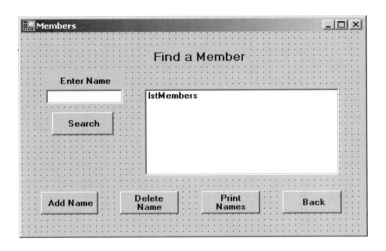

With the new form and added functionality for existing forms, project management becomes an essential feature of application development. Project management involves developing forms with a consistent *look and feel,* so the user can easily understand from previous experience how to use them. There must also be a straightforward navigation pattern between the forms so that the user does not become lost. For example, for the expanded Vintage DVDs project, the two secondary forms should have a similar interface and should be designed so that clicking on a *Back* button will always take the user back to the main form. Project management also requires that the developer be consistent in naming forms and controls and declaring variables; otherwise, debugging the project will quickly become a nightmare.

> **TIP:** You can copy a button from one form to another by selecting it and using the **Edit | Copy** and **Edit | Paste** menu commands You can also use the **Ctrl-C** and **Ctrl-P** keyboard shortcuts.

Modifying the frmDVDs form

In addition to adding a new form, we also need to modify the frmDVDs form to add DVDs and to print a list of sorted DVDs. The resulting form will look as shown in Figure 7-15. We will consider the code for the additional controls in a later section.

FIGURE 7-15.
Modified frmDVDs form

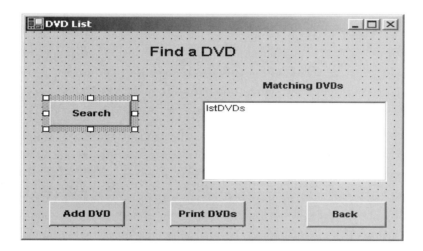

Modifying frmVintage

Because late fees should be included in the amount-due calculation, the main form *(frmVintage)* needs to be modified to include a new text box *(txtLateFees)* that will display them. They must also be included in the calculation of amount due and added to the list box that is printed as a receipt. In addition, there is no longer a need for a combo box with member names *(cboMembers)*, and the Add Name *(btnAdd)* and Delete Member *(btnDelete)* buttons need to be replaced with a single Check Name *(btnCheck)* button. This button should transfer control to the membership management form added earlier and set the focus on the text box used to search for a customer's name. The revised main form is shown in Figure 7-16, with the changes pointed out.

The code for the btnCheck_Click event procedure is shown in shown in VB Code Box 7-12. This code creates a new instance of the frmMembers form and displays it. Note that this code displays the frmMembers form *on top of* the frmVintage form and does not hide it.

FIGURE 7-16.
Revised main form

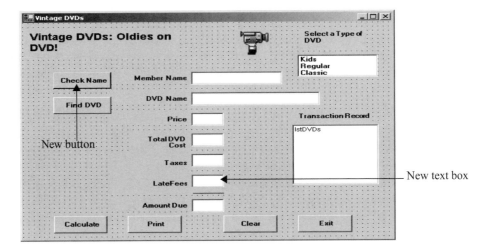

VB CODE BOX 7-12. Code for the btnCheck_Click event procedure	```Private Sub btnCheck_Click(ByVal sender As Object, _ ByVal e As EventArgs) Handles btnCheck.Click Dim frmNewMembers As New frmMembers() frmNewMembers.Show() End Sub```

To include the late fees in the amount due calculation in the btnCalc_Click() event procedure requires that we first validate that there is some value in the txtLateFees text box before making this calculation. If the late fees text box is empty, this means the clerk has not checked to see whether the customer is a member because doing so would result in either a late fee ($0 or some positive value) for an existing member or a zero value for a new member. If the text box is empty, a message should be displayed instructing the user to click the *Check Members* button, and the procedure should be exited.

If the txtLateFees text box is *not* empty, we can proceed with the calculation of amount due. This requires a new variable, decLateFees, to be declared as Decimal. This variable is then set equal to txtLateFees.Text and added to the total cost and taxes to determine the amount due. The contents of the txtLateFees text box should also be added, with an appropriate descriptor, to the transactions list box in the btnPrint_Click event procedure before the amount due is added to the list box.

The new code in the btnCalc_Click event procedure to validate the contents of the txtLateFees text box and to calculate the amount due using the late fees amount is shown in VB Code Box 7-13. The new code in the btnPrint_Click event procedure to display the late fees in the transaction list box is also shown here. Note that the existing code, which is clearly pointed out in this code box, is only shown to provide you with a reference point for adding new code and does *not* need to be added. You should only add the code designated as being "new code".

Using Global Variables with Vintage DVDs

Since at least two forms in the Vintage DVDs scenario need to know about each list—that is, the frmVintage and frmMembers forms need to know about the membership information, and the frmVintage and frmDVDs forms need to know

| VB Code Box 7-13. New code for btnCalc and btnPrint event procedures on frm-Vintage | ```
Private Sub btnCalc_Click(ByVal eventSender As Object, ByVal _
eventArgs As EventArgs) Handles btnCalc.Click (Existing code)
    Const sngTaxRate As Single = 0.07 (Existing code)
    decLateFees As Decimal (NEW CODE)
    Existing Code goes here
    decTaxes = decTotalCost * sngTaxRate (Existing code)
    If txtLateFees.Text = "" Then (NEW CODE)
        MsgBox("Click Check Members button and try again!", _    (NEW CODE)
        vbCritical, "Membership Status")   (NEW CODE)
        Exit Sub   (NEW CODE)
    End If   (NEW CODE)
    decLateFees = cDec(txtLateFees.txt)   (NEW CODE)
    decAmountDue = decTotalCost + decTaxes + decLateFees (NEW CODE)
    txtLateFees.txt = Format(decLateFees, "Currency")   (NEW CODE)
    txtTotalCost.Text = Format(decTotalCost, "currency") (Existing code)
    Existing Code goes here
End Sub (Existing code)


Private Sub btnPrint_Click(ByVal eventSender As Object, ByVal _
eventArgs As EventArgs) Handles btnPrint.Click (Existing code)
    Existing Code goes here
    lstDVDs.Items.Add("Taxes " & txtTaxes.Text) (Existing code)
    lstDVDs.Items.Add("Late fees " & txtLateFees.Text)   (NEW CODE)
    Existing Code goes here
End Sub
``` |

about the DVD information—we need to globally declare the arrays needed to process the membership and DVD lists. For the membership list, we want the number of members and the lists of member names, phone numbers, and late fees to be known to all parts of the project. We also want to pass a customer name and late fees from the frmMembers form back to the frmVintage form, so we also include two variables, strCustName and decCustFee in the global declarations. In this case, after the modVintage module has been added to the project, the declaration statements area is shown in VB Code Box 7-14.

| VB Code Box 7-14. Global declarations for Vintage DVDs project | ```
Module modVintage
    Public strMembers(100) As String, decLateFees(100) As Decimal
    Public strPhoneNumbers(100) As String, intNumMembers As Integer
    Public strDVDs(100) As String, decDVDPrice(100) As Decimal
    Public strDVDLoc(100) As String, intNumDVDs As Integer
    Public strCustname As String, decCustFees As Decimal
End module
``` |

With these declarations, the main and secondary forms will know about the name, phone number, and late fees for the member. They will also be aware of the name, location, and price for each DVD. Because these variables are declared globally, the declaration of the three DVD arrays at the form level in frmDVDs needs to be deleted.

Inputting the Membership and DVD Lists

Since the arrays for the membership and DVD lists are now declared globally, we can input both in the frmVintage_Load event procedure. This will allow us to avoid reloading the DVDs list every time we go to the frmDVDs form to search for a DVD. The easiest way to make this change is to move the code from the frmDVDs_Load event procedure to the frmVintage_Load event procedure. The existing frmVintage Form_Load event procedure also needs to be modified to input the member's phone number and late fees, if any, in addition to the member's name from a new data file, membersnew.txt that is **tab-delimited**, that is, instead the fields being separated by commas as was done in Chapter 6, they are separated by the Tab character. The revised frmVintage_Load event procedure code is shown in VB Code Box 7-15 where the delimiter is set equal to Chr(9) which is the Tab character. Note that we use two StreamReader objects with the Split function as we did in Chapter 6.

| **VB CODE BOX 7-15.** Revised frmVintage_Load event procedure for frmVintage | ```Private Sub frmVintage_Load(ByVal eventSender As System.Object, _
ByVal eventArgs As System.EventArgs) Handles MyBase.Load
  Dim strPathName, strLine As String, strFields() As String
  Dim strDelimiter As String = Chr(9)
  strPathName = CurDir() & "\membersnew.txt"
  Dim srdMembers As System.IO.StreamReader = _
New System.IO.StreamReader(strPathName)
  lstDVDs.Items.Add("Welcome to Vintage DVDs")
  Do Until srdMembers.Peek = -1
     strLine = srdMembers.ReadLine()
     strFields = strLine.Split(strDelimiter)
     ReDim Preserve strMembers(intNumMembers)
     ReDim Preserve strPhoneNumbers(intNumMembers)
     ReDim Preserve decLateFees(intNumMembers)
     strMembers(intNumMembers) = strFields(0)
     strPhoneNumbers(intNumMembers) = strFields(1)
     decLateFees(intNumMembers) = CDec(strFields(2))
     intNumMembers = intNumMembers + 1
  Loop
  srdMembers.Close()
  strPathName = CurDir() & "\DVDs.txt"
  Dim srdDVDs As System.IO.StreamReader = _
New System.IO.StreamReader(strPathName)
  Do Until srdDVDs.Peek = -1
     strLine = srdDVDs.ReadLine()
     strFields = strLine.Split(strDelimiter)
     ReDim Preserve strDVDs(intNumDVDs)
     ReDim Preserve decDVDPrice(intNumDVDs)
     ReDim Preserve strDVDLoc(intNumDVDs)
     strDVDs(intNumDVDs) = strFields(0)
     decDVDPrice(intNumDVDs) = CDec(strFields(1))
     strDVDLoc(intNumDVDs) = strFields(2)
     intNumDVDs = intNumDVDs + 1
  Loop
  srdDVDs.Close()
End``` |

Step-by-Step Instructions 7-3: Revising the Vintage DVDs project

1. Create a new folder within the *Chapter7* folder named **Vintage7** and copy all of the files and folders from the Chapter6\Vintage6 folder into the new folder.

2. Start VB .NET (or use **File|Open**) and open the new *Vintage7* project. Add a new form with a file name of **Members.vb** with a name of **frmMembers.** It should have the controls shown in Table 7-1 and the corresponding labels shown in Figure 7-14.

TABLE 7-1: Controls for frmMembers form

Control	Name	Text Property (if any)
button	btnSearch	Search
button	btnAdd	Add Name
button	btnDelete	Delete Name
button	btnPrint	Print Names
button	btnBack	Back
listbox	lstMembers	

3. Modify the existing **frmDVDs** form to add buttons to print the list of DVDs (**btnPrint**) and to add DVDs (**btnAdd**). The resulting form should look like Figure 7-15. Why is there no problem with using the same names for controls on both forms?

4. Modify the main form by adding the **txtLateFees** text box beneath the *txtTaxes* text box with an associated label. Delete the *Member List* label, the *cboMembers* combo box, the *btnAdd* button, the *btnDelete* button, and any associated event procedures. Also, delete the code in the frmVintage_Load event procedure and btnExit_Click event procedures that pertains to cboMembers. At this point, the *cboMembers* control should not be referenced anywhere in your code (if it is, it will underlined in the code denoting an error).

5. Clear all existing code *except* the **End** command from the btnExit_Click event procedure as it is no longer correct.

6. Add a new button **(btnCheck)** with a text property of **Check Name** and with the code shown in VB Code Box 7-12. The revised frmVintage form should look like Figure 7-16.

7. Modify the btnCalc_Click event procedure to declare a new variable, **decLateFees,** as Decimal and add the *new* code shown in VB Code Box 7-13.

8. Modify the btnPrint_Click event procedure, as also shown in VB Code Box 7-13, to add the text property of **txtLateFees** to the lstDVDs list box with an appropriate descriptor before adding the Amount Due value.

9. Use NotePad to modify the existing *Members.txt* text file to add phone numbers and late fees amounts to existing names as shown in Table 7-2. Separate each item on a line with by pressing the **TAB** key. Note that since we are separating the items with the Tab character, it is no longer necessary to enclose character strings in quotes. .

TABLE 7-2: Data for MembersNew.txt File

Name	Phone Number	Late Fees
Stams, Lonnie	770-555-1294	$2.12
Goodly, Alice	706-555-4244	$3.18
Watson, Betsy	706-555-8590	$0
Arons, Suzy	706-555-3587	$16.00
Carroll, Ann	706-555-3700	$4.26
Triesch, Jimmy	706-555-9021	$10.65
Hyatt, Ashley	706-555-5355	$0
Patrick, Chris	770-555-9238	$3.20
Jones, Sam	770-555-8100	$4.24
Myers, Carolyn	706-555-9475	$0
Dyer, Ben	770-555-4505	$9.60
Kidd, Margo	770-555-1203	$5.30
Sibley, Ben	770-555-1032	$0
Smith, Joe	770-555-0023	$0
Adams, Bill	706-555-8163	$3.20
Brown, Andy	706-555-7096	$19.20

10. While still in Notepad, add the name shown below to the list and then save the file as **MembersNew.txt** in the Bin folder of the Vintage folder in the Chapter7 folder. You may also download the modified *MembersNew.txt* file from the Chapter 7 section of the text Web site.

Smith, Joe	706-555-1234	$12.80

11. Use the **Project | Add Module** menu option to add a module to the Vintage project with a name of **modVintage.vb.**

12. Add the four lines of global declarations shown in VB Code Box 7-14 to the modVintage module. Remove the form-level declarations in frmDVDs.

13. Modify the existing frmVintage_Load event procedure to input the arrays for the membership list; that is, strMembers( ), strPhoneNumbers( ), and decLateFees( ), from the **MembersNew.txt** data file.

14. Move the code from the frmDVDs_Load event procedure to the frmVintage_Load event procedure. The resulting code should look like that shown earlier in VB Code Box 7-15.

15. Modify the **DVDs.txt** file to use the Tab character rather than a comma to delimit items for each record. The easiest way to do this is to use a word processing package to search for and replace commas with the Tab character. Be careful, though; there may be commas in the names of the DVDs. If you use the word processing approach, be sure and safe the file as a *text* file and not a word processing file. You may also choose to download the file from the Chapter 7 section of the textbook Web site.

16. Temporarily add the For-Each loops shown below to the end of the frmVintage_Load event procedure to print the contents of the membership and DVD list arrays to the Output window:

```
Dim intCount as Integer
For intCount = 0 to intNumMembers
   Debug.Writeline strMembers(intCount), _
   strPhoneNumbers(intCount), DecLateFees(intCount)
Next
For intCountr = 0 to intNumDVDs
   Debug.Writeline strDVDs(intCount), _
   decDVDPrice(intCount), strDVDLoc(intCount)
Next
```

Once the input is correct, you can remove this code.

17. Test the revised version of the project to ensure that all the membership and DVD information is being correctly input to the arrays and output to the Output window. Delete the For-Each loops used to test the project, and save all project files under their current names

18. Save all files in your project.

━ ■ ━

It's Your Turn!

1. What is meant by the term *look and feel* when it refers to computer applications?

2. What is a shortcut way to move a button from one form to another?

3. To modify the existing Vintage DVDs project, you should follow Step-by-Step Instructions 7-3.

SEARCHING FOR MEMBER AND DVD NAMES

In the Vintage DVDs application in Chapter 6, we included an event procedure to search for a partial name of a DVD in the list of DVDs and display the DVDs in a list box. In this chapter, we want to carry out the same operation to search for a partial name in the list of members. Because we are carrying out the same operation on two different lists, this is a situation where a sub may be useful to reuse the same code.

Since both the membership and DVD lists use two String arrays and one Decimal array, we can use the same sub to search through both of them. If there had been a different number or different types of arrays, we would have had to use two different subs that use similar logic. In either case, using subs for the search process will reduce the complexity of the programming process.

The common Search sub, which will be stored in the modVintage module, will be invoked in the btnSearch_Click event procedures on the frmD-VDs or frmMembers forms. In this case, the logic used for the Search sub will be similar to that used for the btnSearch_Click event procedure in frmDVDs, which we discussed in Chapter 6. Because the results of the search will be added to list boxes on different forms, we need to pass a variable to the sub that designates the list box to which the matching entries should be added and passes out a string array that contains the information that should be added to the listbox on each form. The pseudocode for this process is shown below:

```
Begin search procedure
    Repeat for each item in list
        If SearchString is substring of list item then
            Increment Number of matches Counter
            If Membership list then
                Add Name, Phone Number and Late Fee to string array
            Else
                Add DVD Name to string array
            End decision
        End decision
    End repeat
End procedure
```

Note in the pseudocode that when a match is found, the counter for the number of matches is incremented and then, depending on which list is being processed, the appropriate matching elements are added to a list box. The actual VB .NET code to implement this Search sub is shown in VB Code Box 7-16.

| VB CODE BOX 7-16. Code for Search sub | ```
Public Sub Search(ByRef strSearchStr As String, ByRef strList1() _
As String, ByRef strList2() As String, ByRef decList3() As _
Decimal, ByVal strWhich As String, ByRef intNumMatches As Integer, _
ByRef strForListBox() As String)
    Dim strFound As String
    Dim intCounter As Integer, strInList As String
    intNumMatches = 0
    For Each strInList In strList1
        If InStr(UCase(strInList), UCase(strSearchStr)) > 0 Then
            If strWhich = "Members" Then
                strForListBox(intNumMatches) = strList1(intCounter) & _
                " " & strList2(intCounter) & " " & _
                Format(strList3(intCounter), "currency")
            Else
                strForListBox(intNumMatches) = strList1(intCounter)
            End If
            intNumMatches = intNumMatches + 1
        End If
        intCounter = intCounter + 1
    Next
    If intNumMatches > 5 Then
        MsgBox("Too many matches! Please try again.", _
        MsgBoxStyle.Exclamation, "Vintage DVDs")
    ElseIf intNumMatches = 0 Then
        MsgBox("No matching entries found! Please try again.", _
        MsgBoxStyle.Exclamation, "Vintage DVDs")
    End If
End Sub
``` |

The Search sub has seven parameters: strSearch, strList1(), strList2(), decList3(), strWhich, intNumItems, and strForListBox. The first parameter is
```

> **TIP:** Internal comments should be used wherever they help a reader understand the code.

the partial DVD name or partial member name being searched for, and the next three parameters are the three lists associated with the membership list or the DVD list. The strWhich parameter is a string that designates the contents of the strForListBox array. Finally, the intNumMatches parameter is the number of elements in the strForListBox array—the number of matches.

In the sub itself, whenever a match is found using the InStr() function between the Search string (strSearch) and an item in the list of names (strList1()), the parameter strWhich is checked to determine what should be added to the strForListBox array—the member name, phone number, and late fees for the frmMembers form or the DVD name for the frmDVDs form. For example, if the membership list is being searched, as indicated by the strWhich variable being equal to *Members*, then elements from all three lists should be concatenated into a string, which is added to the strForListBox array in the follow statement:

```
strForListBox(intNumMatches) = strList1(intCounter) & _
"  " & strList2(intCounter) & "  " & _
Format(strList3(intCounter), "currency")
```

In either case, if no matches are found or if too many matches are found, a message box is displayed.

As mentioned above, the invoking procedures for the Search sub are the btnSearch_Click event procedures in the frmDVDs and frmMembers forms. In both cases, the intNum and strListBox arguments being passed back from the Search sub reference contain the number of matches and the list of matches that should be added to the listbox on that form. For the frmMember form, the btnSearch_Click event procedure is shown in VB Code Box 7-17.

VB CODE BOX 7-17. frmMembers code to invoke the Search sub for members	```Private Sub btnSearch_Click(ByVal eventSender As _```

```
Private Sub btnSearch_Click(ByVal eventSender As _
System.Object, ByVal eventArgs As System.EventArgs) _
Handles btnSearch.Click
    Dim strFindName, strListBox(5) As String
    Dim intNum As Integer, IntCounter As Integer
    lstMembers.Items.Clear()
    strFindName = txtSearch.Text
    Search(strFindName, strMembers, strPhoneNumbers, _
    decLateFees, "Members", IntNum, strListBox)
    If IntNum = 0 Or IntNum >= 5 Then
       Exit Sub
    Else
       For IntCounter = 0 To IntNum - 1
          lstMembers.Items.Add(strListBox(IntCounter))
       Next
    End If
End Sub
```

Note that the event procedure is straightforward because all of the important logic is in the Search procedure. The frmDVDs version of this btnSearch_Click() event procedure will be the same as this one, except that the strFindName variable is set equal to *txtDVDs.Text,* and the last six arguments are replaced with strDVDs(), strDVDLoc(), decDVDPrice(), "DVDs", intNum, and strListBox. The number of matches, intNum, is checked, and if between 0 and 5, the contents of the strListBox array are added to the lstMembers list box.

If the project is run and the *Check Members* button on the frmVintage form is clicked, the new frmMembers form will be displayed. On this form, the *Search* button can be clicked and a partial name, say, "smi", can be entered to search for anybody with a last name beginning with *smi, SMI,* or *Smi.* The results are as shown in Figure 7-18, where two persons named *Smith, Joe* are listed along with their phone numbers and late fees.

FIGURE 7-18. Result of Search sub

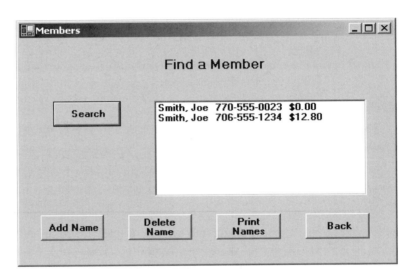

The lstMembers.Selected-IndexChanged Event

Once a list of names has been displayed in the list box on the frmMembers form, the next step is for the user to click on the correct name and display it on the main form along with the late fees associated with this person. If the customer's name is not found, the user can click on the Add Name button to add this person's name and phone number to the membership arrays (since the person is a new member, he or she will not have any late fees). We will consider the lstMembers_SelectedIndexChanged event procedure first and then consider the btnAdd_Click and btnDelete_Click event procedures.

In Chapter 6, we discussed the lstDVDs_SelectedIndexChanged event procedure, which finds the DVD that matches the name selected by the user by searching the DVD name array for an exact match. Unfortunately, we cannot use the same approach for the membership list, because the member names may be exactly the same. However, since each line in the list box is one long character string, we need to extract the information from the list box and transfer it to the main form.

In previous chapters, we have discussed the numerous character string functions available in VB .NET including CStr, UCase, Format, Asc, Chr, and InStr. While these functions are still very useful, VB .NET has created the String class that includes a number of useful properties and methods. These properties and methods are shown in Table 7-3 where the example string variable, strExample, is equal to "Smith, Joe". A key difference between the string functions you have worked with earlier, especially, Instr, is that the first position is equal to zero instead of one as with the functions. So, while Instr(strExample, ",") = 6, the corresponding String class property, Indexof, results in a value of 5.

TABLE 7-3: String Class Properties and Methods

Properties and Methods	Operation	Example
strVariable.Length	Returns number of characters in *strVariable*	strExample.Length = 10
strVariable.Indexof(*substring*	Returns location of *substring* in *strVariable*	strExample.Indexof(",") = 5
strVariable.Substring(*P, N*)	Returns the *N* characters in *strVariable* starting a position P	strExample.Substring(0,5) = "Smith" strExample.Substring(7,3) = "Joe" strExample.Substring(5,1) = ","
strVariable.Chars(*N*)	Returns the character in the *N*th position	strExample.Chars(5) = ","
strVariable.Trim	Trims blank characters from both ends of *str-Variable*	strExample = " Smith, Joe " strExample.Trim = "Smith, Joe"

Before going into the use of these methods and properties to extract the name and late fees from a list box, we first need to look at the structure of the information in the list box. Each line of the list box is composed of the member's name, phone number, and late fees separated by two spaces, as shown below (where **b** indicates a space, *x* represents a character, and *n* represents a digit):

```
xxxxxx,bxxxxxbbnnn-nnn-nnnnbb$nn.nn
```

For example, one of the names shown in Figure 7-18 is

```
Smith, Joe  706-555-1234  $12.80
```

In our case, since the member name is at the left end of the list box character string, we only need to determine where it ends and then use the Substring method to extract it. Similarly, since the late fees amount is at the right end of the character string, we need to determine its length with the Length property and then use the Substring method to extract it (because it counts the actual number of characters, the Length property is the one case with String class properties where counting starts at one rather than zero.) To find where the name ends, we can use the IndexOf property to search for two blanks and use this value as the length of the name (because we starting counting at zero with the IndexOf property, the position of the next character beyond the end of the substring is the same of the number of characters in substring.) Similarly, to find where the late fees amount begins, we can use IndexOf property to find the location of the dollar sign, use its position to determine the length of the late fees substring, and then extract it. Once extracted, both strings should be transferred to the appropriate text boxes on frmVintage form.

For example, if

```
strExample = "Smith, Joe  706-555-1234  $16.80"
```
with two spaces after the name, then to find the two spaces, we would use
```
strExample.IndexOf("  ")
```
which equals 10 indicating we should find the 10 leftmost characters using
```
strExample.Substring(0,10)
```
which equals "Smith, Joe".

Also, since strExample.Length = 32 and strExample.Indexof("$") = 26, the length of the late fees substring (without the dollar sign) is equal to 32 – 27 = 5. Using these values, we can extract the late fees string via the following line:
```
strExample.Subtring(27, 5)
```
which equals "16.80". Note that we start at 27 rather than 26 since we want only the amount and not the dollar sign.

The code for the lstMembers _Click( ) event procedure is shown in VB Code Box 7-18.

| **VB CODE BOX 7-18.** **Code for lstMembers** | ```Private Sub lstMembers_SelectedIndexChanged(ByVal _
eventSender As System.Object, ByVal eventArgs As _
System.EventArgs) Handles lstMembers.SelectedIndexChanged
    Dim strMemberInfo, strMemberName, strLateFeeAmount As String
    Dim intNumChar, intTwoBlankPos, intDollarSignPos, intLen As Integer
    Dim frmNewVintage As New frmVintage
    strMemberInfo = lstMembers.Text
    intLen = strMemberInfo.Length
    intTwoBlankPos = strMemberInfo.IndexOf(" ")
    strMemberName = stMemberInfo.Substring(0, intTwoBlankPos)
    intDollarSignPos = strMemberInfo.IndexOf("$")
    intNumChar = intLen - (intDollarSignPos + 1)
    strLateFeeAmount = strMemberInfo.Substring(intDollarsignPos + 1, _
    intNumChar)
    lstMembers.Items.Clear()
    strCustName = strMemberName
    decCustFees = CDec(strLateFeeAmount)
    Me.Hide()
End Sub``` |

The final step to display the member name and late fees on the frmVintage form is to use its **Activated** event. This event occurs whenever the form is moved to the front or another form in front of it is hidden. Since we are hiding the frmMembers form as a part of the lstMembers_SelectedIndexChanged event procedure, the frmVintage form is now on top and the Activated event is "fired." We don't use the Load event, because it will cause the reloading of all the arrays, which will cause an error as we exceed array limits.

To write code for the Activated event, display the Code window for frmVintage and click in the Class Name list box at the left side of the top of the Code window. From the Class Name list box, select (Base Class Events)—these events are those for the form itself. Then, from the Method Name list box, select the Activated event as shown in Figure 7-19. This will open the sub for the frmVintage_Activated event for the insertion of the appropriate instructions.

The frmVintage_Activated event procedure copies the values of the global variables strCustName and decCustFees into the corresponding text boxes

FIGURE 7-19.
Selecting the
Activated event

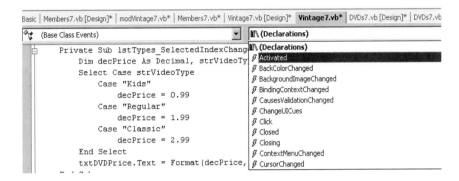

on frmVintage. The code for this event procedure is shown in VB Code Box 7-19.

| **VB CODE BOX 7-19.** frmVintage_Activated event procedure | ```Private Sub frmVintage_Activated(ByVal sender As Object, _
ByVal e As System.EventArgs) Handles MyBase.Activated
    txtCustName.Text = strCustName
    txtLateFees.Text = decCustFees
End Sub``` |
|---|---|

Searching for DVDs

To search for DVDs using the frmDVDs form, we simply replace the existing code for the btnSearch_Click event procedure on this form with code very similar to that shown in earlier in VB Code Box 7-17, with the exception that we are referring to DVD names instead of member names and we are listing them in the lstDVDs list box instead of the lstMembers list box. The code for the btnSearch_Click event procedure on the frmDVDs form is shown in VB Code Box 7-20.

| **VB CODE BOX 7-20.** btnSearch_Click event procedure on frmDVDs | ```Private Sub btnSearch_Click(ByVal eventSender As _
System.Object, ByVal eventArgs As System.EventArgs) _
Handles btnSearch.Click
    Dim strDVDName, strOneDVD As String, intCounter as Integer
    Dim strForListBox(5) As String, intNum As Integer
    strDVDName = txtSearch.Text
    lstDVDs.Items.Clear()
    lstDVDs.Items.Add("DVD Name")
    Search(strDVDName, strDVDs, strDVDLoc, decDVDPrice, _
    "DVDs", intNum,   strForListBox)
    If intNum = 0 Or intNum >= 5 Then
       Exit Sub
    Else
       For intCounter = 0 To intNum - 1
          lstDVDs.Items.Add(strForListBox(intCounter))
       Next
    End If
End Sub``` |
|---|---|

Step-by-Step Instructions 7-4: Searching for Member and DVD Names

1. Use the Solution Explorer to open the **modVintage7** Code module and create the first and last lines of the **Search** sub. Add the code shown in VB Code Box 7-16 to actually create the sub.

2. Switch to the code window for frmMembers and open the btnSearch_Click( ) event procedure. Add the code shown in VB Code Box 7-17 to this event procedure.

3. On the same form, open the lstMembers_SelectedIndexChanged( ) event procedure and add the code shown in VB Code Box 7-18.

4. Switch to the Code window for frmVintage and select **(Base Class Events)** from the Class Name list box at the top-left of the Code window. Then select **Activated** from the Method Name list box at the top-right of the Code window, as shown in Figure 7-19. This will open the sub for the frmVintage_Activated event procedure in which you should enter the code shown in VB Code Box 7-19.

5. Switch to Code window for the frmDVDs form and open the btnSearch_Click event procedure. Add the code shown in VB Code Box 7-20 to create the event procedure.

Mini-Summary 7-5: String class properties and methods

1. Properties and methods of the String class can be used to search for parts of a string or to extract a substring from within a longer string.

2. Useful properties and methods of the string class include Length, IndexOf, Substring, Char, and Trim.

It's Your Turn!

1. Using the IndexOf String class method, create a user-programmed function that, when passed a string and a character, will count the number of times that the character occurs in the string.

2. Describe the purpose and operation of the function that on the next page:

```
Public Function strAFun(strWord As String) As String
  Dim intN As Integer
  Dim strWord = "Georgia", strAFun As String
  strAFun = ""
  Do
    intN = strWord.Length
    strAFun = strAFun & strWord.substring(intN - 1, 1)
    strWord = strWord.Substring(0, intN - 1)
  Loop
End Function
```

3. Follow Step-by-Step Instructions 7-4 to modify the Vintage DVDs application to search for member names or DVDs.

4. Run your modified project and use it to each for names of members starting with "smi". Click on the second name you find to add it and the corresponding late fees to the frmVintage form.

5. Now search for DVDs using the frmDVDs form. Carry out the same search as you did in Chapter 6.

ADDING TO, DELETING FROM, PRINTING, AND SAVING LISTS

It is also desirable to add members and DVDs to the respective lists as well as to delete members. Adding members or DVDs is fairly straightforward, but deleting a member requires more effort.

A straightforward way to add members or DVDs to the lists is to use the InputBox function to request information on the new member or DVD. In the case of a new member, we can assume that after the member name and phone number are entered and added to the membership arrays, the new member name is added to the txtCustName text box on frmVintage. In addition, the variable for the late fees is set equal to zero and copied to the txtLateFees text box on frmVintage. Finally, the current form is hidden. The code for the btnAdd_Click event procedure on the frmMembers form is shown in VB Code Box 7-21.

VB CODE BOX 7-21. Code to add members to the membership list on frmMembers	```
	Private Sub btnAdd_Click(ByVal eventSender As System.Object, _
	ByVal eventArgs As System.EventArgs) Handles btnAdd.Click
	    ReDim Preserve strMembers(intNumMembers)
	    ReDim Preserve strPhoneNumbers(intNumMembers)
	    ReDim Preserve decLateFees(intNumMembers)
	    strMembers(intNumMembers) = InputBox("Enter new name:")
	    strPhoneNumbers(intNumMembers) = InputBox("Enter phone number:")
	    decLateFees(intNumMembers) = 0
	    strCustName = strMembers(intNumMembers)
	    decCustFees = decLateFees(intNumMembers)
	    intNumMembers = intNumMembers + 1
	    Me.Hide()
	End Sub
	``

On the other hand, the staff of the DVD store may need to enter multiple DVDs, so we need an event-driven input loop controlled by the Add DVDs button on the DVDs form. That is, by repeatedly clicking on this button, we can enter multiple DVDs. The code for the btnAdd_Click event procedure on the frmDVDs forms is shown in VB Code Box 7-22.

Deleting a Member

In the previous version of the Vintage DVD application, we were able to delete members from the combo box by using the combo box Item.RemoveAt command. However, now that the membership list is stored in arrays, there is no corresponding command to carry out this activity. For that reason, we must write a procedure to delete members information from the arrays just as we did to sort an array.

Although you may think that deleting an element of an array is nothing more than simply setting the element to be deleted to zero or a blank, this is

| VB CODE BOX 7-22. Code to add DVDs to the DVD list on frmDVDs | ```Private Sub btnAdd_Click(ByVal sender As System.Object, _
ByVal e As System.EventArgs) Handles btnAdd.Click
    ReDim Preserve strDVDs(intNumDVDs)
    ReDim Preserve strDVDLoc(intNumDVDs)
    ReDim Preserve decDVDPrice(intNumMembers)
    strDVDs(intNumDVDs) = InputBox("Enter new DVD name:")
    strDVDLoc(intNumDVDs) = InputBox("Enter DVD Location:")
    decDVDPrice(intNumMembers) = CDec(InputBox("Enter DVD price:"))
    intNumDVDs = intNumDVDs + 1
    Me.ActiveForm.Hide()
End sub``` |

not the case. Setting the element to a zero or blank does not delete it from the array; it just changes the contents of the array element. To delete an array element in a one-dimensional array, it is necessary to move each element *below* it up one position to replace the contents of the array element and then subtract one from the number of elements in the array. Moving the array elements up has the effect of writing over the element to be deleted with the element below it and then repeating the process until the end of the array is reached. In the process, only the element to be deleted is lost. For the decPrices array, the process for deleting decPrices(5) is shown in Figure 7-20. Note that after the deletion, there is no decPrices(9) value because the number of elements in the array has been reduced by one.

FIGURE 7-20.
Deletion of element from array

The pseudocode for the logic behind this process follows, where the index of the element to be deleted is assumed to be known and is equal to a variable called *DeletedIndex*. By setting each array element equal to the array element that comes after it, we *write over* the element to be deleted.

```
Begin deletion procedure
    Repeat for each element starting with DeletedIndex
        ArrayElement(Index) = ArrayElement(Index + 1)
    End repeat
End procedure
```

To delete a member from the strMembers array, we must first find the person to be deleted by using their phone number, which is assumed to be unique. Next, we would delete their name, phone number, and late fees from the appropriate arrays. We can write the first process as a function since it is to return a single value—the array index of the person to be deleted. The second process should be written as a sub procedure that deletes the array elements corresponding to this index. The intFindDelete function to find the array index of the person with the matching phone number is shown in VB Code Box 7-23. Note that it is a Public function that will be saved in the modVintage7 module, because it has been written to be general enough to be used to delete DVDs as well.

VB CODE BOX 7-23. Function to find array index	```Public Function intFindDelete(ByVal strSearchList() As String, _ ByVal strToFind As String) As Integer Dim intCounter As Integer, StrInList As String Dim intFound As Integer For Each StrInList In strSearchList If StrInList = strToFind Then intFound = intCounter Return (intFound) Exit Function End If intCounter = intCounter + 1 Next Return (-1) End Sub```

Note that a string array, StrSearchList, is passed to the intFindDelete function along with a string variable, strToFind. The function then searches for a match between the elements of the array and the variable. If a match is found, the matching array index is returned and the function is exited. If the For-Each loop is completed, then no match has been found and a value of – 1 is returned from the function.

The intFindDelete function is called from the Delete sub procedure. The Delete sub inputs a phone number and passes it and the array of phone numbers to the intFindDelete function, which returns either the array index of the matching phone number or a minus one if no match is found. The Delete sub is shown in VB Code Box 7-24.

In looking at the Delete sub procedure, note that if the returned array index is not negative, then the user is queried about whether they are sure they want to delete the record for this phone number. If they do, then a For-Next loop going from the index to be delete to the next to last record (Int-NumMembers – 2) is used to move the array elements up for the strMembers, strPhoneNumbers, and decLateFees arrays (all of which were declared globally), and the number of elements in the array (intNumMembers) is reduced by one. If the user decides not to delete the record for this phone number, the process is terminated.

A common way to go about this deletion process would be to find the phone number of the member to be deleted using the btnSearch_Click event procedure and then using the btnDelete_Click event procedure to actually delete the record. If this is done, you should be aware that the name will *not* be deleted from the list box since there is no direct connection between the arrays and the search list box. However, if you were to click the *Search* button again, the record would not be displayed. The process of finding a record and then deleting it is shown in Figure 7-21.

| **VB CODE BOX 7-24.** Sub to delete members | ```
Private Sub DeletePhNum()
    Dim intCounter As Integer, strOkToDelete, strPhNumToFind As String
    Dim intFoundIndex As Integer
    strPhNumToFind = InputBox("Input phone number to be deleted", _
    "Vintage DVDs")
    intFoundIndex = intFindDelete(strPhoneNumbers, strPhNumToFind)
    If intFoundIndex >= 0 Then
        strOkToDelete = InputBox("Ok to delete record for " _
        & strPhoneNumbers(intFoundIndex) & " Y or N ?", "Vintage DVDs")
    Else
        MsgBox("No one with that phone number!", MsgBoxStyle.Exclamation, _
        "Vintage DVDs")
        Exit Sub
    End If
    If UCase(strOkToDelete) = "Y" Then
        For intCounter = intFoundIndex To intNumMembers - 2
        strMembers(intCounter) = strMembers(intCounter + 1)
        strPhoneNumbers(intCounter) = strPhoneNumbers(intCounter + 1)
        decLateFees(intCounter) = decLateFees(intCounter + 1)
    Next
    intNumMembers = intNumMembers - 1
    ReDim Preserve strMembers(intNumMembers - 1)
    ReDim Preserve strPhoneNumbers(intNumMembers - 1)
    ReDim Preserve decLateFees(intNumMembers - 1)
    Else
        MsgBox("Record not deleted", MsgBoxStyle.Information, _
        "Vintage DVDs")
        End If
End Sub
``` |

FIGURE 7-21. Form to delete member

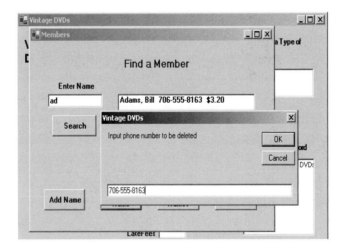

To implement the delete procedure, a single line needs to be added to the btnDelete_Click event procedure:

```
DeletePhNum()
```

Now when the *Delete* button is clicked, the user will be requested to enter a phone number. If this is a valid phone number, they will then be queried as to whether they want to delete this record. If they answer in the affirmative, the member's record is deleted from the arrays.
```

Sorting and Printing a List

To print either list in alphabetical order, we need to sort the corresponding arrays and print them. Because these arrays are not shown in a list or combo box, we need to sort them. Both the membership and DVD lists use three similar arrays, so we can use a single Sort sub (Sort) like that discussed earlier. We can also use a single sub to print the resulting sorted lists (PrintInfo). The btnPrint_Click event procedure for the frmMembers form that invokes the Sort and PrintInfo subs to sort and print the membership information is shown in VB Code Box 7-25. Note that there is also a btnPrint_Click event procedure in the frmDVDs form to sort and print the DVD information event procedure will be the same as this one except for the arguments in each statement invoking the Sort and PrintInfo subs.

| **VB CODE BOX 7-25.** btnPrint event procedure to print sorted membership list | ```
Private Sub btnPrint_Click(ByVal eventSender As system.Object,_
ByVal eventArgs As System.EventArgs) Handles btnPrint.Click
    Sort(strMembers, strPhoneNumbers, decLateFees, _
    intNumMembers)
    PrintInfo(strMembers, strPhoneNumbers, decLateFees, _
    intNumMembers)
End Sub
``` |
|---|---|

If we use the same Reverse and ReverseStr subs that were written for the earlier Sort example but move them to the modVintage7 module and declare them as public, the sub to sort the membership and DVD lists in order of member names or DVD names would be as shown in VB Code Box 7-26.

| **VB CODE BOX 7-26.** Code for Sort sub | ```
Public Sub Sort(ByRef strList1() As String, ByRef strList2() _
As String, ByRef decList3() As Decimal, ByRef intNum As Integer)
    Dim blnNotSwitched As Boolean, intCounter As Integer
    Dim intNextToLast As Short
    blnNotSwitched = False
    Do Until blnNotSwitched
        blnNotSwitched = True
        For intCounter = 0 To intNum - 2
            If strList1(intCounter) > strList1(intCounter + 1) Then
                ReverseStr(strList1(intCounter), strList1(intCounter + 1))
                ReverseStr(strList2(intCounter), strList2(intCounter + 1))
                Reverse(decList3(intCounter), decList3(intCounter + 1))
                blnNotSwitched = False
            End If
        Next
    Loop
End Sub
``` |
|---|---|

The PrintInfo sub to print the sorted lists to the Output window using the Debug object is shown in VB Code Box 7-27. If the membership list is printed, the result is as shown in Figure 7-22.

Modifying the btnClear and btnExit Event Procedures

The final modifications we need to make to the Vintage DVDs project are to change the btnClear_Click and btnExit_Click event procedures. In the first case, we need to add a line to set the late fees textbox to the null character string before starting a new customer.

In the second case, we need to write both the membership and DVD arrays to files using the **StreamWriter** object instead of the method of writ-

| **VB Code Box 7-27.**<br>Code for Print sub | ```
Public Sub PrintInfo(ByRef strList1() As String, ByRef strList2() _
As String, ByRef decList3() As Decimal, ByRef intNumItems As Integer)
   Dim intCounter As Integer
   For intCounter = 0 To intNumItems - 1
      Debug.WriteLine(strList1(intCounter) & "  " & _
      strList2(intCounter) & "  " & Format(decList3(intCounter), "c"))
   Next
End Sub
``` |
|---|---|

Figure 7-22.
Results of printing
the membership list

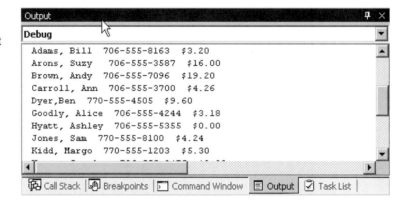

ing to a file as discussed in Chapter 5. The Streamwriter object is very similar to the StreamReader object except that it is writing a stream of characters to a file rather than reading from a file. To do this, we need to create a stream of characters for each line of output including the Tab character as a delimiter. Creating the output stream can be done as one statement or as a series of statements where each new part is concatenated with the existing part to create an entire stream. We will use the latter method as shown in VB Code Box 7-27.

Note that, for each file, we declare a StreamWriter object with a *swr* prefix almost exactly like we did for the StreamReader object. In this way, we create both swrMembers and swrDVDs as StreamWriter objects. We then use a For-Next loop to loop through the items in each array, adding each to the string that will eventually be written to the file with the WriteLine method of the StreamWriter object. After completing the operation, we close the StreamWriter object.

Step-by-Step Instructions 7-5: Adding, deleting, and printing member or DVD information

1. For the frmMembers form, add the code shown in VB Code Box 7-21 to the btnAdd_Click event procedure. For the frmDVDs form, add the code shown in VB Code Box 7-22 to the btnAdd_Click event procedure.

2. Open the code module and create the Integer-valued function named **intFindDelete** shown in VB Code Box 7-23.
```

| VB CODE BOX 7-28. frmVintage code to exit the project | ```
Private Sub btnExit_Click(ByVal eventSender As System.Object, _
ByVal eventArgs As System.EventArgs) Handles btnExit.Click
    Dim intCounter As Integer, strLine As String
    strPathName = CurDir() & "\membersnew.txt"
    Dim swrMembers As System.IO.StreamWriter = _
    New System.IO.StreamWriter(strPathName)
    For intCounter = 0 To intNumMembers - 1
        strLine = strMembers(intCounter) & Chr(9)
        strLine = strLine & strPhoneNumbers(intCounter) & Chr(9)
        strLine = strLine & CStr(decLateFees(intCounter))
        swrMembers.WriteLine(strLine)
    Next
    swrMembers.Close()
    strPathName = CurDir() & "\DVDs.txt"
    Dim swrDVDs As System.IO.StreamWriter = _
    New System.IO.StreamWriter(strPathName)
    For intCounter = 0 To intNumDVDs - 1
        strLine = strDVDs(intCounter) & Chr(9)
        strLine = strLine & CStr(decDVDPrice(intCounter)) & Chr(9)
        strLine = strLine & strDVDLoc(intCounter)
        swrDVDs.WriteLine(strLine)
    Next
    swrDVDs.Close()
    End
End Sub
``` |

3. Go to the Code window for the frmMembers form and add the sub procedure **DeletePhNum** shown in VB Code Box 7-24. For the btnDelete_Click event procedure on this form add the single line of code:

DeletePhNum()

4. Add the code shown in VB Code Box 7-25 to the btnPrint_Click event procedure on the frmMembers form. Modify this code to invoke the same subs with the arguments strDVDs( ), strDVDLoc( ), decDVDPrice( ), and intNumD-VDs, instead of the membership list arguments. Add this code to the btnPrint_Click event procedure on the frmDVDs form.

5. Open the Code module and enter the code shown in VB Code Box 7-26 to create the **Sort** sub. Also, add the code shown in VB Code Box 7-9 to create the **Reverse** sub. Modify this code by changing the Decimal declarations to be String data type declarations to create the **ReverseStr** sub.

6. Add the code shown in VB Code Box 7-27 to the Code module to create the **PrintInfo** sub that will be used to print the two lists.

7. Add a single line to the btnClear_Click event procedure on the frmVintage form to clear the txtLateFees text box.

8. Replace the existing code in the btnExit_Click event procedure on the frmVintage form with the code shown in VB Code Box 7-28.

9. Execute your project and correct any errors you may find. Save all files.

■ ▬ ■ ▬ ■ ▬ ■ ▬ ■ ▬ ■ ▬ ■ ▬ ■ ▬ ■ ▬ ■ ▬ ■ ▬ ■ ▬ ■ ■

Summary of Changes to Vintage DVDs Project

We have made a large number of changes and additions to the Vintage DVDs project in this chapter—so many that a summary table of the new and modified general and event procedures may be helpful to you. Instead of display-
```

ing all of the code for this project, which would take at least four pages, we will use two tables to show you where the code in the various VB Code Boxes should appear, that is, in the code module (modVintage7), the main Vintage DVDs form (frmVintage), the membership information form (frmMembers), or the DVD information form (frmDVDs). Table 7-4 lists each VB Code Box in order and indicates what is new about the procedure, its location, and its status—that is, is it new to this chapter or a modification of previous code? On the other hand, Table 7-5 shows the four elements of the Vintage7 project, that is, the code module, frmVintage, frmMembers, and frmDVDs and lists the VB code boxes that contain code that is new or modified in this chapter for that element. If an event procedure is not shown in either table, it is not changed from previous chapters and remains in the Vintage DVDs project unchanged. You should consider these two tables to be a *roadmap* to the changes and modifications that have taken place in this chapter.

TABLE 7-4: Location of code in VB code boxes

VB Code Box	General or Event Procedure	Location	Status
7-12	btnCheck_Click event procedure	frmVintage	New
7-13	btnCalc_Click event procedure	frmVintage	Modified
7-14	Global variable declarations	modVintage7	New
7-15	frmVintage_Load event procedure	frmVintage	Modified
7-16	Sub Search procedure	modVintage7	New
7-17	btnSearch_Click event procedure	frmMembers	New
7-18	lstMembers_SelectedIndexChanged event procedure	frmMembers	New
7-19	frmVintage_Activated	frmVintage	New
7-20	btnSearch_Click	frmDVDs	Modified
7-21	btnAdd_Click event procedure	frmMembers	New
7-22	btnAdd_Click event procedure	frmDVDs	New
7-23	Function intFindDelete procedure	modVintage7	New
7-24	Sub Delete procedure	frmMembers	New
7-25	btnPrint_Click event procedure	frmMembers	New
7-26	Sub Sort procedure	modVintage7	New
7-27	Sub PrintInfo procedure	modVintage7	New
7-28	btnExit_Click	frmVintage	Modified

TABLE 7-5: Location of new or modified code in Vintage.vbp

modVintage7	frmVintage	frmMembers	frmDVDs
VB Code Box 7-14	VB Code Box 7-12	VB Code Box 7-17	VB Code Box 7-20
VB Code Box 7-16	VB Code Box 7-13	VB Code Box 7-18	VB Code Box 7-22
VB Code Box 7-23	VB Code Box 7-15	VB Code Box 7-21	

TABLE 7-5: Location of new or modified code in Vintage.vbp (Continued)

modVintage7	frmVintage	frmMembers	frmDVDs
VB Code Box 7-26	VB Code Box 7-19	VB Code Box 7-24	
VB Code Box 7-27	VB Code Box 7-28	VB Code Box 7-25	
VB Code Box 7-9			

Mini-Summary 7-6: Adding to, deleting from, printing, and saving lists

1. Adding to an array is simply a matter of increasing the number of elements in the array and copying the new value into the last position in the array.

2. Deleting from an array requires that all elements *below* the element to be deleted be copied up one position and the number of elements decreased by one.

3. The same sort sub can be used to sort different sets of arrays as long as they are the same data types.

4. The StreamWriter object can be used to write arrays to a sequential access file.

It's Your Turn!

1. Follow Step-by-Step Instructions 7-5 to modify the Vintage DVDs project to add, delete, and print names to the membership list and to add and print DVDs to the DVD list.

2. Run your project and test the additional code by adding a new member named **Joe Smith** with the phone number **706-555-1122.** (Remember to add the name in last-name-first form.) Also, add the DVDs shown in Table 7-6 to the list of DVDs.

TABLE 7-6: New DVDs

Name	Location	Price
Easy Rider	Drama	$1.99
A Fistful of Dollars	Western	$1.99
Sleeping Beauty	Kids	$.99

3. Test the project by failing to check a customer name. You should be forced to check a customer name before any calculations can be made.

4. Test your delete procedure by searching for all members with a last name beginning with *Smi.* You should find three names. Now delete the member with telephone number of *706-555-0023.* Search again and you should now see only two names.

5. Test the Print buttons on both forms. Both lists should be printed in alphabetical order by the last name.

6. Finally, use the *Exit* button to exit the project. Now, run it again and click both *Print* buttons. The member and DVDs you added in the previous execution should be displayed. They should have been saved to disk when you exited the project before and then reloaded when you ran it again.

7. Add a **btnDelete** button to the frmDVDs form that can be used to delete lost, stolen, or defective DVDs from the store's inventory. Also, add a **DeleteDVD** sub to this form that is similar to the DeletePhNum sub on the frmMembers form. This sub should search for DVDs by exact name and delete them.

8. Save your project as before.

SUMMARY

At the beginning of the chapter, we said you would be able to do a number of things after reading it. Let's review those things here:

1. Understand the importance of general procedures and modules in programming with VB .NET. General procedures are an important part of programming in VB .NET. Unlike event procedures, general procedures are not associated with a specific event and can be used anywhere on a form or in the project as needed. They increase the capability of dividing up the work in creating a VB .NET project. General procedures also offer the potential to reuse code in multiple locations and to reduce the complexity of event procedures.

2. Describe the difference between the two types of general procedures: sub procedures (subs) and functions. Two types of general procedures—function procedures and sub procedures—are written by the programmer rather than being built into VB .NET. Function procedures return a value through their name, whereas sub procedures (commonly referred to as *subs*) do not return a value. However, subs are very useful for modifying arguments passed to them. Both functions and subs must be invoked by an event procedure or general procedure, and they must be defined in the Code window of the form or in a Code module.

3. Describe the relationship between arguments and parameters in general procedures. When a function or sub is defined, there must be a one-to-one correspondence between the arguments in the calling event or general procedure and the parameters in the function or sub.

4. Understand the difference between passing by value and passing by reference in sub procedures. Arguments can be passed to a sub or function by value or by reference. When an argument is passed by value, any changes in the corresponding parameter are not reflected in the argument. If the argument is passed by reference and the corresponding parameter is changed in the sub or function, this change is reflected in the argument. The ByVal or ByRef keywords are used in the Procedure definition statement to define an argument to be passed by value or by reference. The default is to pass by value.

5. Write functions to return single values and sub procedures to process multiple values. A common use of a function is to create a single value that is assigned to a variable or output. The name of the function must be assigned a value in the function. Functions and subs discussed in this chapter included a function to find the income tax due, a sub to sort an array using another sub to reverse two array values, and a sub to search an array.

A sub is often used for manipulating the arguments passed to it. A sub can invoke another sub; for example, a sub to sort an array can invoke a sub to reverse two array elements. Sorting an array requires that nested loops be used to repeat the comparison-reversal process until the array is sorted.

6. Understand the types of errors that can occur in the use of general procedures. Errors in using general procedures most often involve the number or type of the arguments not matching the number or type of the corresponding parameters. Having the arguments out of order can also result in an error.

7. Use the Code module to declare variables globally or create global general procedures. The use of global variables and general procedures was also discussed in this chapter. Global variables are declared in the Code module of the project and are known to all forms and procedures in the project. However, if a global variable is changed anywhere in the project, this change is reflected everywhere. Global general procedures are also defined in the Code module and are known to all forms and procedures.

8. Understand the use of string functions to work with string constants and variables. String functions were used to search for parts of a string or to extract a substring from within a longer string. They were used here to search for partial names. Useful string functions include UCase, InStr, Len, Microsoft.VisualBasic.Right, Microsoft.VisualBasic.Left, and Mid.

9. Be able to write general procedures to add to arrays, delete from arrays, print arrays in a desired order, and save arrays to disk. Adding to an array is simply a matter of increasing the number of elements in the array and copying the new value into the last position in the array. Deleting from an array requires that all elements *below* the element to be deleted be copied up one position and the number of elements decreased by one. The same Sort sub can be used to sort different sets of arrays as long as they are of the same data types. The StreamWriter object is used to write an array to a sequential access file.

NEW PROGRAMMING STATEMENTS

Statement to reference a programmer-defined function variable = functionName(arg1, arg2, ..., arg*n*)
Statement to reference a programmer-defined sub procedure subName(arg1, arg2, ..., arg*n*)
Statement to create programmer-defined function **Function** *type*FuncName(parameter1 as type, parameter2 as type, ...) as type
Statement to create programmer-defined sub procedure **Sub** SubName(parameter1 as type, parameter2 as type)
Statement to declare a parameter to be passed by reference **Sub** SubName(**ByRef** parameter1 by type)

NEW PROGRAMMING STATEMENTS

Statement to reference a programmer-defined function
variable = functionName(arg1, arg2, ..., arg*n*)

Statement to publicly declare a variable in Code module
Public varName1 as type, varName2 as type, ...

KEY TERMS

Activated event
bubble sort
code module
event procedure
function procedure (function)

function definition statement
general procedure
global declaration
parameter
passing by reference

passing by value
programmer-defined general procedures
reusable code
sub procedure (sub)

EXERCISES

1. For each of the following, write the scope (local, module, or global) of the variables described.

   a. Variable sngY declared inside sub procedure called CalcInterest

   b. Array variable intAge declared using the keyword Dim in the general declaration section of the form frmEmployee.frm

   c. Variable intSize declared using the keyword *Public* in the general declaration section of the code module modSearch.mod

   d. Variable blnStatus declared as a parameter of the function blnCheck

   e. Variable intNumber declared using the keyword Dim in the general declaration section of the module modSort.vb

2. Write function procedures for each of the following:

   a. Write a function that, when passed an array of letter grades and the number of grades, will calculate a grade point average (GPA). Use the scale: A = 4.0, B = 3.0, C = 2.0, D = 1.0, and F = 0.0.

   b. Write a function that will have as parameters a single variable representing degrees of temperature and a string variable representing a code that can be either "F" for Fahrenheit or "C" for Celsius. If the code is F, then the original temperature is in degrees Celsius and should be converted to degrees Fahrenheit. If the code is C, then the original temperature is in degrees Fahrenheit and should be converted to degrees Celsius. The formula to convert from Celsius to Fahrenheit is: $F = (9/5) \times C + 32$.

   c. Write a function that will receive two integer values and return a random number between these values. A formula for doing this using the *Rnd* function may be written as:

```
Int((intUBnd - intLBnd + 1) * Rnd() + intLBnd)
```

   where intUBnd is the higher of the two values passed to the function and intLBnd is the lower of the two values passed to the function. Note: you should always precede the use of the Rnd function with the *Randomize* function to reset the first value in the Rnd function.

3. Write sub procedures or each of the following:

a. Write a sub procedure that will accept an array of names and the number of names, and return a second array with initials. The original array has names in last-name-first format, separated by a comma and a space, for example, "Smith, John." The new array should contain the initials in order with periods, for example, "J. S."

b. Write a sub procedure for a computerized testing program that will receive three variables: a Boolean variable blnAnswer, an integer variable intNumCorrect, and an integer variable intNumTried. When blnAnswer is true, then intNumCorrect should be incremented, and a message should appear saying: "That's correct." When blnAnswer is false, a message should appear saying: "That's incorrect." In either case, the variable intNumTried should be incremented, and a message should appear showing how many answers are correct out of the number attempted.

c. A short-term parking lot charges based on the time a car has been in the lot. Less than 15 minutes there is no charge, the first half hour is $0.50, the second half hour is $0.75, and for every hour thereafter or portion of an hour, the charge is $1. In addition, employees who work in a building adjacent to the lot receive a 20% discount of the total parking charge. Write a sub procedure that will receive a Boolean variable indicating whether or not a patron works in the adjacent building and two time variables, one representing the time in the parking lot and the other representing the time out. Your sub should calculate the amount owed, display the amount owed in a message to the patron, and pass the amount owed back to the calling routine.

4. For each of the following, explain what is wrong with the code. What error messages would you see, if any? What can you do to fix each section of code?

a.
```
Public Sub (sngX As Single) As Boolean
   If sngX >= 0 And sngX < 100 Then
     blnCheck = True
   Else
     blnCheck = False
   End If
End Sub
```

b.
```
Public Function lngCube(ByVal intX As Integer) As Long
   Dim intX As Integer
   lngCube = intX ^ 3
   Return lngCube
End Function
```

c.
```
Public Function intSum() As Sum
  Public intX As Integer
  Public intY As Integer
  Public intZ As Integer
  intSum = intX + intY + intZ
  Return intSum
End Function
```

PROJECTS

Before starting any of these projects, use Windows Explorer to create a folder within the *Chapter7* folder named **Homework.** Store all of the projects in your homework folder.

1. Use Windows Explorer to create a folder named **Ex7-1** in the *Chapter7\Homework* folder and copy the contents of the *Chapter6\Homework\Ex6-1* folder into the new folder. Use VB .NET to rename all of the files as **Ex7-1.** Also, change the name of the form to be **frmEx7-1** and make it the Startup object. Add a button to the form that will invoke a sub to sort and display the student records in *descending order* of the quiz average. Write the corresponding sub(s). Also, write a String data type function to replace the code that assigns a letter grade to each student and a Single data type function to find and display the average of the quiz scores. Finally, write a sub to replace the code to find and display the information on the students with the highest *and* lowest quiz scores. Why could you not write a function for this purpose? Run and test your project with the Student.txt data file.

2. Use Windows Explorer to create a folder named **Ex7-1** in the *Chapter7\Homework* folder and copy the contents of the *Chapter6\Homework\Ex6-2* folder into the new folder. Use VB .NET to rename all of the files as **Ex7-2.** Also, change the name of the form to be **frmEx7-2** and make it the Startup object. Add a button to the form that will invoke a sub to sort the customer names in *descending order* of the sales. Write the corresponding sub(s). Add a button that will invoke a function to find the average sales. Display this value in a text box with an appropriate label. Add a new array that will contain the customer sales status. This status is determined as *high* if the customer sales are more than 20 percent above average, *low* if the sales are more than 20 percent below average, and *average* otherwise. You will need to add a sub to make this calculation and assignment. Finally, replace the code with a sub to find and display the customers with the highest and lowest sales. Run and test your project with the CustSales.txt data file.

3. Use Windows Explorer to create a folder named **Ex7-3** in the *Chapter7\Homework* folder and copy the contents of the *Chapter6\Homework\Ex6-3* folder into the new folder. Use VB .NET to rename all of the files as **Ex7-3.** Also, change the name of the form to be **frmEx7-3** and make it the Startup object. Add a button to the form that will invoke a sub to sort and display the golfer records in *ascending* order of the golf scores. Write the corresponding sub(s). Replace the code that assigns a designation to each golfer with a String data type function. Replace the code that finds and displays the name and score of the golfers with highest and lowest scores with a sub. Run and test your project with the Golfers.txt data file.

4. Use Windows Explorer to create a folder named **Ex7-4** in the *Chapter7\Homework* folder and copy the contents of the *Chapter6\Homework\Ex6-4* folder into the new folder. Use VB .NET to rename all of the files as **Ex7-4.** Also, change the name of the form to be **frmEx7-4** and make it the Startup object. Replace the code used to search for the Zip code for a city name with a function. Also, add a button to the form to invoke a sub to sort the list of cities in alphabetical order and display them and their Zip code in

a list box. Add a Click event procedure for the list box that will invoke the same search function you wrote earlier. Add another function that provides the capability of reversing the search—that is, the capability of inputting a Zip code and displaying the corresponding post office. Test your project with the ZipCodes.txt data file.

5. Use Windows Explorer to create a folder named **Ex7-5** in the *Chapter7\Homework* folder and copy the contents of the *Chapter6\Homework\Ex6-5* folder into the new folder. Use VB .NET to rename all of the files as **Ex7-5.** Also, change the name of the form to be **frmEx7-5** and make it the Startup object. Replace the code used to find an insurance premium with a function. Test your project with the data shown in Chapter 6.

6. Use Windows Explorer to create a folder named **Ex7-6** in the *Chapter7\Homework* folder and copy the contents of the *Homework\Ex7-1* folder into the new folder. Use VB .NET to rename the files as **Ex7-6.** Use the **Project|Add Existing Item** menu selection to add the file named **Ex6-6Two.vb** file to the project from the Chapter6\Homework\Ex6-6 folder. Rename the file as **Ex7-6Two.vb.** Make the following changes and additions:

a. Modify this project so that the student names and quiz score arrays are loaded only *once* and all subs and functions are known to both forms.

b. Replace the code on the second form with a global sub that will display a given student's average and letter grade.

c. Replace the code on the second form with a global sub that will respond to the option button by displaying all student names with quiz scores above the corresponding quiz scores (90-80-70-60).

d. Add a third form, which should be named **frmStudentAdd,** with a filename of **Ex7-6Three.vb.** The user should be able to switch to this form by clicking a button on the main form. The new form should allow the user to add new students and quiz scores to the student list, determine letter grades for the new students as they are added, and print a list of all students, their quiz scores, and their letter grades in alphabetical order (use existing subs wherever possible).

e. Modify the Exit button on the main form so that the revised student name and quiz score arrays are saved to the data file upon exit. Test your project with the Student.txt data file.

7. Use Windows Explorer to create a folder named **Ex7-7** in the *Chapter7\Homework* folder and copy the contents of the *Homework\Ex7-2* folder into the new folder. Use VB .NET to rename the files as **Ex7-7.** Use the **Project|Add Existing Item** menu selection to add the file named **Ex6-7Two.vb** file to the project from the Chapter6\Homework\Ex6-6 folder. Rename the file as **Ex7-7Two.vb.** Make the following changes and additions:

a. Replace the code on the second form with a global function that will display a given customer's sales. Give the module the name **modEx7-7.vb.**

b. Replace the code on the second form with a global sub that will respond to the option button by displaying all customer names with sales less than a designated value in a list box (use the same values as in Chapter 6).

c. Add a third form, which should be named **frmCustomerAdd,** with a filename of **Ex7-7Three.vb.** The user should be able to switch to this form by clicking a button on the main form. The new form should allow the user to add new customers and sales to the customer list and print a list of all customers and their sales in alphabetical order (use existing subs wherever possible).

d. Modify the Exit button on the main form so that the revised customer name and sales arrays are saved to the data file upon exiting the project.

8. Use Windows Explorer to create a folder named **Ex7-8** in the *Chapter7\Homework* folder and copy the contents of the *Homework\Ex7-3* folder into the new folder. Use VB .NET to rename the files as **Ex7-8.** Use the **Project|Add Existing Item** menu selection to add the file named **Ex6-8Two.vb** file to the project from the *Chapter6\Homework\Ex6-6* folder. Rename the file as **Ex7-8Two.vb.** Make the following changes and additions:

a. Replace the code on the second form with a global function that will display a given golfer's score. Give the module the name **modEx7-8.vb.**

b. Replace the code on the second form with a global sub that will respond to the option button by displaying all golfer names with scores above a certain score (use the same values as in Chapter 6).

c. Add a third form, which should be named **frmGolferAdd,** with a filename of **Ex7-8Three.vb.** The user should be able to switch to this form by clicking a button on the main form. The new form should allow the user to add new golfers and scores to the golfer list, determine the status for the new golfers as they are added, and print a list of all golfers, their scores, and their status in alphabetical order (use existing subs wherever possible).

d. Modify the Exit button on the main form so that the revised golfer name and score arrays are saved to the data file upon exiting the project.

9. Validation of user input is an important part of many programs. In addition, much of the necessary validation is similar from program to program—so much so, that you may find yourself writing similar code over and over to perform the same validation tasks. To save time writing future programs, create a VB .NET module file of validation functions. This module can then be added to any project that requires input validation. Each function should receive relevant parameters to perform the validation and then return a Boolean value. The Boolean return value may be true when the input value is correct and false when it is not correct. You will probably need to write different functions for each data type. As a start to your validation library, write functions to validate for the following items:

a. Validate that a string value has been entered into a text box.
b. Validate that an item entered into a text box is a number.

    c. Validate that an integer value falls between an upper and a lower bound.

    d. Validate that a string value contains a specific character.

    e. Validate that an item has been selected from a list box.

To do this, use Windows Explorer to create a folder named **Ex7-9** in the *Chapter7\Homework* folder. Start VB .NET (or select **File|New Project**) and select **Windows Application** with a name of **Ex7-9,** but don't worry about renaming the form because it will only be used to test your functions. Add a module with a name of **modEx7-9.vb** and create all of the validation functions as public procedures in this module. Add a text box and button to the form to use in testing your validation functions. Make sure you test incorrect as well as correct values. When you are completed, delete the form from the project.

10. Currency exchange rates are important for both the world traveler and the investor. But because they fluctuate on a daily basis, it is often difficult to keep up with answers to questions such as: How many pesos are equivalent to 1 U.S. dollar? How many French francs make a Japanese yen? If a pound of tea costs 10 Russian rubles, what does it cost in China? To do this, use Windows Explorer to create a folder named **Ex7-10** in the *Chapter7\Homework* folder. Start VB .NET (or select **File|New Project**) to create a new Windows application with a name of **Ex7-10** with a single form that will be used for input and output. Write a VB .NET project to create a table of equivalent currency values. Include a subroutine that will read a file containing a list of currencies and the equivalent amount in U.S. dollars. Each record in this file will contain a string representing the currency name, and a value representing the amount of the currency equal to 1 U.S. dollar, for example *"Euro"*, *.849* would mean that 0.849 EU Euros are equal to 1 U.S. dollar. Create a second sub procedure that will generate a table like that shown in Table 7-7. By reading across the table, we can read the amount of foreign currency indicated by the column heading that equals one unit of the currency indicated by the row heading. Create two functions to perform your calculations. One function may be used to calculate the exchange values between 1 U.S. dollar and any given foreign currency. The second function may be used to calculate exchange values between two foreign currencies. Note that to find values between two foreign currencies you may need two conversions, the first currency to U.S. dollars followed by converting U.S. dollars to the second currency.

TABLE 7-7: Currency exchange table

	U.S. Dollar	**Euro**	**Jap. Yen**	**English Pound**
U.S. dollar	1	.849	118.65	.60
Euro	1.186	1	138.14	.716
Jap. yen	.00849	.00718	1	.00514
English pound	1.6617	1.1857	193.39	1

11. Chef Lutz has been keeping a recipe collection for years on note cards. He has recently decided to save these recipes in two files. One file will contain a list of ingredients and amounts whereas the other will be a text file containing the step-by-step instructions. He would like to have a VB .NET program to help him manage his recipe collection. An interesting twist to his collection is that some of his recipes were obtained in his homeland of Germany, but others were obtained in the United States. The main difficulty this brings is in converting the various measures from German to U.S. measures and vice versa. He has decided to input each file using its original values and measurements and then incorporate into the program the capability of converting between the measurement scales. An example recipe file is shown in Table 7-8.

TABLE 7-8: Recipe file format

"American Apple Pie"
"Serves:", 8 **"Scale:", "American"** **"Items:", 6** **"White Flour", 2.4, "cups"** **"Sugar", 2, "tbsp""** **"Salt", .25, "tsp"** **"Cold Butter", 0.5, "cups"** **"Vegetable Shortening", 5, "tbsp"** **"water", 8, "tbsp"**

Build a recipe management project for Chef Lutz. Include as many general sub procedures and functions in your code as possible. Your project should allow Chef Lutz to enter a new recipe; retrieve a recipe by selecting it from a list box (you may need another file with a list of recipe names); convert a recipe from American measures to European measures, and vice versa; calculate measures when the required number of people to serve is different from the amount served by a particular recipe; and print a recipe with calculated measures. Conversion factors for some common measurements are found in Table 7-9, as are some internal American conversion factors.

TABLE 7-9: Recipe conversion factors

	American	**European**
Flour	1 cup	125 grams
Sugar or butter	1 cup	250 grams
Liquids	1/4 cup 1 cup 1 quart	5 cL 2.5 dL 1 L
	2 tablespoons = 1 ounce	
	1 cup = 8 ounces	
	3 teaspoons = 1 tablespoon	

To do this, use Windows Explorer to create a folder named **Ex7-11** in the *Chapter7\Homework* folder. Start VB .NET (or select **File | New Project**) to create a new Windows application with a name of **Ex7-11** with a single form of the same name.

12. One way to compute a person's fitness level is based on the time that it takes for the person to walk 3 miles without running. Table 7-10 shows the standards for five general fitness levels for a woman from 20 to 29 years of age. These standards can be extended to men by subtracting 2 minutes from each of the times listed in the table. They can be extended to younger people, aged 13 to 19 years, by subtracting 1 minute from each time.

TABLE 7-10: Fitness level standards (women, 20–29)

Fitness Level	Time to Walk 3 Miles
1	Over 48 minutes
2	Over 44 but less than or equal to 48 minutes
3	Over 40 but less than or equal to 44 minutes
4	Over 36 but less than or equal to 40 minutes
5	36 minutes or less

Write a program that can determine a person's fitness level based on these standards. Your program should allow the user to enter the person's first and last name, age, gender, and time (in minutes) to walk 3 miles. Be sure to validate all input using an appropriate function. The program should store the input information in a fitness profile structure along with the person's fitness level. Create a function that will determine the fitness level based on the input. The fitness profile should also be displayed as a report on the screen. If the person's age is outside of the 13 to 29 age, display a message indicating that the fitness level cannot be determined. Use as many general sub and function procedures as needed. To do this, use Windows Explorer to create a folder named **Ex7-12** in the *Chapter7\Homework* folder. Start VB .NET (or select **File | New Project**) to create a new Windows application with a name of **Ex7-12** with a single form of the same name.

8 Using User-Defined Data Types and Object-Oriented Programming

Learning Objectives

After reading this chapter, you will be able to

1. Understand user-defined data types and their relationship to object-oriented programming.

2. Create and use your own user-defined data types.

3. Understand and discuss the basic concepts of object-oriented programming.

4. Describe the basics of the .NET framework and namespaces.

5. Work with the ArrayList and Hashtable classes.

6. Create and use your own object classes.

User-Defined Data Types and Object-Oriented Programming

As you have seen, there are many components of VB .NET programs, such as forms and buttons, that are thought of as objects. It turns out that the concept of an object is fundamental to a complete programming paradigm known as object-oriented programming. In this chapter, we will explore how object-oriented programming is implemented in VB. NET.

In VB .NET, understanding user-defined data types is the first step in moving towards object-oriented programming. A user-defined data type is a data type that is defined by the programmer and is created using the keyword *Structure*. In addition to data fields, a structure can also incorporate functions that can be called when working with the user-defined data type. In object-oriented programming terminology, the functions of the user-defined data types are known as methods.

In fact, a user-defined data type is a rudimentary form of an object in that it has data definitions and methods, but these are not encapsulated as are true objects. Discussing user-defined data types first will give you a feel for the process of creating your own classes and objects, which is discussed later in the chapter.

Once we understand user-defined data types, we will expand the concept to that of objects and classes. We will see that classes are the basic templates that determine the characteristics of an object and learn how we can declare objects to an instance of a class. Specifically, we will look at how you can use objects from existing classes that are available in the .NET framework. In addition, we will see how you can create and use your own classes and objects.

User-Defined Data Types (UDTs)

One of the shortcomings of arrays is that only one type of data can be stored in a single array. For example, an array might be defined as a String array, an Integer array, or a Single array, but not as all three at the same time. Fortunately, if we are willing to create our *own* data types in VB .NET, we can circumvent this problem. These new data types are commonly referred to as **user-defined data types (UDTs),** although that is something of a misnomer because it is not the person using the program but the programmer creating the project who does this. For this reason, a more appropriate name might be **programmer-defined data types.**

UDTs in Visual Basic are made up of elements, where each element is declared to be a standard data type (String, Integer, and so on) or a previously declared UDT. As we will see in later chapters, UDTs in VB .NET are much like database records. (In fact, in some programming languages, a UDT is referred to as a *record type.*) We will discuss how you can work with databases using VB .NET in the next chapter. For example, a UDT for a college student might include data fields about the student's ID number, last name, first name, middle initial, and GPA. By creating an array of college student data types, we become able to store all this different type of information under one name in memory.

Using UDTs is a two-step process. First, the data type must be declared, and, second, a variable or array must be declared to be of that data type in the procedure in which it is going to be used. You *cannot* use the UDT declaration as the variable; you must declare a variable (or array) to be of that type and then use it in your code.

Declaring a Data Type

The first step in using a UDT is to declare the data type using the **Structure statement.** A common place to make this declaration is in a Code module so the UDT will be available throughout the project. The various elements, fields, and methods, that will make up that data type are then listed. The structure declaration process is terminated with an **End Structure statement.** The form of the Structure statement is

  Structure *UDTname*
   Public *elementname1* **As** *datatype*
   Public *elementname2* **As** *datatype*
   Public *elementnameN* **As** *datatype*
   Public Sub *subname()*
    sub statements
   End Sub
   Public Function *functionname()* **As** *datatype*
    function statements
   End Function
  End Structure

where *typename* and the various *elementname, subname,* and *functionname* values must follow the standard variable-naming rules. Also, the *datatype* values must be standard data types or previously declared UDTs. The elements in a Structure statement can be individual variables or arrays. For our discussion, we will create a UDT with these elements only. We will save discussions of methods for our discussion of objects and classes later in this chapter.

For example, the Structure statement to declare the college student data type discussed earlier in a Code module is shown in VB Code Box 8-1.

VB CODE BOX 8-1. Code to define a data type	```Structure CollegeStudent Public intIDNumber As Integer Public strLastName As String Public strFirstName As String Public strMidInit As String Public sngGPA As Single End Structure```

Using a UDT

Although a UDT can be declared at any level, the best place to do so is at the module level. Once a UDT has been declared globally in a Code module, it can then be used in declaring variables or arrays anywhere in the project, just as any other data type would be used to declare variables. For our example, to declare a variable udtOneStudent to be of the type CollegeStudent, the statement would be

```
Dim udtOneStudent As CollegeStudent
```

Note that the variable prefix for a UDT is *udt*. Now, the variable udtOneStudent is composed of the same five elements that were declared for the type CollegeStudent. This structure is shown in Figure 8-1.

FIGURE 8-1.
Structure of variable
OneStudent

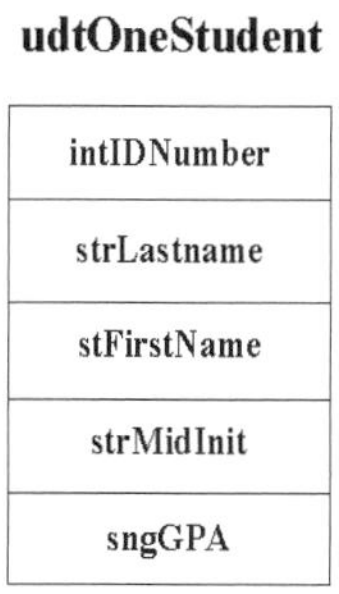

udtOneStudent

intIDNumber
strLastname
stFirstName
strMidInit
sngGPA

To refer to the individual elements of the udtOneStudent variable, we use the **dot notation**—that is, *VariableName.ElementName*. For example, to assign a student name to the strFirstName element of the variable udtOneStudent, the statement would be

```
udtOneStudent.strFirstName = "George"
```

Similarly, to assign a grade point value to the GPA element, the statement would be

```
udtOneStudent.sngGPA = 3.12
```

If the data about a student are being input from text boxes on a form like that shown in Figure 8-2, the complete set of statements to input the data and clear the text boxes would be as shown in VB Code Box 8-2 (where the sub procedure ClearTextBoxes clears the text boxes and sets the focus back to the txtIDNumber text box).

> **TIP:** If two variables are declared as the same user-defined data type, you can assign one to the other. This will assign all of the elements in one variable to all of the elements in the other.

FIGURE 8-2. Student information form

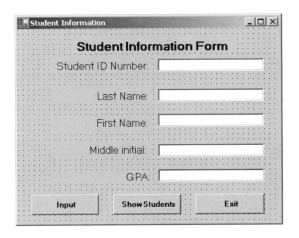

| **VB CODE BOX 8-2.** Code to input student data | ```
Private Sub btnInput_Click(ByVal sender As System.Object, ByVal e _
As System.EventArgs) Handles btnInput.Click
    Dim udtOneStudent As CollegeStudent
    udtOneStudent.intIDNumber = CInt(txtStudentID.Text)
    udtOneStudent.strLastName = txtLastName.Text
    udtOneStudent.strFirstName = txtFirstName.Text
    udtOneStudent.strMidInit = txtMiddleInitial.Text
    udtOneStudent.sngGPA = CSng(txtGPA.Text)
    ClearTextBoxes()
End Sub
``` |

Using the With Statement

To reduce the redundancy in working with data type variables like udtOneStudent, we can use the **With statement,** which allows us to work with multiple elements of a single object or structure. The form of the With statement is

> **With** *udtVariable*
>   *statements*
> **End With**

where all of the statements would normally begin with the *udtVariable* name followed by a period and then the rest of the statement. The With statement allows you to mention the UDT variable name once and then begin each statement with a period. For example, the five statements to input data to the udtOneStudent variable from text boxes, as shown in VB Code Box 8-2, can be replaced using the With statement, as shown VB Code Box 8-3.

The With statement can also be used to assign properties to a control or object. For example, to assign the properties to the txtStudentID text box, the
```

VB CODE BOX 8-3.
Use of With statement
	``
	With udtOneStudent
	    .intIDNumber = CInt(txtStudentID.Text)
	    .strLastName = txtLastName.Text
	    .strFirstName = txtFirstName.Text
	    .strMidInit = txtMiddleInitial.Text
	    .sngGPA = CSng(txtGPA.Text)
	End With
	``

Tip: The With statement can save a great deal of typing of long UDT variable names, and at the same time it keeps all UDT variable fields together.

statements might be as shown in VB Code Box 8-4. Note that the With statement for the Size property can be nested within the outer With statement. Using the Size property you can set the size of a control by specifying values for its width and height. This works only if the element of the inner With structure is a member of the element used in the outer structure.

VB CODE BOX 8-4.
Use of With statement
for setting property
values
	``
	With txtStudentID
	    .TabIndex = 0
	    With .Size
	        .Height = 1500
	        .Width = 2500
	    End With
	End With
	``

If we add a second form (*frmStudentList*) with a list box *(lstStudentList)* to which we want to add the elements of the udtOneStudent variable, it should be declared as the *form* level of the input form using the following:

```
Dim frmStudent As New frmStudentList()
```

The data from the input form can then be added to the list box on this second form using the With statement to reduce the redundancy in the Items.Add method as shown below:

```
With udtOneStudent
    strItem = CStr(.intIDNumber) & "  " & .strLastName _
      & "  " & .strFirstName & "  " & .strMidInit & "  " & _
      Format(.sngGPA, "fixed")
    frmStudent.lstStudentList.Items.Add(strItem)
End With
```

Declaring a new string variable called strItem and adding this code to the revised btnInput_Click event procedure results in the final code to input student information and display it to the list box on the frmStudentList form as shown in VB Code Box 8-5.

If several names are input and added to the list box, and the list is displayed with the *Show Students* button, the result is as shown in Figure 8-3. Adding the code shown in VB Code Box 8-6 to the *Show Students* button results in the user being able to view the list of students that has been input.

More on UDTs

As we said earlier, one reason to use UDTs is to be able to include different types of data within an array. For example, using standard data types, we would need five different arrays to store the five elements of the student

| **VB CODE BOX 8-5.** Revised code to input student information and add to list box | ```
Dim frmStudent As New frmStudentList() 'Declared at form level

Private Sub btnInput_Click(ByVal sender As System.Object, _
  ByVal e As System.EventArgs) Handles btnInput.Click
    Dim udtOneStudent As CollegeStudent, strItem As String
    With udtOneStudent
      .intIDNumber = CInt(txtStudentID.Text)
      .strLastName = txtLastName.Text
      .strFirstName = txtFirstName.Text
      .strMidInit = txtMiddleInitial.Text
      .sngGPA = CSng(txtGPA.Text)
    End With
    With udtOneStudent
      strItem = CStr(.intIDNumber) & "  " & .strLastName & "  " & _
        .strFirstName & "  " & .strMidInit & "  " & _
        Format(.sngGPA, "fixed")
      frmStudent.lstStudentList.Items.Add(strItem)
    End With
    ClearTextBoxes()
End Sub
``` |

FIGURE 8-3. Student information form with several names input

| **VB CODE BOX 8-6.** Code to show student list form | ```
Private Sub btnShowStudents_Click(ByVal sender As System.Object, _
  ByVal e As System.EventArgs) Handles btnShowStudents.Click
    frmStudent.Show()
End Sub
``` |

record with which we have been working. These arrays would include an Integer data type array for the student ID; String arrays for the last name, first name, and middle initial; and a Single array for the GPA. Although it is not difficult to declare these arrays and input data into them, manipulating them would require that we use the same index value for each array—a much more complicated process than if we simply declared an array of type CollegeStudent. If this latter process is done, all of the data are stored in a single array.

An array that uses a UDT is declared in the same way as an array for a standard data type:

Dim *arrayName(max index)* **As** *datatype*

The only difference is that now the *datatype* is a user-defined type. The same is true with regard to passing a UDT variable or array to a sub procedure or function: You replace the standard types with the UDT.

For example, to declare an array to be of type CollegeStudent, the statement is

```
Dim udtManyStudents(100) As CollegeStudent
```

Once an array is declared to be a UDT, we refer to the elements of the array by giving the array name plus the data type element name, separated by a period. For example, to assign a value to the strLastName element of the tenth student record in the udtManyStudents() array, the statement would be

```
udtManyStudents(9).strLastName = "McGahee"
```

Similarly, to display the sngGPA value for the twentieth student in a text box, the statement would be

```
txtGPA.Text = CStr(udtManyStudents(19).sngGPA)
```

> **Tip:** Using UDTs in arrays can cut down on problems associated with working with multiple arrays, especially when they are being updated or sorted.

Just as UDTs can be included in an array, it is also possible to include arrays within a UDT. For example, assume that, in addition to including the student's ID number, name, and GPA data, we wanted to include a list of all courses that the student has taken while in college. This list could include many courses, so clearly we would need an array to handle it. The array declaration for the array should be included within the Structure statement, immediately before the End Structure statement:

```
Public strCourses(60) As String
```

If the array element definition is added to the CollegeStudent Structure statement, and the udtManyStudents is declared as above, we can now add up to 61 courses to each student. To add the third course to the record for the twentieth student, the statement could be

```
udtManyStudents(19).strCourses(2) = "Math 116"
```

It would be fairly easy to extend the small project in which we input information about a student and displayed it in a list box to also include information about the courses the student has completed. Doing this would require adding to the CollegeStudent data type an array that stores the courses for which the student has credit and an Integer type data element that would hold the number of courses completed. By adding such an array, we would be able to display the list of courses in another list box.

> **Tip:** Just as personal information is a subset of student information in the example, programmers can effectively use UDTs by thinking in terms of how larger data sets can use subsets to simplify and standardize programming.

Building upon Existing UDTs

Once the programmer has defined a data type, it enjoys the same status as a standard data type in that it can be passed to sub procedures and functions and can be used in the creation of other UDTs. For example, if we wanted to create a UDT that consists of the personal student information currently stored in variables of type CollegeStudent *plus* financial information on the student, including residency status, fees-paid status, and amount of fines outstanding, the Structure statement might look like that shown on the next page:

```
Structure StudentInfo
    Public udtPersonal As CollegeStudent
    Public strResidency As String
    Public blnFeesPaid As Boolean
    Public curFinesOutstanding As Currency
End Structure
```

Note that the element udtPersonal has been declared to be of the type CollegeStudent, which means that any variable declared to be of type StudentInfo can store *all* of the data that can be stored in a variable of type CollegeStudent *plus* the residency, fees-paid status, and outstanding fines data—a great deal of information under one variable name!

▮▮▮▮▮▮▮▮▮▮▮▮▮▮▮▮▮▮▮▮▮▮▮▮

Step-by-Step Instructions 8-1: Working with UDTs

1. Use Windows Explorer to create a new folder in the Visual Studio Projects folder named **Chapter8.** In this folder, create a folder named **UDTType.** Start VB .NET to begin a new project and give it a name of **StudentInfo** (or use **File | New | Project** to do this). Rename the default form file name to be **StudentInfo.vb.**

2. Modify the default form to appear as shown in Figure 8-2 with the controls shown in Table 8-1, along with appropriate labels or text properties shown in the figure. Give this form a name of **frmStudentInfo.**

TABLE 8-1: Controls for student information system

Control	Control
txtIDNumber	txtGPA
txtLastName	btnInput
txtFirstName	btnShowInfo
txtMiddleInitial	btnExit

3. Use the **Project | Add Module** menu option to add a Code module and, as shown in VB Code Box 8-1, define the CollegeStudent data type in the new code module. Save this module as **StudentInfo.vb.**

4. Add a form called **frmStudentList** to the project and modify it to appear as shown in Figure 8-3 with a list box named **lstStudents** and a button named **btnBack.** Save it as **StudentList.vb.**

5. Add the code shown in VB Code Box 8-5 to the frmStudentInfo form; declare at the *form* level an instance of the frmStudentList form; and create the btnInput_Click event procedure to input student information and add it to lstStudents list box on the frmStudentList form.

6. Write the sub procedure called **ClearTextBoxes** that is referenced in the btnInput_Click event procedure. This sub procedure should clear all text boxes and set the focus back to the txtIDNumber text box.

7. Add the code shown in VB Code Box 8-6 to the btnShowInfo_Click event procedure.

8. Add appropriate code for the btnExit_Click event procedure to terminate the project execution.

9. On the frmStudentList form, add code to the btnBack_Click event procedure to hide the form.

10. Run your project and add the four students shown in Table 8-2 to your project. Your result should look like Figure 8-3.

TABLE 8-2: Student data

ID Number	Last Name	First Name	MI	GPA
1234	Burdell	George	C.	2.50
4321	Bell	Steve	J.	2.80
3912	Patrick	Chris	P.	2.25
1102	Hyatt	Ashley	H.	3.50

11. Click the **Save All** icon to save the files in this project.

■ ■

Mini-Summary 8-1: User-defined data types

1. The Structure statement is used to create a UDT that is composed of standard data types or previously defined data types. UDTs are usually defined in a Code module, so they are known to all modules of the project.

2. Before variables can be used, they must be declared to be a UDT; the type itself **cannot** be used as a variable.

3. By using a UDT, we can create an array that will store multiple data types.

4. The With statement enables the programmer to work with multiple elements of a single structure or object.

It's Your Turn!

1. Denote each of the following statements as true or false:

    a. UDTs are usually defined in a code module.

    b. You can use the UDT name as a variable.

c. It is possible using UDTs to create arrays that store multiple data types.

d. The With statement enables you to refer to UDT fields without repeating the UDT name.

2. Write the statements necessary to create a new UDT with name equal to NewType that has three elements: an Integer type called intElement1, a String type called strElement2, and a Decimal type named decElement3.

3. Write a UDT for the elements of each of the following scenarios:

a. A university bookstore wishes to work with the following information about the textbooks that are sold: title, author, publisher, year of publication, wholesale price, and retail price.

b. A trucking company wishes to store the following information about each truck in its fleet: truck ID, manufacturer, model, year of purchase, and current mileage.

c. A shipping company wishes to work with the following information when tracking packages: invoice number, sender, receiver, send date, and current location.

4. Follow Step-by-Step Instructions 8-1 to create a UDT to store student information.

PROTOTYPE PAYROLL APPLICATION

An application that could be useful to many companies, including Vintage DVDs, is a prototype payroll information system that will use payroll data in the form of employee name, Social Security number, pay status (salaried or hourly), pay rate, and hours worked to compute the gross and net pay for each employee. The gross pay will depend on pay status and hours worked, whereas the net pay will involve subtracting federal payroll taxes, Social Security taxes, and, for salaried employees, health insurance premiums from the gross pay.

To handle these processing needs, we can create a UDT with elements for the first name, last name, Social Security number, telephone number, pay type, and pay rate. If this data type is called EmpRecord, then the structure declaration in a Code module is as shown in VB Code Box 8-7.

VB CODE BOX 8-7. Type and variable declarations in Code module	<pre>Structure EmpRecord
	    Public strFName As String
	    Public strLName As String
	    Public strSSNum As String
	    Public strPhone As String
	    Public strPaytype As String
	    Public decPayRate As Decimal
	End Structure
	Public udtEmployees(100) As EmpRecord
	Public intEmpCntr, intCurrEmp As Integer</pre>

Also shown in VB Code Box 8-7 are declarations of the variable udtEmployees() as an array of this type and of two Integer type variables, intEmpCntr and intCurrEmp, that represent the number of items in the array and the index of the current item in the array, respectively. It should be noted that the array udtEmployees() can grow or shrink as employees join or leave the company by using the ReDim Preserve statement.

Forms for Payroll Project

To create a payroll project for Vintage DVDs, we need three forms:

1. a startup form to load and display a list of employee names, phone numbers, and pay types as well as providing the capability to add new employees and delete existing employees;
2. a dialog form to add data on a new employee and to calculate gross and net pay based on the information stored about a given employee.
3. a form to show employee information and calculate gross and net pay.

The startup form has three primary purposes: loading a list of employees, putting them in order of last name, and adding their names to the list box. This employee information form, named frmPayroll, is shown in Figure 8-4. The code to exit the project uses the End command. The *Add Employee* button will transfer control to a *dialog* form, on which new employees are added to the list box, and to the udtEmployees() array declared globally in the Code module. The Delete Employee button will remove the employee from the array and from the list box. We have also changed the labels and the list box from the default MS Sans Serif **proportional font,** in which different characters take up different amounts of space, to a **monospace font** (in this case, Courier New) in which all characters take up the same amount of space. This will help us in lining up the data items beneath the headings.

FIGURE 8-4.
Employee payroll form

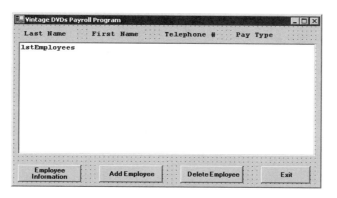

Loading Employees

We will assume that a list of employees is initially stored on a sequential access file. They could just as easily be stored on a database file or a type of file to be discussed in Chapter 10 called a direct access file, but for our purposes, we can use the sequential access file. To load these employee data into the list box, we use the StreamReader object and Split function as we did in Chapters 6 and 7, except that the input will go into the various fields of the elements of the utdEmployees() array. The frmPayroll_Load event procedure to retrieve data for existing employees is shown in VB Code Box 8-8.

VB Code Box 8-8. frmPayroll_Load event procedure	```vb Private Sub frmPayroll_Load(ByVal sender As System.Object, _ ByVal e As System.EventArgs) Handles MyBase.Load Dim strLine, strFields(), strPathName, strItem As String Dim intCounter As Integer = 0 Dim strDelimiter As String = Chr(9) strPathName = CurDir() & "\employeedata.txt" Dim srdEmployee As System.IO.StreamReader = _ New System.IO.StreamReader(strPathName) Do Until srdEmployee.Peek = -1 ReDim Preserve udtEmployees(intCounter) strLine = srdEmployee.ReadLine() strFields = strLine.Split(strDelimiter) With udtEmployees(intCounter) .strFName = strFields(0) .strLName = strFields(1) .strSSNum = strFields(2) .strPhone = strFields(3) .strPaytype = strFields(4) .decPayRate = CDec(strFields(5)) End With intEmpCntr = intEmpCntr + 1 Loop SortEmp() AddItems() End Sub ```

In looking at the frmPayroll_Load event procedure, you should notice three main parts: the code to input the array from file using the StreamReader object; a reference to the *SortEmp* sub procedure that sorts the udtEmployees array in order of last name; and a reference to the *AddItems* sub procedure that adds some of the items from the udtEmployees() array into the list box on the frmPayroll form. We will discuss the first operation here and discuss the other two shortly.

In the case of use the loop that uses the StreamReader object to input data from the file, the first two statements redimension the udtEmployee() array and input the stream of characters. Next, the Split function divides the tab-delimited data up into six fields, one for each of the data types in the EmpRecord data type. Third, we use the With statement to set each value of one element of the udtEmployee() array to one of the strField() array elements created by the Split function. This adds one row to the array for each person's data in the file. The last step in the loop is to increment the employee counter, intEmpCntr.

The SortEmp sub procedure

We need to sort the list of employee names in the lstEmployees list box in order of last name. Although we can easily do this by setting the *Sorted* property of the list box to *true,* a shortcoming of this approach is that there is no way to link the items in the list box to the corresponding items in the array of employee records. This means that without sorting the array, the sorted list box items will not match the items in the array, and we will not be able to select an item in the list box and know the corresponding array element. To maintain the one-for-one match between the items in list box and the corresponding UDT array, we will sort the array and refill the list box after any changes to the array, including loading it from disk, adding employees, or deleting employees. We do *not* set the lstEmployees.Sorted property to *true* because this could lead to a mismatch between the list box and the sorted udtEmployees array.

It would be nice if we could use the System.Array.Sort( ) method to sort the udtEmployees array, but since the array is a UDT array, this requires the use of programming methodologies that are beyond the scope of this chapter. Instead, we will have to write our own sort routine. As it turns out, sorting a UDT array is actually *easier* than working with multiple arrays, since reversing two UDT array elements reverses all fields at one time. The SortEmp sub procedure is shown in VB Code Box 8-9, where we have included the reversal process in the sub procedure because it is so short. Note that this procedure looks just like the sort sub procedure discussed in Chapter 7 except that we are comparing the strLName field of the udtEmployee(intCounter) element of the array to the same field of udtEmployee(intCounter +1) element and reversing the array elements if they are out of order.

Tip: It is possible to use the array.Sort object to sort a UDT array, but it requires an additional object to have the sorting accomplished on the correct field of the UDT array.	

| **VB CODE BOX 8-9.** Sub procedure to sort the udtEmployees array | ```
Sub SortEmp()
    Dim intCounter, intNextToLast As Integer
    Dim blnNotSwitched As Boolean, udtTemp As EmpRecord
    blnNotSwitched = False
    Do Until blnNotSwitched
        blnNotSwitched = True
        For intCounter = 0 To intEmpCntr - 1
            If udtEmployees(intCounter).strLName > _
            udtEmployees(intCounter + 1).strLName Then
                udtTemp = udtEmployees(intCounter)
                udtEmployees(intCounter) = udtEmployees(intCounter + 1)
                udtEmployees(intCounter + 1) = udtTemp
                blnNotSwitched = False
            End If
        Next
    Loop
End Sub
``` |
|---|---|

The AddItems sub procedure

Once the array is input and is sorted in order of last name, the last operation required is to add the last and first names, phone numbers, and pay type of the array elements to the lstEmployees list box. This is accomplished by building a string composed of these udtEmployees array fields by successively concatenating them to the string along with the tab character and then adding each complete string to the list box. This is accomplished in the AddItems sub shown in VB Code Box 8-9.

In looking at the AddItems sub procedure, you will note that we have used a function called *strSpacer* to ensure that the values displayed in the list box are neatly aligned in columns. This function takes a string and a size and then adds spaces to the end of the string to make the total length of the string equal to the desired string size. It does this by using the VB .NET *Space* function to generate a specified number of spaces and then concatenating them
```

| VB CODE BOX 8-10. Sub procedure to add array elements to list box | ```
Sub AddItems()
    Dim intCounter As Integer, strItem As String
    lstEmployees.Items.Clear()
    For intCounter = 0 To intEmpCntr - 1
        With udtEmployees(intCounter)
            strItem =strSpacer(.strLName, 15) & Chr(9)
            strItem = strItem & strSpacer(.strFName, 15) & Chr(9)
            strItem = strItem & strSpacer(.strPhone, 15) & Chr(9)
            strItem = strItem & .strPaytype & Chr(9)
            lstEmployees.Items.Add(strItem)
        End With
    Next
End Sub
``` |

with the existing string. For example, to make a string have 15 characters, the strSpacer function reference would be

```
strItem = strSpacer(strName, 15)
```

The strSpacer function is shown in VB Code Box 8-11, and the result of loading a sequential access file with two employee names is shown in Figure 8-5.

| VB CODE BOX 8-11. Function for adjusting a string length to a fixed size | ```
Public Function strSpacer(ByVal strWord As String, ByVal intSize _
    As Integer) As String
    Dim strSpaces As String
    Dim intNumSpaces As Integer
    Dim intEnd As Integer
    intNumSpaces = intSize - strWord.Length
    strSpaces = Space(intNumSpaces)
    Return (strWord & strSpaces)
End Function
``` |

FIGURE 8-5. Data entry form to add employees

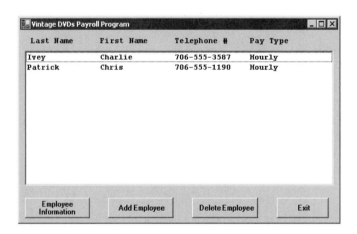

Adding Employees   The next step in creating this payroll prototype project is to write the code to add employees to the list box and the udtEmployees() array. To add the employees, we need a data entry form like that shown in Figure 8-6. Note that the user enters the new employee's first and last names, Social Security number, phone number, and pay rate in the text boxes and selects a pay type from the pay type combo box. Clicking the *Add Employee* command button adds this information to the array of employee records. The *Cancel* button will return to the main form without saving any information in the text boxes.

FIGURE 8-6. Form to use in adding employees

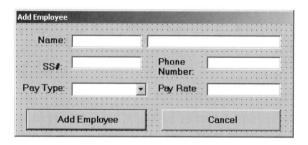

To facilitate the input of employee data, the data entry form for this project has been created as a **dialog box.** Dialog boxes are used to interact with the user and retrieve information. VB .NET has built-in dialog boxes that you can incorporate into your projects, such as the OpenFile Dialog that can be used to work with stored files. You can also build your own custom dialog boxes just like you can build a windows form. In fact, to create a dialog box you start with a form and set the properties as shown in Table 8-3, *FormBorderStyle* property to *FixedDialog*. Since dialog boxes are meant for simple capture of user input, they do not usually include menu bars, window scroll bars, *Minimize* and *Maximize* buttons, status bars, or sizable borders. Set the *ControlBox, MinimizeBox,* and *MaximizeBox* properties of the form to *False.* You can also set the *AcceptButton* property of the form to the btnAddEmployee button. With this setting, the form will act as if the *Add Employee* button has been clicked whenever the user presses **ENTER** while working with the form.

> **Tip:** The dialog form replaces a number of repetitive input boxes and allows the user to check all fields before submitting them.

TABLE 8-3: Form property settings for a dialog box

Property	Name or Value
Name	frmDialog
FormBorderStyle	FixedDialog
ControlBox	False
MinimizeBox	False
MaximizeBox	False
AcceptButton	btnAddEmployee

Just as the dialog form design is kept simple, it is best to keep the code for the dialog simple as well. Buttons on the dialog box often simply close the box and return a status value. Code is written on the main form that reacts to the status from the dialog box in an appropriate manner. This being the case, most of the code that handles the input provided on the frmAddEmployees form will be written on the frmPayroll form.

The next step is to open the Code window for the *Add Employee* command button and add the code necessary to close the dialog and transfer the contents of the various text boxes to the udtEmployees() array and to the lstEmployees list box on the frmPayroll form. To do this, we will use the DialogResult property of the form. When the DialogResult property is set to OK, a dialog box will close while retaining the property values of its controls in memory and set the dialog box status to OK. The code for closing the dialog box in this fashion is

```
Me.DialogResult = DialogResult.OK
```

You can also close a dialog box using other result values such as Yes, No, or Cancel among others. For the *Cancel* button we will simply use the following statement:

```
Me.DialogResult = DialogResult.Cancel
```

The entire code for both of these buttons is shown in VB Code Box 8-12.

VB CODE BOX 8-12. Sub procedures to close dialog box	```Private Sub btnCancel_Click(ByVal sender As System.Object, _ ByVal e As System.EventArgs) Handles btnCancel.Click Me.DialogResult = DialogResult.Cancel End Sub Private Sub btnAddEmployee_Click(ByVal sender As System.Object, _ ByVal e As System.EventArgs) Handles btnAddEmployee.Click Me.DialogResult = DialogResult.OK End Sub```

The majority of the code to handle the input from the dialog box is written for the *Add Employee* button of the main frmPayroll form. When this button is clicked, we first need to display our custom dialog box. Then, when the dialog box is closed, capture and store the data if the status of the dialog box is OK.

We display the dialog box form similar to how we display any other form. First, we declare an instance of the dialog box form and then call its ShowDialog method. The code for this is

```
Dim dlgInput As New frmDialog()
dlgInput.ShowDialog()
```

Here, the dialog box form is named frmDialog and the variable declared as an instance of the form is called dlgInput.

Remember that when the dialog box has been closed with the DialogResult property set to OK, we want to get the data that was input into the dialog. For this, we need to declare a variable of type EmpRecord. Then we can check whether DialogResult of the current form is equal to the OK property of DialogResult. If so, the data can then be stored as needed by setting the field elements of a local variable, *udtEmp,* of type EmpRecord, equal to the text boxes on the frmDialog form. This is done using the dot notation to indicate that these text boxes are on a form other than the current form. For example,

```
udtEmp.strFName = dlgInput.txtFirstName.Text
```

indicates that the value for udtEmp.StrFName is found on the in the Text property of the txtFirstName text box on the dlgInput form. The complete code for the btnAddEmployee_Click event procedure is shown in VB Code Box 8-13.

| VB CODE BOX 8-13. Code for *Add-Employee* button on frmPayroll form | ```
Private Sub btnAddEmployee_Click(ByVal sender As System.Object, _
  ByVal e As System.EventArgs) Handles btnAddEmployee.Click
  Dim dlgInput As New frmDialog()
  Dim strItem As String, udtEmp As EmpRecord
  dlgInput.ShowDialog()
  strItem = ""
  If dlgInput.DialogResult = DialogResult.OK Then
    With udtEmp
      .strFName = dlgInput.txtFirstName.Text
      .strLName = dlgInput.txtLastName.Text
      .strPhone = dlgInput.txtPhoneNumber.Text
      .strSSNum = dlgInput.txtSSNum.Text
      .strPaytype = dlgInput.cboPayType.Text
      .decPayRate = CDec(dlgInput.txtPayRate.Text)
    End With
    ReDim Preserve udtEmployees(intEmpCntr+1)
    udtEmployees(intEmpCntr) = udtEmp
    intEmpCntr = intEmpCntr + 1
    SortEmp()
    AddItems()
    FileSave()
  End If
End Sub
``` |
|---|---|

In looking at this code, you will note that, after the With statement, the size of the array udtEmployees is increased using the ReDim Preserve statement, the employee counter (intEmpCntr) is incremented, and the SortEmp and AddItems sub procedures are called. This is very similar to the logic for loading employee names from file.

In addition, another sub procedure, *FileSave,* is referenced. This sub procedure saves the changes to the udtEmployees array back to the sequential access file using the StreamWriter object in a manner similar to that used in Chapter 7. This ensures that every employee name that is added is also written back to file. The code for the FileSave sub procedure is shown in VB Code Box 8-14 and Figure 8-7 shows the process of adding a name to the employee list and the result of pressing the *Add Employee* button.

Deleting Employees

To delete an employee we will need to delete the record from both the list box and the array. Because we have written the code for this project in such a way that the index of the item in the list box matches the array index of the corresponding employee, we can use the SelectedIndex property of the list box to our advantage. For the code shown in VB Code Box 8-15, we first check to see if an item has been selected. If no item has been selected, the SelectedItem property of a list box control will equal −1 and no action will be taken.

If, on the other hand, an lstEmployees item is selected, the SelectedItem property will be equal to the integer row number in which the item appears
```

| VB CODE BOX 8-14. FileSave sub procedure | ```
Sub FileSave()
    Dim strPathName, strLine As String, intCounter As Integer
    strPathName = CurDir() & "\employeedata.txt"
    Dim swrEmployee As System.IO.StreamWriter
    swrEmployee = New System.IO.StreamWriter(strPathName)
    For intCounter = 0 To intEmpCntr - 1
        With udtEmployees(intCounter)
            strLine = .strFName & Chr(9)
            strLine = strLine & .strLName & Chr(9)
            strLine = strLine & .strPhone & Chr(9)
            strLine = strLine & .strSSNum & Chr(9)
            strLine = strLine & .strPaytype & Chr(9)
            strLine = strLine & CStr(.decPayRate)
        End With
        swrEmployee.WriteLine(strLine)
    Next
    swrEmployee.Close()
End Sub
``` |
|---|---|

FIGURE 8-7. Adding employee (top) and employee list (bottom)

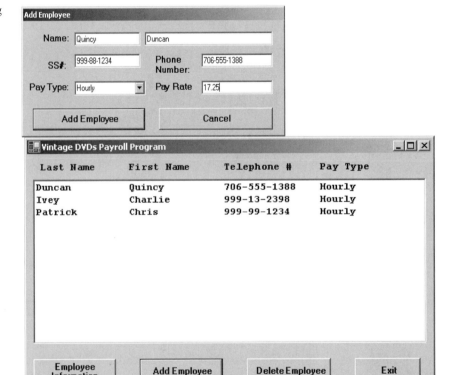

Tip: Trying to delete when no employee has been selected will cause a difficult-to-understand error to be generated by a VB .NET error. Such errors should be avoided if at all possible.

in the list box, where the first row has an index of 0. The SelectedIndex property is then used to find the employee in the udtEmployees array and a loop is used to remove the item from the array in a manner similar to that
```

used in Chapter 7. Recall that this involves simply moving all employee records after the selected one up one position in the array.

As with adding a new employee, the removal of an employee causes the array to be resorted, added back to the list box, and saved to disk. The complete code for the btnDeleteEmployee_Click event procedure is shown in VB Code Box 8-15.

| VB CODE BOX 8-15. Code to delete an employee | ```
Private Sub btnDeleteEmployee_Click(ByVal sender As _
System.Object, ByVal e As System.EventArgs) Handles _
btnDeleteEmployee.Click
    Dim intDeletedIndex,intIndex As Integer
    If lstEmployees.SelectedIndex = -1 Then
        MsgBox("An employee has not been selected.")
    Else
        intDeletedIndex = lstEmployees.SelectedIndex
        lstEmployees.Items.RemoveAt(intDeletedIndex)
        For intIndex = intDeletedIndex To intEmpCntr - 2
            udtEmployees(intIndex) = udtEmployees(intIndex + 1)
        Next
        intEmpCntr = intEmpCntr - 1
        SortEmp()
        AddItems()
        FileSave()
    End If
End Sub
``` |

Step-by-Step Instructions 8-2: Vintage DVDs Payroll

1. Use Windows Explorer to create a new folder in the **Chapter8** folder named **Payroll.** Start VB .NET to start a new project and give it a name of **Payroll** (or use **File|New|Project** to do this). Rename *form1.vb* in this project to be **Payroll.vb** and make sure that the new name is the startup object of the project. Give it a name property of **frmPayroll.**

2. Add a code module named **Structure.vb** to your project using the menu option **Project|Add Module.** Add the code shown in VB Code Box 8-7 to create the structure for the user defined data type *EmpRecord* and declare global variables to be used later.

3. On the frmPayroll form create the form shown in Figure 8-4 with the control names shown in Table 8-4. Make sure that the Sorted property of the list box is *not* set to True; if it is, change it to False.

TABLE 8-4: Control names for frmPayroll form

Control or Menu Item Name	Control or Menu Item Name
lstEmployees	btnEmployeeInformation
btnAddEmployee	btnDeleteEmployee
btnExit	
```

4. Add labels with the text properties shown in Table 8-5 to the form above the list box. Change the Font property for the lstEmployees list box and these labels to be 10-point Courier New. At a later point, adjust the labels to match the positioning of the items in the list box.

TABLE 8-5: Label text properties on frmPayroll

Headings
Last Name
First Name
Telephone #
Pay Type

5. Add in the Code window for the frmPayroll form the code shown in VB Code Box 8-8 for the frmPayroll_Load event procedure. Also, add the SortEmp and AddItems sub procedures shown in VB Code Box 8-9 and VB Code Box 8-10. Finally, add the code for the strSpacer function shown in VB Code Box 8-11.

6. Add a second form to the project with the name **DialogBox.vb** to add employees to the project. Give the form a name of **frmDialog** and assign the form properties shown in Table 8-3 to it. Modify this form to appear as shown in Figure 8-6 by adding the controls shown in Table 8-6. Add the necessary labels for the text boxes and combo box. Finally, add two items to the combo box: **Salaried** and **Hourly.**

TABLE 8-6: Controls for frmDialog

Control Names	Control Names
btnAddEmployee	btnCancel
txtFirstName	txtLastName
txtSSNum	txtPhoneNumber
cboPayType	txtPayRate

7. Add the code shown in VB Code Box 8-12 for the btnAddEmployee_Click and btnCancel_Click event procedures to the Code window for the frmDialog form.

8. Add the code shown in VB Code Box 8-13 to the btnAddEmployee_Click event procedure of the frmPayroll form to switch to the frmDialog form and to retrieve employee data when the dialog form is closed.

9. Add the code for the btnDeleteEmployee_Click event procedure shown in VB Code Box 8-15 to the Code window for frmPayroll.

10. Add the code for the FileSave sub procedure shown in VB Code Box 8-14.

11. Use Notepad to create a sequential access file named **EmployeeData.txt** with the data shown in Table 8-7. Be sure and use the **TAB** key to separate items on the same line. Save this file to the **bin** folder of this project. You may also download this file from the Chapter 8 section of the Web site for this textbook.

TABLE 8-7: Data for EmployeeData.txt file

First Name	Last Name	Phone Number	SSNum	Pay Type	Pay Rate
Charlie	Ivey	706-555-3587	999-13-2398	Hourly	17.75
Chris	Patrick	706-555-1190	999-99-1234	Hourly	22.50

12. Run your project; the results should appear like those shown in Figure 8-5.

13. Click the *Add Employee* button to add the employee data shown in the top of Figure 8-7. Your result should appear as shown in the bottom of Figure 8-7.

14. Add another employee of your choosing and then delete them.

15. When your project is running correctly, click the **Save All** icon to save the files in this project.

■ ■

Mini-Summary 8-2: User-defined data types and dialog boxes

1. It is possible to create an array composed of UDTs. A UDT can be included in other UDTs.

2. Sorting a UDT array is fairly simple because any action to an array element affects all of the fields of the record.

3. You can create custom dialog boxes in VB .NET by setting the FormBorderStyle property to FixedDialog. Also, set the ControlBox, MinimizeBox, and MaximizeBox properties of the form to False.

4. The *AcceptButton* property of a form can be used to set the default button of the form that will click when the **ENTER** key is pressed.

5. Deleting a UDT array element also deletes all fields at one time, thereby avoiding any possible update errors or conflicts.

It's Your Turn!

1. Write a UDT for the elements of each of the following scenarios. Also, write examples of the statements needed to declare a variable of each type:

   a. An online news company wishes to store the following information about each news report on its site: article ID, author, date written, subject category, and an array of 10 keywords.

b. A manufacturing company gathers a set of five measurements at set periods and plots the average on a control chart as part of a quality control program. As part of a VB .NET program the production manager wishes to store the following information: machine number, product ID, date, time, and an array of five measurements (single data type).

2. What is the AcceptButton property of a dialog form used for? Why do we need it?

3. What properties of the list box can be used to add or delete an item?

4. Follow Step-by-Step Exercises 8-2 to create a payroll application for Vintage DVDs.

CALCULATING GROSS AND NET PAY

Once the employee data have been entered, we can view the information for an employee record and compute the gross and net pay. To do this, we want to switch from the frmPayroll form to a third form named **frmShowEmp** when the employee's record in the lstEmployees list box is highlighted and the *Employee Information* button is clicked. The frmShowEmp form for showing employee information and calculating weekly payroll is shown in Figure 8-8.

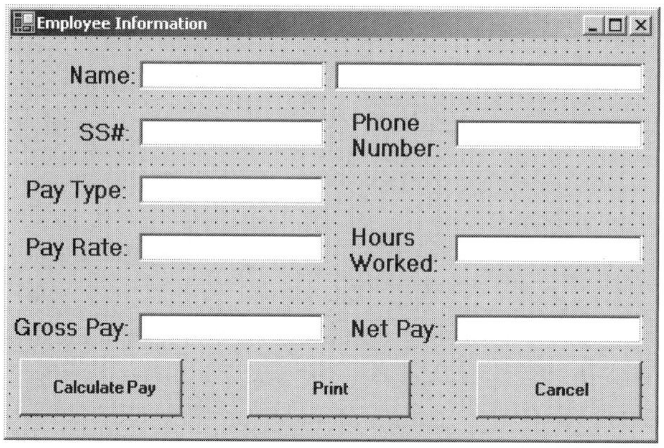

FIGURE 8-8.
Employee
information form

Note that it has text boxes for all of the employee information, and all of the information *except* the hours worked will come from the udtEmployees() array. The user will enter the hours worked for hourly employees and then click the *Calculate Pay* command button to display the gross and net pay. For a salaried employee, it is only necessary to click the button because it won't matter how many hours were worked. The user can also print the contents of the text boxes or cancel the operation and return to the first form by clicking *Print* or *Cancel* buttons at the bottom of the form.

The code for the btnEmployeeInformation_Click event procedure is shown in VB Code Box 8-16. Note that, to ensure that a name is indeed highlighted before an attempt is made to display employee information, it is necessary to check the SelectedIndex property of the list box to make sure it is not equal to −1. If it is not, then we display the frmShowEmp form. Note also that we use a global variable, *udtCurrentEmp*, to pass information about the highlighted employee to the frmShowEmp form.

VB CODE BOX 8-16. Code to call ShowEmployee sub	```
	Private Sub btnEmployeeInformation_Click(ByVal sender As _
	System.Object, ByVal e As System.EventArgs) Handles _
	btnEmployeeInformation.Click
	    If lstEmployees.SelectedIndex <> -1 Then
	        udtCurrentEmp = udtEmployees(lstEmployees.SelectedIndex)
	        Dim frmShEmp As New frmShowEmp()
	        frmShEmp.Show()
	    Else
	        MsgBox("No employee selected")
	    End If
	End Sub
	``

When the frmShowEmp form is displayed, the employee's data should be transferred from the udtCurrentEmp variable to the text boxes of the form in the frmShowEmp_Load event procedure. The frmShowEmp_Load event procedure is shown in VB Code Box 8-17.

VB CODE BOX 8-17. frmShowEmp Form_Load event procedure	```
	Private Sub frmShowEmp_Load(ByVal sender As System.Object, _
	ByVal e As System.EventArgs) Handles MyBase.Load
	    txtFName.Text = udtCurrentEmp.strFName
	    txtLName.Text = udtCurrentEmp.strLName
	    txtSSNum.Text = udtCurrentEmp.strSSNum
	    txtPhone.Text = udtCurrentEmp.strPhone
	    txtPayType.Text = udtCurrentEmp.strPaytype
	    txtPayRate.Text = udtCurrentEmp.decPayRate
	End Sub
	``

Once the employee data are displayed in the text boxes on the form, the next step is to calculate the gross and net pay based on the pay type, pay rate, and, for hourly employees, number of hours worked. To do this, we need to add code to the btnCalculatePay_Click event procedure. If the employee is hourly, we need to make an overtime calculation. If the employee is salaried, we simply divide the annual pay rate by 52 to compute the weekly gross pay. In either case, we compute the net pay by subtracting 22.45 percent of the gross pay (15 percent for federal taxes and 7.45 percent for Social Security taxes). Finally, if the employee is salaried, we subtract an additional $25 per week for health insurance premiums. The btnCalculatePay_Click event procedure is shown in VB Code Box 8-18. If an employee from the list box (Charlie Ivey) is selected and 45 is entered as the number of hours worked, the result of clicking the *Calculate Pay* command button is as shown in Figure 8-9.

The *Print* button should print the contents of the text boxes to the Debug object with appropriate labels, and the *Cancel* button should clear the text boxes and return control to the Payroll form.

FIGURE 8-9.
Calculation of gross
and net pay

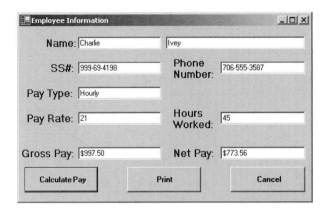

| VB CODE BOX 8-18.<br>Code for btnCalcu-<br>latePay button | ```
Private Sub btnCalculatePay_Click(ByVal sender As System.Object, _
ByVal e As System.EventArgs) Handles btnCalculatePay.Click
    Dim sngHrsWrked As Single, decPayRate, decGrossPay As Decimal
    Dim decNetPay As Decimal, strPayType As String
    strPayType = Trim(txtPayType.Text) 'Remove extra spaces
    decPayRate = CDec(txtPayRate.Text)
    If strPayType = "Hourly" Then
        If txtHrsWrked.Text = "" Then
            txtHrsWrked.Text = InputBox("Please input hours worked")
            Exit Sub
        Else
            sngHrsWrked = CSng(txtHrsWrked.Text)
        End If
        If sngHrsWrked > 40 Then
            decGrossPay = 40 * decPayRate + 1.5 * (sngHrsWrked - 40) _
                * decPayRate
        Else
            decGrossPay = sngHrsWrked * decPayRate
        End If
    Else
        decGrossPay = decPayRate / 52
    End If
    txtGrossPay.Text = Format(decGrossPay, "Currency")
    decNetPay = decGrossPay - (decGrossPay * (0.15 + 0.0745))
    If strPayType = "Salaried" Then
        decNetPay = decNetPay - 25
    End If
    txtNetPay.Text = Format(decNetPay, "Currency")
End Sub
``` |

Step-by-Step Instructions 8-3: Creating the employee information form

1. Open the **Payroll** project and make sure that you declared a global variable called **udtCurrentEmp** as an instance of the EmpRecord UDT in the **Structure.vb** module. If you did not do this earlier, do it now.
```

2. Add the code shown in VB Code Box 8-16 to the btnEmployeeInfo_Click event procedure on the frmPayroll form.

3. Create the form to calculate gross and net pay shown in Figure 8-8, using the control names shown in Table 8-8 and the text properties shown in Figure 8-8. Add appropriate labels to the form and give it a text property of **Employee Information** and a name property of **frmShowEmp.** Save this form as **frmShowEmp.vb** to the **Chapter8\Payroll** folder.

TABLE 8-8: Controls for frmShowEmp

Control Name	**Control Name**
txtFName	txtHrsWrked
txtLName	txtGrossPay
txtPayType	txtNetPay
txtPayRate	btnCalculatePay
txtSSNum	btnPrint
txtPhone	btnCancel

4. Add the code shown in VB Code Box 8-17 to the frmShowEmp_Load event procedure.

5. Add the code shown in VB Code Box 8-18 to the btnCalculatePay_Click event procedure.

6. Add appropriate code to the btnCancel_Click event procedure to return control to the frmPayroll form. In addition, add necessary code to the btnPrint_Click event procedure to print the contents of the text boxes with appropriate labels to the Output window.

7. Click the **Save All** icon to save the files in this project.

■ ■

It's Your Turn!

1. Follow Step-by-Step Exercises 8-3 to create the Employee Information Form.

2. Run your project and enter the names of the employees shown in Table 8-7. Select the record for **Charlie Ivey** and enter a value of **45** for the number of hours worked. Calculate the gross and net pay for this employee. The result should look like that shown in Figure 8-9.

3. Change the number of hours worked for this employee to **30** and recalculate the gross and net pay.

4. Click *Cancel* to clear the text boxes and return to the frmPayroll form. Add some more records of your choosing and select one for which to calculate the gross and net pay *without* entering a value for the number of hours.

VB .NET AND OBJECT-ORIENTED PROGRAMMING

As we mentioned in Chapter 1, VB .NET is an object-oriented, event-driven computer language because it uses objects that respond to events. An **object** is a *self-contained module that can combine data and program code and that cooperates in the program by passing strictly defined messages from one to another.* This may seem like a mouthful, but if you think about it you have been using many objects already. The controls that you add to your form can be called visual objects, that is, objects that can be seen on the screen. These visual objects include data in the form of the property values that you set. They also include program code both in the event procedures that you write and in the methods that are built-in with the control. Finally, what sets controls apart from other objects is that they usually have a graphical user interface that allows the user to interact with the control object by causing events.

As you may have noticed, however, VB .NET is not restricted to visual objects; objects that are not displayed on the screen can also be used. In very general terms, the term *object* can refer to almost any piece of data or code in your application, including variables, controls, procedures, and more. For example, a variable that has been declared as String data type is actually an instance of an object class called String. The String variable will hold data such as the current variable value and the length of the string held in the Length property. The String variable can also execute several methods such as the Insert method, which inserts a string value at a specified index position in this String variable, or the Start method, which determines whether the beginning of the String variable matches a specified string of characters. In general, nonvisual objects cannot be accessed by the user. They only appear in your lines of program code.

VB .NET comes with a huge library of objects that you can include and use in your programs. In addition, you have the ability in VB .NET to create and use your own objects. Commonly referred to as **application objects,** these are objects that the programmer may use to improve the efficiency of the project. Like visual objects, application objects have both properties and methods.

Why is it necessary to understand objects? After all, we've been getting along pretty well so far without knowing much about them. It turns out the objects are the fundamental concept behind an entire programming methodology known as **object-oriented programming (OOP).** The idea of objects came about from the need to model real-world objects in simulation programs. This methodology is easier to work with because it is more intuitive than traditional programming methods, which divide programs into hierarchies and separate data from programming code. To understand why objects are extremely valuable programming tools, it is necessary to understand that all programs consist of data that require processing and procedures for processing that data. As long as the data and procedures remain the same, the program will work; however, if either the data or the procedures change, the program may not work. Object-oriented programming transforms programming by binding data and procedures in objects. A primary advantage of objects is that once created, they can be reused many times. Users can combine the objects with relative ease to create new systems and extend existing ones. Around us is a world made of objects, so the use of objects to create information systems provides a natural approach to programming.

Although Visual Basic has always used some objects, VB .NET is the first version to be fully object-oriented. This is because it is the first version to fully support some important OOP concepts, such as *inheritance.* In 2000, Microsoft introduced its **.NET platform** ("dot-net"). The .NET platform is a set of software components and technologies that allow Web-based applications to be distributed to many types of devices, such as PDAs and cell phones, as well as personal computers. The .NET platform offers a new programming model that allows program components written in different languages to communicate with each other. This means that you can write an application using VB .NET that will declare and use objects created using other languages, such as C++ or C#, and vice versa. To work on the .NET platform, Visual Basic was rewritten from the ground up to comply fully with OOP methodology. The bottom line is that with VB .NET, we can create reusable software objects that can be called from programs written in any language that is compatible with the .NET platform.

Object-Oriented Programming Concepts

To work with objects in VB .NET (or any other computer language), it is necessary to understand some basic concepts. First, an object can be anything about which we want to capture information—things, people, places, events, and even ideas. For example, an object that is important to Vintage DVDs is the Employee object. Objects include properties and methods. *Properties* contain data that describe information about an object. Data such as the employee's last and first names, phone number, Social Security number, pay time, and pay rate may be stored as properties of the Employee object. *Methods* correspond to actions that the object can perform. An Employee object for Vintage DVDs could include methods such as GrossPay and NetPay. A model of the Vintage DVDs Employee object is shown in Figure 8-10.

FIGURE 8-10.
Employee object

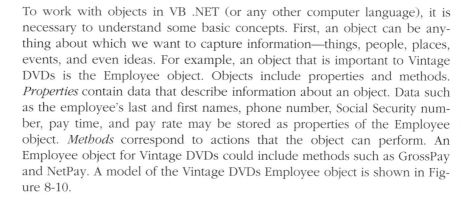

In order to create an object, you must first create a class. A *class* is a *template with data and procedures from which objects are created.* Every object is associated with a class. All of the actual work in creating an object is accomplished in creating the class; an object is created by defining it to be an instance of a class, with the elements of the object known as **instance variables.** An example of a visual class is a form that you create; you can use it to create new forms with the same characteristics as the class form. Similarly, the controls in the toolbox are classes from which you can create instances on a form. However, you cannot use these instances to create similar objects. The Vintage DVDs Employee Class is modeled in Figure 8-11.

FIGURE 8-11.
Employee class and object

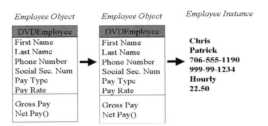

Messages are used to trigger a response from an object. For example, when you write a line of code in your VB .NET program to call the DVDEmployee method GrossPay, the computer will execute your instruction by creating a message for the Employee object. The object will receive and interpret the message and then respond appropriately. Messages are an important part of working with the Windows operating system. Windows is constantly scanning for messages and directing them toward their target objects.

All object-oriented languages, including VB .NET, incorporate three important concepts known as the "pillars of OOP." The first pillar, *Encapsulation,* refers to how well the language hides the internal implementation of an object. It should never be possible to work with instance variables directly; they must be addressed through the object's properties and methods. This implies a *black-box* view of an object, in which the programmer does not need to know what is going on inside the object, but only needs to know how to work with the object's methods and properties. For example, for the last seven chapters you have been using text boxes without knowing exactly how the Focus method moves the cursor to a text box; you just know that it does.

The second pillar in object-oriented programming, *inheritance,* refers to the capability to create classes that descend from other classes—so-called *subclasses.* Inheritance is key in allowing for code reuse. This capability makes it easier to build a new class by having it inherit properties and methods from another class. With inheritance a class will usually have an "is-a" relationship with its heir. For example, we already know that there are two types of employees at Vintage DVDs—hourly and salaried. Both of the types of employees will inherit certain properties and methods from a more general type of employee. In this relationship, the higher-level class, such as Employee, is known as the **parent class** and the subclass, DVDEmployee, is known as the **child class**. The child class is said to inherit all properties and methods from the parent class. This relationship is illustrated in Figure 8-12.

The third pillar of OOP is polymorphism. *Polymorphism* reflects how classes in a language can react to the same message. Using polymorphism you can create child classes that perform the same functions found in the parent class, but the child class may perform one or more of these functions in a different way. For example, the DVDEmployee class will inherit the GrossPay method from the more general Employee class. With Polymor-

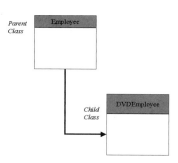

phism, we can redefine the GrossPay method in the DVDEmployee class so that a new DVD employee can, say, receive overtime for more than 35 hours instead of the standard 40 hours per week. An example of this type of polymorphism is illustrated in Figure 8-13.

FIGURE 8-13.
Polymorphism

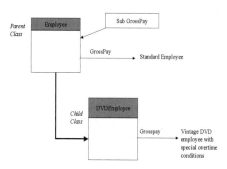

Namespaces

As mentioned earlier, a huge number of object classes are provided as part of the .NET framework. The **.NET Framework Class Library (FCL)** is a comprehensive, object-oriented collection of reusable types that you can use in your applications. Like your local library, the FCL is organized into categories and subcategories. For example, your local library may be organized into sections such as fiction, nonfiction, or periodicals. Further, the fiction section may have various subsections, such as mystery, romance, science fiction, and others. This not only helps the library to organize the volumes and you to find the volumes easier, but it also allows one to make a distinction between books that have the same title but are of different types. One thing to note is that the FCL is the .NET framework library and not the VB .NET library. This means that the FCL is available for all .NET-compatible languages and not just Visual Basic.

In the .NET FCL, the categories are known as namespaces. Formally, a **namespace** is a logical naming scheme that is used by the .NET framework to group related types, classes, and objects under a distinct umbrella. For example, the System.data namespace includes classes that may be used for database manipulation. When you start creating a VB .NET application several namespaces are referenced automatically. To see some of these, open an application in Visual Studio .NET and click on the plus (+) sign next to the References folder. You should see a listing of FCL namespaces that can be referenced by your application similar to that shown in Figure 8-14.

FIGURE 8-14.
Referenced
namespaces

Some common namespaces that may be referenced in your application are described as follows in the Visual Studio .NET help system:

* *System:* contains fundamental classes and base classes that define commonly used value and reference data types, events and event handlers, interfaces, attributes, and processing exceptions.

* *System.IO:* contains classes that are used for input and output operations such as StreamReader and StreamWriter.

* *System.Data:* Consists mostly of the classes that constitute the ADO.NET architecture. The ADO.NET architecture enables you to build components that efficiently manage data from multiple data sources, such as a database.

* *System.Drawing:* Provides access to GDI+ basic graphics functionality.

* *System.Windows.Forms:* Contains classes for creating Windows-based applications that take advantage of the user interface features available in the Microsoft Windows operating system.

    System.XML: Provides standards-based support for processing XML.

Besides the namespaces that are already included in your project, you can use additional namespaces from the FCL. To do this use the *Imports* keyword. For example, if you want to use an object from the System.Collections namespace, which contains interfaces and classes that define various collections of objects, you would include the following statement in your code:

```
Imports System.Collections
```

You can then declare objects in your program that are instances of classes within this namespace, such as the ArrayList or Hashtable classes that we will discuss shortly.

Namespaces can exist and be used other than those that are defined as part of the FCL. For example, every executable file you create with VB .NET automatically contains a namespace with the same name as your project. Each object that you create within this project will be included in this namespace. For example, if you define an object within a project named MyNewProject, the executable file, MyNewProject.exe, contains a namespace called MyNewProject. This particular namespace is known as the **root namespace.** As you create classes of your own, you can also create your own custom namespaces in which to group them. This is easy enough to do: Simply create them in a single project that you name using the desired namespace title. For instance, assume that you create your class in a program that you call MyClasses. This creates a corresponding root namespace of the same name that can be included in any of your projects.

Mini-Summary 8-3: Object-oriented programming

1. OOP is an efficient way to write computer programs that can be easily combined and reused.

2. Objects are self-contained modules that combine data and program code, which cooperate in the program by passing strictly defined messages to one another. Application objects are like visual objects in that they have properties and methods.

3. Key concepts in OOP are classes, encapsulation, inheritance, and polymorphism. A class is a template with data and procedures from which objects are created. Classes are created first, and then objects are created from the classes.

4. Namespaces are basically logical categories for organizing object classes.

It's Your Turn!

1. Why has OOP become a popular way to build applications?

2. What is the difference between an object and a class?

3. Define the following terms: object, class, instance, message, encapsulation, inheritance, and polymorphism.

4. What is a namespace? Why is it important to programming using VB .NET?

5. Open one of your previous applications in Visual Studio .NET. In the Solutions Explorer Window, click on the plus sign next to References. What namespaces are listed? Use Help to find out what each namespace contains.

DECLARING AND USING OBJECTS FROM THE CLASS LIBRARY

The .NET FCL is one of the major resources for programming, using VB .NET and the other languages that can be used with the .NET framework. The library can save you a lot of work if used properly. Classes exist in the FCL for components that are common to many programs. Without the library, you would need to create these objects yourself. Among the advantages of using classes from the library are the following:

* You can save time and effort in programming.

* Code sections have been extensively tested and are thus very reliable when used properly.

* They provide code that may be beyond your ability to program.

* Classes in the library may be used by programs written using any .NET-compatible language—the language is encapsulated.

In this section, we will look at how to use objects that are instances of classes from the library. Although we will focus on two classes in particular—the ArrayList and Hashtable classes—the way in which we use these classes can be generalized to other classes.

The ArrayList class

For three chapters, we have been working with arrays. Recall that arrays allow you to store a list of values under one name. Each specific value in the list is then accessed using an index value. To work with an array, you first declared the array just like any variable, giving it a name and a data type, but you also specified the size of the array by specifying its range of index values. Then, you could assign values at each index in the array, search through the array, sort or rearrange the array, or work with the array in many other ways. To do this, you had to be careful to write code that manipulated or incremented the index value in just the right way. Working with arrays can often be confusing to first-time programmers. In addition, sub procedures that work with and manipulate arrays can get quite lengthy.

The **ArrayList class**, which is part of the Collections namespace, allows you to create objects that act like smart arrays. An ArrayList object will include properties and methods that can make it easier to work with than regular arrays. Among other things, it is easier to load, sort, and search an ArrayList object than an array. Some properties and methods available with the ArrayList class are listed in Table 8-9 and Table 8-10 as they are discussed in the Visual Studio Help documentation. ArrayList objects are fairly flexible in that they can store lists of any type—simple data types, user-defined variables, and even other objects.

TABLE 8-9: ArrayList properties

Property	Description
Capacity	Gets or sets the number of elements that the ArrayList can contain
Count	Gets the number of elements actually contained in the ArrayList
Item	Gets or sets the element at the specified index

TABLE 8-10: ArrayList methods

Method	Description
Add	Adds an object to the end of the ArrayList
Clear	Removes all elements from the ArrayList
Contains	Determines whether an element is in the ArrayList
Insert	Inserts an element into the ArrayList at the specified index
Remove	Removes the first occurrence of a specific object from the Array-List
RemoveAt	Removes the element at the specified index of the ArrayList

TABLE 8-10: ArrayList methods (Continued)

Method	Description
Reverse	Reverses the order of the elements in the ArrayList or a portion of it
Sort	Sorts the elements in the ArrayList or a portion of it

Although the ArrayList class is versatile and easy-to-use, it has one shortcoming—synchronizing two or more ArrayLists is not possible. For that reason, it is best used for working with a single array. Of course, the array can be a list of UDTs containing multiple data types.

Using ArrayList

As an example of using the ArrayList class, assume we have the array of prices we discussed in Chapter 6. Recall that this array had the elements shown in Figure 8-15. To put this list into an ArrayList, we first need to create an instance of an ArrayList object from the ArrayList class. For example, to declare an instance of an ArrayList to store the price data you will use the command

```
Dim mPriceArray As New ArrayList()
```

mPriceArray is now an ArrayList object with a prefix of "m" to denote that this variable is encapsulated within a class. We can use ArrayList properties and methods to work with the data that will eventually be stored there.

FIGURE 8-15. Array of prices

Array decPrices

3.35	decPrices(0)
9.50	decPrices(1)
12.81	decPrices(2)
7.62	decPrices(3)
1.29	decPrices(4)
19.73	decPrices(5)
4.56	decPrices(6)
23.75	decPrices(7)
14.56	decPrices(8)
5.43	decPrices(9)

Before we add data to the ArrayLists, let's take a look at what we will be doing with the lists. In our current application, we work with the mPriceArray Array-List in several ways, including loading it from a text file when the form is loaded, adding and deleting prices, sorting the prices, reversing their order, and clearing the entire array. To work with this ArrayList of prices, we will use a form named *frmPriceArrayList* similar to that used in Chapter 6 (shown in Figure 6-2) but with additional buttons to sort the array, reverse the order of the array, add a price, delete a price, clear all elements from the array, and load the array from the text file. We will show how to carry out all of the new or modified operations using the ArrayList methods. The frmPrice-ArrayList form is shown in Figure 8-16.

FIGURE 8-16. Form to use an ArrayList object

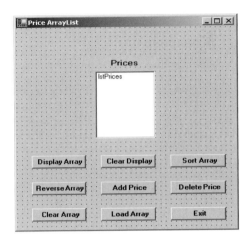

Loading the prices

To load the prices using the frmPriceArrayList_load event, we load data from a text file as we did in Chapters 6 and 7 and then use the ArrayList *Add* method to add each price to the mPriceArray ArrayList object with the following statement:

```
mPriceArray.Add(Price)
```

where Price is a Decimal type variable that is used to transfer the data from the text file to the mPriceArray ArrayList object. The sub procedure to load the ArrayList from the text file, *Sub LoadFile()*, can also be used to load it after it has been cleared. This sub is shown in VB Code Box 8-19.

| VB CODE BOX 8-19. Loadfile sub to load data into ArrayList | ```
Sub LoadFile
    Dim decPrice As Decimal, srdPriceReader As System.IO.StreamReader
    Dim strLine As String
    Dim strPathName As String = CurDir() & "\Prices.txt"
    srdPriceReader = New IO.StreamReader(strPathName)
    Do Until srdPriceReader.Peek = -1
        strLine = srdPriceReader.ReadLine()
        decPrice = CDec(strLine)
        MPriceArray.Add(decPrice)
    Loop
    srdPriceReader.Close()
End Sub
``` |
| --- | --- |

Displaying the prices

Once the prices are loaded into mPriceArray ArrayList object, we can use the For-Each loop to move through the elements in the mPriceArray ArrayList just as we did with arrays. To load the prices into the list box, the For-Each loop is as shown below:

```
For Each Price In mPriceArray
    lstPrices.Items.Add(Format(decPrice, "currency"))
Next
```

As with the frmPriceArrayList_Load event procedure, we actually put this code into a sub called *DisplayList()*, which is called from the btnDisplay_Click event procedure as well as from other procedures. The complete DisplayList() sub is shown in VB Code Box 8-20.
```

| VB Code Box 8-20. Code for DisplayList() sub | ```
Sub DisplayList()
    Dim Price As Decimal
    lstPrices.Items.Clear()
    For Each Price In mPriceArray
        lstPrices.Items.Add(Format(decPrice, "currency"))
    Next
End Sub
``` |
| --- | --- |

Sorting the prices

As you will recall from Chapter 7, sorting an array requires a fairly long sub procedure. On the other hand, sorting an ArrayList is easy, requiring only a single statement. In the case of the mPriceArray ArrayList, to sort the prices you simply call the *Sort* method as

```
mPriceArray.Sort()
```

After this statement is executed, the prices will be sorted in ascending numerical order. If we add a statement to display the list by referencing the DisplayList sub, we will immediately see the effect of sorting the array in the list box.

Reversing the list

If for some reason you need to reverse the current order of prices, you can use the *Reverse* method. The Reverse method simply reverses the current order of the list, sorted or not, as shown below:

```
mPriceArray.Reverse
```

After this statement is executed, the prices will be in reverse order. If we add a statement to display the list, we will immediately see the effect of reversing the array. If we first use the *Sort* button and then the *Reverse* button, the result is shown in Figure 8-17.

FIGURE 8-17. Array-List after sorting and reversing

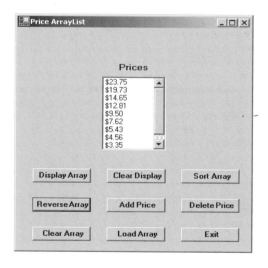

Adding a price

With an ArrayList object such as mPriceArray, adding an element is very easy: You simply use the *Add* method like we did to add prices from the text file. The primary difference is that the new price is entered via an InputBox instead of from a file, as shown in VB Code Box 8-21.

Deleting a price

As you will recall from Chapter 7, deleting an element from an array was complicated by the need to first find it and then to move elements up in the array to write over it. With the ArrayList object, it is much easier. First, to find
```

| **VB CODE BOX 8-21.** btnAdd_Click event procedure | ```
Private Sub btnAdd_Click(ByVal sender As System.Object, _
ByVal e As System.EventArgs) Handles btnAdd.Click
    Dim decPrice As Decimal
    decPrice = CDec(InputBox("Input price to be added.", "Prices"))
    mPriceArray.Add(decPrice)
    DisplayList()
End Sub
``` |
|---|---|

the element, you use the *Contains* method to determine whether the price is in the array. This method returns a Boolean value, which can be checked. If the element is in the ArrayList object, then we can use the *Remove* method to actually delete it from the object. If we know the index of the item, we could use *RemoveAt* method to delete the item. The code to find and remove a price from the mPriceArray object is shown in VB Code Box 8-22.

| **VB CODE BOX 8-22.** btnDelete event procedure | ```
Private Sub btnDelete_Click(ByVal sender As System.Object, _
ByVal e As System.EventArgs) Handles btnDelete.Click
    Dim decPrice As Decimal, blnFound As Boolean
    decPrice = CDec(InputBox("Input price to be deleted.", _
    "Prices"))
    blnFound = mPriceArray.Contains(decPrice)
    If blnFound Then
       mPriceArray.Remove(decPrice)
    End If
    DisplayList()
End Sub
``` |
|---|---|

Clearing an ArrayList

If we wanted to clear an array, we would have had to delete each individual element, requiring significant code. On the other hand, for an ArrayList, this is carried out with the *Clear* method as shown below:

```
mPriceArray.Clear
```

The complete code for project

The complete code for the project is shown in VB Code Box 8-23.

Step-by-Step Instructions 8-4: Declaring and using objects from the class library

1. Use Windows Explorer to create a new folder in the **Chapter8** folder named **NewPrices** and create in this folder the **frmPriceArrayList** form shown in Figure 8-16, using the control names and properties shown in Table 8-11.

2. Declare the ArrayList object **mPriceArray** as a form-level object in the new form.

3. Write the code for the **FileLoad** sub procedure as shown in VB Code Box 8-19. Then, add the code for the frmPriceArrayList_Load event procedure, which consists of the following statements:

```
FileLoad()
DisplayList()
```

4. Add the code for the **DisplayList** sub shown in VB Code Box 8-20. Then, add the code for the btnDisplay_Click event procedure, which consists of a single statement:

| VB CODE BOX 8-23. All code for frmPrice-ArrayList project | ```vb
Dim MPriceArray As ArrayList = New ArrayList()
Private Sub frmPriceArrayList_Load(ByVal sender As _
System.Object, ByVal e As System.EventArgs) Handles MyBase.Load
    FileLoad()
    DisplayList()
End Sub
Sub FileLoad()
    Dim decPrice As Decimal, srdPriceReader As System.IO.StreamReader
    Dim strLine As String,
    Dim strPathName As String = CurDir() & "\Prices.txt"
    srdPriceReader = New IO.StreamReader(strPathName)
    Do Until srdPriceReader.Peek = -1
        strLine = srdPriceReader.ReadLine()
        decPrice = CDec(strLine)
        MPriceArray.Add(decPrice)
    Loop
    srdPriceReader.Close()
    DisplayList()
End Sub
Private Sub btnDisplay_Click(ByVal sender As System.Object, _
ByVal e As System.EventArgs) Handles btnDisplay.Click
    DisplayList()
End Sub
Sub DisplayList()
    Dim decPrice As Decimal
    lstPrices.Items.Clear()
    For Each decPrice In mPriceArray
        lstPrices.Items.Add(Format(decPrice, "currency"))
    Next
End Sub
Private Sub btnClrDisplay_Click(ByVal sender As System.Object, _
ByVal e As System.EventArgs) Handles btnClrDisplay.Click
    lstPrices.Items.Clear()
End Sub
Private Sub btnSort_Click(ByVal sender As System.Object, _
ByVal e As System.EventArgs) Handles btnSort.Click
    mPriceArray.Sort()
    DisplayList()
End Sub
Private Sub btnAdd_Click(ByVal sender As System.Object, _
ByVal e As System.EventArgs) Handles btnAdd.Click
    Dim decPrice As Decimal
    decPrice = CDec(InputBox("Input price to be added.", "Prices"))
    mPriceArray.Add(decPrice)
    DisplayList()
End Sub
Private Sub btnDelete_Click(ByVal sender As System.Object, _
ByVal e As System.EventArgs) Handles btnDelete.Click
    Dim decPrice As Decimal, blnFound As Boolean
    decPrice = CDec(InputBox("Input price to be deleted.", "Prices"))
    blnFound = mPriceArray.Contains(decPrice)
    If blnFound Then
        mPriceArray.Remove(decPrice)
    End If
    DisplayList()
End Sub
``` |
```

| VB CODE BOX 8-24. All code for frmPrice-ArrayList project (cont.) | ```
Private Sub btnLoad_Click(ByVal sender As System.Object, _
ByVal e As System.EventArgs) Handles btnLoad.Click
    LoadFile()
    DisplayList()
End Sub
Private Sub btnClear_Click(ByVal sender As System.Object, _
ByVal e As System.EventArgs) Handles btnClear.Click
    mPriceArray.Clear()
End Sub
Private Sub btnReverse_Click(ByVal sender As System.Object, _
ByVal e As System.EventArgs) Handles Button1.Click
    mPriceArray.Reverse()
    DisplayList()
End Sub
Private Sub btnExit_Click(ByVal sender As System.Object, _
ByVal e As System.EventArgs) Handles btnExit.Click
    End
End Sub
``` |

TABLE 8-11: Controls and properties for frmPriceArrayList form

Control	Name Property	Text Property	Control	Name Property	Text Property
Form	frmPriceArrayList	frmPriceArrayList	Button	btnAdd	Add Price
ListBox	lstPrices		Button	btnDelete	Delete Price
Button	btnDisplay	Display Array	Button	btnClear	Clear Array
Button	btnClrDisplay	Clear Display	Button	btnLoad	Load Array
Button	btnSort	Sort Array	Button	btnExit	Exit
Button	btnReverse	Reverse Array			

```
        DisplayList()
```

5. Add the code for the btnClrDisplay_Click event procedure, which consists of a single statement:

```
lstPrices.Items.Clear()
```

6. Add the code to sort the mPriceArray object to the btnSort_Click event procedure. This code consists of two statements:

```
mPriceArray.Sort
DisplayList()
```

7. Add the code to reverse the order of the mPriceArray object to the btnReverse_Click event procedure. This code consists of two statements:

```
mPriceArray.Reverse
DisplayList()
```

8. Add the code to the btnAdd_Click event procedure to add a new price value to the mPriceArray object, using an InputBox and the Add method of the ArrayList object as shown in VB Code Box 8-21.

9. Add the code to the btnDelete_Click event procedure to delete a price from the mPriceArray object, using the code shown in VB Code Box 8-22.

10. Add the code to the btnClear_Click event procedure to clear the entire mPriceArray object.
```

11. Add the code to the btnLoad_Click event procedure, which consists of the following statements:

```
FileLoad()
DisplayList()
```

12. Add the code to the btnExit_Click event procedure to end the project.

13. Run the project and test all of your buttons on the form. If all work correctly, then Save **all** the files.

▪ ■ ▬ ▬ ▬ ▬ ■ ■ ▬ ■ ▬ ▬ ▬ ▬ ▬ ▬ ■ ■ ▬ ▪

The Hashtable Class

Another useful class provided in the .NET FCL is the Hashtable class. A Hashtable object lets you store items in a list similar to an ArrayList object, but with the Hashtable you give each element that you store a unique name. Then when you want to access a specific element, you can simply refer to its name rather than searching for the appropriate index. The name assigned to each element is actually converted and stored as a number called a *hash*. By associating a hash number with each record, searching the list is more efficient.

For example, assume that we want to store a list of prices in a Hashtable in which each price can be identified by a part identifier as was done in Chapters 6 and 7. To do this, we first need to declare a new instance of the Hashtable class using

```
Dim mParts As Hashtable() = New Hashtable
```

We can then add members to the mParts Hashtable using the Add method. For each part, we would enter the part identifier as the key and the price as the value that is stored there. For example, we could enter several members using

```
mParts.Add("V23-5W", 3.35)
mParts.Add("X37-3K", 9.59)
      :
mParts.Add("R13-8W", 5.43)
```

We can now retrieve any of the entered parts by simply using the part identifier as a key. For instance, to assign the price for the part with an identifier of X37-3K to a Decimal type variable we can use

```
decPrice = mParts("X37-3K")
```

Like ArrayList, a Hashtable object will include some other useful properties and methods. For example, we can use the Count property to ascertain the number of members currently in the table as

```
intNumofParts = mParts.Count().
```

We can also edit a value at a specific key using

```
mParts("R13-8W") = 5.45
```

You can remove all items using the Clear method or remove a specific entry using

```
mParts.Remove("V23-5W")
```

> **Mini-Summary 8-4: Declaring and using objects from the class library**
>
> 1. The .NET FCL has many classes that you can use to create useful objects for your programs. To use an object from the FCL, we need to declare an instance of the object.
>
> 2. The ArrayList class can be used to create objects that work like arrays but can be easier and more powerful to use. It has many useful properties and methods, including Sort, Reverse, Add, Remove, and so on.
>
> 3. The Hashtable class can be used to store a list of objects when we want to easily search based on a key or hash. Searching for an element with a specific key is very easy with the Hashtable class.

It's Your Turn!

1. Why is the .NET FCL important to programming using VB .NET?

2. What are some types of lists for which you might want to use a Hashtable?

3. What are some advantages of using an ArrayList over using a regular array?

4. Follow Step-by-Step Instructions 8-4 to complete the NewPrices project discussed in the text.

CREATING A CLASS AND OBJECTS

In addition to objects based on classes in the .NET FCL, you can create and use your own classes. As an example of creating application objects, we will first create the DVDEmployee class shown in Figure 8-11. In our case, to keep it simple, we will be rewriting the existing code for the Payroll application created earlier to make it an object-oriented project. Recall that in this project, we will have six properties—first and last names, phone number, Social Security number, pay type, and pay rate—as well as two methods—calculate gross pay and calculate net pay—that we would like to create.

Creating a Class

To create a class from which the DVDCustomer object can be generated, we must use a new type of module: the **Class module.** A Class module contains only code with no visual objects. The code in a Class module is used to create the properties and methods for a class.

Creating a Class module involves a six-step process to develop the procedures and functions that carry out the operations for an application object, that is, a programmer-created object derived from this class. These six steps are

1. Add the Class module to the project.

2. Declare local variables to be used in the module.

3. Initialize the Class properties of the object by creating a constructor.

4. Write the statements necessary to enable the class to have values assigned to its properties or to assign its properties to variables outside of the object.

5. Write the methods that will carry out processing within the class.

6. Save the class module.

Steps 2 through 5 provide encapsulation for objects within Visual Basic .NET. Step 2 sets up *local* variables that will not be accessible from outside the class. Step 3 provides initial values for the class properties, and step 4 provides a way for the class's properties to be changed or used without the properties directly interacting with the project. Finally, step 5 creates the functions that will carry out processing within the class without being exposed to the outside world of the project. Once the class has been created, you can declare any number of objects to be of that class. All of these objects will share the same properties and methods created in the class.

Adding the Class Module

You add Class modules to the project using the Project |Add Class main menu option, just like you add a module or a new Windows form. Doing so will display the Add New Item dialog box like that shown in Figure 8-18. You've seen this before when adding a Windows form. This time when the dialog box appears, highlight the Class icon. Like any item that you add to your project, the class should be given a name. In our case, we are adding a class named *DVDEmployee.vb*. After clicking on the *Open* button, the Code window will display the code shown in VB Code Box 8-25.

FIGURE 8-18. Add New Item dialog

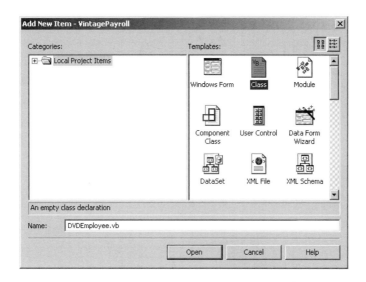

VB CODE BOX 8-25. Class DVDCustomer	``` Public Class DVDEmployee End Class ```

Declaring Local Variables

Since we want to encapsulate objects derived from the Customer class, all variables used in the class should be declared as local variables with the *Private* keyword. We need a local variable for each and every property of the class, because these variables will store the values assigned to the properties. We need to declare local variables for each of the properties of the class shown in the class model of Figure 8-11—that is, customer name, customer phone number, and late fees. For example, for the Name property of this class, we will assign a variable *mName*. (An *m* prefix is used with each variable to signify that it is a *member* of a class.) These variables are declared at the beginning of the Class module that we are creating. The declarations for this example are shown in VB Code Box 8-26.

> **Tip:** To avoid confusion, use an *m* prefix to signify that a variable is a member of a class.

VB CODE BOX 8-26. Declaring local variables for the Class module	```Public Class DVDEmployee Private mLName As String Private mFName As String Private mPhoneNum As String Private mSSNum As String Private mPaytype As String Private mPayRate As Decimal Private decTemp As Decimal```

Constructors

Just as visual objects like the text box have default properties, such as TextBox1 for the Text property, so also do application objects have default properties. The only difference is that, because we are creating the class from which the object is derived, we must set the default properties in a special sub procedure called a **constructor.** Every VB .NET class automatically includes a free default constructor. The default constructor never takes arguments. The constructor creates a new object instance of the class and makes sure that all member variables of the class are set to an appropriate default value. The default constructor is called when an object is declared as an instance of a class with no parameter values submitted. You can include assignment statements and other code in the constructor to initialize your class.

Usually, you will also create one or more additional **custom constructors.** With these, you provide the user a convenient way to initialize a new object's properties at the time the object is created. Each constructor is written as a Public procedure named *New*. Each version of the New method will provide a user with a distinct way of establishing the initial state of an object.

We have only used the default constructor name in our case to define initial values for the Social Security number property, the Pay Type property, and the Pay Rate property, as shown in VB Code Box 8-27. We could also include a second custom constructor that would have allowed us to specify initial values for each of the objects properties at the time the object is created. The initial values would be passed as arguments and then assigned to the member variables. In this manner, the member variables remain encapsulated and are not directly accessed by the user of the object.

VB CODE BOX 8-27. Default class constructor	```Public Sub New() mSSNum = "000-00-0000" mPaytype = "Hourly" mPayRate = 11.5 End Sub```

Creating Properties for the Class

Once the Class module has been added and named and the local variables have been declared and, if necessary, initialized, the next step is to set up the properties for the class. In most cases, a property is a two-way street; it is possible to assign values to these properties from the outside and to determine from the outside the current values of a property. Just as we can change the Text property of a text box or use the current Text property in our code, we should be able to do the same thing with an application object.

Logically, a property is a variable that is contained in a class. So far, we have declared variables to represent properties using the Private statement. But these variables are not directly available to code outside the class as they should be under the rules of encapsulation. In order for a program to get or set properties we need to write **property procedures.** A property procedure is written as follows:

Public Property *propertyname( )* **As** *datatype*
　　property statements
End Property

Notice that the property procedure is declared as *Public* to allow code outside the class to be able to call the procedure. For code outside of the class, the name of the Property procedure is the same as the name of the property.

Working with properties is accomplished using Property procedures with two types of statements: Get and Set. To allow the "outside world" to work with the properties of an object, we need to use the Get statement block within the property procedure. The **Get** statement block assigns the value of the local variable to the property using the following form:

Get
　　Return *mLocalVariable*
End Get

Note that the Get statement block simply returns the property's value, which in this case is represented by the value held in a local variable.

We can change the properties of application objects by setting up a Set statement block in the Class module. A **Set** statement assigns a value to a property using a special type of function. The form of this special type of function is shown below:

Set (ByVal *OutsideVar* **As** *datatype***)**
　　mLocalVariable **=** *OutsideVar*
End Set

In the Set statement block, the value being assigned to the property is passed in through the *OutsideVar* in the Set statement and then assigned to the local variable associated with this property. Notice that the ByVal keyword is used to ensure that the direction of flow is strictly *into* the sub procedure. The *OutsideVar* variable is usually a dummy variable through which the value flows to the local variable; its name has no significance. The code creating all six of the properties for the DVDEmployee object is shown in VB Code Box 8-28.

Creating Methods for the Class

In addition to creating properties for our class, we can also create methods. Methods are added to a class using sub or function procedures. Methods are generally written to work with the properties of the class. The general form of a sub that is written as a method for a class is

| VB CODE BOX 8-28. Class properties for DVDEmployee class | ```
Public Property FirstName() As String
   Get
       Return mFName
   End Get
   Set(ByVal Value As String)
      mFName = Value
   End Set
End Property
Public Property LastName() As String
   Get
       Return mLName
   End Get
   Set(ByVal Value As String)
      mLName = Value
   End Set
End Property
Public Property PhoneNumber() As String
   Get
       Return mPhoneNum
   End Get
   Set(ByVal Value As String)
      mPhoneNum = Value
   End Set
End Property
Public Property SSNumber() As String
    Get
        Return mSSNum
    End Get
    Set(ByVal Value As String)
       mSSNum = Value
    End Set
End Property
Public Property PayType() As String
    Get
        Return mPaytype
    End Get
    Set(ByVal Value As String)
       mPaytype = Value
    End Set
End Property
Public Property Payrate() As Decimal
   Get
       Return mPayRate
   End Get
   Set(ByVal Value As Decimal)
      mPayRate = Value
   End Set
End Property
``` |

Public Sub *MethodName*(**ByVal** *parameter1* **As** *datatype,...*)
   Code to implement method
End Sub

The keyword *Public* is used here to expose the method to the program that is using the object. You can also create Private procedures that are used only within the class. The name of the sub corresponds to the name of the method that will be called. Any parameters that are listed correspond to
```

parameters that should be passed by the calling routine to the method when it is called.

For our current example, we will add two methods: one to compute the gross pay of an employee and one to compute the net pay. The code for these two methods is shown in VB Code Box 8-29. Note that we use the local "m" variables for the computation and pass the computed gross pay value to the computation of the net pay via the local temporary variable, decTemp.

| **VB CODE BOX 8-29.** Creating decGrossPay and decNetPay methods | ```
Public Function decGrosspay(ByVal sngHrsWorked As Single) As Decimal
   If mPaytype = "Hourly" Then
      If sngHrsWorked < 40 Then
         decGrosspay = mPayRate * sngHrsWorked
      Else
         decGrosspay = mPayRate * 40 + 1.5 * (sngHrsWorked - 40)
      End If
   Else
      decGrosspay = mPayRate / 52
   End If
   decTemp = decGrosspay
End Function
Public Function decNetPay() As Decimal
   decNetPay = decTemp - (0.15 + 0.0745) * decTemp
   If mPaytype = "Salaried" Then
      decNetPay = decNetPay - 25
   End If
End Function
``` |

Declaring and Using Your Objects

Once a class is created, the next steps are to declare an application object to be of this class and to then use that object. This is just like what we have already been doing to create instances of VB .NET classes. Objects can be declared at any level just like variables, with one major difference: The **New** keyword is used to denote this as a new object from a class rather than as a variable declaration. The general form of this Declaration statement is

Dim *objectname* **As New** *classname*

For example, to declare an object called objShowingEmp to be of the class DVDEmployee, the statement would be

```
Dim objShowingEmp As New DVDEmployee
```

where the variable name of *obj* is used to define an object.

Once an application object has been declared, its properties are used in much the same way as those of visual objects. That is, properties are assigned values and variables are assigned Object properties. Also, an application's object methods are used to process data and return values, in a similar manner to that used by visual objects. Once created, we use our own objects just like those that already exist in the .NET FCL.

objShowingEmp Object Properties

To demonstrate the use of objects in the frmShowEmp form, we will add another *Display* button to the existing *Calculate*, *Print*, and *Cancel* buttons. This button will display the objShowingEmp object properties. Although this change is not necessary, it will allow you to see the use of the default Object properties created in the New constructor by making the Text properties of the form's text boxes equal to the Object properties in a sub procedure
```

named *ShowProperties*. This sub procedure is called in the Form_Activated event procedure to display the default objShowingEmp object properties when the form is loaded. The declaration of the object, the ShowProperties sub procedure, and the Form_Activated event procedure are shown in VB Code Box 8-30.

VB CODE BOX 8-30. Code to use object properties	```Public Class frmShowEmp
	    Inherits System.Windows.Forms.Form
	    Dim objShowingEmp As New DVDEmployee()
	    Private Sub frmShowEmp_Activated(ByVal sender As Object, _
	    ByVal e As System.EventArgs) Handles MyBase.Activated
	        ShowProperties()
	    End Sub
	    Sub ShowProperties()
	       With objShowingEmp
	          txtLName.Text = .LastName
	          txtFName.Text = .FirstName
	          txtPhone.Text = .PhoneNumber
	          txtSSNum.Text = .SSNumber
	          txtPayType.Text = .PayType
	          txtPayRate.Text = CStr(.Payrate)
	       End With
	    End Sub```

The first time the frmShowEmp form is loaded, several things happen: The objShowingEmp object is defined, the New() event procedure is executed, and the form is displayed with the default properties as shown in Figure 8-19.

FIGURE 8-19. Default Object properties

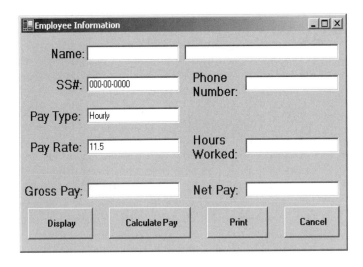

To modify the objShowingEmp Object properties to match those of the employee selected from the lstEmployees list box and to display them on the frmShowEmp form, we use the *Display* button. The code for this button is shown in VB Code Box 8-31, where we have used the ShowProperties sub procedure to display the current Object properties.

| VB CODE BOX 8-31. Code to display object properties | ```
Private Sub btnDisplay_Click(ByVal sender As System.Object, _
ByVal e As System.EventArgs) Handles btnDisplay.Click
    With objShowingEmp
        .LastName = udtEmployees(intCurrEmp).strLName
        .FirstName = udtEmployees(intCurrEmp).strFName
        .PhoneNumber = udtEmployees(intCurrEmp).strPhone
        .SSNumber() = udtEmployees(intCurrEmp).strSSNum
        .PayType() = udtEmployees(intCurrEmp).strPaytype
        .Payrate = udtEmployees(intCurrEmp).decPayRate
    End With
    ShowProperties()
    txtHrsWrked.Text = "0"
End Sub
``` |
|---|---|

Using Object Methods Once the Object properties have been set, the next step is to use the Object methods to compute the gross and net pay when the *Calculate* button is clicked. Since all of the hard work has been done in defining the DVDEmployee Class module, this computation involves only two lines of code that compute the gross pay and net pay and two more to assign them to the appropriate text boxes. The code for the *Calculate* button is shown in VB Code Box 8-32.

| VB CODE BOX 8-32. Code for btnCalculatePay command button | ```
Private Sub btnCalculatePay_Click(ByVal sender As _
System.Object, ByVal e As System.EventArgs) _
Handles btnCalculatePay.Click
    Dim sngHoursWorked As Single, decThisGP, decThisNP As Decimal
    sngHoursWorked = CSng(txtHrsWrked.Text)
    decThisGP = objShowingEmp.decGrosspay(sngHoursWorked)
    decThisNP = objShowingEmp.decNetPay
    txtGrossPay.Text = Format(decThisGP, "c")
    txtNetPay.Text = Format(decThisNP, "c")
End Sub
``` |
|---|---|

Note that the contents of the txtHrsWrked text box are passed to the decGrossPay method, but that nothing is passed to the decNetPay method. If the project is executed and the same employee is selected as before, the result of clicking the *Display* button, entering 45 as the number of hours worked, and clicking the *Calculate* button is shown in Figure 8-20. Note the results are exactly the same as shown before in Figure 8-9 for this same employee.

The only item left is the *Cancel* button, in which we set the contents of the objShowingEmp object back to their default values in preparation for displaying the next employee and show the frmPayroll form by hiding the current form. The code for this purpose is shown in VB Code Box 8-33.

Final Remarks on Objects Although we have given only a brief introduction to objects, we hope it has shown the power of this approach to programming, especially in the area of reusability. For example, the Class module DVDEmployee can be used to create multiple versions of the same type of object in other parts of this current project. On a more global scale, the DVDEmployee.vb file can be transferred to other projects and can be used to create payroll objects there the same as it does here.

FIGURE 8-20. Result of calculating pay

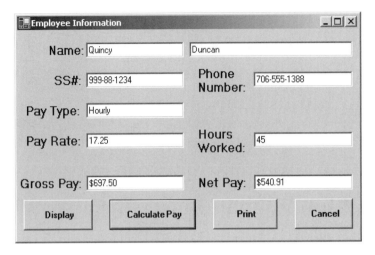

| VB CODE BOX 8-33. Code for btnCancel button | ```
Private Sub btnCancel_Click(ByVal sender As System.Object, _
ByVal e As System.EventArgs) Handles btnCancel.Click
    With objShowingEmp
        .FirstName = ""
        .LastName = ""
        .SSNumber = "000-00-0000"
        .PhoneNumber = ""
        .PayType = "Hourly"
        .Payrate = 6
    End With
    Me.Hide()
End Sub
``` |
|---|---|

Step-by-Step Instructions 8-5: Creating a class and objects

1. Use Windows Explorer to create a new folder in the **Chapter8** folder named **objPayroll.** Copy all of the files from the **Payroll** project into this new folder. Start VB .NET to open the project in the new folder and rename the project file to be **objPayroll.** Leave all other file names and form names as they are. Make sure that the **frmPayroll** form is the Startup object for the project.

2. Add a new button named **btnDisplay** to the frmShowEmp form and give it a text property of **Display.**

3. Next, select **Project|Add Class,** make sure that Class icon is highlighted, and change the name of the class to DVDEmployee. Then click **Open** to begin creating the new class in the Code window.

4. Declare private class member variables for each property of Table 8-12 as shown in VB Code Box 8-26.

5. Add the constructors of VB Code Box 8-27 to your DVDCustomer class.
```

TABLE 8-12: Properties added to EmployeeClass

Property	Member Variable	Data Type
FirstName	mFName	String
LastName	mLName	String
PhoneNumber	mPhoneNumber	String
SSNumber	mSSNum	String
PayType	mPayType	String
PayRate	mPayRate	Decimal

6. Add the property procedures including Set and Get statements for the properties shown in Table 8-12. The code for these procedures is shown in VB Code Box 8-28.

7. Add the methods for calculating gross pay and net pay shown in VB Code Box 8-29 to the class.

8. Open the Code window for the frmShowEmp form and delete all existing code *except* that for the btnPrint_Click event procedure.

9. Insert the first section of code from VB Code Box 8-30 to declare objShowingEmp as a new form-level object of the DVDEmployee class.

10. Insert the bottom two sections of code from VB Code Box 8-30 to create the ShowProperties sub procedure and the Form_Activated event procedure.

11. Add the code shown in VB Code Box 8-31 to the btnDisplay_Click() event procedure.

12. Add the code shown in VB Code Box 8-32 to the btnCalculatePay_Click() event procedure.

13. Add the code shown in VB Code Box 8-33 to the btnCancel_Click() event procedure.

14. Run your project and select **Charlie Ivey** as the employee for whom to calculate gross and net pay. The frmShowEmp form should initially appear like that shown in Figure 8-19. Click the *Display* button to view the properties for this employee. Enter **45** as the number of hours worked and click the *Calculate Pay* button to see the gross and net pay for the employee. It should be the same as shown in Figure 8-20. Finally, click the *Cancel* button to return to the frmPayroll form.

15. Click the Save All icon to save the files in this project.

Mini-Summary 8-5: Creating a class and objects

1. Properties are created in Visual Basic via Property procedures and Set and Get statements. Methods are created by writing procedures that carry out needed processing.

Mini-Summary 8-5: Creating a class and objects (Continued)

2. One or more constructors are required in a class in order to be able to create a new instance of an object.

3. Objects are declared when needed with the Dim...As New... statement. Once declared, an application object's properties and methods can be used just like those of visual and .NET FCL objects.

It's Your Turn!

1. What are the six steps to creating a Class module?

2. What do the Set and Get statements have to do with encapsulation?

3. Why do we use functions to create the methods of a class?

4. What statement is used to declare an object?

5. What is the difference between a visual object and an application object? Do they have any similarities?

6. How are an application object's properties and methods used?

7. Complete the Step-by-Step Instructions 8-5 to create a DVDEmployee Class and an object from that class.

8. Run your project and test it by adding the following name and then calculating gross pay and net pay for that person when they work 42 hours.

    Joe Smith   706-555-1234   999-23-4381   Hourly   18.50

9. Do the same for the individual shown in Figure 8-20.

SUMMARY

At the beginning of the chapter, we said you would be able to do a number of things after reading it. Let's review those things here:

1. Understand user-defined data types and their relationship to object-oriented programming. We can create our own data types known as user-defined data types (UDTs). The Structure statement is used to create a UDT, which is composed of standard data types or previously defined data types. User-defined types are related to objects since, in both cases, the programmer is able to define programming forms beyond those provided by the creators of VB .NET. UDTs are like objects that have only simple properties.

2. Create and use your own user-defined data types. UDTs are defined wherever they are needed, but often in a Code module so that they will be known to all modules of the project. The With statement enables the programmer to work with multiple elements of a single object. It is possible to create an array composed of a UDT, and arrays can be defined as an element of a UDT.

3. Understand and discuss the basic concepts of object-oriented programming. Object-oriented programming (OOP) is an efficient way to write computer programs that are easily combined and reused. Objects are self-contained modules that combine data and program code, which cooperate in the program by passing strictly defined messages to one another. Application objects are like visual objects in that they have properties and methods. Key concepts in OOP are classes, encapsulation, inheritance, and polymorphism. A class is a template with data and procedures from which objects are created.

4. Describe the basics of the .NET framework and namespaces. The .NET Framework Class Library (FCL) includes many different classes that we can add to and work with in our programs. As mentioned earlier, a huge number of object classes are provided as part of the .NET framework. In the .NET FCL the categories are known as namespaces. A namespace is a logical naming scheme that is used by the .NET framework to group related types, classes, and objects under a distinct umbrella.

5. Work with the ArrayList and Hashtable classes. The ArrayList class lets us create objects that act like a smart array. An ArrayList can contain a list of a single data type, a user-defined data type, or other objects. An ArrayList object includes properties and methods that make it easy to find the number of elements, to search through the list, or to sort the list. Another object, called a Hashtable, can be used to sort lists that have a key that can be used to uniquely identify an entry. Hashtables are used when it is desired to easily search for values based on a key value.

6. Create and use your own object classes. Classes are created first, and then objects are created from the classes. Properties are created in Visual Basic via the Let and Get statements. Methods are created by the programmer writing functions that carry out needed processing.

The six steps to create a class are as follows:

1. Add the Class module to the project.
2. Declare local variables to be used in the module.
3. Initialize the Class properties of the object.
4. Write the statements necessary to enable the class to have values assigned to its properties or to assign its properties to variables outside of the object.
5. Write the functions that will create methods that will carry out processing within the class.

Objects are declared at the form level or project level with the *Dim... As New...* statement. Once declared, an application object's properties and methods can be used just like those of a visual object.

NEW VB. NET ELEMENTS

Control/Object	Properties	Methods	Events
Form object (to use as custom DialogBox)	FormBorderStyle ControlBox MinimizeBox MaximizeBox AcceptButton CancelButton		
ListBox object	SelectedIndex		
ArrayList object	Name Count Item	Add Clear Contains Insert Remove RemoveAt Reverse Sort	
Hashtable object	Name Count	Add Remove	

NEW PROGRAMMING STATEMENTS

Statements to define a UDT, including subs and functions

Structure UDTname
    Public elementname1 **As** datatype
    Public elementname2 **As** datatype
    Public elementname*N* **As** datatype
    Public Sub subname()
      sub statements
    End Sub
    Public Function functionname() **As** datatype
      function statements
    End Function
End Structure

With statement

With
    statements
End With

Statement to declare a variable of a UDT

Dim udtVariableName **As** UserDefinedDataType

Statement to declare an array of a UDT

Dim arrayName(max index) **As** UserDefinedDataType

Statements to declare and display form as a DialogBox

Dim dlgName **As New** frmDialog()
dlgName.ShowDialog()

NEW PROGRAMMING STATEMENTS (CONTINUED)

Statements to set the result of a DialogBox **Me**.DialogResult = DialogResult.ResultValue
Statement to import a namespace from the FCL **Imports** System.Collections
Statement to declare an ArrayList object **Dim** ArrayListObject **As ArrayList = New ArrayList**
Statement to declare a Hashtable object **Dim** HashListObject **As Hashtable = New Hashtable**
Statement to define a class **Public Class** ClassName   properties and methods **End Class**
Statements for a class constructor **Sub** New( )   class variable initialization statements **End Sub**

Statements to create a property of an object class
Public Property propertyname( ) As propertytype
  Get
    Return mLocalVariable
  End Get
  Set (ByVal OutsideVar **As** type**)**
    mLocalVariable = OutsideVar
  End Set
End Property

Statements to create a property of an object class **Dim** objectName **as New** ClassName

KEY TERMS

.NET Framework Class Library (FCL)
.NET platform
application object
ArrayList class
child class
Class module
constructor
custom constructors

direct access file
dialog box
dot notation
Hashlist class
instance variables
messages
monospace font
namespace
object

object-oriented programming (OOP)
parent class
property procedures
proportional font
root namespace
user-defined data type (UDT)
visual object

EXERCISES

1. Assume that each of the following is for the same VB .NET program.

   a. Write the statements to create a data type called Player with five attributes: name (a String), weight (an Integer), height (a Single), points per game (a Single), and rebounds per game (a Single).

b. Write the statements to declare a variable, TheBest, to be an instance of the type Player and use a With statement to assign the following values to TheBest: name: M. Jordan; weight: 200; height: 76; points per game: 30.5; rebounds per game: 2.5.

c. Write the statements to define an array called NCAA82 to be of type Player and assign the first element of this array to be equal to TheBest.

d. Write the statements to input other values to the NCAA82 array from a text file.

2. Describe the object class Word.vb that is created with the following code. What are its properties and methods?

```
Public Class Word
Private mvarText As String, mvarSize As Integer
Private mvarNumVowels, mvarNumConsonants As Integer
Private New()
    mvarText = ""
    mvarSize = 0
    mvarNumVowels = 0
    mvarNumConsonants = 0
End Sub
Public Property Text() As String
  Get
    Return = mvarText
  End Get
  Set (ByVal vWord As String)
    mvarText = vWord
  End Set
End Property
Public Property Size() As Integer
  Get
    mvarSize = Len(mvarText)
    Return mvarSize
  End Get
End Property
Public Property NumVowels() As Integer
  Get
    Dim intI As Integer, strW As String
    mvarNumVowels = 0
    If mvarSize > 0 Then
        strW = mvarText
        For intI = 1 To mvarSize
            Select Case UCase(Left(strW, 1))
            Case "A", "E", "I", "O", "U"
                mvarNumVowels = mvarNumVowels + 1
            End Select
            strW = Right(strW, Len(strW) - 1)
        Next intI
    End If
    Return mvarNumVowels
  End Get
End Property
Public Property NumConsonants() As Integer
  Get
    mvarNumConsonants = mvarSize - mvarNumVowels
    Return mvarNumConsonants
  End Get
End Property
```

```
Public Function Upper() As String
    Upper = UCase(mvarText)
End Function
```

3. For each of the following, explain what is wrong with the code. What error messages would you see, if any? What can you do to correct the code?

a. The following should declare a UDT:

```
Structure DataType
    strCompanyName as String
    intCompanyEmp as Integer
    decCompanyRev() as Decimal
End With
```

b. The following code should allow the outside world to work with a Boolean property called ProperNoun for object class Word.cls of exercise 2.

```
Public Property ProperNoun()
    Get
        If Left(mvarText, 1) = UCase(Left(mvarText, 1)) Then
            mvarProperNoun = True
        Else
            mvarProperNoun = False
        End If
    End Get
End Property
```

4. Use the VB .NET Help facility or the MSDN online library to answer the following questions.

a. Can you define properties for a class without using the Property Get and Set statements?

b. What is polymorphism and what does it allow you to do?

PROJECTS

Before beginning these homework exercises, create a folder in the *Chapter8* folder named **Homework.** Save all projects into this folder.

1. Assume that a list of student names, ID numbers, and quiz averages is stored in a direct access file called *Students.txt*. The fields are shown in Table 8-13, where the LetterGrade field is initially blank. You may download the Students.txt file from the Chapter 12 section of the text Web site and save it to the bin folder of project.

TABLE 8-13: Fields for Students.txt

Field
StudentName (last-name-first form)
StudentID
QuizAverage
LetterGrade

Create a project named **Ex8-1** and save it in the *Chapter8\Homework* folder to input data into this UDT structure and to process the data. Your project should use multiple forms and programmer-defined types to carry out the following operations.

a. Display the list of students in a list box sorted on the name field. Highlighting a student name and clicking a button should display information on that student on a second form in text boxes with appropriate labels.

b. On the second form, the professor should be able to implement a 90-80-70-60 scale to determine the letter grade for the current student and add the grade to the Letter Grade field for that student.

c. The professor should be able add or delete student records as necessary and save the result of this action. It should also be possible to print the list of students.

2. Assume that customer information in the form of names, telephone numbers, and sales amounts is stored in a direct access file called *CustSales.txt*. You may download the CustSales.txt file from the Chapter 8 section of the text Web site and save it to the bin folder of your project. The fields are shown in Table 8-14, where the SalesCategory field is initially blank.

TABLE 8-14: Fields and field names for CustSales.txt

Field
CustomerName (in last-name-first form)
PhoneNumber
SalesAmount
SalesCategory

Create a project named **Ex8-2** and save it in the *Chapter8\Homework* folder to input data into this UDT structure and to process the data. Your project should use multiple forms and programmer-defined types to carry out the following operations.

a. Display the list of customers in a list box sorted on the name field. Highlighting a customer name and clicking a button should display information for that customer in text boxes with appropriate labels on a second form.

b. Display on the second form information for each customer in text boxes with appropriate labels.

c. Enable the user to use the scale shown in Table 8-15 to determine the sales category for a single customer and add it in the Category field for that customer.

d. Add, delete, or edit customer records as necessary, and save the result of this action. It should also be possible to print the list of customers or the results of the computation.

TABLE 8-15: Sales amounts and categories

Sales Amount	Category
$1,000 or less	Light
$1,001 to $5,000	Average
Greater than $5,000	Heavy

3. Assume that a direct access file *RealEstate.txt* exists with the name, Social Security number, a withholding percentage, year-to-date sales, and year-to-date withholding for real estate agents at the Champions Real Estate agency. You may download this file from the Chapter 8 section of the text Web site. The withholding percentage is the percentage of each transaction that the salesperson wants withheld for income tax purposes. When a transaction occurs, the salesperson is paid on the type of transaction—that is, listing, sale, or both, and the percent to be withheld. If the transaction involved a listing by the agent, he or she receives 1.5 percent of the sales amount; if the transaction was a sale by the agent, they receive 2 percent of the sales amount. Finally, if the agent both listed and sold the property, they receive 4 percent of the sales amount (1.5 percent for listing, 2 percent for selling, and 0.5 percent as a bonus for doing both).

For example, assume that Howard Ellis has specified that 20 percent of any amount coming to him is to be withheld. If Howard both lists and sells a property for $100,000, then his gross amount due is $100,000 × 0.04 = $4,000. His net amount due is then $4,000 × (1 − 0.20) = $3,200.

Create a project named **Ex8-3** and save it in the *Chapter8\Homework* folder to input data into this UDT structure and to process the data. Your project should use multiple forms and programmer-defined types to carry out the following operations.

a. Your project should allow the managing partner for the firm to click on a name whenever a sale occurs and display the name, Social Security number, and withholding percentage on a second form. He or she should then be able to determine the agent's gross and net amounts and print this information with appropriate labels.

b. At the same time that the information is printed, the year-to-date sales and withholding fields should be updated based on the latest sale, and the file should be saved to a disk.

c. The manager should be able to add data on new agents, delete agents who have left the firm, print a list of agents, and edit information on agents whenever they change their withholding percentage.

4. Universal Widgets sells a variety of specialized products to a small group of rather large customers, each of which has negotiated its own discount arrangement with Universal. For example, GoodBuy receives a 12 percent discount, whereas BigMart receives a 13 percent discount. Assume that the names of the customers, corresponding discount rates, and year-to-date gross and net sales values are stored on a direct access file named *Universal.txt*. You may download this file from the Chapter 8 section of the text Web site.

Create a project named **Ex8-4** and save it in the *Chapter8\Homework* folder to input data into this UDT structure and to process the data. Your project should use multiple forms and programmer-defined types to carry out the following operations.

a. Your project should display the customer names in sorted order. The sales manager for Universal should be able to click the name of a customer to transfer it and the discount rate to a second form where he or she can enter the number of units to be sold and their price. They should then be able to compute the gross amount due, the retailer's discount retailer, and the net amount due Universal. He or she should be able to print this information with appropriate labels.

b. At the same time that the information is being printed, the year-to-date gross and net sales values for this customer should be updated based on this transaction, and the file should be saved to a disk.

c. The sales manager should be able to add data on new customers, delete customers when necessary, print a list of customers, and edit information on customers whenever the negotiated discount rate changes.

5. Assume that Bulldog Computers has a variety of computer combinations that they sell to both businesses and individuals. A combination typically includes everything the user will need to start work—CPU, hard, floppy, media (CD-ROM/DVD/CDRW) drive, monitor, modem, printer, associated cables, and personal productivity software. The price of each combination depends on the speed of the CPU, the size of the hard drive, the quality of the printer, the size of the monitor, and the type of media drive. Assume that the information of these computer combinations is stored on a direct access file named *BulldogCombos.txt*. Also, assume that the total number of each combination sold to date are stored on this file. You may download this file from the Chapter 12 section of the text Web site. This information includes the SKU number, the name given it by Bulldog, the price of the combination, and the number sold.

Create a project named **Ex8-5** and save it in the *Chapter8\Homework* folder to input data into this UDT structure and to process the data. Your project should use multiple forms and programmer-defined types to carry out the following operations.

a. Your project should allow a Bulldog salesperson to click the name of a combination and display the name, SKU number, and price on a second form. They should then be able to input the number of units sold and applicable tax rate to determine the gross price and the price including taxes on the purchase. They should be able to print this information with appropriate labels.

b. At the same time as this information is being printed, the number of units of this combination should be updated on the file, and the file should be saved to disk.

c. A sales manager should be able to add data on new combinations, delete combinations no longer being sold by Bulldog, print a list of combinations, and edit information on combinations whenever prices change (a frequent occurrence).

6. Assume a list of college mascots is stored in a data file named *Mascot.txt*. Create a project named *Mascots* in the *Chapter8\Homework* folder that uses an ArrayList object to store these mascot names when the main form is loaded. You may download this file from the Chapter 8 section of the text Web site.

Create a project named **Ex8-6** and save it in the *Chapter8\Homework* folder to input data into this UDT structure and to process the data. Your project should use multiple forms and programmer-defined types to carry out the following operations.

a. Display the current list of mascots with a button click.

b. Sort the list in alphabetical order and display it in the list box on the project form when a button is clicked.

c. Sort the list in reverse alphabetical order and display it in the list box when a button is clicked.

d. Input the *number* of a mascot to be removed from the list when a button is clicked. Redisplay the list in alphabetical order after removing the mascot.

e. Input the *name* of a mascot to be removed from the list when a button is clicked. Redisplay the list in alphabetical order after removing the mascot name.

f. Display the current number of mascots on the list in a text box by clicking a button.

g. Clear the mascot list and re-enter it from the text file with a button click.

7. Assume a list of employee names is stored in a data file named *Emp-Name.txt* that can be downloaded from the Chapter 8 section of the text Web site. Create a project named **Ex8-7** in the *Chapter8\Homework* folder. The project should use an ArrayList object to store these employee names when the main form is loaded. Your project should carry out the following operations.

a. Display the current list of employees with a button click.

b. Sort the list in alphabetical order and display it in the list box on the project form when a button is clicked.

c. Sort the list in reverse alphabetical order and display it in the list box when a button is clicked.

d. Input the *number* of an employee to be removed from the list when a button is clicked. Redisplay the list in alphabetical order after removing the mascot.

e. Input the *name* of an employee and then add it to the list when a button is clicked. Redisplay the list in alphabetical order after adding the employee name.

f. Display the current number of employees on the list in a text box by clicking a button.

g. Clear the employee list and re-enter it from the text file with a button click.

h. Save the current employee list back to the text file upon exiting the project.

8. Assume a list of employee ID numbers and salaries is stored in a data file named *EmpID.txt* that can be downloaded from the Chapter 8 section of the text Web site. Create a project named **EX8-8** in the *Chapter8\Homework* folder. The project should use a Hashtable object to store these employee IDs and salaries when the main form is loaded. In this case, the employee ID is the *key,* and the employee salary is the *value.* Your project should carry out the following operations.

a. Input the *ID number* of an employee to be removed from the list when a button is clicked.

b. Input the *ID Number* and *Salary* of an employee and then add that employee to the list when a button is clicked.

c. Display the current number of employees on the list in a text box by clicking a button.

d. Clear the employee list and re-enter it from the text file with a button click.

9. Modify Exercise 1 to use OOP techniques. To do this, first use Windows Explorer to create a folder named **Ex8-9** in the *Chapter8\Homework* folder and copy the contents of the *Homework\Ex8-1* folder into the new folder. Use VB .NET to rename all of the files. Also, don't forget to make the main form the startup object.

10. Modify Exercise 2 to use OOP techniques. To do this, first use Windows Explorer to create a folder named **Ex8-11** in the *Chapter8\Homework* folder and copy the contents of the *Homework\Ex8-2* folder into the new folder. Use VB .NET to rename all of the files. Don't forget to make the main form the startup object after renaming it.

11. Modify Exercise 3 to use OOP techniques. To do this, first use Windows Explorer to create a folder named **Ex8-12** in the *Chapter8\Homework* folder and copy the contents of the *Homework\Ex8-3* folder into the new folder. Use VB .NET to rename all of the files. Don't forget to make the main form the startup object after renaming it.

12. Modify Exercise 4 to use OOP techniques. To do this, first use Windows Explorer to create a folder named **Ex8-13** in the *Chapter8\Homework* folder and copy the contents of the *Homework\Ex8-4* folder into the new folder. Use VB .NET to rename all of the files. Don't forget to make the main form the startup object after renaming it.

13. Use OOP techniques to create a class called **Dataset.cls.** Each instance of the Dataset object represents a list of numerical data with related properties and methods. The dataset object should allow the user to maintain a set of values with no limit to the number of items in the list. Begin by placing the following declaration at the module level of the class:

```
Private sngData() as Single
```

Your object should include the following properties: a Count property that represents the total number of values in the data set; a Minimum property that represents the smallest value in the data set; a Maximum property that represents the largest value in the data set; an Average property that represents the average of all values in the list; and a Range property that represents the difference between the minimum and maximum values in the list. Use appropriate data types for each property that you define.

Also include the following methods for working with the dataset class: an Initialize method that sets the original Count to zero; an Add method that provides a mechanism for adding an item to the data set; an Update method that is used to recalculate property values; a GetItem method that allows for retrieval of a specific item from the data set; a DeleteItem method that allows for the deletion of a specific item from the data set; and a Clear method that will erase the entire data set when invoked. Save your class so that it may be used as part of future projects.

What additional properties and methods could you add to the Dataset class?

14. Use OOP techniques to a create a class called **MyData.cls.** Each instance of the MyData object represents a list of numerical data with related properties and methods. The MyData object should allow the user to maintain a set of values with no limit to the number of items in the list. Begin by placing the following declaration at the module level of the class:

```
Private sngData() as Single
```

Your object should include the following properties: a Count property that represents the total number of values in the data set; a Minimum property that represents the smallest value in the data set; a Maximum property that represents the largest value in the data set; an Average property that represents the average of all values in the list; and a Range property that represents the difference between the minimum and maximum values in the list. Use appropriate data types for each property that you define.

Also include the following methods for working with the MyData class: an Initialize method that sets the original Count to zero; an Add method that provides a mechanism for adding an item to the data set; an Update method that is used to recalculate property values; a GetItem method that allows for retrieval of a specific item from the data set; a DeleteItem method that allows for the deletion of a specific item from the data set; and a Clear method that will erase the entire data set when invoked. Save your class so that it may be used as part of future projects.

What additional properties and methods could you add to the MyData class?

9 WORKING WITH DATABASES IN VB .NET

LEARNING OBJECTIVES

After reading this chapter, you will be able to

1. Understand how databases are used to store business data and how they differ from arrays.

2. Describe the parts of a database and understand database operations, including working with ADO.NET and the Dataset.

3. Add oleDBDataAdapter and DataGrid controls to a form and configure them to display records from a database table.

4. Use the DataGrid control to display records.

5. Add the necessary code to find and display records that match some criterion.

6. Add programming instructions and controls to edit database records, add new records, delete existing records, and print records in the Dataset.

7. Use VB .NET and an ADO.NET database to carry out the rental of a DVD.

DATABASE CONCEPTS

So far in this text, we have used arrays to process lists of data and files to permanently store that data. However, today, most data storage is in the form of databases. For that reason, in this chapter, we will introduce the use of VB .NET to access databases. To start this discussion, we need to formally define a database: A **database** is *the storage of different types of data in such a way that the data can be easily manipulated and retrieved by a user.* Every database is composed of a series of elements, beginning with fields. A **field** is *a single fact or data item; it is the smallest unit of named data that has meaning in a database.* Examples of fields include a name, address, or phone number on a membership list; a product number in an inventory list; or a price in a price list. Fields are given **field names** that are used to identify them. *A collection of related data that is treated as a unit* is referred to as a **record.** Basically, records are collections of fields that pertain to a single person, place, or thing. For example, we might have a membership list record that contains numerous fields, including name, phone number, street address, city, state, Zip code, and other information of interest.

A related collection of records, all having the same fields, is referred to as a **table.** For example, a table for the Vintage DVDs membership list would have a record for each person on the list, with each record referring to a different person but having the same fields. In a table, the records are commonly referred to as the **rows** of the table, and the fields are the **columns** of the table. Figure 9-1 shows the first few records of the Vintage DVDs Members table. Note the rows and columns of this table and that our table only includes the name, phone number, and late fees for each member because this is all of the data we need. We might have another table with additional information, but we won't consider that here.

FIGURE 9-1.
Members table

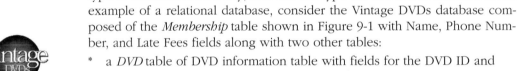

	Name	Phone_Number	Late_Fees
+	Smith, Joe	706-555-0012	$0.00
+	Mullins, Janice	706-555-0777	$1.07
+	Smith, Joe	706-555-1234	$0.00
+	Randall, Ray	706-555-3214	$3.20
+	Arons, Suzy	706-555-3587	$0.00

Relational Databases

Finally, if we have multiple tables that are related, we then have a special type of database known as a **relational database.** This is the most common type of database used today, and it is the type we will use in this text. As an example of a relational database, consider the Vintage DVDs database composed of the *Membership* table shown in Figure 9-1 with Name, Phone Number, and Late Fees fields along with two other tables:

* a *DVD* table of DVD information table with fields for the DVD ID and name, the rental price, and the location in the store;

* a third *Rental* table that contains information on each rental, including fields for the DVD ID number, the phone number of the person renting the DVD, and the date the DVD is to be returned.

In this case, the Membership table is related to the Rental table through the customer phone number that is common to both tables, and the DVD table is related to the Rental table through the DVD ID number that is common to both tables. Because both the Membership table and the DVD table are related to the Rental table, they are also related to each other. These relationships are shown in Figure 9-2.

FIGURE 9-2.
Relationships in
Vintage DVDs
database

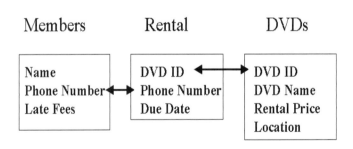

You may ask, Why are these particular fields related, rather than some others? It has to do with ensuring that there is no ambiguity about the records being referenced. If we assume that every Vintage DVDs member has a phone and that there is only one membership per household, then the phone number is a unique identifier for each member with no two members having the same phone number; in database terminology, the phone number is the **primary key** for the Membership table. Similarly, the DVD ID is the primary key for the DVD table. In the Rental table, these two keys become what is known as **foreign keys,** because they identify records from another table in this database. However, note that each transaction is now uniquely identified by the phone number of the person renting it and the DVD ID of the DVD being rented. Through this relationship, for example, we will be able to find out information about the rental status of a DVD or the number of DVDs that a person has rented at any one time. In many database packages, the table is automatically sorted on the primary key. For example, Figure 9-1 is arranged in ascending order of telephone numbers, since this is its primary key.

> **TIP:** When entering a new record into a database, you must provide a value for the primary key field, and the value must not duplicate the primary key value of any other record in the table.

Since this is not a textbook on database design, we will not go any further into the manner in which the tables and keys are designed and selected. For further information on this topic, you may wish to refer to a book on relational databases.[1]

Database Operations   The primary use of a database is to enable the user to obtain information from it in a usable form by constructing **queries** to the database. For a relational database, these queries are written in a special language known as **SQL** (for *structured query language*), and they enable database users to find records from a table that meet some stated criterion or to create composite records from multiple tables that meet the criterion.

Once a query has been used to find a database record, it is then possible to edit the record—that is, make changes to the contents of one or more fields—or to delete a record if it is no longer needed in the database. It is also possible to add new records to the database or to print all or some of the records in a table.

For example, if a member paid his or her late fees, we would want to query the Membership table for this member's record and edit the late fees amount to make it zero. We will also want to edit the record to add late fees when the renter returns a DVD after the due date. Similarly, if a new person joins Vintage DVDs, we would want to add a record for that person to the Membership table. Finally, if a DVD is removed from stock, we would need to find the record in the DVDs table and delete it.

---

1. An excellent discussion of relational databases can be found in *Data Management,* 4th edition, by Richard T. Watson (New York: John Wiley and Sons, 2004).

Databases vs. Arrays   A question that may come to you in reading this discussion is this: Why are databases so superior to the file and array system we have been using? Although arrays are very useful for working with moderate-sized lists and tables in computer memory, databases are superior for the type of processing faced by Vintage DVDs and countless other organizations for several reasons:

1. A database table can store multiple types of data in the same table, whereas arrays are restricted to a single data type.
2. Any changes to the database are immediately saved to disk as they occur.
3. We can use a sophisticated database engine to handle the processing.
4. It is very easy to connect multiple computers to the same database, so that any changes are immediately known to all computers.

In the first case, instead of having to work with multiple arrays, each holding a different type of data or even arrays of UDTs, we can work with a single table that stores different types of data. For example, the Membership table shown in Figure 9-1 has String, Numeric, and Decimal data types in it. In the second case, by storing changes in the database as they occur rather than waiting until the end of the processing period, we avoid potential losses in data due to power outages or other problems. In the third case, instead of the programmer having to develop the logic and write the code to search for a specific record, we can depend on the database engine to handle this operation. The programmer has to be concerned only with ensuring that the correct request is passed to the engine. Finally, an array can reside on only one computer, and any changes to it are not known to other computers, even if those computers have a similar array on them. This means that changes such as new members or rented DVDs would have to be reconciled between computers at the end of the day—an onerous job at best! For all of these reasons, in this chapter we will discuss converting the Vintage DVDs transaction processing application to a database system.

Databases in VB .NET   The VB .NET approach to working with a relational database is termed **ADO.NET,** which is an object-oriented architecture. The name "ADO" comes from *ActiveX Data Objects,* which was an older approach to working with databases. There are a number of ADO.NET object classes that are available to the programmer from the Data toolbox that make carrying out database operations quite easy.

In our case of working with a database in VB .NET, we will assume that it has already been created either by someone else or by you using Microsoft Access or some other database software package. ADO.NET is equipped to work with databases created by virtually any personal computer software as well as databases that are stored on another computer. For the purposes of this text, we will assume that a Microsoft Access relational database already exists and that we will be working with it. As you may know, Microsoft Access files have an *.mdb* (Microsoft database) extension. In VB .NET we will be using the Microsoft Jet database engine to work with databases just as if we were using Microsoft Access. It should be noted that the individual tables in a Microsoft Access database are *not* saved separately—they are all saved in a single .mdb file. In this chapter, you will work with an Access database named Vintage.mdb, which can be downloaded from the Web site associated with this text. The three tables of this database are shown in Figure 9-3, where the symbols on each link between the tables indicate the number of possible matches. The infinity sign on the link between the Members and the Rental tables indicates that each member can rent many DVDs, whereas the link between DVDs and the Rentals indicates a 1-to-1 relationship such that a single DVD can have only one rental associated with it, and vice-versa.

FIGURE 9-3. Vintage DVD database model

TIP: The primary key for the Members table is the Phone_Number field, and an *Auto Number* field is used for the primary key for the DVDs. This avoids the database creator remembering the last number used for the ID_Num field.

One of our goals in using VB .NET to work with a database is to provide users with a friendly front end to the database that will allow them to carry out operations on the database without having to know the appropriate SQL instructions. For example, if we want to find all members with late fees greater than a certain amount, the VB .NET front end should make it possible to enter the amount and click a button to have this list generated. Or, if we want the DVD store clerk to be able to rent a DVD, this should be an easy and intuitive operation.

Using Databases with the Vintage DVDs Application

To help you understand databases, we will modify the DVD rental system from previous chapters to use a database rather than a sequential access file. If you will recall, our previous system had three forms: one to use in renting DVDs and calculating the amount due at the end of the transaction; one to carry out membership operations (find, add, delete, print, and so on), and one to carry out operations on the list of DVDs. In this case, we will start our discussion on the membership operations form and then move to the main form to show how databases can be used there. We will leave the modification of the DVD form to the reader as a part of the exercises.

Recall that we now have three forms in the project: frmVintage, which is the main form; frmDVDs, which is used to work with the various DVDs for rent; and frmMembers, which is used to manage the membership list. The three forms are shown in Figure 9-4, with the connections between frmVintage and the other two forms pointed out.

FIGURE 9-4. Forms
making up the
Vintage DVDs
project

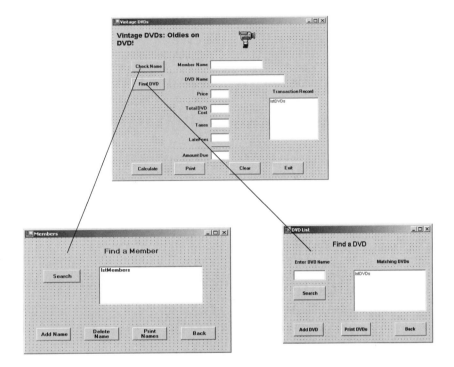

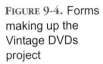

Step-by-Step Instructions 9-1: Starting the database project

1. Use Windows Explorer to create a new folder in the Visual Studio Projects folder named **Chapter9.** In this folder, create a new folder named **Vintage9** and copy all of the folders from the *Chapter7\Vintage7* folder into it.

2. Go to My Computer and then to the C:\ drive. Create a new folder named **VBDB** in which we will store the Vintage.mdb database file.

3. Go to the **Student** section of the text Web page, download the Vintage.mdb database from the Chapter 9 area, and save it in the **VBDB** folder you created in the previous step.

4. If you have access to Microsoft Office, use the Access database program to view the Members table in the database; it should look like that shown in Figure 9-1.

It's Your Turn!

1. List the key elements of any database. Why is a relational database so named?

Mini-Summary 9-1: Database concepts

1. A database is a way of storing different types of data so that the data can be easily manipulated and retrieved by an end user.

2. Databases are composed of fields, records, and tables, where fields are single facts or data items that have field names. A collection of related data that is treated as a unit is referred to as a record, and a related collection of records all having the same fields is referred to as a table.

3. Tables in a relational database are related through fields that contain the same information. The primary key is a field that is unique to each record. A primary key that is used as a field in another table is a foreign key.

4. Database operations include querying to find specific records as well as adding, editing, and deleting records. Some or all of the records can also be printed.

5. Databases have some advantages over arrays, including permanence as well as the ability to store multiple types of data, to use database engines, and to use the same information on multiple computers.

2. What is the difference between a primary key and a foreign key in a relational database table?

3. What are databases typically used for? What is SQL?

4. How is using a database for processing superior to using files and arrays?

5. Why would you want to use a VB .NET front end instead of just allowing users to access the database using a database management system such as Microsoft Access?

6. Follow Step-by-Step Instructions 9-1 to copy the Vintage7 application to the Vintage9 folder and rename it. Also follow them to download the **Vintage.mdb** database to the Bin folder in your application folder.

VB .NET DATA OBJECTS AND WIZARDS

VB .NET provides a large number of objects to use in your work with databases—so many that it can be confusing as to which one you should be using. Luckily, along with objects, VB .NET provides a number of wizards to help you with your work by leading you step-by-step through a series of actions to accomplish the desired task and, once it is completed, to move on to another task. You are probably already familiar with wizards from working with other Microsoft products, such as Microsoft Office. We will be using both database objects and wizards to create the desired project.

The primary object with which you will be working in this chapter is the **data adapter object,** which acts as an intermediary between the database on disk and the disconnected in-memory representations of the database called DataSets and DataTables. A **Dataset** can be made up of one or more database tables along with their relations, whereas a **DataTable** is one table from the database. These are referred to as *disconnected* because they are created from the database in computer memory, manipulated there, and the results are used to update the original database.

The data adapter control acts as a link between the VB .NET project and the database stored on disk. There are two types of data adapters in VB .NET:

FIGURE 9-5. Data
toolbox

the oleDbDataAdapter and the sqlDbDataAdapter. The **oleDbDataAdapter**
control is designed to work with a number of types of databases, including
Access databases. On the other hand, the sqlDbDataAdapter is specifically
designed to work Microsoft SQL Server databases. Since we are working with
Access databases, we will be using the oleDbDataAdapter control.

The oleDbDataAdapter control is added to a project by opening the Data
tab on the toolbox and double-clicking the control. However, since the ole-
DBDataAdapter need not be visible on the form, an instance of it named
oleDBDataAdapter1 is added to the tray beneath the form. Figure 9-5 shows
the Data tab of the toolbox, with the oleDBDataAdapter selected. Figure 9-6
shows the resulting oleDBDataAdapter control as it appears in the tray
beneath the form, after it has been renamed *MembersAdapter* using the Property window. This is the only property you need to change for the oleDB-
DataAdapter.

You will also notice in Figure 9-6 that we have replaced the list box used
in the file-based application with a new control—the **DataGrid control,**
which is a table of cells that is very useful for working with databases. In our
case, it will be renamed *dgrMembers.*

FIGURE 9-6. Form to
find members by
using database

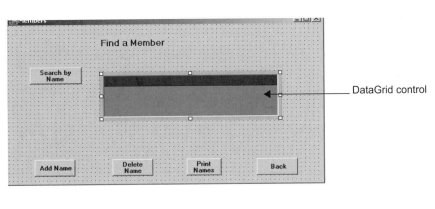

DataGrid control

oleDBDataAdapter control

When the oleDBDataAdapter control is added to the form, the Data
Adapter Configuration Wizard automatically starts. This wizard helps you
configure the data adapter you added to automatically display data from a
database on the form. You can choose to configure the adapter immediately
after adding it to the form or at some time later by clicking the "Configure
Data Adapter..." hypertext link below the Properties window for the data
adapter. However, it *must* be configured at some time to make your work
with a database possible. It is also possible to configure it programmatically,
but we will not discuss that approach here.

When you choose to configure the data adapter, the configuration wizard opens with a splash screen like that shown in the left side of Figure 9-7,
from which you can choose to continue the configuration or to cancel the
process. If you choose to continue the process by clicking the *Next* button,
you will need to follow a series of steps to make it possible for you to display
data from the database on a VB .NET form.

The three primary steps doing this are
1. Set up database connection.
2. Generate SQL to display fields from a table of the database.
3. Generate a Dataset.

We will discuss each step in some detail.

Setting up Database Connection

Setting up the database connection begins with you clicking the *Next* button on the adapter configuration wizard splash screen. This will display the initial screen in the data connection process like that shown in the right side of Figure 9-7.

FIGURE 9-7. Data Adapter Configuration Wizard (left) and Data Connection (right) screens

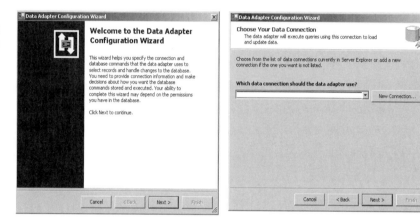

Since you should not now have a data connection set up, you should choose the *New Connection* option to create one. Clicking this button displays the initial Data Link Properties screen as shown in Figure 9-8 (left). However, you cannot use this screen without first selecting the Provider tab on it to display a second Data Link Properties screen, as shown in Figure 9-8 (right).

FIGURE 9-8. Data Link Properties (left) and OLE DB Providers (right) screens

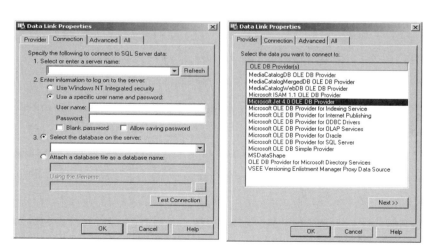

The screen on the right shows a list of OLE DB providers from which you can choose one to use. In our case, we want to choose the "Microsoft Jet 4.0 OLE Data Provider" option because this is the one that works for Microsoft Access 2000. Double-clicking this option or selecting it and clicking the *Next* button displays a different form of the initial Data Link Properties screen from which you can select a database to use in your work. Clicking the ellipsis button (...) to the right of the database name input box results in a dialog window being displayed from which you can select a database. You should navigate to the C:\VBDB folder in which you should have saved the Vintage.mdb database you downloaded earlier, as shown in left side of Figure 9-9. Selecting the Vintage.mdb database and Clicking the *Open* button or double-clicking the database name will redisplay the previous Data Link Properties screen but with the path of the database displayed. Clicking the *Test Connection* button should display the message shown in the right side of Figure 9-9.

FIGURE 9-9. File dialog box (left) and Data Link Properties window (right)

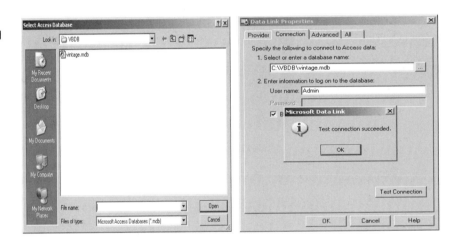

Clicking the *OK* button on the Test Connection box and then again on the Data Link Properties window will complete the data connection process and redisplay the Data Connection screen originally shown in Figure 9-6 (right) but with the path to the database displayed in the input box.

Creating the SQL to Display Fields

You are now ready to continue the process of working with the database for the Vintage DVDs application by clicking the *Next* button on the Data Connection screen. This will display the screen from which you can choose the type of query you will use to connect to the database, as shown in Figure 9-10 (left). Typically, the only type of query available to you is the SQL Query option, so you can simply press the *Next* button to display the SQL Generation screen shown in Figure 9-10 (right), with which you can generate needed SQL statements.

Rather than forcing you to know SQL, VB .NET has included a **Query Builder** facility that allows you to graphically create the SQL query you need to connect to the database. Clicking the *Query Builder* button on the SQL generation screen will display the Query Builder screen with the Add Table dialog box listing the tables in your database. In our case, three tables are

FIGURE 9-10. Query Type (left) and SQL Generation (right) screens

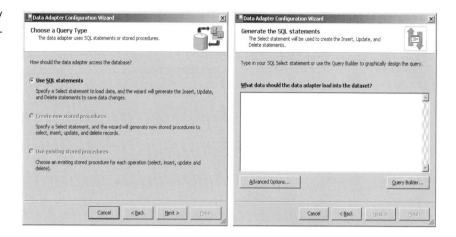

listed—Members, Rental, and DVDs. Since we want to work with the Members tables initially, the *Members* option should be selected and the *Add* button clicked. The result of this operation is shown in Figure 9-11 (left). Note that all of the fields in the Members table—Late_Fees, Name, and Phone_Number—are displayed in alphabetical order in a box in the Query Builder screen. Clicking the *Close* button on the dialog box causes it to disappear, leaving only the Query Builder screen. You can now click each of the fields in the Members box to select them to be displayed. Note: It is very important to click the fields you wish to display in the exact order in which you want them to be displayed in the DataGrid. Simply clicking the *All Columns* box will cause all of them to be displayed in alphabetical order, that is, the same order as they are displayed in the Members box.

In our case, we want to display all three fields in the DataGrid on the frmMembers form in the order of their phone numbers. Figure 9-11 (right) shows the three boxes for the Name, Phone_Number, and Late_Fees fields after they have been clicked in that order and with the *Sort Type* box clicked for the Phone_Number field. This has generated an SQL statement in the SQL box at the bottom of the screen:

```
SELECT Name, Phone_Number, Late_Fees FROM Members
ORDER BY Phone Number
```

which will display these three fields for all records in the Members table in order of the Phone_Number field. Clicking *OK* on this screen and then *Finish* on the next one will complete the process of linking to the database for Vintage DVDs.

Once you have connected the database to one or more fields in a table in the database, it is possible to preview the data in that table by clicking the "Preview Data" hypertext link below the Property window with *either* the form or the data adapter selected. For example, if the form is selected by clicking anywhere in it and the "Preview Data" hyperlink is clicked, the Data Adapter Preview window is displayed as shown in Figure 9-12 (left). Clicking the *Fill Dataset* button in the top portion of this window displays the contents of the Members table as shown in Figure 9-12 (right).

FIGURE 9-11. Query Builder (left) and completed query (right) screens

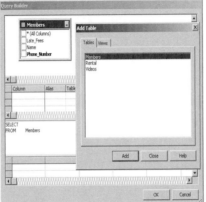

FIGURE 9-12. Preview form unfilled (left) and filled (right)

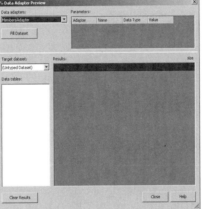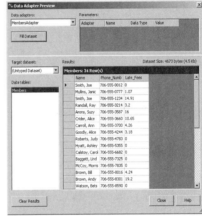

Step 3: Generating the Dataset

After closing the Data Adapter Preview window, the last step in making it possible to display data on a VB .NET form is generating a Dataset. This is accomplished in one of two ways:

* by clicking the "Generate Dataset" hyperlink below the Property window when either the form or data adapter control is selected;

* selecting the **Data | Generate Dataset** menu option.

In either case, a dialog box is displayed like that shown in the left side of Figure 9-13 from which you can choose to use an existing dataset or to create a new one. Note that the bottom window of this dialog box shows that we will be adding the Members table from the database using the Members-Adapter data adapter control. Because there are no existing datasets, you should choose to create a new one with an appropriate name, say, **DsVintage.** Doing this will generate an instance of this Dataset named *DsVintage1,* which is added o the tray beneath the form and corresponding *DsVintage1.xsd* file in the Solution window. The tray icon and the line in the Solution Explorer file for this Dataset are shown in the right side of Figure 9-13.

FIGURE 9-13. Dialog box to generate Dataset and Dataset icon in tray

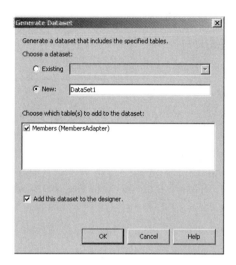

Tray icon for Dataset

DSVintage.xsd

New line in Solution Explorer

Removing Existing Code

Because our approach to programming the Vintage DVDs application is now based on a database rather than on files and arrays or ArrayLists, the best way to make the changeover is to start by deleting *all* of the existing code that involves processing from the three forms and the module. ListBox controls should be deleted as well. This will enable us to start with a clean slate in which to add code for the project. There is no need to delete code that is used to transfer between forms or to exit the project. Table 9-1 shows the event procedures and sub programs from which all code should be deleted.

TABLE 9-1: Event procedures and sub programs from which code should be deleted

frmVintage	frmMembers	frmDVDs	modVintage
btnCalc_Click	Delete *all* code for this form *except* for the btnPrint_ Click and btnBack_Click event procedures.	btnSearch_ Click	Global variable and sub declarations
frmVintage_Load		btnAdd_Click	Sub Search
frmVintage_ Activated		lstDVDs (control and related code)	Function IntfindDelete
lstDVDs (control and related code)			Sub Sort
lstTypes (control and related code)			Sub PrintInfo

Step-by-Step Instructions 9-2: Connecting to the database

1. Start VB .NET and open the new **Vintage9** application. Double-click the **Members9** file in the Solution Window to display the **frmMembers** form. Click the **lstMembers** list box to select it and then delete it. Select the Data-Grid control from the Windows Forms toolbox and add an instance to the frmMembers form. Give it a name of **dgrMembers.**

2. Click on the **Data** tab on the toolbox and select the **oleDBDataAdapter** control to add to the frmMembers form as **oleDBDataAdapter1** (don't worry about renaming it; we will do that later).

3. When the Data Adapter Configuration Wizard splash screen is displayed, click **Next** to continue it. If you decide not to do so at this time, you can always start it by clicking the "Configure Data Adapter..." hyperlink below the properties window for the data adapter.

4. On the Data Connection screen shown in Figure 9-7 (right), click **New Connection** and then click the **Provider** tab on the resulting Data Link Properties screen shown in Figure 9-8 (left). In the Providers list shown in Figure 9-8 (right), click **Microsoft Jet 4.0 OLE DB Provider** and then click **Next.**

5. In the resulting File dialog box shown in Figure 9-9 (left), navigate to the **C:\VBDB** folder and select the **Vintage.mdb** database and click **Open.** From the resulting Data Link Properties window shown in Figure 9-9 (right), click **Test Connection** to ensure that your connection has been made. Click **OK** to move to the next screen.

6. On the Query Type screen, shown in Figure 9-10 (left), simply click **Next** to move to the SQL Generation screen shown in Figure 9-10 (right). On this screen, click **Query Builder** to move to the next screen.

7. From the resulting Query Builder dialog box shown in Figure 9-11 (left), select **Members** and click **Add** to display the Members table on Query Builder screen. Click **Close** to close the Add Table dialog box.

8. Select *in order,* the **Name, Phone_Number,** and **Late_Fees** fields. *Do not select All Columns.* Click **OK** to close the Query Builder screen. Click **Next** and **Finish** to return to the form view.

9. Click the **Preview Data** hyperlink below the Property window with *either* the form or the data adapter selected to display the Data Adapter Preview window. Click the *Fill Dataset* button in the top portion of this window to display the contents of the Members table as shown in the right side of Figure 9-12. Click **Close** to close the Preview window.

10. You are now connected to the Vintage.mdb database, and an instance of the oleDBConnection control (*oleDBConnection1*) has been added to the tray along with the instance of the oleDBDataAdapter.

11. Click the oleDBDataAdapter1 control and use the Property window to change its name to **MembersAdapter.** Also, change the name of the **oleDBConnection1** control to **MemberConnection.**

12. Either click the "Generate Dataset" hyperlink beneath the Property window with the form or data adapter control selected or choose the **Data | Generate Dataset** menu option to display the dialog box shown in the left side of Figure 9-12. Enter **DSVintage** as the name of a new Dataset and click **OK.** A Dataset icon with a name of *DsVintage1* will be displayed in the tray along with the other icons, and the *DsVintage1.xsd* file is added to the Solution Explorer.

13. Open the code window for each of the forms and delete **all** of the code in the event procedures and sub programs as well as deleting the controls shown in Table 9-1.

14. Save all files.

Mini-Summary 9-2: VB .NET data objects and wizards

1. Working with databases in VB .NET is made easier through the use of data objects and wizards. The primary data object is the data adapter object, which acts as an intermediary between the database on disk and the disconnected in-memory representations of the database called DataSets and DataTables.

2. The data adapter is added from the Data toolbox. Since we will be working with an Access database, the oleDBDataAdapter control will be used and added to the tray below the form.

3. The DataGrid control is very useful for displaying the contents of a Dataset when you set its DataSource property to the Dataset.

4. The three steps to working with a database in VB .NET are
    a. Set up database connection.
    b. Generate SQL to display fields from a table of the database.
    c. Generate a Dataset.

5. Setting up the database connection involves choosing a data provider and the actual database using the Data Connection wizard.

6. Generating SQL to display the fields from a database table involves using the Query Builder wizard. The result of creating this query can be previewed by clicking the "Preview Data" hyperlink.

7. Once the database connection is set up and the SQL has been generated, the last step is to generate a Dataset by either clicking the "Generate Dataset" hyperlink or the Data | Generate Dataset menu option. Doing this adds a Dataset icon to the tray and an *xsd* file to the Solution window.

It's Your Turn!

1. What is the purpose of the data adapter control?

2. Why do we use the oleDBDataAdapter rather than the sqlDBDataAdapter?

3. What control do we use to display the contents of a Dataset? Why do we not select the All Fields option in the Query Builder wizard?

4. Follow Step-by-Step Instructions 9-2 to add a data adapter and DataGrid to the frmMembers form, link the data adapter to the Members tables of the Vintage.mdb data, preview the results, and generate a Dataset.

DISPLAYING RECORDS IN THE DATAGRID

The *dgrMembers* DataGrid control you added earlier will be our primary method of displaying some or all of the records in the database. To do this, we must set its **DataSource** property using the Property window. When you select the DataSource property after configuring the data adapter and generating the Dataset, you are presented with a drop-down list from which to select a Dataset as the source of the data for the DataGrid, as shown in Figure 9-14. In our case, the options on the drop-down list include the entire Dataset, *DsVintage1*; the part of the Dataset relating to the Members table, *DsVintage1.Members*; and None. Because we want to work specifically with the Members table, we select the second option, *DsVintage1.Members* as the data source for drgMembers.

FIGURE 9-14.
Setting DataSource property

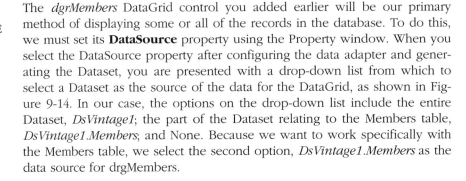

When DsVintage1.Members is selected as the data source, dgrMembers immediately displays the three fields of the Members table—Name, Phone_Number, and Late_Fees–that were selected in the Query Builder as headings for columns, as shown in Figure 9-15.

FIGURE 9-15.
DataGrid after setting the DataSource property

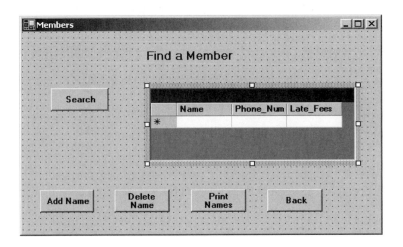

Although you might think you are ready to execute the project and display the contents of the database table in the DataGrid, that is not quite the case. In fact, we need to write some code to actually "fill" the Dataset with the records from the database. To do this we need to add one line of code to the frmMembers_Load event procedure, as shown in VB Code Box 9-1. Note that the line of code uses the Fill method of the MembersAdapter control to put data into the Members table of the DsVintage1 Dataset whenever this form is loaded. If you now execute the project and click the *Check Members* button on the main form (frmVintage), the frmMember_Load event procedure is executed and the DataGrid will be filled with the records from the database, as shown in Figure 9-16. This occurs because the Members table of the DsVintage1 Dataset is filled using the query you created earlier for the MembersAdapter oleDBDataAdapter control using the Query Builder wizard.

VB CODE BOX 9-1. frmMembers_Load event procedure	```Private Sub frmMembers_Load(ByVal sender As System.Object, _ ByVal e As System.EventArgs) Handles MyBase.Load MembersAdapter.Fill(DsVintage1, "Members") End Sub```

FIGURE 9-16. Filled DataGrid

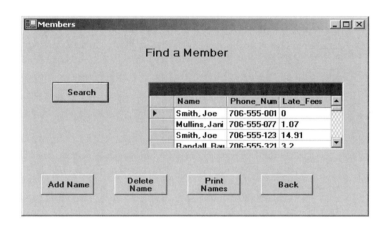

Note that the DataGrid has a vertical scroll bar to enable you to view additional records. It is also possible to enlarge the fields to show all of a field. For example, you can position the cursor over the right-hand side of the Phone_Number field name and use it to drag the border to the right, exposing the complete field name and the contents of the field. You can also do this for *all* fields by setting the **PreferredColumnWidth** property of the DataGrid to a larger value than the default value of 75 (in pixels). In our case, setting it to 100 will display the complete Phone_Number field. Although you will not see the effect of this change at design time, you will at run time. However, because all fields are enlarged at the same time, now you may not be able to see the complete Late_Fees field and will need to enlarge the form and DataGrid to do so.

Searching for Records   To display records in the DataGrid that match a certain criterion, say, a phone number, a whole or partial member name, or those with late fees greater than some amount, we need to use an SQL query that searches for matching records in the Members table of the database. In this case, the SQL query that we create in the code replaces the one we built with the Query Builder wizard when we were designing the application.

However, before we get into using the query, we need a brief explanation of SQL queries.

All SQL queries are of the same general form:

SELECT *fieldnames* **FROM** *tables* **WHERE** *condition*

ORDER BY *fieldname*

where the *condition* part of the SQL statement has it own special form in that it is usually a combination of a database field name, a comparison operator, and a value or string to which the field name is being compared. In fact, it is very similar to the decision comparisons with which you are already familiar. For example, if you wanted to find the first record in the Members table of the Vintage database with late fees greater than, say, $10, the *condition* portion of the SQL statement would be

```
Late_Fees > 10
```

where the condition string is "Late_Fees > 10". In this case, the field name is Late_Fees, the comparison operator is the greater-than symbol, and the contents of the Late_Fees field are being compared to 10.

The complete SQL query in this example would then be

```
SELECT * FROM Members WHERE Late_Fees > 10
```

where the asterisk in the *fieldnames* location indicates that all fields should be displayed.

Compare this with the SQL query you created with the Query Builder wizard:

```
SELECT * FROM Members ORDER By Phone_Number
```

In this case, there was no *WHERE* comparison, so all records in the Members table were displayed but there was an *ORDER BY* clause that indicated the order in which the matching records were listed.

Finding a string, say a phone number, is a little more complex in that we have to denote that the phone number is a string by surrounding it by apostrophes within the query string. For example, to search for a member with a phone number of, say, *706-555-1234*, the SQL query would be

```
SELECT * FROM Members WHERE Phone_Number = '706-555-1234'
```

Failure to include the apostrophes will lead to an error in the SQL query because it will try to compare the field name, *Phone_Number,* which is of type text, to the undecipherable arithmetic expression, *706-555-1234.*

When we are using SQL to search for records in a VB .NET application, the entire SQL query must be treated as a string and is usually stored in a string variable, say, strSelectString, which is then used to modify the data adapters and the Dataset. It is also usually the case that the value of the field being searched for is a variable. For example, instead of searching for all records with a late fee greater than $10, we might be searching for all records with late fees greater than the Decimal variable decAmount. Similarly, instead of searching for the record with a phone number of *706-555-1234*, we may be searching for a record with a phone number matching the string variable strPhNum. In both cases, it is necessary to concatenate the variable with the remainder of the SQL query to create the complete query string.

For example, the assignment statement to assign the SQL query to find all records greater than the Decimal variable decAmount to the string variable, strSelectString, is

```
strSelectString = "SELECT * FROM Members WHERE Late_Fees > " _
& Cstr(decAmount)
```

If the value of decAmount is $10, then the contents of strSelectString will look exactly like the one shown earlier for the late fees.

If, on the other hand, we are searching for the matching record for a phone number that is stored in strPhNum, we have to be careful to include the apostrophes in the query string. This usually requires a second concatenation to add the trailing apostrophe to "build" the complete query string as shown below:

```
strSelectString = "SELECT * FROM Members WHERE Phone_Number = '" _
& strPhNum & "'"
```

Note that the first apostrophe is included as a part of the Select/From/Where part of the SQL statement, but that the second apostrophe has to be added by concatenating it at the end. If the value of strPhNum is *706-555-1234*, then the resulting contents of strSelectString would look just like that displayed earlier for this phone number.

Now that you have a basic understanding of SQL and how SQL statements can be "built" by including variable values and then assigned to a string variable, you are ready to search for records matching various criteria. We will start by searching for records with late fees exceeding some amount because those queries are the easiest to build. We will then learn how to search for the record matching a phone number and then finish with searching for whole or partial names.

Searching Based on Late Fees

To search for late fees and phone numbers in addition to searching by partial name, as was done in previous chapters, we need to begin by modifying the existing frmMembers form to add new buttons to search by late fees and to search by phone numbers. We also need to modify the text property of the existing button to distinguish it from the other buttons. The resulting frmMembers form is shown in Figure 9-17 where we have added two new buttons, btnLateFeeSearch and btnPhNumSearch, and changed the text property of the existing btnSearch button.

To carry out the search for late fees, we need to first write the code for the btnLateFeeSearch_Click event procedure, which inputs the dollar amount that will be input for the search process using an InputBox. The event procedure is shown in VB Code Box 9-2. Note that the amount to be used in the search process is saved in a Decimal variable, decLateFeeAmt, which is then passed to a sub program, FindLateFees, that actually queries the database.

The sub program, FindLateFees, carries a number of actions including

1. clearing the Dataset;
2. creating the query string using the amount entered by the user (the amount is passed to the query string as a parameter);

FIGURE 9-17. Form with added buttons

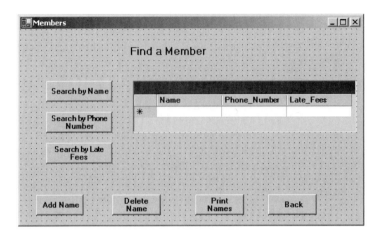

| VB CODE BOX 9-2. Event procedure for btnLateFeeSearch_ Click | ```
Private Sub btnLateFeeSearch_Click(ByVal sender As _
System.Object, ByVal e As System.EventArgs) Handles _
btnLateFeeSearch.Click
    Dim decLateFeeAmt As Decimal
    decLateFeeAmt = CDec(InputBox("Input the late fee amount", _
    "Vintage DVDs"))
    FindLateFees(decLateFeeAmt)
End Sub
``` |
|---|---|

3. modifying the data adapter to use the new query string rather than the one created with the Query Builder wizard during the data adapter configuration process.

The statement to modify the MembersAdapter data adapter sets the CommandText property of the SelectCommand object equal to the query string and then fills the DsVintage1 Dataset using the modified data adapter in the last statement in the sub program. The resulting subprogram is shown in VB Code Box 9-3.

| VB CODE BOX 9-3. Sub program to search for late fees | ```
Sub FindLateFees(ByVal decAmount As Decimal)
    Dim strSelectString As String
    DsVintage1.Clear()
    strSelectString = "Select * from Members where Late_Fees >" _
    & Cstr(decAmount)
    MembersAdapter.SelectCommand.CommandText = strSelectString
    MembersAdapter.Fill(DsVintage1, "Members")
End Sub
``` |
|---|---|

When the application is executed and the *Check Members* button is clicked on the frmVintage form and the *Search by Late Fees* button clicked on the frmMembers form, the btnLateFeeSearch_Click event procedure is executed and an InputBox is displayed. This InputBox requests an amount be input to which all member late-fee amounts will be compared. The records for those members with late fees greater than that amount will be displayed in the dgrMembers DataGrid. For example, Figure 9-18 shows the case where all members with late fees greater than $10 are displayed in the dgrMembers DataGrid.

FIGURE 9-18. Result of searching for late fees > $10

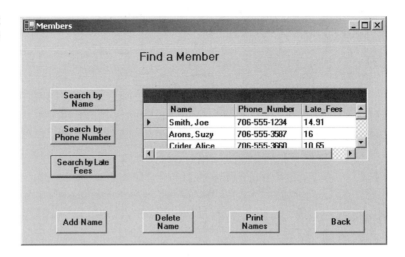

Searching by Phone Number

To search for a member by using his or her telephone number, the code is very similar to that used to search for late fees. The only differences are that the SQL query involves searching for a string instead of a number and, because the phone number is the primary key for the Members table, only one matching record will be found. The code for the btnPhNumSearch_Click event procedure is shown in VB Code Box 9-2. Note that the phone number to be used in the search process is saved in a String variable, strPhoneNumber, which is then passed to a sub program, FindPhoneNumber, that actually queries the database. The code for the btnPhNumSearch and FindPhone-Number sub programs is shown in VB Code Box 9-4.

VB CODE BOX 9-4. Code for event procedure and sub program to search by phone number	<pre>Private Sub btnPhNumSearch_Click(ByVal sender As _
	System.Object, ByVal e As System.EventArgs) Handles _
	btnPhNumSearch.Click
	    Dim strPhoneNumber As String
	    strPhoneNumber = InputBox("Input the phone number", _
	    "Vintage DVDs")
	    FindPhoneNumber(strPhoneNumber)
	End Sub
	
	Sub FindPhoneNumber(ByVal strPhNum As String)
	    Dim strSelectString As String
	    DsVintage1.Clear()
	    strSelectString = "Select * from Members where " & _
	    "Phone_Number = '" & strPhNum & "'"
	    MembersAdapter.SelectCommand.CommandText = strSelectString
	    MembersAdapter.Fill(DsVintage1, "Members")
	End Sub</pre>

When the application is executed and the *Check Members* box is clicked on the frmVintage form and the *Search by Phone Number* button is clicked on the frmMembers form, the btnPhNumSearch_Click event procedure is executed and an InputBox is displayed. This InputBox requests a phone number be input to which all member phone numbers are compared. The record for the member with a matching phone will be displayed in the dgrMembers DataGrid. For example, if a phone number of *706-555-1234* is input, the record for "Smith, Joe" with that phone number and late fee of $14.91 is displayed.

Searching by Name

In Chapter 7, we used the Instr() function to search for names of members that matched partial or whole names and displayed them in a list box. By clicking a specific name, we could transfer information about the corresponding member to the frmVintage form. We can use a SQL query to search for records of members that matched partial or whole names and display them in a DataGrid. We will not repeat the transfer operation because it will be handled on the frmVintage form itself.

To find member names that match the search string that is input via an InputBox, we will use a new type of comparison operator: the **LIKE operator.** This operator type allows us to look for DVD names that partially match a search string input by the user. The query combines the LIKE operator with the SQL percent-sign, wild-card character (%) to search for records containing the search string regardless of what precedes or follows the search string.

The general form of the query using the LIKE operator is

```
SELECT * FROM Table WHERE FieldName LIKE '%SearchString%'
```
with both the percent signs (%) and the search string being enclosed within apostrophes in the query string. For example, if the search string is "jon", then the query would look like

```
SELECT * FROM Members WHERE Name LIKE '%jon%'
```
This query would find "Jones, Ben", "West, Jon", and "Sajon, Chris".

To create the string variable that contains the SQL query, the assignment statement should be of the form

```
strSelectString = "SELECT * FROM Members WHERE Name LIKE '%" _
& strSearch & "%'"
```
where strSearch is the search string passed from the event procedure. The code for the btnSearch event procedure and the FindName sub program are shown in VB Code Box 9-5, and Figure 9-19 shows the outcome of searching for the partial name "smi" resulting in all three individuals with a last name of "Smith" being displayed.

| VB CODE BOX 9-5. Event procedure and sub program to search for names | ```Private Sub btnSearch_Click(ByVal sender As System.Object, _
ByVal e As System.EventArgs) Handles btnSearch.Click
    Dim strSearchName As String
    strSearchName = InputBox("Input the whole or partial name", _
    "Vintage DVDs")
    FindName(strSearchName)
End Sub

Sub FindName(ByVal strSearch As String)
    Dim strSelectString As String
    DsVintage1.Clear()
    strSelectString = "SELECT * FROM Members WHERE Name LIKE '%" _
    & strSearch & "%'"
    MembersAdapter.SelectCommand.CommandText = strSelectString
    MembersAdapter.Fill(DsVintage1, "Members")
End Sub``` |

FIGURE 9-19. Result of searching for names containing "smi"

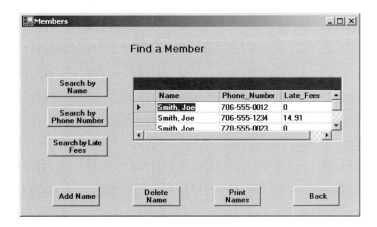

Tip: If you use a database system other than MS Access, remember that not all are created equal. SQL is case sensitive on some systems, some do not support the Like operator, and wildcard characters may vary from system to system.

Step-by-Step Instructions 9-3: Displaying records in the DataGrid control

1. Select the dgrMembers DataGrid control and set the **DataSource** property equal to the Members table of the Vintage database, that is, **DsVintage1.Members.** The field names for this table should be shown in the DataGrid as shown in Figure 9-15.

2. Double-click anywhere in the frmMembers form to open the Code window for the frmMembers_Load event procedure and add the code shown in VB Code Box 9-1. If you then run the Vintage9 project and click the btnCheck button on the main form, the frmMembers form should be displayed with the dgrMembers DataGrid filled with the records from the Members table of the database ordered by phone number.

3. Switch back to the main form and terminate the project. Display the frmMembers form and select the drgMembers DataGrid. Choose the **PreferredColumnWidth** property and change the value from 75 to **100** to enlarge the fields in the DataGrid. Although you will not immediately see the result of this change, you will see it after you run the project. You will probably also need to expand the width of the form to accommodate the wider DataGrid.

4. Add two new buttons beneath the existing search button on the frmMembers form and change the text property of the existing button. The properties for all three buttons are shown in Table 9-2.

5. To search for late fees greater than some input value, double-click the btnLateFeeSearch button and add the code shown in VB Code Box 9-2 to the btnLateFeeSearch_Click event procedure to input a late fee value to be used to search for records by calling the FindLateFees sub program.

TABLE 9-2: Buttons on frmMembers form

Purpose of Button Control	Name Property	Text Property
Search for records matching partial or complete names	btnSearch	**Search by Name**
Search for record matching a phone number	btnPhNumSearch	**Search by Phone Number**
Search for records with late fees greater than a value	btnLateFeeSearch	**Search by Late Fees**

6. Press **ENTER** at the end of the btnLateFeeSearch_Click event procedure to open space for adding the code shown in VB Code Box 9-3 and for creating the FindLateFees sub program. This sub program will use value input in the event procedure to carry out the search.

7. Run the project, click the *Search by Late Fees* button, and enter a value of $10. The result should be the same as shown Figure 9-18.

8. Terminate the project and add the code shown in the top of VB Code Box 9-4 to create the btnPhnNumSearch_Click event procedure. Press **ENTER** at the end of any event procedure to open space for adding the code shown in the bottom half of the VB Code Box 9-4 to create the FindPhoneNumber sub program. This sub program will use the string input in the event procedure to carry out a search for matching records.

9. Run the project, click the Search by Phone Number button, and enter a phone number of **706-555-1234.** This should display a name of "Smith, Joe" with late fees of $14.91.

10. Terminate the project and delete any existing code in the btnSearch_Click event procedure. Now add the code shown in the top of VB Code Box 9-5 to this event procedure. Press **ENTER** at the end of any event procedure to open space for adding the code shown in the bottom half of the VB Code Box 9-5 to create the FindName sub program. This sub program will use the string input in the event procedure to carry out a search for matching records.

11. Run the project, click the *Search by Name* button, and enter a partial name of "smi". The result should be three matching names like that shown in Figure 9-19.

12. All of the *new* code for the frmMembers form is shown in VB Code Box 9-6.

■ ■

It's Your Turn!

1. To cause a DataGrid to display records from a database, what property of the DataGrid must be set? To what must it be set?

2. What is the general form of an SQL query?

3. How do we "build" a query string using constants and variables?

| VB CODE BOX 9-6. New code for the frm-Members form | <pre>Private Sub frmMembers_Load(ByVal sender As System.Object, _
ByVal e As System.EventArgs) Handles MyBase.Load
    MembersAdapter.Fill(DsVintage1, "Members")
End Sub
Private Sub btnLateFeeSearch_Click(ByVal sender As _
System.Object, ByVal e As System.EventArgs) Handles _
btnLateFeeSearch.Click
    Dim decLateFeeAmt As Decimal
    decLateFeeAmt = CDec(InputBox("Input the late fee amount", _
    "Vintage DVDs"))
    FindLateFees(decLateFeeAmt)
End Sub
Sub FindLateFees(ByVal decAmount As Decimal)
    Dim strSelectString As String
    DsVintage1.Clear()
    strSelectString = "Select * from Members where Late_Fees >" _
    & Cstr(decAmount)
    MembersAdapter.SelectCommand.CommandText = strSelectString
    MembersAdapter.Fill(DsVintage1, "Members")
End Sub
Private Sub btnSearch_Click(ByVal sender As System.Object, _
ByVal e As System.EventArgs) Handles btnSearch.Click
    Dim strSearchName As String
    strSearchName = InputBox("Input the whole or partial name", _
    "Vintage DVDs")
    FindName(strSearchName)
End Sub
Private Sub btnPhNumSearch_Click(ByVal sender As _
System.Object, ByVal e As System.EventArgs) Handles _
btnPhNumSearch.Click
    Dim strPhoneNumber As String
    strPhoneNumber = InputBox("Input the phone number", _
    "Vintage DVDs")
    FindPhoneNumber(strPhoneNumber)
End Sub</pre> |

| VB CODE BOX 9-6. New code for the frm-Members form (continued) | <pre>Sub FindPhoneNumber(ByVal strPhNum As String)
    Dim strSelectString As String
    DsVintage1.Clear()
    strSelectString = "Select * from Members where " & _
    "Phone_Number = '" & strPhNum & "'"
    MembersAdapter.SelectCommand.CommandText = strSelectString
    MembersAdapter.Fill(DsVintage1, "Members")
End Sub
Sub FindName(ByVal strSearch As String)
    Dim strSelectString As String
    DsVintage1.Clear()
    strSelectString = "SELECT * FROM Members WHERE Name LIKE '%" _
    & strSearch & "%'"
    MembersAdapter.SelectCommand.CommandText = strSelectString
    MembersAdapter.Fill(DsVintage1, "Members")
End Sub</pre> |

4. What SQL keyword and what wildcard characters are used to find items similar to a string?

Mini-Summary 9-3: Displaying records in the DataGrid control

1. The DataGrid control is very useful for displaying data in a tabular form. This is especially true for database records.

2. To link a DataGrid to a database table, you must make the corresponding Dataset the Data-Source property for the DataGrid. Whatever the Dataset is filled with will appear in the DataGrid.

3. One way to use the DataGrid is to fill the Dataset on the Load event. The Dataset can also be filled depending on queries that are generated by user input.

---

5. Follow Step-by-Step Instructions 9-3 to add the drgMembers DataGrid to the frmMembers form and to automatically fill it. Continue following the instructions to add buttons and code that will enable the user to search by late fee amount, phone number, and exact or partial name.

RECORD OPERATIONS

Once you have searched for records in the Vintage DVDs database, you may wish to carry out a number of operations on records in the database including

* editing a record in the DataGrid by changing one or more fields and saving the results back to the database;
* adding a new record to the database;
* deleting an existing record;
* printing the records in the DataGrid.

We will consider each of these operations in a separate section.

Editing Records

Editing a record that appears in the DataGrid and saving the changes back to the underlying database table is a two-step process:

1. Make changes directly into the cell in the DataGrid.
2. Update these changes to modify the database.

The first step is very easy: Simply position the cursor in the cell to be changed and use the standard word processing editing keys—**DELETE**, **INSERT**, and so on, to change the cell contents. To handle the second step, we need to add a new button named btnUpdate with a text property of *Update Database* to the frmMembers form, as shown in Figure 9-20. The code for the Click event procedure for this button is shown in VB Code Box 9-7, where the Update method of the MembersAdapter object is used to update the DsVintage1 Dataset.

> **TIP:** It is important to note that changing the contents of a cell in the DataGrid but failing to use the Update method will have *no* effect on the actual database.

Adding a New Record

Adding a record to a table in the database is also a multistep process:

1. Use a dialog form like that discussed in Chapter 8 to input multiple items of data and transfer them to variables in the btnAdd_Click event procedure in the frmMembers code window.

FIGURE 9-20.
Adding btnUpdate
button to
frmMembers form

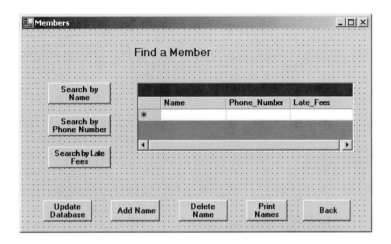

| VB CODE BOX 9-7. Code for btnUpdate button | ```
Private Sub btnUpdate_Click(ByVal sender As System.Object, _
ByVal e As System.EventArgs) Handles btnUpdate.Click
    MembersAdapter.Update(DsVintage1)
    MsgBox("Database updated!", MsgBoxStyle.Information, _
    "Vintage")
End Sub
``` |
| --- | --- |

2. Create a new row of the Dataset table composed of the variable contents from Step 1.

3. Add the new row to the Dataset table and update the database.

In the process of adding the new row to the Dataset table, we need to check to ensure that there is not already a record in the database with the same primary key.

In the first step, we need to create a dialog box form just like we did in Chapter 8. To review that process, recall that we start by using the **Project|Add Windows Form** menu selection or the **Add New Item...** toolbar icon to add a new windows form to the project. To make this into a dialog form, we need to set some properties as shown in Table 9-3. In this case, the first *six* properties create a dialog box form, and the last two properties are standard for any new form.

TABLE 9-3: Property values to create dialog form

Property	Value
FormBorderStyle	FixedDialog
ControlBox	False
MinimizeBox	False
MaximizeBox	False
AcceptButton	btnOk
CancelButton	btnCancel
```

TABLE 9-3: Property values to create dialog form (Continued)

Property	Value
Name	frmDialog
Text	New Record

To this form, we then need to add two text boxes and labels, one pair for each input item: name and phone number. We don't need a for the late fees because they are zero for a new member. We also need to add two buttons: one to accept the input and one to cancel it. These eight controls and their properties are shown in Table 9-3, and the resulting frmDialog form is shown in Figure 9-21. Note that we have included the TabIndex property because this will facilitate the speed at which data can be input.

TABLE 9-4: Controls for frmDialog form

Control	Name	Text Property	TabIndex	Control	Name	Text Property
TextBox	txtNameInput		0	Label	lblNameInput	Name
TextBox	txtPhNumInput		1	Label	lblPhNumInput	Phone Number
Button	btnOk	OK	2			
Button	btnCancel	Cancel	3			

FIGURE 9-21.
frmDialog form after adding controls

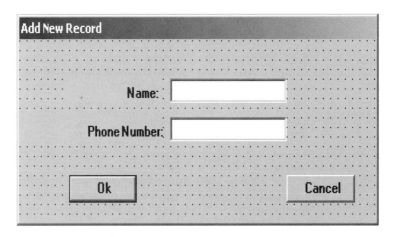

The final properties we need to set for the frmDialog form are the AcceptButton and CancelButton properties. These designate the control, which if clicked, will accept the input or cancel it. In our case, we want to set the AcceptButton property to *btnOk* and the CancelButton property to *btnCancel.* By designating a button to be the "Accept Button," this button is activated by pressing the **ENTER** key. Similarly, the Cancel Button is activated by pressing the **ESC** key. The code for these two buttons is shown in VB Code Box 9-8. Note that pressing **ENTER** or clicking the *OK* button closes the dialog form and sets the DialogResult property of the dialog form to "OK". On the other hand, pressing **Esc** or clicking the *Cancel* button will close the dialog form and set the DialogResult property to "Cancel." We will check the DialogResult property on the frmMembers form prior to adding a new record.

VB CODE BOX 9-8. Code for btnOk and btnCancel buttons	```Private Sub btnCancel_Click(ByVal sender As System.Object, _ ByVal e As System.EventArgs) Handles btnCancel.Click Me.DialogResult = DialogResult.Cancel End Sub Private Sub btnOk_Click(ByVal sender As System.Object, _ ByVal e As System.EventArgs) Handles btnOk.Click Me.DialogResult = DialogResult.OK End Sub```

On the frmMembers form, we need to add code to the btnAdd_Click event to instantiate frmDialog on this form as **dlgNew** and then show it using the ShowDialog method. Next, we need to check that the *Ok* button was clicked instead of the *Cancel* button; otherwise, we might add a blank record to the database. The final code in the btnAdd_Click event procedure sets two string variables equal to the contents of the text boxes on the dialog form and calls a sub program to add them to the database. The names of the text boxes on the dialog form now include the instance name of the dialog form, dlgNew, plus the text box name combined with dot notation. For example, the statement

```
strNewName = dlgNew.txtNameInput.Text
```

transfers the contents of the txtNameInput text box from the frmdialog form to the strNewName variable on the frmMembers form. The btnAdd_Click event procedure is shown in VB Code Box 9-9.

VB CODE BOX 9-9. btnAdd_Click event procedure	```Private Sub btnAdd_Click(ByVal sender As System.Object, _ ByVal e As System.EventArgs) Handles btnAdd.Click Dim strNewName, strNewPhoneNumber As String Dim dlgNew As New frmDialog() dlgNew.ShowDialog() If dlgNew.DialogResult = DialogResult.Ok then strNewName = dlgNew.txtNameInput.Text strNewPhoneNumber = dlgNew.txtPhNumInput.Text() AddMembers(strNewName, strNewPhoneNumber) End If End Sub```

The AddMembers sub procedure handles the actual addition of a new row to the Members table. To do this, it is first necessary to create a variable, **Member_Row**, of type DataRow and set it equal to a new row of the Members Table of the DsVintage1 Dataset by using its NewRow method. Each field of this new row is then set equal to the value that we input using the frmDialog form or, in the case of the Late_Fees field, it is set equal to zero. This row is then added to the Members table using the Add Method of the Rows object of the Dataset. If the Add method works, then the database is updated with the new Dataset contents using the Update method of the data adapter. The resulting code is shown in VB Code Box 9-10.

| **VB CODE BOX 9-10.** AddMembers sub program | ```
Sub AddMembers(ByVal strName As String, ByVal strPhoneNumber As String)
   Dim Member_Row As DataRow
   Member_Row = DsVintage1.Tables("Members").NewRow
   Member_Row("Name") = strName
   Member_Row("Phone_Number") = strPhoneNumber
   Member_Row("Late_Fees") = 0
   Try
      DsVintage1.Tables("Members").Rows.Add(Member_Row)
   Catch e As System.Data.ConstraintException
     MsgBox("Phone number is already in the database!", _
     vbExclamation, "Vintage")
     Exit Sub
   End Try
   MembersAdapter.Update(DsVintage1, "Members")
End Sub
``` |

In looking at VB Code Box 9-9, you should notice a new structure—the **Try-Catch** structure. This is an error-catching programming structure that does exactly what looks exactly like its name implies: It tries a statement and then catches any errors *thrown* by the statement. The complete form of the Try-Catch structure is

Try
   Programming statement to be tested
Catch *variable* **As** *exception error*
   Programming statement to be executed if error is caught
Finally
   Programming statements to be executed in all cases
End Try

In this structure the programming statement that has the potential to generate an error comes after the *Try* statement. The *Catch* statement uses a variable to accept the exception error, and the statement following it is executed if an error occurs. The *Finally* statement is executed regardless of whether or not an error is caught and is not included in our case.

In VB Code Box 9-9, we are using the Try-Catch programming structure to catch errors that may occur when a new row is being added to an existing table. It is necessary here to avoid adding a row with the same primary key as an existing row. If that error occurs, a message is displayed and the sub is exited without trying to update the database.

> **TIP:** The Try-Catch structure is a great way to catch errors in all kinds of programming situations beyond just working with databases!

For example, if we want to add a new record for John Lister, with phone number of 770-555-2579, we would click on the *Add Name* button to display the frmDialog form. The user can then enter the pertinent information and press **ENTER** to transfer it back to the frmMembers form, where it is added to the database and the database updated. It should be noted that the new record is saved as the *last* record in the database, but when the database is
```

reopened later, it will be resorted to put the new record in its appropriate location. If we wanted to cancel the process of adding a new member, we could simply click the *Cancel* button on the frmDialog form or press **Esc.**

Deleting a Record

In addition to editing existing records and adding new records, we need to provide the capability to delete an existing record using the btnDelete_Click event procedure. As with the other features, VB .NET has provided the **Delete** method to remove a record from the database. Once the pointer is positioned on the record to be removed, the Delete method automatically handles the delete operation. However, we first need to make this record the only record in the Dataset and then ask the user whether they are sure they want to delete this record, because once a record is deleted, it cannot be undeleted.

To make the record to be deleted the only record in the Dataset, we use the same FindPhoneNumber sub program that we used to find the member with a specific phone number. We then need to check to make sure that there is indeed a member with that phone number, since trying to delete a nonexistent record will cause an error to occur. We do this check using the **Count** property of the Rows object of the Dataset, which will return the number of rows in the Dataset. If it is zero, then there was no member matching the phone number that was input, and the btnDelete_Click event procedure is terminated.

Once we have ascertained that there is a matching record for the phone number, we use the MsgBox function, which returns a value depending on which button the user clicks. The statement to check whether the user really wants to delete the record would be

```
intResponse = MsgBox(strDelete, vbYesNoCancel + _
    vbCritical + vbDefaultButton2, "Delete Record")
```

where

    intResponse = an Integer variable that will be checked to determine which button was clicked

    strDelete = a user-defined constant with the message "Are you sure you want to delete this record?"

    vbYesNoCancel = a VB .NET constant resulting in the Yes, No, and Cancel buttons being displayed

    vbCritical = a VB .NET constant resulting in an "X" in a red circle being displayed

    vbDefaultButton2 = a VB .NET constant that makes the second (No) button the default button (the one with the focus)

    "Delete Record" = the title for the message box

This Msgbox will cause a window to be displayed like the one shown in Figure 9-22.

As discussed in Chapter 6, if the user clicks "Yes" to delete the record, then the value of Response is equal to 6; if the user clicks "No," the value of intResponse is 7; and if the user clicks "Cancel," the value is 2. However, it is not necessary to remember these values, because there are vbYes, vbNo, and vbCancel constants that are equal to them. If intResponse is equal to the vbYes constant, then the record is deleted; otherwise, the event procedure is terminated. Note that if the user selects "Yes" to delete the record, the Rows

FIGURE 9-22. Delete Record message box

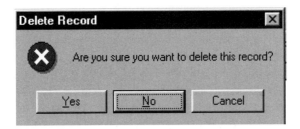

object Delete method is executed, and the record pointer is deleted. However, to make this deletion permanent, we need to use the Update method on the Dataset.

The code for the btnDelete_Click event procedure is shown in VB Code Box 9-11, where we start by creating a string constant to hold the message to go into the message box and then declaring variables. Next, we input the phone number of the person to be deleted, using the FindPhoneNumber sub program to search for it. The Count property is checked to make sure that there is a matching record, and the user is queried about deleting it. Finally, the Delete method is called to remove the record, and the Dataset is updated.

| VB CODE BOX 9-11. Code to delete a record | ```
Private Sub btnDelete_Click(ByVal sender As System.Object, _
ByVal e As System.EventArgs) Handles btnDelete.Click
    Const strDelete As String = "Are you sure you want to " _
    & "delete this record?"
    Dim strPhoneNumber As String, intNumRows, intResponse As Integer
    strPhoneNumber = InputBox("Input phone number of person " & _
    "to be deleted.")
    FindPhoneNumber(strPhoneNumber)
    intNumRows = DsVintage1.Tables("Members").Rows.Count
    If intNumRows = 0 Then
        MsgBox("Nobody with that telephone number!")
        Exit Sub
    End If
    intResponse = MsgBox(strDelete, vbYesNoCancel + _
    vbCritical + vbDefaultButton2, "Delete Record")
    If intResponse = vbYes Then
        DsVintage1.Tables("Members").Rows(0).Delete()
        MembersAdapter.Update(DsVintage1, "members")
    Else
        MsgBox("Record not deleted", vbInformation, "Vintage")
    End If
End Sub
``` |

Printing Matching Records

To print the contents of the Dataset, we need to make use of two new objects, the **oleDBCommand** object and the **oleDBDataReader** object. The oleDBCommand object is used to generate the oleDBDataReader object, which is used to read the contents of the Dataset and place them in a string. The string is then sent to the Output window. Because of this relationship between the two objects, an instance of the oleDBCommand object must be created first by dragging it from the Data panel of the toolbox to the form. Like the other data controls, it appears in the tray beneath the form and has a
```

default name of oleDBCommand1, but we will change its name to *Member-sCommand* using its Property window. We will also use the existing Members-Connection instance of the oleDBConnection object that was automatically created when we configured the data adapter as the Connection property of the MembersCommand object, as shown in Figure 9-23.

FIGURE 9-23. Setting the Connection property of the MembersCommand object

Finally, the CommandText property is created in the same way that you created the query using the Query Builder wizard to configure the data adapter, except that in this case you start the Query Builder wizard by clicking the CommandText property line to highlight the property and then clicking the ellipsis icon at the right side of the property window. The resulting CommandText property will be a query *exactly* like that you created when you configured the data adapter, that is

```
SELECT Name,Phone_Number,Late_Fees FROM Members
ORDER BY Phone_Number
```

(You can also type in this query directly if you wish.) To summarize, the ole-DBCommand object's properties are shown in Table 9-5.

TABLE 9-5: oleDBCommand object properties

Property	Value
Name	MemberCommand
Connection	MemberConnection
CommandText	Select Name, Phone_Number, Late_Fees from Members Order by Phone_Number

Once the properties for the oleDBCommand object have been set, you can use it in your btnPrint_Click event procedure to generate a oleDBDataReader object named *datReader* with the following statement:

```
datReader = MembersCommand.ExecuteReader
```

The datReader object now has all the contents of the Members table of the DsVintage1 data set. We can use a While loop to iterate through the Read method of the datReader object, creating a string composed of the contents of the fields in the Members table. This string can then be written to the Output window using the Debug.Writeline command. The complete btnPrint_Click event procedure is shown in VB Code Box 9-12. Note that we are using the vbTab constant to space the items and are formatting the Late Fees as currency. If the project is run and the btnPrint button on the frm-Members form clicked immediately after the form is loaded, the result is as shown in Figure 9-24.

VB CODE BOX 9-12. Code for the btnPrint_Click event procedure	```Private Sub btnPrint_Click(ByVal sender As System.Object, _```

```
Private Sub btnPrint_Click(ByVal sender As System.Object, _
ByVal e As System.EventArgs) Handles btnPrint.Click
   Dim datReader As OleDb.OleDbDataReader, strOutput As String
   MembersConnection.Open()
   datReader = MembersCommand.ExecuteReader
   While datReader.Read()
     strOutput = datReader("Name").ToString() _
     & vbTab & datReader("Phone_Number").ToString() _
     & vbTab & Format(datReader("Late_Fees").ToString, _
     "currency")
     Debug.WriteLine(strOutput)
   End While
End Sub
```

FIGURE 9-24. Printing the contents of the Dataset

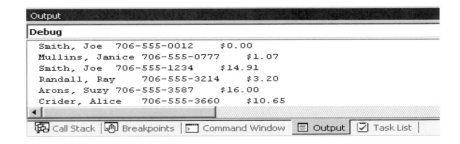

Step-by-Step Instructions 9-4: Record operations

1. Add a new button to the frmMembers named **btnUpdate** with a text property of **Update Database.** Double-click this button and add the code shown in VB Code Box 9-7 to the btnUpdate_Click event procedure.

2. Run the project and switch to the frmMembers form. Using the vertical scroll bar to display the record for **Janice Mullins** and change her phone number to **706-555-0778** instead of 706-555-0777. Click the *Update* button to make the change permanent. Go back to the frmVintage (main) form and then return to the frmMembers form. The change should be displayed when you move to the record for Janice Mullins.

3. Use the **Project|Add Windows Form** or the **Add New Item...** toolbox icon to add a new Windows form. Give this form the name **frmDialog** and add the controls shown in Table 9-4 to the frmDialog form. Change the properties for this form to match those shown in Table 9-3.

4. Add the code shown at the top of VB Code Box 9-8 to the btnCancel_Click event procedure. Add the code shown at the bottom of VB Code Box 9-8 to the btnOk_Click event procedure.

5. Display the frmMembers form and add the code shown on VB Code Box 9-9 to the btnAdd_Click event procedure for this form. This code will call the frmDialog form, check that the user clicked *OK*, and, if they did, input the values from the two textboxes on that form.

6. Add the code shown in VB Code Box 9-10 to create the AddMembers sub program in the code window for the frmMembers form.

7. Run your project and add the new member discussed in the text (**John Lister,** with phone number of **770-555-2579**). Go back to the frmVintage (main) form and then return to the frmMembers form. The new record should be displayed when you scroll down the DataGrid.

8. On the frmMembers form, add the code shown in VB Code Box 9-11 to the btnDelete_Click event procedure.

9. Run your project and use the *Delete* button to delete the new member you just added (**John Lister**, with phone number of **770-555-2579**). The first time you do this, do NOT accept the deletion. Then click the *Delete* button again and accept the deletion. Go back to the frmVintage form and then return to the frmMembers form. The absence of this record should be displayed when you scroll down the DataGrid.

10. Add an oleDBCommand control to the frmMembers form (it will appear in the tray beneath the form.) Modify the properties of this command control to match those shown in Table 9-5. Add the code shown in VB Code Box 9-12 to the btnPrint_Click event procedure.

11. Go back to the frmVintage (main) form and then return to the frmMembers form. Click the *Print* button to display all records in the Members table of the database.

12. All of the *new* code for the frmMembers form is shown in VB Code Box 9-13.

■ ▬ ■

Mini-Summary 9-4: Record operations

1. Record operations include editing, adding, and deleting records.

2. Records in a DataGrid can be edited by adding, deleting, or typing over characters in a cell. To be made permanent, the changes must be updated using the data adapter Update method on the Dataset.

3. Adding records to a table uses a dialog form for input and a variable of type DataRow to hold the new row. The new row is created using the NewRow method of the Tables collection of the Dataset. This row is added to the Dataset using the Add method from the Rows object of the Tables collection.

4. The Try-Catch structure is used to catch errors and is very useful for catching errors generated by database operations.

Mini-Summary 9-4: Record operations (Continued)

5. A database record can be deleted with the Delete method after it has been made the only record in the Dataset. The Count property of the Rows object can be used to ensure that there is a matching record before trying to delete it and making the deletion permanent using the Update method of the data adapter. Querying the user before making the deletion is a good idea.

6. Printing records in the Dataset requires that you use the oleDBCommand object to generate the oleDBDataReader object. The Read method of the oleDBDataReader object is used to read the records.

| **VB CODE BOX 9-13.** New code for frm-Members form | ```
Sub AddMembers(ByVal strName As String, ByVal strPhoneNumber As String)
    Dim Member_Row As DataRow
    Member_Row = DsVintage1.Tables("Members").NewRow
    Member_Row("Name") = strName
    Member_Row("Phone_Number") = strPhoneNumber
    Member_Row("Late_Fees") = 0
    Try
        DsVintage1.Tables("Members").Rows.Add(Member_Row)
    Catch e As System.Data.ConstraintException
        MsgBox("Phone number is already in the database!", _
        vbExclamation, "Vintage")
        Exit Sub
    End Try
    MembersAdapter.Update(DsVintage1, "Members")
End Sub
Private Sub btnUpdate_Click(ByVal sender As System.Object, _
ByVal e As System.EventArgs) Handles btnUpdate.Click
    MembersAdapter.Update(DsVintage1)
    MsgBox("Database updated!", MsgBoxStyle.Information, "Vintage")
End Sub
Private Sub btnCancel_Click(ByVal sender As System.Object, _
ByVal e As System.EventArgs) Handles btnCancel.Click
    Me.DialogResult = DialogResult.Cancel
End Sub
Private Sub btnOk_Click(ByVal sender As System.Object, _
ByVal e As System.EventArgs) Handles btnOk.Click
    Me.DialogResult = DialogResult.OK
End Sub
Private Sub btnAdd_Click(ByVal sender As System.Object, _
ByVal e As System.EventArgs) Handles btnAdd.Click
    Dim strNewName, strNewPhoneNumber As String
    Dim dlgNew As New frmDialog()
    dlgNew.ShowDialog()
    If dlgNew.DialogResult = DialogResult.Ok then
        strNewName = dlgNew.txtNameInput.Text
        strNewPhoneNumber = dlgNew.txtPhNumInput.Text()
        AddMembers(strNewName, strNewPhoneNumber)
    End If
End Sub
``` |
```

| VB CODE BOX 9-13. New Code for frm-Members form (Continued) | `Private Sub btnDelete_Click(ByVal sender As System.Object, _`
`ByVal e As System.EventArgs) Handles btnDelete.Click`
`    Const strDelete As String = "Are you sure you want to " _`
`    & "delete this record?"`
`    Dim strPhoneNumber As String, intNumRows, intResponse As Integer`
`    strPhoneNumber = InputBox("Input phone number of person " & _`
`    "to be deleted.")`
`    FindPhoneNumber(strPhoneNumber)`
`    intNumRows = DsVintage1.Tables("Members").Rows.Count`
`    If intNumRows = 0 Then`
`        MsgBox("Nobody with that telephone number!")`
`        Exit Sub`
`    End If`
`    intResponse = MsgBox(strDelete, vbYesNoCancel + _`
`    vbCritical + vbDefaultButton2, "Delete Record")`
`    If intResponse = vbYes Then`
`        DsVintage1.Tables("Members").Rows(0).Delete()`
`        MembersAdapter.Update(DsVintage1, "members")`
`    Else`
`        MsgBox("Record not deleted", vbInformation, "Vintage")`
`    End If`
`End Sub`
`Private Sub btnPrint_Click(ByVal sender As System.Object, _`
`ByVal e As System.EventArgs) Handles btnPrint.Click`
`    Dim datReader As OleDb.OleDbDataReader, strOutput As String`
`    MembersConnection.Open()`
`    datReader = MembersCommand.ExecuteReader`
`    While datReader.Read()`
`        strOutput = datReader("Name").ToString() & vbTab _`
`        & datReader("Phone_Number").ToString() & vbTab _`
`        & Format(datReader("late_fees").ToString, "currency")`
`        Debug.WriteLine(strOutput)`
`    End While`
`End Sub` |

It's Your Turn!

1. How can database records be edited in the DataGrid? How are the changes made permanent?

2. What is a good way to handle data input for a new record? How do you check to ensure that the user did not cancel the input operation?

3. What collections, objects, and methods are used to actually add a record to an existing database table?

4. Why do we use the Try-Catch error-checking structure rather than just letting the user deal with an error?

5. Why do you not need to remember the integer values of the "Yes" and "No" responses to the message box query?

6. What collections, objects, and methods are used to delete a record from an existing database table? (Be sure to include any used to ensure that there is a record to delete!)

7. What new objects are needed to print the records in a Dataset to the Output window? What object is used to generate the other?

8. Follow Step-by-Step Instructions 9-4 to create the code necessary to edit, add, delete, and print records in a database table.

9. Save your form and project under the same name.

RENTING A DVD

To rent a DVD using the Vintage.mdb database, we need to make it easy for the store clerk to access information from the Vintage.mdb database on the member and on the DVDs they wish to rent and to display this on the main form. For the member, they need to be able to use the member's phone number to display their name and late fees, if any. For the DVDs they wish to rent, the clerk must be able to repeatedly enter the identification numbers from the DVDs being rented to display their names and prices. Since this repetition is a type of event-driven loop, it is carried out by clicking the *Calculate* button once for the Member's name and first DVD rented and then clicking it again for each DVD that is rented.

In terms of database operations, renting one or more DVDs requires a number of operations using all three of the tables: Rental, DVDs, and Members tables. These operations are

1. *Rental table:* When each DVD is rented, a new row is added to the Rental table containing the DVD ID number, the phone number of the person renting it, and the date it is due back (two days from the day it is rented).

2. *Members table:* We will also assume that all existing late fees are paid at the time of the rental of any DVD, so we need to retrieve the late fees to the frmVintage form to be used in calculating the amount due. We also need to update the Members table to set the Late_Fee field for the current members record to zero.

3. *DVDs table:* We must retrieve the price of the DVD being rented to the frmVintage table to be used in calculating amount due.

Adding and Configuring Adapters

To make this process work, we need to add and configure three instances of the oleDBDataAdapter object to the frmVintage (main) form: one each for the Members, Rental, and DVDs tables of the Vintage.mdb database. The name properties will be, respectively, MembersAdapter, RentalAdapter, and DVDAdapter. In each case, the configuration involves linking the data adapter to the Vintage.mdb database in the C:\VBDB folder. However, the SQL query for each adapter will be created differently using the Query Builder wizard. In addition, the Dataset table must be generated for each data adapter that is configured, and it should be tested before preceding.

For the MembersAdapter, this process will be carried out in a manner similar to that described in Step-by-Step Instructions 9-1 for creating the data adapter for the frmMembers form. For the DVDAdapter, the DVDs table should be added to the Query Builder and all four fields—ID_Number, DVD_Name, Price, and Location—checked to add them to the query, which should be ordered by ID_Number. Generating the data set for this adapter simply involves ensuring that the DVDs table is selected as a part of the DsVintage1 Dataset.

For RentalAdapter, the Rentals table should be added to the Query Builder and all three fields—DVD_ID, Phone_Number, and Date_Due— should be checked to add them to the query, which should be ordered by DVD_ID. As with the DVDAdapter, generating the Dataset for the Rental-Adapter simply involves ensuring that the Rental table is selected as a part of the DsVintage1 Dataset. This information for each of the three data adapters is shown in Table 9-6.

TABLE 9-6: oleDBDataAdapter properties on frmVintage form

Adapter Name	MembersAdapter	RentalAdapter	DVDAdapter
Provider Type	Microsoft Jet 4.0 OLE DB	Microsoft Jet 4.0 OLE DB	Microsoft Jet 4.0 OLE DB
Database	C:\VBDB\Vintage.mdb	C:\VBDB\Vintage.mdb	C:\VBDB\Vintage.mdb
Table Added	Members	Rental	DVDs
Fields Selected	Name, Phone_Number, Late_Fees	DVD_ID, Phone_Number, Date_Due	ID_Num, DVD_Name, Price, Location, Rented
Ordering	Phone_Number	DVD_ID	ID_Number
DataSet	Members table added	Rental table added	DVDs table added

Finding the Matching Member and DVDs Being Rented

To make this rental process work on the frmVintage (main) form, we need to replace the code in the btnCalc_Click event procedure, which we deleted earlier, with code to find information on the member and the DVDs being rented. We also need to add a row to the Rental table and mark the DVD as being rented in the DVDs table.

The general idea of this code is to enter a telephone number of a customer and query the Members table in the Vintage.mdb data to find their name and late fees, if any. Once this information is found, it can be displayed in the appropriate text boxes. In both cases, we need to carefully check for errors in the input to ensure that we are searching for a valid phone number or DVD ID number and that a match was found in each case. Because of this error checking, the code will be somewhat longer than otherwise, but it is very important to do the checking to avoid strange error messages.

As an example of this DVD rental process, assume that the member with telephone number *770-555-1010* is renting three DVDs *A Few Good Men* (DVD ID = 3), *Bambi* (DVD ID = 7), and *To Kill a Mockingbird* (DVD ID = 63).

Let's start with displaying the name and late fees for the member who is renting the DVD in the text boxes on the form using the member's telephone number. This will require creating a new btnCalc_Click event procedure, as shown in VB Code Box 9-14, where the FindNumber sub is virtually the same as was used in the frmMembers form. The strPhoneNum *must* be declared at the form level because it will be needed each time the *Calculate* button is clicked as well as later when the row is added to the Rental table.

| **VB Code Box 9-14.** Beginning lines of revised btnCalc_Click event procedure | ```Dim StrPhoneNum As String, decTotalCost As Decimal
Private Sub btnCalc_Click(ByVal sender As System.Object, _
ByVal e As System.EventArgs) Handles btnCalc.Click
    Const sngTaxRate As Single = 0.07
    Dim decPrice, decAmountDue, decTaxes As Decimal
    Dim intCounter As Integer, decLateFees As Decimal
    Dim intDVDNumber As Integer, strDVDNumber As String
    If txtCustName.Text = "" Then
        strPhoneNum = InputBox("Enter the customer phone number", _
        "Vintage DVDs")
        If strPhoneNum = "" Then 'Check for Cancel
            btnCalc.Focus()
            Exit Sub
        End If
        FindNumber(strPhoneNum)
        If strPhoneNum = "" Then 'Check for Cancel
            btnCalc.Focus()
            Exit Sub
        End If
    End If
``` |

Note that in the btnCalc_Click event procedure, the member phone number is input from an InputBox and then checked to ensure it is not a blank (which would occur if the *Cancel* button is clicked on the InputBox dialog box). If it is a blank, the event procedure is terminated and the focus is put back on the *Calculate* button.

If a nonblank phone number is entered, the FindNumber sub shown in VB Code Box 9-15 is called and the phone number is passed to it by *reference* so it can be passed back to the calling procedure.

| **VB Code Box 9-15.** FindNumber sub program | ```Private Sub FindNumber(ByRef strPhNum As String)
    Dim strSelectString As String
    DsVintage1.Clear()
    strSelectString = "Select * from Members where Phone_Number = '" _
    & strPhNum & "'"
    MembersAdapter.SelectCommand.CommandText = strSelectString
    MembersAdapter.Fill(DsVintage1, "Members")
    Try
        txtCustName.Text = _
        DsVintage1.Tables("Members").Rows(0).Item("Name")
    Catch e As System.IndexOutOfRangeException
        MsgBox("No match for that phone number; please try again.")
        strPhNum = ""
        Exit Sub
    End Try
    txtLateFees.Text = _
    DsVintage1.Tables("Members").Rows(0).Item("Late_Fees")
    DsVintage1.Tables("Members").Rows(0).Item("Late_Fees") = 0
End Sub
``` |

As mentioned before, the FindNumber sub is very similar to the FindPhoneNumber sub in the frmMembers form code, so we won't explain it again here other than to note that, when a match is found, the text property of the txtCustName text box is set equal to the Name field of the matching record and the text property of the txtLateFees text box is set equal to the Late_Fees field. If no match is found for the phone number, the matching parameter is set to the null string ("") and passed back to the btnCalc_Click event procedure, where it is again checked. The two checks are necessary because the first looks for an empty input string and the second looks for a no-match situation in the database. In either case, the event procedure is terminated.

For our example, the store clerk would start the rental process by clicking the *Calculate* button and entering the member's telephone number in the input box as shown in Figure 9-25, with the resulting member name (Todd Martin) and late fees of $5.94 shown in the bottom portion of the figure.

FIGURE 9-25.
InputBox for phone number and resulting rental form

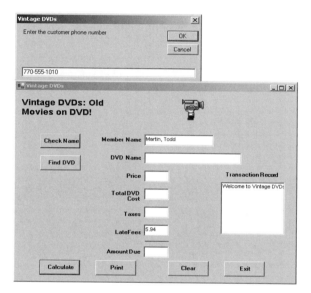

The next step is to find the DVD that matches the identification number of the one being rented. The logic for this is similar to that used to find the phone number, except that the sub program used to find the DVD matching the identification number refers to the DVDAdapter instead of the Members-Adapter, and to the DVDs table instead of the Members tables. As with the FindNumber sub program, we use the Try-Catch structure to ensure that no errors are generated by erroneously entered DVD ID numbers. The *additional code* in the btnCalc_Click event procedure to find the matching DVD name and price is shown in VB Code Box 9-16.

| **VB CODE BOX 9-16.** Continuation of btnCalc_Click event procedure | ```
strDVDNumber = InputBox("Enter the DVD number", _
"Vintage DVDs")
If strDVDNumber = "" Then
    btnCalc.Focus()
    Exit Sub
End If
intDVDNumber = CInt(strDVDNumber)
FindDVD(intDVDNumber)
If intDVDNumber < 0 Then
    btnCalc.Focus()
    Exit Sub
End If
``` |
|---|---|
```

Note that the DVD number is initially saved in a string variable, which is checked to make sure it is not empty (the same as was done for the input phone number). If the ID number is not blank, it is converted into an integer variable, which is passed to the FindDVD sub program. You should note that this same ID number is checked after the FindDVD sub program to determine if it has been set to –1 in the sub program, indicating that there was no DVD matching that number (probably through an input error). If it is less than zero, the event procedure is terminated, and the focus is set back to the *Calculate* button.

The FindDVD sub program that actually carries out the search is shown in VB Code Box 9-17. In this sub program, a logic similar to that used in the search for a matching phone number is used, with a few differences. First, the intNumber parameter is passed by *reference* instead of by value, so we can pass its value back to the calling event procedure where it is checked. Second, the Try-Catch structure is used to check for a nonexistent DVD ID number. If the DVD ID number is nonexistent, then a message is generated, the intNumber parameter is set to minus one, and the sub is exited.

| **VB Code Box 9-17.** FindDVD sub program | ```
Private Sub FindDVD(ByRef intNumber As Integer)
    Dim strSelectString As String
    DsVintage1.Clear()
    strSelectString = "Select * from DVDs where Id_Num = " & intNumber
    DVDAdapter.SelectCommand.CommandText = strSelectString
    DVDAdapter.Fill(DsVintage1, "DVDs")
    Try
        txtDVDName.Text = _
        DsVintage1.Tables("DVDs").Rows(0).Item("DVD_Name")
    Catch e As IndexOutOfRangeException
        MsgBox("No DVD with that number; please try again.")
        intNumber = -1
        Exit Sub
    End Try
    txtDVDPrice.Text = _
    DsVintage1.Tables("DVDs").Rows(0).Item("Price")
End Sub
``` |
|---|---|

TIP: The Try-Catch structure will also generate an error if you happen to have the database open in Access while you are working with it in VB .NET.

The next-to-last operation in the rental process is to fill in the various text boxes on the frmVintage form and to save their values as variables. This is the part of the btnCalc_Click event procedure that is the same as before, so we will simply show it again without comment in VB Code Box 9-18.

The RentDVD Sub Program

The last step in this process is to carry out the rental process by adding a row to the Rental table of the Vintage.mdb database corresponding to each DVD that is rented. This action is carried out using the RentDVD sub program, to which we pass the ID number of the DVD to be rented and the phone number of the customer. The fields of the Rental table include the ID number for
```

| VB CODE BOX 9-18. Completion of btnCalc event procedure | ```decPrice = CDec(txtDVDPrice.Text)
decTotalCost = decTotalCost + decPrice
decTaxes = decTotalCost * sngTaxRate 'Compute taxes
decLateFees = CDec(txtLateFees.Text)
decAmountDue = decTotalCost + decTaxes + decLateFees
txtLateFees.Text = Format(decLateFees, "Currency")
txtTotalCost.Text = Format(decTotalCost, "currency")
txtTaxes.Text = Format(decTaxes, "currency")
txtAmountDue.Text = Format(decAmountDue, "currency")
txtDVDPrice.Text = Format(decPrice, "currency")
lstDVDs.Items.Add(txtDVDName.Text & " " & _
txtDVDPrice.Text)
RentDVD(intDVDNumber, strPhoneNum)
btnCalc.Focus()
End Sub``` |

the DVD, the phone number of the person renting the DVD, and the due date for the return of the DVD. In this case, we have all of the information except the due date, but that is easily found.

The due date is found by first creating a variable of type Date, TodayPlus2, and then initializing it to the date of the rental. This is accomplished by setting the TodayPlus2 variable equal to the Today function. To add two days to this variable, we use the AddDays(2) method of the Date data type. The two lines of code to do this are shown below:

```
Dim TodayPlus2 As Date = Today
TodayPlus2 = TodayPlus2.AddDays(2)
```

Once the Date type variable is set, we then add a row to the Rental table in the same manner that we did to add a new member to the Members table, that is, using the NewRow method of DataRow object and then adding the DVD ID number, customer phone number, and due date to the new row.

Since we are assuming that the customer has presented the DVD from the shelf to the store clerk to rent and there are no duplicate DVDs in the store, there *should* never be a case where the same DVD is rented twice. However, because there is always the chance of an error on input, we will use the Try-Catch structure to make sure that we catch any problems with the addition of the new row to the Rental table. The complete RentDVD sub program is shown in VB Code Box 9-19.

After entering the member's phone number as shown earlier, the store clerk would enter the first DVD ID number (3) as shown in the top portion of Figure 9-27.

With the entry of the DVD ID number, the DVD name and price will be shown on the form along with the taxes and total amount due, as shown in the left side of Figure 9-27. Also, the DVD name and price are shown in the transaction record list box. Clicking the *Calculate* button for each additional DVD that is to be rented will update the taxes, amount due, and transaction record list box as shown in the right side of Figure 9-27.

Setting Late Fees to Zero

When the member rents a DVD, he or she must pay any late fees in addition to the rental costs for the current DVDs. This payment of the late fees must be recognized in the database by modifying the Late_Fees field in the Members table to set it to zero when the receipt is being printed and the transac-

| **VB Code Box 9-19.** RentDVD sub program | ```
Sub RentDVD(ByVal intNum As Integer, ByVal strPhNum As _
String)
    Dim TodayPlus2 As Date = Today
    TodayPlus2 = TodayPlus2.AddDays(2)
    Dim Rental_Row As DataRow = _
    DsVintage1.Tables("Rental").NewRow
    Rental_Row("DVD_ID") = intNum
    Rental_Row("Phone_Number") = strPhNum
    Rental_Row("Date_Due") = TodayPlus2
    DsVintage1.Tables("Rental").Rows.Add(Rental_Row)
    Try
        RentalAdapter.Update(DsVintage1, "Rental")
    Catch e As System.Data.OleDb.OleDbException
        MsgBox("There was an error renting that DVD.")
        Exit Sub
    End Try
End Sub
``` |
|---|---|

FIGURE 9-26. Entry of DVD ID number

FIGURE 9-27. Result of entering DVD ID number (left) and multiple rentals (right)

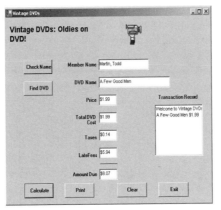 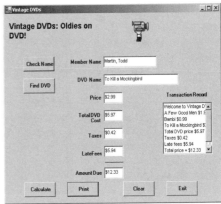

tion is completed. The easiest way to do this is to use the Update SQL command instead of the Select command in the strSelectString query string as shown in the following code:

```
strSelectString = "Update Members Set Late_Fees = 0 " & _
"where Phone_Number = '" & strPhoneNum & "'"
```

If this strSelectString is used as the CommandText property of the MembersAdapter, and the MembersAdapter updated as with the Select SQL statement, the result is that the member's late fees are set to zero. The appropriate location for these additional statements is at the end of the btnPrint_Click event procedure because this completes the transaction. The complete set of new statements to be added is shown in VB Code Box 9-20.
```

| VB CODE BOX 9-20. Setting late fees to zero in btnPrint_click event procedure | ```strSelectString = "Update Members Set Late_Fees = 0 " & _
    "where Phone_Number = '" & strPhoneNum & "'"
MembersAdapter.SelectCommand.CommandText = strSelectString
MembersAdapter.Fill(DsVintage1, "Members")``` |
|---|---|

Adding these statements to the btnPrint_Click event procedure and clicking the *Print* button will print the transaction record to the Output window, as shown in the top of Figure 9-28, and set the late fees to zero.

FIGURE 9-28. Output of rental activity (top) and additions to Rental table (bottom)

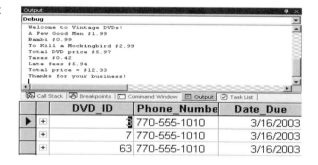

As a result of these actions, if you looked at the Rental table of the Vintage.mdb database, you would see three new records corresponding to the three DVDs that were rented. The bottom of Figure 9-28 shows the Rental table if these are the only three DVDs that have been rented and they were rented on March 14, 2003, resulting in a due date of March 16. Finally, as before, clicking the *Clear* button will clear the form. If you were to enter the same telephone number as before (*770-555-1010*), you would see that the late fees are now zero.

Step-by-Step Instructions 9-5: Renting a DVD

1. Display the frmVintage form in Design mode and add three oleDBDataAdapter controls to the form (they will appear in the tray beneath the form). Modify the properties of these adapters to match those shown in Table 9-6. In each case, remember to generate the Dataset by adding tables to the existing DsVintage1 Dataset.

2. Make sure all of the code in the btnCalc_Click event procedure has been deleted. Begin writing the code for the rental process by adding the code shown in VB Code Box 9-14 to the btnCalc_Click event procedure. This code will handle the process of the store clerk entering a telephone number to display the member's name and late fees, if any, using the FindNumber sub program.

3. Add the code shown in VB Code Box 9-15 to create the FindNumber sub program that will use the telephone number to display the member's name and late fees.

4. Add the code shown in VB Code Box 9-16 to the existing code in the btnCalc_Click event procedure to handle the process of the clerk entering one or more DVD ID numbers to display their names and prices on the form by calling the FindDVD sub program. Also add the code shown in VB Code Box 9-17 to create the FindDVD sub program.

5. Add the code shown in VB Code Box 9-18 to complete the btnCalc_Click event procedure by carrying out the processing of the rental. This includes calling the RentDVD sub program to add a row to the Rental table. Also add the code shown in VB Code Box 9-19 to create the RentDVD sub program that actually adds the row for the DVD being rented to the Rental table. Finally, add the code shown in VB Code Box 9-20 to the end of the btnPrint_Click event procedure.

6. Test your project by executing it and entering a telephone number of **770-555-1010** to display a name of "Todd Martin" with late fees of $5.94. Then enter a DVD ID number of 3 to rent the DVD *A Few Good Men*. Your form should now appear like that shown in the left side of Figure 9-27.

7. Repeat the rental process for the DVDs with ID numbers of 7 (*Bambi*) and 63 (*To Kill a Mockingbird*) and click the *Print* button to display a form like that shown in the right side of Figure 9-27. If you choose to view the Output window in the VB. NET MDE, it should look like that shown in the top of Figure 9-28. Finally, if you use Microsoft Access to view the Rental table of the Vintage.mdb database, it should look like the bottom of Figure 9-28.

8. Click the *Clear* button and test your project by entering the same phone number as before. You should now see that the late fees are zero. Click the *Clear* button and enter information for another member and set of DVDs. Be sure to also check all of the error-checking code by failing to enter appropriate telephone numbers or DVD IDs or by clicking the *Cancel* button on the InputBoxes.

9. Save all files. All of the *new* code for the frmVintage form is shown in VB Code Box 9-21

Mini-Summary 9-5: Renting a DVD

1. Renting a DVD entails working with all three tables in the Vintage.mdb database. This requires adding new oleDBDataAdapters to the frmVintage form and configuring them.

2. One adapter will be used to query the Members table using a telephone number to display a member's name and late fees, if any. Another adapter will be used to query the DVDs table using an ID number to display a DVD name and price. The last adapter will be used to add a row to the Rental table for each DVD rented.

3. Querying the Members and DVD tables is accomplished in a manner similar to that used on the frmMember form.

4. Adding a row to the Rental table involves using the NewRow method of the Tables collection of the Dataset, as was done in the Members table to add a new member. Finding the due date involves using the AddDays method of a Date type variable.

| VB CODE BOX 9-21. New code for frmVintage form | <pre>Dim strPhoneNum as String, decTotalCost as Decimal

Private Sub btnCalc_Click(ByVal sender As System.Object, _
ByVal e As System.EventArgs) Handles btnCalc.Click
   Const sngTaxRate As Single = 0.07 'Use local tax rate
   Dim decPrice, decAmountDue, decTaxes As Decimal
   Dim intCounter As Integer, decLateFees As Decimal
   Dim intDVDNumber As Integer, strDVDNumber As String
   If txtCustName.Text = "" Then
      strPhoneNum = InputBox("Enter the customer phone number", _
      "Vintage DVDs")
      If strPhoneNum = "" Then 'Check for Cancel
         btnCalc.Focus()
         Exit Sub
      End If
      FindNumber(strPhoneNum)
      If strPhoneNum = "" Then 'Check for Cancel
         btnCalc.Focus()
         Exit Sub
      End If
   End If
   strDVDNumber = InputBox("Enter the DVD number")
   If strDVDNumber = "" Then
      btnCalc.Focus()
      Exit Sub
   End If
   intDVDNumber = CInt(strDVDNumber)
   FindDVD(intDVDNumber)
   If intDVDNumber < 0 Then
      btnCalc.Focus()
      Exit Sub
   End If
   decPrice = CDec(txtDVDPrice.Text)
   decTotalCost = decTotalCost + decPrice
   decTaxes = decTotalCost * sngTaxRate 'Compute taxes
   decLateFees = CDec(txtLateFees.Text)
   decAmountDue = decTotalCost + decTaxes + decLateFees
   txtLateFees.Text = Format(decLateFees, "Currency")
   txtTotalCost.Text = Format(decTotalCost, "currency")
   txtTaxes.Text = Format(decTaxes, "currency")
   txtAmountDue.Text = Format(decAmountDue, "currency")
   txtDVDPrice.Text = Format(decPrice, "currency")
   lstDVDs.Items.Add(txtDVDName.Text & " " & _
   txtDVDPrice.Text)
   RentDVD(intDVDNumber, strPhoneNum)
   btnCalc.Focus()
End Sub</pre> |

| **VB CODE BOX 9-21.** New code for frmVintage form (Continued) | ```
Private Sub FindNumber(ByRef strPhNum As String)
   Dim strSelectString As String
   DsVintage1.Clear()
   strSelectString = "Select * from Members where Phone_Number = '" _
   & strPhNum & "'"
   MembersAdapter.SelectCommand.CommandText = strSelectString
   MembersAdapter.Fill(DsVintage1, "Members")
   Try
      txtCustName.Text = _
      DsVintage1.Tables("Members").Rows(0).Item("Name")
   Catch e As System.IndexOutOfRangeException
      MsgBox("No match for that phone number; please try again.")
      strPhNum = ""
      Exit Sub
   End Try
   txtLateFees.Text = _
   DsVintage1.Tables("Members").Rows(0).Item("Late_Fees")
End Sub
Sub RentDVD(ByVal intNum As Integer, ByVal strPhNum As _
String)
   Dim TodayPlus2 As Date = Today
   TodayPlus2 = TodayPlus2.AddDays(2)
   Dim Rental_Row As DataRow = _
   DsVintage1.Tables("Rental").NewRow
   Rental_Row("DVD_ID") = intNum
   Rental_Row("Phone_Number") = strPhNum
   Rental_Row("Date_Due") = TodayPlus2
   DsVintage1.Tables("Rental").Rows.Add(Rental_Row)
   Try
      RentalAdapter.Update(DsVintage1, "Rental")
   Catch e As System.Data.OleDb.OleDbException
      MsgBox("There was an error renting that DVD.")
      Exit Sub
   End Try
End Sub
Private Sub btnPrint_Click(ByVal eventSender As System.Object, _
ByVal eventArgs As System.EventArgs) Handles btnPrint.Click
   Dim intNumber, intCounter As Short, strSelectString
   lstDVDs.Items.Add("Total DVD price " & txtTotalCost.Text)
   lstDVDs.Items.Add("Taxes " & txtTaxes.Text)
   lstDVDs.Items.Add("Late fees " + txtLateFees.Text)
   lstDVDs.Items.Add("Total price = " & txtAmountDue.Text)
   lstDVDs.Items.Add("Thanks for your business!")
   intNumber = lstDVDs.Items.Count - 1
   For intCounter = 0 To intNumber
      Debug.WriteLine(lstDVDs.Items(intCounter))
   Next
   DsVintage1.Clear()
   strSelectString = "Update Members Set Late_Fees = 0 " & _
   "Phone_Number = '" & strPhoneNum & "'"
   MembersAdapter.SelectCommand.CommandText = strSelectString
   MembersAdapter.Fill(DsVintage1, "Members")
End Sub
``` |
```

It's Your Turn!

1. Why do we need three oleDBDataAdapters added to the frmVintage form in order to handle the DVD rental process?

2. What method of the Dataset tables collection is used to add a new row to the Rental table?

3. How do we create the due date for the DVD that is being rented? How would we change the code if the due date was three days after the rental date?

4. Follow Step-by-Step Instructions 9-5 to write and test the code for the DVD rental process.

SUMMARY

At the beginning of the chapter, we said you would be able to do a number of things after reading it. Let's review those things here:

1. Understand how databases are used to store business data and the parts of a database. A database stores different types of data in such a way that an end user can easily manipulate and retrieve the data. Databases have some advantages over arrays, including permanence and the ability to store multiple types of data, to use database engines, and to be used on multiple computers. Databases are composed of fields, records, and tables, where *fields* are single facts or data items that have field names. A collection of related data that is treated as a unit is referred to as a *record*, and a related collection of records all having the same fields is referred to as a *table*. Tables in a relational database are related through fields that contain the same information. The *primary key* is a field that is unique to each record. When a primary key appears in another table, it is a *foreign key*.

2. Describe the parts of a database and understand database operations, including working with ADO.NET and the Dataset. Database operations include querying to find specific records as well as adding, editing, deleting, and printing records. ADO.NET, which is an object-oriented architecture, is used in VB .NET to access and work with a database. There are a number of ADO.NET object classes that are available to the programmer from the Data toolbox that make carrying out database operations quite easy.

3. Add oleDBDataAdapter and DataGrid controls to a form and configure them to display records from a database table. The primary object for working with databases in ADO.NET is the data adapter object, which acts as an intermediary between the database on disk and the disconnected in-memory representations of the database, called DataSets. A DataSet can be made up of one or more database tables along with their relation. Datasets are referred to as disconnected because they are created from the database in computer memory, manipulated there, and the results used to update the original database link between the VB .NET project. Data adapter objects are configured in VB .NET using wizards that guide the programmer through the process of linking it to a database table or relation. This includes creating the initial query to the database table. Once the data adapter is configured, the

Dataset is generated using the table that was referenced in the configuration process. Although there may be multiple adapters on different forms, there is only one Dataset being referenced by all of them.

4. Use the DataGrid control to display records. Once the data adapter has been configured and the Dataset generated, the next step is to display records using the DataGrid control. This tabular control can be configured to automatically display all of the records or only those that meet some criterion. This is accomplished by setting the DataSource property of the Data-Grid equal to a table in the Dataset and then filling that Dataset from the data adapter control. The columns of the DataGrid automatically take on the field names of the database table.

5. Add the necessary code to find and display records that match some criterion. For a relational database, finding or querying records is carried out in a special language known as SQL, which enables database users to select records from a table that meet some stated criterion or to create composite records from multiple tables that meet the criterion. In VB .NET, these operations are carried out by creating the query as a composite string composed of string constants and variables. The resulting query string is then used in combination with the data adapter to fill the Dataset with the matching records, which are automatically displayed in the DataGrid control.

6. Add programming instructions and controls to edit database records, add new records, delete existing records, and print records in the Dataset. Record fields can be edited by changing them in the Data-Grid and then updating the database. New records can be added using a DataRow type variable and setting it equal to a new row of the Dataset table using its NewRow method. Each field of this new row is then set equal to some value. This new row is then added to the Dataset table using the Add Method from the Rows property of the table and then updating the Dataset. Records can be deleted from the database by first making them the only record in the Dataset and then using the Delete method to actually remove them. When records are added or deleted, it is a good practice to use the Try-Catch error-checking mechanism to catch errors before they reach the user. Printing records in the Dataset requires that you use the oleDBCommand object to generate the oleDBDataReader object. The Read method of the oleDBDataReader object is used to read the records.

7. Use VB. NET and an ADO.NET database to carry out the rental of a DVD. Renting a DVD entails working with all three tables in the Vintage.mdb database requiring and configuring three new data adapters on the rental form: one to query the Members table to display a member's name and late fees; one to query the DVDs table to display a DVD name and price; and one to add a row to the Rental table for each DVD rented. The only unique operation of the three is finding the due date, and that involves using the AddDays method of a Date type variable.

NEW VB .NET ELEMENTS

Control/Object	Collections	Properties	Methods	Events
oleDBDataAdapter		SelectCommand CommandText	Fill Update	
DataSet	Tables	Rows Count	Clear NewRow Add Delete	
Dialog Form			ShowDialog	
oleDBCommand		Name Connection CommandText	ExecuteReader	
oleDBDataReader		ToString	Read	

NEW PROGRAMMING STATEMENTS

Try-Catch Structure
Try
    Programming statement to be tested
Catch variable **As** exception error
    Programming statement to be executed if error is caught
Finally
    Programming statements to executed in all cases
End Try

KEY TERMS

ADO.NET
column
data adapter object
DataGrid control
Dataset
DataTable
DataSource property

database
field
fieldname
foreign key
oleDBDataAdapter
primary key
query

Query Builder wizard
record
relational database
row
structured query language
(SQL)
table
Try-Catch structure

EXERCISES

1. Suppose that the database table, Food.mdb, is as shown in Table 9-7 with a single table, *Food*. Describe what each procedure does in the code on the next page.

TABLE 9-7: The Food.mdb database

ItemID	Item	Item Price
1	Hamburger	1.50
2	Hot Dog	0.95

TABLE 9-7: The Food.mdb database (Continued)

ItemID	Item	Item Price
3	French Fries	0.85
4	Soda	0.90
5	Milk Shake	2.10
6	Pizza	2.75
7	Wings	3.55
8	Gyro	4.25

```
Private Sub btnCompleteOrder_Click(ByVal sender As _
System.Object, ByVal e As System.EventArgs) Handles _
btnCompleteOrder.Click
    Dim sngTax As Single, decTotal As Decimal
    sngTax = 0.05 * CDec(txtTotal.Text)
    decTotal = CDec(txtTotal.Text) + sngTax
    txtTotal.Text = Format(decTotal, "Currency")
End Sub
Private Sub btnFood_Click(ByVal sender As System.Object,_
ByVal e As System.EventArgs) Handles btnFood.Click
    Dim strQuery As String, decTotal, decPrice As Decimal
    Dim Index As Integer
    Index = CInt(InputBox("Input the food items #"))
    strQuery = "Select From Food where ItemID = " _
    & CStr(Index)
    FoodAdapter.SelectCommand.CommandText = strQuery
    FoodAdapter.Fill(DsFood1, "Items")
    decPrice = DSFood1.Tables("Items")._
    Rows(0).Item("Item_Price")
    decTotal = CDec(txtTotal.Text) + decPrice
    txtTotal.Text = Format(decTotal, "Currency")
End Sub
Private Sub btnNewOrder_Click(ByVal sender As _
System.Object, ByVal e As System.EventArgs) _
Handles btnNewOrder.Click
    txtTotal.Text = Format(0, "Currency")
End Sub
Private Sub Form1_Load(ByVal sender As System.Object, _
ByVal e As System.EventArgs) Handles MyBase.Load
        txtTotal.Text = Format(0, "Currency")
End Sub
```

2. Write query strings for each of the following:

a. For the Vintage DVD Membership table (shown in Figure 9-1), write a query string to find all customers with no late fees at all.

b. For the Food database in Table 9-7, write a query string to find all items that cost less than $1.

c. For the Mystery Book database of Table 9-8, write the necessary code to create a query string that will find books by an author name provided by the user. The user enters the author name in a text box called txtAuthor.

TABLE 9-8: Mystery database

BookID	BookTitle	BookAuthor	Detective	Pages
1	Free Fall	Crais	Elvis Cole	265
2	Hush Money	Parker	Spenser	239
3	Murder on the Orient Express	Christie	Hercule Poirot	188
4	Purple Cane Road	Burke	Dave Robicheaux	320
5	Lullaby Town	Crais	Elvis Cole	287
6	Family Honor	Parker	Sunny Childs	225
7	A Is for Alibi	Grafton	Kinsey Milhone	185
8	Hunting Badger	Hillerman	Joe Leaphorn and Jim Chee	238
9	Sacred Clowns	Hillerman	Joe Leaphorn and Jim Chee	255
10	The Murder of Roger Ackroyd	Christie	Miss Marple	190
11	I, the Jury	Spillane	Mike Hammer	215
12	Stalking the Angel	Crais	Elvis Cole	320
13	Pastime	Parker	Spenser	250
14	The Secrete of Annex Three	Dexter	Inspector Morse	210
15	Murder After Hours	Christie	Miss Marple	256

d. For the Stocks database described in Table 9-9, create a query string to find stocks with a purchase price between $20 and $50.

TABLE 9-9: Fields and field names for Stocks.mdb database

Field	Field Name
Sticker Symbol	Symbol
Company Name	CompName
Purchase Date	PDate
Purchase Price	PPrice
Current Price	CPrice
Number of Shares Owned	Shares

3. For each of the following, explain what is wrong with the code. What error

messages would you see, if any? What can you do to correct the code?

a. The code shown on the following page should find the first item with a price that satisfies the query string using the Food database of Table 9-7.

```
Private Sub btnGo_Click()
  Dim strQuery As String
  strQuery = "Select Where Item_Price > 1"
  FoodAdapter.SelectCommand.CommandText = strQuery
  FoodAdapter.Fill(DsFood1, "Items")
  TxtDisplay.Text = DsMystery1.Tables("Items")._
  Rows(1).Item("Item_Price")
End Sub
```

b. The following code should find all items that satisfy the query string using the Mystery Book database of Table 9-8.

```
Private Sub btnGo_Click()
  Dim strQuery, strAuthor As String
  strAuthor = txtAuthor.Text
  strQuery = "Select From Mystery Where BookAuthor = "
  MysteryAdapter.SelectCommand.CommandText = strQuery
  MysteryAdapter.Fill(DsMystery1, "Detectives")
  Text2.Text = DsMystery1.Tables("Detectives")._
  Rows(0).Item("BookAuthor")
End Sub
```

PROJECTS

1. For the Vintage DVDs project discussed in the text, modify the existing frm-DVDs form to enable the store clerk to search for DVDs to determine whether they are carried by the store. This search should be by DVD name or partial name and result in the display of the name, price, and location in the store. It should also be possible to search for DVDs of a certain type, that is, drama, comedy, and so on, resulting in the display of all DVDs that match that type.

2. For the Vintage DVDs project discussed in the text, add a new form that will enable the store clerk to search for rented DVDs by entering their ID number and displaying a message regarding their rental status. If the DVD is rented, the form should display the due date for return of the DVD and the telephone number of the member who has rented it. Hint: This is very similar to the process carried out on the frmMembers form except that the data adapter should be linked to the Rental table.

3. Assume that you wish to create a project to process a list of student names, ID numbers, and quiz averages that is stored in a database called *Students.mdb*. Create a new project in VB .NET in your Chapter9 folder named *Grades,* download the Students.mdb file from the text Web site, and save it in the Bin folder. The fields and field names are shown in Table 9-10, where the Letter_Grade field is initially blank.

Your project should access this database and process the data using a single form to carry out the following operations:

a. Display information on each student in a DataGrid on the main form.

TABLE 9-10: Fields and field names for Students.mdb database

Field	Field Name
Student Name	Name
Student ID Number	ID_Number
Quiz Average	Quiz_Average
Letter Grade	Letter_Grade

b. Enable the user to use a 90-80-70-60 scale to determine the letter grade for a student based on their student ID number and add the grade to the database in the Letter_Grade field for that student.

c. Enter a quiz average value using an InputBox and display the information on all students with a quiz average *higher* than the value you entered.

d. Enter an ID number and display the name and information for the corresponding student.

e. Add, delete, or edit student records as necessary, and save the result of this action.

4. Assume that customer information in the form of names, telephone numbers, and sales amounts is stored in a database file called *CustSales.mdb*. Create a new project in VB .NET in your Chapter9 folder named *Customers,* download CustSales.mdb file from the text Web site, and save it to the Bin folder of project. The fields and field names are shown in Table 9-11, where the Category field is initially blank.

TABLE 9-11: Fields and field names for CustSales.mdb database

Field	Field Name
Customer Name	CustName
Telephone Number	PhoneNum
Sales Amount	Sales
Sales Category	Category

Create a project to access this database and to process the data. Your project should use a single form to carry out the following operations:

a. Display information on each customer in a DataGrid control.

b. Enable the user to use the scale shown in Table 9-12 to determine the Sales Category for a single customer based on their telephone number (which is unique) and add it to the database in the Category field for that customer.

c. Enter a sales value and display the information on all customers with sales values *lower* than the value you entered.

d. Enter a telephone number and display the information for the corresponding customer in the DataGrid.

TABLE 9-12: Sales amounts and categories

Sales Amount	Category
$1,000 or less	Light
$1,001 to $5,000	Average
Greater than $5,000	Heavy

e. Add, delete, or edit customer records as necessary, and save the result of this action.

5. Assume that Jane has created a database of her favorite mystery novels using the data shown earlier in Table 9-8. Create the same database and create a VB .NET application that return the following information:
   a. List all books with more than some number of pages.
   b. List all books by a specific author.

6. Create a project named *ZipFind* that will allow the user to input a city name and find that city's Zip code. Assume that the name and Zip code for each city are stored in a database named *ZipCode.mdb*. Download the ZipCode.mdb file from the text Web site and save it to the Bin folder of project. The two field names for this database are City and Zip_Code. The user should also be able to browse through all of the city–Zip code pairs using the DataGrid.

Also make it possible for a user to make a selection regarding entering a city or a Zip code and then find the other one. Depending on the user's selection, a dialog form is displayed asking the user to enter the appropriate information (there are two different dialog forms). Once the user has entered the appropriate information, the city and Zip code are displayed in text boxes on the main form. The user should also be able to add, delete, or edit city–Zip code records and save the results.

7. Assume that the FlyByNite Insurance company wishes to use a database to store information on its customers. This information should include the customer's name, Social Security number, age, and insurance premium. Assume that this information is stored in the *Insured* table in a database named *Insurance.mdb*. In addition, this database has a *Life* table that has two fields: Age and Premium. Create a project named *LifeInsurance* and download the Insurance.mdb file from the text Web site into the Bin folder of this project. The fields and field names for the Insured table are shown in Table 9-13, where the Amount field is initially blank.

TABLE 9-13: Fields and field names for CustSales.mdb database

Field	Field Name
Name of insured	Name
SS number	SSNum
Age	Age

TABLE 9-13: Fields and field names for CustSales.mdb database (Continued)

Field	Field Name
Does insured smoke?	Smoker
Premium amount	Amount

Your project should display information about the company's customers in the Startup form in a DataGrid. There should be another form that computes the premium amount using the Insured and Life tables. A customer is assigned the premium in the Life table that has the first Age field higher than his age; that is, age 31 and below have a premium of $65, but age 32 jumps to $95 (see Exercise 5 in Chapter 6). If the insured smokes, there is a surcharge equal to 30% of the premium amount. The second form should show the insured's name, age, and smoker status (yes or no) from the main form; it should calculate the premium from the Life table, the surcharge, if any, and the amount due using the Smoker status and the Life table. There should be a way to print this information and to return to the main form. When the command is given to return to the main form, the second form should be cleared and the amount due should be saved in the Amount field of the Insured table.

8. For the Vintage DVDs project discussed in the text, add a new form that will enable the store clerk to handle the returns of DVDs. This form should enable them to repetitively enter ID numbers for DVDs that have been returned by members. For each DVD ID number, the corresponding row should be deleted from the Rental table and, if the DVD is late, late fees equal to the rental price times the number of days overdue are added to the late_fees field of the Members table. Hint: This is the reverse of the process used to rent a DVD described in Step-by-Step Instructions 9-5.

9. Annie Morebucks is attempting to increase her personal wealth by investing in stocks. To aid in her struggle, she has created a database to store information about the stocks in her portfolio. The fields in her database are shown earlier in Table 9-9. Create a VB .NET program that Annie can use to manage her database. The program should include all functions needed to manage the database, that is, browse, add, delete, and update records. In addition, provide controls for calculating and displaying the following statistics for the stocks:

    a. Change in Price = Current Price – Purchase Price

    b. Current Position = Shares × (Change in Price)

    c. Total Value = Sum of (Shares × Current Price) for all stocks

    d. Also, provide features that allow Annie to query the database. This should include a search for stocks that have been purchased before or after a particular date, a search for stocks that have a negative or positive current position, and a search for stocks that have increased in value by a given percentage.

e. Notice that this database is set up under the assumption that all shares of a particular stock are purchased at a single time. How would you change the database to allow for multiple purchases of the shares from the same company?

10. Scott Aficionado spends a lot of time managing his fantasy baseball team. In order to use his time more efficiently and hopefully improve his standing in the league, he has decided to create a database with a VB .NET front end. He hopes to use the program to help him search through and analyze baseball statistics. He can then use the results of his analysis to build a formidable team. He begins by creating a database table with fields shown in Table 9-14. This table contains information that can be used to analyze a player's success at batting. Scott will be able to populate this table using information available at many sites on the Web. Create a VB .NET program to manage Scott's database. The program should include all functions needed to manage the database, that is, browse, add, delete, and update records. In addition, provide controls for calculating and displaying the following statistics for the players:
   a. Batting Average = Divide the number of hits by at-bats.
   b. Slugging Percentage = Divide the total bases of all hits by the total times at bat, where single = 1 base, double = 2 bases, triple = 3 bases, home run = 4 bases.
   c. On-Base Percentage = Divide the sum of hits plus walks plus number of times hit-by-pitch by the total number of plate appearances.

For an additional challenge, provide features for Scott to search for players who have a minimum value for one of the three calculated statistics.

TABLE 9-14: Fields and field names for Baseball.mdb database

Field	Field Name
Player ID	PLID
Player Name	Name
Team Name	Team
Player Position	Pos
At Bats	AB
Runs Scored	Runs
Total Hits	Hits
Doubles	Doubles
Triples	Triples
Home Runs	HR
Runs Batted In	RBI
Walks	BB
Hit-By-Pitch	HBP
Sacrifice	SF

11. Chance Ivory conducts simulation studies for a leading manufacturer of video-gaming machines. Since simulation studies often require multiple runs, Chance would like to develop a method that would allow him to store the results of many simulations in a database.

For a prototype he decides to conduct simple simulations of rolling a single, standard die. Each simulation run will consist of multiple throws of the die. Each time a simulation is conducted, Chance wants to save a simulation ID, the number of throws of the die for the simulation, and counts of how many times each possible die value appears. The fields and field names for the Simulation table are shown in Table 9-15.

Initially, all records are blank. New records are added when each simulation is conducted. Your form should contain a data control for linking to the database; a DataGrid control; one button for running the information and storing the results in the database; and one button to end the program.

When the button is pressed, a record should then be added to the database and the user should be prompted to enter the number of rolls to be conducted during the current simulation. As the simulated rolls are executed, counts for each possible die roll are stored in an array. When the total number of rolls has been executed, the die counts are assigned to the text boxes and the new record in the database is updated. Finally, the values for the current simulation are displayed in the text boxes.

TABLE 9-15: Fields and field names for Simulation.mdb database

Field	Field Name
Simulation ID	SimID
Number of ones that occurred in each simulation	Ones
Number of twos that occurred in each simulation	Twos
Number of threes that occurred in each simulation	Threes
Number of fours that occurred in each simulation	Fours
Number of fives that occurred in each simulation	Fives
Number of sixes that occurred in each simulation	Sixes

10 SECURITY, MENUS, FILES, AND GRAPHICS

LEARNING OBJECTIVES

After reading this chapter, you will be able to

1. Require a password to protect the information system from unauthorized access.

2. Create a menu for a project using the MainMenu control and add code to the menu items to execute actions when an item is selected.

3. Work with direct access data files

4. Add and use the SaveFileDialog and OpenFileDialog controls to save and open files.

5. Use Graphics objects in your projects to draw figures on a form.

6. Use Graphics objects to add print and print preview capabilities to a project.

7. Add the MS Chart control to the Toolbox and then to a form to use in charting data.

INTRODUCTION

In this chapter, we are completing our introduction to the VB .NET computer language by taking up a number of topics that either help us to improve existing projects or are useful in other ways. These include including a password system to provide security for our project, changing from a button-oriented interface to one that uses menus, using a new type of data file, working with files using a special control designed specifically for that purpose, and, finally, using graphics in our projects.

In the first case, passwords continue to be the most prevalent form of security system for information systems today, and we will discuss their use with the Vintage DVDs rental system. Similarly, menus are widely used along with buttons to carry out many operations, and we will discuss their use to give our projects a more professional "look and feel." The new type of file we will be introducing this chapter, the direct access data file, uses UDTs to create a record that can be manipulated directly rather than through a database system. To make this work even easier, we will discuss the file dialog box that enables us to manipulate files with VB .NET in much the same way you do in the Windows operating system. Finally, graphics are useful for portraying important data and information, so we will take a brief look at their use in VB .NET.

USING PASSWORDS FOR SECURITY

Security is an important concept in information systems that is aimed at protecting them from unauthorized entry. Virtually every day you hear about a hacker breaking into a computer system for "fun" or with criminal intent. One of the most widely used (and abused) systems for providing protection for an information system is to require a password that is known only to an authorized user. The user is typically given some number of chances to enter his or her password, which is compared to the password associated with the user's account ID number. If the user does not enter the correct password within the allotted number of tries—say, three—then the user is "kicked off" the system. In this section, we will illustrate how to create a very basic password system using VB .NET.

> **TIP:** Passwords should be at least six characters long and should not be anything that can be easily guessed, like Test, Password, or first or last names of family members.

Password Security System for Vintage DVDs

To create a password validation system for Vintage DVDs, we need to add a form that will request the user to enter a password when the project is started. The sequence of characters entered by the user should be checked against the correct password and, if the sequence is correct, the frmVintage form should be displayed. The user should be given three chances to enter a correct password before the project is automatically terminated.

To add a password form, you should either click the *Add New Item* icon and select *Windows forms* or select the *Project|Add Windows Form* menu option. In either case, a new form is added to the project. Table 10-1 shows the properties for this form that should be set at design time.

TABLE 10-1: Password form properties

Property	Value
Name	frmPassword
Text	Password
FormBorderStyle	Fixed Single
ControlBox	False

You should be familiar with all of these properties from previous applications, with the FormBorderStyle and ControlBox properties coming from Chapter 8. The only difference between a password form and a dialog form is that the FormBorderStyle property is set here to *Fixed Single* instead of *Fixed Dialog,* as it was in the dialog form. Setting it to *Fixed Single* prevents the user from moving or resizing the form. Also, since we do not want the user to close the box without entering a valid password, we set the Control-Box property to False. This presents an immovable form that cannot be resized or closed without the user entering a valid password.

> **TIP:** To create a secure password that is easy for you to remember, make up your own rule for creating your password based on something you can remember and using a variety of keyboard characters.

We also need to include a single text box, *txtPassword,* and two buttons: one to accept the password that has been entered in the text box (*btnAccept*) and one to cancel the password process and exit the project (*btnCancel*). The resulting password form is shown in Figure 10-1. Note that since there is no control box in the upper left-hand corner of the form, a user cannot bypass the form without entering a password.

FIGURE 10-1.
Password form

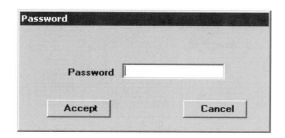

When the password form shown in Figure 10-1 is displayed, the user must enter the correct password in the text box and click the *Accept* button (or press **ENTER**). If they want to terminate the password entry process and exit the project, they would click the *Cancel* button (or press **ESC**).

Making frmPassword the Startup Object

Since we do not want the user accessing our application unless they know the appropriate password, we want the Password form to be the *Startup Object.* Recall from previous chapters that a specific form or module is made the Startup Object by selecting the .sln file in the Solution Explorer window and clicking the properties icon to display the Project Properties dialog box. Using the drop-down list box in this dialog box, we can change the Startup object to frmPassword. The combination of making frmPassword the Startup object and giving it a fixed border with no control box means that the user must go through it to reach any other forms in the project.

Setting Other Properties for the Password Form

The txtPassword text box has two very useful properties for checking whether the user has entered a valid password: the Tag and PasswordChar properties. The **Tag** property is a string that can be associated with a text box (and other controls) at design time and is not available to the application's user at run time. This property is useful for storing extra data needed for the project. By using the Tag property of the text box to store the password at design time, we have an easy way to check whether the user has entered the correct password.

The **PasswordChar** property for a text box sets the character that will be displayed when the user types characters into the text box. For example, if we set the PasswordChar property to the asterisk (*), this character will be displayed in place of every character, while the Text property for the text box is still whatever the user typed. This provides protection from someone reading the password off the screen as it is being input.

As with the dialog form discussed in Chapter 8, there are two important properties of the password form, frmPassword, that need to be set: the AcceptButton and CancelButton properties. If we set the AcceptButton property of frmPassword to *btnAccept*, then we are setting this button as the default button of the form. This means that if the **ENTER** key is pressed while the form is active, the Click event of the btnAccept button will be executed. On the other hand, if the CancelButton property of frmPassword is set to btnCancel, then the Click event of the btnCancel button is activated by the **ESC** key. In both cases, to avoid conflicts, only one button on the form can be set to be the AcceptButton and only one button can be set as the form's CancelButton. This enables the user to enter a password and press **ENTER** to accept it, or to press **ESC** to cancel the password entry process. The properties for the controls on the password form are summarized in Table 10-2.

TABLE 10-2: Controls and properties for password form

Control	Property	Value
frmPassword	AcceptButton	btnAccept
frmPassword	CancelButton	btnCancel
txtPassword	Text	(nothing)
txtPassword	Tag	i81Apple
txtPassword	PasswordChar	* (asterisk)

Adding Code to the Password Form

The code for the btnAccept_Click event procedure compares the contents of the text box to the Tag property of the text box. If the user has entered the correct password and there is a match, this form is closed with the Me.Hide command, and the focus is shifted to the customer name text box on the main form.

> **TIP:** While you are testing your password system, set the Text property of the password text box to the password to avoid repeatedly entering the password. Be sure to clear the text box Text property before using the project.

On the other hand, if the user has entered an incorrect password, there is no match, and the user is requested to try again. After three attempts to enter the correct password, the user is not allowed any more attempts and the project is terminated. The number of attempts at entering a correct password is saved in the Static variable *intNumTries,* so it is not reset between Click events of the btnAccept button. The code for the btnAccept_Click event procedure is shown in VB Code Box 10-1, and the dialog when an incorrect password (*morris*) is entered is shown in Figure 10-2 (the correct password is *i81Apple*).

FIGURE 10-2. Entry of incorrect password

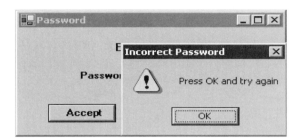

VB CODE BOX 10-1. Code to check a user's password.	```Private Sub btnAccept_Click(ByVal sender As System.Object, _```

```
Private Sub btnAccept_Click(ByVal sender As System.Object, _
 ByVal e As System.EventArgs) Handles btnAccept.Click
    Static intNumtries As Integer
    If txtPassword.Text = txtPassword.Tag Then
        Dim frmVintage As New frmVintage()
        frmVintage.Show()
        Me.Hide()
    Else
        intNumtries = intNumtries + 1
        If intNumtries >= 3 Then
            MsgBox("Too many attempts", MsgBoxStyle.Critical, _
             "Access Denied")
            End
        Else
            MsgBox("Press OK and try again", _
             MsgBoxStyle.Exclamation, "Incorrect Password")
            txtPassword.Text = ""
            txtPassword.Focus()
        End If
    End If
End Sub
```

Step-by-Step Instructions 10-1: Adding password security

1. Use Windows Explorer to create a new folder in the Visual Studio Projects folder named **Chapter10.** In this folder, create a folder named **Vintage10** and use Windows Explorer to *copy* all of the folders from the *Chapter9\Vintage9* folder into this new folder.

2. Add a new Windows Form called **Password.vb** to this project. Set the Text property to **Password** and set the Name property of the form to **frm-Password.**

3. Make the new password form the project's startup form by adjusting the project startup form property.

4. Add a label and a text box to the form. The label should read **Enter Password.** Give the text box the name **txtPassword.** Delete the Text property so that the text box appears empty when the form loads. Set the PasswordChar property to the **asterisk** (*).

5. Add two buttons: the btnAccept button with the text property **Accept** and the btnCancel button with the text property **Cancel.**

6. Set the AcceptButton and CancelButton properties of the Password form to **btnAccept** and **btnCancel,** respectively.

7. Add the code from VB Code Box 10-1 to the Click event of the btnAccept button. Add code to the Click event of the btnCancel button to end execution of the project.

8. Run the project and test the password form by entering the correct password (**i81Apple**). Exit the project and run it again entering an incorrect password three times. What happens?

9. Click the **Save All** icon to save the files in this project.

Mini-Summary 10-1: Password security

1. Passwords are a common method of providing security for information systems.

2. Password protection can be added to a Visual Basic project with the Tag property of a text box and a startup form to which the user must respond.

3. The user's input to the text box can be compared to the Tag property; if the user fails to match the Tag property in three tries, the project is terminated.

It's Your Turn!

1. Why is the system exited after three attempts at entering the password?

2. Why do we use an asterisk as the password character?

3. How can you avoid having to enter the password during the development and testing process?

4. What property is set to True for a button to cause its Click event to be executed when the **ENTER** key is pressed?

5. What is the Static keyword used for?

6. Would the tag property be appropriate for storing passwords for multiple users? Why or why not? What could you do differently?

7. Add a password form to the Vintage project by following Step-by-Step Instructions 10-1.

CREATING A MENU SYSTEM FOR VINTAGE DVDs

Menus from which users select an option have been a part of computer programs for many years, going back to the days when the text-oriented DOS operating system controlled the majority of personal computers. Menus are easy to use, while providing the user with a wide variety of options. You have been using a menu system since we first introduced you to VB .NET back in Chapter 2. Although buttons are useful for many operations and are widely used on Windows toolbars, menus are able to provide many more choices in a more compact manner. In this section, you will learn how to design, create, and write code for menus in your VB .NET programs.

Designing Menus for Windows Programs

In addition to the obvious advantages of menu systems, you may also wish to make your programs appear like the professionally developed software that you have used. Take a look at just about any program that is available for Windows and you will find a menu system. If you compare the menus of two different programs, you will also see that menus have similar look and feel. The menus of two different programs for Windows, MS Word and MS Excel, are shown in Figure 10-3. Notice that several of the menus in both programs have the same name and are positioned near the same location on the menu bar. For example, each program includes the File, Edit, View, Insert, Format, Tools, Window, and Help menus. Notice also that menus from each program may have several similar options. The File menus shown in the figure both include the New..., Open..., Close, Save options as well as others.

FIGURE 10-3.
Menus in Windows software

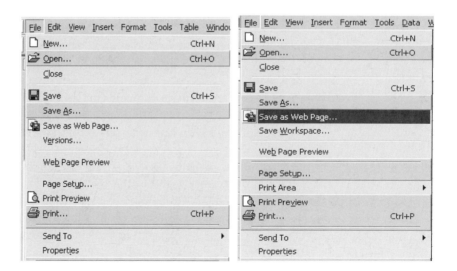

Creating menus that have common options, such as those shown in Figure 10-3, is part of a software design concept known as a **common user interface.** A common user interface provides us with two major advantages. From a user's perspective, common elements make it easier to learn and use software. Once you learn how to save a file that you have created using MS Word, you also know how to save a file that you create with MS Excel, and most other Windows software for that matter. From a programmer's perspective, common elements allow for reuse of controls and code. It turns out that the code and objects used to save a MS Word file are basically the same as the code and objects used by MS Excel.

There are a several other characteristics that we can learn about menus from the examples in Figure 10-3. First, notice how all of the options in the File menu are somehow related to working with a file. If you were to browse through other menus you would find that they are also set up in this way. The Help menu contains options that are all related to obtaining help in using the software. The Windows menu contains options that are all related to adjusting the Window in which the software appears on the screen.

Second, notice that there are a couple of menus that are different in the two programs. For example, MS Word includes a Table menu that is not available on the MS Excel menu bar. Likewise, MS Excel includes a Data menu that is not available on the MS Word menu bar. Given that the two software applications are created to perform different tasks, it is not very surprising that they would each include different menus with different options. In fact, it may be more surprising that the two menu bars have so many menus in common.

Finally notice that the menus include more than a simple listing of options in text. Graphical icons are incorporated to link the menu option with shortcut buttons available on toolbars. Arrows are used to indicate that a submenu with additional options will appear when a menu item is selected. The ellipsis (...) is used to indicate that a dialog box will appear when a menu item is selected. Also, shortcut keys are indicated to show how a menu option may be executed using the keyboard instead of the mouse.

Our brief tour of Windows menu systems provides us with several rules of thumb to keep in mind when adding menus to our VB .NET programs:

* Endeavor to keep main menus similar to the menus in other Windows programs.

* Group together related commands under a main menu heading that reflects the overall relationship of those commands.

* Use unique menus when necessary but try to keep their use to a minimum.

* Use common elements to give the user an idea of what will happen when a menu option is selected.

* Use common elements to show the user what alternatives exist for accessing the command on toolbars or from the keyboard.

Designing the Menu System

To see how menus can be used in a VB .NET application, we will convert some of the existing buttons on the Vintage DVDs application into menu items and add new functionality through menus. To start any such use of menus and buttons, we need to decide the menu structure for the main Vintage DVDs form that was created in Chapter 9. This form is shown in Figure 10-4.[1]

---

1. The Vintage DVDs main form shown here is very similar to that used in Chapter 7, with the exception of the removal of the DVD types list box. For that reason, this discussion also applies the main form created in Chapter 7.

FIGURE 10-4.
Vintage DVDs main
form

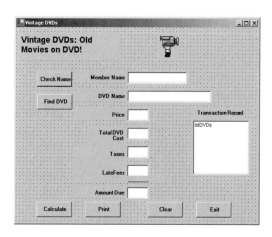

One criterion for deciding which operations should remain as buttons and which should be converted to menu items is frequency of use with more frequently used controls being buttons. In our case, as seen in Figure 10-4, there are six buttons with only the *Calculate* button being used for every DVD. Three others—the *Check Name* button to check a members name, the *Print* button to terminate the transaction and print the transaction record, and the *Clear* button to clear the form—*may* be used for each customer. The *Find DVD* button to find a DVD is used only when a customer asks whether the store carries a particular DVD, and the *Exit* button is used only at the end of the day. Based on this frequency of use, we should leave only the calculation operation as a button and convert all other operations to menus. In summary, Table 10-3 shows the various operations and whether they will be buttons or menu items.

TABLE 10-3: Operations and type of control

Operation	Type of Control
Calculate	Button
Print	Menu item
Clear	Menu item
Exit	Menu item
Check Name	Menu item
Find Video	Menu item

Once the type of control for each operation is decided, the next step is to decide on the number of main menu items under which the menu items will fall. Although we could put all five operations on the menu bar, this would quickly clutter it. Instead, we need to include the operations in submenus that are displayed whenever a menu bar item is selected. Of the five operations, the operations to print the transactions, clear the form, or to exit the project fall under the *File* main menu option, and the operations to check a member or to find a DVD fall under a menu bar item of *Members/DVDs*.

Table 10-4 shows the menu bar headings and the submenu items that will fall under each one.

TABLE 10-4: Main menu headings with submenu items

Menu Bar Item	Submenu Items
File	Print Clear Exit
Members/DVDs	Check Member Find DVD

> **TIP:** A rule of thumb is that frequently used operations should remain as buttons, since they are easier to find and click than menu items.

Using the MainMenu Control

Compared to many tasks that you've learned to do with VB .NET, creating a menu system is relatively easy. To get started, you simply add the **Main-Menu control** that is available in the Toolbox to your program. This control will then let you create your menu system visually in a similar manner to the way you created the rest of the user interface. To illustrate, we will work with our Vintage DVDs program to begin converting most of the buttons into menu options.

To add the MainMenu control to your program, double-click its icon in the Toolbox. When you do, your screen should appear like that shown in Figure 10-5. There are three things to notice in this figure. First, the Main-Menu control appears in the **component tray** below the application's form as the various database objects did in Chapter 9. You can tell that it is currently the selected object because it is surrounded by a dotted box. Second, a box has appeared with the words *Type Here* just below the title bar of the form. This box is known as the **Menu Designer,** and it is where you will begin to enter the menu headings and options. Third, the properties for the MainMenu control appear in the Properties Window. We will change the Name property of our MainMenu control to *mnuVintage*. The mnu prefix is commonly used when naming menus.

For the frmVintage form, we will create two menus: *File* and *Members/ DVDs*. The *File* menu will include the menu items *Print, Clear,* and *Exit*. The second menu will have the heading *Members/DVDs* and will include the menu items *Check Member* and *Find DVD*. These two menus will replace the functionality provided by some of buttons on the form.

To begin creating the menus, type *File* in the Menu Designer box to replace the words *Type Here*. Your menu designer will now appear as shown in Figure 10-6. When you do this, notice that your Properties Window changes to include more properties. In particular, the Name property is listed as *MenuItem1*. These properties are specific to the menu item that you have just entered. It turns out that the MainMenu control is an object that contains other objects. Each of the menu items that you add to the control are objects themselves with their own properties. We will explore some of these proper-

FIGURE 10-5.
Adding the
MainMenu control

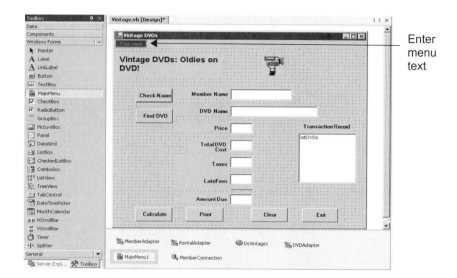

ties in the next section after we have added all of the menu items for this form. For now, we will use a Name property of *mnuFile*.

FIGURE 10-6.
Adding menus with
the Menu Designer

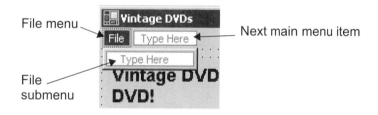

To continue building the File menu, click on the words *Type Here* just under the File menu and type the next command, *Print*. After typing the new menu item, change the name for the new item to *mnuPrint* in the Properties window. The results of typing this new menu item are shown in Figure 10-7. Notice that two new boxes have appeared, both filled with the words *Type Here*. The box below the Print menu item provides the next location for a new item to be added to the File menu. The box to right of the Print menu item provides a location for a submenu that can be accessed when the Print menu item is clicked.

As seen above, to add menu items to the MainMenu control simply type the name of the new item into the desired location on the control. In Figure 10-8 we see the results of adding all of the desired menu items for the frm-Vintage form.

Notice that there is a line, called a **separator,** in between the Clear and Exit menu items. A separator is easy enough to include in your menus. You simply need to type a dash (-) as the menu item text, as shown in Figure 10-9. Alternatively, in the Menu Designer, you can right-click the location where you want a separator bar and choose *New Separator*.

FIGURE 10-7.
Adding menu items

File|Print item

New file submenu item

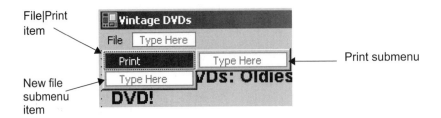

Print submenu

FIGURE 10-8. File menu items

FIGURE 10-9.
Adding a menu separator

> **TIP:** Separators make it much easier for the user to find groups of menu items with similar operations.

A couple of other tasks that are nice to know about when creating your menus is how to move or delete a menu item at design time. To move a menu within the Menu Designer, click the desired menu item and drag it to its new location. You can place it in a top-level menu position along the menu bar, insert it between other menu items on a menu, or add it as a new submenu of an existing menu item. To delete a menu item at design time, simply right-click the desired menu item in the Menu Designer, and choose Delete.

Setting Menu Properties

As mentioned above, each menu item that you add to the MainMenu control has its own set of properties. You can set these properties in the Properties window to control how the menu item will look and behave. The most commonly used properties of the menu item are listed in Table 10-5.

TABLE 10-5: Menu item properties

Property	Meaning
Name	Indicates the name used in code to identify the menu item
Text	The caption displayed by the menu item

TABLE 10-5: Menu item properties (Continued)

Property	Meaning
Checked	Indicates whether the menu item is checked
Enabled	Indicates whether the menu item is enabled
Shortcut	Indicates the keyboard shortcut for the menu item
ShowShortcut	Determines whether the shortcut for the menu item will be displayed
Visible	Indicates whether the item is visible

Besides the Name property, the Text property is the most commonly used property of the menu item. Although the Text property is usually set automatically as you add the items to the MainMenu control, there are a couple of special things that you can do with the Text property. We have already seen in Figure 10-9 how you can create a menu separator by entering a dash as the Text property for the menu item. Separator bars are used to group related commands within a menu and make menus easier to read. You can also use the Text property to set an Access key for the menu item.

Access keys allow the user to navigate menus from the keyboard. To add an access key to a menu item, enter an ampersand (&) prior to the letter in the Text property that you want to be underlined as the access key. For example, typing &File as the Text property of a menu item will result in a menu item that appears as File with the "F" underlined. To navigate to this menu item, the user can press **ALT** to give focus to the menu bar and then press the access key of the menu name, "F" in this case.

Another way to allow keyboard access to menu commands is through the use of shortcut keys. **Shortcut keys** are keyboard commands to access menu items within an application. To add a shortcut key to a menu item at design time, select the menu item within the Menu Designer. In the Properties window, set the Shortcut property to one of the values offered in the drop-down list. You can control whether or not the Shortcut key is visible on the menu by setting the ShowShortcut property. For example, you might set the Shortcut property of the Print submenu item to Ctrl+P. The user may then execute the Print submenu command by pressing the Ctrl and P keys simultaneously.

> **Tip:** Access and shortcut keys make working with menus easier for users who do not wish to remove their hands from the keyboard to use a mouse.

You may also wish to add check marks to your menus. **Check marks** can be used to designate whether a feature is turned on or off. Two methods are available for adding a check mark to a menu item at design time. With the menu item selected within the Menu Designer, click the area to the left of the menu item. A check mark will appear indicating that the Checked property has been set to true. Alternatively, with the menu item selected within the Menu Designer, set the Checked property to true in the Properties window.

Adding Code to Menu Items

Creating a menu system for a VB .NET application is just the first step in using menu items to execute procedures in response to events. The second step is to write the code for the menu item Click event procedure. This step is similar to that used to add code to the event procedures we discussed earlier. To display the corresponding default event procedure, you double-click the menu item to display the Code window. Keep in mind that there will be no code for menu bar items that have submenus; all of the code will be associated with the submenu items. For example, there will be no code for the mnuFile menu bar item, since it has a submenu. There will be code for mnuExit item, since it is a menu item with no additional submenu.

If the code being added to menu or submenu items contains totally new code, then the code is entered the same as for any other event. On the other hand, when an application like Vintage DVDs is being converted from using buttons or other controls to using a menu system, many of the code procedures for the buttons can be transferred to the menu items without having to be retyped.

Converting Event Procedures

In the Vintage DVDs application, the buttons are being converted to submenu items. Although we could retype the code for these event procedures, it is much more efficient to use the Editor capabilities of VB .NET to *cut and paste* the code from each button event procedure to the corresponding menu item event procedure. This entails a six-step process (all at design time):

1. Open the Code window by double-clicking the button for which the code is to be transferred.
2. Use the mouse to highlight the code for that event procedure. Do not include the first statement (starting with "Sub") and the last (*End Sub*) statements.
3. Cut the code using the *Edit | Cut* menu option (use *Ctrl+x* as a shortcut for this operation) and delete the first and last statements of the empty event procedure.
4. Open the Code window for the corresponding submenu item Click event by clicking it *once* or by just changing to the menu item in the Code window.
5. Paste the code into the submenu item Click event procedure using the *Edit | Paste* menu option (use *Ctrl+v* as a shortcut for this operation).
6. Delete the button control from the form.

For example, to transfer code from the Click event procedure for the *Find DVD* button to the Click event procedure for the *Find DVD* submenu item at design time, here are the six steps:

1. Open the btnFindDVD_Click Code window by double-clicking the *Find DVD* button.
2. Highlight the code for this event procedure with the mouse, as shown in Figure 10-10.
3. Use *Edit | Cut* to remove the highlighted code and delete the first and last statements of the now-empty event procedure.

4. Open the Code window for the mnuFindDVD procedure by clicking the *Members/DVDs* menu bar option and then clicking the *Find DVD* submenu option.

5. Use *Edit | Paste* to paste the code into the event procedure.

6. Display the frmVintage form, highlight the *Find DVD* button, and delete it.

These same operations should be carried out for the other buttons on the form.

FIGURE 10-10.
Highlighted code in btnFindDVD_Click() event procedure

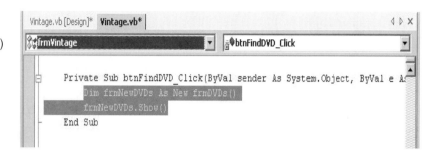

In addition to transferring code from button event procedures to menu item event procedures, we must revise any references to the button event procedures. To make sure that we find and revise all references to a control event procedure, we can use the *Edit | Replace* menu option to search for the button references and replace them with menu item references. A look at frmVintage after the buttons have been converted to menu items is shown in Figure 10-11.

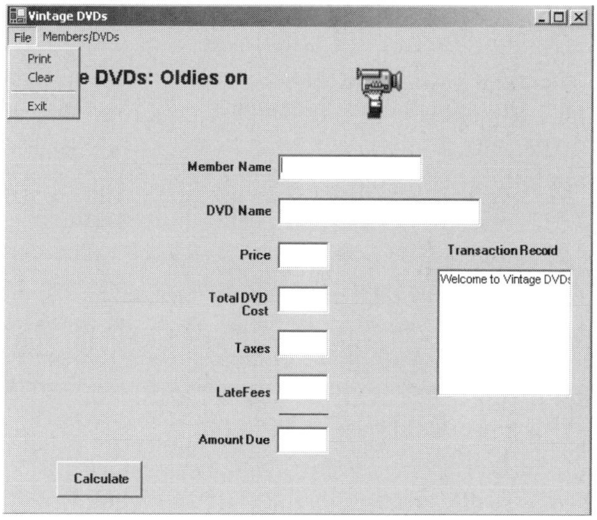

FIGURE 10-11.
frmVintage after conversion to menus

Step-by-Step Instructions 10-2: Adding menus to a VB .NET project

1. Start VB .NET (or use **File|Open|Project**) to open the Vintage DVD project from the folder **Vintage10.**

2. Double-click the MainMenu icon in the Toolbox to add a MainMenu control to the project in the component tray. Change the Name property of the control to mnuMain.

3. Add the menu items listed in Table 10-6 using the Menu Designer of the MainMenu control.

4. Set the properties of each menu item as shown in Table 10-6.

TABLE 10-6: Menus for frmVintage

Menu Name	Text	ShortCut
mnuFile	&File	None
mnuFilePrint	&Print	Ctrl+P
mnuFileClear	C&lear	F10
mnuFileSep1	-	None
mnuFileExit	E&xit	None
mnuMembersDVD	Members/DVD	None
mnuCheckMember	Check &Member	Ctrl+M
mnuFindDVD	Find &DVD	Ctrl+D

5. Using **Edit|Cut** and **Edit|Paste,** move the code from the Click event procedure for each button being converted to a menu item to the corresponding menu item Click event procedure.

6. Delete the buttons being converted from the form and adjust the look of the form as desired.

7. Browse through the code using **Edit|Replace** and change any references to button controls that have been deleted to the corresponding menu item.

8. Click the **Save All** icon to save the files in this project.

Mini-Summary 10-2: Using the MainMenu control

1. The MainMenu control makes it easy to create menu system for any VB .NET application by entering Text, a Name, and setting other properties for each menu item.

3. Access keys can be assigned by including an ampersand (&) in the Text property, and shortcut keys can be assigned by selecting from a drop-down list box.

4. Code can be added to a menu item Click event by double-clicking the menu item to open the Code Editor window.

It's Your Turn!

1. Why would we replace buttons with a menu system?

2. What are the menu options that most often appear in a Windows-based menu system?

3. What is the difference between access and shortcut keys?

4. What shortcut keys are standard for Windows applications?

5. Follow Step-By-Step Instructions 10-2 to add menus to frmVintage.

6. Run your project and test the menus.

USING DIRECT ACCESS FILES

As mentioned in the introduction, this chapter serves two purposes: first, to make it possible for you to improve the security and the look and feel of your VB .NET projects, which you accomplished in the two previous sections; second, to introduce you to the use of direct access files and graphics, which will be discussed in this section and the next. To start with, a **direct** (or **random**) **access file** is a new type of data file in which data are assumed to be stored as fixed-length records. It has similarities to both types of data files that we have discussed so far, sequential access files and database files, but has distinct differences as well. Direct access files are similar to sequential access files because they can be read and written to directly from VB .NET. On the other hand, direct access files are similar to database files in that the data are stored as records that can be accessed directly. Direct access files are different from sequential files, since data in a sequential access file is stored in the same order that they were written, and they are read back in that same order. It is not possible with a sequential access file to access a record of data directly, making it cumbersome to use when the order of processing records on a file differs from the order in which those records are physically stored or when records are being added or deleted during the processing. On the other hand, although data can be accessed directly using database files, they require a separate database engine and language like SQL.

To understand the use of direct access files, recall the Vintage DVDs Payroll application from Chapter 8, in which we used UDTs to work with employee data. In that application, it was possible to load employee data from a sequential access file, display it in a list box, process employees to calculate gross and net pay, add new employees, and save new employee data back to the sequential access file. Although a sequential access file worked for this application, given the use of fields and records in this application, storing the data in a direct access file is more appropriate. In fact, the UDT structure matches up so closely to direct access files that it is sometimes referred to as a *record type*. For that reason, we will store the payroll data in a direct access file.

Pictorially, a direct access file would appear as shown in Figure 10-12. Note the similarity to a table in a database file with records and fields. Note also that all records in a direct access file are assumed to have the same fields and to be of the same size. To make sure that records are the same size, we will need to adjust our user-defined type to include fixed-length strings. Direct access files are so named because the user can access any record on this type of file directly, without going through any other records.

FIGURE 10-12.
Depiction of the
direct access file

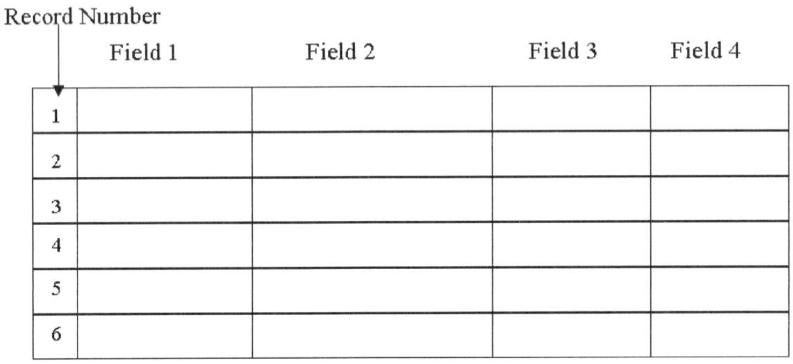

The key parameter for a direct access file is the **record number.** This is a positive integer value that is assigned to the record when it is written onto the file. Once a record is written onto a file with a given record number, it can always be identified for processing. The record number of a direct access file is analogous to the subscript on a one-dimensional array, in which each record corresponds to an element in the array. Although the order of the records on a direct access file is the same as the order of their record numbers, any record, regardless of its physical position, can be written, read, or rewritten by having the user simply specify its record number. Given the flexibility and ease of use of the direct access file, we will use it to save the records created in the employee payroll system to secondary storage.

You are probably asking yourself, Why not use a database? Although a database provides major advantages and is a requirement for many applications, there are times when we would prefer not to become involved in working with one. For example, the amount of data that we want to store may not justify the extensive design requirements needed for a full database. Or, we might want to quickly create a **prototype** information system that has some of the features of a database system but without the effort to write the required SQL. In both cases, the direct access file system can work quite well. The payroll example is a case where we are only storing a few records (Vintage DVDs has less than 10 employees), so a direct access file will be used.

UDTs Revisited

Recall that UDTs in Visual Basic are made up of elements, where each element is declared to be a standard data type (String, Integer, and so on) or a previously declared UDT. Also recall that the Structure statement is used to create a UDT. The current Structure statement that defined the EmpRecord UDT is shown in VB Code Box 10-2.

The EmpRecord structure works fine when simply working with the information in memory, but it requires some changes if we wish to use that structure when storing the data in a direct access file. As stated above, all records in a direct access file are assumed to have the same fields and to be

VB Code Box 10-2.
EmpRecord UDT
	``
	Structure EmpRecord
	  Public strFName As String
	  Public strLName As String
	  Public strSSNum As String
	  Public strPhone As String
	  Public strPaytype As String
	  Public decPayRate As Decimal
	End Structure
	``

of the same size. Although all data stored using the current EmpRecord structure will have the same six fields, we cannot guarantee that they will require the same storage size.

Remember from our discussion of data types in an earlier chapter that the amount of storage used by a variable is determined by its data type. We saw that the numeric data types each have a fixed amount of storage used no matter what variable value is stored. This is not the case with a String variable. With the String data type, the amount of storage required is based on the number of characters. Each character will require about 1 byte of storage. For example, assume we have a variable strName that currently holds the value *Nicolas.* Then strName will require about 7 bytes of storage, one byte for each character. If we changed the value of strName to *Nick,* it would then use only 4 bytes of storage since this string has only four characters in it. So to ensure that each record is the same size using the EmpRecord UDT, we need a way to make sure each String variable uses a constant length, that is, a **fixed-length string.** Fortunately, VB .NET provides us with a way to define fixed-length strings. To declare a fixed-length string, we use a statement of the following form:

<VBFixedString(n)> Public *VariableName* **As String**

In this statement, the value n determines how many characters will be used to store a value. If the value to be stored is less than n, spaces will be added to the end of the value to make a string of length n. If the value to be stored is greater than n, the value will be truncated after the nth character. Obviously, if the variable is being declared at the form or procedure level, we would substitute *Dim* for *Public* in the declaration statement. For example, to declare publicly the String variable strFName to be a fixed-length string variable holding 15 characters, the declaration statement would be

```
<VBFixedString(15)> Public strFName As String
```

In declaring a fixed-length string, it is important to choose an appropriate value for n in each declaration statement. For some data, such as phone numbers or social security numbers, you can choose a value that matches exactly the number of characters you will need to store. For others, such as names of people or cities, you may need to estimate a value that is higher than the largest value that you might want to store.

To adjust the EmpRecord UDT for our application, we simply need to convert all of the String variables to fixed-length strings. Recall that this is carried out in a module in which we also declare the array udtEmployees to be of the data type EmpRecord and use it in our processing. The result is shown in VB Code Box 10-3.

VB CODE BOX 10-3.
EmpRecord UDT with
fixed-length strings
	``
	Module structures
	    Structure EmpRecord
	        <VBFixedString(15)> Public strFName As String
	        <VBFixedString(20)> Public strLName As String
	        <VBFixedString(11)> Public strSSNum As String
	        <VBFixedString(12)> Public strPhone As String
	        <VBFixedString(10)> Public strPaytype As String
	        Public decPayRate As Decimal
	    End Structure
	    Public udtEmployees(), udtCurrentEmp As EmpRecord
	    Public intEmpCntr, intCurrEmp As Integer
	End Module
	``

Creating a Direct Access File

Creating a direct access file in VB .NET is very similar to creating a sequential access file. The major difference is the manner is which we store and retrieve information from the file. With direct access files we use the **FilePut** command to write data to the file. When data or information is being retrieved from a direct access file, we use the **FileGet** command.

In either case—adding data to or retrieving data from a direct access file—the file must first be opened, just as was done with sequential access files. The **FileOpen** statement for a direct access file has the following form:

FileOpen(*FileNumber, FileName,* **OpenMode.Random,** _
OpenAccess.*Access,* **OpenShare.***ShareMode, RecordLength*)

where the various parameters for this FileOpen statement are described in Table 10-7.

TABLE 10-7: FileOpen parameters for a direct access file

Parameter	Possible Values	Explanation
File Number	1–255 (Use FreeFile function)	Same as with sequential access file
File Name	Any valid file name	Same as with sequential access file
OpenMode.*Type*	Random	Declares this to be a direct (random) access file
OpenAccess.*Access*	Read, Write, or ReadWrite but most common value is ReadWrite	Determines whether the file is being read from, written to, or both
OpenShare.*ShareMode*	Shared, Lock Read, Lock Write, or Lock ReadWrite but most common value is Shared	Determines the operations restricted on the open file to other processes
Recordlength	The number of bytes required to write a record to storage	The same for all records

In regard to the *FileNumber* parameter, once you start working with multiple files at the same time, you may not always be able to recall which file numbers have already been used. To help you with this, the **FreeFile function** returns the next available file number. By setting an Integer variable (intFileNum) equal to the FreeFile function and using it everywhere we would have had to use a value for the file number, we no longer have to worry about what actual file number is being used.

Similarly, rather than having to determine the *Recordlength* parameter manually, we can rely on the VB .NET Len() function, which returns the number of bytes required to store a variable or record. For example, since Len(udtEmp) returns the number of bytes in the variable udtEmp, which was declared to be an EmpRecord data type, we can open a direct access file to store the employee records created by the employee payroll system discussed earlier with the statements shown in VB Code Box 10-4. Note that the FileName parameter is equal to strFileName, which must be assigned prior to opening the file. We will discuss that more shortly.

VB CODE BOX 10-4. Code to open a direct access file	`intFileNum = FreeFile()`
	`FileOpen(intFileNum, strFileName, OpenMode.Random, _`
	`OpenAccess.ReadWrite, OpenShare.Shared, Len(udtEmp))`

The **FileClose(***FileNumber***)** statement is used to close a direct access file, just as it was for sequential access files. The value used for FileNumber should be the same for both the FileOpen and FileClose commands as well as for other commands that work with the file.

Once a direct access file is opened, the next step is to write data on the file. As mentioned earlier, this is accomplished with the **FilePut** command, which has the following form:

FilePut(*file number, variable name, record number***)**

where the *record number* parameter is optional. The first record in a file is at record number 1, the second record is at record number 2, and so on. If you omit the record number, the next record after the last FileGet or FilePut command is written. If the length of the data being written is greater than the length specified in the RecordLength clause of the FileOpen function, an error message will be generated that will need to be caught with the *Try-Catch* error-checking mechanism. For example, to write the udtEmployees array to the direct access file opened earlier, the statements are shown in VB Code Box 10-5, where we use For-Next loop to put each record in the array udtEmployees to the direct access file. The counter, intCurrent, is increased by one to become the record number, since record numbers start with one, whereas array indices start with zero.

VB CODE BOX 10-5. For-Next loop to write records to file	`For intCurrent = 0 To intEmpCntr - 1`
	`  FilePut(intFileNum, udtEmployees(intCurrent), intCurrent + 1)`
	`Next`
	`FileClose(intFileNum)`

Retrieving Data from a Direct Access File

For records on a direct access file to be useful, they must be retrievable. As with writing to the file, the file must first be opened with the FileOpen statement. The records then are retrieved with the FileGet command, the form of which is shown below:

FileGet(*file number, variable name, record number***)**

where the parameters are the same as with the FilePut command. As with the FilePut command, the record number is optional. If we are retrieving records in sequence and the record number parameter is omitted, the next record in order is retrieved.

Just as the FilePut statement is often found in a loop, so too is the FileGet statement since we must retrieve the records one-at-a-time. For example, to retrieve records from the file that was opened and written to in VB Code Box 10-4 and VB Code Box 10-5, the necessary code is shown in VB Code Box 10-6 (assuming that the strFileName variable has had a value assigned to it and that the udtEmployees() array has been appropriately declared and dimensioned).

| **VB CODE BOX 10-6.** For-Next loop to read records from file | ```intFileNum = FreeFile()
FileOpen(intFileNum, strFileName, OpenMode.Random, _
OpenAccess.ReadWrite, OpenShare.Shared, Len(udtEmp))
For intCurrent = 0 To intEmpCntr - 1
  FileGet(intFileNum, udtEmployees(intCurrent), intCurrent + 1)
Next
FileClose(intFileNum)``` |
| --- | --- |

Step-by-Step Instructions 10-3: Direct access files

1. Use Windows Explorer to create a folder named **Payroll10** in the **Chapter10** folder, and use Windows Explorer to *copy* all of the folders from the *Chapter8\Payroll* folder into this new folder.

2. Convert the Payroll form to use menus instead of buttons by adding **File** and **Employee** main menu options. Use the menu items shown in Table 10-8 with the underlined letters indicating access keys for each menu item.

TABLE 10-8: Menu properties for payroll application

File Menu Items	Name	Employee Menu Items	Name
Open	mnuFileOpen	Employee Information	mnuEmpInfo
Save	mnuFileSave	Add Employee	mnuEmpAdd
Save As	mnuFileSaveAs	Delete Employee	mnuEmpDel
Print	mnuFilePrint		
Separator			
Exit	mnuFileExit		

3. Convert all the code for items that were previously buttons from button Click event procedures to menu item event procedures.

4. Convert the structure of the EmpRecord UDT to include fixed-length strings, as shown in VB Code Box 10-3.

Mini-Summary 10-3: Direct access files

1. A direct (or random) access file is a record-oriented file in which records can be accessed and manipulated in any order through their record number.

2. Direct access files are opened with the FileOpen statement, with the record length being defined by the Len( ) function.

3. The FilePut statement is used to write records to a direct access file, and the FileGet statement is used to read records from the file.

It's Your Turn!

1. How does a direct access file differ from a sequential access file? Why is it often also referred to as a random access file?

2. Why do we need the record number and record length parameters when working with a direct access file?

3. What statement is used to write information to a direct access file? Read information from it?

4. Assume that each of the following statements applies to the same program. Also, assume that the following data type has been declared with a record length of 78 bytes.

```
Public Type Speaker
  <VBFixedString(15)> strFName as String
  <VBFixedString(25)> strLName as String
  <VBFixedString(30)> strTopic as String
  dtmLectureDate as Date
End Type
```

a. Write a statement that opens the file Schedule.rnd for random access. Each record uses the Speaker UDT.

b. Write a statement that retrieves the 34th record from the file Schedule.rnd. The values retrieved should be assigned to the variable udtGuest that has been declared as data type Speaker.

c. Write a statement that writes the values stored in the variable udtGuest that has been declared as data type Speaker to the next available location in the file Schedule.dat

4. Why do we use fixed-length strings in the UDT that is being stored in a direct access file?

5. Follow Step-by-Step Instructions 10-3 to convert the payroll application to use menus and to convert the EmpRecord UDT to use fixed-length strings.

USING FILE DIALOG BOXES

In this section, we will discuss the use of direct access files for saving and retrieving payroll data. To do this, we will continue the payroll application started in Chapter 8 and modified in the previous section. We will start our discussion on how to save the employee payroll records that we have cre-

Saving Records to Direct Access Files

ated in the payroll application and then move to retrieving the saved records and displaying them in the list box. In both cases, you should already have converted the payroll application to use menus and to fixed-length strings.

Saving the data to a direct access file in the payroll application should be possible with either the *File | Save As...* or *File | Save* or menu options, with the difference being that with the first option, we need to display a dialog box automatically so the user can enter a file name or change the file name. In the second case, the file will be saved under an existing file name (if one exists), or a dialog box will be displayed if no file name exists. In either case, we need to do three things:

1. Add a form-level String variable *(strFileName)* that saves the name of the file (if one exists).
2. Add a form-level Boolean variable *(blnSaved)* that indicates whether the file has been saved or not after it has been changed.
3. Add a new control, the **SaveFileDialog** control that enables us to select a filename from a list of existing files or enter a new name for a file.

The first two items are straightforward, so we will concentrate on the use of the SaveFileDialog control, since it will be required for the *Save As* option. This control is in the Toolbox, but you will probably have to scroll down to find it. When added to the form, it is displayed in the component tray just like the Database and MainMenu controls you added earlier. When added, it has a name of *SaveFileDialog1,* indicating that it is an instance of the SaveFileDialog object. The name can be changed using the Property window to a more manageable one, such as *dlgSave.*

Once we have added the SaveFileDialog control to the form and renamed it, we need to add code to the appropriate submenu item Click event to *connect* the event to the FileSaveDialog control. This is accomplished with the **ShowDialog** method of the control. For example, to display the dlgSave dialog box to save a file, the instruction is

```
dlgSave.ShowDialog()
```

Before using the ShowDialog method to connect the common dialog control to a form, we need to display a list of file types from which the user can select a type to save the file as. This is done with the **Filter** property of the SaveFileDialog box with the following syntax:

dlgName.Filter = "description1 | filter1 | description2 | filter2 | etc."

where *descriptionN* is a description of the file type (All Files, Text files, and so on), and *filterN* is the actual filter (*.*, *.txt, and so on) for the *Nth* description and filter. Also, the pipe symbol (|) is required to separate descriptions and filter strings. For example, the filter instruction to display all types of files and text files for the dlgSave dialog control is

```
dlgSave.Filter = "All files(*.*)|*.*|Data files(*.dat)|*.dat"
```

To indicate the default type of file—that is, the type that the file will automatically be saved as a certain type—we use the **FilterIndex** property (this is also the type of file that is displayed in the dialog box). This property has the following form:

*dlgName.*FilterIndex = *N*

where *N* equals the number of the type of file in the Filter property statement. For example, to make text files the default file type for the dlgMemo common dialog control, the statement is

```
dlgSave.FilterIndex = 2
```

where data files are the second file type in the filter statement.

If the three statements shown in VB Code Box 10-7 are included in the mnuFileSaveAs_Click event procedure, a File|Save As dialog box similar to the one shown in Figure 10-13 will be displayed. Note in the figure that we are creating a new file named *Employees.dat* in the bin folder of the project.

VB CODE BOX 10-7. Code to set up Filter property	```dlgSave.Filter = "All Files (*.*)|*.*|Data Files(*.dat)|*.dat"```
	```dlgSave.FilterIndex = 2```
	```dlgSave.ShowDialog()```

FIGURE 10-13. Save As dialog box

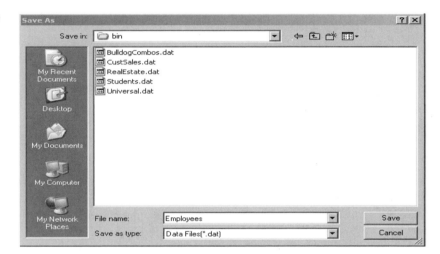

Note also in Figure 10-13 that only files with a .dat extension are shown in the list box. Users can select one of these files as the file name for the memo, thereby writing over the previous contents, or they can enter a new file name in the File Name text box at the bottom of the dialog box. Finally, note that the *Save as type* drop-down list box shows that the file will be saved as a data file.

Once we have entered a file name in the File Name text box, either by typing or by selecting an existing file, this becomes the **FileName** property for the SaveFileDialog control. If we assign a String variable, *strFileName*, to the FileName property of the dialog control, it can be used in the FileOpen statement. The String variable, strFileName, should be declared at the form level so that the name of the file can be shared by the Save, SaveAs, and Open event procedures.

Error Checking

Handling errors is especially important when opening and closing files. Common errors occur when users attempt to open a file that does not exist or when they try to open a file on a diskette that is not in the drive. We need to anticipate file errors and include code to handle related problems when they occur. In our case, there are two types of errors to check for: errors in with an existing file with the same filename and errors in the FileOpen process. In the first case, we need to check for the existence of a file with the same name and, if there is one, delete it to avoid any file conflicts. In the second case, we can use a the Try-Catch structure like that discussed in Chapter 9 to check for errors.

The first type of error with an existing file could occur in the Payroll example because we are writing the entire udtEmployees array to the file each time the procedure executes. This action could result in a logical error if deleted records remain in the file to be reloaded the next time that the file is used. In order to prevent this logical error, we need to clear out the stored values before saving the new array values to the file. To do so, we first need to check to see if the file exists and, if it does, use the **Kill function** to remove it. The file will be recreated when the FileOpen statment is executed.

To carry out both of these operations, we need to create a new type of object: the **FileInfo object.** The FileInfo class is useful for retrieving information about a file, such as its existence, path, or memory size. To make the FileInfo class available to the project, we need to import the **System.IO namespace** of which it is a member. To do this we need to add the following statement at the form level:

```
Imports System.IO
```

To actually use the class, we then declare an object variable to be an instance of the class with the following statement:

```
Dim objFileInfo As New FileInfo(strFileName)
```

This declaration should be made after a value has been assigned to the str-FileName variable from the FileName property of the SaveFileDialog control.

Once the instance of the object has been created, we can use its *Exists* property to check whether the file already exists and, if it does, use the Kill function to remove it. The statements to carry out this operation are shown in VB Code Box 10-8. If the file does not exist or it has been deleted, we may go ahead and open the file with the FileOpen statement.

VB Code Box 10-8. Checking for existence of file and deleting it	`If objFileInfo.Exists Then`
	`    Kill(strFileName)`
	`End If`

To use the Try-Catch structure to check for errors in the FileOpen statement, we attempt to open the file after the Try statement. The Catch statement is used when an error occurs and will display a message to the user and exit the event procedure as shown in VB Code Box 10-9. If no errors are found, the file is created, and the file is closed with the FileClose statement.

VB Code Box 10-9. Using the Try-Catch structure to avoid file errors	`Try`
	`    FileOpen(1, strFileName, OpenMode.Random, _`
	`    OpenAccess.ReadWrite, OpenShare.Shared, Len(udtEmp))`
	`Catch x As System.ArgumentOutOfRangeException`
	`    MsgBox("Error in opening file", "Vintage DVDs Payroll")`
	`    Exit Sub`
	`End Try`

Putting It All Together

So far in this section and the last, we have shown you a number of code segments to use in creating a new direct access file. The next step is to put all of them together in a single sub procedure named *SaveAs* that is shown in VB Code Box 10-10. We put this code in a sub procedure so we can call it from multiple event procedures.

In this code, notice that we chose to include the record number in the FilePut statement, but this was not required. If we had left it out, each udtEmployee array value would be written to the end of the current direct access file immediately after the last record written to the file. Once the file is saved, a form-level Boolean variable *blnSaved* is set equal to True. This variable will be used in the mnuFileExit event procedure to determine if the data file has been saved before closing the project.

VB CODE BOX 10-10. Code to save a direct access file	

```
Private Sub SaveAs()
    Dim udtEmp As EmpRecord, intCurrent, intFileNum As Integer
    dlgSave.Filter() = "All Files(*.*)|*.*|Datailes(*.dat)|*.dat"
    dlgSave.FilterIndex() = 2
    dlgSave.ShowDialog()
    strFileName = dlgSave.FileName
    Dim objFileInfo As New FileInfo(strFileName)
    If objFileInfo.Exists Then
        Kill(strFileName)
    End If
    Try
        intFileNum = FreeFile()
        FileOpen(intFileNum, strFileName, OpenMode.Random, _
        OpenAccess.ReadWrite, OpenShare.Shared, Len(udtEmp))
    Catch x As System.ArgumentOutOfRangeException
        MsgBox("Error in opening file", "Vintage DVDs Payroll")
        Exit Sub
    End Try
    For intCurrent = 0 To intEmpCntr - 1
        FilePut(1, udtEmployees(intCurrent), intCurrent + 1)
    Next
    blnSaved = True
    FileClose(intFileNum)
End Sub
```

Saving a File

The purpose of the *File|Save* menu option in the Payroll application is to save the current direct access file using the name under which it was previously opened or saved as. The code to handle this operation is much like that for the *File|Save As* operation, except that there is no need to display the Save As dialog box because the file name is already known. (Recall that the file name was saved earlier as the form-level String variable *strFileName*.) However, there can be a problem: What happens if a user tries to use the Save procedure when the file has not been previously given a name in the Save As operation? Since the variable strFileName has nothing in it, this will generate an error. One way to avoid this error is to check whether the file named strFileName exists using the objFileInfo object in the same way we did in the SaveAs sub procedure. If it does exist, then the previous version of the file needs to be deleted with the Kill function. On the other hand, if the file does not exist, then the SaveAs sub procedure is called, and the user can enter a file name using the Save As dialog box. The complete mnuFileSave_Click() is shown in VB Code Box 10-11, where we have used the Try-Catch structure to ensure the file is opened properly. Also, as in the SaveAs sub procedure, the form-level Boolean variable *blnSaved* is set to True to indicate that the file has been saved.

| **VB CODE BOX 10-11.** Code to write text to a file | ```
Private Sub mnuFileSave_Click(ByVal sender As System.Object, _
ByVal e As System.EventArgs) Handles mnuFileSave.Click
    Dim udtEmp As EmpRecord, intCurrent, intFileNum As Integer
    Dim objFileInfo As New FileInfo(strFileName)
    If objFileInfo.Exists Then
        Kill(strFileName)
    Else
        Saveas()
        Exit Sub
    End If
    intFileNum = FreeFile()
    Try
        FileOpen(intFileNum, strFileName, OpenMode.Random, _
        OpenAccess.ReadWrite, OpenShare.Shared, Len(udtEmp))
    Catch x As ArgumentOutOfRangeException
        MsgBox("Error in opening file", "Vintage DVDs Payroll")
        Exit Sub
    End Try
    For intCurrent = 0 To intEmpCntr - 1
        FilePut(intFileNum, udtEmployees(intCurrent), intCurrent+1)
    Next
    blnSaved = True
    FileClose(intFileNum)
End Sub
``` |
| --- | --- |

Retrieving Data from a Direct Access File

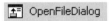

Opening an existing file involves adding the **OpenFileDialog control** to the project and renaming to *dlgOpen* in our case. The ShowDialog method of this control will display an Open File dialog box in which an existing file can be highlighted or a file name entered and the strFileName variable assigned to the Filename property of the control. If the user tries to open a blank file name in the Open File dialog box, nothing happens. The user must either select or enter a file name to open the dialog box or click the *Cancel* button to close it.

Much of the code to display the Open File dialog box is the same as that for the Save As operation, with the same Filter and FilterIndex property statements being used. The key difference is that the contents of the file are input from the file to an array and displayed in a list box instead of being written to a file. The resulting Open File dialog box is shown in Figure 10-14, where we have selected the file we created earlier, *Employees.dat,* as the file to open.

In our case, the objective is to input the employee records, add them to the udtEmployees() array, and display them in the lstEmployees list box. If the number of records on the file is known, a For-Next loop can be used to retrieve them. Fortunately, just as the record length can be determined with the Len function, the total length of the file (in bytes) can be found with the **LOF** (length of file) **function.** Once this value is known, we can find the number of records on the file by using integer division to divide the LOF value by the record length as returned by the Len function. For example, if
```

FIGURE 10-14.
Dialog box to open
a file

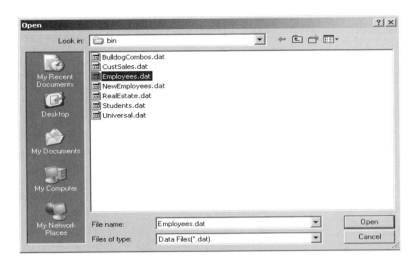

the LOF value is 1,000 and the record length value is 100, then there are 1,000\100 = 10 records on the file. The number of employees, intEmpCntr, is also set equal to this value.

Using the number of records on the file, which we found by using the LOF and Len functions, we can input each one, add it to the udtEmployees( ) array, and display it in the lstEmployees list box in a For-Next loop. We use the Spacer function described in Chapter 8 to control the format of each line added to the list box. The code to open a file and read it into the udtEmp array and the lstEmployees list box is shown in VB Code Box 10-12.

In looking at the mnuFileOpen_Click event procedure, note that after the Filter and FilterIndex properties are set, the ShowDialog method is compared to the Cancel property of the DialogResult object. If this comparison is true, the user clicked the *Cancel* button on the dialog box and the event procedure should be terminated. Next, the file name and number are determined, and the Try-Catch structure is used to open and read from the file into the udtEmp array and the list box. This includes first determining the number of records in the file. The result of opening the *Employees.dat* file, which we created earlier, is shown in Figure 10-15.

Using the blnSaved Variable

We noted that the blnSaved Boolean variable would be useful to inform us whether or not a file has been saved and suggested that it be declared at the form level with an initial value of *True*. We have already added statements to the mnuFileSave and mnuFileSaveAs event procedures to set this variable to True so that we know the file has been saved. We also need to add statements to the mnuEmpAdd and mnuEmpDel event procedures because data are changed in those procedures, and whenever data are changed, the user needs to be alerted whenever they initiate the process to exit the project. To do this, we first need to add the statement

```
blnSaved = False
```

at the end of the procedures where employee records are added or deleted.

Next, we need to check the status of the blnSaved variable in the mnuFileExit_Click event procedure. If it is true, nothing is required since either the data are unchanged during the execution of the project or, if the

| VB CODE BOX 10-12. Code to read records from a direct access file | ```
Private Sub mnuFileOpen_Click(ByVal sender As System.Object, _
ByVal e As System.EventArgs) Handles mnuFileOpen.Click
    Dim udtEmp As EmpRecord, strItem As String
    Dim intCurrent intNumEmp, intFileNum As Integer
    dlgOpen.Filter() = "All Files(*.*)|*.*|Data Files(*.dat)|*.dat"
    dlgOpen.FilterIndex() = 2
    If dlgOpen.ShowDialog() = DialogResult.Cancel Then
        Exit Sub
    End If
    strFileName = dlgOpen.FileName
    intFileNum = FreeFile()
    Try
        FileOpen(intFileNum, strFileName, OpenMode.Random, _
        OpenAccess.ReadWrite, OpenShare.Shared, Len(udtEmp))
        intEmpCntr = LOF(1) / Len(udtEmp)
        lstEmployees.Items.Clear()
        For intNumEmp = 0 To intEmpCntr - 1
          FileGet(1, udtEmp, intNumEmp + 1)
          ReDim Preserve udtEmployees(intNumEmp)
          udtEmployees(intNumEmp) = udtEmp
          strItem = Spacer(Trim(udtEmp.strLName), 15)
          strItem = strItem & Spacer(Trim(udtEmp.strFName), 15) & Chr(9)
          strItem = strItem & Spacer(Trim(udtEmp.strPhone), 15) & Chr(9)
          strItem = strItem & udtEmp.strPaytype & Chr(9)
          lstEmployees.Items.Add(strItem)
        Next
        lblNumberofEmployees.Text = "Number of Employees: " & intEmpCntr
    Catch x As System.ArgumentOutOfRangeException
        MsgBox("File Open Error: Please check that the file exists", _
        MsgBoxStyle.Critical, "File Open Error")
    Finally
        FileClose(intFileNum)
    End Try
End Sub
``` |
|---|---|

FIGURE 10-15.
Result of opening the Employees.dat file

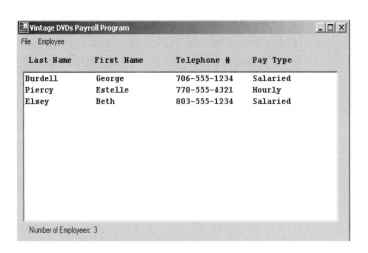

data are changed, the file has been saved. If it is false, then we need to call the SaveAs sub procedure so the user can save it prior to exiting and losing the changes. The statements to do this are shown in VB Code Box 10-13, where we first check the value of blnSaved. If it is false, then we ask the user
```

if they want to save their changes to the data. If they answer in the affirmative, then the SaveAs sub procedure is called; otherwise, the project is exited without saving the data.

| VB CODE BOX 10-13. Modified mnuFileExit event procedure | ```
Private Sub mnuFileExit_Click(ByVal sender As System.Object, _
ByVal e As System.EventArgs) Handles mnuFileExit.Click
    Dim strSaveData As String
    If Not blnSaved Then
        strSaveData = InputBox("Save changes to data?", _
        "Vintage DVDs Payroll System")
        If UCase(strSaveData) = "Y" Then
            SaveAs()
        End If
    End If
    End
End Sub
``` |
|---|---|

■ ■

Step-by-Step Instructions 10-4: Using file dialog boxes

1. If it is not already started, start VB .NET and retrieve the payroll application project from the Chapter10 folder.

2. Add the statement **Imports System.IO** at the form level of the frmPayroll form so that your project may use the FileInfo class to check for the existence of a file.

3. Declare a String variable, **strFileName,** and a Boolean variable, **blnSaved,** at the form level of the frmPayroll form. Initialize blnSaved to be **True.**

4. Double-click the mnuFileSaveAs menu option and enter the code shown in VB Code Box 10-10 to save employee payroll data to a *new* direct access data file.

5. Double-click the mnuFileSave menu option and enter the code shown in VB Code Box 10-11 to save an existing employee payroll data file over a previous version of the same file.

6. Double-click the mnuFileOpen menu option and enter the code shown in VB Code Box 10-11 to read employee data from an existing direct access file.

7. Edit the mnuEmpAdd and mnuEmpDel click event procedures to add the statement

```
blnSaved = False
```
at the end of each procedure. This will alert us that the data has changed and needs to be saved.

8. Modify the mnuFileExit_Click event procedure to the statements shown in VB Code Box 10-13 to check the status of blnSaved and save the data if the user wishes.

9. Click the **Save All** icon to save the files in this project.
```

Mini-Summary 10-4: Using file dialog boxes

1. To save data to a new direct access file, we use the SaveFileDialog control to find an existing file name or to enter a new name. The ShowDialog method of the control displays a dialog box that can be used to save a file.

2. The Filter and FilterIndex properties of the SaveFileDialog control are useful for displaying specific file types in the dialog box.

3. The FileInfo class in the System.IO namespace makes information about file and file operations available to us. In particular, we can determine if a file exists and delete it if so desired.

4. The OpenFileDialog control is useful for opening an existing direct access file to retrieve data.

5. We can find the number of records in a direct access file by dividing the number of bytes in the file, which is found through the LOF( ) function, by the length of one record.

6. File errors are common, which makes it particularly important to write code to handle file exceptions.

It's Your Turn!

1. Why do we need to import the System.IO namespace to work with direct access files?

2. Why do we need to declare a Boolean variable that informs us whether or not the file has been saved?

3. What is the difference between the Save and Save As menu options? Why do we call the SaveAs sub procedure from within the mnuFileSave_Click event procedure?

4. Why do we need both the Len and LOF functions to work with direct access files.

5. Follow Step-By-Step Instructions 10-4 to be able to store employee information in direct access files using the Payroll Application.

6. Run the project and, after correcting any errors, repeatedly use the Employee|Add Employee menu option to add the data shown in Figure 10-15 to the list box. Now try to use the File|Save menu option. What happens? Go ahead and save the data as Employees.dat (no need to enter the file extension as it will be added by the dialog box).

7. Use the Employee|Delete Employee option to delete one of the employees, and then attempt to exit the program without saving the data. What happens? Do not save the data, and exit the program.

8. Start the program again and use the File|Open option to retrieve the data you saved earlier as Employees.dat. Now repeat the above exercise, but add a new employee and attempt to exit without saving. In this case, go ahead and save the data and then exit.

WORKING WITH GRAPHICS OBJECTS

As you have seen in previous chapters of this book, lists and tables are very useful in displaying numeric and textual information. However, they do not always do a good job of helping a business decision maker find trends or make comparisons between groups of numbers, especially when there are a large number of values to consider. On the other hand, **graphics** are very useful for handling data or information visually. Mathematicians and scientists have been using graphics for years to display equations. Similarly, engineers use graphics to design a wide variety of machines and structures using CAD (computer-aided design) graphics, and artists use graphics to create images for both business and artistic purposes. Graphics are also an important part of improving the aesthetics and user-friendliness of the user interface.

VB .NET offers the capability to create a wide variety of graphics. For instance, you have already seen the use of the image control to display a logo for Vintage DVDs. It is also possible to include a variety of shapes or to draw freehand pictures in a VB .NET project. Animated graphics are also possible with VB .NET.

In this section, we will discuss the object classes provided by VB .NET. These classes allow you to declare objects that you can use to create custom graphics for your projects. These tools are primarily provided in the **System.Drawing** namespace of the FCL. The System.Drawing namespace also contains special object classes that can be used for printing both text and graphics. We will see how we can use these printing objects to preview and print formatted output from our applications.

Introducing GDI+

VB .NET provides tools for you to create graphics by using an implementation of the Windows graphics design interface (GDI) called **GDI+**. GDI+ provides classes that allow you to create vector graphics, draw text, and manipulate graphical images. A **vector graphic** is represented by a set of mathematical properties called vectors rather than as a grid of pixels. **Vectors** describe the graphic's size, properties, and position. Vector graphics are most often used for items that can be represented by line drawings, such as simple pictures and charts. Vector graphics will typically incorporate lines, shapes, colors, and text that are drawn on the background of a control. You can use GDI+ to draw graphics on Windows forms and controls.

You can get access to GDI+ basic graphics functionality with the classes that are available in the System.Drawing namespace mentioned above. Objects created from the **Graphics** class provide methods for drawing to the forms or controls of your project. The **Pen** class can be used to draw lines or curves, and the **Brush** class can be used to fill the interiors of shapes. The System.Drawing namespace also includes other classes that we will use to create various shapes, specify the color of graphics, and set the font of the text. To gain access to System.Drawing classes, we need to reference the namespace in our project using the following statement:

```
Imports System.Drawing
```

Be sure to place this statement at the beginning of the code for your form.

Once the Graphics class is available to us, there are two main steps to create graphics on a VB .NET control:

1. Create a Graphics object using the Graphics class.

2. Use the Graphics object to draw lines, shapes, text, or images.
The Graphics object is the primary object that is used to create graphical images. You can think of the Graphics object as representing a GDI+ drawing surface.

When we want to create and add a Graphics object to a form or other control, we can call the **CreateGraphics** method of the form or control as shown here:

Dim *objName* **As Graphics** = *controlname*.**CreateGraphics( )**

In this case, *controlname* is the name of the control on which the graphic will be displayed, and *objName* is the name of the Graphics object. While a form can be used, the **Panel control** can be used to group items on a form. Typically, you use panels to divide the form into identifiable groupings of controls. Grouping some controls can provide a visual cue to users that the controls are related. For example, the statement to create a graphics object named objGraphics on a Panel control named PnlGraphicsDisplay is shown below:

```
Dim objGraphics As Graphics = pnlGraphicsDisplay.CreateGraphics()
```

The Coordinate System

An important concept when drawing with a Graphics object on a VB .NET control is the coordinate system. The **GDI+ coordinate system** uses a pair of integer values to identify every point on the control on which the graphic will be drawn. Each pair of values includes an x-coordinate and a y-coordinate and are often expressed as (x,y). The **x-coordinate** represents the horizontal distance of a point from the origin. The **y-coordinate** represents the vertical position of a point from the origin. In VB .NET, coordinate values are expressed in **pixels.** For example, the point (5,10) represents a location 5 pixels away along the horizontal or x-axis and 10 pixels away along the vertical or y-axis. The coordinate systems used on VB .NET controls are set up as shown in Figure 10-16. Notice that the origin of the system, point (0,0), is located on the upper-left corner of the control.

FIGURE 10-16. VB .NET graphics coordinate system

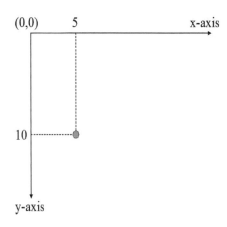

Graphics Example

Once you have created a Graphics object on a control, you can use its methods to draw various shapes, such as lines, circles, rectangles, or other shapes. Here we will create a simple example to illustrate how you can work with the Graphics object to make these shapes. To demonstrate creating graphics, we will use a form named frmGraphics with two main menu options: *File* and *Graphics*. The File menu contains an Exit option, and the Graphics menu has options for drawing a rectangle, circle, and polygon. To draw the graphics, we will use the Panel control mentioned above. The properties of the Panel control are shown in Table 10-9, and the resulting form is shown in Figure 10-17. Note that the panel is distinguished by dashed lines and a lighter color.

TABLE 10-9: Properties for Panel control

Property	Value
Name	pnlGraphicsDisplay
Height/Width	300 pixels
BackColor	Window

FIGURE 10-17.
Form for the Graphics menu using the Panel control

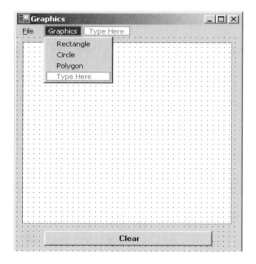

To draw the rectangle, we use two drawing objects. The first is the Graphics object, objGraphics, which is declared using the CreateGraphics method of the pnlGraphicsDisplay Panel control. The second is a Pen object created from the Pen class that is used to draw lines and curves. The general format for creating a Pen object is

Dim *objName* **as Pen = New Pen(Color.***color***)**

The Color object is used here to set the color of the line drawn by the Pen object.

For example, the following statement creates a Pen object named objPen that uses red to draw with:

```
Dim objPen As Pen = New Pen(Color.Red)
```

After these objects are available, we can use the DrawRectangle method of the objGraphics object to draw a rectangle as shown below:

objGraphicsObject.**DrawRectangle(***objPen, x, y, width, height***)**

where *x* and *y* represent the coordinates for the upper-left corner of the rectangle to be drawn. The *width* and *height* specify the dimensions of the rectangle. Using the dimensions shown in VB Code Box 10-14, a square 250 × 250 pixel rectangle is drawn with the upper-left corner located at the position (25,25), as shown in Figure 10-18. You should experiment with the draw parameters to see how they affect the rectangle, but remember that the total dimensions of the Panel control are 300 × 300 pixels. In addition to rectangles, draw methods for several common shapes are available.

VB CODE BOX 10-14. Code for drawing a rectangle	```Private Sub mnuGraphRectangle_Click(ByVal sender As System.Object, _ ByVal e As System.EventArgs) Handles mnuGraphRectangle.Click Dim objGraphics As Graphics = pnlGraphicsDisplay.CreateGraphics() Dim objPen As Pen = New Pen(Color.Red) objGraphics.DrawRectangle(objPen, 25, 25, 250, 250) End Sub```

FIGURE 10-18. Drawing a rectangle

Keep in mind that anytime we want to work with the graphics on a control we will need to declare a new Graphics objects. For example, you might expect that we could simply use a method of the Panel control to clear the graphics. Instead, we need to declare a Graphics object and then use its Clear method. The code for the Clear button is shown in VB Code Box 10-15.

VB CODE BOX 10-15. Code for clearing a Graphics object	```Private Sub btnClear_Click(ByVal sender As System.Object, _ ByVal e As System.EventArgs) Handles btnClear.Click Dim objGraphics As Graphics = pnlGraphicsDisplay.CreateGraphics() Dim objColor As Color objColor = pnlGraphicsDisplay.BackColor objGraphics.Clear(objColor) End Sub```

Note that the Graphics object Clear method clears the control of all graphics and then sets its background to the color specified. In order to set the Panel control back to its original color, we have declared objColor as a

Color object and set it to the BackColor property of pnlGraphicsDisplay. The objColor object was then used as the parameter for the Clear method of obj-Graphics.

We can easily adjust the code to draw a solid circle. In this case, instead of a line figure, we have drawn a solid object. To do this, we declare a graphics object as before, but in this case, instead of a Pen, we declare a Brush object. A **Brush object** is used to draw solid objects. In general, a Brush object is declared in this manner

Dim *objName* **As** *BrushType* **= New** *BrushType*(**Color.***color*)

The SolidBrush type fills the Graphics objects with a single color. Other Brush types exist, such as a TextureBrush, which uses an image to fill the interior of a Graphics object. For example, to create a Brush object, the statement would be:

```
Dim objBrush As SolidBrush = New SolidBrush(Color.Blue)
```

To create a circle, we use the **FillEllipse method** of the Graphics object instead of a DrawRectangle method. Fill methods are used instead of Draw methods when you wish to draw a filled Graphics object. The general format for the FillEllipse method is

objName.**FillEllipse(***objBrush, x, y, width, height***)**

The parameters of the FillEllipse method are very much like those of the DrawRectangle method where the coordinates *x* and *y* specify the upper left-hand corner of a rectangle, whereas *width* and *height* specify the rectangle's dimensions. The object uses the rectangle specified by these values as the boundary in which to draw the ellipse. Since we wish to draw a circle, we would set the *width* and *height* to equal values.

For example, to draw a solid blue circle, the statements are

```
Dim objBrush As SolidBrush = New SolidBrush(Color.Blue)
objGraphics.FillEllipse(objBrush, 20, 10, 100, 100)
```

The code for the mnuGraphicsCircle_Click event procedure is shown in VB Code Box 10-16, and the resulting graph is shown in Figure 10-19.

VB Code Box 10-16. Code for drawing a solid circle	```Private Sub mnuGraphCircle_Click(ByVal sender As System.Object, _ ByVal e As System.EventArgs) Handles mnuGraphCircle.Click Dim objGraphics As Graphics = pnlGraphicsDisplay.CreateGraphics() Dim objBrush As SolidBrush = New SolidBrush(Color.Blue) objGraphics.FillEllipse(objBrush, 20, 10, 100, 100) End Sub```

As we can see, regular shapes such as squares, rectangles, and circles are not too difficult to create using the Draw and Fill methods of the graphics objects. As it turns out, drawing irregular shapes is only slightly more involved.

To draw irregular shapes, the **FillPolygon method** is used. As you might expect by now, there is also a **DrawPolygon method** that is not solid. Both methods require that we provide an array of points defining the location of the corners, or vertices, of the shape. To create this array, we create five **Point objects** and then assign them to an array called objPolyPoints. The general format for using the FillPolygon method is

objGraphicName.**FillPolygon(***objBrushName, objPointArrayName***)**

Most of the work is in determining the appropriate coordinates for the corners of the shape.

FIGURE 10-19.
Drawing a circle

To add text to the Graphics object, we use the **DrawString method**. The general format for this method is

*objGraphicName.***DrawString(***string, objFontName, objBrushName, x, y***)**

where *x* and *y* are the coordinates of the upper-left corner at which to draw the text. Notice that for each label coordinates were selected to set the label at an appropriate distance from the shape.

For example, to generate an irregular polygon with text, the code is shown in VB Code Box 10-17, where we have declared the Graphics and Brush objects as before. In addition, we have declared a **Font object** called objFont. The Font object is used to hold the characteristics of text that will be added to the graphic. The resulting polygon is shown in Figure 10-20,.

VB CODE BOX 10-17. Code for drawing a labeled polygon	```Private Sub mnuGraphPolygon_Click(ByVal sender As System.Object, _
ByVal e As System.EventArgs) Handles mnuGraphPolygon.Click
Dim objGraphics As Graphics = pnlGraphicsDisplay.CreateGraphics()
Dim objBrush As SolidBrush = New SolidBrush(Color.Blue)
Dim objFont As New Font("Times New Roman", 8)
Dim objPoint1 As New Point(90, 55)
Dim objPoint2 As New Point(160, 120)
Dim objPoint3 As New Point(92, 210)
Dim objPoint4 As New Point(30, 118)
Dim objPoint5 As New Point(80, 80)
Dim objPolyPoints As Point() = {objPoint1, objPoint2, _
objPoint3, objPoint4, objPoint5}
objGraphics.FillPolygon(objBrush, objPolyPoints)
objGraphics.DrawString("(90, 55)", objFont, objBrush, 80, 45)
objGraphics.DrawString("(160, 120)", objFont, objBrush, 163, 110)
objGraphics.DrawString("(92, 210)", objFont, objBrush, 82, 215)
objGraphics.DrawString("(30, 118)", objFont, objBrush, 0, 98)
objGraphics.DrawString("(80, 80)", objFont, objBrush, 40, 70)
End Sub```

A summary of some of the other methods that you can use to draw shapes on a VB .NET Graphics object is provided in Table 10-10.

FIGURE 10-20.
Drawing a labeled polygon

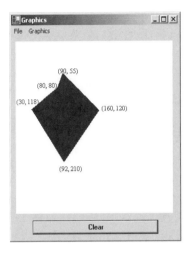

TABLE 10-10: Methods of the Graphics class

Graphic Element	Method	General Statement Format
Arc	DrawArc draws an arc representing a portion of an ellipse specified by a rectangle structure.	*objG*.DrawArc(*objPen, x, y, width, height, startAngle, sweepAngle*)
Curve	DrawCurve draws a curve through a set of points specified by the user.	*objG*.DrawCurve(*objPen, objPoints*)
Line	DrawLine draws a line connecting a pair of coordinate points.	*objG*.DrawLine(*objPen, x1, y1, x2, y2*)
Pie	DrawPie and FillPie draw a wedge of a pie given a start angle and the size of the wedge in degrees.	*objG*.DrawPie(*objPen, x, y, width, height, startAngle, sweepAngle*)

Step-by-Step Instructions 10-5: Working with Graphics objects

1. Start a new VB .NET project and store it in a folder named **GraphicsExample.**

2. Create the form shown in Figure 10-17 by adding a Panel control with the properties shown in Table 10-9. Create the menus shown in Table 10-11.

TABLE 10-11: Menu for graphics example

Menu Option	Name Property
File	mnuFile
File | Exit	mnuFileExit
Graphics	mnuGraphics
Graphics | Rectangle	mnuGraphicsRectangle
Graphics | Circle	mnuGraphicsCircle
Graphics | Polygon	mnuGraphicsPolygon

3. Add the code in VB Code Box 10-14 to the mnuGraphicsRectangle_Click event procedure.

4. Add the code in VB Code Box 10-15 so that you can clear the Panel control. Run your program and test it by selecting the **Graphics \| Rectangle** option. The results should appear as shown in Figure 10-18. Clear the graphic display and then redisplay the rectangle.

5. Experiment with drawing a rectangle by adjusting the various parameters of the objPen declaration and the DrawRectangle method. Try converting the DrawRectangle method to a FillRectangle method and the Pen object to a Brush object to see what happens.

6. Add code shown in VB Code Box 10-16 for drawing a circle to the mnuGraphicsCircle_Click event procedure. The result of clicking the **Graphics \| Circle** menu option should appear as shown in Figure 10-19.

7. Experiment with drawing circles and ellipses as you did in Step 6 above.

8. Add code shown in VB Code Box 10-17 for drawing a polygon to the mnuGraphicsPolygon_Click event procedure. The result of clicking the **Graphics \| Polygon** menu option should appear as shown in Figure 10-20.

9. Experiment with drawing polygons as you did in Step 6 above. Also, experiment with placing text labels on your drawing.

10. Modify your code to experiment with other Draw and Fill methods shown in Table 10-10.

11. Click the **Save All** icon to save the files in this project.

I ▬ I

Mini-Summary 10-5: Working with Graphics objects

1. Graphics object classes are part of the System.Drawing namespace of the .NET FCL and are compatible with GDI+.

2. GDI+ uses a coordinate system with the origin located in the upper-left corner of the Graphics objects and measures location in pixels.

3. To draw graphics, you can declare a Graphics object and associate it with a control that is capable of displaying graphic images. You can think of the Graphics object as the paper or canvas on which your code will draw the graphic.

Mini-Summary 10-5: Working with Graphics objects (Continued)

4. Pen and Brush objects are used to draw lines, line figures, filled shapes, and text of various colors on a graphics object.

5. Several Draw and Fill methods are members of the Graphics class that you can use to draw common graphic elements.

It's Your Turn!

1. What statement would you need to write for your program to have access to the System.Drawing namespace? Where would you put it?

2. Write statements for each of the following:

    a. Declare a Graphics object to be drawn directly on a form called frm-Main.

    b. Declare a blue Pen object.

    c. Declare a green Brush object.

    d. Declare a Font object using bold, 14 point, Courier New.

3. Write a statement or statements for each of the following:

    a. Draw a green, filled rectangle 20 pixels wide and 10 pixels high.

    b. Draw a red, unfilled circle with a radius of 20 pixels.

    c. Draw a blue, filled section of pie that begins at a 30 degree start angle and uses a 45 degree sweep.

    d. Draw the text "Welcome" in center of the Graphics object. Use an underlined, 12-point, Times New Roman font.

4. Follow Step-By-Step Instructions 10-5 to experiment with the techniques for drawing graphics.

ADDING PRINTING AND PRINT PREVIEW CAPABILITIES

Up to this point in this textbook, we have output our results to the Output window. Now, by adding graphics capabilities, we are able to print to paper through the default printer linked to your computer. As an illustration of using the graphics capabilities to print your results to a printer, we will add printing capability to our Vintage DVDs Payroll program. This will include a print preview capability that will enable the user to view what will be printed prior to it actually being printed.

Using the PrintDocument Object

Most software provides the capabilities of printing output to a printer and previewing what you are going to print before printing. As usual for common software features, controls are available in the VB .NET toolbox, and classes are available in the .NET FCL that you can use to add these capabilities to your programs.

    The primary object that is used for printing is called the **PrintDocument** object, and its class is available in the System.Drawing namespace. A

PrintDocument object will include properties and methods that allow you to work with and print your output. It is basically a Graphics object (its in the same namespace as the Graphics object), and you can think of the PrintDocument object as a piece of paper on which you will draw graphics and text just like you would on a Panel control or form. To do this, you use the same Drawing objects that we discussed in the previous section.

To make sure that we have access to the PrintDocument object, add the following line at the beginning of the program:

```
Imports System.Drawing.Printing
```

A PrintDocument can cause a **PrintPage event** to occur. This event occurs whenever the **Print** method of the PrintDocument object is called. You can write the code that specifies the format of the printed document in the event procedure for the PrintPage event. For the Vintage DVDs Payroll program, we will print a simple report listing the employee names and payroll types that are shown in the list box. We will keep it simple with only a few enhancements, such as a report title and column heading.

In general, we follow four steps when writing text or graphics to the PrintDocument.

1. Create the item that we want to print.
2. Set the location on the document where it should be printed.
3. Select style, font, color, and so forth of the item that you want to print.
4. Use the appropriate method to draw the item on the PrintDocument object.

For example, going back to our Vintage DVDs payroll application, we have previously printed information to the Output window using the mnu-FilePrint menu option. Now we want to print to the printer instead. The code to do this is shown in the PrintDocument's PrintPage event, shown in VB Code Box 10-18.

First, notice in this code that the name of the sub procedure is *objPrintDocument_Print*. Recall from the preceding paragraphs that PrintDocument is an object. As such, we will need to declare an instance of the object each time we want to use it. Once declared, we can use its members—properties, methods and events—to link code in the form of event procedures to the object. We will create an instance of a PrintDocument object in procedures that you will see on the next few pages. For now, assume that we will use the name *objPrintDocument* and that this code will be associated with the PrintPage event of the object.

Also note that in the sub statement we have the parameter *e* that is passed as PrintPageEventArgs object. The Graphics property of this object lets you specify what you want to print. The Graphics property includes most of the graphics methods that we discussed in the previous section, such as DrawString and FillRectangle.

The first statements in the code of the objPrintDocument_Print sub project shown in VB Code Box 10-18 are used to declare local variables and objects. The variables sngX and sngY are used as the coordinates where we will want to place things on the PrintDocument object. Using variables instead of simply typing exact values allows us to use equations to determine the next location to draw an item. Several variables, including sngLeftMargin,

| **VB CODE BOX 10-18.** Code to specify the format of the print document | ```
Private Sub objPrintDocument_Print(ByVal sender As Object, _
ByVal e As PrintPageEventArgs)
  Dim sngX As Single, Dim sngY As Single
  Dim sngLeftMargin As Single = e.MarginBounds.Left
  Dim sngRightMargin As Single = e.MarginBounds.Right
  Dim sngTopMargin As Single = e.MarginBounds.Top
  Dim objTitleFont As New Font("Courier New", 14, FontStyle.Bold)
  Dim objHeadingFont As New Font("Courier New", 12, FontStyle.Bold)
  Dim objRecordFont As New Font("Courier New", 12)
  Dim objBrush As SolidBrush = New SolidBrush(Color.Black)
  Dim objpen As Pen = New Pen(Color.Black)
  Dim strLine, strName As String, intCounter As Integer
  strLine = "Employees"
  sngX = sngLeftMargin + 10
  sngY = sngTopMargin + 5
  e.Graphics.DrawString(strLine, objTitleFont, objBrush, sngX, sngY)
  strLine = "Name" & Space(26) ' write column headings
  strLine = strLine & "Phone" & Space(10)
  strLine = strLine & "Pay Type"
  sngY = sngY + 34
  e.Graphics.DrawString(strLine, objHeadingFont, objBrush, _
    sngX, sngY)
  sngY = sngY + 24
  e.Graphics.DrawLine(objpen, sngX, sngY, sngRightMargin - 10, sngY)
  For intCounter = 0 To intEmpCntr - 1 ' print records
    strName = Trim(udtEmployees(intCounter).strFName) & _
      " " & Trim(udtEmployees(intCounter).strLName)
    strLine = Spacer(strName, 30)
    strLine = strLine & _
     Spacer(Trim(udtEmployees(intCounter).strPhone), 15) & Chr(9)
    strLine = strLine & udtEmployees(intCounter).strPaytype _
     & Chr(9)
    sngY = sngY + 24
    e.Graphics.DrawString(strLine, objRecordFont, objBrush, _
      sngX, sngY)
  Next intCounter
  sngY = sngY + 36 ' print total employees
  strLine = "Number of Employees = " & CStr(intEmpCntr)
  e.Graphics.DrawString(strLine, objHeadingFont, objBrush, _
    sngX, sngY)
End Sub
``` |
| --- | --- |

sngRightMargin, and sngTopMargin, are declared and immediately set to the margin values of the PrintPageEventArgs object. These can be used as reference points to ensure that our graphic elements are drawn within the margins of the page. Next, we declare several Font, Brush, and Pen objects. These will be used to draw graphics and text on the PrintDocument. Finally, we declare several processing variables.

The first example of this processing occurs in VB Code Box 10-18 when we want to print the title of the report. Going back to our four-step process, for step 1, we assign the text for the title of the report, *Employees,* to the String variable strLine. Then, for step 2, we assign coordinate values to the variables sngX and sngY using the left and top margins for reference. We select the appropriate style for step 3 by choosing the desired Font object that we want to use for the title. Here we use the objTitleFont object that we declared earlier. Finally, we use the DrawString method to draw the word
```

Employees to the PrintDocument object in Bold, 14-point, Times New Roman font.

A careful reading of the rest of VB Code Box 10-18 should show you that these same four steps are followed for each item that is drawn to the Print-Document object. There are a few things that you should notice in the rest of the code. First, we can set the location of our next item to draw by using the previous location as a reference. We do this by simply adding the appropriate value, representing a distance in pixels to either the sngX or sngY variables. Keep in mind that coordinate values are measured in pixels. Also keep in mind that sngX and sngY represent the location of the upper-left corner of a rectangle in which the item will be drawn. The bottom-left corner of a text item that uses a 14-point font will be approximately 14 pixels farther down the *y*-axis than the upper-left corner. This fact can be important in deciding how much to add when determining the next location.

Second, notice that we can draw graphics as well as text. We add a line under the column headings using the DrawLine method. Third, since each record of our udtEmployees array contains similar data, we can use a loop to print these items to the PrintDocument object. Here again, the use of variables for our coordinates comes in handy since we can easily make adjustments each time an item is to be drawn.

Previewing and Printing the PrintDocument Object

To use the PrintDocument object and its PrintPage event, we need to add a few controls to our program. Although we already have a Print option on the payroll applications File menu, a **Print Preview** option needs to be added as shown in Figure 10-21.

FIGURE 10-21. Print Preview and Print Menu options

Next, we need to add the *PrintPreviewDialog* control to the program. Once the option for this control is clicked in the Toolbox, the control will appear below the form in the component tray just like a Menu or Database control. We will set the control name to *dlgPreview* and set the UseAntialias property to True. The *UseAntiAlias* property will make the text look better on the screen. A PrintDialog control is available for use when you want to be able to select a printer. To keep the example simple, we have decided not to use it here.

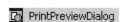

With the addition of the proper controls, we are ready to add the code for previewing and printing the document defined by the objPrintDocument_Print sub procedure, as shown in VB Code Box 10-19. First, we declare an instance of a PrintDocument called objPrintDocument. Recall that we wrote code for the PrintPage event of this object already. Next, we use an *AddHandler* statement to let VB .NET know which procedure will handle the PrintPage event of the object. The general format of the AddHandler statement is

AddHandler *ObjectName.Event*, **AddressOf** *ProcedureName*

Here, we assign the procedure objPrintDocument_Print to handle the objPrintDocument.PrintPage event.

We next use an If statement to make sure that a printer is available. The goal is to allow our program to keep control of any errors that could result from no printer being available. Finally, we call the Print method of the Print-Document object, objPrintDocument. Calling this method causes the Print-Page event to occur.

VB Code Box 10-19. Code for printing the document	<pre>Private Sub mnuFilePrint_Click(ByVal sender As System.Object, _
	  ByVal e As System.EventArgs) Handles mnuFilePrint.Click
	    Dim objPrintDocument As New PrintDocument()
	    AddHandler objPrintDocument.PrintPage, _
	      AddressOf objPrintDocument_Print
	    If PrinterSettings.InstalledPrinters.Count = 0 Then
	      MessageBox.Show("No printers are currently installed", _
	        "Print Error", _
	        MessageBoxButtons.OK, _
	        MessageBoxIcon.Information)
	      Exit Sub
	    End If
	    objPrintDocument.Print()
	End Sub</pre>

The code for previewing the document is provided in VB Code Box 10-20. This code is practically the same as that shown for printing the document. The difference occurs in the last two lines. Instead of calling the Print method, here we first assign the PrintDocument object to our dlgPreview control. Then, we call the ShowDialog method of this control. The results of this code showing the preview of the document are shown in Figure 10-22. For this figure, the Zoom option was set to 100%, and the window was resized. Note the buttons and menu options that are available with this control.

VB Code Box 10-20. Code for previewing the document	<pre>Private Sub mnuFilePrintPreview_Click(ByVal sender As _
	  System.Object, ByVal e As System.EventArgs) Handles _
	  mnuFilePrintPreview.Click
	    Dim objPrintDocument As New PrintDocument()
	    AddHandler objPrintDocument.PrintPage, _
	      AddressOf objPrintDocument_Print
	    If PrinterSettings.InstalledPrinters.Count = 0 Then
	      MessageBox.Show("No printers are currently installed", _
	        "Print Error", _
	        MessageBoxButtons.OK, _
	        MessageBoxIcon.Information)
	      Exit Sub
	    End If
	    dlgPreview.document = objPrintDocument
	    dlgPreview.ShowDialog()
	End Sub</pre>

FIGURE 10-22.
Previewing the
document

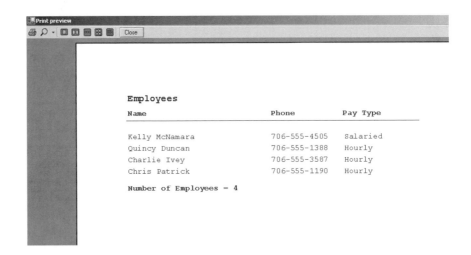

![Print preview window showing Employees list]

Employees		
Name	Phone	Pay Type
Kelly McNamara	706-555-4505	Salaried
Quincy Duncan	706-555-1388	Hourly
Charlie Ivey	706-555-3587	Hourly
Chris Patrick	706-555-1190	Hourly

Number of Employees = 4

Step-by-Step Instructions 10-6: Adding print and print preview capabilities

1. Open the Vintage DVDs Payroll application in your *Chapter10\Payroll* folder.

2. In the Code Window for the Payroll form, add the **objPrintdocument_Print** sub procedure shown in VB Code Box 10-18.

3. On the form itself, modify the Menu control to include the **Print Preview** option as shown in Figure 10-21. Also, add the **PrintPreviewDialog** control to the component tray and rename it as **dlgPreview.**

4. Add the code shown in VB Code Box 10-19 for the mnuFilePrint_Click event procedure.

5. Add the code shown in VB Code Box 10-20 for the mnuFilePrintPreview-_Click event procedure.

6. Run your program and test its new features by using the **File | Open** command to open the **Employees.dat** file from the Bin folder of your project. Select the **File | Print Preview** option and your screen should appear like that shown in Figure 10-22. If you have a printer connected to your computer, select the **File | Print** option to print the list of employees to the printer.

7. Save all of your files.

Mini-Summary 10-6: Adding printing and print preview capabilities

1. VB .NET provides a PrintDocument class in the System.Drawing namespace. Use the Import statement to access the namespace when needed.

Mini-Summary 10-6: Adding printing and print preview capabilities

2. You can treat a PrintDocument object similar to a Graphics object—it is laid out using a coordinate system enabling you to place graphics and text on the PrintDocument using the Draw and Fill methods.

3. The PrintPreview Dialog control can be used to preview a document before it is printed.

It's Your Turn!

1. Write statements for each of the following items:

   a. Provide access to the PrintDocument class for your program.

   b. Use an AddHandler statement to associate the procedure MySub with the objPrintDocument.PrintPage.

   c. Assign the location of the left and right margins in pixels to two variables.

   d. Call a method of a PrintDocument object that will cause the PrintPage event to occur.

2. Follow Step-By-Step Instructions 10-6 to add printing to the Payroll application.

3. Add some employees to your project and use the File|Print Preview and File|Print option to see the result.

WORKING WITH THE MS CHART CONTROL

Another nice enhancement for our Payroll project is to add a charting capability. Although we could use a Graphics object and its corresponding methods to draw the lines, text, and shapes that we want on the chart, this can get to be a long and complicated process. Fortunately, charting is also a very common software feature, especially for software designed to work with data. Because charting is so common, Microsoft has created the MS Chart control and made it available to VB .NET programmers.

The **MS Chart control** provides the capability of displaying two-dimensional graphs on a form. Data is supplied to the control using a two-dimensional array. The MS Chart control can display several types of charts including line, scatter, bar, and pie charts. It is fairly simple to use. Primarily, you just need to add the control to your form, set desired properties, and write code to assign the values to the control. We will see how this is done by adding a simple bar chart to the Payroll form.

Adding the Chart Control to the Toolbox

The MS Chart control is not a part of the standard Toolbox. To use it in your projects, you will need to first add the control to the Toolbox. First, make sure your form is selected in the main window of Visual Studio and view the Toolbox. Right-click on the Windows Forms tab near the top of the Toolbox as shown in Figure 10-23.

FIGURE 10-23.
Adding a new
control to the
Toolbox

Select the "Customize Toolbox..." option from the menu that appears. After clicking the menu option, the Customize Toolbox dialog box shown in Figure 10-24 will appear. This dialog box is filled with many other controls that you can add to your Toolbox. Make sure that the COM Components tab is selected. Scroll down until you find the item *Microsoft Chart Control 6.0,* and check the box next to it. Click the *OK* button, and the control will be added to your Toolbox. Make a note to come back later and check out other controls that might be useful to add to your Toolbox.

FIGURE 10-24.
Customize Toolbox
dialog box

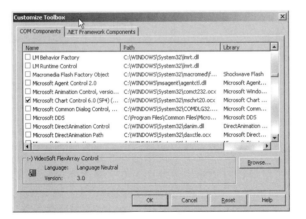

Scroll down through your Toolbox until you find the newly added control. It will probably have been added at the bottom of the list. Select the control and add it to your form as shown in Figure 10-25. We also add a menu option named *mnuChart* with a submenu option of *mnuChartEmp-Type* to click when we want to see the chart.

Setting Chart Properties

Click on the MS Chart control to select it and then take a look at the Properties Window as shown in Figure 10-26. As with any other control, we can use the Properties Window to set property values at design time. We will first set the Name property to chBarChart. Notice that the MS Chart control appears with a sample chart already in place. Unfortunately, this sample chart also appears when we run the program. To keep the chart hidden until it is ready to be shown to the user, we set the Visible property to False.

But what about the other Chart properties? Although we could go ahead and set them using the Properties Window, there is a little more user-friendly

FIGURE 10-25.
Payroll form with
Chart control

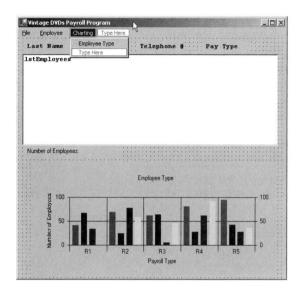

FIGURE 10-26. MS
Chart control
properties

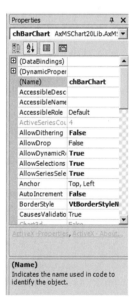

way to set MS Chart properties. Notice at the bottom of the Properties Window a link that reads *ActiveX - Properties*. The meaning of this text is too long a story to go into here. For our purposes, it means that we have another means of setting properties for the MS Chart control.

Clicking on the *ActiveX - Properties* link will cause the dialog box in Figure 10-27 to be displayed. Using this dialog box is easier than the Properties window because the chart properties are logically grouped by function. In addition, you may be familiar with charting dialogs similar to this one used in programs like MS Excel.

To navigate the dialog box shown in Figure 10-27, you click on a tab to display the page that you want to see. Then you can set properties by clicking option buttons, checking check boxes, selecting from lists, or typing text in

FIGURE 10-27. MS Chart ActiveX Properties dialog box

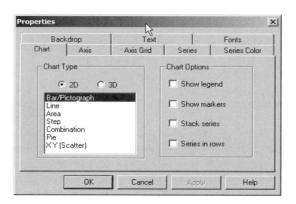

text boxes. We will use these pages to design our chart according to the items listed in Table 10-12. All other properties will be left a their default values.

TABLE 10-12: Chart properties

Tab	Property	Value
Chart	Chart Type	Bar/Pictograph
Series Color	Series	C1
	Series Color	Red
Text	Title	Employee Type
	X-Axis Title	Payroll Type
	Y-Axis Title	Number of Employees (oriented vertically)

Next, we need to add the code for the mnuChartEmpType menu option. This code is shown in VB Code Box 10-21. There are three main activities occurring in this procedure. First, a loop is used to look at all of the records in the udtEmployees array and count the number of hourly and salaried employees. These values are stored in intHourly and intSalaried, respectively. Second, the two-dimensional array is loaded with the data for the chart. The MS Chart control does not use the first "row" elements of the array. We use these elements as simple reminders of the values in each "column." For each remaining "row" we load the payroll category as the first element and the number of employees of that payroll type in the other. Third, we chart the data by setting the ChartData property of the MS Chart control equal to the data array. Before the procedure is over, we remember to set the Visible property to True so that the user may actually see the chart.

The results of selecting the mnuChartEmpType menu option are displayed in Figure 10-28. Keep in mind that you can alter the type and format of the Chart by using the dialog box to change Chart properties.

VB CODE BOX 10-21. Code for making the chart	```Private Sub mnuChartEmpType_Click(ByVal sender As System.Object, _```

```
Private Sub mnuChartEmpType_Click(ByVal sender As System.Object, _
ByVal e As System.EventArgs) Handles mnuChartEmpType.Click
    Dim intCounter, intHourly intSalaried As Integer
    Dim strEmployees(2, 1) As String
    For intCounter = 0 To intEmpCntr - 1
        If Trim(udtEmployees(intCounter).strPaytype) = "Hourly" Then
            intHourly = intHourly + 1
        Else
            intSalaried = intSalaried + 1
        End If
    Next intCounter
    strEmployees(0, 0) = "Payroll Type"
    strEmployees(0, 1) = "Number of Employees"
    strEmployees(1, 0) = "Hourly"
    strEmployees(1, 1) = CStr(intHourly)
    strEmployees(2, 0) = "Salaried"
    strEmployees(2, 1) = CStr(intSalaried)
    chBarChart.ChartData = strEmployees
    chBarChart.Visible = True
End Sub
```

FIGURE 10-28. Results of clicking the Charting| Employee type

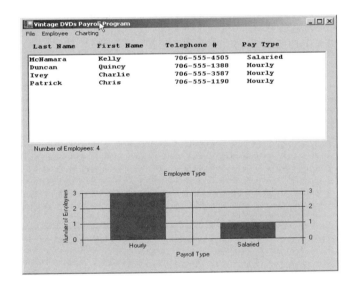

- -

Step-by-Step Instructions 10-7: Working with the MS Chart control

1. Open the Vintage DVDs Payroll application in your Chapter10\Payroll folder.

2. Add the MS Chart control to your Toolbox following the steps illustrated in Figure 10-23 and Figure 10-24.

3. Add the MS Chart control and menu options shown in Figure 10-25 to the Payroll form. Name the menu options **mnuChart** and **mnuChartEmpType,** respectively.

4. Use the ActiveX Properties dialog box to set the properties listed in Table 10-12.

5. Type the code shown in VB Code Box 10-21 for the mnuChartEmpType-_Click event procedure.

6. Run your program and open the Employees.dat direct access file to test the Chart feature. Add some new employees and test the Chart feature to ensure it has changed.

7. Afterwards, adjust some of the properties of the Chart control and experiment with the Chart format.

8. Click the **Save All** icon to save the files in this project.

Mini-Summary 10-6: Working with the MS Chart control

1. You can add more controls to your Toolbox when needed by accessing and using the Customize Toolbox dialog box in Visual Studio .NET.

2. The MS Chart control can be used to easily add business graphics in the form of charts to your projects.

3. Data are entered in the Chart control via an array.

It's Your Turn!

1. Follow Step-By-Step Instructions 10-7 to add charting capabilities to the Payroll application.

2. Run your project and retrieve the Employees.dat file from the Bin folder and chart the number in each category. Add and delete employees from the list and ensure that the chart changes to match the revised list

SUMMARY

At the beginning of the chapter, we said you would be able to do a number of things after reading it. Let's review those things here:

1. Require a password to protect the information system from unauthorized access. Passwords are a common method of enforcing security for information systems. Password protection can be added to a VB .NET project by using the Tag property of a text box and a startup form to which the user must respond. The user's input to the text box can be compared to the Tag property, and if the user fails to match the Tag property in three tries, the project is terminated.

2. Create a menu for a project using the MainMenu control and add code to the menu items to execute actions when an item is selected. The MainMenu control makes it easy to create a menu system for any VB .NET application. The MainMenu control appears in the component tray below the application's form. The actual menu is designed with the Menu Designer, and this is where you will begin to enter the menu headings and options. Menu item names include a prefix of *mnu,* whereas submenu items also include any menu and submenu names to which the item belongs. Access keys can be assigned by including an ampersand (&) in the caption, and shortcut keys can be assigned by selecting from a drop-down list box.

For menu items to work, you must add code to them in the same way you added code to buttons or other controls. It is easy with VB .NET's editing options to move code from other controls to menu items. Help/About forms are commonly found in most commercial software.

3. Work with direct access data files. A direct (or random) access file is a record-oriented file in which records can be accessed and manipulated in any order through their record number. This type of file is similar to both sequential access and database files. Direct access files are opened with the FileOpen statement and the OpenMode parameter set to Random. The record length parameter is commonly set to the Len() function. The FilePut statement is used to write records to a direct access file, and the FileGet statement is used to read records from the file. As with sequential access files, direct access files are closed with the FileClose statement.

4. Add and use the SaveFileDialog and OpenFileDialog controls to save and open files. The SaveFileDialog and OpenFileDialog controls make working all types of files, including direct access files, easier by displaying dialog boxes from which a file name can be selected or entered. The Filter and FilterIndex parameters can be used to determine the type of files to be listed in the dialog box and the type to be displayed by default. In both cases, the System.IO namespace has the FileInfo class that can be used to determine information about a file, including whether or not it exists. It can also be used to delete a file. To save a direct access file, a name is entered into the dialog box and used as the FileName parameter in the FilePut operation. A For-Next or For-Each loop can be used to write an array onto the direct access file. To open a direct access file for input, a name is selected from the dialog box. The number of records in the file can be determined from the LOF and Len functions and used in a For-Next loop.

5. Use Graphics objects to draw figures on a form. Graphics object classes are part of the System.Drawing namespace of the .NET FCL and are compatible with GDI+, which uses a coordinate system with the origin located in the upper-left corner of the Graphics objects and measures location in pixels. To draw graphics, you can declare a Graphics object and associate it with a control that is capable of displaying graphic images. You can think of the Graphics object as the paper or canvas on which your code will draw the graphic. Pen and Brush objects are used to draw lines, line figures, filled shapes, and text of various colors on a Graphics object. Several Draw and Fill methods are members of the Graphics class that you can use to draw common graphic elements.

6. Use Graphics objects to add print and print preview capabilities to a project. VB .NET provides a PrintDocument class in the System.Drawing namespace. The Import statement is used to access the namespace when needed. A PrintDocument object can be treated similarly to a Graphics object—it can be laid out using a coordinate system, enabling you to place graphics and text on the PrintDocument using Draw and Fill methods. The

PrintPreview dialog control can be used to preview a document before it is printed. You can add more controls to your Toolbox when needed by accessing and using the Customize Toolbox dialog box in Visual Studio .NET.

7. Add the MS Chart control to the Toolbox and then to a form to use in charting data. MS Chart is a control that can be used to create business charts from data. Although it is not on the default Toolbox, you can add it to the Toolbox by accessing and using the Customize Toolbox dialog box in Visual Studio .NET. It then can be linked to a Click event to read data from the project and generate a chart.

NEW VB .NET ELEMENTS

Control/Object	Properties	Methods	Events
TextBox	PasswordChar Tag		
MainMenu	Name Text Checked Shortcut ShowShortcut		Click
FileInfo (from System.IO)	Exists		
SaveFileDialog/OpenFileDialog	Name FileName Filter FilterIndex	ShowDialog( )	

NEW PROGRAMMING STATEMENTS

Statement to open a direct access file
FileOpen(FileNumber, FileName, OpenMode.Random, _
OpenAccess.*Access*, OpenShare.*ShareMode*, RecordLength**)**

Statement to write data on a random access file
FilePut (FileNumber, variable name, record number**)**

Statement to input data from a random access file
FileGet(FileNumber, variable name, record number**)**

Function to find available file number
FileNumber = **FreeFile( )**

Statement to delete a file (must import System.IO first)
Kill(FileName**)**

Statement to find the number of characters in a file
intNumChar = **LOF**(intFileNum**)**

KEY TERMS

access keys
checkmarks
common user interface
component tray
direct access file

fixed-length string
graphics design interface
(GDI)
menu designer
password
prototype

random access file
record number
separator
shortcut keys

EXERCISES

1. Which of the following would be considered unacceptable passwords for Harry Jones, who has a spouse named Lisa Knight and a dog named Mutt? In each case, explain why it is unacceptable.

   a. MyDogMutt

   b. M77TT

   c. LisaK

   d. HJones

   e. L11S88

2. Design a project that contains one upper-level menu with the name **Appearance.** Include in this menu two submenus, **Color** and **Size.** For the color submenu, write a series of menu items such as **Black, White, Green,** and so on. When each Color menu item is selected, the BackColor property of the form should change to the corresponding color. In addition, the selected menu item should be checked. For the Size submenu, create three menu items, **Big, Medium,** and **Small.** When each of these is selected, the size of the form should adjust to match the selected menu item and the menu item should be checked. Select appropriate access and shortcut keys for each menu item.

3. One way to save time when developing VB .NET projects is to begin by using an existing form or template that already contains standard features that you may use for most of your projects. Create a template form with standard, functioning menu items. At a minimum, include a **File** and **Help** menu. On your file menu include the submenus **Open, Close, Save, Save As...,** and **Exit.** Write code for each of these and set appropriate access and shortcut keys. On the Help menu, include a submenu with the caption **About.** For this submenu, have it generate a message box for which the message may be easily edited to describe the current project.

4. Write the statements to create a data type called *BestDVDs* with four attributes: Name (a string with 30 characters), Year (an integer), Price (a decimal), and Category (a string with 20 characters.) Declare a variable called *DVDsInStock()* to be an array of type BestDVDs and then write statements to input a list of DVDs from a direct access file called *OurDVDs.*

5. For the above exercise, write statements for the following:

   a. Define a filter for all files, data files, and text files, with data files being the default.

b. Open the file to save data from the DVDsInStock array to the a direct access (.dat) file.

c. Save the array data to the file.

d. Close the file.

PROJECTS

1. Assume that a random access file *RealEstate.dat* exists with the name, Social Security number, withholding percentage, year-to-date sales, and year-to-date withholding for real estate agents at the Champions Real Estate agency. The withholding percentage is the percentage of each transaction that the salesperson wants withheld for income tax purposes. When a transaction occurs, the salesperson is paid on the type of transaction—that is listing, sale, or both—and the percentage to be withheld. If the transaction involved a listing by the agent, he or she receives 1.5 percent of the sales amount; if the transaction was a sale by the agent, they receive 2 percent of the sales amount. Finally, if the agent both listed and sold the property, he or she receives 4 percent of the sales amount (1.5 percent for listing, 2 percent for selling, and 0.5 percent as a bonus for doing both).

For example, assume that Howard Ellis has specified that 20 percent of any amount coming to him is to be withheld. If Howard both lists and sells a property for $100,000, then his gross amount due is $100,000 × 0.04 = $4,000. His net amount due is then $4,000 × (1 − 0.20) = $3,200.

Create a project named **Ex10-1** in the *Chapter10\Homework* folder to input data from the *RealEstate.dat* direct access file into this UDT array and to process the data. (If you have completed Exercise 3 in Chapter 8, you can modify it to complete this exercise rather than starting over.) In all cases, your project should use menus to carry out the operations, and there should be a password form with a password of *Real8state* that is the startup form. Use the following specifications to create the project:

a. The project should display the data in a list box and allow the managing partner for the firm to click a name whenever a sale occurs and display the name, Social Security number, and withholding percentage on a second form.

b. It should be possible to determine the gross and net amounts due the agent and print this information with appropriate labels.

c. At the same time, the year-to-date sales and withholding fields should be updated based on the latest sale and the file should be saved to disk.

d. The manager should be able add data on new agents, delete agents that have left the firm, print a list of agents, and edit information on agents whenever they change their withholding percentage.

e. It should be possible to save all of the salesperson records back to the original file or to a new file depending on the user's needs.

f. The project should have the capability to print preview a list of salesperson records and then to print them to the default printer.

g. Add the MS Chart control to the your Toolbox and then to this project. Your project should be able to generate a bar chart that shows the number of employees with 20 percent or more withholding as compared to those with less than 20 percent withholding.

2. Universal Widgets sells a variety of specialized products to a small group of rather large customers, each of which has negotiated its own discount arrangement with Universal. For example, SuperStore receives a 12 percent discount whereas GiantStore receives a 13 percent discount. Assume that the names of the customers, corresponding discount rates, and year-to-date gross and net sales values are stored on a text file named *Universal.dat*. You may download this file from the Chapter 10 section of the text Web site.

Create a project named **Ex10-2** in the *Chapter10\Homework* folder to input data from the *Universal.dat* direct access file into this UDT array and to process the data. (If you have completed Exercise 4 in Chapter 8, you can modify it to complete this exercise rather than starting over.) In all cases, your project should use menus wherever appropriate to carry out the operations, and there should be a password form with a password of *uni555x* that is the startup form. Create the project according to the following instructions:

a. The data should be displayed in a list box, and the sales manager for Universal should be able to click the name of a customer to transfer it and the discount rate to a second form where he or she can enter the number of units to be sold and their price.

b. They should then be able to compute the gross amount due, the discount due the retailer, and the net amount due Universal. He or she should be able to print this information with appropriate labels.

c. At the same time that the information is being printed, the year-to-date gross and net sales values for this customer should be updated based on this transaction, and the file saved to disk.

d. The sales manager should be able add data on new customers, delete customers when necessary, print a list of customers, and edit information on customers whenever the negotiated discount rate changes.

e. The data should be written back to the original file or to a new file, depending on the user's wishes.

f. The project should have the capability to print preview a list of customer records and then to print them to the default printer.

g. If you have not already done so, add the MS Chart control to the your Toolbox. (In any case, MS Chart should be added to this project.) Use it to generate a bar chart showing the number of customers with discounts of 10 percent or more as compared to those with less than 10 percent discount.

3. Assume that a list of student names, ID numbers, and quiz averages is to be stored and processed using a UDT array. The fields for the UDT structure are shown in Table 10-13, where the LetterGrade field is initially blank.

TABLE 10-13: Fields for UDT Array

Field
StudentName (lastname-first form)
StudentID

Table 10-13: Fields for UDT Array (Continued)

Field
QuizAverage
LetterGrade

Create a project named **Ex10-3** in the *Chapter10\Homework* folder to input data into this UDT structure and process the data. (If you have completed Exercise 5 in Chapter 8, you can modify it to complete this exercise rather than starting over.) Assume the data are stored in a file called *Students.dat* direct access file, which you may download from the Chapter 10 section of the text Web site and save to the Bin folder of the project folder for this exercise. In all cases, your project should use menus wherever appropriate to carry out the operations, and there should be a password form with a password of *Stu30nt* that is the startup form. Your project should use multiple forms to carry out operations based on the following instructions:

a. The project should input the data from the direct access file and display it as a list of students in a list box on the main form. Double-clicking a student name or highlighting it and clicking a button should display information on each student in text boxes with appropriate labels on a individual student form.

b. The professor should be able to implement a 90-80-70-60 scale to determine the letter grade for the current student and add the grade to the LetterGrade field for that student and to a text box on the individual student form.

c. The data on all students processed so far should be displayed in a list box on a another form, which can be accessed from the main form. It should be possible to return to the main form.

d. It should be possible to save new or modified data back to the original data file to a new one, depending on the user's wishes.

e. The project should have the capability to print preview a list of student records and then to print them to the default printer.

f. If you have not already done so, add the MS Chart control to the your Toolbox. (In any case, MS Chart should be added to this project.) Use it to generate a bar chart that shows the number of students receiving grades of A, B, C, D, or F.

4. Assume that customer information in the form of names, telephone numbers, and sales amounts is to be processed in a UDT structure. The fields for the UDT structure are shown in Table 10-14, where the Sale Category field is initially blank.

Create a project named **Ex10-4** in the *Chapter8\Homework* folder to input data into this UDT structure and to process the data from a direct access file called *CustSales.dat*. You may download the CustSales.txt file from the Chapter 10 section of the text Web site and save it to the Bin folder of the project folder for this exercise. (If you have completed Exercise 5 in Chapter 8, you can modify it to complete this exercise rather than starting over.) In all

TABLE 10-14: Fields and field names for CustSales.dat

Field
CustomerName (in lastname-first form)
PhoneNumber
SalesAmount
SalesCategory

cases, your project should use menus wherever appropriate to carry out the operations, and there should be a password form with a password of *cust00er* that is the startup form. Your project should use multiple forms to carry out operations based on the following instructions:

a. The project should display the list of customers in a list box. Double-clicking a customer name or highlighting it and clicking a button should display information on that customer in text boxes with appropriate labels on a separate form.

b. The user should be able to use the scale shown in Table 10-15 to determine the sales category for a single customer and add it in the Category field for that customer.

TABLE 10-15: Sales amounts and categories

Sales Amount	Category
$1,000 or less	Light
$1,001 to $5,000	Average
Greater than $5,000	Heavy

c. The user should be able to add, delete, or edit customer records as necessary, and save the result of this action. It should also be possible to print the list of customers or the results of the computation.

d. Save the resulting data back to the original file or to a new file of the customer's choosing.

e. Add the capability to print preview a list of customer records and then to print them to the default printer.

f. If you have not already done so, add the MS Chart control to the your Toolbox. (In any case, MS Chart should be added to this project.) Use it to generate a bar chart showing the number of customers in each category.

5. Assume that Bulldog Computers has a variety of computer combinations that they sell to both businesses and individuals. A combination typically includes everything the user will need to start work—CPU; hard, floppy, and DVD drives; monitor; printer; associated cables; and personal productivity software. The price of each combination depends on the speed of the CPU, the size of the hard drive, the quality of the printer, the size of the monitor,

and whether or not a CD writer is included. Assume that the information of these computer combinations is stored on a direct access file named *Bulldog-Combos.dat*. Also, assume that the total number of each combination sold to date are stored on this file. You may download this file from the Chapter 10 section of the text Web site. This information includes the SKU number, the name given it by Bulldog, the price of the combination, and the number sold. In all cases, your project should use menus wherever appropriate to carry out the operations, and there should be a password form with a password of *Go03Dogs* that is the startup form. Your project should use multiple forms to carry out operations based on the following instructions:

a. The project should load the data from the direct access file and display it in a list box on the main form. A Bulldog salesperson should be able to click on the name of a combination and display the name, SKU number, and price on a second form.

b. They should then be able to input the number of units sold and applicable tax rate to determine the gross price and price including taxes on the purchase. They should be able to print this information with appropriate labels.

c. At the same time as this information is being printed, the number of units of this combination should be updated on the file and the file saved to the direct access file.

d. A sales manager should be able to add data on new combinations, delete combinations no longer being sold by Bulldog, print a list of combinations, and edit information on combinations whenever prices change (a frequent occurrence).

e. The project should have the capability to print preview a list of computer combination records and then to print them to the default printer.

Index